MANY MASKS

A LIFE OF FRANK LLOYD WRIGHT

BRENDAN GILL

Ballantine Books • New York

Part of one chapter first appeared as "Optimistic Ziggurat" in *The New Yorker*
in a slightly different form.

Library of Congress Catalog Card Number: 87-91901

ISBN: 0-345-35698-5

This edition published by arrangement with G. P. Putnam's Sons.

Cover design by Richard Aquan
Cover photo © Omba, courtesy of the Frank Lloyd Wright Memorial
Foundation

Manufactured in the United States of America

First Ballantine Books Edition: November 1988

10 9 8 7 6 5 4 3 2 1

OTHER BOOKS BY BRENDAN GILL

Death in April
The Trouble of One House
The Day the Money Stopped
Cole (with Robert Kimball)
Tallulah
Happy Times (with Jerome Zerbe)
Here at The New Yorker
Ways of Loving
Summer Places (with Dudley Witney)
Lindbergh Alone
The Dream Come True (with Derry Moore)
Wooings

ACKNOWLEDGMENTS

My first and most profound thanks go to Susan Woldenberg, architect, writer, and photographer, whose several skills have made this book, save in respect to the delectable labor of authorship, as much hers as mine.

I wish also to thank Ellis Amburn, Felicity Ashbee, Lois Bagel, Barbara Ballinger, Victor Barcilon, A. Radford and Gladys Barton, Mary Bell, Donald Brace, Joseph Brewer, Gus Brown, Rigo Cardenas, Richard Carney, Jeff Chusid, Alan Crawford, Nicole Daniels, Jim Dennis, Chris Densmore, William and Janet Dring, Shonnie Finnegan, Phil Feddersen, Ray Fischer, Pedro Guerrero, Paul and Jean Hanna, Joy Harris, Wilbert Hasbrouck, Thomas S. Hines, Henry-Russell Hitchcock, Elizabeth Wright Ingraham, Elsie Jacobsen, Jean Johnson, Philip Johnson, Elaine Wright Jones, Sally Jungers, Don Kalec, Edgar J. Kaufmann, Jr., Roger Kennedy, Walter H. Kilham, Jr., Nancy Knechtel, Emily Landau, Jonathan Lipman, Philip Lyman, Stanley Marcus, Hedy Margolies, Cliff May, Esther McCoy, Herb McLaughlin, Lillian Melgin, Mrs. David Michaels, Larry Millett, Herbert Mitchell, Maya Moran, Nora Natoff, John O'Hern, Donald Oresman, William Wesley Peters, Bruce Brooks Pfeiffer, Franklin Porter, Harold Price, Jack Prost, Roland Reisley, Milt Robinson, Hope Rogers, Nicholas and Mary Sahlas, Tim Samuelson, Elizabeth Nelle Jones Sanford, Nancy Schmid, Walter Bill Schmidt, Nils Schweitzer, Margaret Scott, Warren Scott, William Shawn, Joel Silver, Geraldine Strey, Dale Smirl, Edgar Tafel, Roy Thurman, William and June Walker, Robert Weil, David and Gladys Wright, Eric and Mary Lloyd Wright, William Zeckendorf, Jr., and John Zukowsky.

A key to the abbreviations that accompany the illustrations is to be found on pages 517–518.

MANY MASKS

1

FRANK LLOYD WRIGHT died well over a quarter of a century ago and yet he remains a lively figure among us. Indeed, he strikes me as being almost as intensely present in the world today as he was in his vivid, passionate old age, when his fame—and his evident delight in his fame—seemed to double and redouble with every passing year.

As a friend of Wright's in that late, sunny period of his life, I find it easy to imagine how pleased he would be to learn that his name was still capable of provoking headlines in our contemporary press. He pretended to dislike reporters (it was as a reporter that I first met him), blaming many of his early troubles on their pesky, incessant pursuit of him, but the fact was that he lured them on as ardently as they followed after; the relationship amounted to a lifelong love-affair, disguised from time to time as antagonism. I used to tell Wright that he had no true antagonists except himself, and he would shake his superbly coiffed old head in mock-chagrin: had all his ruses, all his succession of masks, all his recklessly reiterated falsehoods—one outrageous whopper after another, from his teens to his nineties—been so damnably easy to see through?

It is a paradox characteristic of Wright that even as a corpse he has been able to stir up a considerable measure of excitement among the living. When his widow Olgivanna died, in 1985, it turned out that one of her last wishes was that Wright's body be dug up out of the little family burying ground in the valley below Taliesin, his famous house near Spring Green, Wisconsin, and brought to Taliesin West, Wright's tawny-red, stone-and-concrete fortress in the Arizona desert. There his ashes and Olgivanna's were to be mingled and buried together in a new grave-site. This grotesque transaction—based in large part on Olgivanna's justified sense of grievance over the treatment that she and Wright had received at the hands of their Spring Green neighbors when they first settled down at Taliesin as unmarried lovers—became the occasion for innumerable front-page stories throughout the country. One cynical editorial writer suggested that the adventitious doubling of the number of grave-sites of a great man, however sentimental the reason for its having occurred, would be sure to have the favorable effect of increasing the crowds of tourists who pay substantial sums to visit one or the other of the two Taliesins.

A shrine at least as important to tourists as the two Taliesins is Wright's home and studio in Oak Park, Illinois. Over the past few years, at a cost of two million dollars, the intricately joined buildings have been made to look much as they did in 1909; that was the year in which Wright abandoned his wife and children and decamped with his mistress, Mamah Cheney, the wife of a client and friend, Edwin Cheney. Some sixty thousand people

The Oak Park house and studio that FLW incessantly added to and tinkered with for over twenty years.

a year come to visit this shrine, located in a setting of quiet, leafy streets in the still enviably serene and prosperous suburb of Oak Park, just west of Chicago. (One glimpses at the vanishing point of many an Oak Park avenue the Sears tower in downtown Chicago, rising against the horizon like a child's crudely drawn cartoon notion of a skyscraper.) Even the most sympathetic feats of restoration carry the taint of an embalmment; nevertheless, the little house and the much larger studio beside it continue to bear plausible witness to Wright's high spirits and inventiveness. He was celebrated for the frequency with which, ignoring some task whose completion was already long past due, he would set about reorganizing the furniture in the house and studio, or would knock down walls and ceilings to gain some new and more pleasing aesthetic effect. In those days, the state of both house and studio was one of incessant, fruitful dishevelment, and the hushed decorum of the rooms through which the contemporary public is invited to pass serves to remind us that the mischievous genius who provided the reason for enshrining this house and studio was but a ghost in them for many decades before he died.

Wright left Oak Park over three-quarters of a century ago, in a veritable firestorm of scandal, and yet the power of his presence is to be felt everywhere in the town to this day. Some forty houses were designed by him in Oak Park and in the neighboring communities of River Forest and Riverside, and to the owners of these houses he exists as a sort of invisible resident despot, whose disapproval they dread incurring. Even the slightest changes in the layout or appearance of a Wright house are undertaken with fear and trembling; where previous owners have had the temerity to install modern improvements in kitchens and bathrooms, true devotees of Wright are quick to rip them out. Tours of Wright houses are a conspicuous feature of the cultural life of Oak Park; stories about Wright, equally relished whether true or false, abound among the natives. Mostly, the stories concern his unconventional sexual life or his no less unconventional business life, which is to say his habit of running up enormous bills and then not paying them.

To own a Wright house is a sufficient distinction anywhere in the United States; in Oak Park it is a form of aristocracy, the various levels of which are determined by what one's house contains—the possession of half a dozen pieces of furniture designed by Wright for the very rooms in which they stand is roughly equivalent to possessing a dukedom. A few fortunate people not only live in Wright houses but actually knew Wright as well. Warren Scott has lived in such a house for over thirty years: the enchanting little lattice-windowed cottage that Wright designed in 1908 for the office manager of the Oak Park studio, Isabel Roberts. (Half a dozen variations on the Roberts cottage were to come from Wright's hand in later years.) According to gossip still prevalent in River Forest, Wright's horse would be seen tethered on weekends outside Miss Roberts's house, to the scandal—and ill-concealed delight—of pious Sunday-morning churchgoers. Wright was then deeply involved with Mrs. Cheney and, despite his manic energy, is unlikely to have been carrying on two strenuous love-affairs at the same moment. Adding to the unlikelihood of the romance is the fact that the house was occupied not only by Miss Roberts but by her mother and sister, who would not have served as complaisant onlookers. Nevertheless, it is only fair to say that Scott favors the hypothesis of a romance, and he has reasons. In the nineteen-fifties, he and his wife asked Wright to redesign portions of the house and to make certain much-needed repairs. On arriving in River Forest, Wright seated himself at the Scotts' piano, provided them with a brief, vehemently improvised concert, and then walked them through the house, indicating with his cane a score of mistakes in its construction.

During that visit, Wright spoke candidly to the Scotts of Miss Roberts— "I couldn't bear to be without her"—and of the irritating economies he had been obliged to practice in building the house. Scott says, "Wright was overflowing with comments about what a mess he had made of it. I got the impression that he had done the job as cheaply as possible because it was a secret gift to Isabel. He must have had his usual hard time finding the money. When I bought the house, the beam holding up the balcony in the living room had come loose and was hanging almost free; Wright blamed its condition on the fact that he had let the carpenter use one-inch nails to fasten the beam to its adjacent supports instead of using the more expensive three-inch nails. Imagine remembering a thing like that after almost fifty years! The roof overhangs that are cantilevered out beyond the two-story-high bay window in the living room had sagged by as much as a foot; Wright was delighted to have me fit some long steel beams into the overhangs, in place of the failed wood. He also arranged for us to gain a sizable coat closet by the front door—in Isabel's day, he hadn't provided for any closet at all. More important to Isabel and him at the time, I suppose, was the pretty wrought-iron balcony that he placed outside

© SUSAN WOLDENBERG

The house that FLW designed for Isabel Roberts in 1908. A big tree on the property was left untouched, to grow amiably up through the porch roof. This was a favorite architectural prank of Wright's.

© SUSAN WOLDENBERG

The little wrought-iron "Romeo and Juliet" balcony of Miss Roberts' bedroom.

the French doors of her bedroom; on the balcony were two little iron seats—one for Romeo, surely, and one for Juliet?"

According to Scott, Wright had his "boys" at Taliesin prepare working drawings for the restoration of the house and rendered no charge for his services; Scott attributes this unexpected gesture to Wright's recalling, at eighty-eight, an amorous episode of his early middle age—one that, if it took place at all, may well have seemed to require expiation, having induced in him a triple guilt for betraying his wife Catherine, her already chosen successor Mrs. Cheney, and Isabel Roberts (who, for whatever the fact may be worth, never married).

A further proof of Wright's presence among us is the increasing frequency with which his name appears in newspaper and magazine accounts of art auctions and real-estate sales. Weekly, if not daily, we read of a Wright art-glass window or a Wright article of furniture—even, say, one of those hideous chairs so unstable that nobody can sit upright in them for more than a few seconds at most—bringing a couple of hundred thousand dollars at auction. A house designed by Wright and well worth preserving as a residence may be worth half a million dollars if put on the market for that purpose alone, but a Wright house has come to be worth far more as a quarry for Wright artifacts than for itself; demolished with care and sold off as so many windows, doors, and lighting fixtures, it may well bring a total of a couple of million dollars. (The wall-supported toilets that Wright designed for the Larkin Administration Building appear to have disappeared without a trace when the building was demolished in 1950; today, they would bring a high price indeed.) The Wright heritage is more vulnerable to this crass and highly profitable exploitation than to the conventional greed of real-estate developers, for whom in the past a Wright house or office building was simply an obsolete nuisance, standing in the way of progress. Entrepreneurial scavengers prowl the country in search of Wrightiana, and because the supply of authentic Wright objects cannot possibly keep up with the demand a thriving commerce in Wright fakes has sprung up, the fakes being peddled much as portions of the True Cross were peddled to credulous Christians during the Middle Ages. From the point of view of serious admirers of Wright, peddlers of Wright fakes are ethically no more deplorable than peddlers of authentic Wright pieces; it could even be argued that peddlers of fakes are less deplorable, since what they peddle is of no intrinsic value, while the peddlers of the real thing dissipate and consume the very essence of Wright, which is his work in place, precisely where Wright intended it to be. Collectors of Wright, whether dealers earning a living, or curators in museums gaining a reputation, or ignorant millionaires acting as vacuum cleaners in the wake of fashion, by no means escape confronting an ethical problem and having ethical judgments passed upon them. They may claim to be saving Wright, but often enough they are destroying him.

A few years ago, Max Protetch, a New York City dealer in architectural drawings, arranged with the Frank Lloyd Wright Foundation to sell a certain number of authentic Wright drawings, at prices that are reputed to reach as high as two hundred thousand dollars. The success of Protetch and a few other respected dealers in architectural drawings has led inevitably to emulation; drawings that are known not to be by Wright, or by any of his draftsmen, turn up in galleries throughout the world and bring a handsome price from beginning collectors. (Architectural drawings are particularly difficult to authenticate, because for the past century or more architects have employed skilled renderers to prepare, for clients unable to comprehend elevations and plans, pleasing views of buildings in their projected settings. A Wright drawing is considered authentic if it was signed by him; in some cases, he may actually have drawn it, but in most cases he will have caused it to be drawn and will have indicated his approval of it by his signature. Many of the most distinguished American architects of our day have never made a drawing in their lives.) Because so many thousands of letters by Wright, either written in his own hand or dictated to a typist, are known to exist, they remain comparatively cheap to buy and therefore don't yet invite faking; no doubt some enterprising forger is already practicing his skills against the days of scarcity to come. If so, he will have to prove himself to be a very gifted writer as well as a gifted forger; it will be far harder to imitate Wright's exuberant epistolary style than to imitate his scratchy penmanship.

Perhaps the most convincing evidence of Wright's uncanny contemporary popularity is the fact that people are eager to go on commissioning Wright houses: houses that are genuinely from the master's hand and that happen not to have been built in his lifetime. When an architect dies, it is nearly always the case that he leaves behind a number of projects that for one reason or another—difficulties with a budget, changes in a client's personal life, a nationwide depression—have remained unexecuted. It is also nearly always the case that these projects not only remain unexecuted but are quickly forgotten except by scholars, blueprints and renderings seeming in some mysterious fashion to lose much of their attractiveness because the maker of them is no longer living. The great exception to this commonplace is Wright, a great exception to all commonplaces. To an extent that Wright himself, despite his vanity, might well have been willing to be awed by, his work, both built and unbuilt, impresses us as being of even more significance today than it was during his lifetime; the result is that the houses Wright designed and yet failed to find a suggestible client for are at last being realized in brick, wood, and stone: a circumstance probably without parallel in architectural history.

Thus it has happened that several Wright houses have been completed since his death. One of them was commissioned by Bruce Brooks Pfeiffer, Director of Archives at the Frank Lloyd Wright Foundation, and was built on the grounds of Taliesin West in 1971. It is a single-story house consisting of three loosely joined circular pavilions, from one of which extends a low-roofed wing containing a garage and storage space. Smoothly finished concrete terraces fill the interstices between the pavilions; at the outer

The house, designed by FLW, that Bruce Brooks Pfeiffer and his father built on the grounds of Taliesin West many years after FLW's death.

15

edge of a grassy terrace raised above the desert floor to the east of the house is a small pool, big enough to splash in if not swim in, and behind the house rises the formidable shouldering presence of the Mount McDowell Range. As a means of tempering the fierce desert sunlight, a continuous band of windows less than three feet high circles the main living rooms at a point approximately halfway between the floor and ceiling; one looks out at the view from a seated position, much as one might look out at the ocean through the portholes of a ship.

The Pfeiffer house had been designed in the first instance for Ralph Jester, in 1938, for a site in Palos Verdes, California. The exterior was to have been of plywood, whose flexibility lends itself readily to a circular form. Nevertheless, building contractors were leery of the difficulties posed by the detailing of circular rooms and their estimates of the cost of building such a house were always radically high. Over the course of eighteen years, Wright sought to persuade no fewer than nine prospective clients (Huntington Hartford among them) to build the house, always in vain. As a former Taliesin apprentice and as its official archivist, Pfeiffer didn't fear to carry out the designs according to Wright's intentions, modifying them only in order to gain a greater interior height.

Other houses designed by Wright have been built since his death, in Minnesota, California, and Michigan. One of the most recent new/old Wright houses was completed two or three years ago on a stony hilltop on the outskirts of Santa Fe. The design, Wright's only essay in adobe construction, was whimsically nicknamed by him "the pottery house" (its walls bulge outward and then inward much as a pot is shaped by the potter's hand) and was initially designed for friends of his in El Paso, in 1929. The plan of the house, which consists of two curved wings embracing a central patio, is intended to protect its occupants from the high winds and extremes of heat and cold that are to be met with in western Texas. A developer in Santa Fe, happening to run across a published drawing of the house, decided that it would be every bit as suitable for Santa Fe as for El Paso. In the knowledge that any Wright house was highly salable, he reasoned that a brand-new Wright house might be even more salable than an old one. He got in touch with the Frank Lloyd Wright Foundation, at Taliesin West, and arranged to lease the plans of the house and to employ T.A.A.—the acronym stands for Taliesin Associated Architects, who are in commercial practice and whose fees help to fund the teaching aspects of the Taliesin Fellowship—to adapt the house to the site chosen and to make sure that the plans met the current building codes of the community.

The architect who took charge of the project on behalf of T.A.A. was Charles Montooth, who first served as an apprentice under Wright forty-odd years ago and who, like all his colleagues at Taliesin, finds it natural to this day to speak of "Mr." Wright. As a friend of Wright's, I had been accustomed to calling him "Frank," but whenever I speak of him in that fashion at either of the Taliesins I suspect that I am looked upon as having committed a serious breach of decorum. Wright's former associates are too polite to mention it, but if Wesley Peters, who was once Wright's son-in-law, as well as an early recruit to the Fellowship, continues to refer to "Mr." Wright, then surely it is an impertinence for me to do otherwise. The fact is that I came early in our acquaintanceship to calling Wright "Frank," largely at his insistence: first names are among the most convenient of bridges between age and youth. Given my admiration for Wright, at first I found his informality of address startling; when he came to New York, he would ring me up from the Plaza Hotel and say, "Hello, Brendan, this is Frank," and I felt as if George Washington were telephoning me from Mount Vernon and saying, "Hello, Brendan, this is George."

In the course of going through the Taliesin files, Montooth concluded that Wright was still tinkering with the El Paso plans as late as 1941. "Mr. Wright had a habit of putting different dates on his drawings at different times," Montooth says. "If his purpose was to confuse scholars, he has certainly succeeded. The Second World War put a stop to house construction and the plans were set aside. Originally, the house was to have been pretty small—twenty-four hundred square feet. Adding to the width of the wings, we managed to expand it to just under five thousand feet, but we took care to preserve the same proportions. This was something that Mr. Wright often had to do in the reverse direction, shrinking the scale of a house to meet a client's limited budget. What he always wanted more than anything else was to get a house *built*, though not at the sacrifice of his principles. We've also added a swimming pool and a three-car garage, but we tucked the garage underground and gave it an earth roof, so it doesn't interfere with the appearance of the house as Wright imagined it."

Wright's novel "pottery" manipulation of conventional adobe building practices was characteristic of him; so was his use in the house of ordinary clay drainage tiles, which he set high in its walls like portholes to provide natural light and ventilation. Montooth has pointed out that Wright designed the house before air conditioning had become popular and comparatively inexpensive; he must have intended the tiles to allow the prevailing winds to blow through the rooms and help carry off excessive heat. That was natural air conditioning, which Wright believed in; artificial air conditioning he considered "a dangerous circumstance," though for the Larkin building, erected in Buffalo just after the turn of the century, Wright devised a system of air conditioning that was among the first to be invented. "In 1985, our client understandably wanted the latest in air conditioning," Montooth says, "so we decided that Mr. Wright wouldn't mind our blocking off the ends of the tiles with glass. Mr. Wright loved fireplaces, the more the merrier, and we have eight of them in the house. Air, fire, water, and earth—the classic four elements were what he liked to work with and play with, and here they are in Santa Fe, as you find them at Fallingwater and Wingspread and all his other houses. You could say that this pottery house was brand-new, or you could say it was fifty years old, or you could say it was five thousand years old—it would all be the same to Mr. Wright. He enjoyed the feeling of being outside time."

The truth of that observation is quickly made clear to anyone paying his first visit to the pottery house. Climbing the hill, he finds himself trapped inside an odd and yet agreeable time-warp. He would be delighted but not in the least astonished if a certain insouciant figure in a broad-brimmed, vanilla-colored hat and tweed cape were to come sauntering down the path to greet him. But we are entitled to wonder what this figure would say upon learning that the Taliesin Associated Architects had permitted the licensing of not one posthumous pottery house but two. For while Montooth was busy supervising an adaptation of the El Paso house for a speculator-builder in Santa Fe (who is said to have sold the house for something like two million dollars), another T.A.A. architect, Charles Robert Schiffner, was supervising a second adaptation of the house in Phoenix. This house was built for a man and wife who believed themselves to be the sole beneficiaries of the design—who, indeed, had chosen the design because the wife was a potter and wished a house appropriate to her vocation. The T.A.A. defends the transaction partly on the strength of Mrs. Wright's having sanctioned it, her sanction being based in turn on the fact that Wright had drawn a number of versions of the original. Perhaps Wright himself would also have given it his approval, since in his lifetime so many near-duplications of his favorite designs were dispatched to grateful clients throughout the country; nevertheless, the hazard of a carelessly monitored licensing of Wright designs to help fund the varied (and unpredictable) future activities of the Frank Lloyd Wright Foundation is a disturbing one.

Wright having been turned into a commodity more "commercial" than he ever succeeded in being in life, some of the products that he lent his talent and name to in the nineteen-fifties are today being manufactured and profitably marketed by several firms; and this, too, is a disturbing fact, because it is so hard to determine what is truly Wright's and what is mere contemporary "adaptation." The well-known fabric house of Schumacher, in New York City, currently offers for sale not only certain designs that Wright himself licensed but designs recently licensed by the Frank Lloyd Wright Foundation and taken from sources—concrete blocks, leaded-glass windows—that Wright might well have deplored and would certainly have ridiculed. In his dealings with Schumacher, in the fifties, he was often at his worst (at luncheons given in his honor, he would be overbearing and overtalkative) and it was plain that he had consented to work with the firm only in order to make money for the Foundation, whose prospects after his death gave him reason for concern. In the introduction to a current Schumacher catalogue, one reads:

> The archives of Taliesin West . . . have inspired the collection shown here. The wallcoverings, borders, print and woven fabrics, custom area rugs, and sheer window panels represent adaptations of just a few of the many details exhibited in the work of this prolific architect. . . . To be sure, there are patterns that will prompt a familiar, knowing nod. Others will delight you with their freshness.[1]

It is the patterns that will delight us with their freshness that are likely to distress guardians of Wright's reputation; these purists are also likely to be distressed by the fact that the Frank Lloyd Wright Foundation licenses designs, or adaptations of designs, for books, posters, calendars, china, glassware, silver, and stationery. (In 1986, Tiffany's sold twenty-five hundred Wright-designed silver candlesticks.) Replicas of the Froebel building-blocks that Wright played with as a child are on sale at the Wright Home and Studio. Moreover, the Foundation is engaged in a real-estate development located just outside the gates of Taliesin and all too aptly called "Taliesin Gates." Land in the development sells for many thousands of dollars an acre, and purchasers of property in the development are expected to employ Taliesin architects. To the astonishment of his friends and family, Wright in death has become an industry—one that, as it prospers, is likely to be running more and more recklessly out of control.

In the case of Wright and two or three other exceptionally gifted people that I have known, I find that they are not content to exist as figures among a host of other figures in my memory, capable of being summoned up or passed by according to my momentary wishes. They exercise an active influence, even an aggressively disruptive one, over any attempt I make to give them not only a just place in my life (in their eyes, surely a matter of little importance) but a just place in the history of our time as well. It is as if history were still a matter of concern to them, and for that reason, in a fashion hard to credit unless one has experienced it, they go on playing a role of advocacy in their own behalf. They are restless, vehement ghosts, urging upon us that their version of the lives they have led be seen to be the only accurate one; the masks that they created and that sufficed to disguise them successfully throughout their careers are to be accepted by the world as their true countenances.

Nobody in my experience has been a more artful dodger in this respect than Wright. The prodigious lies he told in his autobiography and the still more prodigious lies that he related in conversation are easy to trace back to the often anguished ignominy of his boyhood and adolescence, most of the events of which he pretended to have forgotten, but the fact is that he went on continuously inventing and reinventing himself, and the smiling, irresistible divinity that he impersonated in his seventies and eighties was but the latest of many similar masterpieces. It was this master-piece that I encountered on the occasion of our last meeting: the commence-ment exercises held at Sarah Lawrence College, in Bronxville, New York, in June of 1958, less than a year before he died.

The campus of Sarah Lawrence occupies what used to be the suburban estate of William Van Duzer Lawrence, a pharmaceutical magnate and real-estate developer, who on his death, in 1927, left funds with which to establish a college in his wife's name. (Lawrence's intention was that the college should turn out well-mannered young ladies wholly unlike the short-skirted, cigarette-smoking "flappers" that some of his nieces had dis-mayingly degenerated into during their undergraduate years at Vassar. Lawrence's intention was, of course, never to be realized.) The campus runs along the spine of a rocky hillside densely planted with dogwood, oaks, pines, and maples; the weather being fine on that particular day, the graduation ceremonies were being conducted on the terrace and lawn of Westlands, a red-brick, Westchester Tudor mansion that has always served as the administrative headquarters of the college.

Along one side of the Westlands lawn runs a rickety wooden pergola, garlanded in early summer with spikes of white and lavender wistaria. As I entered the pergola, I saw two men in academic gowns approaching me. One was Dr. Harold Taylor, then president of the college; the other was Wright. A handsome man in his early forties, Dr. Taylor was wearing a red gown that but for his companion would have served to make him the most conspicuous sight for miles around, but Wright had disposed of all imaginable competition by wearing a scarlet-and-purple gown so rich and soft that it might have been run up out of fuchsia blossoms. Erect, bright-eyed, and in high spirits, he received with some skepticism my compli-ments on his attire. "You don't think it makes me look like a rather question-able old lady?" he asked. "I acquired it a couple of years ago, when the University of Wales gave me a Doctorate of Laws. Don't get much chance to wear it, in my line of work."

Taylor said that it was time they were joining the academic procession that had formed at the far end of the pergola, and Wright affected not to hear him. "My wife and I flew in from Wisconsin last night," he said. "Before that, I was in Baghdad. Got work under way all over the world— churches, temples, synagogues, public buildings, office buildings, houses! Forty houses going up in this country alone! Never have I had so much to do, and though I can't keep at it as long as I used to, never have I done so much good work." Wright's indirect reference to age put me in mind of the fact that his birthday was only a few days off. According to *Who's Who,* I told him, he was about to be eighty-nine, but according to certain other authorities he was already ninety and about to be ninety-one.

Wright shook his head as if in despair. "Authorities!" he said. "There are no official records, but my mother always said that I was born in 1869, and if she didn't know, who would? I'm starting my ninetieth year next week and I feel as strong and fresh as a boy."

Taylor coaxed Wright into place at the rear of the procession, which then marched slowly across the lawn and onto the broad, flagstone-paved terrace of Westlands. While some preliminary speakers were at the microphone, Wright set off unexpectedly into the house and Taylor darted after him, plucking at his gown. "Want to go to the bathroom?" Taylor whispered. "Certainly not! No bathroom for me!" Wright said, in a loud voice. "Just biding my time till my turn comes." Taylor hadn't intended the great man of the day to disappear at that critical moment in the exercises, but

FLW in his eighties. Pretending to deplore the eagerness with which people sought to take his picture, he would then pose tirelessly for them.

© OBMA

he accepted Wright's explanation with perfect good humor. "Whatever suits you, Buster," Taylor said. ("Buster" to Frank Lloyd Wright? And to think that I had once had difficulty saying "Frank"!)

When the time came for Wright to be introduced, he slipped out of the house and, brushing Taylor aside with a buoyant gesture, without any introduction launched into his talk. Knowing Wright's reputation as an iconoclast, a good many people in the audience had expected him to make an effort to shock them, and so had steeled themselves against the terrible things he might say about Westchester, about Westchester Tudor architecture, or even about the college itself. And shock them he did, in spite of themselves, by dint of not being an iconoclast at all.

"Greetings to the young womanhood of America," he said. "Green womanhood, I suppose—beautifully green, the way your school buildings are here. It is a very happy occasion for an architect to be asked to say something to the young womanhood of America before it's too late, before they have, I think they call it, 'hired' an architect, and if there is any advice I would like to give . . . it is to beware of architects. . . . Architecture is really the blind spot of our nation. . . . The things we have to depend on for our culture, if we are ever to have one that is indigenous, are art, architecture, and religion. . . . You know we have no religion to go with the Declaration of Independence, to go with the sovereignty of the individual. None! The only thing we have to go with it and assure us and encourage us in that connection is the saying of Jesus that the Kingdom of God is within you. That greatest of all poetic students of human nature gave us the key to the religion that would be ours someday and be appropriate to the brave status we have taken before the world. . . . The principles that build the tree will build the man. . . . That's why I think Nature should be spelled with a capital 'N,' not because Nature is God but because all that we can learn of God we will learn from the body of God, which we call Nature. Thank you!"

Another buoyant wave of the hand and, as the green young womanhood applauded, the fuchsia-robed old man strode vigorously away from the dignitaries gathered on the terrace, with Taylor in smiling, vain pursuit of him. It struck me then that surely, like any divinity, he was beyond the tiresome necessity of dying.

2

WHEN, THAT PLEASANT afternoon under the pergola at Sarah Lawrence, I raised the question of the year of Wright's birth and he replied that he saw no reason to doubt his mother's recollection that the year was 1869—"if she didn't know, who would?"— his jocular dismissal of the matter was, I have come to perceive, not nearly so offhand as he may have wished me to suppose it was. In the years that have passed since that occasion, a number of official records have been uncovered, which Wright and his mother are sure to have known about, and these records indicate that he was born on June 8th, 1867.

Presumably with the mother's knowledge and consent, the son chose to falsify the date of his birth, and the motive may have been nothing more obscure than the conventional one of desiring to be thought younger than one is. No doubt this was the case with Wright's mother, Anna Lloyd Jones Wright, who earlier had taken care to tamper with the year of *her* birth as well. Most biographies of Wright state that his mother was born in Wales in 1842, coming with her family to this country in 1845. The fact is that she was born in 1839 and, by the standards of those days, was already considered an old maid at the time of her marriage to William Cary Wright, which took place in 1866. Though she was twenty-seven, she let it be thought that she was twenty-four.

Oddly enough, her son in his autobiography muddles matters still further, making both of his parents older than they were instead of younger. He writes that in 1866 his mother was twenty-nine and his father was seventeen years her senior, which would make him forty-six; actually, the father was forty-one. Still more oddly, the son gets his father's name wrong, calling him William Russell Cary Wright; there was no "Russell" in his name. (The mistake may have arisen as an echo of a family tradition to the effect that the Wrights were related to James Russell Lowell, which it appears they were not. The mistake could also have arisen from the fact that William had a brother named Russell.) The autobiography states that the father came from Hartford, Connecticut, implying that he was born there; in fact, he was born in Westfield, Massachusetts, in 1825, at a time when his father, the Reverend David Wright, was serving as a Baptist preacher in that community, and he was named after the celebrated missionary to India, William Carey (1761–1834). David Wright was later called to preach in Hartford, where he spent the rest of his life and where William spent a portion of his youth and early manhood. David Wright lived to the sufficiently remarkable age of ninety-three; drawing the longbow as usual, his grandson boasted that he had lived to be ninety-nine.

This mishmash of chronological errors, in many cases intentional and in other cases obviously a consequence of carelessness or faulty memory, might be considered of trifling importance except that it is so characteristic of Wright's lifelong habit of turning facts into fiction. He was a virtuoso at bearing false witness, which is to say that he sometimes lied in the name of self-promotion or self-protection and at other times he seems to have lied simply for the pleasure it gave him. Certain fabrications of his have taken years to detect; others have been successfully contradicted within moments of his having spoken them. Once, for example, at a luncheon of architects in New York City in the nineteen-forties, Wright began to expatiate upon his contribution to the handiwork of a number of his fellow architects—a favorite topic of his, though understandably not a favorite topic of the architects to whom he chose to call this unflattering attention. Of Raymond Hood, who had died some years earlier and who was therefore presumably past challenging anything Wright said, he mentioned that he had visited Hood at his office while the latter was engaged in designing the Daily News building, on East Forty-second Street. It is a building celebrated in architectural history for being among the first skyscraper towers to dispense with finial embellishments in its upper stories—its straight shaft ends as abruptly as if it had been cut off with a knife. Wright explained to his auditors just how this novelty had come about: "I studied the elevation," he said, "and I told Ray, 'Ray, you just stop the whole thing right here,' and I drew a line across the elevation with the tip of my cane. And that's why the Daily News building looks the way it does."

An architect named Walter H. Kilham, Jr., happened to be seated at the table. An admirer of Wright but an even greater admirer of Hood, Kilham leaped to his feet and broke in upon Wright's discourse with, "Mr. Wright, sir! Mr. Wright! I'm Walter Kilham, and I want you to know that I was Ray Hood's head draftsman all the time the News building was in our office. Every one of the News elevations was drawn under my supervision and I can assure you and everybody at this table that from the start the building was designed exactly the way it was built." Wright stared at the excited Kilham. The room fell silent, awaiting Wright's response. Smiling, supremely self-confident, in his exquisite voice Wright said, "Well, there you are!" and proceeded to complete his remarks. Seemingly, it had cost the old charmer nothing to be found out.

"Well, there you are!" might be his response to certain mysteries that, though small in themselves, cast an instructive light over Wright's entire career. His genius as an architect and his talent for public relations have made his name one of the most famous on earth—all the more interesting, then, that it may not have been his name at all. At birth and for some years afterward, he was called Frank Lincoln Wright, and the reason he bore that name and the reason that it was abandoned are fairly easy to guess at. When Wright was born, his parents were living in Richland Center, Wisconsin, a prosperous market town a few miles north of Spring Green. (The house in which he was born remains a matter of dispute among local Wright authorities; Wright himself was characteristically vague on the subject, telling different people different stories at different times, according to the satisfaction he assumed it would give them.) Wright's father, who was sometimes concurrently and sometimes consecutively a lawyer, a preacher, a school superintendent, and a music teacher, was also known throughout the region as an orator. In the mourning that followed President Lincoln's assassination, in 1865, many public eulogies were pronounced throughout the country; William Cary Wright was chosen to deliver the eulogy in Richland Center, in ceremonies held on the courthouse lawn. Speaking from an improvised platform on the courthouse steps, he gave what the local newspaper described as "an eloquent address."

The following year, Wright married Anna (then called Hannah) Lloyd Jones, and their first child was born some ten months later; what more natural than to name him after the martyred President, as many thousands of other male babies were being named at that time? At least two Wright family documents of the period record his middle name as Lincoln and family oral tradition to this day favors Lincoln over Lloyd, in part because of the suspicion that the name was altered by Anna Lloyd Jones after her relationship with William Wright had deteriorated into open warfare; she confirmed her possession of her especially favored son—she appears to have felt comparatively little affection for the two daughters that followed him—by substituting a portion of her name for the name that (one surmises) her husband had chosen for him.

Students of the giving of names would be rightfully hesitant to stop at this juncture: what is one to make of the name "Frank"? If it were true—which I will be arguing that it wasn't—that Anna Lloyd Jones Wright wished even before his birth for her first and only son to become a great architect, why on earth would she have been content to give him a name so common, so humbly down-to-earth, so totally unrelated to the names of great architects of the past as . . . Frank? On both the Wright and

FLW at three. [AU]

Lloyd Jones sides of the family, there were many strong Biblical names to be drawn upon, as well as the names of many kings and nobles, but not Frank. It is a possibility, if not a likelihood, that the infant was named Franklin, after Benjamin Franklin, who was held in high regard at that period in our history. By an irony, many years later the elder of Frank Lloyd Wright's two sisters, Jane Porter, had a son whom she named Frank Porter in honor of her famous brother; after a falling-out with him, she changed her son's name to Franklin, which he contentedly bears to this day.

It is Franklin Porter who has reason to rue the powerful influence that his uncle had upon all members of the family, whether he was on good terms with them or not. When at an early point in his life Wright abandoned his authentic birth-year of 1867 in favor of 1869, he usurped the birth-year of his sister Jane. As she lay dying, she kept insisting to her son that the year of her birth was 1869. So in awe of his Uncle Frank was Franklin Porter that he took it for granted that his mother must be mistaken; when she died, he provided her with the wrong birth-year.

Wright's manipulation of the facts in respect to his name and the year and place of birth springs from a wish to devise, as much for his mother's sake as for his own, an appropriately mythic entrance into the world. This entrance glorified mother and son and tended to diminish the father, to the point where he could be seen to have performed a service not much loftier than that performed by St. Joseph. The view of William Cary Wright that we are given in the autobiography is radically unfair to him. We read, "After their son was born something happened between the mother and father. Sister [sons and daughters in the Lloyd Jones family were always addressed as "Sister" and "Brother"] Anna's extraordinary devotion to the child disconcerted the father. He never made much of the child, it seems."[1] The harsh judgment uttered in the last sentence is obviously the mother's and not the son's; the phrase "it seems" is tacked on as a mitigating filial afterthought.

That the father was disconcerted may well be true, but it is only a small fraction of the truth; the autobiography is an extended apologia—a fabrication that takes the form of a bittersweet romance, with Frank Lloyd Wright as its hero. Being self-contradictory often from one page to the next, it must be read almost literally between the lines. Wright told me once that he had written the 1943 version of the autobiography because *The New Yorker* had sharply criticized the quality of the writing in the first version, published in 1932. There is no evidence that *The New Yorker* ever said anything, favorable or unfavorable, about the 1932 version, though it certainly might have: Wright's was just the sort of overheated prose that E. B. White, James Thurber, and other *New Yorker* writers of the period continuously mocked. It is possible that a friend like Lewis Mumford or Alexander Woollcott (whose own prose often appeared to have been composed in fudge on a lace doily) wrote to Wright on *New Yorker* stationery, urging him to improve his style, and that Wright remembered the advice as having come straight from the pages of the magazine; be that as it may, the advice was in vain. The second version of the autobiography is far longer than the first, but the style remains the same; though Wright asserts that he has become less angry in the decade between the two versions and therefore no longer takes what he calls "a worm's eye view of the world," he continues to ignore accuracy in the course of paying off his mother's grudges and setting the stage for his nativity. In a celebrated passage that follows immediately after the three sentences quoted above, he writes:

> No doubt his wife loved him no less but now loved something more, something created out of her own fervor of love and desire. A means to realize her vision.
>
> The boy, she said, was to build beautiful buildings. Faith in prenatal influences was strong in this expectant mother. She kept her thoughts on the high things for which she yearned and looked carefully after her health. There was never a doubt in the expectant mother's mind but that she was to have a boy.
>
> Fascinated by buildings, she took ten full-page wood-engravings of the old English cathedrals from "Old England," a pictorial periodical to which the father had subscribed, had them framed simply in flat oak and hung them upon the walls of the room that was to be her son's.
>
> Before he was born, she said she intended him to be an Architect.[2]

A couple of other family mysteries emerge from these lines, the first and more important one being the question of how it came about that a young woman growing up on an isolated farm in the Middle West in the middle years of the nineteenth century hit upon architecture as the most desirable profession for her sure-to-be-incomparably-gifted son. For in those days architecture was scarcely a profession at all; it lacked the prestige attached to medicine, the ministry, teaching, and the law (professions that, as it happened, William Cary Wright had proved himself adept at). Many who called themselves architects were in fact building contractors, who in most cases would have begun their careers as carpenters. The first school of architecture in the United States opened its doors at the Massachusetts Institute of Technology only a year after Frank Lloyd Wright was born and boasted a total of four students. The handful of architects practicing in Chicago—the one big city within easy reach of Spring Green—were certainly unknown to fame and therefore unlikely to be known to Anna Lloyd Jones. (It wasn't until the period devoted to the rebuilding of Chicago after the great fire of 1871 that the city became a mecca for architects.) The structures that Sister Anna's eyes fell upon in the Wisconsin countryside were all carpenter-built; to this day, save for Taliesin itself, the man-made environment there is pitifully meagre.

In respect to those English cathedrals, wood engravings of which were supposed to have graced the walls of little Frank's room, as a devout Welsh Unitarian Sister Anna ought to have despised them; she and her family were accustomed to speaking to God in small wooden meeting-houses, which deliberately shunned ecclesiastical embellishment. To Unitarians, English Gothic architecture hinted strongly at the Red Whore of Babylon, which is to say the diabolical Roman Catholic Church; was it not the Roman Catholic hierarchy that had scattered cathedrals throughout England in the first place? Religious prejudice aside, there are other reasons to be skeptical of Wright's charming tribute to his mother's preemptive architectural strike on his behalf. Several years ago, Edgar Kaufmann, Jr., pointed out in the pages of the *Journal of the Society of Architectural Historians* that the engravings in question were almost certainly published not in *Old England* but in *Harper's Weekly*, sometime between 1878 and 1881. (It was Kaufmann who as an apprentice at Taliesin in the nineteen-thirties introduced his father to Wright and so set in train the designing of the masterly woodland retreat called Fallingwater.) As for the flat oak frames that surround the engraving, Kaufmann asks where Anna could have purchased them—was Wright, he wonders, imposing his taste unconsciously upon his recollections? Kaufmann goes on to speak of "the Wright nursery," but I am fairly confident that such a nursery, like Anna's prenatal ambitions for her son, never existed. Wright was born in a very small house, which cannot have had more than two bedrooms on the second floor and perhaps a single makeshift bedroom on the ground floor; already living in the house at the time of Wright's birth were his father and mother and three children from William Cary Wright's earlier marriage. There was no space available for a pretty little nursery decorated with pictures; baby Frank no doubt occupied a cradle beside his parents' bed, conveniently close to his mother when he needed to be nursed, and there may well have been at least one other child in the room. For a baby to sleep alone in a nursery is an upper-middle-class notion, realized but rarely in America in the nineteenth century; it is characteristic of Wright's uncanny power over us that we are quick to accept his fantasies as fact and challenge them only with reluctance.

Another feat by Wright the hypnotist: his lifelong rhapsodizing over the German educator Friedrich Froebel and the Froebel kindergarten blocks that had, he claimed, such a profound effect on his development as an architect. He often told me (as indeed he told everyone else, with an accompaniment of illustrative gestures) that he could still feel in the palms of his hands the Froebel blocks that his mother had brought home to him as a result of having encountered them—and presumably, along with them, the Froebel principles of child education—at the Philadelphia Exposition of 1876. Their shapes, he said, had become instinctive to him, giving him his first strong perception of the meanings of volume and form. Kaufmann, who knew Wright intimately and who is always more amused by Wright's whoppers than distressed by them, has sought to put the record straight in regard to Froebel, as he has in regard to those wood engravings of English cathedrals. If Anna Wright, a teacher, hadn't heard of Froebel before the Centennial, then she was many years behind hundreds of her countrywomen, teachers and lay persons alike. Kindergartens employing Froebel's principles had been in operation throughout the East and even in Anna's home state of Wisconsin since the eighteen-fifties.

A young apprentice at Taliesin in Wright's late middle age, Kaufmann over the years has succeeded in reversing their roles: he speaks of Wright as a kindly father might speak of an errant son, not to debunk him but to ensure that his beguiling exaggerations be kept in perspective. Gently, Kaufmann notes that most of Froebel's teaching paraphernalia has little relevance to architecture, especially in respect to volume and form, while in respect to function it has no relevance whatever. I will be speaking at greater length in the next chapter of Wright's relationship to Froebel; I mention Froebel here as a participant in one of the small but surely significant mysteries with which Wright chose to surround his mother in the course of exalting her.

One reads the early chapters of the autobiography with mounting suspicion, because they so thoroughly misrepresent the personalities of the mother and father. It is a commonplace of history that great men tend to be what are vulgarly called "mama's boys," but rarely in history has a son devoted himself so sedulously to the celebration of his mother and the derogation, in part by omission, of his father. Freud's apothegm to the effect that no man who has been his mother's favorite knows what it is to fear failure has much biographical evidence to support it, including (as cynics would be eager to point out) the case of Freud himself, who even as a white-haired, world-famous old man was expected week after week to pay a dutiful Sunday call upon his ancient mother, to whom since childhood he had remained *"mein goldener Sigi."* Everyone has heard of Caesar's mother, of Napoleon's mother, of Washington's mother; few have heard of their fathers. In our time, we think of Franklin Delano Roosevelt's mother, who, like Anna Wright, appears to have regarded her son as the consequence of a sort of virgin birth, for which she deserved and took all credit. In words I quoted earlier, Wright said of Anna that she saw her son as "something created out of her own fervor of love and desire." What of William Wright's physiologically indispensable share in that fervor and desire? In the autobiography, no hint.

Wright's parents proved to be singularly ill-matched, though at the time of their wedding the auspices must have seemed favorable. True that the Lloyd Jones family either disapproved of the marriage or claimed to have done so after it broke up, and they had their reasons: for one thing, William Wright was a Baptist and the Lloyd Joneses were ardent Unitarians and, for another, he was forty-one and a widower, with three small children on his hands. Moreover, he had already demonstrated a quite exceptional versatility in respect to occupations and—perhaps more ominously—in places of residence as well. Following the old adage, it might be suspected of him that, being a jack-of-all-trades, he was master of none, and that his incessant peregrinations might have behind them the energy not of success but of failure.

However likely this suspicion may have been, there was no question of William Wright's affectionate nature, his good looks, his charm, his talent for musical composition, his oratorical prowess, and his high intellectual capacity. He had matriculated at Amherst College at the age of fourteen (not so remarkably youthful an age then as it would be today), had dropped out of college, probably for financial reasons, had several times begun and abandoned medical training under doctors who held him in high esteem, and had eventually graduated from Madison College—now Colgate University—in 1849, when he was twenty-four. In 1850, he was teaching music in Utica, New York, and the following year he married one of his pupils, Permelia Holcomb, who lived with her family in the nearby hamlet of Litchfield. The newlyweds soon moved to Hartford, where William's father was an admired preacher and where William read law, being admitted

William Cary Wright and his first wife, Permelia Holcomb. [HR]

to the bar in 1859. By then, the young couple had had two children, the first of whom had died in infancy. Their second child, Charles William, was born in Hartford, in 1856; as if to prove that William's wanderlust was already well established, we learn that their third child, George Irving, was born in Providence, in 1858, and their fourth, Elizabeth Amelia, was born in Belle Plaine, Iowa, in 1860. A year or so later, the little family settled in Lone Rock, Wisconsin, where Wright immediately made a very favorable impression, though without achieving an income sufficient for the family's needs. Permelia took in boarders in order to help out financially, and among these boarders was Anna Lloyd Jones, who was teaching school in Lone Rock.

To Anna, William must have seemed an ideal figure. She longed to better herself in respect to the kinds of cultural activities that were particularly hard to come by in that pioneer setting. Think of encountering, in this village of unpaved, unlighted streets and gross country manners, a brilliant Easterner, college-educated, trained in the law, who composed music, sang, and played half a dozen musical instruments (some of which he fashioned with his own hands). He had moved at ease in the society

One of W. C. Wright's hobbies was the fashioning of musical instruments. A label inside this violin reads, "Gulielmo C. Artigiano (nomme [sic] de plume pour W. C. Wright) id faciebat A.D. 1877 in imitazione Stradivarii Cremonensis 1704." Family tradition holds that the great Norwegian violinist Ole Bull once played this instrument. [EWJ]   Pieces by W. C. Wright, attributed mostly to fictional composers, whose names are playful mistranslations of his own—Wilhelm Kehri for William Cary, etc. [EWJ]

of Hartford, which did not flinch from describing itself as a second Boston. His only defect was his short stature; like all the Lloyd Joneses, Anna was tall and broad-shouldered, obliging her to glance down as if from a manly height upon the diminutive William. When in 1864 Permelia, having given birth to a dead child, herself died two weeks later, of childbed fever, the strong-minded Anna set her cap for William. To have been a boarder in his house gave her certain advantages; in less than two years the erstwhile boarder had become his wife. By then, William, who had been ordained a Baptist minister in Lone Rock in 1863, had been called to serve as the minister of a struggling little Baptist church in Richland Center.

It was a commonplace in the nineteenth century for wives to die young, leaving behind a number of forlorn children; for that reason, the role of stepmother was also a commonplace, to be undertaken as cheerfully as possible. Anna appears to have found the role onerous, especially after the birth of her worshipped Frank. Among Permelia's descendants, there has been handed down evidence of how harshly Anna dealt with her stepchildren—with Charles, who was nine, with poor little George, who at seven or eight was a persistent bed-wetter, and with Elizabeth, who was only five: a pretty, rosy-cheeked, intelligent child, who resembled her mother and was her father's favorite.

In an unpublished account of her life that Elizabeth wrote in old age, she tells of her first encounters with Anna:

> . . . folks said she angled for him; she was very sweet to us children till after they were married. Then she grew worse and worse each year. She had a terrible temper and seemed to make no effort to control it. She vented it upon me mostly, because she was jealous of Father's affection for me, and the boys could keep out of her sight, but she wouldn't allow me to. As I grew older, she used to tell me that she hated me and all my Mother's people. All my early life, I was always told what a sweet and lovely girl and woman my own Mother had been and how everyone loved her, what a beautiful character she had, and how they hoped I would grow up to be like her. So the contrast must have been pretty hard for Father. . . . While we lived in McGregor [after the birth of her half-brother Frank] . . . she not only beat me till I was black and blue all over but threatened me with some terrible things, and especially if I should tell my father about her treatment. I had no wish to make him any more trouble than he had already, so I kept things to myself. . . .[3]

It appears that Anna was already in a perilous mental state at the time of her marriage (though the Lloyd Joneses would admit only that she had "a most tremendous temper") and that her conduct grew steadily more alarming under the pressure of a domestic setting more impoverished and physically more exhausting than she had expected. Fearing for the children's safety, Permelia's mother eventually arranged for them to be farmed out to various Holcomb relatives and so they grew up at a great distance from their father. Over the years, he did his best to keep in touch with them; they were his first family, the fruit of a loving marriage, and in his late years he rejoiced to be cared for by them. For Anna, they ceased to exist; as for Frank, apparently he made no effort in adult life to establish contact with his father and made little effort to establish contact with his half-brothers and half-sister and with their children and grandchildren. In middle age, Elizabeth Wright was invited by Jane Porter to visit Spring Green; she met Frank on that occasion and he invited her to attend a lecture that he would be giving that evening. She appears to have declined the invitation.

Left, FLW's younger sister, Margaret Ellen, whose name was shortened first to Maggie Nell and then to Maginel. [HR] *Right, FLW's half-sister, Elizabeth Wright, as a school-girl.* [HR]

Nine years after Jane's birth, Anna bore a third child, Margaret Ellen, whose double-barreled name was quickly reduced to the affectionate diminutive Maggie Nell and then to Maginel. The year was 1878; arriving so long after Frank and Jane, Maginel was a fragile infant, for many years in peril of her life; she was almost certainly an unlooked-for addition to the family, for during this period Anna was treating her husband with open contempt and in a few years would be announcing that she hated the ground he walked on and would no longer consent to have sexual relations with him.

William Wright and his daughters were left in no doubt that the son was the mother's favorite; Frank himself accepted his position as the be-all and end-all of her life with understandable satisfaction. For her sake, he would be as much a Lloyd Jones and as little a Wright as possible. He was often to quote with pride the Lloyd Jones's family motto, "Truth against the world," without noticing its intrinsic fatuity. Mottoes are not composed under oath, but for a family to see itself as the embodiment of some grandly undefined truth that pits itself against the entire world implies arrogance on a colossal scale. A motto more appropriate to Wright as he was growing up would have been, "Me Against the World With Mother Always Right Beside Me." His autobiography reveals clearly enough that Mother ruled his days and nights with unusual strictness, but it is Father who is recorded as being too hard on him, rapping his knuckles when he strikes a wrong note on the piano and forcing him, at the age of seven, to pump a church organ until, weeping bitterly, he all but faints from fatigue. When the father finally breaks off his organ-playing and observes his son's suffering, he takes him by the hand and leads him home without speaking a word. The autobiography continues:

> When they got there, his mother, seeing the state the boy was in, looked reproachfully at the father.
> It was always so. The differences between husband and wife all seemed to arise over that boy. Mother always on the defensive, father taking the offensive.
> So the lad grew, afraid of his father.[4]

Plainly, "that boy" feels something akin to pleasure instead of pain at being the cause of friction between his parents. He is grateful to have his mother as a protectress; rather grudgingly, he goes on to say that he was proud of his father, in part because "everybody listened and seemed happy when father talked" and in part because his father taught him "to see a symphony as an edifice—of sound!" (William Wright may have been paraphrasing for his son's benefit Browning's then newly written poem, "Rabbi Ben Ezra," in which the relationship between music and architecture is explored.) Wright wrote in his autobiography that music was his father's friend "when all else had failed," and it is this image of William Wright as a failure, dolefully comforting himself at the piano because the world at large has rebuffed him is one that has been generally accepted as accurate. I take a contrary view. From conversations with a number of his descendants, I get the impression that William Wright, though in age he spoke of having been unlucky, was far from being a failure, either in his own eyes or in the eyes of friends and relatives, with the predictable exception of Anna Wright and her defenders.

By an irony, the charm, the playful wit, and the evangelical eloquence of Frank Lloyd Wright, along with his short stature, physical grace, and fine-boned facial features, were inherited from his father; so were his eupeptic disposition, his gregariousness, and his disregard for the practical side of life—a disregard that was often a reason for distress to members of the households of both father and son but that appears to have cost them scarcely a moment of regret or remorse. Temperamentally and physically, the two were very alike, and Anna Wright's awareness of this resemblance must have caused her many a rueful shake of the head: no matter how vehemently she pressed her claim to a total possession of Frank, genetically he was a Wright and not a Lloyd Jones.

When William Wright was born, in January, 1825, Jefferson was still alive and a number of people among whom William grew up had once been subjects of King George III. Members of his family had been settled in New England since early in the seventeenth century and were often mentioned in local histories as being among the leaders of their respective communities. William belonged to a generation that saw the opening up of the West on a prodigious scale; he was one of the comparatively small group who accepted the opportunity to pioneer not as a means of growing rich but as a means of serving his fellow men, in occupations—teaching and preaching—that would almost certainly guarantee him a lifetime of genteel poverty. Not everyone in the period of national corruption following the Civil War sought to participate in the gaudy nights and days of the Gilded Age; the accumulation of wealth by whatever means had not yet been certified to be the American Dream, and William Wright gave no sign of bitterness at being obliged to go on working hard into his late seventies.

William Wright's dissatisfaction with careers in medicine and the law is evidence not of failure but of idealism. Medicine struck him as being closer to witchcraft than to science, and the law seemed to pit the rich successfully against the poor; his intention was to inspire people, to lead them away from evil and toward good, as so many of his preacher-ancestors had done before him. He attempted this feat first as a Baptist and afterward as a Unitarian; having preached hundreds of sermons upon such texts as "The Nature of True Religion" and "What Must I Do to Be Saved?", in his sixties he drifted away from the pulpit and into the full-time teaching of music. Still optimistic and full of energy, he became Director of the Central Conservatory of Music, in Stromsburg, Nebraska; he left this position only because of financial reverses suffered by his employer, as the following encomium reveals:

Professor William C. Wright, A.M., was connected with our school for three years . . . and it is with great pleasure that I testify to his nobility of life and efficiency of work. Prof. Wright is a man of unusually broad education and a master in his special profession. He brings to his work the freshness of youth, the force and learning of a philosopher, and the experience of a veteran. As a piano and vocal trainer and skillful instructor of singing classes his equal would be difficult to find east or west. His ability, energy, and fidelity while at this place brought constantly increasing prosperity to his work, which was terminated directly and solely by a long continued drouth. It was with great regret that I saw his connection with our school severed and I cheerfully recommend him to the confidence and favor of the public.[5]

In his last years, William Wright presided over an establishment in Des Moines, Iowa, proudly bearing his name: Wright's School of Music and Oratory. He died of a stroke in June, 1904, in Jeannette, a small town near Pittsburgh, at the home of his son Charles. By that time, he had lived in upwards of twenty towns in seven states; again and again, we read in the local newspapers of the welcome he received upon arriving in one or another of these communities and the universal regret felt by the community upon his departure. Wherever he went, he was much loved and much admired; over eighty years after his death, there are families

William Cary Wright entertaining a granddaughter. [DB]

in the Middle West that still speak fondly of him, recalling the pleasure he gave them by his visits. To them and to his first family, he was a musical genius, and Frank Lloyd Wright was of but little consequence beside him.

William Wright never lost interest in his second set of children and did his best to follow their careers without Anna Wright's knowledge. He visited the World's Fair in Chicago, in 1893, where the gorgeous Transportation Building would surely have caught his eye; Adler & Sullivan were the architects, but William's son Frank was Sullivan's "pencil" at the time, and it would be pleasant to think that William was aware of the fact. All that we know for certain is that in some jottings of a somewhat later period William Wright wrote, "Frank is an architect—gets a good income and spends it fast."[6] He then lists with care the names and birth-years of the four children that Frank had fathered up to that time and that he was never to be permitted to see. It appears that he corresponded occasionally with his daughter Jane, and it was she to whom his son George Wright is likely to have sent word of their father's death. William Wright's body was brought to Lone Rock, Wisconsin, to be buried beside that of his first wife, Permelia. Lone Rock is only a few miles north of the Lloyd Jones cluster of farms at Hillside, which Frank enjoyed running up from Oak Park to visit; he was often at Hillside during that summer of 1904 and could easily have attended his father's burial service, but there is no evidence that he did so. (The week William Wright was buried, Anna Wright and daughter Jane were reported in the local press to be attending social events in and around Spring Green.) In his will, William Wright

Left, Brown Church Cemetery in Bear Valley, near Lone Rock, Wisconsin. [DB] *Right, The beloved music-master, as natty a dresser as his son.* [EWJ]

took pains to be as fair as possible to both his families, ordering the assets of his small estate to be divided equally among his six children. Many years later—once in the nineteen-twenties, shortly after Anna Wright's death, and once in the forties—Frank drove to Lone Rock to visit his father's grave. Whatever his thoughts may have been on the first of those occasions (perhaps a sense of disloyalty to his mother? a reluctance to deal with her as harshly as she deserved?), he was perversely unwilling to come to terms with the truth. Though by then he must have been well aware of the nature of his parents' marriage, in the autobiography that he was soon to begin writing he would give the world his mother's false version of the events that led to its dissolution.

From our late twentieth-century point of view, William Wright's zigzag journey through life smacks of eccentricity, but it would not have been thought to be especially eccentric by his contemporary Mark Twain, who moved in and out of almost as many towns as Wright did. An admirer of Emerson, Thoreau, and Whitman, William Wright dared to espouse the practice of individual self-fulfillment that all three writers constantly urged upon their readers (taking care, for their part, to remain more or less conventional-seeming homebodies. From the snug recesses of the Old Manse, "Give all to love!" Emerson cried, doing no such thing.). In a long lifetime, William Wright made but a single irremediable error—that of consenting to marry the ambitious, half-mad, sexually cold, and drearily self-righteous Anna Lloyd Jones.

3

IN HIS AUTOBIOGRAPHY, Frank Lloyd Wright sings the praises of his mother in terms that could be almost as fittingly applied to one or another of her many stalwart brothers. We are told of her that she was tall and handsome, that she was a willing worker, that she walked with a free stride like a man, and that much fire gave her temper beneath her self-possession. As a young teacher, she rode horseback over the hills of Spring Green and its adjacent villages. In rainy weather she wore a blue soldier's cape with brass buttons and a hood; otherwise, she went about bareheaded. She never wore corsets and she avoided bright colors in her dress. According to Wright, Anna used to say that Nature's most precious gift to mortals was a beautiful head of hair. Throughout their lifetimes, mother and son devoted a good deal of attention to their hair; Wright always wore his hair unusually long, whether long hair was in fashion or out.

Much that we read in the autobiography in praise of Anna has its source in the son's choosing the mother's side against the father's, but there is far more to the matter than that; Wright's fictions in her behalf are at least partially in expiation of his own treatment of her, which was much less kindly in fact than he pretends it was. She was a pious, cold-blooded disciplinarian, who sought to keep Frank bound forever to her apron strings, and since he was temperamentally a Wright and not a Lloyd Jones her constant reiteration of the importance of the conventional virtues, as espoused by her, must have proved extremely irksome to him; when he could stand her garrulous nagging no longer and ran off to seek his fortune and his freedom in Chicago, she pelted him with daily letters of rebuke and exhortation.

What Wright has not told us about Anna has come down to us in the form of what historians call oral tradition, which is what lay people call family gossip. Generations of Wrights have reported that Anna at twenty-seven felt, as most Victorian women did, a dread of failing to find a husband, of failing to have children. Moreover, she is reputed to have grown tired of the drudgery of teaching. In Permelia Wright's lifetime, she had been a boarder in the Wrights' house; after Permelia's death, either William asked her to return to the house to serve as a sort of nurse-governess to his children or she volunteered to do so. Nothing that we know of Anna would lead us to suspect her of being a temptress; nevertheless, it is the case that she proved sufficiently seductive or sufficiently useful to the household for a marriage to take place—one that the Wright family has always described as a marriage of convenience. In the divorce proceedings, William asserted that the marriage had been unhappy from its beginning, in part because his wife had been jealous of his children by Permelia. One surmises that another difficulty was that Anna, though she longed for children, found distasteful the means by which they were produced; she resisted carrying out what were then discreetly referred to as "wifely duties."

With characteristic good cheer, William, answering a call to a Baptist church in Pawtucket, Rhode Island, moved his little family east. There they occupied a house with a big basement kitchen, where the family took its meals. Water was pumped by hand to the kitchen sink from a cistern dug in the earth beneath the kitchen floor, and it was in the kitchen that Elizabeth suffered a further misadventure at the hands of her stepmother:

I remember one time in the winter when Mother was in one of her tantrums, she got mad about something and as usual vented it on me; she jumped up and down and pumped water as fast as she could and threw it over me and yelled with every jump. Father had his study on the third floor but he heard the racket and came down to see what was up. He told me to go upstairs but I was afraid to go past her to the stairway and my clothes were dripping wet, but I slipped out the front door and went around to the back and up the outside stairs. My clothes froze on me before I could get in the house.

One other time when he was at home and up in his study, she was frying meat at the stove with a long two-tined fork that goes with a carving set. She got at me for something or nothing and grabbed me by the hair and held my head back and jabbed that fork at my face and said she would put my eyes out. I screamed, "Papa!" with all my might and he came running down and stopped her, but I had the worst fright of my life. . . . I think those were the only two times when Father was home. . . . I remember one time she was pounding beefsteak with a heavy hardwood roller with sharp ridges all over it, made for the purpose, and she pounded me all over my back with it until I was black and blue and sore, but not bleeding. I suppose those things relieved her feelings, but they certainly didn't relieve mine any. . . . I never could please her, no matter how hard I tried. She admitted sometimes that she hated me and all my mother's relatives; she said she would like to have all our heads laid over a log and take an ax and chop them off. I do not know whether her mind was just right or not. She seemed to have periodical spells when she got "mad hysterics" and raved like a maniac. Then she would be sick in bed for a day or two and I would have peace.[1]

William Wright arranged for Elizabeth to be taken in by relatives, with whom she spent several years; meanwhile, he received still another call, to a Baptist church in Weymouth, Massachusetts. Wright's autobiography omits the Pawtucket period entirely, making the years in Weymouth his first experience in the East. This omission allows him to exclude any reference to Elizabeth's sufferings, of which he cannot have failed to be a witness. Nowhere in the autobiography is there the slightest hint of his mother's mental condition, which may well have been one of the reasons that William Wright was so often on the move. For eighteen years, Frank was a constant observer of his mother's fits of madness—including physical attacks not only upon Elizabeth but upon his father as well—and of her subsequent fits of remorse (she sometimes cried out pitifully to be placed in an asylum); all of this aspect of her nature is suppressed in the course of his inventing a saintly mother bent upon the nurture of a genius.

Weymouth in the eighteen-seventies was a prosperous suburb of Boston; as a minister's son, Frank was entitled to attend a private school there, which he remembered as snobbish and peopled by Little Lord Fauntleroys. As for Anna, whatever her relations with William may have been at the time, she was grateful to find herself within reach of Boston, which was then indisputably the intellectual center of the country. If the Wrights were poor (and it was no disgrace for a minister's family to be poor), she was nevertheless able to buy the latest books, which she mailed to her teacher-sisters in Spring Green, and to attend lectures and concerts. In 1876, the family undertook a holiday journey to Philadelphia, to visit the Centennial Exposition being held there; according to the autobiography, it was in the course of this visit that Anna is supposed to have encountered for the first time the charming educational toys invented by Friedrich Froebel and immediately upon the family's return to Boston purchased a set of them.

As we have seen, Edgar Kaufmann, Jr., has effectively demonstrated that Anna Wright would have had to be unusually ill-read not to have encountered word of Froebel many years before the Centennial Exposition. In fact, she was unusually well-read; her embrace of Froebel principles that had long been familiar to her may have had more to do with the quality of teaching that her children encountered in Weymouth than with any purported discovery of these principles. Friedrich Froebel was a German teacher and theorist who early in the nineteenth century originated the term "kindergarten" and who devised a system of preliminary schooling

Left, Anna Lloyd Jones Wright at Weymouth, near Boston, enjoying with a certain grimness the fruits of Eastern culture. Right, FLW as a schoolboy, coolly distancing himself from his fellow Lord Fauntleroys. [AU]

that was intended to encourage children to learn through natural play. Though Frank at nine and his sister Jane at seven were well beyond the usual kindergarten age, they took with delight to the Froebel method.

From the autobiography, I excerpt a passage worth calling attention to not only for the information that it contains but also as an example of Wright's highly individual writing style—impressionistic, non-grammatical, and oracular. The many exclamation points hint that the words preceding them will prove more effective if spoken rather than read, which leads one to suspect that the words were dictated by Wright and not written by him. Several stenographers having been employed at different times, differing degrees of skill are manifested in setting down the typed drafts that Wright would look over, seemingly in haste, and then expand upon. The method invites howlers, which exist in profusion. Many gross errors in the 1932 version appear uncorrected in the 1943 version—for example, the British organization known in its early days as "The National Trust for Places of Historic Interest and Natural Beauty" becomes "The Natural Trust for Planes of Historic Interest," etc., etc. The book was accumulated in bits and pieces over a considerable period of time; as one might expect, the earliest passages, like this one on the Froebel "gifts" (as the Froebel play materials were called) are the most lyrical and are neither more nor less reliable than any of the later passages:

The strips of colored paper, glazed and "matt," remarkably soft brilliant colors. Now came the geometric by-play of those charming checkered color combinations! The structural figures to be made with peas and small straight sticks: slender constructions, the joinings accented by the little pea-green globes. The smooth shapely maple blocks with which to build, the sense of which never afterward leaves the fingers: *form* becomes *feeling*. The box had a mast to set up on it, on which to hang the maple cubes and spheres and triangles, revolving them to discover subordinate forms.

And the exciting cardboard shapes with pure scarlet face—such scarlet! Smooth triangular shapes, white-back and edges, cut into rhomboids with which to make designs on the flat table top. What shapes they made naturally if only one would let them!

A small interior world of color and form now came within the grasp of small fingers. Color and pattern, in the flat, in the round. Shapes that lay hidden behind the appearances all about.

Here was something for invention to seize, and use to create. These "Gifts" came into the gray house in drab old Weymouth and made something there that had never lived there before. Mother would go to Boston, take lessons of a teacher of the Froebel method and come home to teach the children. When her housework was done mother and the two children would sit at a low mahogany table with polished top, working with these "Gifts."

Fra Angelico's bright-robed angels, some in red, some in blue, others in green; and one—the liveliest of all—in yellow, would come and hover over the table. From their golden harps simple rhythms were gently falling on child minds like flying seeds carried on the wings of the wind to fertile ground. Giotto standing in the shadow at the mother's elbow would have worn a smile beneath his Florentine cap; musing smile prophetic of seed-time and harvest other than his but eternally the same. Again—architecture.[2]

What a curious non-sequitur the phrase "Again—architecture" is! Wright's highfalutin rhetoric is applicable to painting and indirectly to interior design and decoration but is remote indeed from architecture.

The fact that Wright spoke repeatedly in age of Froebel's influence offers a possible explanation for the presence in the late work of so many fairy-tale–like shapes—shapes that may have come drifting up out of the depths of his unconscious, where they had lain largely undisturbed since those hours spent around the mahogany table in Weymouth. If, as is well known, the nightmares of childhood return to haunt the sleep of the old, should not the fantasies of childhood return to give the old a waking pleasure? The many-colored forms that enchanted the innocent Wright are especially conspicuous in those unbuilt projects of the nineteen-fifties that appear destined for some benign Cloud-Cuckoo-land—the Arizona

State Capitol Project and the Baghdad Cultural Center. I may be pressing the point too hard (something Wright himself would never have hesitated to do), but is it not perhaps significant that many of the renderings of projects commissioned in Wright's old age show the projects as they would look by night instead of by day? They are beautiful simply as drawings; they may also be instructive in regard to the sources of Wright's inspiration on the threshold of his tenth decade; though executed in the middle of the twentieth century, they put us in mind of nineteenth-century magic-lantern shows, which Frank as a child would have been captivated by. Geniuses have a more tenacious hold on youth than ordinary mortals do; as Henry James says, we are all young to life, but it is geniuses who find it possible to remain creatively playful up to the moment of death.

Certain events that took place at about the time young Frank was experimenting with his Froebel blocks and that he recounted in the 1932 version of the autobiography were omitted from the version that was published eleven years later. One of the passages concerned a comic experiment with smoking, conducted by Wright and a neighbor's boy, Allan Hunt:

> Son of a petted, languid, aristocratic mother and a wealthy father who smoked big, black cigars, it was Allan's ambition to smoke them too. In the glass cupola of the Hunt house "learning" began and how long it lasted is out of memory. But the leaden, sunken sense of the scene, and all connected with it, remains. The novice slid backward down the attic stair believing himself dying, a trail of interior decoration all the way down, to go with the work of the capable inferior desecrators who had just finished the setting for this debacle.
>
> Got the front door open, crawling along the sidewalk he got up the steps to the minister's house. Managed to pull the bell. The sight that mother saw may be imagined.[3]

Wright plainly enjoyed telling this Twain-like story, so careless in its grammar that it must bear a close resemblance to a number of earlier oral versions and was certainly dictated and then ill transcribed. I find it hard to understand why he would elect to drop it, unless it was at Olgivanna's urging. Wright gave her credit for having encouraged him to begin his autobiography, and with her European upbringing she may have felt entitled to protest some of its native American vulgarities, which would probably include any reference to vomit. ("Inferior desecrators" was, by the way, a cherished pun of Wright's, which he used far too often, but which is expressive of his lifelong antagonism to interior decorators.)

Another passage may have been dropped from the autobiography because it tended to give away the fact that he was two years older than in middle age he claimed to be; the passage had to do with the first stirrings of an interest in girls, more appropriate to a nine-year-old than to a seven-year-old:

> At this time the mystery that was "girls" began to intrigue a lively imagination. There was something mysterious, between himself and the mystery. But he was so shy he never dared speak to a girl for fear of spoiling that something.[4]

In a passage published in approximately the same form in both versions of the autobiography, Wright's usual headlong prose is brought to a stumbling halt by an unexpected display of Victorian reticence, couched in polysyllabic latinisms; the subject is sex:

> Let the delicate psychology of biological unfoldings in boys under eleven, important, but so much the same, stand as on record by able artists with a taste for psychological anatomy. In public schools the susceptible little animals encounter and learn things that mothers promptly try to make their boys unlearn and protect them from. So well was this done with him that until marriage in his twenty-first year, personal biological experience was exactly nothing at all, left probably too innocent for his own self-guidance.[5]

Translation: "Thanks to my mother's constant surveillance, I remained a virgin until I was married and I would have been far better off if I hadn't remained one."

The mother who kept Wright sexually prim was at the same time on her guard lest he become a sissy. She feared that her son dwelt "too much in the imaginative life of the mind." He preferred reading to playing with other boys and he would rather listen to music, draw, and "make things" than sleep. Above all, he liked to dream, shut away in a world of his own devising, and the hovering mother saw, according to Wright, "which way her man-child was going. She was wise and decided to change it. And change it she did."[6]

On the surface, these words seem intended to introduce the fact that, in order to make sure that her man-child prove manly, Anna asked her brothers to let Frank spend his summers in arduous labor on the family farm in Hillside; beneath the surface, the words hint at the fact that by early in 1878 the William Wrights were again on the move. William gave up his Baptist berth in Weymouth (to the accompaniment of the usual heartfelt expressions of regret by members of the community), switched his allegiance from Baptist to Unitarian—a sop to Anna and her family?—and purchased in Madison, Wisconsin, a modest house having the advantage for the children of a big open lot running down to the shore of Lake Mendota.

W. C. Wright (extreme left, rear row) in a late reunion with his brothers and sisters. All tiny folk, like their minister-father; when he preached, he was often obliged to stand outside a pulpit in order to be seen by the congregation. [EWJ]

The Lloyd Jones family was now readily accessible, thanks to the trains running between Madison and Spring Green. Her brother James drove a horse and wagon the forty miles between Hillside and Madison with a cow hitched on behind the wagon, to provide the Wright children with plenty of fresh milk. Weeping, Anna cut off Frank's golden curls and entrusted him to Uncle James: one of those brawny, bearded Lloyd Jones giants beside whom William Cary Wright appeared almost dwarfish—men whose size induced in Frank a lifelong self-consciousness in respect to his stature. (In maturity, he claimed to be five feet, eight and a half inches tall, but in reality he was probably closer to five feet, six or seven inches tall—he wore built-up heels on his shoes and carried himself so superbly that even at ninety he gave the impression of being far taller than he was.)

Writing in middle age of his summers on the James Lloyd Jones farm, Frank struck a lyrical, nostalgic note, very much in the mode practiced so compulsively by Louis Sullivan in *The Autobiography of an Idea.* It was a note that bore little relationship to the revulsion that Frank had actually felt as a child in regard to the experiences to which those summers repeatedly exposed him—experiences that he chose to run away from several times, always in vain. As we read, we perceive an unbridgeable gap opening between the beauties of nature as he summons them up in a Whitmanesque chant and the ugliness of the daily tasks that he recalls having been obliged to perform. Alarmed by what she took to be the rather girlish delicacy of her son's preoccupations, the mother had sought to strengthen and harden his body and mind by the sort of labor that had strengthened and hardened the bodies and minds of her five brothers. Wright pretends to be grateful for having undergone the mindless drudgery of farming, but in truth he remained a wary outsider, eager to leave Adam's delving to others.

Every morning at four Frank is roused by his Uncle James and led out to the barn to help with the milking: "The strange smells sickened him, but he dutifully began milking as shown, until his hands ached."[7] Back and forth the author goes between pleasure and pain, now celebrating the richness of nature ("he went through the moist woods that in their shade were treasuring the rainfall for the sloping fields below"[8]), now spelling out his distaste for "adding tired to tired and adding it again." When the hired man at breakfast poured sorghum over his pork fat, the sight took Frank's appetite away. Feeding the calves with his Aunt Laura was "a nasty business." Chopping the heads off superfluous roosters, slitting the throats of hogs, gaining a headful of lice from hens, scrubbing manure off the cow's slimy udders before milking—it was all disgusting to Frank, fastidious son on his father's side of generations of city-bred, college-educated preachers. Many years later, he summed up his view of farm life in a conversation with Edgar Tafel, then an apprentice at Taliesin. "It's all pulling tits and shoveling shit," Wright said—a sentence that Olgivanna would never have permitted to appear in the autobiography and that Tafel himself, thirty years later, was unable to persuade the publisher of his delightful volume of reminiscences to print.

And yet it was country life—that country life at Taliesin of open fields and starlit skies glimpsed from comfortable terraces, of summer storms observed from within the shelter of a vast, sturdy house, of long icicles dangling in winter from the broad eaves of many roofs, while fires roared on a dozen stone hearths—that Wright came to cherish as his ideal after a hasty, disorderly retreat, at forty, from the city and suburbs. The country life of sweat, manure, lice, and physical exhaustion shrank in importance as what had once been half a dozen Lloyd Jones farms became, over the years, a single grand country estate, a small part of which was a working farm that existed to supply food for the great house and its many occupants. The master of Taliesin was inspired to sing of pastoral joys because the labor required to create them was being carried out by others—not least the apprentices in the Fellowship. By that time, his were the pleasures of the grandee: riding horseback, driving fast cars, entertaining international notables. If it amused him to try his hand at some of the farm implements employed by the Fellowship, it was because farm implements, especially when they are new and brightly colored, amount to toys in the eyes of adult males. Wright in age especially liked steering a big steel scraper

The fiercely bearded, fiercely fertile Lloyd Jones clan, gathered in Spring Green at the farm of the patriarch Richard Lloyd Jones (with white beard and cane). In the back row, Anna Lloyd Jones Wright stands to the left of her diminutive husband. In front of them is their daughter Jane; seated at Jane's left is FLW, with Maginel on his knee. [HS]

over the gravelly back roads of Taliesin, not so much in order to accomplish anything of value as to provide a visible sign of his close ties with the Fellowship. In a long lifetime, Wright put on and discarded many masks; that of a dedicated manual laborer would be sure to rank among the least plausible.

For some five years, the William Wright family made a practice of spending the summers at Hillside with the Lloyd Joneses—nicknamed by their neighbors "the God-Almighty Joneses" because of the air of self-congratulatory distinction with which they presided over the countryside— and spending the winters in Madison. Relations between husband and wife were worsening throughout the period. Elizabeth, now in her teens, had rejoined the family and was attending high school in Madison. "I liked school very much and my teachers, as usual," she wrote in her memoirs, "but did not enjoy my stepmother nor my half-brother, Frank, who was his mother's idol and badly spoiled by her."[9] How much young Frank took in of the progressive breakup of his parents' marriage we cannot know, because his autobiography at this juncture is a feat of calculated misrepresentation. The likelihood is that he knew a great deal, but most of what he knew would have run counter to a major fiction that his mother was preparing and that he embraced, in his published recollections, as the truth:

> By now, family life was not so well at the small town house by the blue lake. There was no longer much agreement between father and mother.
>
> The father on this eve of the entrance of his son into the university was himself deep in learning to write Sanskrit. Mother for some years had been ailing. Poverty pinched. . . .
>
> The lad was his mother's adoration. She lived much in him. Probably that didn't help either.
>
> For some disobedience about this time [Frank was sixteen], the father undertook to thrash the young man. It had happened in the stable and the young rebel got his father down on the floor, held him there until his father promised to let him alone. He had grown too big for that sort of thing. "Father ought to realize it," said the boy, as he went into the home, white, shamed, and shaken, to tell his mother.
>
> The youth hardly had known himself as his father's son. All had gone well enough on the surface that was now broken. The son had sympathy for his talented father as well as admiration. Something of that vain struggle of superior talents with untoward circumstance that was his father's got to him, and he was touched by it—never knowing how to show Father. Something—you see—had never been established that was needed to make them father and son. Perhaps the father never loved the son at any time.[10]

For a son to suggest that his father never loved him is sufficiently extraordinary; still more extraordinary is the fact that Wright offers this suggestion not once but several times. Plainly, the purpose is to account for his having chosen to side with one parent against the other, and since the mother's account of the failure of the marriage consists mainly of lies, Frank must justify his implicit endorsement of these lies with a damning accusation against his father. Still, his unease is readily detectable; he closes the paragraph cited above with the statement, "Memories would haunt the youth as they haunt the man." And these memories were all the more haunting because, at the time of composing the autobiography, both mother and father were dead; there was no longer any need to deny the truth about his relationship to his mother, which, throughout most of their lives was continuously adversarial. If he was a "mama's boy," he was one who fought Mama at almost every opportunity. She irritated him beyond endurance with her suffocating pieties, and once he had made good his early escape from her—one that she struggled hard to prevent—his irritation turned little by little into impatient boredom. For twenty years, she lived in a house in Oak Park next to him and his wife, quarreling with them and intimidating their children; no word of that in the autobiography. In the course of designing and supervising the construction of the Imperial Hotel, in Tokyo, Wright fell seriously ill and his mother insisted on journeying across the Pacific to help nurse him back to health, to the displeasure of his then mistress, Miriam Noel; only a hasty reference to that in the autobiography. The duty of caring for his mother in her tiresome, complaining old age he left to others, especially to his sister Jane and her family. When she died, in February, 1923, Frank, his Japanese adventure at an end, was again a resident of this country, but he appears not to have taken the trouble to attend her funeral.

4

ONE OF THE MAJOR inventions of the autobiography is to be found in the pages dealing with the William Wrights' divorce, which took place in 1885. Frank writes that his mother one day said to his father, "Well, Mr. Wright, leave us. I will manage with the children. Go your way,"[1] upon which the father vanished and was never seen again by his wife or children. The truth was more complex and more painful, as Frank well knew. Again, we have the valiant Elizabeth Wright bearing witness; in late 1881, she had come back to the little house in Madison in order for her father to preside over her marriage to John Heller. William Wright spent a subsequent Thanksgiving with the young couple and with his son George in Omaha and he confessed to them that his relations with Anna were growing steadily worse. Elizabeth wrote in her autobiography, "John said it was bad enough to run the risk of hell in the next world without living in hell in this one, and George gave him a lot of advice. He told him to come out and practice law with him. . . . And so it came about that finally Father fixed things up and gave Mother the home in Madison, which was very nice, and near the lake, and got a divorce and left the three children with her. He started out for himself with nothing but his violins and a few other things, including the old mahogany bookcase or secretary as we used to call it."[2]

Reluctantly because of the children but weary under the weight of eighteen years of domestic misery, in 1884 William Wright brought a divorce action against Anna, on the grounds of her having willfully deserted him. When the case of Wright versus Wright reached court, William's sworn statement provided ample evidence of Anna's misconduct:

> Since my marriage to my second wife, I have treated her kindly and so far as I know have performed my marriage vows. I have provided for her as well as my means would permit; during the last two or three years, she has had the handling of the largest share of my income.
>
> About three years ago . . . she refused to occupy the same bed with

me. I have since then repeatedly solicited her to occupy the same room and bed with me. Since she left me as stated she has not occupied a bed with me and for the two years last past she has not occupied the same room with me at night. . . . She sometimes said she did not love me and sometimes she said she hated me. . . . Her language during the last three years has not been kind and I do not know of any kind word or expression that she has used toward me during the past three years. Her conduct and temper toward me is ungovernable. . . .

When after suffering violence, indignity, and abuse for years, I was represented as being the prime offender I could endure it no longer. . . . I had the suit brought for desertion, believing it could be maintained on that ground. There was other neglect and abandonment of her duties as a wife. . . . A larger part of my mending I did myself or carried away because when I requested her to do anything it was often neglected, never cheerfully done, and when it was done, often thrown in my face or on the floor. The room that I slept in was the coldest room in the house. . . .[3]

In his deposition, Wright admitted that he had once inquired confidentially of Anna's brothers whether there was a history of insanity in the family. The brothers had indignantly denied that possibility; word of his inquiry had got back to Anna and had made William's life still more intolerable. (Being far bigger than Wright, she was not beyond beating him up on occasion.) Wright testified that their married life had been unhappy from the start; that Anna had always been jealous of his three children by Permelia; that he had had to send the children away as soon as possible after the wedding; and that Anna's brothers had agreed with him that the marriage must be brought to an end.

Acting on the advice of her brothers, Anna did not contest the divorce. She received custody of the children and possession of the house and most of its contents. This sorry tale of marital discord, as conventionally grim after a hundred years as if it had been plucked from a present-day soap opera, is important to history not so much because of the light it throws upon William and Anna as because of the light that it throws upon Frank, both at the time of the divorce and at the time that he was recounting the episode in his late fifties. It has been assumed by many readers of the autobiography that, taking his mother's side, he believed her version of the events that occurred at this critical juncture in the life of the Wright family, but of course he didn't believe it at all—as an especially intelligent and sensitive teen-ager, how could he have failed to observe and respond to every sickening detail of what was going on?

Other readers of the autobiography have assumed that Frank, having been bound to know the truth, deliberately concealed it out of loyalty to the mother. On the contrary, I believe that he was indignant with both parents for the suffering that they caused him to undergo during the

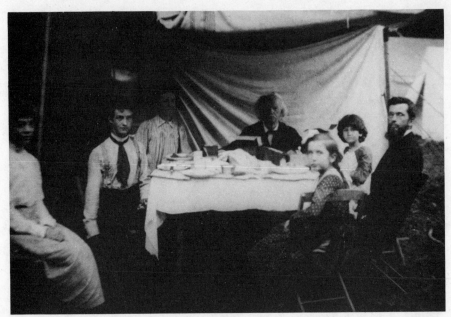

W. C. Wright at a picnic with his son George and George's family. Trained as a lawyer, George later entered the ministry, as his father and a dozen or so other ancestors had done before him. [EWJ]

difficult years of his adolescence, and that it was this indignation that he found it necessary to conceal in his autobiography, not for his mother's sake but for his own. Though he would never afterward admit it, for many years he was struggling harder against his mother than against his father; the falsehoods that he heaped up in respect to Anna's relationship to the divorce were a match for the falsehoods that he heaped up in respect to her desire for him to become a great architect: they were a means for him, in middle age, to expiate the guilt he had felt as a young man in having ruthlessly outwitted her in the succession of tyrannies that she attempted to impose on him. Doting upon him from birth, she had soon enough become not his ally but his adversary; at every turn of his adolescence and early manhood, she sought to force upon him the fate of being her protector, her support spiritual and material, and in every sense except the sexual her indispensable consort.

If this hypothesis is correct, then the passages in the autobiography that describe the immediate aftermath of the divorce amount to a smoke screen of intentionally unanswerable questions, behind whose stridency something of importance may be seen to be going on; to wit, a preliminary, indirect defense against the social ostracism that he himself would be faced with when, many years later, he set about dissolving his own marriage ties. Reading of one situation, we anticipate another:

So the boy himself, supersensitive, soon became aware of "disgrace." His mother was a "divorced woman." His faith in her goodness and rightness did not waver. Therefore there was injustice to her. Did this injustice to her serve some social purpose?

The wondering resentment grew in him. It became a subconscious sense of false judgement entered against himself, his sisters Jennie and Maginel, innocent of all wrong-doing. His mother's unhappiness—was it a social crime? Why must she, as well as they, be punished? Just what had they all done?

He never got the heavy thing straight, and just accepted it as one more handicap—grew more sensitive and shy than ever. And he began to be distrustful—of what he could not have told you then.[4]

Confronting the eighteen-year-old Frank, we confront as well a puzzle that he himself has hitherto glanced at and then peremptorily thrust aside—the question of his education, or, rather, of his astonishing lack of one. Again and again, he protests that he has no recollection of what he was supposed to have learned in elementary school and high school. Such records as exist indicate that he did badly; despite his high intelligence and the tradition on both sides of the family that education was a virtue akin to godliness, he earned low grades and was a recurrent dropout. At the same time, he must have been reading voraciously. Adolescence is a time when many of us ransack books as we will never have the time or the inclination to do again, and Wright was no exception to this practice; in his adult years, he was able to quote from an astonishing variety of books, some of which were of that cranky sort only the self-taught seem to stumble upon in the course of their intellectual rummagings.

Having failed to graduate from high school, Frank entered the University of Wisconsin, in Madison, in the guise of a special student; there, too, he did badly, even in courses that he might have been expected to enjoy and profit from. Afterward, he took care to pretend that he had spent three and a half years at the University, leaving it in the spring of senior year, a few weeks before graduating. The fact is that he spent only three terms at the University, which he entered at the comparatively late age of eighteen and a half and which he quit at twenty. The chronological deceptions that he practiced in the autobiography appear to have remained necessary to him throughout his life; instead of being proud of having achieved a remarkable education on his own, it would seem that he was ashamed of it. Unconventional as he was, he wished to be thought to have been conventionally distinguished from the cradle. The domestic misery that he participated in and avoided writing about must have been one of the chief sources of his failure as a student; he preferred any lie to entering upon that treacherous ground.

In the Wright family, events tend to repeat themselves from one generation to the next, with a regularity that hints at some unconscious, age-old, rhythmic turbulence in the blood (or so a few present members of the family believe, not without evidence). William C. Wright parted from his second family in a fashion that cost his children much anguish and that they were never wholly able to forgive; many years later, Frank Lloyd Wright was to part from his family in a fashion that cost his children much anguish and that *they* were never wholly able to forgive. Frank was a dropout whose only academic degrees were honorary ones; according to his son David, most of Frank's seven children were also dropouts. "Like Dad, we've all been individualists," David has said. "We've wanted to do things our way, no matter what. We've been individualists in our relationships as well. As a family, we like each other well enough, but it seems as if we couldn't stand each other's company for more than a day at a time."

During his brief stay at the University, Wright held a job as a student assistant to Allan D. Conover, a professor of engineering there. Conover, whom Wright described as "a cultivated and kindly man," had recently opened an architectural office in Madison; having hired Wright as a favor to Anna Wright, he paid him thirty-five dollars a month to perform a variety of more or less menial tasks, at the same time teaching him the rudiments of civil engineering and draftsmanship. Where the formal education of the University "meant nothing so much to him as a vague sort of emotional distress, a sickening sense of fear," Conover's architectural practice stood for action out in the real world and was therefore truly "educational," prompting Wright to think of quitting Madison and setting out for Chicago and the career in architecture that he hoped would be awaiting him.

Characteristically, his mother opposed the move. She had no intention of surrendering her darling to a host of strangers, but she couched her arguments in terms of Frank's being too young, too innocent, too little prepared for the boisterous temptations of Chicago. Reluctantly, she consented to write and seek the advice of her brother Jenkin Lloyd Jones, who was one of the leading preachers in Chicago and was engaged at that moment in building a new church there. Back from the Reverend came the message: "On no account let the young man come to Chicago. He should stay in Madison and finish his education. That will do more for him than anything else. If he came here, he would only waste himself on fine clothes and girls."[5]

Anna Wright was relieved by her brother's response, while Frank was infuriated by it; how dare his uncle cheapen the nature of his ambitions by referring to fine clothes and girls (to both of which he was partial, which made the slur all the more unbearable)? He decided that, without a word of farewell to his mother and sisters, he would run away to Chicago,

Chicago in the eighteen-eighties, at the time of FLW's arrival there. A cable car makes its way down the middle of the street; it being summer, the car is an open one.

as earlier he had run away from his Uncle James's farm, and this time there would be no turning back. Pawning some moderately valuable old books that his father had left behind, he got together enough money to buy a railroad ticket to Chicago; seven dollars were left, to provide him with food and shelter until he obtained a job. It was the spring of 1887 and brawling, booming Chicago was full of wonders—Frank saw his first electric light and his first cable car and went for the first time to a ballet performance at the Chicago Opera House. Admission, one dollar. As he was later to boast (and as was to prove customary throughout his life, no matter how parlous his financial situation happened to be), he was always quick to afford luxuries, on the assumption that necessities would sooner or later be sure to take care of themselves.

Wright's prevarications about his past came to him so readily and are so outrageous that one ends by admiring them, which is to say that one is helpless not to forgive them. According to the autobiography, he spent four days trudging the streets of Chicago seeking work. He gives us the names of the architects whose offices he visited and recounts, word for word, the conversations he held with them; on the fourth day, he goes to the office of J. L. Silsbee, the architect of his Uncle Jenkin's new church, "All Souls." He had resolved earlier, he tells us, not to take advantage of his family connection with Silsbee, and so he approaches him as a stranger and is hired as a stranger, upon the strength of some drawings that he has brought along with him and upon the recommendation of one of Silsbee's draftsmen, Cecil Corwin. How well deserved a reward to a supremely gifted young man, who, he claims, has been surviving the rigors of Chicago on a banana a day!

The difficulty with Wright's highly circumstantial account is that there appears to be not a word of truth in it. In his 1973 biography of Wright, Robert C. Twombly points out that Wright supervised the building of the Jones family chapel on the family property in Hillside in 1886 and may even have helped with the design of it; he certainly prepared a rendering of the chapel for Silsbee and signed the drawing "F. L. Wright, Del." ("Del." for "delineator"). Early in 1887, Wright designed a little Unitarian chapel for a congregation in Sioux City, Iowa, possibly thanks to Uncle Jenkin as well as to Silsbee. In a book dealing with Wright's life and work up to 1910 (a book that was published in Wright's lifetime and was researched with his personal assistance), Grant Manson calls this chapel Wright's first independent assignment and adds that "to this day [it remains] his *bête noire*"—a term employed presumably in order to indicate that Wright was ashamed of it. The chapel bears a marked resemblance to the Jones family chapel, being a picturesque stone-and-shingle structure, with a conical tower and an informal floor plan; it is nothing for a twenty-year-old at the beginning of his career to be ashamed of, but Wright disliked being seen to have borrowed any vestiges of style from identifiable predecessors. The one exception to this rule is Louis Sullivan, by whom Wright pretends to have been far more influenced than he actually was, unless that influence had its beginnings in conversations now lost to us.

In his autobiography, Wright makes no mention of the Sioux City chapel and in order to preserve the fiction that he was hired by Silsbee on the basis of talent alone he describes the Jones family chapel, in Hillside, as having been in existence many years before 1886; indeed, he records that it was his duty as a child to decorate the pulpit on Sundays with wild flowers gathered by the armful from nearby fields and hedgerows. Also of the Silsbee period was the residence that Wright claimed to have designed for his Aunts Jane and Nell at the Hillside Home School and which many authorities on Wright are satisfied to designate as his first commission. To me, the building looks to be pure Silsbee, and no harm in that—a big, bluff, high-roofed, and self-confident house, which dominated the landscape instead of accommodating to it. Hints of Silsbee, whom Wright declared that he "adored" and whose Queen Anne romanticism gave Silsbee's clients just the kind of cozy domestic grandeur (and social prestige) that they felt in need of are to be found in Wright's work throughout the rest of his life; for all his preaching to the contrary, he, too, often permitted his structures to dominate a landscape instead of accommodating to it.

Much as Wright enjoyed working in Silsbee's office, after a few months he felt that he had learned all that could be of value to him there; he also felt, like all beginners, that he was underpaid. He secured a position with the architect W. W. Clay, where, for a wonder, he confesses in his autobiography that he found himself beyond his depth; he returned to Silsbee, who appears to have been amused by the prodigal's fleeting abdication and who not only took him back but gave him a small raise. Soon feeling more restless than ever, he applied for an opening in the drafting room at Adler & Sullivan. The firm, which was then engaged in preparing designs for the Auditorium building, was in Wright's eyes the foremost in the city, unrivaled except by Burnham & Root.

UNITY CHAPEL, HELENA, WIS.

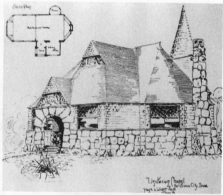

Left above, the Jones family chapel in Helena, a now vanished hamlet near Spring Green. The chapel was designed by J. Lyman Silsbee, in 1886; the drawing is by FLW, who may have been working informally for Silsbee during this period. Right above, project for an unbuilt chapel in Sioux City, designed and drawn by FLW. Below, the Jones family chapel as it looks today.

It used to be commonly said that Louis H. Sullivan was the partner primarily in charge of design, while Adler was primarily in charge of engineering and the management of the office. The architectural historian Tim Samuelson, who is a leading authority on the firm, holds that this division of activities is unfair to both partners. He has written, "Dankmar Adler and Louis H. Sullivan shared responsibility for the design of the Auditorium and other structures to an extent that prevents us from identifying their individual roles. Wright always said that he thought of them as one. Adler's contribution to the success of the partnership having been markedly undervalued in the past, there have been several recent attempts to grant him greater recognition, usually at the expense of the complementary nature of the firm. For his part, Sullivan had a keen sense of the technical aspects of his architectural compositions and he continued to develop technically sound design concepts after Adler and he broke up."[6]

It was certainly the case that Adler, being a dozen years older than Sullivan and having a wider range of social and business connections in the prosperous Jewish community of that day, secured most of the commissions for the firm. Temperamentally, Adler was methodical, Sullivan mercurial; still, it must be said of Adler that he brought to problems in engineering solutions of a highly imaginative nature. (The calculations by means of which he made sure that the enormous weight of the Auditorium building would find adequate support in the soggy soil of Michigan Avenue are, of their kind, as lyrical as an ode by Keats.) Son of a well-known Chicago rabbi, Adler would have been thought to be an insider, while Sullivan was a born outsider, with a fastidious dislike for his fellow Irish-Americans, lace-curtain or otherwise.

When Wright entered the firm, Sullivan was only thirty-one—a small, tense, handsome man, with extraordinarily large brown eyes, which radiated high intelligence and also, often enough, a hot temper. Wright was to become famous for his arrogance; it is safe to say that he learned it at the feet of a master. Indeed, it was as beloved master—"Lieber Meister"— that Wright customarily referred to Sullivan. So familiar is this appellation to us from Wright's employment of it that nobody appears to have noticed its oddity. Given Sullivan's training at the Beaux-Arts, why would Wright not have preferred to call him "Cher Maître"? When I put this question to Henry-Russell Hitchcock a few months before his death, he suggested that there were many German architects practicing in Chicago at the time, including, of course, Sullivan's own partner, and that "Lieber Meister" may then have been a term in common use among them. This reverent salutation, implying that at least a generation separated student from master, has caused many people to gain the impression that Sullivan was a middle-aged man when Wright arrived at his doorstep. Although there was a gap of almost eleven years in age between them—approximately the same

When FLW joined the architectural firm of Adler & Sullivan, the partners (Louis H. Sullivan, left, and Dankmar Adler, right) were hard at work upon the commission that made them famous—the Auditorium building. [AI]

gap that existed between Sullivan and Adler—the physical differences between Adler and Sullivan (Sullivan a lively, quick-moving athlete, Adler stolid and going to fat) caused Sullivan and Wright to seem, by contrast, a couple of go-getting young contemporaries, with many attributes in common. They both loved to draw and so adept did Wright become at imitating Sullivan's drawings of ornaments—those infinitely complicated arabesques of natural forms that were never to be found in nature—that the time came when neither of them could be sure, glancing at a sheet, which of them had executed it. They both loved music, Wright having inherited a perhaps greater measure of talent from his father and mother than Sullivan had done. The two young men were ardently bookish and they sought to attain for themselves a superior writing style; neither of them succeeded in doing so, remaining eccentric amateurs in writing as they remained eccentric amateurs in philosophizing as well. They were admirers of Emerson and Thoreau and especially of Whitman. Plainly, the world was much in need of changes, and plainly they were the geniuses who had been born to bring those changes about.

The differences between Sullivan and Wright were as notable as the likenesses. The twenty-year-old Wright was an exceptionally lovable person and he was eager to love the world in return; Sullivan, though he contracted a brief, childless marriage and was attended in age by a faithful slavey who was at least nominally his mistress, appears to have loved nobody but himself. Probably the closest to affectionate relationships that he ever

61

The virginal FLW in the days when he was learning to become "the pencil in Sullivan's hand." [WMF]

achieved were those with Adler and Wright; in each case, he peevishly and with a wounding abruptness broke off the friendship. Adler attempted a reconciliation, which Sullivan angrily rebuffed; they remained on speaking terms, however, and might have resumed their partnership (Adler was retained as a consulting engineer on Sullivan's Schlesinger & Mayer project) but for Adler's premature death at the age of fifty-six. In Wright's case, he reconciled himself with Sullivan after an estrangement of seventeen years. Some saw this as a gesture of compassion on Wright's part; others saw Wright as staging a grandstand play at a time when Sullivan was a dying, down-and-out alcoholic, with whom the world at large had long since lost patience.

5

WHAT WRIGHT AND SULLIVAN felt
for each other at the time of their first meeting amounted to an infatuation.
As the other men in the drafting room at Adler & Sullivan were quick to
notice (and as Wright recorded many years later, not without satisfaction),
Wright instantly became Sullivan's favorite, working side by side with him
and spending long hours in conversation with him after the office had
closed for the day. If Sullivan had been less consummately narcissistic, he
might have fallen in love with Wright, and Wright, for all the indurated
heterosexuality of his upbringing (those burly, philoprogenitive Welsh uncles of his!), might well have responded in kind. Wright was a virgin—a
virgin, moreover, with smooth, beardless skin and long brown hair clustering
almost to his shoulders—and he was soon to fall in love with the first
marriageable girl that he had encountered on arriving in Chicago. Pretty
and saucy and delightful as Catherine Tobin was, she was nothing like so
dazzling an apparition as Sullivan, but the possibility of the sophisticated
and already celebrated architect seducing the country apprentice never
arose. And this was not because it was unthinkable in sexual terms but
because Sullivan, far from seeing Wright as an object of desire outside
himself, evidently saw Wright as himself at a somewhat earlier stage of
his life—for him, a condition closer to self-infatuation than infatuation.
Nevertheless, that there were powerful sexual overtones in the relationship
may be deduced from the fact that Wright, composing in some haste for
an architectural magazine an obituary notice of Sullivan shortly after his
death, in 1924, saluted him in the following ardent words:

> To know him well was to love him well. I never liked the name Frank
> until I would hear him say it and the quiet breath he gave it made it
> beautiful in my ears and I would remember it was the name of freemen—
> meant free. The deep quiet of his temper had great charm for me. The
> rich humor that was lurking in the deeps within him and that sat in his
> eyes whatever his mouth might be saying, however earnest the moment

might be, was rich and rare in human quality. He had remarkable and beautiful eyes—true windows for the soul of him. Meredith's portrait of Beethoven—"The hand of the Wind was in his hair—he seemed to hear with his eyes," is a portrait I have never forgotten. If someone could give the warmer, different line, that would give the Master's quality! I have tried—but I cannot write it.[1]

It is a common failing of twentieth-century autobiographers to devote an excessive portion of their lives to childhood. Sullivan's case is particularly noteworthy in this respect; writing in old age *The Autobiography of an Idea* (published in 1924), Sullivan is obsessively longwinded over the sublime baby he was from the moment he issued into the world. We get the impression that his birth, like Wright's, was surrounded by portents well worth our paying attention to. Indeed, we do well to suspect that Wright was encouraged to fabricate certain portents associated with his birth by Sullivan's extravagant assertions in respect to his own. Wright admitted that Sullivan had read aloud to him certain chapters of the *Idea* as he was writing them, but he cannily denied having read the published work, on the grounds that his only copy of it, presented to him by Sullivan on his deathbed, had been lost in the second of the fires at Taliesin, in 1925. Is it likely that he had failed to read this precious gift from the *"Lieber Meister"* in the course of the year that he had it in his possession—a year that he happened to have spent largely in uncharacteristic idleness—and that after the fire there was no way for him to obtain another copy of the book? On the contrary: Wright's autobiography is a direct imitation of Sullivan's, as Sullivan's was of Henry Adams's. In apostrophizing nature, Sullivan was a convincing Celtic bard, Wright an unconvincing one.

Sullivan's *Idea* begins with a phrase—"Once upon a time"—common to many folktales, thus striking a universally seductive note; also seductive is the setting he describes, which is a paradisal country retreat, presided over by loving elders:

Once upon a time there was a village in New England called South Reading. Here lived a little boy of five years. That is to say he nested with his grandparents on a miniature farm of twenty-four acres, a mile or so removed from the center of gravity and activity which was called Main Street. . . . Eagerly the grandparents had for some time urged that the child come to them for a while; and after a light shower of mother tears—the father indifferent—consent was given and the child was taken on his way into the wilderness lying ten miles north of the city of Boston. . . .

To the neighbors, he was merely another brat-nuisance to run about and laugh and scream and fight and bawl with the others—all bent on joy and destruction. The peculiar kink in this little man's brain, however, was this: he had no desire to destroy—except always his momentary mortal enemies. His bent was the other way.[2]

One notes the ominous proviso—he had no desire to destroy anyone "except always his momentary mortal enemies." Sullivan appears not to have observed that, far from this being a peculiar kink in his brain, it is an attribute that he shares with every member of the human race, though few act upon it with the vehemence that Sullivan was seemingly ready to manifest from the moment he could make a fist. His story proceeds in what affects to be a self-deprecatory vein, but it takes care to remind us of the birth of many other distinguished people, including even Jesus Christ:

> Now lest it appear that this child had come suddenly out of nothing into being at the age of five, we must needs authenticate him by sketching his prior tumultuous life. He was born of woman in the usual way [which is for Sullivan to confess, with some disappointment, not as Christ was] at 22 Bennett Street, Boston, Mass., U.S.A., on the third day of September, 1856. . . .
>
> The long interval of passing years has made it clear that this pink monstrosity came into the world possessed of a picture-memory. He remembers, even now, certain cradle indiscretions; and from that same cradle . . . he remembers that one night in mid-winter, he was lifted from his warm, cozy refuge, bundled up and taken to the third floor. Grandpa was already there, scraping the heavy frost from one of the small square window panes; finally, after the ecstasies of Mama and the awed tones of Grampa, the child was lifted up and held close to the pane to see what?— a long, brilliant, cloud-like streak, which, he dimly fancied, must be unusual. . . . This streak in the sky was Donati's comet of 1858.[3]

Exceptional two-year-old, to hold an opinion as to the rarity of comets piercing the New England sky! Facetiously, he describes himself as being of "mongrel" origin, having an Irish father and a French-Swiss mother, fellow immigrants arriving a few years apart in the port of Boston. As Wright was later to do in his autobiography, Sullivan glorifies his artistic and musically gifted mother, Andrienne List, and derogates the father, Patrick Sullivan, who ran a successful dancing academy in Boston. But wait—the father is by no means the foppish charmer we expect him to be; he is a peasant, tough in mind and body, and his good manners have been hard won:

> It seems strange at first glance that these highly virile and sensitive powers should be embodied in one so unlovely in person. His medium size, . . . his small repulsive eyes—the eyes of a pig—of nondescript color and no flash, sunk into his head under rough brows, all seemed unpromising enough in themselves until it is remembered that behind that same mask resided the grim will, the instinctive ambition that had brought him alone and unaided, out of a childhood of poverty.

Naturally enough he had not found time to acquire an "education," as it was then called and is still called. He, however, wrote and spoke English in a polite way, and had acquired an excruciating French. Hence by the standards of his time in England he was no gentleman as that technical term went, but essentially a lackey, a flunkey, or social parasite. Perhaps it was for this reason he revered book-learning and the learned. He knew no better.[4]

It is surely an odd thing for a notably bookish man, himself a writer of books, to mock his father for having revered book-learning. Odder still is his account of his father's relationship to the flawless mother:

> The young Irishman, keen through training in the hard school of experience and self-discipline, was always wide awake; and this is what happened; he met the young girl, Andrienne, in the conventional way, was attracted by her grace of manner, her interesting broken English, her skilled piano playing; paid his court to her, professed love for her; they became engaged, and on the 14th of August, 1852, they were married. What is more likely is this; that he heard her playing of Chopin, Beethoven, *et al.*, with approval, for he was fond of music; that he asked her to substitute dance music; that after the first few bars he was electrified—he had found a jewel without price. Her sense of rhythm, of sweep, of accent, of the dance-cadence with its reenforcements and languishments, the *tempo rubato*—was genius itself. He lost no time in marrying her as a business asset. She was lovable and he may have loved her. It is possible but hardly probable; for there is nothing in the record to show that he loved others, or that he loved himself. He was merely self-centered—not even cold.[5]

If, as I have surmised, Louis loved himself with the passion of a monomaniac, how harsh of him to deny his father an equal opportunity for self-love—to take away from him even the opportunity of being thought cold! When Wright's turn came to exalt the mother and betray the father, he had at the very least the decency to express misgivings about the accuracy of his account: "Something—you see—had never been established that was needed to make them father and son."[6]

Wright's desire for history to see him as having been more of a prodigy than he actually was (a desire that, as we have noted, led him to usurp his younger sister Jane's birth-year as his own, to Jane's understandable irritation) was almost certainly prompted by the discovery, early in the course of his friendship with Sullivan, that Sullivan really *was* a prodigy. As he sought to liken himself to Sullivan in drawing, in dress, in manner of speaking, in a sedulously acquired arrogance, and even (years later) in the tone and method of composition of his autobiography, so he wished to be like him in having taken the world by storm, at the earliest possible opportunity.

And this Sullivan assuredly had done. A child to whom all learning came easy, he announced to his father at the age of thirteen that he had decided to make architecture his career. Impressed by the maturity of this decision, the father, for all his presumed Irish cloddishness, agreed to back his son to whatever financial extent might be necessary. Having established a reputation as a brilliant scholar at the Boston English High School, Sullivan impatiently transferred himself at the age of sixteen to the Massachusetts Institute of Technology, which, founded only a few years before, had among its departments the first school of architecture ever to be established in the United States. The training provided at M.I.T. was based upon that of the School of the Beaux-Arts, in Paris, then widely held to be the best training available anywhere, but Louis's classes struck him as being a tiresome mishmash. In the *Idea* he writes:

> Louis had gone at his studies faithfully enough. He learned not only to draw but to draw very well. He traced the "Five Orders of Architecture" in a manner quite resembling copper plate, and he learned about diameters, modules, minutes, entablatures, columns, pediments, and so forth and so forth . . . as time passed he began to discover that this school was but a pale reflection of the Ecole des Beaux-Arts; and he thought it high time that he go to headquarters to learn if what was preached there as a gospel really signified glad tidings. . . . Louis made up his mind that he would leave "Tech" at the end of the school year. . . . He knew what he wanted very well. It behooved him he thought before going to the Beaux-Arts, to see what architecture might be like in practice. He thought it might be advisable to spend a year in the office of some architect of standing, that he might see concrete preparations and results; how, in effect, an actual building was brought about.[7]

Obedient to this ambitious program, the insouciant teen-ager set out to pay a visit to his uncle and grandfather in Philadelphia. On his way south from Boston, he stopped off in New York City for a few days and had the temerity, so he asserts, to drop in without introduction upon Richard Morris Hunt, whom the *Idea* accurately describes as being "the architectural lion there, and the dean of the profession." At that moment in the early eighteen-seventies, Hunt was unquestionably the leading architect in the country, busy with a score of projects. In his 1986 biography of Sullivan, Twombly doubts that Sullivan would have dared to visit Hunt unless, as Twombly guesses, he came armed with a letter of introduction from his professor at M.I.T., William Robert Ware, who had worked in Hunt's office. Certainly Hunt himself would have been unlikely to interrupt his frantic schedule for the sake of a chat with a totally unknown adolescent. Whatever the truth may have been, Hunt is described as giving the audacious little whippersnapper a warm welcome, regaling him with stories of his

Frank Furness's gorgeous polychromatic confection, the Pennsylvania Academy of the Fine Arts (1871–1876).

happy days at the Beaux-Arts (where, under Lefuel, he had helped to design and supervise the construction of a wing of the Louvre), and then passing him along to a young architect in the office, Sidney Stratton, himself a recent student at the Beaux-Arts and eager to sing its praises.

Stratton urged Sullivan to visit the architectural firm of Furness & Hewitt upon his arrival in Philadelphia and seek a position with them; like Ware, Frank Furness had been among the young men whom Hunt had trained in his New York office and was already highly regarded in the profession. Characteristically, Sullivan had—or wrote that he had—a different approach in mind: far from pleading humbly for a job with Furness, he would look about in Philadelphia, choose the architect whose work he found most appealing, and arrange to get a job with him. As it happened, one of the first buildings that he admired in the course of his perambulations through the streets of Philadelphia was a dwelling on Broad Street that turned out to have been designed by Furness & Hewitt. The events that followed this discovery show Sullivan at his best, as raconteur and writer; for once, we encounter him in an altogether benign, self-mocking mood, and we sense how captivating a mentor and companion the young Wright must have found him and how eagerly Wright must have sought to use him a model. Long as the following excerpt is, it gives us not only an invaluable glimpse of Sullivan but also of Furness, who was one of a group of nineteenth-century American architects more vivid in their robust eccentricities than any American architect since Wright has dared to be:

He made up his mind that next day he would enter the employ of said Furness & Hewitt, they to have no voice in the matter, for his mind was made up. So next day he presented himself to Frank Furness and informed him that he had come to enter his employ. Frank Furness was a curious character. He affected the English in fashion. He wore loud plaids, and a scowl, and from his face depended fan-like a marvelous red beard, beautiful in tone with each separate hair delicately crinkled from beginning to end. Moreover, his face was snarled and homely as an English bulldog's. Louis's eyes were riveted, in infatuation, to this beard, as he listened to a string of oaths yards long. For it seems that after he had delivered his initial fiat, Furness looked at him half blankly, half enraged, as at another kind of dog that had slipped in through the door. His first question had been as to Louis's experience, to which Louis replied, modestly enough, that he had just come from the Massachusetts Institute of Technology in Boston. This answer was the detonator that set off the mine which blew up in fragments all the schools in the land and scattered the professors headless and limbless to the four quarters of earth and hell. Louis, he said, was a fool. He said Louis was an idiot to have wasted his time in a place where one was filled with sawdust, like a doll, and became a prig, a snob, and an ass.

As the smoke blew away he said: "Of course you don't know anything and are full of damnable conceit."

Louis agreed to the ignorance; demurred as to the conceit; and added that he belonged to that rare class who were capable of learning, and desired to learn. This answer mollified the dog-man, and he seemed intrigued that Louis stared at him so pertinaciously. At last he asked Louis what in hell had brought him there, anyway? This was the opening for which Louis had sagaciously been waiting through the storm. He told Frank Furness all about his unaided discovery of the dwelling on Broad Street; how he had followed, so to speak, from the nugget to the solid vein; that here he was and here he would remain; he had made up his mind as to that, and he looked Frank Furness in the eye. Then he sang a song of praise like a youthful bard of old to his liege lord, steering clear of too gross adulation, placing all on a high plane of accomplishment. It was here, Louis said, one could really learn. Frank Furness admitted as true a part of what Louis had said, waving the rest away as one pleasantly overpraised, and said: Only the Greeks knew how to build.

"Of course, you don't want any pay," he said. To which Louis replied that ten dollars a week would be a necessary honorarium.

"All right," said he of the glorious beard, with something scraggy on his face, that might have been a smile. "Come tomorrow morning for a trial, but I prophesy you won't outlast a week." So Louis came. At the

end of that week Furness said, "You may stay another week," and at
the end of that week Furness said, "You may stay as long as you like."
Oh, what a joy![8]

During several months of incessant hard work in the office of Furness
& Hewitt, Sullivan acquired the skills necessary to a professional architect.
In September, 1873, the failure of the banking house of Jay Cooke &
Co., located only a few blocks away from Furness & Hewitt, launched a
financial panic; by November, a serious depression had set in, and the
practice of architecture was, as usual, the first among the professions to
suffer. One day Furness said, "Sullivan, I'm sorry, the jig is up. There'll
be no more building. The office now is running dry. You've done well,
mighty well. I like you. I wish you might stay. But as you were the last to
come it is only just you should be first to go."[9] And pressing a bill into
Sullivan's hand, Furness wished him "Farewell and better days."

Ignoring the financial depression as something outside the range of
his intellectual and aesthetic interests (all his life, Sullivan cultivated an
ignorance of money matters that helped to leave him destitute as he lay
dying), he set out at once for Chicago, where his parents then lived. Chicago
was feverishly rebuilding itself after the conflagration that had destroyed
much of the city in 1871, and in spite of the depression there was plenty
of work for architects—work whose value lay more in the quantity of structures designed than in their quality. (Architects actually boasted of the
number of miles of buildings they had put up since the fire.) True to his
principles, Sullivan looked about, noticed a building that seemed to possess
some merit, learned that it had been designed by Major William Le Baron
Jenney, presented himself to Major Jenney, and was hired on the spot.

In the *Idea* Sullivan gives a hilarious account of the Major as a party-
giver and party-goer, a connoisseur of food and wine, and a crackerjack
storyteller. We are entitled to suspect that the degree of hilarity that Sullivan
wished us to feel is the degree to which his description of the Major is
partial, if not unfair. It is even possible to suspect that the reason Sullivan
felt obliged to make fun of Jenney is that the Major was one of the sources,
whether direct or indirect, of a concept that Sullivan wished to have thought
entirely his—the cherished dictum to the effect that form follows function.
A well-born and wealthy Easterner, Jenney had enrolled in the Lawrence
Scientific School, at Harvard, and—like Charles McKim many years later—
had found its engineering courses unsatisfactory; he went off to Paris and
entered the Ecole Centrale des Arts et Manufactures, from which he graduated with honors in 1856. Sullivan dismisses Jenney as a mere engineer,
but the Ecole Centrale enjoyed a prestige every bit as great in Europe as
the Ecole des Beaux-Arts; during his three years at the Ecole Centrale
Jenney took courses in architecture as well as engineering and was unques-

Left, Frank Furness (1839–1912). For half a century, a leading Philadelphia architect, notable for the exuberance of his designs. Right, William Le Baron Jenney (1832–1907). Trained as an engineer in Paris, Jenney was a pioneer in skyscraper construction in Chicago. He was also a celebrated party-giver and party-goer. [WH]

tionably as well qualified to practice architecture as any American of his time. Indeed, his only rival might be said to be Richard Morris Hunt, the first American to study at the Ecole des Beaux-Arts, whose years in Paris coincided with those that Jenney spent there. Given that they were both New Englanders of the same social class and with the same professional interests, it would have been odd for them not to have met as members of the small American colony then established in Paris, but there is no record of their having done so. Forty years later, they worked together upon the design of the World's Columbian Exposition of 1893, in Chicago; by then, Jenney had become one of the leading architects of the West, as Hunt was the leading architect of the East, if not of the entire country.

As Carl W. Condit tells us, at the Ecole Centrale Jenney attended the lectures on architecture by Professor Louis Charles Mary, a disciple of Jean Nicolas Louis Durand, of the Ecole Polytechnique, who, half a century earlier, had formulated the doctrine that "the structural system embodied in a building and its formal architectural dress are interdependent aspects of the building art." The process of architectural design, according to Mary, "must as a consequence represent a unification of planning and formal expression with structural techniques, which in turn must evolve from the materials of construction and the function for which the building is intended." Condit deduces "that the empirical and pragmatic spirit that Jenney later brought to architectural practice in Chicago was instilled in him directly or indirectly by French theorists."[10] Durand, shaped by the culture of the eighteenth century (he was Boullée's most celebrated student), believed in a modular architecture based on symmetry and repetition, and these principles were also to manifest themselves in Jenney's work as he and his colleagues began to experiment with the bolted iron and/or steel frame and the non-bearing wall as among the necessary attributes of the skyscraper. Sullivan's "form follows function" has ancestral roots in Boullée, Durand, Mary, and Jenney, among others; despite this distinguished ancestry, it could not, as we shall see, be taken very seriously by Sullivan himself or by his devout disciple, Wright. It wasn't so much an aphorism as a slogan and, like most slogans, its ability to arouse interest bore little relationship to its intellectual content. (A somewhat similar failed aphorism of a later generation was Thomas Hastings's "Style is the problem solved." At first one thinks, "How wonderful!" And then one thinks, "Yes, of course, but what does it *mean?*")

Sullivan at seventeen, hard at work among delightful companions in the Jenney office, was content for a time, but only for a time—with his usual impatience, he felt that he had gained a sufficient taste of the commercial practice of architecture and he wished now to approach what he assumed to be the fountainhead of the theory of architecture, the Ecole des Beaux-Arts. Off he went to Paris in the late summer of 1874. There a tutor who was helping him to prepare for his entrance examinations to the Ecole startled him with a simple and yet overwhelming pronouncement. Urging his American student to throw away his textbook on descriptive geometry because the theorems and cases printed in it all required the memorizing of a number of exceptions, the tutor said, "Here our demonstrations shall be so broad as to admit of no exception." Louis was aghast with admiration—if this could be accomplished in mathematics, why could it not be accomplished in architecture as well? As he was to write many years later of that unforgettable epiphany, "The instant answer: It can and it shall be! No one has—I will! . . . I shall live for that!" And so to the practicalities of design and construction taught by Professors Durand and Mary and acquired by Sullivan at second hand through Major Jenney was added a philosophical basis for the concept that he became obsessed by and was eventually to reduce to a single phrase—"form follows function" needed no exceptions and permitted none.

Sullivan passed his Ecole exams with ease and spent much of the following year as a student in Paris and as a traveler seeking out the conventional aesthetic monuments of France and Italy. He wandered about Florence bedazzled by its wonders and he felt, in the Sistine Chapel in Rome, a close affinity with Michelangelo—still in his teens, Sullivan put himself on terms of immediate comradeship with "the man of super-power, the glorified man, of whom he had dreamed in his childhood. . . . Now was he in that veritable dreamed-of Presence. Here was that great and glorious personality. Here was power as he had seen it in the mountains, here was power as he had seen it in the prairies, in the open sky, in the great lake stretching like a floor toward the horizon, here was the power of the forest primeval."[11] In short, here was Michelangelo meeting the American Middle West in the mind of a lad eager to preside over the introduction. And not the lad only, for it was Sullivan at sixty-six who wrote with such passion of that brief Roman encounter and who saw nothing comically egotistical about his young self's easy entrance into the soul of Michelangelo.

Emile Vaudremer, the architect in whose atelier Sullivan chose to work, was a champion of the Romanesque style, with its emphasis upon stone arches and barrel vaults. This emphasis occupied a lifelong and substantial place in Sullivan's architectural vocabulary, and it was certainly a factor in the approval he bestowed upon his elder contemporary, H. H. Richardson, one of the few architects about whom Sullivan found it possible to speak a favorable word. Much as Sullivan enjoyed the companionship of the atelier and its accompanying *vie de bohème*, he soon discovered that the Beaux-Arts was not the lofty idea he had sought but "a method, a state of mind, that was local and specific; not universal." Once again, he was in pursuit of a means of transmuting base metal into gold—of a rule that would admit of no exceptions and that would account for everything. This time, the pursuit would lead from the Old World back to the New, for he perceived that "he must go his way alone, that the Paris of his delight must and should remain the dream of his delight, that the pang of inevitable parting was at hand."[12]

Sullivan's words are far more peculiar than they appear at first glance. Why has this marvelous boy already decided that he must go his way alone? Are we right to believe that the boy did indeed make such a decision, or is the explanation the least painful that could be contrived by an old man, setting down in defeat an account of his victorious beginnings? Given the unpredictable vicissitudes of life, we might consent to the notion that Paris "must" remain the dream of his delight, but why "should" it do so? What reason is there to strike this minatory, moralizing note? As for "inevitable parting," surely that is the strangest phrase of all. Sullivan wishes us to see him in a romantic light, confronting the doom that any man of super-power must expect to face in order to fulfill himself. Throughout his life, Sullivan presided over many partings—from Adler, from Wright, from his wife, and from a dozen or more clients and friends—but the inevitability of the partings was a consequence of his nature and not of theirs. He had what amounted to a dark gift for breaking off relationships; alcoholism and what I assume was an uneasy sexual orientation help to account for the gift, but they leave much to be explained.

Returning to Chicago, Sullivan went to work in a number of nondescript architectural offices. Between jobs he devoted himself to reading (Darwin,

Near-twins in the Sullivan oeuvre. Left, the Wainwright building, St. Louis, 1890–1892. Upper right, detail of Wainwright building. Lower right, detail of Guaranty building, Buffalo, 1894–1896.

Huxley, Spencer, Whitman, and the like) and to excursions on foot—twenty miles a day was but a trifle to the young athlete—throughout the length and breadth of the ever-expanding city. As he noted in his autobiography, "His plan was in due time to select a middle-aged architect of standing and established practice, with the right sort of clientele; to enter such an office, and through his speed, alertness, and quick ambitious wit, make himself so indispensable that partnership would naturally follow."[13] A friend, John Edelmann, introduced Sullivan to Adler, who in 1879 had parted company with a well-known Chicago architect, Edward Burling, and had established an independent practice. According to Samuelson, it was in the spring of 1880 that Adler invited Sullivan to join the firm, then known as Dankmar Adler, Architect, and assume full design responsibility for all its projects. The nature of the firm's designs underwent an immediate change; by 1881, a newspaper article was praising a certain design as being by "Mr. Adler and his talented assistant, Mr. Sullivan." From May, 1882, to May, 1883, Sullivan was a partial partner in the firm of D. Adler & Company; at that time Sullivan was given a full partnership and the firm name was changed to Adler & Sullivan. From 1880 until the breakup of the firm in 1895 the partners worked in close and, in spite of Sullivan's hot temper, apparently amicable collaboration. Sullivan writes that he found in Adler

> a most congenial co-worker, open-minded, generous-minded, quick to perceive, thorough-going, warm in his enthusiasms, opening to Louis every opportunity to go ahead on his own responsibility, posting him on matters of building technique of which he had a complete grasp, and all in all treating Louis as a prize pet—a treasure trove. Thus they became warm friends.[14]

When Wright arrived on the doorstep of Adler & Sullivan in 1887, it was Sullivan who hired him, because it was Sullivan who was in need of a talent for drawing that would come as close as possible to resembling his own. Wright was hired as a draftsman but from the beginning he was intended to function as an artist. Sullivan was working at fever pitch upon the plans and drawings for the Auditorium building, which would make Adler & Sullivan famous from coast to coast; it was the ideal moment for Wright to enter the firm and become Sullivan's other self.

WRIGHT AT TWENTY was quick to assume his role as "a good pencil in the Master's hand." And this despite the fact that their styles of drawing were essentially unlike, with Sullivan devoting himself to freehand leafy convolutions and Wright preferring his T-square and triangle to express his sense of form. "Whenever the Master would rely upon me for a detail," Wright noted in his autobiography, "I would mingle his sensuous efflorescence with some geometric design, because, I suppose, I could do nothing else as well. And, too, that way of working to me seemed to hold the surface, give needed contrast, be more architectural. Again—less sentimental. But I couldn't say this to him and I wasn't sure."[1]

Wright was setting down these words many years after his period of apprenticeship to Sullivan and his uncharacteristic modesty ("I could do nothing else . . . I wasn't sure") is more than merely touching—to my mind, it hints, however indirectly, at something about the sexual natures of the two men that they appear to have left as nearly unexamined as possible throughout their lives. The difference in their styles of drawing certainly sprang from something far deeper than professional skill on the part of the older man and a lack of professional skill on the part of the younger one. Sullivan's imagery was unbridled in the voluptuousness of its natural shapes; Wright's imagery was inhibited to the point of a total suppression of any natural shape whatever. Wright has told us that he was a virgin at the time, brought up by a mother who regarded any sexual activity as a contamination. At just past thirty, Sullivan may also have been a virgin, though the odds are surely very much against it: he boasted of having shared the merry bohemian life of the Beaux-Arts students in Paris, and the merriment could perhaps have confined itself to drinking and the usual student horseplay—he was, after all, a native of Boston and a product of a doting Victorian household—but Wright was afterward to complain of his master's whoring, along with his drinking and smoking, and Wright was in a position to observe his conduct at close range. (If

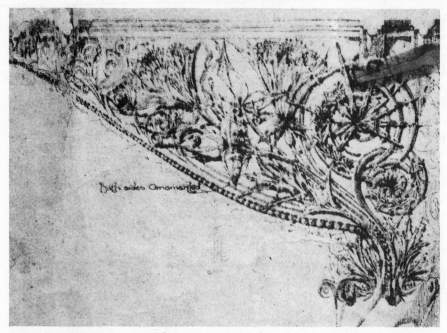

A drawing by Sullivan, probably inked in by FLW, for a voluptuous corbel in the Auditorium building. [AI]

Sullivan's whoring was a fact and involved men, Wright was unlikely to have mentioned it; a number of Wright's friends and associates were homosexuals, but convention used to require that something capable of being readily talked about wasn't for that reason capable of being readily written about.) In any event, Sullivan's graphic work seems charged with a frustrated sexuality; some of his designs, in their twisting, anguished exuberance, appear to be making love to themselves. This sexuality threatens to break through at any moment into some sort of figurative equivalent of a primal scream. Passing from ornament to structure, we note how eager Sullivan was to respond to the aggressively masculine shapes that he found in Richardson; the brutal primordial chunkiness of Richardson's stonework affected him as an adult in something like the same fashion that he claimed to have been affected, at five or six years of age, by "the big, strong men who did wonderful things such as digging ditches, building walls, cutting down great trees, cutting with axes, and splitting with maul and wedge for cord wood, driving a span of great workhorses. He adored these men. He felt deeply drawn to them, and close to them."[2] He felt passionately drawn to trees as well: "[the] lovely elm was his infatuation—he had adopted her at first sight, and still gazed at her with a sweetness of soul he had never known. He became infiltrated, suffused, inspired with the fateful sense of beauty. He melted for an instant into a nameless dream. . . .

Was there nothing in common [between them]? Did she not know he was there?"[3]

In a lively, crankily speculative book about Sullivan, published in 1985, David S. Andrew suggests the possibility that "the effort Sullivan devoted to his career had its source in deflected or sublimated autoeroticism," and he quotes Wright's illuminating summary of Sullivan's handiwork: "Ah, that supreme erotic adventure of the mind that was his fascinating ornament!"[4] I think Andrew is correct in assuming that Sullivan's autoeroticism was deflected from masturbation, for which the nineteenth century felt, or claimed to feel, a horror at least as great as it felt, or claimed to feel, for homosexuality. This horror was much heightened for men like Sullivan, who took pride in their athletic prowess; what the Victorians called the "solitary pleasure" that led to "nocturnal pollution" was the enemy of bodily fitness—it was said to drain one's energy as well as eventually to soften the brain and induce blindness. In their ardent rowing, swimming, cycling, and the like, Sullivan and his comrades celebrated the puissance of their male sexuality and simultaneously denied that puissance any of its normal outlets.

Andrew goes on:

> His preoccupation with the business tower would seem an almost laughably obvious expression of this facet of Sullivan's character. In "The Tall Office Building Artistically Considered" (1896), he says that it should be "every inch a proud and soaring thing." One wonders if the ithyphallic aspect of the skyscraper ever occurred to him. Evidently not, for he speaks of the tall building as one who believes himself to possess the most serious, sacerdotal role in its behalf.[5]

Samuelson would argue, *pace* Andrew, that Sullivan wasn't preoccupied with the business tower; far from whiling away his time with fantasies about proud and soaring things, Sullivan responded to commissions for towers as they happened to come into the office (similar commissions were coming into other architectural offices at the same time), and his celebrated essay was one of the few that he ever devoted to the question of the tall building. It is true that few writers on architecture worry the question of whether Ernest Flagg (the Singer building) or Cass Gilbert (the Woolworth building) harbored ithyphallic obsessions; it appears that Sullivan's unconventional life and unconventional ornament invite unconventional explanations. If Andrew is right in supposing that the ithyphallic nature of the skyscraper may not have occurred to Sullivan on a conscious level, he is surely wrong to propose that this would account for his seeing his role as sacerdotal. On the contrary, it would hint strongly at Sullivan's unconscious awareness of the skyscraper's true meaning for him: the priest is, after

Left, a carved birch capital in the banquet hall of the Auditorium building, 1890. Sixty-six years later, FLW was attempting to distinguish the capitals that he had designed from those designed by his "Lieber Meister." With his cane, he indicated first one column and then another, saying to his companion, Crombie Taylor, "Look over there—Sullivan designed that one. No, maybe I did. . . ." At last, in good-humored vexation, he gave up: "To tell you the truth, I can't even see the god-damned things!" [CCL] Right, fret-sawn mahogany door grille from Auditorium Hotel dining room. [CCL]

all, a male who remains chaste as a sacrificial act of worship. From Samuelson's point of view, it would also hint strongly that plain facts are sometimes only plain facts: the tall building and Sullivan's career coincided and Sullivan, faced with a novel design problem, solved it more brilliantly than anyone else.

Nevertheless, one cannot resist seeking to discern the sexual message implicit in Sullivan's architecture and ornament; he is as tempting in that respect as his pro tem employer, Frank Furness, some of whose buildings are so recklessly tumescent as to seem to threaten the safety of innocent passersby. Also tempting to read is the underlying message conveyed by Sullivan's prose and poetry. It is a message worth glancing at for a moment because of the degree to which Wright, imitating Sullivan, fell into the same treacherous gaucheries of style. Wright wrote as badly as he did in part because Sullivan wrote as badly as *he* did. In each case, their worst excesses have to do with vulgarly overexcited apostrophes to nature; in these apostrophes Sullivan reveals the degree to which his apparent identification with the natural world amounts, in fact (using Andrew's word), to a "deflected" orgasm. Discussing the decorative work that Sullivan designed for the Auditorium building, Andrew cites the opening passage of Sullivan's "Spring Song," composed at approximately the same time. An examination of the passage tells us even more about Sullivan's use of words as a sublimated sexual activity than it does about his use of ornament for that purpose. Within the space of a few lines, we encounter such phrases as "large,

Left, Getty tomb, 1890. [CCL]   *Right, detail of the exquisite blue-green bronze gates.*

abundant nature . . . clothed in fresh filigree of tender green . . . fresh from every nook springs forth new life . . . the swelling anthem of rejuvenated life, to mate with birds and flowers . . . to pulsate ardently with hope, rich in desire so tremulously keen . . . open wide the portals . . . hail the new-born world . . . quick-melted . . . gush forth . . . wildly leap, tumultuous . . . fall in gentle spray . . ."[6]

"Sentimental" is a mild word to apply to this passionate lyrical spasm, but Wright nearly always uses "sentimental" not as it is defined in dictionaries but as he chooses to define it, different occasions producing different definitions. (He practiced the same Alice-in-Wonderland liberality in defining such key words as "romantic," "organic," and "plastic.") For example, when he writes that he came to Chicago as a boy seeking information that no member of his family appeared able to impart to him, he describes himself as "this young sentimentalist already in love with the truth! Is there a more tragic figure on earth—in any generation?" In such a context, what does Wright mean by "sentimentalist" and "tragic," unless it be that a sentimentalist is someone who will never discover the truth that he purports to be in love with? According to this formulation, it was Sullivan who remained a sentimentalist all his life and failed in life precisely because he was a sentimentalist, while Wright views himself as having discovered truths that eluded Sullivan and that made it possible for him to outdistance Sullivan. He had begun as Sullivan's proto-son and he ended as Sullivan's proto-father—indeed, by an unwelcome irony, Wright became his *Lieber Meister*'s *Lieber Meister,* as Sullivan himself acknowledged, writing to him in age as "my dear Frank" and begging him, in humble terms, for handouts.

Wright boasted all too often of having revolutionized twentieth-century architecture. He did so, he said, by means of his genius, aided by certain technical innovations for which he was always quick to take credit. Many of these innovations required hitherto untested engineering solutions, and it is one of the oddities of Wright's voluminous documentation of his work that he has comparatively little to say about the sources of his engineering skills. As we have seen, he studied for a few months under Allan D. Conover, Dean of Engineering at the University of Wisconsin. In the Silsbee office, he was mostly engaged in the ordinary tasks of draftsmanship—the inking in of working drawings and the like—and it was at least nominally for the same purpose that he was hired by Adler & Sullivan, then hard at work on the Auditorium project.

Sullivan and Wright possessed a gift in common that was innate and unteachable and that Sullivan therefore cannot be said to have taught Wright but that, on discovering it in his new employee, he must have been eager to encourage. (That putative discovery would help to account for the speed with which Wright became Sullivan's favored assistant.) The rare gift that I speak of was the ability to conceive plan and elevation as one—to move mentally in three dimensions through the volumes of space that a given project called for and to perceive the proportions of those volumes so directly that almost as if by magic—certainly without prolonged and painful effort—plan and elevation could be set down in the two dimensions of a sheet of paper. And so thoroughly could Sullivan and Wright envisage a project that even the methods of construction that would be required and the materials that would be made use of in the course of construction emerged simultaneously with its design. It was usually the case with a Sullivan design that it was translated into working drawings with few appreciable differences from his first studies on paper. Wright worked in a similar fashion, bragging that once he had a building on paper he was ready to set about furnishing it.

When a Sullivan or Wright building failed, the failure was one of concept and not a failure to reconcile plan and exterior design. For example, the house that Sullivan designed in 1912 for Mr. and Mrs. Carl Bennett, in Owatonna, and which the Bennetts never ventured to build, was a successful intellectual exercise but would have been impossible to live in, because, as William Gray Purcell pointed out, "Mr. Sullivan simply had no concept whatever of American family life." Sullivan in the days of his glory wisely turned aside from the complex trivialities of domestic commissions; I am not making a gloomy joke at his expense when I say that he appeared more at ease designing tombs than designing houses.

Inspired by the new warehouse that H. H. Richardson had just designed for Marshall Field, Sullivan gave the Auditorium building a Richardsonian shape and dress—a bulky stern stoniness on the exterior that contrasted

Above, Marshall Field & Company Wholesale Store, 1885–1887, H. H. Richardson, architect. [CCL]   *Below, Auditorium building, 1887–1890, Adler & Sullivan. It is plain that Sullivan was bowled over by Richardson's virile style.* [CCL]

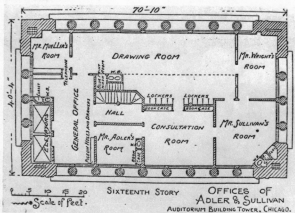

SIXTEENTH STORY OFFICES OF ADLER & SULLIVAN
AUDITORIUM BUILDING TOWER, CHICAGO.

The Adler & Sullivan offices at the top of the tower. Wright boasted of having been given a private "office" next to Sullivan's, but in fact it was simply a glassed-in portion of the main drafting room, as the drawing makes clear. [TS]

uneasily with the exotic decorations that Sullivan designed for the interior. The disparity between the interior and the exterior of the building was criticized at the time, and with reason, although Samuelson and other admirers of Sullivan hold that the disparity was Sullivan's "honest" response to a particular design problem: giving appropriate expression to the fact that the exterior of the structure consisted of bearing wall masonry and the interior consisted in large part of freely molded plaster. A somewhat similar disparity was pointed out between the main façade, opening upon Michigan Avenue, and the façades that open upon Congress Parkway and Wabash Avenue. Looking uncomfortably out of place as a feature of the main façade is a pillared second-story open portico (now glassed in)—a leftover from earlier elevations that Sullivan had been working up before he saw and was enraptured by the Field warehouse. The lovely, slender tower toward the Wabash Avenue end of the building leaps up unexpectedly out of the blunt Richardsonian cube and is at such a distance from the Michigan Avenue façade as to seem, to the eye of the casual passerby, another building altogether. In Wright's vocabulary, the tower is "inorganic" and "non-plastic," though in conventional aesthetic terms it is a bolder and more radical manipulation of the Romanesque mode than even Richardson might have been capable of designing. High up in the tower, we observe what appears to be a second pillared open portico, though in fact it is a band of deeply recessed windows, from which one looks out over the city and the great blue inland sea of Lake Michigan. Initially, an open-air observatory had been planned for that space; enclosed, it became the offices of Adler & Sullivan.

Wright was happy to share the frantic hurly-burly with which, under pressures that brought Sullivan close to a nervous breakdown, the Auditorium building proceeded from drawing board to construction. By the time the building was finished, in 1890, and the firm had installed itself in its romantic quarters at the top of the tower, Wright had been appointed

The auditorium, which seats over four thousand people and is celebrated for its excellent acoustics. The arches spanning the vault anticipate those of the Radio City Music Hall at Rockefeller Center. [CCL]

head draftsman, with a total of thirty draftsmen working under him; moreover, as an unprecedented privilege, he was assigned a private office immediately adjacent to Sullivan's. (Not so private, to be sure, as Wright afterward pretended: it was simply a small partitioned-off space, but the staff correctly took Wright's occupancy of it as a sign of grace and favor.) The instant public approval of the Auditorium building brought a number of sizable commissions into the office, and I assume that it was during those years of the late eighties and early nineties that Wright acquired much of his knowledge of engineering. This knowledge came to him not only from the two partners but also from Paul Mueller, a young engineer in the firm; Mueller was later to supervise the construction of several of Wright's most important projects, including the Larkin building, in Buffalo, and the Imperial Hotel, in Tokyo. Following the usual nineteenth-century custom, Wright learned by doing—a method that does not meet with general approval in the late twentieth century. Throughout his career he was accustomed to making changes in the design of a building even when it was under construction. Some of these changes were for artistic reasons; others were necessitated by Wright's overly optimistic engineering calculations. No doubt it was partly in order to protect himself against unwelcome and perhaps embarrassing surprises in the course of construction that

Wright insisted upon having a personal representative—a sort of "clerk-of-the-works"—on duty at each of his building sites, to guide local contractors through any Wrightian intricacy of design that appeared to them unbuildable. For example, in framing a roof that would prove of requisite strength and yet have a look of exceptional lightness, Wright would often fall back upon flitches, a flitch in his usage consisting of a thin steel plate invisibly bolted, in a sandwichlike fashion, to a pair of wooden members. Sometimes the flitch was called for in the plans; sometimes, for safety's sake, it had to be inserted at the last possible moment. (As one speaks of a pride of lions, in Wright's case one may speak of "an improvisation of flitches.") Many a Wright cantilever has required adjustment over the years; it was a part of his long-cultivated architectural bravado to defy gravity, and it was only to be expected that gravity would occasionally strike back.

Like Sullivan, Wright tended to look down his nose at the profession of engineering as being a necessary but earthbound handmaiden of architecture. In the nineteen-thirties, writing of his desire to introduce "aesthetic continuity" into the physical method of constructing a building, Wright complained that "the changes came along slowly because, to eliminate the post and beam as such (the old order), I could get no help from the engineer." He went on harshly:

> By habit, engineers reduce everything in the field of calculation to post and girder before they can calculate anything or tell you where and just how much of what. Walls that were part of floors and ceilings all merging together, reacting within upon each other, the engineer had never met in buildings. And so the engineer had not yet enough scientific formula in any handbook to enable him to calculate at all for continuity. Even slabs stiffened and used over supports as cantilevers to get planes parallel to the earth, such as were now necessary to develop emphasis of the "third dimension" (as I myself had been calling it), were yet new. But the engineer soon mastered the element of continuity, which we call the cantilever, in these floor slabs. The cantilever thus became a new feature in architectural form. As used in the Imperial Hotel in Tokio it was one of the several features that insured the life of that building in the subsequent terrific temblor. After that "practical" demonstration a great new *economic stability* had entered building construction proving the new *aesthetic* not only safe but also *sound economics of structure.* Form and function were one.[7]

"Form and function were one" is Wright's transformation of Sullivan's supposed "rule that shall permit of no exception," to wit, the rule that "form follows function." Both phrases have less in them than meets the eye, though they proved convenient sticks with which Wright could rap his opponents' knuckles in arguments over the nature of architecture. What matters to us at this early stage of Wright's career is not the intellectual distance he had established between himself and Sullivan by the time he was writing about it in the nineteen-thirties but the practical experience he was acquiring at Adler & Sullivan. Much of that experience had to do with helping the partners to design what Wright was later to excoriate as the box. Indeed, although he would often claim to have destroyed the box as a permissible convention in architecture, during the period in which he served as Sullivan's alter ego he devoted much of his time and talent to the design and decoration of boxes on an exceedingly large scale. Despite Wright's protestations, it wasn't the obtuseness of engineers that stood in the way of his artistic development but, rather, the hours-long, late-at-night blarneying of his beloved master.

Once Wright was securely established as Sullivan's favorite, he asked Sullivan to invite over from the Silsbee office a gifted young artist-draftsman named George Elmslie, whose role would be that of understudy to Wright. Wright was later to bear a grudge against Elmslie as one of a number of architects who became known to the world as members of the Prairie School of Architecture; in Wright's not unjustified view of the matter, there was no such thing as a Prairie School—there was Frank Lloyd Wright, architect of genius and the inventor of the Prairie House, and behind him a host of imitators: William Gray Purcell, George Maher, Dwight Perkins, and the like. In his autobiography, Wright introduces Elmslie in a peculiar way, saying of him, "George wasn't a minister's son but ought to have been."[8] Given that Wright and his then closest friend Cecil Corwin were both ministers' sons, it is hard to tell whether he is praising Elmslie or sneering at him; Elmslie assumed that it was a sneer. Wright goes on, "George was a tall, slim, slow-thinking, but refined Scottish lad who had never been young. Faithful, very quiet and diffident. I liked him. I couldn't get along without somebody—ever."[9]

One would never guess from this description of Elmslie that he was no less truly a pencil in the Master's hand than Wright was. After Wright was fired by Sullivan, Elmslie took his place by Sullivan's side and remained there throughout the long, painful years of Sullivan's decline, until in 1909, penniless and with scant prospects of any future work, Sullivan was obliged to let him go. Elmslie joined forces with Purcell, a wealthy Chicagoan, who had grown up in Oak Park (members of his family were friends of Wright) and who had founded an architectural firm in Minneapolis. In a book entitled *The Curve of the Arch,* Larry Millett describes Elmslie's relationship with Sullivan, Wright, and Purcell over many years, and an exceptionally sympathetic figure he proves to be. He was victimized by Sullivan and Wright and consoled in his solitariness and fiscal ineptitude by Purcell and by his chief benefactor, a banker named Carl Bennett.

Defiantly unlike the stereotype of a banker, Bennett was scholarly and tenderhearted; he commissioned from Sullivan and Elmslie a bank building in Owatonna, Minnesota, that was to become famous throughout the world—a small structure in a small town, to which over several generations a path has been beaten as if to a mousetrap of pure gold. As Millett tells us, Elmslie could put up with Wright's offhand dismissal of him, but he was determined to defend Sullivan against Wright at all costs, saying of the former that he "walked in the sun like a man," and of the latter that he preferred devious ways.

In his imperious fashion, Wright took over Sullivan after Sullivan's death and devised a legend of which he was characteristically the hero and Sullivan the beneficiary. The legend wasn't altogether false; after their long estrangement (in the course of which Sullivan is known to have described Wright as an arrogant ass), Wright and Sullivan indeed embraced and from that moment, though himself financially and psychologically hard-pressed, Wright did everything in his power to keep Sullivan alive. Still, there was little room in the legend for such self-effacing friends of Sullivan's as Elmslie. Millett tells of how Elmslie was finally driven to defend himself when, in 1936, Wright referred to him as having been merely the "backwash" of Sullivan's late career. With a forbearance rare in an injured party, Elmslie wrote a letter to Wright defending his work and that of Sullivan and ending, "You, of course, *are* a great genius, and no one knows this better than I. But I do bespeak entrance into your mind of the still, small voice of truth, of fair play, of dignity, and high honor, and the exit of your strange claims of omniscience when you come to write on a great Master and an infinitely greater man than yourself."[10]

Almost half a century earlier, how eagerly young Wright and Elmslie had worked together, their fortunes seeming at that moment indissolubly joined to that of their incandescent mentor! They stood on tiptoe in his presence, and they were right to do so.

Even for that prim Victorian period, Wright in the opening months of 1889 was an unusually innocent twenty-one-year-old. He neither smoked nor drank nor had as yet any sexual experience of women. He was surely old enough to have occupied what were then known as "bachelor digs" in Chicago; instead, in the name of economy but for reasons more complex than that of economy, he was living with his mother and sisters in a little middle-class house in the conventional suburb of Oak Park. For of course the fretful and possessive Anna had had no intention of being left behind in Madison while her runaway darling confronted the dangers of what was said to be the most wide-open city in the country. She and her daughters would do their best to protect him even as he would do his best to serve as the breadwinner of the fatherless little family.

Like most of the other dutiful breadwinners in Oak Park, Wright attended church services on Sunday mornings and attended edifying lectures and concerts throughout the week. If he was beginning to enjoy

Oak Park in the eighteen-eighties. A utopian suburb, carved out of forest and prairie and readily accessible to Chicago.

Armed with a box camera, a local bicycle repairman of the period, Philander Barclay, devoted his spare time to photographing Oak Park street by street. The village had many churches and no saloons. This is the Unitarian church, which the Wrights attended; its burning gave FLW the opportunity to design Unity Temple.

© PHILANDER BARCLAY

intimations of the degree to which his intelligence, talent, and good looks were to set him apart from a quintessentially domestic environment, he was also attempting to make use of that environment as a means of escaping Anna's tedious tyranny. The most obvious means of escape available to Wright at that time and place was one that happened to coincide with his long-suppressed biological needs: that is, to fall in love. The name of the girl that Wright fell in love with was Catherine Tobin. When they met, in the course of a "social" held at his Uncle Jenkin's church, she was seventeen and a student at the Hyde Park High School. Her father was a successful businessman in Chicago and Catherine was "the idol of the family, [who] had pretty much her own way about everything."[1] She was tall and blue-eyed, with pink cheeks and reddish, curly hair, and Wright described her in his autobiography as walking with a kind of lighthearted gaiety. Their courtship was disapproved of by the Tobins, by Mrs. Wright, and by his friend Cecil Corwin, who protested that Wright mustn't commit himself to the only girl he had ever kissed, if indeed he had gone even that far. Wright and Catherine persevered: "With no knowledge at all, we had come to the boy and girl intimacy, no longer satisfied with sheepish looks and perfunctory visiting or playing or talk or music."[2]

Wright explained the situation to Sullivan, noting that among the innumerable parental objections to Catherine's and his longed-for marriage was his small, uncertain income. As Wright tells us, Sullivan was, as usual, decisive; he shouted for Adler:

> Adler came.
> "Wright wants to get married—no visible means of support. What do you say to a five-year contract?"
> "All right," said Adler. "You fix it, Sullivan!" And he went out—his usual exit—as though suddenly remembering something that demanded instant attending to.[3]

Having gained the advantage of a contract (one that made him, according to Sullivan, the highest-paid draftsman in Chicago), Wright pressed for a further advantage. He needed, he said, five thousand dollars with which to buy a plot of land and build a house. Almost a hundred years later, we cannot fail to be impressed by the brass of the young man:

"Mr. Sullivan, if you want me to work for you as long as five years, couldn't you lend me enough money to build a little house, and let me pay you back so much each month—taken out of my pay envelope?"

Mr. Sullivan—it seemed—had a good deal of money of his own at the time. He took me to his lawyer, Felsenthal. The contract was duly signed, and then the Master went with me—"the pencil in his hand"—to Oak Park to see the lot I knew I wanted. It was Mr. Austin's gardener's, the plain lot, the lovely old tanglewood. The lot was on Forest and Chicago Avenues. The Master approved the lot and bought it. There was $3500 left over to build a small home on that ground planted by the old Scottish landscape-gardener.

"Now look out, Wright!" said Mr. Sullivan, "I know your tastes . . . no 'extras.' "

I agreed. "No, none."

But there was $1200 more to be paid toward the end. I kept this dark, paid it in due course as best I could out of what remained of my salary.[4]

Wright's account of the wedding ceremony is succinct and hilarious. The day was rainy, the atmosphere funereal. The mother of the groom fainted. The father of the bride was in tears. So was the minister performing the ceremony—no less a person than Wright's Uncle Jenkin. The young couple went off to Wisconsin, to the "Valley of the God-Almighty Joneses," for their honeymoon. Catherine may have found her encounter with so many new relatives an ordeal; no doubt there were further showers of tears to be got through—the Welsh weep at least as readily as they laugh— and much advice given by the bridegroom's doting aunts as to his proper care and feeding. After a few weeks, they returned to Oak Park; in the course of the journey, changing trains in Chicago, they had their first quarrel, and Wright's account of it is worth quoting because the candor of his confessing to a brattish arrogance is so rarely encountered elsewhere in his writings:

On the way across town . . . came the first *meum* and *tuum*.

I wanted to carve mottoes on the panels of the doors of the rooms of the new house. The decided Kitty, with better sense, accustomed to having her own way, too, said, "No, no mottoes." But the reason she gave was not good. "Didn't like mottoes."

I—new husband, lugging a heavy suitcase, tired and tried by the useless effort to keep the damned thing off my legs—was surprised to find my superior taste in matters pertaining to my own work disputed. And I was caught red-handed in my own "sentimentality." It was forever claiming me and every time it did I would not only lose face, but my patience: find someone or something to blame.

I put the suitcase down, wiped the sweat from my face, more indignant to be caught sentimentalizing than anything else. Picked it up again and refused the offer of help. Not in those circumstances. Thank you. We walked wide apart.[5]

Catherine's better sense prevailed in respect to carving mottoes on doors, but Wright had his way in respect to carving a motto on the oak slab above the fireplace in the living room of the cottage he had designed for them. The motto read "Truth Is Life!" and he saw, too late, that it made little sense and that "Life Is Truth!" might well have come closer to the mark; whether Catherine pointed this out to him his autobiography fails to say. His weakness for hortatory apothegms never left him, though he resisted the temptation successfully in his later years, symbols blessedly ambiguous in their nature taking the place of words.

For a couple in many respects scarcely more than children the Oak Park cottage was a by no means humble abode; in today's money, the cost of the land, building, and furnishings would probably approach a hundred thousand dollars. To this sum must be added the cost of remodeling a small Gothic-style frame house already on the property as a residence for his mother and sisters. Having lost the struggle to keep her son unmarried, Mrs. Wright was reluctant to surrender more than a grudged portion of him to another woman; she would be keeping watch on him at a range conveniently close for her and inconveniently close for Catherine. From having almost no possessions, Wright had assumed the responsibilities—and perhaps some of the airs—of a country squire. Which is to say that at the very beginning of his career he was living, as Sullivan had suspected he would ("I know your tastes . . ."), well beyond his means.

As originally designed and built, the cottage was a simple six-room cube, clad in brown cedar shingles, with a high, triangular gable and casement windows. If not quite a plagiarism of the cottages being built in Tuxedo Park and elsewhere by Bruce Price and other Eastern architects, it was at the very least (to use a euphemism of the present day) an act of homage to them. Without the protection of a vestibule, the front door led into a small hallway containing a flight of stairs and giving onto a living room whose chief feature was a fireplace in an inglenook. Inglenooks were all the rage in England at the time and they became the rage in Wright's early work as well. If he was studying photographs of Price's work in American architectural magazines, he was no less diligently studying

The Oak Park house as FLW designed it in 1889; many people took it for a "seaside" cottage, whose advanced style FLW had imported from the fashionable East Coast.

the work of Shaw, Voysey, Mackintosh, and others in British architectural magazines. Guessing at proportions from a magazine photograph is a risky business; the Voysey-like inglenook in the Oak Park house is deep but narrow, with pinched-looking upholstered benches on either side of an arched fireplace in Roman pressed brick: a hideaway for children to play house in but not a place for the conversation of adults.

From the moment that he and Catherine moved into the house, Wright was busy tinkering with it. One of the first changes had to do with the windows; Wright replaced plain glass with diamond panes of leaded glass, which greatly increased the picturesque charm of the exterior but which were also, in terms of style, a self-conscious step backward—and this from an architect who was so soon to denounce and repudiate the past! Casement windows were rare in America at that time and common in Europe; it is likely that Wright borrowed the use of them from Voysey and Mackintosh in the British Isles and from Olbrich and others in Austria. They have much to recommend them aesthetically but are less efficient than double-hung sash at keeping out the cold of a Middle Western winter and the insects of a hot Middle Western summer, since storm windows and screens are only with difficulty accommodated to them. In championing the cause of casement windows, Wright was, as usual, quick to use words

A family group gathered on the front terrace, before or after tennis. FLW, unexpectedly mustachioed, is at right; his wife, Catherine, holds their firstborn, Lloyd; behind Lloyd is seated Anna Lloyd Jones Wright. FLW's sister Jane holds a tennis racket and his sister Maginel peeps over his right shoulder. An Oriental rug has been dragged out of the house to be posed upon. The picture was almost certainly taken by FLW. [HS]

as weapons. He called double-hung sash "guillotine" windows; what gently brought-up householder, fearful of the sight of blood, would willingly occupy a house with guillotine windows?

Within a year, the Wrights' first child was born and given the name of Frank Lloyd Wright, Junior, later prudently shortened to Lloyd. Five other children followed, seemingly at random, over the course of some thirteen years—John, Catherine, David, Frances, and Llewellyn—and the house expanded to embrace them and their multifarious activities. The house and the studio that Wright built adjoining the house served as a sort of laboratory for Wright's experiments with concepts of space and with the uses of materials, some of them new to the marketplace and not to be recommended to clients without testing. As a bride, Catherine ruefully complained that her young husband was more interested in the house than in her and to some extent the accusation appears to have remained a legitimate one throughout their marriage; for example, it amused him to add an exquisite—and practical—playroom to the house for the sake of the children, but if he and Catherine had been childless, the room

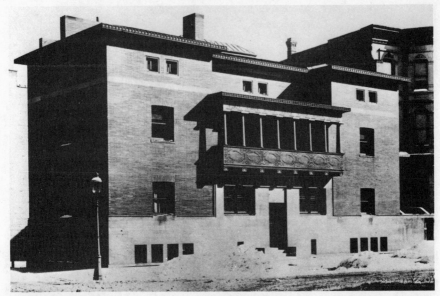

The Charnley townhouse (1891), on fashionable Astor Street, in Chicago. [CCL]

would almost certainly have come into existence under some other pretext, perhaps as a ballroom or private art gallery.

"Now went along these matchless early years of master and apprentice. Louis Sullivan, the Master, and I, the open-eyed, radical and critical but always willing apprentice."[6] So Wright's autobiography sums up the period in which he found himself as an architect, thanks in part to having thrust upon him tasks that the firm of Adler & Sullivan was too busy to undertake. Neither partner was interested in designing houses; when clients of the firm or personal friends of the partners asked them to design a house, the project would be turned over to their youthful head draftsman, who would carry out the work after regular business hours and on weekends. Sullivan and his friends the James Charnleys having purchased adjacent parcels of land in Ocean Springs, Mississippi, on the Gulf of Mexico, it fell to Wright to design a couple of cottages for them there. The residential commissions that he executed in the name of Adler & Sullivan and the residential commissions that he executed during the same period without the firm's knowledge, in order to pick up a little extra money (what he called his "bootlegged" houses), are, with one or two exceptions, very Silsbee-like in inspiration, whether embodying the Queen Anne style that Silsbee had long favored or the neo-Colonial style that he and other fashionable architects had recently imported from the Eastern coast.

The first of the exceptions amounts in my view to an unresolvable mystery. It is the Charnley townhouse, on Astor Street, in Chicago, designed in 1891. Almost every authority gives the house to Wright, as does Wright

A house designed by Ledoux for his projected ideal "Salt City" in the Jura mountains.

himself. With the Master coaching him, Grant Manson in his 1958 book *Frank Lloyd Wright to 1910* seeks to place the structure once and for all: "Although it is officially an Adler & Sullivan design, it is in reality the first great monument of Frank Lloyd Wright's career. It was in every sense a miraculous accomplishment. Wright justly says of it, 'It is the first modern building.' . . . It owes no debt to anyone but its designer, much of whose coming development it forecasts, and it carries us in one amazing leap into the spirit of the next century."[7] This judgment strikes me as preposterous. The building owes far more to Sullivan than to Wright, and so far from being "the first modern building" is patently a clever pastiche, by way of Sullivan and his Beaux-Arts teachers, of Ledoux (1736–1806). One sees at a glance its strong resemblance to certain residences that Ledoux proposed to have constructed at Chaux. Instead of carrying us "in one amazing leap into the spirit of the next century," it carries us at one amazing leap backward into the eighteenth century, a period that Wright was soon utterly to repudiate. The open second-story loggia is a favorite device of Sullivan's, used by him in the Auditorium, Schiller, and other buildings, and is, of course, a borrowing from Ledoux; so are the pairings of the basement and third-floor windows. As Hitchcock suggests, the cladding of limestone ashlar and Roman brick is no doubt also a borrowing, in this case from the firm of McKim, Mead & White, which had already successfully introduced that shape and coloring of brick in the East. The fretsawn detailing of the loggia is Sullivanesque in principle and, according to Samuelson, unquestionably Wright's in design, being based on a complex geometric matrix that Wright often employed at that period. Samuelson assumes that Sullivan, as a favor to his friend Charnley, sketched a basic plan and elevation, then turned his sketches over to Wright to complete under his supervision; this has always been a conventional practice in big firms, and if all the detailing of the house is Wright's, then he may well have come to think of the house as his. Nevertheless, to me the impression conveyed by the house is inexpungeably that of Sullivan; the uncompromising—indeed, the relentless—rigidity of the façade bears his stamp and so does the no less rigid interior. One steps through the front door into a square vestibule and then into a rectangular hall, with a stairway rising along the wall opposite the entrance. Square alcoves the size of the vestibule open off the hall at either side of the vestibule; to the left, an arched entrance leads into a rectangular living room, and to the right a similar arched entrance leads into a dining room whose end wall takes the form of a bay. A door leads into a serving pantry, from which a flight of stairs gives access to a basement kitchen.

The alcoves are totally non-functional, being too small to sit in and too open to serve as closets. (Some time after the house was built, a shallow closet for hats and coats was fitted into an arched recess under the stairs.) The two upper floors are laid out with an equally rigid matter-of-factness into bedrooms and bathrooms; the only easygoing note struck in the house is the open stairwell, rising like a miniature atrium to a skylight in the roof. Sullivan was a devotee of arches, and the six archways that one encounters on the ground floor are repetitive to the point of obsession. Manson is so determined to give the house to Wright that he finds Wright-like attributes in the house where none exist; for example, he mentions its

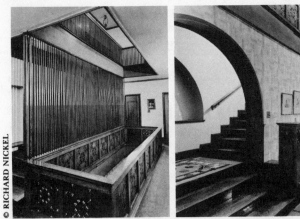

© RICHARD NICKEL
© RICHARD NICKEL

Left, the second-floor hall of the Charnley house, with an open stairwell rising to the third floor. Right, the entry hall of the Charnley house, displaying a Sullivanesque multiplicity of arches.

The Henry Babson residence, Riverside, 1908. The second-floor loggia echoes that of the Charnley house. Babson gave Sullivan the commission for the house after overhearing some architects at Vogelsang's restaurant, in Chicago, say of Sullivan, "He is the best of us and he has no work."

low chimneys as among the features that anticipate Wright's Prairie Houses; in fact, those Prairie Houses were to be distinguished by conspicuous chimneys. To me, the most convincing evidence of Sullivan's hand in the Charnley house is the resemblance the floor plan bears to the floor plan of Sullivan's Babson house and, still more strikingly, to the floor plan of the Bennett house in Owatonna. The Charnley, Babson, and Bennett houses all have a boxy, agglutinative linearity of plan that comes straight out of Beaux-Arts teachings in respect to the social utility of the enfilade and that Wright learned early to oppose.

I mentioned earlier that with two exceptions most of the work that Wright executed during this period reflected his training under Silsbee rather than his training under Sullivan and Adler. The first exception is the Charnley house and the second exception is the Harlan house of 1891, on the south side of Chicago, which is indeed Wright's and is that "amazing leap into the spirit of the next century" that Manson wrongly hailed the Charnley house as being. The face it presents to the street is deliberately not a welcoming one; a blank wall guards a terrace between the house and the street and the front door is located to one side; a stranger would seek it out with some diffidence. A short flight of stairs leads into an open hall, from which, through wide openings, one gains access to a many-windowed living room and a dining room that leads to an exceptionally large breakfast room. The plan takes care to avoid a formal axis and hints at the beginning of the centrifugal, pinwheel-shaped plan that Wright was later to develop in a score of different ways. A balcony, cantilevered out from the second floor of the house, is sheltered by the broad eaves of a hip roof, through which emerges a dormer unexpectedly grand in scale, containing three sets of casement windows crowned by openwork crestings. The Harlan house is a radically original work, which Hitchcock long ago singled out as Wright's best house of the nineties. It has always been identified (by Wright himself, among others) as one of the "bootlegged" houses that was the occasion for Sullivan's dismissing Wright, just as his five-year contract with Adler & Sullivan was reaching its end, but I find it hard to believe that Sullivan was not aware of its existence in the many months required to design and build it. As Twombly points out in his life of Sullivan, the house was announced in 1891 in a local paper as being about to be constructed according to designs by C. Corwin, Wright's close friend and presumed "cover," but since Corwin had been an employee of Adler & Sullivan he would surely have proved a very inadequate cover indeed. It seems to me more plausible to assume that Corwin was described in the press as the architect of record for the Harlan house (and later for the Blossom and McArthur houses as well) not so much because an attempt was being made to deceive Sullivan as because Corwin, Wright's senior by several years, had set up an independent architectural practice and

A rare view of the "bootlegged" Harlan house (demolished), which FLW designed in 1891, while still in the employ of Adler & Sullivan. The apartment house at right, built to the lotline, is characteristic of the largely unregulated real estate practices of the period. [HS]

Wright had not. It is fairly clear that the Harlan house cannot have been the primary reason for Sullivan's quarrel with Wright since the house was constructed and occupied at least a year and a half before the moment of dismissal in 1893.

The likelihood is that Sullivan knew of the bootlegged houses for an extended period of time and simply waited until the moment came when it was convenient for him to lose his temper with Wright and make a scene over something in which Wright could be legally perceived to be in the wrong. Wright's version of the episode is an ambiguous one. Of the three houses, he writes:

> I did not try anything radical because I could not follow them up. I could not follow up because I did these houses out of office hours, not secretly. And Mr. Sullivan soon became aware of them. He was offended and refused to issue the deed to the Oak Park house; the deed was due because the little house was now paid for. But, although I had not realized this, I had broken my contract by doing this outside work. So I protested. I asked the Master if I had been any less serviceable in the office lately.
>
> "No," he said, "but your sole interest is here, while your contract lasts. I won't tolerate division under any circumstances."
>
> This seemed unjust to me. If I could work over-hours at home for Adler & Sullivan and keep up my work in the office what harm in doing likewise for myself to relieve my own necessities? All the same I was wrong— I saw it, but angered now by what seemed the injustice of the Master—it was the first time he had said harsh words to me—I appealed to Dankmar Adler.
>
> Mr. Adler interceded, which more deeply offended the Master than ever and—more offensively still—he refused to issue the deed.
>
> When I learned this from the Master in none too kindly terms and with the haughty air now turned toward me, it was too much. I threw my pencil down and walked out of the Adler & Sullivan office never to return. Within a few months my five-year contract would have expired. This five-year term added to the previous time would make more than six years with Adler & Sullivan.
>
> Again I was in the wrong. More so than my Master. But again out on my own, this time to stay.
>
> Nor for more than twelve years did I see Louis Sullivan again or communicate with him in any way. The deed to the home duly followed, by Mr. Adler's hand.[8]

The undertone of these angry confrontations is that of a lovers' quarrel, so one ought not to expect a high degree of reasonableness to prevail; still, how did Sullivan dare to confuse the matter of the contract, which he had arranged for in order to help Wright get married, with the matter of the deed to the house, which he held because he had lent Wright the money with which to buy the Oak Park land and build the house? These were separate transactions and were surely to be recognized as such, especially among friends. And if, as Wright says, he had already paid off his debt to Sullivan, how did it happen that Sullivan hadn't turned over the deed to him before the problem of the contract arose? Is it possible that Wright's account of the dispute conceals an altogether different agenda? For example, that Sullivan had encouraged Wright to take on the outside work in order to help him pay off his debt to Sullivan, had then grown envious of Wright's increasing reputation, and had sought to find a moment at which it would appear appropriate to break off relations with him? Or

FLW with his friend Cecil Corwin, who was the architect of record of some of the "bootlegged" houses. [PF]

was it Wright who, in the light of his increasing reputation, chose to provoke the quarrel, which provided him with a welcome opportunity to leave the firm? Still another possibility exists, knowledge of which Elmslie hinted at strongly in later years, both to Wright and to others: that Wright had been asked to carry out certain purchases of Oriental rugs and other household valuables in Sullivan's behalf and had embezzled a sizeable portion of the funds that Sullivan had entrusted him with. A gentle, honest man, Elmslie would never have entertained such a notion, much less spoken of it, without some basis in fact, but it is in the nature of such an embezzlement, if indeed it ever took place, that the guilty party will claim that it was all the result of an unfortunate misunderstanding.

Whatever the truth of the matter may be, it is fairly certain that Sullivan and Wright were equally eager to set themselves free, each from the other. They succeeded in doing so, but only in anger and with recriminations that threatened to make the break between them a permanent one. How would their careers have developed if they had managed to remain friends and colleagues? A not quite idle speculation: my guess is that Sullivan would have had far more to gain from Wright than Wright from him. Although Sullivan would never have enjoyed designing "mere" houses as much as Wright did, Wright would have had more big buildings to put up at an earlier stage of his career and might even have succeeded in bringing into existence his proposed "mile-high" building, "a proud and soaring thing," over the problem of whose foundations Dankmar Adler in heaven would no doubt have spent many a contentedly sleepless night. (Engineers tell me that Wright's so-called "tap-root" foundation remains an excellent solution to that problem.) Certainly in extreme old age Wright permitted the façades of his buildings to pullulate with exotic decorative elements, some of them reminiscent of the Wolf Lake Amusement Park project that he designed within a decade of leaving Adler & Sullivan. He came to love and praise Sullivan when he could afford to do so, in the security of his own hard-won fame, but if he had loved him enough in youth to go on practicing architecture with him, what wonders they might have brought into the world!

Given the great age that Wright attained and the variety of masks that he assumed from one decade to the next, we tend to think of his years of domesticity with Catherine and the children in Oak Park as amounting to a comparatively brief episode; in fact, the episode embraced what for many people amounts to an adult lifetime—almost nineteen years. One can say of the Wrights without gushing that they were, at the start, an irresistible couple, handsome and energetic and with a touching eagerness to play the role of distinguished grown-ups, though they were but newly emerged from their teens. In spite of how hard he was working and in spite of the numerous children that Catherine bore (and appeared content to bear), they were bent upon making a mark in the proud little cultural group that had established itself in Oak Park—"Saints' Rest," as it was mockingly referred to, thanks to its profusion of churches and its aspiration to lofty moral standards.

The young Wrights were conventional in every respect save that of money, which according to Oak Park standards was to be spent only after it had been earned, with a certain portion of it first to be put aside in the form of savings. The Wrights not only failed to accumulate savings, they lived habitually beyond their means, running up bills all over town in a way that made them the occasion of much head-shaking among their neighbors. According to the divorce petition prepared by William C. Wright, Anna Wright had been an extravagant woman, unwilling to remain within the bounds of his admittedly small income, and it is curious that their son, having observed at first hand the sorry consequences of the debts that had helped to cause the breakup of his parents' marriage, should have been so willing to plunge into the same vexatious sea of debt himself, and yet he did so with an uncanny blitheness—one that he retained even into his eighties and nineties. He pretended to deplore his always perilous financial condition, but he took care to see that the perils remained real. The reputation he earned in his early twenties in Oak Park of being slow to pay his bills—of being capable, indeed, of never paying them at all—

© PHILANDER BARCLAY

*Despite revolutionaries like FLW, time may be said to move slowly in Oak Park. Above,
typical Oak Park houses of the eighteen-nineties, as photographed by the indefatigable Philander. Below, a photograph taken almost a hundred years later.*

© SUSAN WOLDENBERG

Above, the playroom, used with equal success by the Wright children and their youthful parents, who liked giving parties there. Below, Catherine Wright reading to Lloyd and John, while baby Frances sleeps in the cradle. [HS]

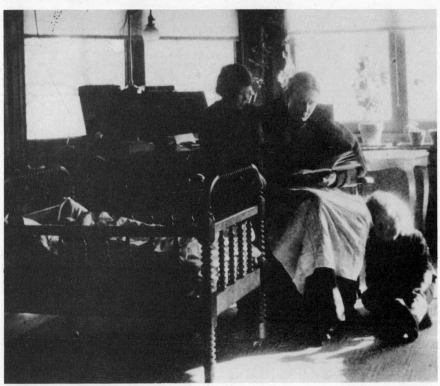

was still his at the time of his death. To this day in Spring Green one hears stories not of Wright's greatness but of his purported fiscal skulduggery.

If the Wrights' attitude toward money was a notable aberration in the Oak Park of the nineties, so was their profligacy in respect to childbearing. Few of the ambitious young couples in that community were hurling child after child into the world; the white Protestant upper-middle-class world had achieved a few more or less successful methods of birth control by that time and six or more children were beginning to be regarded as evidence of a deplorable carelessness, not to say lubricity. The eccentric nature of the ever-burgeoning Wright family is much heightened for us by Wright's repeated claim to have had no vocation for fatherhood. In his autobiography, he wrote, "Is it a quality? Fatherhood? If so, I seemed born without it. And yet a building was a child. I have had the father-feeling, I am sure, when coming back after a long time to one of my buildings. That must be the true feeling of fatherhood. But I never had it for my children. I had affection for them. I regarded them as with me—and play-fellows, comrades to be responsible for." Wright notes that Catherine insisted upon the children calling him "Papa," which he disliked. "There is a stuffy domesticity about the sound applied to the male that was always intolerable to me," he wrote. And added, more benignly than one might have expected, " 'Father' is tolerable after fifty. Papa never!"[1]

Catherine played her several roles as wife, mother, kindergarten teacher, party hostess, patroness of the arts, and dutiful daughter-in-law to the dragonish Anna Lloyd Wright with remarkable competence. Long afterward, Wright complained that she hadn't known the names of his clients, but how on earth was she to accomplish that feat in the midst of accomplishing a dozen others? She had never known any other man and it is plain that she loved Wright ardently and from early in their lives together was willing to put up with a good deal of nonsense from him, including his dandified public preening and posturing, his pursuit of fame along with his pursuit of business, and his increasing attractiveness to other women. In the running of the household, she depended much upon her mother and her maternal grandmother, both of whom, it appears, were not above enjoying an occasional bitter quarrel with Anna Wright. The children, intelligent and energetic, were encouraged to express themselves, and the turmoil in the house was continuous; some clients found the experience of visiting Wright in Oak Park nerve-wracking, others found it hilarious. What did Catherine make of the circumstances that she had helped to invent and over which she was obviously losing control? Perhaps she chose not to examine them, or perhaps, only half-examining them during the few moments of any day that she may have been able to claim for taking thought, she perceived that domestic commotion was the only means at her disposal for tethering, at least for the time being, the hypnotic genius that fate had brought her into passionate collision with.

Immediately after quitting Adler & Sullivan, Wright and his friend Cecil Corwin had rented quarters for the practice of architecture in the tower of the Schiller building, on Randolph Street, in Chicago. Wright divided his time between this downtown office, convenient for prospective clients, and the studio at his home in Oak Park. Ironically, the Schiller building had been designed by Adler & Sullivan a couple of years earlier and Wright had had a hand in its design, though probably not so great a hand as he was afterward characteristically to claim. To my mind, the Schiller building (demolished in 1961) is an even greater achievement than the Auditorium building; no ghost of Richardson hovers over its strong and slender tower, which leaps up off the street like a fantasy more Byzantine

© RICHARD NICKEL

Left, a window embrasure of the Schiller building, the detailing of which is said to have been carried out by FLW under Sullivan's eye. Right, the Schiller building, by Adler & Sullivan, 1890. In many respects a more successful design than the Auditorium building. Wantonly thrown down in 1961. [CCL]

© RICHARD NICKEL

Left, a terra-cotta detail on the Schiller building. The heads are said to be German cultural heroes, so far unidentified. Right, a plaster panel from the interior, probably designed by FLW. [CCL]

than Teutonic, concealing behind its graceful façade what were then unprecedented feats of engineering on Adler's part. Wright was proud of the simple and straightforward decoration that he imposed upon his Schiller building offices: plain walls, plain square chairs, simple oak chests, clear plate-glass doors, and indirect lighting. As Manson notes, Wright's description of the offices puts one in mind of his description of the decoration that his mother had imposed on their little Gorham Street house in Madison, even down to the simple transparent glass globe placed in the middle of a seven-foot-square conference table and containing flowers of the season. By conventional Victorian standards, the decoration was Spartan; it was also at odds with the romanticism of the ornament that Sullivan and Wright had lavished upon the building itself.

In the residences that Wright designed while still working for Adler & Sullivan, whether they were "bootlegged" as Wright claimed or are more accurately to be described as acts of "moonlighting," informally recognized as such by Sullivan, we see him as being still very much under the influence of Silsbee. Wright himself blamed the appearance of these residences in part upon the fact that he had not been in a position to supervise their construction; he might have claimed that his clients at that time were also under the prevailing Silsbeean influence—Silsbee was one of the most popular architects in the Middle West and a novelty introduced by him would be far more acceptable to clients than the same novelty introduced by Wright. The neo-Colonial style manifested in the Blossom house and the Dutch Colonial style of its next-door neighbor, the McArthur house, were something comparatively new under the Chicago sun, but Silsbee had sanctioned their advent and so Wright's clients, though brave, were

Two bootlegged houses, both built in 1892—the Blossom house on the left, the McArthur on the right. FLW appears to be demonstrating his youthful architectural virtuosity by the houses' unlikeness to each other; it may be, however, that the clients insisted on this unneighborly lack of comity.

not being foolhardy. The Blossom house was a miniature scion of the grand Taylor house that the fashionable Eastern firm of McKim, Mead & White had recently designed in Newport, Rhode Island. Except for its combined dining room and conservatory, the Blossom house is so "correct" in the formal symmetry of its ground-floor plan as to defy being comfortably lived in; designed and built in the same period, the ground-floor plan of the McArthur house is informally asymmetrical and downright cozy. The parlor, living room, and dining room all boast large bay windows at their outside corners (an early anticipation of Wright's suppression of post-and-beam in favor of an invisible cantilever) and the entrance hall, though rather pinched in scale, has the eccentric charm of something that has turned out well through inadvertence.

The earliest Oak Park houses, "moonlit" as they were, are more backward-looking in their Queen Anne façades than Wright's own house, itself a borrowing from the fashionable East and accused by some of his neighbors of being "seaside." Nevertheless, the floor plans of these houses show a certain venturesomeness, especially in respect to the placing of entrance doors and stairways. Wright's first major independent commission came to him from W. H. Winslow, a manufacturer of ornamental iron works, who had long enjoyed a close business relationship with Adler & Sullivan. Knowing how little interest the partners had in designing residences, Winslow found it natural to commission one from their gifted former head draftsman; a choice into which convenience entered, since the land on which he was intending to build was in River Forest, a village adjacent to Oak Park and only a few minutes away from Wright's own house.

A portion of the Edward Waller estate in River Forest had been set aside for real-estate development and Winslow had purchased a choice parcel in the development, on Auvergne Place, across from the Waller house. Waller was a highly successful entrepreneur in Chicago and an admirer of Wright; he had Wright remodel the dining room of his house (now demolished) and commissioned a house from him that was never built. Winslow was an aesthete as well as a businessman, interested in fine printing and prepared to entertain novel ideas in respect to domestic architecture. The façade of the house that Wright designed for him and his family was a shrewd mingling of Sullivanian formality with Wrightian emphasis upon shelter. Hints of the Charnley house and even of the Wainwright tomb, which Sullivan had designed a couple of years earlier, are visible as one approaches the house, but what makes the most profound impression is the immense, broad-eaved hip roof, uninterrupted by dormers and silently announcing the Prairie Houses to come. Although there is a large third floor to the Winslow house, reached by a stairway more richly detailed than the stairway connecting the first and second floors, the space is rendered almost uninhabitable by the deliberate suppression of natural light and ventilation except through a single small dormer set high in the rear roof; this is a formidable price to pay for the cavelike, primordial protectiveness that the front roof gives us promise of.

Manson writes that Wright's design "precludes any thought of using attic space as living space; ushering household domestics out of cramped, airless quarters under the rafters was Wright's most humanitarian contribution, in an age when domestic service was still taken for granted, to the progress of the American dwelling."[2] In fact, the third floor of the Winslow house, far from being an attic, is fully finished off, with plastered walls and wood trim, and the elaborate stairway leading to it, enclosed in a

A little Queen Anne house in Oak Park, 1893, typical of those that FLW was more or less secretly turning out for friends while still under contract to Adler & Sullivan.

© SUSAN WOLDENBERG

many-sided brick tower, encourages us to see that it was indeed intended for human occupancy and was so employed by the Winslows—there was nowhere else in the house to fit their servants. Moreover, the peculiar positioning of the stairs, to which one gains access from a narrow, secondary hall on the ground floor, made it possible for the servants to reach their dark eyrie without entering the family portions of the house. In Wright houses of the period, the stairway is usually a feature in the design as important as the hearth; in the Winslow house the stairway, though wide, is shut away behind doors and so low-ceilinged that a six-foot-tall person instinctively ducks his head in climbing it. There are other oddities in the plan, betraying the youthful uncertainty of the architect. Not the least of these is an iron fluestack that emerges from the flat roof of the kitchen, makes a right-angle turn, and enters a brick chimney at a point a few inches above the roof: a miscalculation that Wright could find no way to disguise.

The major oddity of the façade is a dwarfish front door, lower in height than the rectangular windows balancing it on either side. A similar dwarfishness afflicts the entrance to the Charnley house and the entrances to several houses designed by Maher, a follower of Wright. In every case the effect is largely an optical illusion; the doors prove to be of normal height. In one form or another, Wright was often to practice this psychological blackmail upon anyone taller than he. William Wesley Peters, universally known as Wes, became in 1932 one of the first of the Taliesin apprentices. Being something over six feet, four inches tall, he underwent constant teasing by Wright. "Sit down, Wes," Wright would call out to him, year after year and decade after decade, "you're spoiling the scale!" Living to this day in grottolike quarters at one or the other of the Taliesins, Peters admits to have lost perhaps half an inch in height, though his friends reckon that the loss is far more substantial than that.

Having admired the tranquil Sullivanian symmetry of the front of the house, one passes through the equally Sullivanian arch of a porte cochere on the north side of the house to encounter the unexpectedly complex, not to say incoherent, massing of the rear elevation. Writing in Wright's lifetime, Hitchcock was kind enough to say of the rear that its "fine composition . . . with its bold conjunctions of horizontal and vertical elements, its contrast of solid and void and of rectangular and polygonal forms was hardly understood by early imitators."[3] To which I would add, "How fortunate for them!" since at that point Wright had plainly lost control of the design, surrendering the tranquility of the front of the house to the exigencies of its plan, which he correctly saw were of paramount importance, but to which, at that stage of his career, he was unable to make an appropriate exterior accommodation. Matters might only have been made worse if a covered gallery, which was intended to connect the porch to a freestanding octagonal pavilion south of the house, had actually been built.

In the entrance hall, a couple of shallow steps lead up to a platform that has the feeling of a miniature stage. A screen consisting of eight wooden colonnettes with carved capitals is reminiscent of the eight-pillared loggia that is the main feature of the façade of the Charnley house. Behind the screen is an inglenook and a fireplace of Roman brick. Surprisingly, there is no fireplace in the living room, its focal point being a bay window opening from still another stagelike area—an elevated and railed platform, suitable for the giving of musicales. The dining room is large and handsome, with a fireplace at its inner end and a semicircular bay window—itself as big as a room—with exquisite leaded-glass casements and an upholstered window seat filling the garden end.

The stable of the Winslow house in its early years boasted a big tree growing through its roof—a trick that Wright rejoiced to play not only in his own house but in the Isabel Roberts house and other houses as well. Where the tree emerged from the roof, a crudely fashioned gasket of rubber and cloth would keep the roof from leaking—or, rather, from leaking more than the average amount for a Wright building. The stable provided ample room for a hobby of Winslow's, the Auvergne Press, which published elegant hand-set limited editions of books of a non-commercial nature. One of the books printed by the press was *The House Beautiful*, by William C. Gannett, a Unitarian minister whom Wright and Winslow admired. Like Edward W. Bok, editor of the *Ladies' Home Journal*, who was later to commission designs for ideal, inexpensive houses from Wright, Gannett believed in the private house as a citadel of family love, virtue, and culture; he also believed that such a house should be well made, well ventilated, sunny, and sanitary. Wright designed Gannett's book, drew individual page decorations for it, and wrote its preface. Copies of *The House Beautiful*, which upon publication were given away to friends as keepsakes, are being offered for sale today for $25,000.

The Wrights, Winslows, and Wallers made an intimate social set inside their suburban community and were soon to be joined by another "W" couple, the Chauncey Williamses, who came from Madison and were already acquainted with Wright. Like the Winslows, the Williamses purchased a parcel of land from the Wallers in River Forest and commissioned Wright to design a house for them; to put it bluntly, the Williams house is a freakish-looking structure, with none of the serenity of façade that Wright had achieved apparently with so little effort in the Winslow house. Its mansardlike roof and gigantic chimneys, which may well echo a Wrightian memory of something he had encountered in his perusals of Viollet-le-Duc, threaten to crush a ground floor whose exterior is a melange of disparities; it boasts a Roman-arched front entrance with Sullivanesque

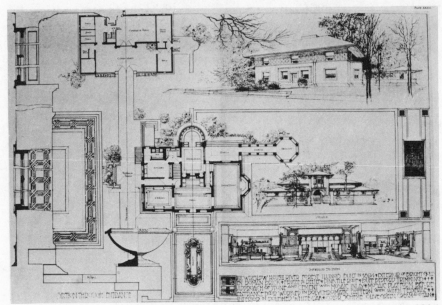

Illustration from The Architectural Review *of the Winslow house, River Forest, 1894.*

detailing, a Spanish baroque bull's-eye window immediately adjacent to it, and a heaping up of boulders on either side of the door. One might suppose, as Hitchcock did, that the boulders betray a Japanese influence, but it appears that they embody as well a certain pleasing Middle Western sentimentality, for Manson tells us that they were dragged up out of the nearby Des Plaines River on summer weekends by the four "W" couples and were supposed to symbolize that period of glaciation during which the Illinois prairies were formed.

Wright fails to mention the Williams house in his autobiography, and I am not surprised; too many experiments are being conducted within the structure at the same moment and the consequence isn't merely eccentricity but incoherence. As originally designed, the dormers were so peculiar that they have long since been subsumed into moderately less peculiar ones, also designed by Wright. Even in the presence of failure, Wright rarely gave up altogether on an experiment; the steeply pitched roof of the Williams house turns up later in, among other places, the Lake Tahoe project of 1922, in the Richard Davis residence of 1950, and in the Beth Sholom Synagogue of 1954.

An architect just launching himself in the world is subject to the whims of clients, and even Wright, for a time, may have been no exception. Manson cites the case of the Frederick Bagley house of 1894, which Wright designed in the Dutch Colonial style that he had already toyed with in

A photograph of the Winslow house under its now long vanished elms. [WW]

the McArthur house. Mr. Bagley happened to be in the marble business and like any businessman wished to display a sample of the source of his wealth to guests in his house. Having in stock a couple of Ionic marble colonnettes that he had yet to find a purchaser for, Bagley asked Wright to incorporate them in the design of the house. Wright succeeded in doing so, using the colonnettes to frame a chimney breast sheathed, no doubt to Bagley's intense pleasure, in red marble. Wright repeated the colonnettes in wood to support the roof above the front porch. A charming anomaly

Left, the complex rear façade of the Winslow house. [WW] *Right, the entry hall, with its delicately arcaded inglenook. Note the chic slantwise display of the Oriental rug on the steps.* [WW]

Left, the Williams house, River Forest, built somewhat later than the nearby Winslow house and remarkable for its variety of ill-digested details. Right, an essay in the Tudor manner for FLW's Oak Park neighbor, Nathan Moore. Erected in 1895 and remodeled by FLW (who added a few Japanese touches to the Tudor) after a fire in 1922. Far right, a bay window in the Moore house, designed around 1914 by the architect William Fellows.

in the Bagley house is an octagonal library wing, lit by clerestories; it was apparently inspired by a circular library wing in a Dutch Colonial house designed by Silsbee and it anticipated the octagonal library that Wright was to design for his Studio building a year or so later.

Manson takes seriously the notion, which Wright voices in his autobiography, that he intensely disliked having to give in to his clients' preference for conventional styles. Some contemporary students of Wright's life doubt whether this dislike was as intense in his youth as he pretended it had been by the time he had reached middle age. Though he later jeered at columns, colonnettes, and pilasters, he employed them profusely even in houses where he was totally in charge of the design, as in the Winslow, Heller, and Husser houses. Some of these columns and pilasters owe their configurations to architectural sources in Vienna and elsewhere on the continent, which Wright would have seen in *The International Studio* and other magazines.

Another client who was able to impose his wishes upon the beginning architect was Nathan G. Moore, a lawyer who lived across the street from the Wrights in Oak Park. Mr. and Mrs. Moore turned up at Wright's office in the Schiller building with some photographs, evidently clipped out of magazines, of English Tudor houses with full half-timbering—a style then coming into vogue in suburbs throughout the country. The Winslow house had created a sensation in and around River Forest, with many people regarding it as a welcome step forward in domestic architecture and with others heaping ridicule upon it. In true lawyerly fashion, Mr. Moore was balanced between these extremes. He admired Wright and yet he told him, "We don't want you giving us anything like that house you did for Winslow. I don't fancy sneaking down back streets to my morning train just to avoid being laughed at."[4]

© SUSAN WOLDENBERG

© SUSAN WOLDENBERG

Partly (so Wright subsequently claimed) because he needed the money and partly because he felt challenged by the opportunity to produce something of value in a style basically repugnant to him, Wright designed a handsome Tudor mansion for the Moores. To his dismay, the Moore house was considered every bit as successful as the Winslow house; the appetite for Tudor houses proved so strong that it threatened to turn him into just the sort of conventional architect that he was determined not to become. "Anyone could get a rise out of me," he wrote, "by admiring that essay in English half-timber. . . . I could have gone on unnaturally building them for the rest of my natural life. It was the first time, however, an English half-timbered house ever saw a porch."[5] That wholly American porch helped to reconcile him to the hypocrisy of the essay; when, some twenty years later, the house was gutted by fire, the Moores called upon Wright to rebuild it for them and on that occasion he created an exuberantly bastard form, elements of Japanese architectural grammar mingling with remnants of the Tudor and the American porch remaining a triumphant solecism.

For an architect still in his twenties, Wright was gaining an exceptional degree of attention. Colleagues many years older than he commended his designs and began to take seriously his utterances on arts and crafts and their relationship to the machine. Daniel H. Burnham, known to colleagues of all ages as "Uncle Dan," was the most prominent architect in Chicago in that period. (Outside Chicago, his firm designed such celebrated structures as the Flatiron building, in New York City, and the Union Station, in Washington, D.C.) His design partner, John Wellborn Root, had died in 1891, at the tragically early age of forty-one; the cause of his death was pneumonia, which he contracted in the course of entertaining a group

Panorama of the Chicago World's Fair of 1893—a classical daydream imposed on an astonished nation largely by Richard Morris Hunt and "Uncle Dan" Burnham. [TS]
The Transportation building at the Fair, designed by Sullivan (with FLW "a pencil in his hand"). The gorgeous polychromy of its entrance was radically at odds with the rest of the "white city," as Sullivan was almost always radically at odds with Burnham. [TS]

of Eastern architects who had come to Chicago to discuss the proposed World's Columbian Exposition of 1893. Root was succeeded as Burnham's design partner by a brilliant but erratic young architect named Charles B. Atwood, who in 1895, overworked and incapacitated by drugs, was invited to "retire" from the firm; ten days later he was dead, at the age of forty-six. One evening after dinner at the Wallers', Uncle Dan turned to Wright and made him an astonishing offer: he would send him and his wife and three children to Paris for the three years that it would take Wright to complete his courses at the Beaux-Arts; he would then treat the Wrights to a two-years' residence in Rome, after which Wright would be brought into the Burnham firm as a design partner. To the disappointment of Uncle Dan and Waller, Wright rejected the offer, saying that Sullivan had poisoned his mind against the Beaux-Arts and adding, "I know how obstinate and egotistic you think me, but I'm going on as I've started. I'm spoiled, first by birth, then by training, and . . . [finally] by conviction."[6]

Despite Wright's penchant for exaggeration, especially in telling anecdotes of which he is the hero, the Burnham offer strikes me as having the ring of truth, in part because Wright ends it with the rueful confession, "I helped Catherine on with her things and we went home. I didn't mention to her what had happened until long afterward."[7] No wonder he kept silent, for Catherine, coming from a far wealthier background than Wright's, would presumably have welcomed that fashionable thing, a European sojourn; moreover, she would have foreseen that, the sojourn ended, a position for Frank high up in the ranks of D. H. Burnham & Company would have spelled a lifetime of security for her and her growing family.

Instead, the Wrights remained in Oak Park, with Wright growing ever busier, ever more socially ambitious, and ever more spendthrift in his tastes. "So long as we had the luxuries," he would write later, half boasting, half in contrition, "the necessities could pretty well take care of themselves. . . . This love for beautiful things—rugs, books, prints, or anything made by art or craft or building—especially building—kept the butcher, the baker, and the landlord always waiting. . . . I felt remorse. . . . I would resist the next adventure into art and craft, perhaps resist for several months. But this self-denial would not last. . . . It was my misfortune . . . that everybody was willing to trust me. I don't know why they were willing, either, because I don't imagine my appearance or my way of life would appeal to a businessman any more than my buildings appealed to the local bankers a little later on."[8]

Wright was continually laggard in paying his rent in the Schiller building, and when Cecil Corwin decided to begin a new career in the East, Wright moved his quarters to Steinway Hall, sharing space in a loft there with several young architects, among them Robert Spencer, Dwight Perkins,

The Roloson row-houses, Chicago, 1894. FLW's only executed row-house design and a highly successful one.

and Myron Hunt. Most of his designing was done in the Studio in Oak Park, which he built in the late nineties and where he gradually accumulated a band of young assistants, not unlike the Fellowship that would one day come into existence at Taliesin; Steinway Hall was for the conduct of business. The first additions to the Oak Park house had proceeded one by one out of family needs—a new dining room and kitchen, a servant's room, a playroom. The Studio, with its entrance terrace immediately off Chicago Avenue, its complex double entrance and hall, its two-story-high drafting room (with a balcony at the clerestory level, held in place in part by a seemingly miraculous disposition of heavy iron chains), its private office, and its octagonal library, is of an altogether different order of architectural ambition. It is laid out with a debonair disregard for the difficulty of its incommodious site and the equal difficulty of attaching it to the house proper. The mazelike entry to the Studio, decorated with sculptures by Richard Bock, implies that the effort of mastering it will provide visitors with a sufficient reward. The building as a whole possesses a dignity unlooked-for in the handiwork of a thirty-year-old; one is reminded that genius rejoices to play tricks with time and that Wright, if he was capable of being grave in youth, was no less capable of being playful in old age.

A structure comparatively trifling in size and cost (less than thousand dollars) but of great emotional significance to Wright throughout his lifetime was the so-called Romeo and Juliet windmill that he designed and built for his Aunts Nell and Jane Lloyd Jones at the Hillside Home School. The two maiden aunts, who to ensure the continued success of the school they had founded had promised each other that they would never marry, doted upon Frank almost as much as his mother did, and they turned to him for assistance whenever the school needed to expand its facilities. In 1896, to ensure an adequate supply of water for the school, a reservoir was dug out of the solid rock at the top of the hill that rose behind the school. To pump water up out of an artesian well into the reservoir, the aunts intended at first to purchase a light metal windmill of the sort commonly used on farms in the days before the advent of electric pumps, but it occurred to them that Frank might be able to design something prettier for them, which would be more in keeping with the aesthetic ambitions of the school. The aunts' five brothers, all of whom had farms in the neighborhood and would have the windmill within their purview, were fearful of giving their gifted nephew a chance to show off; a conventional windmill would be cheaper and would no doubt last longer than any newfangled contraption cobbled up by him.

When Wright's design for the windmill arrived at Hillside, the local builder, a man named Cramer, mocked it as a structural monstrosity, sure to blow down in the first big storm. Sixty feet high, with a wheel fourteen feet in diameter at the top, and hammered together out of nothing but timber and shingles—well! The builder and the five uncles were all scandalized, and the aunts telegraphed Wright in Chicago: CRAMER SAYS WINDMILL TOWER SURE TO FALL. ARE YOU SURE IT WILL STAND? To which Wright replied: BUILD IT. Cramer and the uncles grumbled, but the aunts held fast. Wright sent them a reassuring letter, which also served to explain why he had nicknamed the windmill Romeo and Juliet, an appellation that may have caused the uncles to fear the worst. In form, the windmill was an octagon, penetrated in one plane by a diamond shape that Wright labeled on the plans a "storm prow," calculated to deflect the fierce winds that, among those hills and valleys, would be most likely to assail the tower from the southwest. To the aunts he wrote:

Of course you had a hard time with Romeo and Juliet. But you know how troublesome they were centuries ago. The principle they represent still causes mischief in the world because it is so vital. Each is indispensable to the other . . . neither could stand without the other. Romeo, as you will see, will do all the work and Juliet cuddle alongside to support and exalt him. Romeo takes the side of the blast and Juliet will entertain the school children. Let's let it go at that. No symbol should be taken too far. As for the principle involved, it *is* a principle but I've never seen it in this form. No. But I've never seen anything to go against it, either.[9]

© SUSAN WOLDENBERG

Left, the drafting room of the Studio is a two-story-high octagon, with a fireplace and ample space for eight or ten draftsmen. Right, the library in which FLW entertained clients is also an octagon, handsomely paneled and with high clerestory windows.

He added a postscript:

> Romeo and Juliet will stand twenty-five years, which is longer than the iron towers stand around there. I am afraid all of my uncles themselves may be gone before "Romeo and Juliet." Let's go.

In his autobiography, Wright ends the story on a note of triumph:

> Now nearly forty-four years have gone by since the amateur windmill tower—Romeo and Juliet—took its place on the hill in the sun overlooking the beloved valley. I, the author of its being, hair getting white now as Aunt Nell's was when, before the tower was built, she first walked to the window to see its wheel spinning there among the trees. . . . Seemingly good as ever the wooden tower that was an experiment still stands in full view. Shall I take it down, faithful servant serving so long, so well? Or shall I let it go until it falls just as I myself must do—though neither tower nor I show any signs of doing so.
>
> The tower is weatherbeaten. My hair is gray. One never knows. But when we fall, there will surely still be those to say, "Well, there it is—down at last! We thought so!"[10]

Romeo and Juliet still crowns the hill behind the Hillside Home School buildings, which at present are occupied by the drafting room and other facilities of the Taliesin Fellowship. By now, not forty-four years but almost ninety years have passed since the windmill was built and it remains as stormproof as ever and as romantic an object as ever against the sky.

120

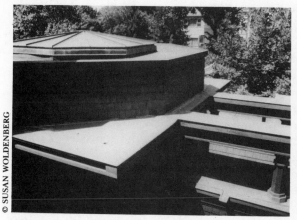

© SUSAN WOLDENBERG

© SUSAN WOLDENBERG

Left, roof of the Studio as seen from the house. Right, humorously sculpted creatures guarding the entrance to the Studio. Sketched by FLW and executed by Richard Bock, they are thought by some to be storks, by others to be secretary birds. In either case, what is the message?

Besides the satisfaction that Wright took in its beauty, the tower was important to him for reasons that go back far into his childhood. Its construction justified his aunts' confidence in him and at the same time (for the aunts were but women) demonstrated his superiority over his five skeptical uncles, especially over Uncle Jenkin, the preacher, who was the leading male member of the family in his generation and a particular thorn in Wright's flesh.

The evident delight with which Wright relates the story of Romeo and Juliet—a story that he attempted to sell for magazine publication through his friend Darwin D. Martin long before it appeared in his autobiography—springs in part from his having outwitted the intimidating patriarchs of his youth and in part from a characteristic falsifying of his age; he always sought to be younger than he was and in this instance he disguises his true age by many years. He was nearing thirty, married, and with several children when he designed the tower, yet he portrays himself in terms more appropriate to a twenty-year-old. The uncles always refer to him as "the boy," and even Aunt Jane, in a moment of doubt, exclaims, "Poor boy! What a pity his tower won't stand up." As for Cramer, the builder, Wright puts into his mouth a veritable aria of derogation; he is made to say of Wright, "It beats heck the way those two old maids dance around after that boy. He comes up here with his swell duds on, runs around the hills with the school girls and goes home. You wouldn't think he had a care in the world nor anything but something to laugh at."[11]

At almost the same time that the windmill was helping to establish Wright's credentials within the family and possibly as a direct consequence of his having thus established them, the prickly Uncle Jenkin invited Wright to design for him a new church in Chicago, to take the place of "All Souls," the church that Silsbee had designed for Jenkin Lloyd Jones a few years earlier and that had proved too small to accommodate the success of his ministry. The new church, to be called by the deliberately non-sectarian name of the Abraham Lincoln Center, was to have the appearance of an ordinary multistory office building and would contain auditoriums, assembly rooms, kitchens, gymnasiums, and living quarters for Uncle Jenkin and his family, along with retail shops at street level, the rents from which would contribute to the support of the church.

This revolutionary concept of what a church building might be must have struck Wright as the greatest opportunity yet offered him to test his mettle, and he set about producing many designs on paper and models in plaster, none of which proved satisfactory to the Reverend Lloyd Jones. Uncle and nephew clashed repeatedly over the project during a period of five years; perhaps they were too alike in temperament not to end up far apart, or perhaps there was a certain Oedipal taint in the relationship.

Left, the Romeo and Juliet windmill, 1896, designed to pump water for his aunts' school at Spring Green. In later years, FLW replaced its shingle cladding with board-and-batten siding. [UA] Right, the windmill still stands on its hilltop, obscured by trees.

Be that as it may, in 1902 Wright turned the project over to his young colleague Perkins, who also quarreled with Lloyd Jones and, walking away from the job, scribbled in red crayon on one of the final blueprints, "bldg. completed over protest of architect." Opening in 1905, the Abraham Lincoln Center bore little resemblance to Wright's original designs and is never included in any list of his works. Wright always called his unbuilt projects "office tragedies," but Uncle Jenkin's brainchild never attained even that degree of recognition; he makes no mention whatever of this embittering episode in his autobiography, and one is inclined to suspect that the happy episode of the windmill is intended to conceal its absence.

9

LIVING SO LONG, Wright saw much
of his handiwork vanish over the years, including several masterpieces.
He was more cheerful about this than one might have expected, in part
because he was always preoccupied with producing new designs and in
part because, as his fame spread, many projects that had long remained
merely furled blueprints and pretty renderings were at last translated into
brick and stone. Two of my favorite Wright houses of the late nineties
are those of Isadore Heller and Joseph Husser, both in Chicago; the Heller
house is still standing and the Husser house has been demolished. The
Heller house provides an exceptionally attractive solution to the problem
of the long and narrow city lot. The house fills its constricted sleeve of
space with deceptive ease, the rooms flowing into one another and the
three full stories mounting skyward as if from choice and not necessity.
We tend to think of Wright's mastery of the horizontal in his domestic
architecture as defining a personal preference, but his equal mastery of

*In the Joseph Husser house of 1899, FLW took advantage of the site's superb view out
over Lake Michigan by putting all the important living quarters on the second and third
floors, the first floor serving in place of a basement. In a few years, the open land between
the house and the lake was usurped by big apartment houses; hemmed in and viewless, the
house was eventually demolished.*

the vertical implies that when the occasion called for it he took pleasure in creating what Sullivan called "a proud and soaring thing." On its small scale, the Heller house soars; the structure is dominated by a romantically pillared open loggia on the third floor, set in a frieze of hand-holding maidens, modeled by the sculptor Richard Bock; the setting might as easily be thought to be central Europe as Chicago.

Still more romantic was the Husser house, which enjoyed a site looking out over Lake Michigan. In describing the advantages of his Prairie Houses, Wright noted that "a little height on the prairie was enough to look like much more—every detail as to height becoming intensely significant, breadths all falling short."[1] This "little height" was of measurable importance on the lakeshore as well and for that reason Wright conceived of the second floor as a true piano nobile, with the living room, the dining room, the kitchen, and a vast covered porch all gaining unobstructed views of the lake, as did the bedrooms on the floor above. The ground floor provided room for an entrance hall and for the utilities usually sequestered in basements. Like the loggia of the Heller house and the decorative cupola on the roof of the Schiller building, the detailing of the windows of the Husser house puts one in mind of the amusing little domed minarets that Sullivan and Wright designed to flank the Golden Doorway of the Transportation building at the World's Columbian Exposition.

If the plan of the Husser house looked forward to the Willits and Robie houses, still some years in the future, the elevations looked backward to Sullivan and, at least from the landward side, had an air of having been accumulated part by part and never successfully stitched together into a rational whole—of being, in short, by Wright's own definition "inorganic." Arriving by automobile or carriage, one gained access to the house through a porte cochere, above which rose a two-story wing of the house; this wing, windowless on the second-floor level, contained the grand main staircase and was crowned by a roof with exceptionally wide eaves. Arriving on foot, one gained access to the house by means of a long pergola, running parallel to the driveway on one side and the house on the other and offering convenient shelter but no view. Wright was far from being what in the nineteen-eighties is called a "contextual" architect. He pretended to pay great attention to the siting of a house, and sometimes he did so, but he rarely paid any serious attention to the relationship of his houses to their immediate neighbors; he had no reason to practice this courtesy, since by his standards they were houses "that lied about everything. . . . To take any of those so-called 'homes' away would have improved the landscape and cleared the atmosphere. . . . It is not too much to say that as an architect my lot in Oak Park was cast with an inebriate lot of sinners hardened by habit against every human significance. . . . I will venture to say that the aggregation was the worst the world ever saw—at the lowest aesthetic

The Isadore Heller house, Chicago, 1897. A free-standing house on a narrow city lot would seem to present insuperable difficulties in respect to generous interior space, but not at all—FLW's floor plan (below) flows with unconstricted ease from room to room.

level in all history. Steam heat, plumbing, and electric light were coming in as its only redeeming features."[2]

This noisy bombast, written in the nineteen-twenties, is so exaggerated as to prompt us to guess that it has little to do with architecture and a great deal to do with the community that Wright had early sought to become a prominent member of and had then outraged by his scandalous misconduct in the years 1909 and 1910. A town nicknamed Saints' Rest, which boasted that, thanks to a total prohibition of alcoholic beverages, was the point where "the saloons stop and the steeples start," is hardly likely to have been populated by "an inebriate lot of sinners"; moreover,

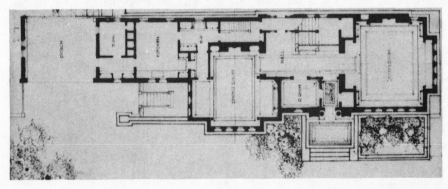

© SUSAN WOLDENBERG

© SUSAN WOLDENBERG

The exterior of the Heller house reveals FLW's interest in current European architectural experiments, especially in Vienna; the plaster frieze by the sculptor Richard Bock strikes an unexpectedly lyrical note in a city then known as the "hog-butcher to the world."

a great many of the houses occupied by those reputed sinners had been designed by Wright and were only marginally better than the conventional second-rate Queen Anne work that his architectural colleagues were producing.

It was an aspect of Wright's arrogant genius to perform his feats as if they were a series of solos; each house being a separate act of creation, each house was expected to stand on its own, refusing to acknowledge its role as one unit among many tens of thousands of units in a complex urban mass. For example, the Blossom and McArthur houses are built upon adjacent lots; their side walls are but a few feet apart. They were on Wright's drawing board together and the clients commissioning the houses were friendly with one another, as well as with their architect. It would seem the most natural thing in the world for Wright to have designed for Blossom and McArthur a pair of complementary houses, which would gain an increased sense of space surrounding them (to say nothing of an increased sense of dignity) by being seen to be related. Instead, the two houses are experiments in different styles and therefore appear at first glance to be aggressively at odds with one another; impossible, one would say, that they could have been designed by the same architect at the same time!

According to the famous aphorism of Robert Frost, "Good fences make good neighbors"; it is perhaps a negative corollary of this aphorism that radically dissimilar houses do not make good neighbors. Whatever excellence of design they may happen to possess is altered for the worse by the amount of individuality they embody. Fascinating as Richardson's Glessner house was—and is—it had no business being built on the corner of Prairie Avenue and Eighteenth Street, in what was then the heart of a fashionable residential district in Chicago. Its courtyard provided a highly agreeable degree of intimacy for the family, but to a passerby the grim façade was a presence as inimical as any medieval fortress; it said not merely "Keep out!" but also "Go away!" Many of Wright's houses must have created in certain benignly undistinguished neighborhoods an effect of interruption and even of bullying domination. Surely the Husser house came as a shock to its neighbors on the lakefront; it was twice as big and ten times as strange as anything else in the area, and this was to be the case with Wright houses for the ensuing half-century.

The currently faddish word "contextualism" may therefore be defined as almost everything that Wright took care not to be. Like Wright himself, his houses were manifestations of a Whitmanesque originality ("narcissism" would be the harsher term), and if the immediate neighborhood could not accommodate to them, so much the worse for the neighborhood. Originality in literature, on no matter how grandly egotistic a scale, need do little harm to one's fellow human beings—a book is likely to be of roughly the same size whether it is original or unoriginal and must be read in order to give offense—but a house is an inescapable physical presence; if nothing like it has ever been seen before, it may cause irritation to the public, as in our time certain large and overbearing sculptures (Serra's *Tilted Arc,* for example) have caused irritation. Wright would have called contextualism a fancy word for compromise, or even for hypocrisy; by definition his houses were what all houses ought to be and every other kind of house was a lie. Like Sullivan, Wright believed that the world was perversely out of step with him, not he with the world; Sullivan destroyed himself in the course of asserting this belief, as Wright again and again threatened to destroy himself. In the light of his innumerable autumnal triumphs, people tend to forget how close he came to meeting Sullivan's fate.

By just past the turn of the century, Wright's practice was expanding geographically as well as aesthetically into areas far beyond the geographic and aesthetic boundaries of Oak Park and Chicago. Not that it was necessary for him, in any adulatory fan-magazine sense, to "outgrow" either that suburb or that city. Chicago was then, as it is today, one of the greatest cities on earth and it could perfectly well have served as a sufficient base of operations for Wright throughout his lifetime; it was Wright who aban-

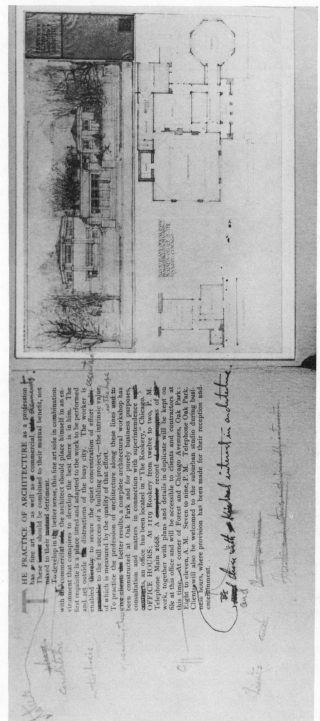

A proof, emended in FLW's hand, of the announcement in 1898 that he is establishing a studio adjoining his house in Oak Park; he will also be maintaining a "downtown" office in the Rookery building. [AL]

Family portrait, taken by FLW. At the time, he was an ardent amateur photographer and took many self-portraits. Later, he came to despise photography as a falsifier of architecture, though he continued to enjoy having his picture taken. [WS]

doned Chicago, for reasons personal and not professional, and I consider it a question worth speculating on for a moment whether Wright's genius might not have been even more richly fulfilled if it had rooted itself in a single place crowded with enviable opportunities instead of enduring the heterogeneous misadventures of those long middle years. So many disappointing false starts, so many occasions for heartbreak during that period when, as Wright often said, he was taking "a worm's eye view of the world"! And what is true of turn-of-the-century Chicago is true, obviously to a lesser degree, of Oak Park itself, which commentators on Wright tend to sneer at as the quintessence of overambitious bourgeois culture—a genteel trap that a gifted superman like Wright was understandably eager to seek an early escape from. It happens that Oak Park was not like that, and neither was Wright.

William Stearns Walker, who owns and occupies the Winslow house and whose family has lived in River Forest and Oak Park for several generations, says of Oak Park that from its founding it was altogether different from any other suburb of Chicago; like Llewellyn Park, in New Jersey, and Lawrence Park, in Bronxville, New York, it was conceived of as a utopian suburb. It drew its high intellectual aspirations from New England and, indeed, thought of itself as a sort of transplanted New England town. Most of the first settlers were Congregationalists, members of a notably democratic Protestant sect, in which every congregation has the right to elect its own minister. Throughout history, Congregationalists have been known to conduct their affairs in much the same open and vociferous fashion as a New England town meeting; they have also been known for the emphasis they place upon public education. Further evidence of continuing bias in favor of New England can be found in the names of a number of Oak Park grammar schools: Whittier, Longfellow, Emerson, Holmes, Lowell, and Hawthorne. From Oak Park schools over the years came such well-known Americans as Ernest Hemingway, Edgar Rice Burroughs, Charles MacArthur, and Bruce Barton.

As Wright gained in reputation and traveled farther and farther afield, the actual preparation of designs and working drawings continued to be carried out at the studio that Wright affixed to the house and that, through constant remodeling and expansion, ended by being far bigger than the house itself. Despite a hubbub of domestic disorder (six high-spirited and undisciplined children were more or less continuously underfoot) and the added burden of the busy social life that Wright and his wife pursued at that time, he was approaching a period of unprecedented creativity.

Of the many remarkable works of this period, the most unexpected is a charming little Japanese cottage that Wright designed, in 1900, for an attorney, S. A. Foster, in a new real-estate development called West Pullman, located in open countryside to the southwest of Chicago. Foster, one of the backers of the development, resided in Chicago and intended the cottage as his summer place. The vogue for things Japanese that followed exhibitions of Japanese architecture and decorative arts at the Philadelphia Centennial Exposition, in 1876, and the Columbian World's Fair, in Chicago, in 1893, was especially manifest in the design and decoration of summer places, from Newport on the Atlantic to Pasadena on the Pacific.

© SUSAN WOLDENBERG

The S. A. Foster house and stable, in the West Pullman district of Chicago, 1900. The client wished a summer cottage where it would be possible to ride horseback, and FLW appears to have convinced him that this meant a pretty little house in the Japanese vein. Almost ninety years later, the Foster stable remains as charming as ever, though it has been long since the neighborhood has seen an equestrian except on television.

Even in the heart of the Adirondacks, one would come upon Japanese parasols hanging from shaggy hemlock rooftrees and tatami lining closet floors. What is unexpected, then, in Wright's design is not so much that it borrowed motifs from the Japanese as that he assimilated them so convincingly into a parti otherwise conventionally Queen Anne. An enchanting structure, to this day it conveys an impression of sunny, summery ease, even though it has long been maintained as an all-the-year-round residence in a densely built-up community. It sits in the midst of a large lawn, with a stable at the rear of the property, giving onto a paved alley (the stable has been converted into a garage, but the location of stalls, a tack room, and a hayloft are still readily detectable). A remnant of grape arbor—

The Thomas house of 1901, in Oak Park. FLW felt no hesitancy in extending his newfangled Prairie House to within a few feet of its Queen Anne neighbor.

that inescapable feature of a summer place at the turn of the century— extends from the southerly portion of the old stable. The interior of the cottage is as simple in plan as Wright's own cottage in Oak Park, with a fireplace serving as the focus of a large combined living room and dining room. The bedrooms are lit by dormers peaked at their tips; the gable ends of the roof are similarly peaked. Wright was still several years away

A comparatively lavish Prairie House in Oak Park, commissioned by Arthur Heurtley (1902). The main living quarters are on the second floor.

from paying his first visit to Japan, but he had already begun collecting Japanese prints and he had studied with care a half-scale replica of a Japanese temple of the Fujiwara Period, erected at the Chicago Fair.

In the Hickox and Bradley houses, built in the same year in Kankakee, the Japanese influence is still present, oddly but successfully mingled with hints of the Swiss Chalet style, which was enjoying a certain vogue throughout the country at that time, and the Tudor style, which Wright had already made use of in the Moore house. One might have expected these three styles to clash; if they don't, it is partly because by tradition they all employ exceptionally heavy methods of framing (which Wright pretends for appearance's sake to imitate in the plaster-and-board cladding of the Hickox and Bradley houses) and partly because the stamp of a contemporary, highly individual personality has been placed so strongly upon them. And that

Right, the walls of the Heurtley house are laid up in tawny Roman pressed brick, with the courses of brick projecting at regular intervals to form a pattern. Left, a close-up of brickwork at the Robie house, showing a favorite Wright practice: a deep raking out of the horizontal joints, with the vertical joints made as nearly invisible as possible.

stamp we recognize as identifying what Wright came to call his Prairie Houses.

Other early Prairie Houses were designed by Wright for two Oak Park friends, Frank Thomas and Arthur Heurtley. As in the Husser house, the main rooms of these houses are on the second floor, the ground floor taking the place of the old-fashioned basement that Wright deplored as violently as he did the equally old-fashioned attic. (I recall his faithful colleague, Wes Peters, irreverently saying that if basements and attics hadn't existed in Wright's day, Wright would have been proud to have invented them.) In the Husser house, the second floor offered an enviable view out over Lake Michigan; in the Thomas and Heurtley houses, the second floors offer little in the way of views—in Oak Park, houses are built on small plots of level land and have only each other to look at—but they provide much-needed privacy. The roof of the Thomas house comes within a few feet of touching the roof of the house next door, and yet members of the household seated on the open second-floor veranda feel agreeably isolated from both the nearby street and from their neighbors. With its exotic arched entry and raised living quarters, the Thomas house was at once nicknamed "The Harem," which passed in Oak Park for a fairly daring jest.

The Heurtley house is especially handsome, with a broad, sheltering roof almost identical to those of the Thomas and Winslow houses and with brick walls of a striking, tawny-orange hue, laid in bands of regularly projecting and receding courses that create a powerful horizontal effect. The front entrance is reached through a Romanesque arch similar to the Romanesque entrance arches in the Thomas and Dana houses. In each case, the arches strike me as a belated borrowing from Richardson; nevertheless, there can be no doubt that this overemphatic arch was firmly fixed in Wright's hand and heart and it returned with undiminished vigor in many of his late designs. (In some of the buildings of his extreme old age, a sort of squashed Roman arch became a favorite motif; Wright must have approved of it, but I suspect that it didn't originate with him.) The Heurtley house is almost square in plan and would strike us as being excessively dense in volume if it were not for the way in which Wright has crimped its exterior walls with prowlike bay windows and pierced them with a ground-floor loggia and a second-floor veranda. To indicate the scale of the house, it may be noted that the veranda measures approximately fifteen feet wide by fifty-two feet long, while the living room and dining room, which function almost as a single room, have a floor area of something over a thousand square feet.

The Heurtley house is ideal for party-giving. In his 1969 book about Wright and Howard Van Doren Shaw (the Chicago "society" architect who was a contemporary of Wright), Leonard K. Eaton notes that Mr. Heurtley was extremely gregarious and that Mrs. Heurtley was a homebody, whose only known pleasures were cooking and needlework. Although the Heurtleys gave many parties, Eaton thinks that Mrs. Heurtley failed to enjoy them—"the Heurtleys," he says, "must have been among the least contented of the couples for whom Wright built."[3] A judgment hard to verify: what are the criteria for marital contentment? Be that as it may, Wright frequently attended parties at the Heurtleys'; he was himself an ardent party-giver as well as a party-goer, and few architects in history have provided spaces more agreeable to entertain in. Even in the smallest of his houses, one feels that there is plenty of room in which to dance and sing; we have

The rear of the Willits house, in Highland Park, 1901. A prosperous businessman, Willits financed FLW's first visit to Japan, in 1905.

reason to regret all the more bitterly Wright's loss of the McCormick commission, in 1907, when we consider that it might well have been the most delightful party-giving house ever built in America.

What Hitchcock calls "the first masterpiece among the Prairie Houses" is the Ward W. Willits house, in Highland Park, Illinois, but to my mind it is much less adventurous in plan and elevation than the Thomas and Heurtley houses, which it accompanies in time, or than the Tomek, Coonley, and Robie houses to come, all five of which employ the second floor as a *piano nobile*. The Willits house is set in an ample lot, well planted with trees, and presents a formal, almost symmetrical façade to the street; a long, low-roofed porte cochere at the front entrance balances a long, low-roofed porch off the dining room, and bands of windows are fitted into a rigid wood-and-plaster grid. The plan makes conventional use of the ground floor, with living room, dining room, butler's pantry, and kitchen pinwheeling off a massive central chimney and two servants' bedrooms, a bathroom, and a flight of service stairs grouped behind the kitchen. The second floor is even more tightly organized than the ground floor—off a narrow corridor are fitted three bedrooms, two bathrooms, a large nursery, and a linen room. The main stairway rises through a grand double-height space; a small library opens off the landing and below the library is a reception room. (To judge by the plans of so many of Wright's early houses, reception rooms were still obligatory in the Middle West at the turn of the century, though who was to be received within those stiff little boxes has become something of a puzzle to later generations.)

Despite the rather too obvious efficiency of its plan, the Willits house has the warmth and charm that Wright was able to introduce into all his best houses by dint of their detailing—the bejeweled art-glass windows, the peek-a-boo wood screens that lure one on from room to room, the broad brick hearths that promise the primordial consolations of firelight and tribal gatherings. It was not the actual prairie that these houses summoned up, but the expression of some essential goodness in family life that could be imagined as existing (or as having once existed) on the American prairie. This goodness that Wright evoked and so persistently championed is all the more touching when we consider the family life that Wright himself had experienced in childhood and had made his necessary early escape from.

A freakish structure that, though often listed as a Prairie House, has nothing to do with the prairie either physically or emotionally, is the Susan Lawrence Dana house, in Springfield, Illinois. Urged on by a goodhearted client of seemingly unlimited wealth and equally unlimited eccentricity, Wright went much further than he needed to go in performing feats of gorgeous, self-indulgent showmanship in the course of carrying out the biggest commission he had received up to that time. Wright was thirty-five, his client five years older; like Aline Barnsdall many years later, Mrs. Dana was an "advanced" woman, being a suffragette, a friend of Jane Addams (who may have helped to arrange the commission), and a philanthropist. Her husband had been killed some years earlier, while inspecting a mining property in which he held an interest; a few months later, her father, a self-made railroad and mining magnate, also died. Mrs. Dana kept in touch with "darling Papa" through a spirit "control" in the other world, asking his advice on such practical matters as whether a family relative was likely to die soon and, if the answer was yes, whether she should take out life insurance on him. (If Darling Papa answered the first question in the affirmative, surely as a successful businessman he must have answered the second question in the affirmative as well.)

What had begun as the remodeling and expansion of a sturdy Victorian

© SUSAN WOLDENBERG

The Dana house, in Springfield, Illinois, 1902. Carried away by the chance to remodel and improve a Victorian mansion, FLW effectively obliterated it.

mansion in the Italianate style ended with the total exterior obliteration of the mansion. (Papa's study was preserved in the depths of the interior, where it was hoped that Papa would continue to feel at home.) Usurping much of the land on which the mansion had been built, a sequence of grand rooms—an art gallery, a library, a two-story-high dining room— were designed to permit social gatherings of a lofty cultural nature, often attended by hundreds of guests. (For the less loftily inclined, a bowling alley was fitted into the basement.) The mansion stood on an eminence several feet higher than Fourth Street, upon which it faced; Wright cut an entrance at street level into the new wing of the house, which one now approaches from a side street, named Lawrence Street after the family. A visitor passes through two overscaled Romanesque archways, the vaulting between them filled with art glass in the colors of certain late-blooming wild flowers common to the Middle West—purple aster, goldenrod, and sumach—that Wright chose for the autumnal palette of the house. On the entrance landing, poised halfway between the basement and the first floor, stands a statue designed by Wright and executed by Bock—a bizarre obelisk in creamy-white terra cotta, called, after a line in a poem by Tennyson, "Flower in the crannied wall." The obelisk as it tapers transforms itself into an idealized nude woman, visible from a point just above the pubic region and thereby avoiding any dangerous hint of the erotic. She is daintily placing a capstone on the uppermost finial of an idealized skyscraper (an early version of the "Mile-High" tower of Wright's old age?) and seems far from recognizing the phallic nature of the object whose tip she fondles. The landing presents a choice: descending the steps, one

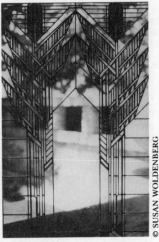

© SUSAN WOLDENBERG

© SUSAN WOLDENBERG

Main entrance to the Dana residence and one of its stylized "sumac" windows.

would reach cloakrooms and lavatories and a long passage leading to the library; climbing the steps, one would reach the salon and from there the dining room, the drawing room, Papa's study, Mama's bedroom (Mama died shortly after the house was completed), and the art gallery. Another flight of stairs, this one very grand, leads to a modest upper floor, with Mrs. Dana's bedroom, two guest bedrooms, two servants' bedrooms, several bathrooms, and a narrow balcony overlooking the vaulted, two-story-high dining room. Between the house and the old Lawrence stables, which were left largely untouched behind a two-story-high masonry and wood screen, was a garden and a reflecting pool.

The distinction of the Dana house owes much to Wright's having been given a free hand to design (and with what youthful exuberance!) every detail of the exterior and interior: art glass, woodwork, tilework, copper guttering, bronze lighting fixtures, carpets, draperies, and furniture; it also owes much to the superb craftsmanship with which these details have been executed. But it is possible to argue that Mrs. Dana's open purse had proved a danger to Wright as well as an opportunity; the note of excess is struck again and again in what amounts, after all, to a gargantuan folly—a sort of Springfield San Simeon. (The state of Illinois now owns the folly and has authorized the expenditure of several million dollars upon its not very necessary restoration.) Wright cannot have been unaware of the likelihood that the house might someday be described in unflattering terms; he spoke of it afterward in an equivocal fashion as having been "somewhat elaborately worked out," and although it was one of the major events of his architectural career, he omits it altogether from his autobiography.

When within a year or so Wright undertook to design houses for the two Martin brothers, the difference between having just enough money at his disposal (the W. E. Martin house) and having too much (the Darwin D. Martin house) ought to have become even more apparent to him than in the case of the Dana house, but no—mad about money and always short of it (as his father had written, "Frank . . . spends it fast"), Wright was the last man on earth to notice such a difference. And if he had, he would have paid it no attention.

10

THE PERIOD OF CREATIVITY of which I spoke in the last chapter embraces the several buildings that Wright was soon to design in Buffalo under the patronage of one of the most generous, percipient, and lovable of all his clients—Darwin D. Martin. A self-made businessman of exceptional intelligence and energy, Martin had set about making his fortune at the age of twelve, peddling Larkin Company soap on the streets of Brooklyn. Since in maturity he was a short, rather roly-poly man, as a child he must have cut a particularly waiflike figure, but his spirit was a merry and aggressive one and he was bound to make good. He read voraciously (his letters to Wright are peppered with quotations from the classics) and made so favorable an impression upon his employers that they soon summoned him to the Larkin Company headquarters in Buffalo. The Larkin Company had been founded as a mail-order house by John Larkin and Elbert Hubbard, who married one of Larkin's sisters and who, once the firm was well launched, transferred his skills as a promoter to the development of an arts-and-crafts and publishing enterprise known as The Roycrofters, in East Aurora, New York. Martin advanced to the post that Hubbard had relinquished; he had a bent for figures that was ideally suited to the needs of a mail-order house (he was a compulsive keeper of records of all kinds, for which students of Wright have reason to be grateful to him), and as he married, prospered, and moved upward in Buffalo society, he and his wife felt a desire to manifest their good fortune by means of a new house.

Martin had an older brother, W. E. Martin, with whom he was a partner in the E-Z Polish Company, in Chicago, manufacturers of shoe and stove polish. W. E. was as ebullient as Darwin and, it appears, more volatile. He lived in Oak Park and was about to commission a house there from Wright. W. E. had been bowled over by Wright, as the following letter to Darwin (written in anticipation of Darwin's thirty-seventh birthday) indicates:

Mr. and Mrs. Darwin D. Martin. Isabelle Martin was less impressed by FLW's genius than her husband was. A sensible woman, she wished for a bedroom that would provide space for a normal-sized bed and normal-sized closets. FLW was irritated by such requirements. Martin acted as a pacifying go-between, but nearly always sided with Wright. [UA]

10–02–02

Dear Dar:

37—Sat.—eh!—quite a ways to 40. I have been—seen—talked to, admired, one of nature's *noblemen*—Mr. Frank Lloyd Wright. He is an athletic-looking young man of medium build, black hair (bushy, not long) about 32 yrs. old. A *splendid* type of manhood. He is not a *freak*—not a "crank"—highly educated and polished, but *no dude*—a straightforward business-like man—with high ideals. I met his mother, a *beautiful type* of woman.

He says that the way labor and materials are now, that he would not care to try for anything in his line *under* 5000.00—but thinks a design that would please me could be made.

I told him of your lot—he says it would be a pity for you to build on a 75 foot front, unless the houses on each side of you stood well to one side (which is unlikely). . . . He would be *pleased* indeed to design *your* house—and further he is *the man* to build has had *large* experience in large office buildings with Adler & Sullivan, was educated as a civil engineer, was head man in A.&S., and stood next to Mr. S. He says it is strange that he is only known as a residence architect—when his best and largest experience was in large buildings—I suppose that if you discover this man—that Mr. L. would never consent to his drawing the plans—yet I am sure he is *the* man you want, and if some way could be devised so that Mr. L. could first discover him that he would be tickled to death with his find. Mr. Wright says he don't want any man to accept his ideas just because they are *his*—he proposes to furnish a *reason* for his ideas and wants judgements made solely *on the merits.*

You will *fall* in *love* with him—in 10 min. conversation. He will build you the *finest,* most *sensible* house in Buffalo. You will be the envy of every rich man in Buffalo, it will be published in all the Buffalo papers, it will be talked about all over the East. You will never grow tired of his work, and what more can you ask? When will you come to see him?

Can you not manage to have him first *discovered* by Mr. L. An office such as Wright can build will be talked about all over the country. It would be an ad. that money spent in any other way cannot buy. I am not too enthusiastic in this—he is *pure gold.* . . .[1]

This is indeed an astonishing letter; one gains a glimpse of the powerful effect that the young Wright had upon businessmen, presumably trained to be on their guard against the notorious irresponsibility of "artistic" types. Granted that W. E. Martin was more suggestible than his brother (and that he was later to denounce Wright in terms every bit as extreme as the terms in which he praises him here), his prophecies in respect to the Darwin D. Martin house and the Larkin administration building, extravagant as they must have seemed at the time, proved to be precisely on the mark. Evidently, Mr. Larkin, who was a generation older than the Martins and by temperament more hard-bitten and more skeptical, had to be dealt with carefully. In a letter from Darwin D. Martin to Larkin, written several months after the letter excerpted above, one observes with amusement how the process of conversion is carried out:

At the risk of appearing to have been made intoxicated by my contact with Frank Lloyd Wright, I do not hesitate to say at the outset of this, my report of my interview with him, which lasted all day March 18th, and of my visit to his houses on Mar. 14th, 15th, and 11th, that I believe we have all greatly underestimated our man. This because of his youth, the newness of our acquaintanceship and its limitations, and also because of the adverse things we have heard about Wright, which are due to his radical departure from conventional lines.

The glory of the firm of Adler & Sullivan has forever departed. They failed at the end of the panic and Mr. Adler died three years ago. Mr. Sullivan is a true artist, who now, not having the companionship of a business man, does not cut as large a figure as formerly. When this house was in their palmy days, however, Mr. Wright was the right-hand man. . . . Mr. Sullivan's and Mr. Wright's offices [were] side by side. In these two rooms all their work was created, and during much of the time Mr. Sullivan was away because of poor health.

Mr. Adler was a Structural Engineer and a business man. The $500,000 Wainwright Building and the Union Trust Building of St. Louis; the Schiller

Theatre and the Stock Exchange in Chicago; the Seattle and Pueblo Opera Houses, all Adler & Sullivan work, were, I inferred from Mr. Wright, largely his creations. He also had as much to do with the Auditorium as a young man, just past twenty, could be expected to have. . . .[2]

Thanks to what Martin calls "the newness of our acquaintanceship," he was in no position to detect the whopper Wright was telling when he claimed so substantial a part in the design of Adler & Sullivan's greatest works. (The most reckless portion of Wright's whopper was the reference to the Seattle Opera House, which, as it happened, had never been built.) Wright was in his middle thirties and eager to test his mettle on projects grander in scale than houses for neighbors in Oak Park, and exaggeration, not to say downright lying, was to him a natural means of furthering his career. Martin goes on to say that he and Mrs. Martin had visited five of those neighbors' houses and had talked with four of the owners:

You never witnessed such enthusiasm. Not one will admit a fault in their house. They will admit faults in other of Wright's houses but not in theirs. That, Mr. Wright says, is because he studies his client and builds the house to fit him.[3]

The remainder of the letter deals with arrangements to be concluded between Wright and the Larkin Company in respect to the new administration building that he was about to design for the company on a plot of ground adjacent to their complex of factories and warehouses in downtown Buffalo. The Martin brothers' surrender to Wright's talent and charm was complete—so complete, indeed, that it led to the commissioning of a total of nine major structures: the W. E. Martin house, in Oak Park; the E-Z Polish factory building, in Chicago; and the Larkin administration building, the Darwin D. Martin house, the George Barton house (Barton was Martin's brother-in-law), the W. R. Heath house (Heath was Larkin's brother-in-law), the Alexander Davidson house (Davidson was Treasurer of the Larkin Company), and a gardener's cottage adjoining the Martin property, all in Buffalo; and a summer residence for the Darwin D. Martin family, in Derby, New York.

Two of the most pleasing houses that Wright was ever to design were the W. E. Martin house and the Heath house, and by an irony that may be instructive in respect to all relationships between architects and clients, they appear to have been built with little or no friction because the clients let the architect have his way; meanwhile, poor Darwin D. Martin, sharing every moment of the design and building process with Wright, ended up with a house much less pleasing than his brother's or Heath's. W. E. Martin was to quarrel fiercely with Wright over the E-Z Polish factory building but had never a cross word to say about the house; although Heath protested

© SUSAN WOLDENBERG

the constant escalation in the cost of his house as it was going up, he and his numerous family were delighted with the results. They lived happily in the house for many years; one of the Heath daughters, now in her nineties, speaks of it with remembered joy to this day.

The W. E. Martin house made exceptionally cunning use of a large level lot in Oak Park. Placed close to the northern boundary of the lot, the house as Wright designed it (and as it is delineated in the Wasmuth *Ausgeführte Bauten und Entwürfe von Frank Lloyd Wright*) rose to a full three stories, but its verticality was modified by long horizontal wings on the ground floor, two of which were open porches. One of the porches was joined to a wooden pergola running almost to the southern boundary of

Above and below, two views of the W. E. Martin house, in Oak Park (1902). Though called a Prairie House, its vertical massing owes something to Secessionist Vienna.

© SUSAN WOLDENBERG

the lot, with gardens on either side and a lawn tennis court occupying the eastern portion of the property. The interior of the house has a feeling of snugness; the fireplace end of the living room is one of the most successful of Wright's "caves" and in mounting the stairs from floor to floor one might be climbing to the top of some thick-walled ancient Rhenish tower. The gardens and lawn tennis court have long vanished, but the house, which at one time was turned into three apartments, has been admirably restored and contains much of the furniture that Wright designed for it.

The Heath house is much larger in scale than the W. E. Martin house and fills most of the plot of ground upon which it is placed. Its ground-floor plan is reminiscent of the Heller house plan "flipped"; in its siting, it prefigures the Robie house, with its long axis running parallel to the street and with an adjacent public park serving—in the same fashion that the pasturelike Midway was intended to serve the Robie house—as a substitute for the ample grounds that a house of such considerable size would ordinarily be expected to possess. Though it stands only a few feet from

Two views of the Fricke house (1901), closely related to the W. E. Martin house and like it striking a European note that, though alien to the prairie, was not unwelcome there. FLW spent a lifetime preaching horizontality and violating it.

the sidewalk and street, the house achieves a remarkable degree of privacy by being set on a grassy terrace raised above the level of the street; this privacy is heightened by Wright's having cut the aperture for the front door into a solid red-brick wall at right angles to the street and adjacent to an immense chimney wall of the same red brick. It takes something of an effort to find this front door and an almost equal effort to find a secondary front door, presumably for family use, which has been tucked into the façade—again at right angles to the street—a few feet away from the kitchen door, which boldly confronts the street head-on. The façade terminates in a wing containing a servants' living room, two servants' bedrooms, a bathroom, a three-car garage (commodious for the period), and a stable. Opening off the living room at the park end of the façade is a big open

The Heath house, Buffalo, 1905. The Darwin D. Martin house, built at about the same time, cost its owners and FLW much anguish. The Heath house cost its owners and FLW no anguish at all: it is all sunniness and high spirits.

porch whose hip roof generously overhangs the brick parapet of the porch, protecting it from rain in summer and, in the notoriously brutal Buffalo winters, from heavy falls of snow. On the interior, the living room and dining room flow together with so little interruption that one can glance diagonally from room to room over a distance of something like seventy feet. Throughout his life, Wright found it difficult to resist painting or incising cautionary maxims or snatches of verse on any available flat surface; into the large sandstone lintel of the living-room fireplace in the Heath house are cut the words:

> The reality of the house is order
> The blessing of the house is community
> The glory of the house is hospitality
> The crown of the house is godliness

On the second floor are a master bedroom, a sewing room or study, four children's bedrooms, two guest bedrooms, and two bathrooms. The master bedroom is like a glass birdcage, looking out in three directions over parkland. In the basement is what we would now call a recreation room or rumpus room; it has a fireplace and plenty of sunlight from a large, south-facing lightwell, and in stormy weather the children of the house were known to play football there.

Given the charm and livability of the W. E. Martin and Heath houses, it is saddening to turn to the long-drawn-out misadventure of the Darwin D. Martin house, intended by architect and client alike to be Wright's greatest achievement. It is part of the Martin family lore that Martin, being well known for the astuteness he practiced in the world of business, must have been literally mesmerized by Wright; there was no other way to account for his compliance with the demands that Wright made upon his time, purse, and sympathy. Mrs. Martin appears to have done what she could to exercise a certain degree of discipline over her husband, but in vain; nearly always it was the case that when Martin had to make a choice between his wife's wishes and Wright's, he favored Wright's. As the house-building project began, Mrs. Martin may have consented to a good many things out of admiration for Mrs. Wright, who in raising six children and playing a prominent role in the cultural life of Oak Park matched her husband in energy and high spirits and set (as people said in those days) a splendid example to her sex. The Martins and the Wrights became good friends; a few years later, when Wright abandoned his family and set off on his travels with Mamah Cheney, the Martins remained close to Mrs. Wright. (Like her friend Mrs. Martin, Mrs. Heath suspected Wright of having a bad character; even before he abandoned his wife, he revealed his untrustworthy nature by expressing doubts about the existence of Mrs. Heath's God. Although her husband and her children liked having Wright visit the house, Mrs. Heath feared his influence upon them.)

The house that Wright designed for the Darwin D. Martins in 1903 bears a striking resemblance to the house he designed for publication in the *Ladies' Home Journal* in 1901, under the title "A Home in a Prairie Town." The house was part of a project launched a year earlier by Edward Bok, of the Curtis Publishing Company, in Philadelphia, who was bent upon improving the design of American houses, especially in regard to efficiency and hygiene. Bok was a champion of sleeping porches, sanitary bathrooms and kitchens, and servants' bedrooms of a humane size; he invited architects to publish in the *Journal* houses that could be built at a cost within reach of its hundreds of thousands of readers, a complete set

Left, the south façade of the Heath house; right, the mingling of living room and dining room areas provides a diagonal vista of some seventy feet.

of working drawings for such houses being offered for sale at a price of five dollars a set. Many architects refused Bok's invitation, as being beneath the dignity of the profession, but not Wright; already he was determined to provide the best possible housing for the largest possible number of people at the lowest possible cost.

Not for the first time and not for the last, Wright found himself purveying his utopian designs to the wealthy instead of to the masses. The big, luxurious, and extremely costly Martin mansion began as a house to be built in some imaginary prairie town for seven thousand dollars. (No doubt the house, if it had been built, would have cost at least half as much again as Wright estimated; he was always to be criticized for the fact that his arithmetic was at the mercy of his desire to create.) Except for the front entrance, which in the *Journal* house echoes the Romanesque arch of half a dozen earlier Wright designs, the Martin house and the *Journal* house have almost identical façades, with shallow, broad-eaved hip roofs

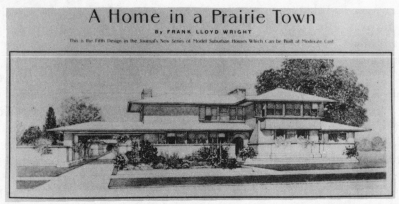

A Home in a Prairie Town

By FRANK LLOYD WRIGHT

This is the Fifth Design in the Journal's New Series of Model Suburban Houses Which Can be Built at Moderate Cost

The source of the Darwin D. Martin house plan. The Ladies' Home Journal *design of February, 1901, had as an option a two-story-high living room, which would have assured an abundance of much needed light from the second-story windows. As built, the living room is darker than it should have been, and Mrs. Martin never tired of saying so.*

running parallel to the street and squarish windows gathered into bands under the eaves. In plan, the Martin house repeats most of the ground floor of the *Journal* house; the library, living room, and dining room open into one another on an extended cross-axis to the main axis of the house, the living room opens onto a very large covered porch (depriving the living room of adequate natural light—a flaw corrected in an alternative set of plans for the *Journal* house, in which the living room rises two stories and gains additional light from windows in the second story). The porch at one end of the main axis is balanced at the opposite end by a porte cochere of almost equal size.

What is labeled a hall in the *Journal* plan becomes, in the Martin

The exterior of the Martin house, with its innumerable urns. Mr. Martin wanted a grand house, symbolic of his success in the world, and he got it. [BEC]

plan, a reception room, which the family used as a secondary living room; a small office beyond it, known to the family as "the bursar," was for Mr. Martin's use. An awkward failure in the Martin plan—the fact that there is no direct connection between the kitchen and the dining room, thus obliging servants to thread their way across the pillared entrance hall in the course of carrying dishes back and forth between the two rooms, is explicable only in terms of the earlier *Journal* plan, where kitchen and dining room are joined by a conventional serving pantry. In order to provide access to the glass-enclosed pergola that connected the Martin house to a conservatory and an adjacent garage and stable, Wright was obliged to give up the pantry altogether; the view from the front hall down the great length of the pergola to where a large plaster cast of the Winged Victory of Samothrace stood embowered at the entrance to the conservatory must have been a breathtaking one, but it was attained at the cost of visitors' also gaining a glimpse of servants passing back and forth between kitchen and dining room surely not to be encountered in any other mansion in the country. One suspects that Mrs. Martin objected strongly to this aspect

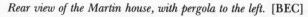

Rear view of the Martin house, with pergola to the left. [BEC]

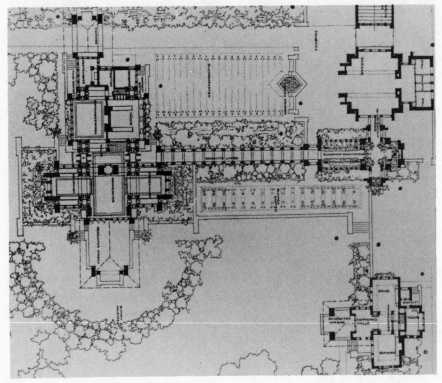

Floor plans of the Martin house, pergola, conservatory, stable, and garage, along with the Barton house at the lower right-hand corner. (Martin built the house for his sister and brother-in-law to rent.)

of the plan and was overruled by Mr. Martin, as she was when, looking over the plans and observing the construction of the house, she complained of other readily detectable inconveniences. She struggled to obtain a bedroom appropriate to her needs and failed. She warned that the house would prove dark; in age, she began to lose her sight and the shadowiness of the house became an increasing nuisance to her. From first to last, Wright breezily brushed aside her objections; in his view, the Martins were the fortunate custodians of a work of art that had sprung from his brain and was his in all but ownership.

The first of the Buffalo projects to be built was the Barton house, which was tucked away in a corner of the Martin property facing a side street. Mrs. Barton was Mrs. Martin's sister, and one gets the impression that she and her husband lived in the shadow of the Martins and were content to find themselves there. So modest was the siting of the Barton house that Nikolaus Pevsner and other European scholars, relying on the widely published plans of the Martin property, assumed that the Barton house contained the servants' quarters. (In the nineteen-sixties, the then owner of the property tore down the pergola, conservatory, and garage and sold the land between the Martin house and the Barton house to developers, who put up a conventional apartment building on the site. Fortunately, the two houses remain intact.) It had been arranged for the Bartons to rent the house; they had little to say in respect to its design. Manson thinks that Wright paid scant attention to it, being eager to get on with the planning of the main house, but the fact is that the Barton house is a small and nearly perfect jewel, a shelter cozy and yet filled with light, and most people who have visited both houses are apt to prefer it to the Martin house, which is grand but gloomy, bearing on the ground floor an ineradicable taint of the institutional.

Martin got an early taste of the difficulties he was to face as a consequence of commissioning works from a spellbinding young genius when the first estimates came in from a contractor named Lang, whom he had chosen to undertake the construction of the Barton house. On August 14th, 1903, Martin wrote to his wife, who was away on holiday:

My dear:

Mr. Lang made his report last night on the Barton house. The bids aggregate at first sight, including architect's fees, $10,000. Isn't it awful?

Instead of a little house, every man who figured on it referred to it as a big house, Lang constantly reminding them that it was a little house. . . . It would not be safe to assume that we can build the house as planned for less than $9,000. This does not include the hot water heater for heating purposes or that flower pot. . . .[4]

What Martin calls "that flower pot" (one can almost hear a suppressed "damned" in front of "flower") is evidently one of those big, flattened concrete urns that were an unavoidable feature of almost every house that Wright was designing at the time. I suspect that the Martins had their doubts about the appropriateness of the urn to Buffalo—it was perhaps one "artistic" touch too many for the community they were becoming prominent members of—and they may have hoped to eliminate it in the name of expense rather than be accused by Wright of philistinism. Simple and straightforward as the little Barton house was, it cost far more than Martin had intended it to. When it came to the main house, the sums required almost from one day to the next exceeded his preliminary calculations by many tens of thousands of dollars, and the cry uttered in this first letter— "Isn't it awful?"—was to be uttered again and again, with increasing anguish, over the next couple of years.

The most orderly of men—one whose success in business was achieved through a passion for numerical exactitude and for whom punctuality

To the right, the delightful little Barton house. Right, below, a view from the hall of the Martin house along the enclosed pergola to the conservatory—a distance of well over a hundred feet. Left, below, the porch of the Martin house: in summertime, it became an outdoor living room. [UA]

© SUSAN WOLDENBERG

was among the highest of virtues—found himself trapped in the whirligig life of a man who regarded numbers as a nuisance and time as his slave. One glimpses the mounting frustration of the Martins in this letter from W. E. to Darwin, dated May 20th, 1904:

Dear Brother:

Your telegram requesting stable plans was received, and I called up Wright that evening, when I found that he had gone to Hillside for three or four days; this, notwithstanding that he came to town with me that morning and did not say that he was going out of town but led me to think that he would give some of my matters his attention that day and inform me of proceedings—so I was much surprised to find that he had gone away that evening.

If you discover any way in your dealings with him, whereby you are able to keep tabs on him, I would like to know how you do it.

I called at his office yesterday morning, and one of the draftsmen said that he had been working on the plans, and mailed them to you Thursday, but knew nothing regarding the brick. He said that when Mr. Wright returned from Buffalo, he threw the plans into one corner of the office—which, by the way, has been torn up from stem to stern for the last two weeks—and said nothing about any alterations until Wednesday or Thursday morning, when he inquired if the plans had been altered, and, much to his surprise, he was told that nothing had been done, as nothing had been said about it by him. They then got busy, and by working all day and part of the night were able to return the plans, as stated.

Certainly, if Wright's plans appear to be "queer," his business methods are more so. Probably his loose methods are a mere indication of his great genius—because if a man is a genius, he must be a little off in other respects (?) I have fully concluded that while I thoroughly appreciate his plans and ideas, I would not give two cents for his superintendence of a job. As a matter of fact, the superintendence ought to be on *his* part of the work, to get him to do the right thing at the right time—and when I take him to task about his dilatory practices, he lays it all on the "boys" and says they are to blame for the whole "show."[5]

W. E. Martin's exasperated letter faithfully catches his speaking voice. A couple of months later, Wright writes to Darwin Martin, again in respect to some tardily drawn-up plans, and again we hear the voice of the speaker; as usual, Wright takes command, acting as if the client and not he were in the wrong:

My dear D. D. Martin:

Your plans you have by this time, no doubt. I think you understood me to say that the plans had to be figured before they could be printed and that it would be done right away as soon as I got home. As but one man could work on each plan at a time and as they have been working so continuously since the plans returned, from eight in the morning until seven at night, and then a special messenger took them in to the blue-printer's and waited there for them to send them to you with the least possible delay, I have that modest assurance of conscious worth that makes W. E. M.'s onslaughts and your own harmless.

If the making of plans were as simple and as quickly to be performed as you think I for one should be glad.

The steel schedule the boys are now working at, and they will stick at it until done. We hope to have it off today, but don't declare a broken promise if you don't get it tomorrow. Do try and have faith that we will serve you as we best can, for we will so serve you, but drawings are not going to leave this office for your buildings until they are right and fit to use as nearly so as we can make them at least, even if you wander homeless for the rest of your mortal days. Write us your needs and rest assured that we will hasten to give you whatever you require but if you don't receive it next day don't assume neglect, default, or unnecessary delay. It takes some time to arrive at correct information.

You fellows down there put a Chicagoan to shame in your get-there-gait, but be persuaded that the best results in buildings don't come with that gait. . . .[6]

Wright's reference early in the letter to his having a "modest assurance of conscious worth" is just the sort of arrogant claim that would have delighted and disarmed Martin, who was a truly modest man; it has the ring of being a quotation (perhaps an inadvertent scrambling of a phrase out of Milton's *Paradise Lost*—"the conscience of her worth"?) and if so Martin would no doubt have recognized it and been pleased to do so. He would try to forgive Wright, but Wright disdained forgiveness; in any event, there was obviously no changing him, because a couple of months later Martin was in greater distress than ever in respect to the stable and its doors, writing as follows:

> Have you any idea by this time how exceedingly aggravating it is to a client to have to tease and coax and wheedle for past due details? For details that obviously require only concentrated industry, not courting of the Muse, to produce. You do not have to court a Muse to produce detail for our stable doors. We want to hang the doors soon and we don't want to wait much longer for brains. We will make them without 'em.
>
> The same is true for details for basement light steel frames, concerning which Mr. Lang wrote you Sept. 13th. We should not be waiting for the Intelligence Department for this feature; instead, we ought to have the steel frames manufactured and on the site, as we are ready to place them and some work will be delayed for lack of them. . . .[7]

Though the Martins had had doubts about the single flowerpot at the Barton house, it would appear that Wright had assuaged all doubts; the main house was to have a host of them, and the only question was how many:

> . . . I presume there are to be flower pots on the piers at front porch, carriage porch, veranda steps (2), front wall of front terrace (2), and pier at southeast corner flower garden, making seven more than Mr. Lang counted. How many flower pots are there? How many flower pots need water connection? . . .
>
> Do you remember that Mrs. Martin wants soft wood floor in kitchen for linoleum?
>
> I have repeatedly asked to see detail of greenhouse glass??[8]

And then that kindly man cannot resist tempering his wrath with a good-humored jest at his own expense; after his signature, he adds a postscript:

> The stone wall southside of bursar's den has a fine crack from top down 4 ft. Lang swears struck by lightning. Better not further disclose purpose of this room.

Toward the end of September, Martin is writing to Oak Park about further lapses on the part of his ever-lagging architect:

Getting closer to the question of a gardener, I come to a realizing sense
that you have not filled my order for one greenhouse, but instead have
substituted a building which in a pinch will answer for a conservatory.
We will have to build a greenhouse, that is, a growing house, elsewhere
on the premises or depend on outside resources.

Be this as it may, I do not understand why you have entirely omitted
part of your job, i.e., the provision for ventilation. You have either begged
the question or neglected it, I do not know which.

Martin goes on to explain that he and his contractor, Mr. Lang, have
been taking matters into their own hands:

I have before protested against the prodigal waste of the only sure-enough
greenhouse space we have, i.e., that directly under the long skylight, and
you have scorned my protest. Now the worm has turned and we are
going to utilize that space and this is the way we are going to do it unless
the architect steps in and helps us.

Martin describes a concrete "aquarium" that he and Lang have designed
to be built in the floor of the conservatory under the long skylight, which
will supply water of the proper temperature for the watering of flowers;
above the aquarium will be a bench upon which potted flowers can be
grown to a height of at least five feet. He adds:

For your further edification, I enclose cross section of my plan, which is
copyrighted. You cannot dissuade me, for I swiped this idea from the
greenhouse of J. J. Albright, who has the champion private gardener of
Buffalo, and, by the way, I have a fair chance of having his freshly imported
brother-in-law, now on the water, for my gardener. . . . When will we
receive instructions on chimney building? . . . When will I hear what?
From whom? About interior trim?[9]

After further correspondence back and forth, to which Martin's brother,
W. E., is an agitated party, Wright in mid-October answers a number of
questions about gutters, copings, bathroom windows, and the like, and
ends his letter by firing off a defensive salvo:

W. E. M. will be rather late at this end to stop the carnage now. He
would better organize himself into a red-cross society and help save the
pieces at the Buffalo end. No quarter, no! Not until D. D. M. has the
most perfect thing of its kind in the world—a domestic symphony, true,
vital, comfortable. A real something to show for his years of hard work,
and a translation of those hard, faithful years into a permanent record
that will proclaim him to subsequent generations as a lover of the good!
the true! the beautiful! For did he not consider the lilies of the field?

"For I say unto thee that Solomon in all his glory was not arrayed like one of these."

Was his home not as a lily of the field? The field? The human soul. There now—will you be good?[10]

Wright letters of this sort exist by the thousands. The Martin correspondence provides us with samples of Wright in many moods and has been chosen for that purpose, but it must be remembered that what is quoted here is only an infinitesimal fraction of a mountainous whole and that beyond the Martin range lie further mountain ranges of equal or greater breadth and height. To publish the complete Wright correspondence would require many stout volumes; one marvels at the energy that Wright was able to devote to writing, in the early days almost always in longhand. Like all first-rate correspondents, he seems to have felt himself in the presence of the recipient of a letter even at the moment of writing it; whatever the nature of the emotion with which it was composed, the act in his eyes was akin to an embrace and he was genuinely astonished to discover, from time to time, that his uninhibited candor had given offense.

In the summer of 1905, the correspondence was still in spate; having completed certain necessary tasks, Wright was in high spirits:

My dear D. D. M.:

The cartoon for windows over sideboard is finished—very pretty!

The cartoon for the fireplace complete is also finished—superb!

Giannini has a considerable section of the design worked out in gold for your approval—ship it tomorrow—great piece of work!

Furniture drawings and gas fixture details are my daily trouble—dream of them at night!

Linden has all the drawings that he has a right to expect from us—jump on him!

Spencer I have tried to get some reliable information from [name indecipherable] and failed, but have O.K.'d drawing for hook-fast and told him to go ahead with adjusters—think he lied about condition of same in letter to you—blow him out of the water!

Have detail finished for lily pond in circular hollow—the proper scheme at last!

Going to New York Sunday night—returning to Buffalo Wednesday—will see you then, a complete walking compendium with a panacea for interrogation points.

Gaily,
Wright[11]

By September, the mercurial W. E. had totally lost confidence in Wright. The factory building that Wright had designed for the Martins' E-Z Stove and Shoe Polish Company, in Chicago, was being built at the same time as the D. D. Martin house and the Larkin Company headquarters building, in Buffalo, and Wright, who never showed anything like as much respect for W. E. as for D. D., goaded him beyond endurance with his unbusinesslike methods. Poor W. E. finally erupted:

Dear Brother:

If you or the Larkin Co. owe Frank Lloyd Wright any money, please refuse to pay until you have heard further from me. He has served me a *dirty, mean trick,* for which he *ought to pay,* but it would be useless to sue him unless there is something due him in Buffalo, as he is not worth a dollar and probably never will be.

At this writing, I can only say that he is not a man that I would ever have any dealings with.

Sincerely yours,
W. E. Martin[12]

A few days later, Darwin D. Martin was in receipt of a letter from Wright:

My dear Mr. Martin:

I am more than sorry to say to you that the friendly relation between your brother, W. E. Martin, and myself is a closed episode—so far as either is concerned.

This will be a disagreeable surprise to you, I know, and of course will affect (whether we will it so or not) our own relations with each other. He gives me a character blacker than the ace of spades and far less symmetrical. His adherence was not temperate—I could not live up to it and the reaction is even more intemperate. The facts I will relate when I have an opportunity "viva voce." They look ugly on paper.

The past two years have given me both respect and admiration for your character and a warmth of personal regard that has been a real pleasure—a possession I have been proud of, and that alone should have made this rupture with your brother impossible. I have often wished for your strength in similar circumstances but I have broken finally, where I am sure you would have triumphed in the interest of all concerned.

I want to bring Mrs. Wright to Buffalo with me next week and would like to have her spend a day with Mrs. Martin just as though nothing had happened, and then, if we must, we can succumb to the inevitable.[13]

On the very same day, W. E. was writing a long letter to D. D., the opening paragraphs of which imply both that his grievance against Wright was a just one and that he may nevertheless have overreacted to it:

You were, no doubt, nonplussed on reading my note regarding Wright, and awaiting developments before venturing to remark?

I am myself only just getting my breath, for he struck me below the solar-plexus, but after all perhaps he hurt himself more than he did me.

The trouble was this, as nearly as it can be put on paper—it would have had to be experienced to fully comprehend the situation.[14]

He goes on to say that, at the moment when the contractor (Wright's ally and colleague from the Sullivan office, the engineer Paul Mueller) began to excavate for the foundations of the E-Z Polish factory building, no blueprints or final specifications had been made ready by Wright's office. The trenches for the foundations were being scooped out of the black soil on the site to what W. E. considered an insufficient depth; moreover,

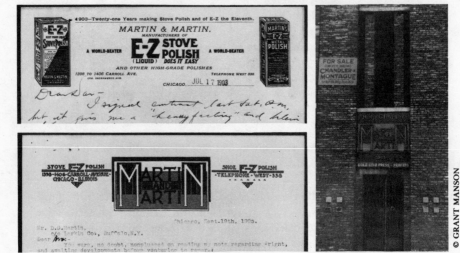

E-Z Stove Polish was manufactured by a company jointly owned by Darwin D. and W. E. Martin. Upper left, its letterhead before the advent of FLW; lower left, its letterhead as designed by FLW. [UA] At right, the Martin & Martin factory in Chicago, also from Wright's hand during this period.

the basement, which W. E. had assumed would have a clear height of eight feet, was apparently to have a height of only seven feet, six inches. Still without blueprints or specifications, W. E. telephoned Wright and was told that if he wanted an eight-foot clearance it would cost an extra four hundred and sixty-five dollars. This led to a quarrel in which Wright "in his most insulting tones and manner" declared that he would prefer to drop the entire job then and there. Still more insultingly, Wright hinted that W. E. could not be trusted to pay the extra amount.

This from a man [W. E. writes] whom everyone knows I had befriended in every instance possible since I had known him and it was *too much* for him to insinuate that I might repudiate the bill for extras, unless the blueprints were first signed and sealed.

I once loaned him $1000.00 on his unsecured note to keep his old Aunts from going into bankruptcy and this was the treatment he accorded me at the first opportunity. . . . Hence my note to you. I have since recovered myself and am seeing somewhat clearly that the error manifested by Wright is not his.

Wright was conducting matters as though he was to superintend the job, but I had not spoken to him in any way to lead him to so conclude. It is his superior claim to knowledge that makes him deal so with clients.

To show that my contention that the trenches were not deep enough [was correct], Mueller told me that he had noticed that the black dirt was scarcely removed and had called up Wright and told him that he wanted his O.K., so it seems that to have made the trenches deep enough for a good foundation Wright's calculations were "off" and the basement ought to have been deeper in the first instance.

I enclose all that has passed between Mr. Wright and myself since our conversation on the 'phone, above mentioned. He disrupted Mueller's organization of men, which are hard to get; lost his foreman; and they only got well started again today.

The blueprints and specifications were not ready until last Thursday, around 8:30 P.M. Mr. Mueller brought them to my house that evening after having spent the entire afternoon at Wright's office, when the whole force were working under high pressure to complete the work so Mueller could proceed.

Mr. Wright knows that our friendship has been dissolved until he sees fit to apologize for his insult and the trouble he unnecessarily caused me.

Incidentally, Mr. Mueller probably does not think any more of him for his action, which was unprecedented and scandalous; all sorts of rumors being afloat as to why the job was stopped.

You will draw your own conclusions as to how you had best deal with such a man.[15]

To which he adds, in a handwritten postscript:

Better take warning and be *very* careful in your dealings with him. If he is sane, he is *dangerous*.

With his usual tact and goodness of heart, D. D. Martin dispatched a joint letter to the litigants; startlingly, he dared to address them both as brothers (one wonders how welcome such an imposed fraternity may have seemed to W. E., no doubt still nursing his wounds):

Dear Brothers:

I am in receipt this morning of your letters of the 19th. I will lay off from my own busy job and write you a dissertation (on what, we will learn as we proceed). If I were only wise enough to rise to the occasion, there are enough nice things said by each of you of the other to make all as merry as a marriage bell (this simile seems to be in order here, there were so many marriages yesterday of Larkin employees), but I know no better than to just say to you that if I had you both in the woods of Oak Park I would bump your heads together a few. But my wife says I cannot drive out our boy's faults by licking him.

When two men deal together, each will recognize minus or plus (as it may be) characteristics and enliven their dealings with a row, they only get what is coming to them, don't they? I have cussed myself more than once, and have come dangerously near cussing Wright as often for his aggravating shortcomings. I have tried to hold myself always, though, recalling that I knew in advance something of them and might have known them all, and so have tried as best I could to smother my indignation. Besides, I have been helped always by the possession of the healthiest kind of a counter-irritant in the form of my superintendent, so it will be a real Godsend for W. E. M. to have, like I have, a superintendent on whom to divide his wrath.

Mr. Wright knew, at least in advance of any connection with the factory building for W. E. M., of the latter's weaknesses and intemperate temper and knows, too, and deplores as much as any of us (probably more—it hits him harder) his own lack of the faculty to consummate and so he hasn't much right to explode when the medicine coming to him is administered by a man too intemperate to pour it in the sewer—where all medicine belongs.

I have noted carefully W. E. M.'s points of disagreement, which he pleads as his justification for exploding, and I think he scores—if he wants to. There isn't much reason in conceding to Wright a law unto himself, but we do it when we begin operations and might therefore be consistent in it. There isn't any justification, however, for vituperation or recrimination among men, so when a man employs it he loses his whole case, and when an attempt is made to settle a case by its use I will back a Martin for doing his share, and therefore willingly concede that when Wright was talking and acting like a boy, Martin was responding with 150%.

You both know as well as I each other's good qualities and your individual personal loss by allowing the other's weakness to blot out and deny you access to the greatly predominating good, and I trust that ere this letter reaches you that good will have demonstrated its supremacy.

It is always better to conduct business in writing. It is even more important between men who have other than ordinary business relations. I hope you will both learn to do business in writing as a principle and not as an expedient—and be happier.

I prefer to keep the smoke and din of battle away from my domicile and so my wife knows nothing of your vaudeville stunts (not continuous, we will hope), so our social relations all round will, so far as we here can make them, be just what they have been. We are both looking forward with great pleasure to Mr. and Mrs. Wright's visit next week. I suppose it will be inevitable that Mr. Wright and I will hold a post-mortem unless the little affair is buried in the Carroll Ave. trench or the drainage canal before.[16]

And then D. D. M. added a postscript—indeed, two postscripts:

Postscript #1. Mind, I haven't excused either of you. I think you have both been cussed and like as not Wright "begun it"—but I'll bet he got the worst of it and so in the end W. E. M. has the most to answer for.

Postscript #2. Meanwhile, Mr. Mueller is ground between the obstreperous millstones and smiles and smiles, attributing no preponderance of blame to either party, amiable and well-poised gentleman that he is!

By Christmas of 1905, the D. D. Martins were settled in their house and content to be there, though many details remained to be completed and Mrs. Martin, according to her husband, was finding "the protraction of the completion of the house almost beyond endurance." Pleading that he had spent far more time in Buffalo resolving problems connected with

For years, Wright found it hard to resist adding one or more urns to his designs; other architects followed his practice, leading to an epidemic of urnomania throughout the Middle West. Top left, Heller house, Top right, Wright Home and Studio. Lower left, Dana house. Lower right, Robie house.

the construction of the Martin house than he had on the simultaneous construction of the Larkin administration building and on the Heath residence, Wright sought extra payments from Martin, most of which Martin consented to, though he felt them to be unreasonable. "I am willing to strain every point in your favor," he wrote, "in recognition of the high quality of your work," but he beseeched Wright to adopt certain principles, "necessary to the possibility of success in every business" and likely to render Wright's future much smoother than his past. The principles are worth recounting, in part because of the cheerful fashion in which Wright received them and in part because of the degree to which he failed to live up to them throughout the remainder of his long life:

1st. Follow the precedent you have already established for yourself in the Unity Church, of building within the appropriation, or approximately, not as in Mr. Heath's case, way beyond, or in my case, way, way beyond.

2nd. FIX your plans.

3rd. Make adequate drawings and specifications. I am aware that you never have agreed with me that you have ever failed on this point, and I am aware that when you deliver you give full measure and running over, but the stubborn fact remains that in our case at least a very great deal of planning was verbal.

4th. Be punctual. Though the heavens fall, be punctual. Delays of months running into years are killing. Only an unlimited supply of enthusiasm will live down such adverse conditions.

5th. Be mejum [medium]. As Samantha said to Josiah, "If you cannot be mejum, be as mejum as you can." You get nothing but rebuffs and bumps from all sides when you are extreme. Take your wise and good wife into your plans. When she tells you you have overdone 100%, believe her 10% at least and modify your plans in the direction of conservatism. Eschew your overelaborate simplicity. It is the extremes that are expensive to you and to your clients and profit the least in the end. It is the extreme things only in our house that we would change. Take as an example the elaborate light units. Believe me, they are a dream, i.e., the realization is not all that you saw in your imagination. And again, No. 1 bedroom. It is the extremes only that scare people.

6th. Keep alive every day your perfectly evident capacity for letter-writing. You can encompass your wonderful ability with all the common-sense practice necessary to fill your office with business to overflowing. Do not sacrifice so much to your exaggerated idea of the province of an architect to be the arbiter of the aesthetic, for your only return will be reproach, whether candidly expressed or not, for a selfish gratification of riotous invention.[17]

Wright replied by return mail, on January 2nd, 1906, that he would accept Martin's six "articles"—significantly, he didn't refer to them as "principles"—as his profit in the Martin job. He protested disingenuously that to the "architecturally initiated" he was already considered a conservative and that he didn't want his capabilities hedged about with the practice of so-called common-sense people. "I am not cut out," he wrote, "for a 'successful architect.' I don't like the kind I have seen who enjoy that distinction. I am used to rebuffs and bumps—they don't count so very much except to make a fellow look kind of battered up, but as long as his wife loves him what's the difference?" In conclusion, Wright pointed out that his letter was proof that he was in accord with "Article Six" and then set down an apologia for his wayward financial practices that managed to strike a note of unselfish heroism:

> I have never yet made an investment of any nature, from the food I put into my children's mouths to the multitude of Japanese prints I give away, that I have not miscalculated my means and my obligations to my creditors and I don't suppose (though still I hope) that the day will ever come when it will be otherwise—for I sell something I have no right to sell. I ought to give it. There is no unearned increment in my business, not even the advantage of "repetition," nothing but the unceasing effort of emptying myself of my best and highest qualities for hire, from day to day, whenever someone wants a little beauty and nobility "mixed in" with the theatre of his animal habits.[18]

This is the High Victorian view of the artist as a sort of combined priest and prostitute, and Wright states the case with exceptional eloquence— "the theatre of his animal habits" is a phrase that Ruskin might have envied. Half a century later, Wright was still miscalculating his means and still emptying himself, for hire, in order to provide what he called a little beauty and nobility to his commonsensical fellow men.

IN THE FIRST of the six principles that Darwin D. Martin set down in his fatherly letter of advice to Wright—fatherly, though in fact he was but three years older than Wright—he made reference to Unity Church, in Oak Park, for whose design Wright had recently won the commission. Martin indirectly congratulated Wright on his determination to design a structure that was capable of being built at least "approximately" within the limits of a given budget. In his reply to that letter, Wright ignored the implied rebuke to his unbusinesslike, budget-defying practices, but it was a rebuke that he was to be unhappily familiar with throughout his life and one that he found particularly galling because it was so closely bound up with his desire to accomplish the best possible results for his client as well as for himself. The client's pocketbook might be at stake; also at stake was Wright's reputation as an architect—the greatest living American architect, which he early came to believe himself to be. (Over the years, he also came to believe that "American" and "living" were unnecessarily restrictive modifiers: "the greatest architect who ever lived" had to his ear in old age the ring of an unchallengeable authenticity.) Again and again, he struggled to remain inside the terms of a budget that he had reluctantly consented to or had perhaps helped to devise as the necessary fiction that would bring a project to the point of his being able to break ground; again and again, he failed.

Martin and Wright had tussled over the cost of the Barton and Martin houses for more than two years; given that Martin's success in business was based on his paying an exceptional degree of attention to budgets and inventories, it was indeed curious that he appears never to have pinned Wright down to any hard-and-fast estimates. (The two houses probably cost a total of something over a hundred thousand dollars, which in today's money would amount to at least a million dollars; Martin had expected to spend only a small fraction of that amount.) During the same two years, Martin had been a party to the budgetary difficulties that Wright had undergone in the course of designing and constructing the Larkin Company's administration building. As vice-president of the company, Martin had strongly recommended Wright to Mr. Larkin and the other officers of the company, and his heart must have alternated between soaring and sinking as his young protégé gave proof of architectural genius on the one hand and financial irresponsibility on the other.

The Larkin administration building is one of the most important of Wright's works and as such one goes on speaking of it in the present tense, though in fact it was thrown down in 1950. By then, it had long since outlived its usefulness, as the Larkin Company itself had outlived its prosperity. Wright is said to have been less troubled by the demolition of the building than one might have expected him to be, and for a reason sufficiently doleful: he felt that the Larkins had never really comprehended the nature of his handiwork. In his autobiography he wrote that the building was "too severe for the fundamentalist English tastes of the Larkin family. They were distracted, too, I imagine, by so many experiments, some of which, like the magnesite, delayed the completion of the building. A few minor failures annoyed them and made them think the whole might be— merely queer? They did not really know. They never realized the place their building took in the thought of the world, for they never hesitated to make senseless changes in it in after years. To them it was just one of their factory buildings, to be treated like any other. And I suppose that from any standpoint available to them, that was all it was. In architecture they were still pallbearers for the remains of Thomas Jefferson and subsequently all built colonial houses for themselves in Buffalo."[1] The last sentence is unexpectedly revealing. Wright had good reason to be disappointed by the Larkin family's treatment of his famous building, but it appears that what really irritated him was their failing to ask him to design houses for them; a cluster of big red-brick Georgian ("colonial") Larkin houses still stand in Buffalo, looking handsomer to the contemporary eye than

A single desolate and crumbling pier remains upright to mark the location of the once world-celebrated Larkin Administration building, in Buffalo.

© SUSAN WOLDENBERG

Wright would wish them to. The executive offices having been moved elsewhere, for a long time Wright's building was used simply for storage. Nothing remains of it today except some foundation walls of red sandstone and a rosy brick pier, but the site is well worth visiting, because it explains much about the exterior appearance of the building.

Unlike Sears Roebuck and other big mail-order houses of that day, the Larkin Company manufactured the products that it sold and distributed. Its catalogues boasted that the Larkin factories covered over sixty acres of floor space in downtown Buffalo and that the company was "the world's largest manufacturers of soaps, perfumes, and toilet preparations. The entire output goes direct from factory to family without tribute to middlemen." Interstate trucking was then unheard-of; goods were shipped throughout the country by rail, which required factories and warehouses to have easy access to freight trains; these trains were powered by coal-fired steam locomotives, and the dust, stench, and noise that accompanied their incessant comings and goings led to notoriously unhealthy working conditions. When Wright was invited to design a new administration building for the Larkin Company and was shown the only land available to construct it on—a trapezoidal plot bordered on one side by the New York Central railroad tracks and on two other sides by streets crowded with horse-drawn vehicles—he perceived at once that he must devise a structure totally sealed off from its environment. Such a sealing off is a commonplace readily achieved today, but at the turn of the century it would have been considered a technical impossibility—one of those pipe dreams that wild-eyed inventors were always promising to turn into reality, to the open derision of their neighbors.

The Larkin administration building was designed to dominate and lend an air of grandeur to the quite ordinary factory buildings that made up the rest of the Larkin complex. The façade on Seneca Street rose skyward like some pagan temple carved millennia ago out of the rocky banks of the Upper Nile; in an idealized drawing that served to illustrate the Larkin Company catalogue, it was the most prominent object visible in the foreground, with a smoking factory chimney—the classic symbol of prosperity in nineteenth-century business iconography—relegated to a minor position in the background. The Larkin Company prided itself upon the many economies it practiced in order to save its customers (known to the company, for public-relations purposes, as "the Larkin Family") a penny of unnecessary expense, and upon the completion and occupancy of the new administration building, in 1906, its architect was asked to write an article for the company's house organ, *The Larkin Idea,* accounting for the unprecedented nature of its design and justifying its high cost. This was a welcome task to Wright; he begins the article in his usual racy high spirits, with a mocking, self-deprecatory reference to the fact that the exterior of the building consisted of ordinary, dark-red paving bricks, and with an exaggerated compliment to its owners:

> The architect has been asked to tell the "Larkin Family" why the big pile of brick across the street from the Larkin factories is an economical headpiece to house the intellectuals of a great industry. . . . Has the Larkin Company in this instance been true to its traditions and "saved all cost which adds no value"? Perhaps not, if all values are to be reckoned in money. Real values are subjective and more difficult to estimate than the more obvious ones of the balance-sheet.

Wright rarely allowed a visitor to enter one of his buildings head-on, and the Larkin building was no exception: its entrances were not where one looked for them, between the great piers of the façade, but in a wing attached to the atrium pictured above. As members of what was known as "the Larkin Family," many hundreds of workers filled out mail orders in the atrium, under the benign, unblinkingly efficient eye of management. [BEC]

The piers of the façade supported only themselves and some ill-scaled ornamental stone globes; they appear to have been inspired by a preliminary sketch that Joseph Maria Olbrich made for the Secessionist Art Gallery, in Vienna. (See photograph, page 179.) [BEC]

And yet, if over-and-above the mere house-room required by 1800 workers, clean, pure, properly tempered air for them to breathe whatever the season or weather or however enervating the environment may be worth "money" to young lungs and old ones, we have that—the best in the world.

If ideal sanitary conditions and toilet facilities are worth "money" we have those—perfect.

If the positive security insured by the use of permanent fireproof materials throughout an isolated building and its fittings and furnishings is valuable—we have that.

If a restful, harmonious environment, with none of the restless, distracting discords common to the eye and ear in the usual commercial environment, promoting the efficiency of the 1000 or more young lives whose business home the building now is can be counted an asset, why, we have that too, together with that total immunity from conditions outside the building which are entirely the reverse. . . .

In short, if the incentive that results from the family-gathering under conditions ideal for body and mind counts for lessened errors, cheerful alacrity, and quickened and sustained intelligence in duties to be performed, we have created some very real values.[2]

Wright goes on to enumerate the many innovations that the "cliff-like" mass of the building contains. The list of innovations is indeed extraordinary: double-glazed windows to help control heat and cold and reduce exterior sounds; an early form of mechanical air-conditioning, employing fans and jets of cool water; subfloor electric-light and telephone connections; a vacuum-cleaning system concealed in the walls; wall-hung toilets and ceiling-hung toilet partitions; built-in metal file-cabinets and metal desks, with seats attached to the desk-uprights and giving full access to the floor; and desk tops and floors all composed of a then new commercial product called magnesite, a synthetic fireproof material as durable as concrete but softer to the touch. The design of the interior was also novel, consisting of a five-story-high atrium capped by an immense skylight. The dark brick of the exterior walls had been chosen to accept as inconspicuously as possible the soiling that was certain to occur in that industrial environment; the interior walls were lined with a hard, semi-vitreous, cream-colored brick, which reflected light and was easy to clean.

Wright objected to the deceptiveness of architectural photography except when it happened to serve his purpose. This was his favorite representation of the Larkin building, which flatteringly distorted its proportions. [BEC]

The Larkin Company letterhead gave pride of place to its fortresslike administration building.
[BEC]

Like the Larkin Company executives themselves, Wright took delight in striking an evangelical note. In *The Larkin Idea,* he writes of how his building promotes "the health and cheerfulness of its official family at comparatively a very low cost." What he doesn't mention is that he and the Larkin Company were eager to establish a closed society in that closed environment; what the former Larkin Company advertising genius, Elbert Hubbard, was seeking to establish at The Roycrofters, a few miles away, and what Wright would one day also seek to establish at his two Taliesins was a way of life dictated from above according to principles not in the least democratic but pretending to espouse democracy at its best. (An old friend of Wright's, Carleton Smith, was once visiting Taliesin and with a wink Wright said to him, "You know, Carleton, a perfect democracy flourishes here at the Fellowship. When I get hungry, we all eat.") The Larkin administration building was architecturally and technically a welcome wonder; for its employees it may have come to seem a sort of prison. The soot and smells and even the very sight of the industrial wasteland in which it was placed were certainly excluded; the windows, for example, were too high to be looked out of by employees either seated or standing and the building was entered and left by means of what Wright called a "convenience annex," which also contained the dining rooms, the kitchens, the library, and the toilet facilities. The roof of this annex was supposed to serve as an open-air garden but appears never to have done so. The building was efficient and yet penitentiary-like, especially when viewed from a distance. This defect was partly a function of its dark color and partly a function of its shape: the structure was twice as long as it was high and, looked at from either of its long sides, seemed much more like a conventional factory building than when looked at head-on, from either

Seneca Street or Swan Street. Wright appears to have been well aware of the disparity of effects that the building produced. As Jack Quinan has pointed out in the *Journal of the Society of Architectural Historians,* he always preferred photographs and drawings of the building that emphasized the formidable massing of its façades and foreshortened its length.

When, in 1908, the architect and critic Russell Sturgis, writing in the *Architectural Record,* described the Larkin building as "extremely ugly" and "a monster of awkwardness," Wright dashed off an indignant riposte, which was probably intended for the *Record* but which the *Record* never published (perhaps, so Quinan reasons, because Sturgis died early the following year and editorial tact preferred a benign silence to controversy). Wright in eruption:

> I make no plea for ugliness, nor is ugliness necessary—although I think the buildings Mr. Sturgis in an unguarded moment permitted himself to build are very ugly. But I recognize what Mr. Sturgis evidently does not recognize, and that is that ugliness exists in the eye of the beholder rather than inheres in the thing beholden. As to just what constitutes ugliness all men differ—as they should. For me, meretricious ornament, devoid of significance, and manufactured for its own sake is ugly, honesty seldom

The smiling fathers of "the Larkin Family." The white-bearded patriarch is John Larkin, founder of the company; Darwin D. Martin stands at his left; and W. R. Heath is the tall man at Larkin's extreme right. [BEC]

is. Ugliness is a matter of the false and of discord. Awkwardness may be only undigested greatness. . . . The Larkin Building is not pretty; it was not intended to be. But it is not discordant and it is not false. . . . It may be ugly, certainly it may appear so to some; but it is noble. It may lack playful light and shade, but it has strength and dignity and power. It may not be "Architecture," but it has integrity, and its high character is a prophecy. . . . It is a bold buccaneer, swaggering somewhat doubtless, yet acknowledging a native god in a native land with an ideal seemingly lost to modern life—conscious of the fact that because beauty is in itself the highest and finest kind of morality so in its essence must it be true.[3]

Darwin D. Martin's kindly admonition, cited at the beginning of this chapter, to the effect that Wright should make every effort to keep "approximately" within a budget, reminds us that Martin had made the mistake of allowing Wright to design his house without a budget. In the case of the Larkin building, there was certainly a budget, but it is also certain that Wright kept exceeding it. In his entertaining memoir, *Apprentice to Genius: Years With Frank Lloyd Wright* (1979), Edgar Tafel tells of a visit that Wright and he paid to the Larkin building in the middle nineteen-thirties, in the course of a leisurely, indirect journey between Spring Green and Bear Run, Pennsylvania, where Fallingwater was under construction:

Our first visit was to the Larkin Building—unannounced, naturally. As we walked in, Mr. Wright described the air-conditioning system he had devised: air blown over ice to cool it, then circulated through the rest of the building. It was also here that Mr. Wright first used one of his favorite inventions—the wall-hung toilet, along with ceiling-hung stall partitions. He was so proud of this that he charged into the nearest rest rooms to show us. It happened to be the ladies room and it was quite busy. Ignoring the astonished ladies, Mr. Wright went directly to the closest ceiling-hung stall, swung open the door with his cane, and exclaimed, "There it is! The first wall-hung water-closet!"

The executive offices of the Larkin Company had been moved across the street. After our tour of the original building, Mr. Wright crossed to the other building and announced to the receptionist that he wanted to see the Larkins. A son of Mr. Wright's 1903 client was president at the time, and other members of the family were still in the company. We were asked to lunch in the executive dining room, where perhaps fifteen of us, altogether, met around one big table. A most cordial reception. . . . We finished our lunch and relaxed into conversation. Mr. Wright told the Larkins a story about their father, the founder, who had asked him to design a great building. Mr. Wright said that after working on the design for some time, he'd decided to pull the stair towers out of the building center and place them in outside corners, in a strongly articulated way. Larkin senior asked if this would be more costly. Mr. Wright answered, "I don't think it would be more than an additional $26,000." "All right, then. Build it like that, with the extra $26,000," said Mr. Larkin. Mr. Wright went on to praise Mr. Larkin's understanding and foresight. . . . "Mr. Wright," interrupted one of the Larkins, "your story is true as far as it went. But according to Dad, when the building was completed, the additional cost wasn't $26,000, it was $62,000." A great quiet ensued.[4]

In the case of the Larkin building, however much it may have exceeded the initial budget and however unhappy the Larkins may have been with their fiscally irresponsible young genius, they soon came to see that the building would pay for itself over and over as a symbol of the company's virtuous business practices—it became a semiological equivalent of the Prudential Insurance Company's Rock of Gibraltar and as such was beyond price.

With Unity Temple, in Oak Park, the financial restrictions were not to be taken lightly. The Unitarian congregation was in need of a new church because their old church had burned down; the amount of money available for the task was forty thousand dollars. Much more than money was at stake in the Unity Temple commission. To begin with, the building committee that had been appointed to choose an architect for the new building had not been altogether sure that it wished to settle on Wright,

The Larkin building in 1949, in the course of its demolition. FLW took some satisfaction (as he did in the case of Midway Gardens as well) in learning how difficult—and therefore how expensive—the Larkin building was to destroy. [BEC]

who, though a distinguished member of the congregation, was already well known for having second (and third and fourth) thoughts that led to delays and the overrunning of budgets. A competition had been considered and then abandoned, perhaps through Wright's having discreetly furnished his objections to the principle of a competition to the Chairman of the

© PHILANDER BARCLAY

The smoking ruins of the Gothic Revival Unitarian Church in Oak Park, 1905. Despite his reputation as a financially reckless architectural iconoclast, FLW was chosen to design its replacement.

Building Committee, Charles E. Roberts, an inventor and strong individualist, who was Wright's champion. (Throughout his career, Wright steadfastly refused to enter competitions, arguing that a jury, itself the product of averaging, will invariably choose a design based upon averaging, which will lead in turn to a building that is well behind the times before it has been begun.) Moreover, it was the case that the pastor, Dr. Rodney F. Johonnot, had rather set his heart upon a white Colonial church, with a pretty steeple and green shutters, and most of the congregation probably shared his preference. Nevertheless, Roberts had prevailed in committee, Wright had been chosen, and it was up to him to be on his best behavior and to give the congregation a building they could be happy with.

As usual, Wright had something else in mind, which was to give the congregation a building that *he* could be happy with. At once, he set about convincing the building committee that his wishes embodied theirs. Why build a conventional church, with a spire pointing literally to heaven? "Why not build a temple to man," Wright in his autobiography recalls arguing, "appropriate to his uses as a meeting place, in which to study man himself

for his God's sake? A modern meeting-house and a good-time place?"[5]
He then describes how he arrived at the design of the structure, with
one portion of it to be called Unity Temple, where worship would occur,
and the other portion called Unity House, the "good-time place," in which
the lay activities of the congregation would occur. A pamphlet published

© SUSAN WOLDENBERG

Instead of ecclesiastical gloom, sun from the sky. To its amazement, the congregation was
offered what FLW called "a meeting-house and a good-time place."

for fund-raising purposes while the building was under construction—a
pamphlet purportedly written by Dr. Johonnot but with Wright's hand
plainly visible behind the doctor's hand—gives a summary of its location
and plan:

> The site of the building is a corner lot having a frontage of 100 feet on
> Lake Street, the main street of Oak Park, and a depth of 170 feet on
> Kenilworth Avenue.
>   The Temple is a cruciform building, 67 feet on each axis and 47
> feet high. The form of the cross, however, is made less apparent externally,
> owing to the spaces between the arms being filled with square stairchambers
> which rise nearly to the roof. The Temple stands in the center of the lot
> at the front. In the rear, with its main axis crossing the lot, is Unity House,
> 50 × 90 feet. These two buildings are knit together into one integral
> structure by a large Entrance Hall standing between the two buildings.
> The depth of the whole structure on its main axis running through the
> Entrance Hall is 143 feet. The two buildings are still further integrated

by parapets extending forward from the ends of Unity House and enclosing in their broad arms the rear of the Temple and connected with it by wide flights of steps facing the main street.

Both the Temple and Unity House are lighted mainly from the top through large skylights shielded beneath by glass ceilings. A crown of windows also extends around the Temple beneath the broad projecting roof. Taking the light from above is an ideal method for practical purposes and it also embodies a fine religious idea. With the exception of narrow windows set deeply into recesses between the cruciform mass and the stairchambers, the lower portion of the Temple is unbroken by doors or windows, save where it opens into the Entrance Hall. This preserves the mass of the building and by means of quiet surfaces and unbroken lines gives great dignity to the structure. This method of construction serves the further purpose of keeping out the noise of the street cars, thus securing a quiet and restful interior. At the height of 22 feet the wall of the Temple is recessed to carry columns extending up the roof, thus affording the necessary ornamentation and beauty to what would otherwise be a too severely simple façade. Behind these columns is a continuous sweep of windows. At a lower level the ends of Unity House are recessed and set with columns backed by windows in the same way.[6]

Now, this was indeed a marvelous structure, but it bore no resemblance to any church building with which the congregation, or indeed the residents of Oak Park in general, can have been familiar, and to this day it strikes me as astonishing that it was allowed to go forward, for to this day it remains an unexpected presence in that leafy suburban setting. When Wright took a new friend, the designer Norman Bel Geddes, on a stroll through Oak Park in the early nineteen-twenties, Bel Geddes mistook (or pretended to mistake) the church for a library, and Wright was not amused. Other people have made harsher comparisons, at least in respect to its exterior: the gatehouse to a prison, a Mayan handball court, an ice-making plant. The walls, which are of poured concrete, are certainly forbidding. (The walls were resurfaced a few years ago; prior to that time their pebbled aggregate plainly revealed the accumulation of the separate "pours" as from day to day the concrete was tamped into place between movable wooden forms.) The interiors of both the temple and the "good-time place" are flooded with light and lift one's spirits not in any conventionally Christian fashion; no ritual symbolizing a bloody sacrifice to a god or the sacrifice of God Himself is intended to be carried out there. An epigraph on the walls proclaims that the building is "For the worship of god and the service of man," and plainly Wright wished the emphasis to be upon service rather than worship.

For the purpose of getting the church built, Wright affected a piety

A monolithic structure of poured concrete was a rarity at the turn of the century, especially if the structure was a church. To leave the marks of each day's concrete pour permanently exposed was also a bold aesthetic gesture. Many parishioners prayed for ivy and were happy when ivy came.

sufficiently conventional to keep the Building Committee from becoming alarmed, but in fact it was the structure itself, rather than any use to which it might be put, that was of the highest possible concern to him. Though Wright would have been quick to deny the truth of the assertion, the inspiration for the Larkin building and for Unity Temple had the same source: the Secession building, in Vienna, designed by Joseph Maria Olbrich in 1898. Its function was to provide exhibition space for the art works of the so-called Secessionist *Kunst Haus* school, then commanding much attention throughout Europe and, to a lesser extent, in America as well. Olbrich was Wright's exact contemporary, having been born in 1867, and in something like the way that Wright was able to establish a relationship with Sullivan as his favorite disciple and proto-son, so Olbrich was able to achieve that relationship with Otto Wagner. Wright was familiar with Olbrich's work through the magazines to which he and his Chicago colleagues subscribed and observed at first hand, with admiration, Olbrich's contributions to the German pavilion at the St. Louis World's Fair, in 1904; it was some years later that he took pains to conceal this familiarity.

The eagerness with which Wright and his generation of Chicago architects followed the latest experiments of their colleagues in Vienna and Glasgow and the lack of interest in these experiments manifested by architects in cities along the Eastern seaboard is a rarely commented-on oddity of American architectural history. It was as if the latest aesthetic news from Central Europe, having leapt over the Atlantic, had unexpectedly leapt over the Alleghenies as well, to find a welcome up and down the Mississippi valley. Certainly the news received little enough welcome from McKim, Mead & White and the other fashionable Eastern architectural nabobs, committed as they were to the verities of the Beaux-Arts. Scores of Secessionist borrowings are to be found in Chicago and almost none in New York City. A possible exception is the interior of the St. Regis Hotel (1901–1904), designed by Trowbridge and Livingston. Though the exterior of the building is in a neo-classical Parisian vein, one observes hints of racy, decadent Vienna in the voluptuously oleaginous bases of the marble columns in the lobby. They appear to be melting, and the effect is a pleasingly erotic one.

As Wright gained a surer sense of his greatness, he began to surround it with what he took to be the appropriate fictions. He wished history to record that his pioneering handiwork in the New World had bowled over the architects of the Old World (and to be sure it did so) but he didn't wish history to record that the Old World's pioneering handiwork had previously bowled over Wright, not alone with its buildings but with its revolutionary furniture as well. On the occasion of his first visiting Germany, in 1909, Wright claimed that he was astonished to hear himself introduced

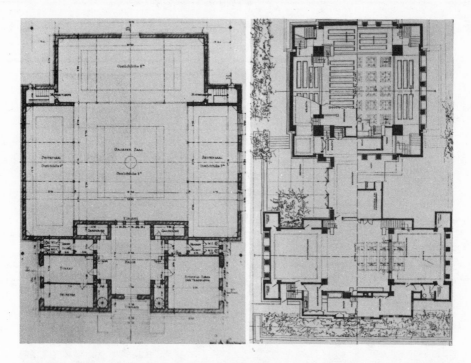

Like the Larkin building, "the good-time place" had its precedent in an art gallery in Vienna, skylit, with few internal supports, and with massive, boxy corners. Left, the floor plan of Olbrich's Secessionist Art Gallery. [IL]   Right, the floor plan of Unity Temple. Olbrich's preliminary sketch for the Art Gallery, which on Gustav Klimt's recommendation was abandoned in favor of the design for the building as it was actually constructed. [IL]

in Berlin as "the American Olbrich." He dared to write that his curiosity was aroused by this appellation and that he then set about discovering Olbrich's work; he visited the arts and crafts community at Darmstadt, in the hope, so he notes, of meeting Olbrich, only to learn that Olbrich had died unexpectedly, at the age of forty-one, almost a year earlier. It is hardly possible for Wright not to have known of this tragic event at the time it took place; his disingenuousness in regard to dates nearly always disguises some factual awkwardness that he must hasten past.

The Secessionist building was—and is—an extraordinary feat, with the ability even today of astonishing the unprepared passerby. Its white stucco façade rises from the Friedrichstrasse like some royal tomb of un-

Left, Joseph Maria Olbrich (1867–1908). Olbrich was an exact contemporary of FLW and had the misfortune to die young. [IL]   *Right, FLW at about the time of Olbrich's death.* [HS]

known origin, enigmatically ignoring its neighborhood as the Larkin building ignores Seneca Street and Unity Temple ignores Kenilworth Avenue; at every point, however, the ancient touch-me-not mortuary note is modified—indeed, exuberantly contradicted—by playful decorative details, beginning with the urns that stand on plinths on either side of the flight of red marble steps leading up to the entrance. Four substantial piers embrace (and appear to support) an immense dome fashioned of gilded bronze laurel leaves, which has long borne the affectionate nickname of "the golden cabbage." A pattern of stylized laurel leaves heightens key areas of the

© SUSAN WOLDENBERG

Left, Unity Temple. Right, the Secessionist Art Gallery, with its globe of gilded bronze laurel leaves—soon nicknamed "the golden cabbage."

façade; modeled in plaster above the entrance are three female masks, from which depend six entwined snakes. Olbrich saw to it that the large volume of space within the building suffered the least possible obstruction; the iron-trussed, skylit roof was supported by six widely separated columns, with provision for the erection of temporary walls wherever they might prove convenient for exhibition purposes. Stairs were placed in the corners of the structure, just as they were later to be placed in the Larkin building and in Unity Temple. (In this respect, Wright has improved on Olbrich, transforming a necessity into an advantage by treating the corners of his buildings as among the most important aspects of their design. Having

Unity Temple today.

© SUSAN WOLDENBERG

© SUSAN WOLDENBERG

Above, a church in Chicago by Hugh Garden, designed for the Third Church of Christ, Scientist, in 1900. The detailing has unexpected touches of Middle European belle-epoque chic. Below, a residence in Oak Park (1908) by the architectural firm of Tallmadge & Watson, also carrying hints of Viennese high fashion.

© SUSAN WOLDENBERG

hit upon this motif, Wright couldn't resist profiting from it even where it made little functional sense: in the Unity "good-time place" the massive corner piers contain nothing but closets.) The two massive piers that give emphasis to the central portions of the front and rear façades of the Larkin building and terminate with sculptured ornaments in lieu of capitals, there being no structure above them in need of support, appear in Olbrich's preliminary drawings for the Secessionist building but are not part of the final design. Psychologically as well as aesthetically, the Secessionist building manifests a release of energy in a form that Wright must have recognized at once as having been somewhere within his reach but hitherto beyond his grasp; though the entrance to the Transportation Building at the Chicago World's Fair, which Wright had worked on with Sullivan in the nineties, had hinted at a similar release of energy, the building itself had amounted to scarcely more than a grotesquely overextended cowshed. It was a shell and only a shell; the Secessionist building was also a shell, but with what a difference! It could be made fit for any purpose, and with breathtaking virtuosity Wright created in its image both a factory and a church.

Evidence that the creation of a particular kind of space rather than the creation of a particular kind of building led Wright to the design of Unity Temple may be found in a letter that Elmslie wrote to Wright in 1932, shortly after the publication of the first version of Wright's autobiography. Elmslie was justifiably indignant over the slurs that Wright directed at him and other early comrades of the Adler & Sullivan days, but with his usual good temper managed to praise Wright for what he called "unquestionably a great performance." In the course of the letter, he writes eloquently of Wright's genius and then proceeds with a gentle firmness to note certain attributes that this genius appears to lack:

> Even in some of your best work there is yet missing, to me at least, a large part of that element perhaps best qualified by the word overtone. Somehow I want always, from you, a radiant quality of expression to the point of contagion; a fairness, a simple serenity unqualified and unruffled; and I expect it. The unsatisfactory elements may arise from a lack of basic mobility, at times, coupled with a desire to do something to the problem instead of allowing it to breathe more clearly and cleanly through your mind, untrammeled.
>
> In connection with this thought it may amuse you to have recalled to your mind a comment you made to me, long ago, in connection with Unity Church in Oak Park. I made some general comment about the use to which the building was to be put, and your reply was, "I don't give a damn what the use of it is; I wanted to build a building like that." It may be added that in general scheme and with minor modifications it

would serve equally well as a counting house. I admire it immensely. It gives me a thrill. It ages with an austere glamour that is very compelling, be it meeting house or counting house![7]

12

U

NITY TEMPLE WAS several years in the making; meanwhile, there were many other commissions for Wright and his disciples to busy themselves with at the Studio. What was later to be given a formal structure in the system of apprenticeship established at Taliesin North and Taliesin West had already come into informal existence in Oak Park, where young admirers of Wright would be brought into what amounted to the family circle. They would work long hours under continuously discombobulating circumstances, at one moment enjoying Wright's close supervision, at another not knowing where on earth he had disappeared to. If their hours were erratic, so was their pay; often enough, Wright would be borrowing a few dollars from them at a time when he already owed them considerable sums in unpaid salaries. As was to be the case in respect to the Taliesin Fellowship, the draftsmen at the Studio counted on receiving a certain amount of financial assistance from their families, and Wright was not above taking advantage of this source of funding. For example, when Ward Willits invited the Wrights to accompany his wife and him on a holiday trip to Japan, in 1905, Wright borrowed five thousand dollars from Walter Burley Griffin to help make the trip possible. (Much of the money may have gone to pay pressing local debts; his many creditors would probably have prevented him from leaving town for an extended period unless at least a portion of their bills had been taken care of.) Later, Wright and Griffin quarreled over the loan, which Wright kept finding reasons not to repay; the quarrel was finally settled by Wright's handing over to Griffin a large number of Japanese prints— part of the vast treasure-trove of prints that he accumulated in the course of his first visit to Japan.

What a gifted and ambitious group of young folk they were! It was no wonder that they crowded round Wright and championed him among their more conventional comrades and then, inevitably, broke with him in order to find a place for themselves somewhere outside his formidable shadow. The principle of the atelier, which is that of a master encouraging

Marion Mahony (1871–1962), the most gifted of FLW's delineators. Like her Irish contemporary Maud Gonne, she was tall and sharp-tongued and possessed a gaunt, beaky beauty. Marrying Walter Burley Griffin, in 1911, she sacrificed her career to his and lived to regret it. [NY] Walter Burley Griffin (1876–1937) was spunky and talented; rightly, he chafed at being under FLW's domination and soon set up practice for himself. In 1912 he won a competition for the design of a new capital city in Canberra, Australia, and his settling "down under" brought his American career to a close. [NY]

ignorant beginners to follow his example, has the defect of requiring in such a master the opposing attributes of egotism and selflessness. The relationship of father and son is notoriously difficult; there are reasons that the relationship of teacher and student is even more difficult, since the inescapable rivalry between them cannot be mitigated by family pride. Wright was to experience this problem at first hand, both in regard to his disciples and in regard to the two of his four sons who became architects. As a self-proclaimed genius, he could scarcely be expected to manifest selflessness; the egotism he manifested was crushing, even when it was expressed—as surprisingly often it was—in terms of affection.

The roster of disciples who worked under Wright at the Studio during those opening years of the century is an impressive one. Griffin, the most prominent of them, should perhaps be described as a colleague rather than as a disciple. He contributed to the design of several of Wright's most distinguished houses and supervised their construction; he also maintained an architectural practice of his own. Clients often preferred dealing with the quiet and civil Griffin to dealing with the short-tempered Wright. In the case of the Willits house, for example, Willits was often irritated with Wright, whom he could rarely reach when a question arose in respect

© SUSAN WOLDENBERG

The Beachy house of 1906, although canonically FLW's, is thought to be largely by Griffin. The Wrights were off in Japan while the house (a remodeling of a house already on the site) was being designed; the job may have been handed to Griffin as part of a deal by which FLW borrowed enough money from Griffin to make the Japanese jaunt possible.

to plumbing lines, electric wiring, and the like; Willits would turn to Griffin to get a proper answer. Given the difficulties that arose in the course of building the house, it is odd that Willits would have proposed the Japanese adventure to the Wrights; the friendship between the two men certainly cooled immediately afterward, in part because of Wright's neglect of his wife and the Willitses while the group was in Tokyo (Wright made a practice of running off by himself to explore the city, often in native garb) and in part because Wright borrowed money from Willits that he failed to repay; Mrs. Willits expressed the opinion that Wright was a boor, and in after years Willits would have nothing to do with Wright, though in their seventies and eighties the two men were often within hailing distance of each other in Phoenix.

Shy and introspective and yet determined to make his name known in the world, Griffin was pursued for several years by Marion Mahony, a tall young woman of Irish ancestry, in appearance and disposition much like Yeats's beloved Maud Gonne. She had an aquiline nose, a sharp tongue, and a gift for delineating Wright's work that was far greater than Wright himself possessed. Mahony, the second woman ever to graduate from the Massachusetts Institute of Technology with a degree in architecture, is one of the few people whom Wright appears not to have dared to patronize, at least to her face. Behind her back, he was braver; when, praising her

A rendering by Mahony of the Adolf Mueller residence, designed by von Holst and her. [NY]

art, somebody compared it to Japanese printmaking, Wright said at once that, while Mahony *copied* Japanese prints, he was inspired by them. Wright and Mahony were also strongly influenced by the drawing techniques being practiced by Mackintosh in Glasgow and the Secessionists in Vienna; the "M.M." that she often affixed to her drawings seems a direct and playful inversion of the "W.W." that stood for "Wiener Werkstätte" (Viennese Workshop). She was several years older than Griffin, who appears to have found her intimidating; not without some difficulty, she would talk him into going off on weekend canoe trips with her, in the course of which they would bivouac chastely in the same tent. This virtuous conduct was evidently Griffin's idea, and Mahony at last outwitted it by a proposal of marriage accompanied by an architectural proposal: if they were to marry, she would make all his presentation drawings for him. Griffin accepted the proposal and after their marriage Mahony was as good as her word; the exquisite drawings that she prepared to accompany his entry in the competition for a new Australian capital city at Canberra are said to have played a large part in his winning that competition.

Mahony was at Wright's side in the Studio for a total of eleven years (though with many undocumented interruptions), Griffin for five. Also present for varying lengths of time were William Drummond, Barry Byrne, and John Van Bergen, with George Elmslie, Hugh Garden, and others (friends rather than disciples) occasionally helping out in an emergency. Often enough, they would work all night, falling asleep at their drafting tables or curling up on the drafting room floor, in front of an open fire. It was said to have been the case that the newly married wife of one of these overworked and ill-paid young architects came to the studio late at night, in search of her husband, and ended by quarreling with Wright and attempting to beat him up.

It was in Wright's nature to invent emergencies when they failed to develop of their own accord, and the size of the contribution that a given disciple would make to a design was a function of how hard-pressed Wright had caused himself to become; like any busy architect, he would rough out a design, turn it over to others, criticize and revise their handiwork, and so arrive at a design sufficiently detailed to present to a client, always with the proviso in Wright's case that no design could be called complete until the building itself was complete; to him the process of construction was a process of refinement as well. Many a client felt his pulse quicken with distress as Wright joyously stayed the carpenter's hand and improvised an alteration to a plan, at a cost that the dismayed client had had no reason to anticipate. (The Johnson Wax administration building cost several times as much as Wright had predicted it would; as a hardheaded business-man, Hibbard Johnson asserted that he would never be able to forgive Wright for having plunged him and the company into such a state of fiscal uncertainty, but Wright's hypnotic powers were invariably heightened by adversity; soon enough, Johnson not only forgave Wright but was happy to commission further work from him.)

Over the years, Wright developed a knack for treating clients like

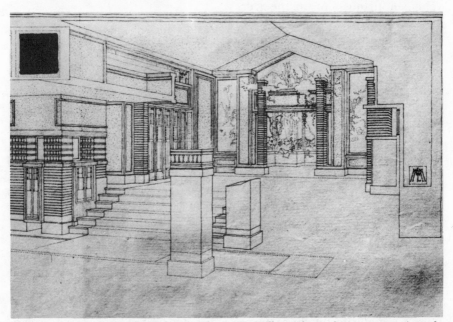

A portion of a rendering by Mahony of the C. H. Wills residence; her monogram is at the extreme right. In old age, she inked out the name of the architect (black square at upper left of the drawing). [NY]

apprentices, or, rather, like gifted children who might one day aspire to the condition of apprenticeship; the fees a client paid Wright were in their nature not unlike the fees that his apprentices paid. What a client acquired was far more than a building, distinguished as that was sure to be and lucky as the client was to have come into possession of it; he had also gained the boon of a relationship with the Master and that boon was beyond price. Nor was Wright's lofty view of the matter inaccurate: his clients really *were* fortunate to find themselves in his presence. For many of them, the relationship proved the most rewarding experience of their lives. I have spoken to elderly men and women throughout the country who, almost thirty years after Wright's death, continue to bear witness to the intensity of emotion that he generated in them, whether the emotion was joy, exasperation, or despair. However anguished the feat of constructing—and paying for—a Wright house, again and again a client would return and ask for a second or even a third Wright house. Of the small number of clients who claim to be sorry that they ever had anything to do with him, one is a very old woman in the South, who spoke with indignation of Wright's attempt to "sell" her the notion of building an entire theatre for music when what she had requested of him was a simple music room. As I stood listening to her, she seemed to shed twenty years; her eyes sparkled, blood rushed into her cheeks, and her voice regained the vehement firmness of middle age.

Among Wright's ideal clients in the early stages of his career one thinks of his neighbors the Winslows, the Moores, the Robertses, and the Gales, and especially of the Coonleys, who, telling Wright that they perceived in his houses "the countenance of principle," commissioned from him the house in Riverside that, at the time he was writing his autobiography, he considered his finest work. Fallingwater, Wingspread, Taliesin West, and many another great house were then far in the future, but the Coonley house and its attendant structures are of their company; serenely, unmarked by age, they rise out of lawns and trees by the banks of the meandering Des Plaines River, and although four families now occupy the little estate, Wright's boldly articulated plan of joined pavilions remains in large measure unaltered. The main house has survived not only a major fire but a radical change in the so-called life-style of its occupants. The Coonleys would have had many in help both indoors and out; they came from well-known families (Mrs. Coonley was a Ferry) and they entertained with a formal elegance that one would be unlikely to encounter anywhere in the United States in the nineteen-eighties, but the house adapts itself readily to the more easygoing hospitality of the present owner, a Greek-born businessman, who takes an appealing pride in his possession of a masterpiece.

By the time Wright was designing the Coonley house, he had pro-

© SUSAN WOLDENBERG

The Coonley house in Riverside (1907), one of the grandest of FLW's residential designs. As in so many Prairie Houses, the ground floor is, in effect, a basement, and not without a basement's usual gloom.   Below, the floor plan of the Coonley house and its appurtenances is ravishingly complex and inefficient, as befits a rich client.

claimed that what he called the Prairie House would be characterized by its abandonment of both basement and attic. As the quintessence of a Prairie House, the Coonley residence has a ground floor that amounts to a basement, providing space for the usual utilities and a large playroom that opens onto a paved terrace and reflecting pool; an insignificant doorway, squeezed into place under a porte cochere, leads into a dark entrance hall, from which one climbs a stairway to the second floor, containing the living room, dining room, kitchen, and family bedrooms and bathrooms.

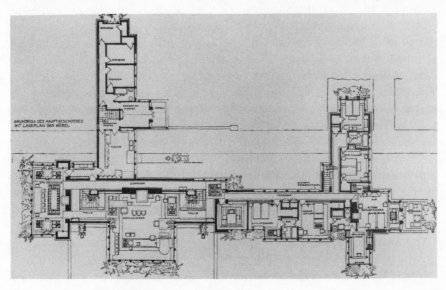

The delight one feels in the airy openness of the living and dining spaces has no doubt been heightened by the crepuscular gloom through which one has been obliged to pass in approaching them; as for the playroom, its penitential severity must have been all the more notable as it was originally designed and built, with small, deep-set, square windows offering the only available natural light; these windows were subsequently replaced by French doors.

The Tomek house, in the same town and of the same period as the Coonley house, is like the Coonley in being without a basement or attic and in having a ground floor that one instinctively hurries through on the way to the hospitable, many-windowed, light-filled spaces of the second floor. The house is related not so much to its site as to the sky; like an ingeniously elaborated tree house, it looks out over a rectangle of green lawn to a house by Wright's early mentor, Silsbee. Despite Wright's championship of the autochthonous bond that ought to exist between a house and its setting, Silsbee's sturdy handiwork appears far more securely tethered to mother earth than Wright's Tomek house does. Accepting the Tomek design as characteristic of Wright's so-called "prairie" style, we may glance for a moment, not without a degree of malicious amusement, at Wright's success in popularizing a term that has very little to do with the kind of architecture to which he applied it. The word "prairie" is charged with romantic allusions to the American past, and Wright did well to take advantage of them, as did those contemporaries of his who came to be loosely grouped under the rubric of "The Prairie School"— Maher, Elmslie, Purcell, and the rest. But the proper definition of the word "prairie" is "an extensive area of flat or rolling grassland," and scarcely a single one of Wright's houses occupied such a site. Wright spoke of Oak Park and the adjacent River Forest as if they had been founded on the prairie, but as the names of the towns imply, they consisted largely of forest in their early days; also heavily forested were Riverside, Highland Park, Wilmette, and the ravines of Glencoe, all sites of "Prairie" Houses. The Robie house, in the heart of Chicago, is a so-called prairie house, as is the Gilmore house, in a conventional residential quarter of Madison, and the Martin and Heath houses, both in Buffalo. European architects— Gropius among them—who learned to admire Wright through the Wasmuth edition of his works, published in 1910, assumed from the lithographs published in that volume that his Prairie Houses stood in open country, in the Wild West of the Old World's imagination, with Buffalo Bill and perhaps even Sitting Bull hallooing in the middle distance.

In an early chapter of his autobiography, Wright asks rhetorically, "What was the matter with the kind of house that I found on the prairie?", to which a possible answer might be, "Well, for one thing it wasn't on the prairie at all." For many years, Wright's domestic architecture concerned itself almost exclusively with city and suburbs, and many of the problems that he claimed to be able to solve by employing "prairie" architecture were, in fact, problems related to city life—problems that Wright sometimes solved and more often ignored.

To ensure privacy in the Robie house, occupying its conspicuous street-corner in Chicago, the main living quarters have been placed on the second floor, behind a cantilevered balcony with a solid brick parapet. At the time that the house was built, the second floor also provided a considerable view to the south, over the unbuilt-upon land of the Midway, but only a romanticist like Wright would have been able to detect the grand sweep of the prairie in that false *rus-in-urbe* prospect. (In his book about the Robie house, Donald Hoffmann quotes Frederick Law Olmsted, the de-signer of the Midway, as calling the environs a flat and mostly treeless terrain, "not merely uninteresting, but, during much of the year, positively dreary.") Fred C. Robie was a wealthy young manufacturer of bicycle and automobile supplies, married to a graduate of the University of Chicago

© SUSAN WOLDENBERG

Because the Gilmore house (1908) was perched on a hilltop in Madison and looked as if it might be about to take off, it was nicknamed "the airplane house"—early cultural homage to the Wright Brothers. The cantilevered roof of an upstairs porch having threatened to give way, the owners inserted two stout posts that seem intended merely to support a hammock.

and the father of two small children. He had a strong mechanical bent and had invented an automobile called the Robie Cycle Car, which never went into commercial production. Robie was eager to build a house that would take advantage of the many efficient industrial products developed in the early twentieth century and would omit what he called the dust-gathering "doodads" of architectural fashion. He had made sketches for such a house, and whenever he showed them to builders, they would say, "Oh, you want one of those damn Wright houses!"

Like its contemporary the Coonley house, the Tomek house in Riverside boasts a ground-floor "basement." On blueprints, FLW liked to identify the main room of this basement as a billiard room, whether or not the client ever played billiards. The eaves of the Tomek house rival in their cantilevered breadth those of the Robie house.

Acting on this tip, Robie got in touch with Wright and at once proved himself to be an ideal client. Between them, they contrived a house unlike any ever seen before, of brick, stone, steel, concrete, glass, and tile, with the latest and most efficient electric lighting, telephone equipment, burglar and fire alarm systems, and even an industrial vacuum-cleaning system, whose pipes would be threaded throughout the house and would have outlets in every room; no doodads, in short, except industrial doodads. For Robie, Wright would provide an attached three-car garage; for Mrs. Robie, there would be balconies and terraces and window boxes filled with flowers; for the children, there would be a large ground-floor playroom opening onto a walled playground.

The house as it went up, with its maze of bolted steel beams supporting cantilevers of breathtaking length, created a sensation. Many people likened it at once to a steamship—a *"Dampfer,"* as the local German-speakers called it. The Robies were enchanted with their unprecedented toy, and for once Wright had no difficulty with the financial aspects of the project. Robie paid a total of sixty thousand dollars for the house and its furnishings (perhaps six hundred thousand dollars in today's money). Fifty years later, he told his son, "Nobody knew, except my father, how much money I was going to spend for a house, and he didn't think I was such a damned fool as that."[1] But Robie was far from considering himself a fool for having helped to bring into existence what he correctly perceived to be a master-piece. All the sadder, then, to set down the fact that within a couple of years the young Robies were divorced (Mrs. Robie charged her husband, accurately as it turned out, with infidelity) and the house passed into other hands. Shortly thereafter, Robie's father died, leaving heavy debts that the son felt honor-bound to pay. Almost a million dollars having been used up in the carrying out of that task, Robie found himself a poor man. He never recovered from this financial misadventure but lived on cheerfully into the late nineteen-fifties. According to Hoffmann, Wright met Robie's son by chance in 1956 and inquired after the father. "A good house," Wright said, "for a good man."[2]

The ravishing little Davidson house, which Wright designed for a Larkin Company executive in 1908, is a near twin of the Isabel Roberts house, in River Forest; it occupies a small, level plot of ground on a quiet side street in Buffalo. Here Wright has made no effort to accommodate to the site, whether in respect to privacy, to orientation, or to Buffalo's winters. (The present owners, mindful of Wright's dislike of draperies, keep the pretty, latticed windows of the little house undraped and have grown accus-tomed to being observed by passersby, as well as to winter drafts that the unobtrusive addition of storm windows cannot wholly outwit. Previous owners, lacking the protection of storm windows, simply abandoned the two-story-high living room in winter, hanging blankets between it and the dining room, which they sought to make habitable by borrowing heat from the adjoining kitchen.) The Davidson house deserves an isolated prairie setting, or perhaps a setting on some benign southern savanna—anywhere, indeed, except Buffalo, but then Wright built his houses wherever he could find a client, not wherever they were fit to go.

If the Prairie House had little to do with an actual prairie, it had a great deal to do with how Wright believed people should live, not only as members of a family, but as citizens of a democracy, and its plan is therefore far more significant than its exterior appearance. Over the years, he man-aged to convince many people that his wide-eaved low roofs and massive chimneys, his open porches and garden walls running out from the house proper in order to marry it to the ground, were outward and visible signs of the principles upon which the nation was founded. It was these principles that he saw his floor plans as reflecting; rooms opened into one another without the usual peremptory boundaries of walls and doors, and a family was united by sharing spaces as well as activities.

The hierarchical nature of conventional Victorian architecture, with servants segregated in attics by night and in cellars for much of the day,

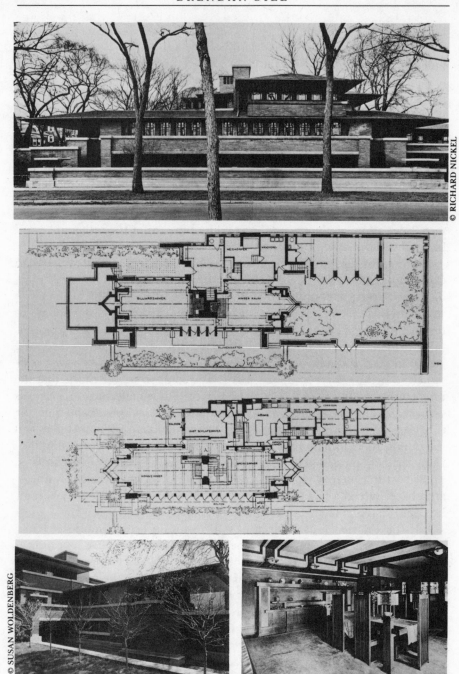

© RICHARD NICKEL

© SUSAN WOLDENBERG

Despite the fact that it occupies a narrow street-corner strip of land in one of the most populous cities on earth, the Robie house (Chicago, 1909) is considered the classic Prairie House. When it was new (and there were still such things as transatlantic sailings and German-speaking Chicagoans), it was known as "der Dampfer"—that is, "the steamer."

was replaced in Wright's designs by something approaching an equality between masters and servants in respect to physical comfort; moreover, his houses looked forward with equanimity to the day when there would be no servants. Even in his youth, in Oak Park, Wright took care to have a couple of servants in his house, and in later years he had the use of an army of servants, disguised as apprentices, farm workers, family members, admirers, and hangers-on, but he was able to imagine other people living without them, and in his Usonian houses the kitchen, however small, rivals the living-room fireplace as the very heart of the house.

"The countenance of principle"—that was what the Coonleys saw in Wright's houses and presumably what they saw in Wright's countenance as well, for they were people who set high moral standards for themselves and their friends. They would never readily abandon these standards, especially if the temptation to do so involved sex. At the time that Wright was designing the Coonley house, he had already gained a reputation as something of a ladies' man, known to go "automobiling" with married women; Wright justified this activity, highly unusual in Oak Park if not in the racier purlieus of Chicago, on the grounds that the women were clients and that he was engaged in the professional task of showing them houses of his design. He certainly made no effort to go unnoticed on these expeditions; he drove about in a Stoddard Dayton sports roadster that had been custom-made to his design. It had (of course) a cantilevered convertible canvas top, which extended well out in front of the dashboard; shiny brass fittings; a body enameled bright yellow; and brown leather seats. It was nicknamed "The Yellow Devil" and was capable of speeds of up to sixty miles an hour; Wright paid many fines for exceeding the Oak Park speed limit of twenty-five miles an hour.

In most cases, whether with or without the assistance of the Yellow Devil, Wright may have contented himself with flirtations; having been adored from the cradle by innumerable women—his mother, his maiden aunts, and his sisters, to say nothing of his wife—he was accustomed to being made much of and of being pursued. Indeed, throughout his life Wright appears to have taken a comparatively passive role in respect to beginning an affair; in his autobiography, we encounter a curious passage having to do with the novelist and playwright Zona Gale, a close friend of members of the Wright family. Wright disliked the Gale house (a pillared, imitation Colonial mansion) in Portage, Wisconsin, upriver from Spring Green, where Gale lived with her elderly father. He wrote, "I hated her environment as utterly unworthy of her. . . . I hadn't met Olgivanna and I thought Taliesin would be a much more appropriate place for the author of 'Lulu Bett.' But I had been spoiled, or something. Perhaps I had always expected the women to make love to me. I just didn't know how to make love to Zona Gale."[3] From which we may deduce either that Zona Gale lacked the aggressive temperament of Mamah Cheney, Miriam Noel, and Olgivanna Milanov, or that Wright had been rebuffed by Gale and is here paying back an old score.

Many people have professed to be puzzled by the seemingly abrupt fashion in which Wright's life broke in two when, in the fall of 1909, he

Left, Catherine Wright. [EWI] *Right, FLW.* [HS] *It was at about this time that he was undertaking his affair with Mamah Cheney.*

abandoned his wife and six children in Oak Park and hastened off to Europe with Martha Borthwick Cheney. (Mrs. Cheney was always affectionately known as Mamah, pronounced "May-mah." "Cheney" was pronounced "Chee-ny.") It is the extreme confusion at the moment of Wright's actual departure that is puzzling and not the break itself. Nowadays, we speak glibly of something called midlife crisis as being the occasion for the separation or divorce of many couples hitherto supposed to have been ideally suited to one another, and it was certainly true that Wright at just past forty was ready for a change and had been ready for some time. Donald Hoffmann cites an unbuilt project of 1903, for an architect's studio house, as a possible hint that Wright was thinking even then of moving into bachelor quarters.

At about the same time, Wright was designing a house in Oak Park for Mamah, her husband, Edwin, and their children. Under a single immense low-pitched hip roof, from whose peak emerged a massive central chimney, Wright provided them with what appears to be a one-story-high bungalow. Like the Tomek and Coonley houses, the Cheney house is, in fact, two stories high, with the first story serving as a sort of raised basement, artfully concealed within a terraced platform. To reach the front door from the street, a visitor makes a number of left and right turns along a garden path and up a series of steps into a small entry: a classic example of Wright's way of deliberately withholding easy access to a structure—of transforming the simple act of entering a building into a complex rite, with overtones of the sacred (whether consciously experienced or not). Hitchcock says of the plan of the Cheney house that it is "unusually compact and original." The main floor consists of a library, living room, and dining room, flowing unimpededly into one another; a kitchen; and four bedrooms and two bathrooms. In the raised basement are more bedrooms, a bathroom, a garage, and the large room that Wright so often identified on his plans as "billiard room," though his clients may never have played, or wished to play, billiards. On the main floor, a skylight, indetectable from the exterior of the house, ingeniously throws light down through the unused attic space into a corridor behind the central chimney. The house is indeed what Wright liked to call "a good-time place," and if he and Mamah Cheney fell in love in the course of his designing it, then we may think of it sentimentally as a not unworthy prelude to the greater wonders of the first Taliesin.

Mamah Cheney was an exceptionally spirited and intelligent woman. She had been born in Boone, Iowa, in June of 1869, one of four children of Marcus Borthwick, a carriage builder and railway machinist, who in the eighteen-seventies moved with his family to Oak Park. (Having been born in June, 1867, Wright may have usurped 1869 as his birth-year in order to establish the closest possible contemporaneity with his beloved. By coincidence, it was also the birth-year of Mamah's successor, Miriam Noel.) Mamah attended the public schools in Oak Park and graduated from the University of Michigan in 1892, earning in the following year a master's degree in teaching. She gained a working knowledge of German, French, and Italian, along with some Latin and Greek. Her future husband, Edwin Cheney, still another child of June, 1869, was in the same class. Presumably he and Mamah met as undergraduates, though Cheney was taking his degree in electrical engineering (to which he devoted his professional career) and not in the humanities. Mamah was always to be remembered for her infectious laugh, her gregarious nature, and her intellectual aspirations; Edwin, far more reserved, had as his chief undergraduate interest the glee club. She accepted a position in the public library of Port Huron, Michigan, where she spent five years.

Edwin is said to have proposed to Mamah a number of times during this period; she accepted him at last and they were married in 1899, in Oak Park. Her reluctance to marry Edwin may have been mitigated by a

The Cheney house in Oak Park (1903). Seemingly a one-story bungalow, it is in fact a full two stories in height and has ample bedrooms and bathrooms for the large number of Cheneys and assorted family members who occupied it. Its open plan and many windows made it all the more difficult a setting for lovers hoping to remain clandestine.

shortage of suitors in Port Huron, by the advent of her thirtieth birthday, or by her mother's death, in 1898. Other deaths followed with unusual swiftness: her father died in 1900 and her sister died in 1901, after giving birth to a daughter, for whom the Cheneys assumed responsibility. A son was born to them in 1903 and a daughter in 1905.

Wright was subsequently to give the impression that there had never been anything furtive about his falling in love with and beginning a sexual relationship with Mrs. Cheney, but it appears that, like most couples in such circumstances, they were making love for a considerable period before they were found out; having been found out, they became, by the standards of that time, brazen in their conduct, being observed by playmates of the Cheney children "spooning" on a couch in the Cheney library (ironically, Wright had designed the house in such a fashion as to make secret observation of its occupants easy, if not downright irresistible). Wright and Mrs. Cheney, both champions of "advanced ideas," saw fit to discuss their affair at length with Catherine Wright and Edwin Cheney, in what must have been a series of exceptionally painful encounters for all of them.

Wright's affair with Mamah Cheney was certainly the immediate occasion of his departure from Oak Park, but the temptation to separate himself from much of his past life, both personal and professional, had long occupied his mind. He was just over forty and had twenty years of incessant hard work behind him. He had been a husband and father for the same period of time and the rewards of domesticity had long since grown meagre, especially for a man who claimed that he had no knack for raising children, had never loved his wife as she deserved, and had struggled daily to keep afloat in an ever-rising sea of household expenses. (Or so he depicted his situation; the fact was that the grand pianos, automobiles, horses, and fine clothes that he found indispensable to his self-regard cost him far more than Catherine and the children ever did.) He was in need of a holiday, or, rather, something more lasting and more radical in its nature than a holiday, and the coming together of several events encouraged him to make a decision.

Kuno Francke, a professor at Harvard who, though of German birth had long been an American citizen, came to see Wright at Oak Park, was greatly impressed by him, and at once urged him to pay an extended visit to Germany and Austria, where so much design work of interest to Wright was being accomplished. In his autobiography, Wright has Francke arguing that Wright must bring the message of his organic architecture to the Germans, who were only fumbling their way clumsily toward what Wright had already seized. On the contrary, it is likely that what Francke said was, "My dear Wright, why not go and take in with your own eyes the work that you and your colleagues have been drawing inspiration from at second-hand, out of exhibition catalogues and magazines?" Wright protested to Francke that he was too busy to leave Oak Park, but some time later he received a letter from the German publisher Ernst Wasmuth (presumably on Francke's recommendation), offering to publish a complete monograph of his work; Wright would have only to prepare the necessary perspective drawings and floor plans. Wright accepted the offer and set his staff to work on the project, but he longed to go over to Europe and finish the job on the spot. For almost a decade, he had been corresponding with C. R. Ashbee, an English architect, designer, and lecturer, whom he had met in the course of Ashbee's several visits to the United States; having enjoyed Wright's hospitality in Oak Park, Ashbee was eager to entertain Wright at his country house in Chipping Campden, in Gloucestershire. Again and again, he had pressed Wright to pay his first visit to the Old World; what better reason could there be than the Wasmuth project?

So matters stood in October, 1909. It appears that everyone in Oak Park was observing—no doubt with relish and yet not without sympathy—the progress of the Wright-Cheney affair. Earlier in the year, Catherine Wright had written to her friend Mrs. Ashbee in England, "I know that peace will come out of all this turmoil and distress," but it was not to be. The prescient Mrs. Ashbee had long since written in her journal, "There is something tender and loveable about Mrs. Wright. . . . Every tone of her voice rings with fearless honesty. . . . I feel in the background somewhere difficult places gone through—knocks against many stone walls—and brave pickings up from sloughs of despond to a serener brightness (it is never gaiety—rather, a hard-won happiness)—and I am certain I hear too beginnings of a different kind of sadness—a battling with what will be an increasing gloom and nervousness (spite of success) in her husband. If her children do not comfort her, she will be hard-pressed. As yet she is almost a girl still—slender and lovely . . . and when she laughs you forget the tragic lines round her mouth. But people do not kiss one in that way unless they are lonely in the midst of plenty."[4]

And that was Catherine's plight. Wright had informed her that he would never relinquish Mamah and was therefore requesting a divorce. According to Wright's later account, Catherine asked that he remain married to her for a year and if at the end of that period he still wished a divorce she would give him one. As for Cheney, he played the role of wronged husband with exceptional tact; given that he had pursued Miss Borthwick with ardor, that it had taken several proposals in order for him to win her hand in marriage, and that they had had two children together, he gains a certain distinction in history by dint of his seeming never to have raised his voice.

A photograph by FLW of the English architect C. R. Ashbee. A social reformer and champion of the arts and crafts movement in the Great Britain, Ashbee came to the United States to raise money for his assorted causes by giving lectures. He and FLW met in Chicago and became fast friends. Ashbee was homosexual (which appears to have escaped FLW's attention) and in proposing marriage to a proper young English maiden he left her almost totally in the dark as to how little their sexual relationship might be expected to amount to. [FA]

This photograph of Ashbee's mother and wife is said to have been taken by FLW during a trip to the States in which Ashbee was imprudent enough to bring along both his mother, whom he doted upon and who doted upon him, and his wife, whom his mother snubbed. Mrs. Ashbee eventually gained a certain revenge by insisting that Ashbee perform in a husbandly fashion and produce issue. Somewhat to his distress, they had four daughters and no sons. [FA]

Symptomatic of the turmoil and distress of which Catherine Wright had written to Mrs. Ashbee, and which was every bit as visible in the Studio as in the home, was a meeting at this period between Wright and Henry Ford. Already on his way to becoming one of the richest men who had ever lived, Ford was an ignorant and eccentric crank of humble origin; he was much less interested in social climbing than most of his Detroit and Pittsburgh contemporaries, but his wife and son Edsel felt that it was time for the Fords to have a suburban estate on a scale commensurate with their wealth. Apparently at Edsel's urging (for it was nearly always members of the younger generation that would urge their parents to take a chance on Wright), Ford came to Oak Park for an interview with Wright. Ordinarily, Wright would have rejoiced at the opportunity of spellbinding this most advantageous of possible patrons, and if he had done so he would have won a commission at least as valuable in dollars and as important to his career as the failed McCormick commission, but alas! Wright was too distraught to make one of his usual dazzling presentations. Bewildered and disappointed—no doubt he held Edsel to blame for wasting his time on a long-haired freak—Ford began to look elsewhere for an architect.

One day in October, something happened that brought the relationship to a sudden climax—something that we call mysterious simply because the facts have so far eluded us but that may not have been mysterious at all. Since late June, Mamah and the children had been visiting with a friend in Colorado. In October, the friend died in childbirth and shortly after this shocking event Mamah notified her husband to come and pick up their children and take them back to Oak Park. By the time Cheney arrived in Colorado, Mamah had departed, perhaps for New York and perhaps to utter an ultimatum to Wright. Certainly his conduct was that of a lover who, after long delays, had been forced to make an irrevocable choice.

According to Manson, Wright had "fought for many years the mounting sense of outrage at being possessed" by what he considered "marital slavery"; at last a point was reached when "the pent-up pressure could not be controlled," which is to assert that Wright was scarcely to be blamed for the subsequent explosion. Manson gives the "official" view of Wright's departure:

> It was an overnight decision. The following morning, he made frenzied rounds of his current clients in Chicago, collecting fees in advance and selling fistfuls of Japanese prints, but explaining his purpose to no one. That afternoon he took a train to New York, where he was joined by Mrs. Edwin Cheney (Mamah Borthwick). A few hours later, they were on a ship bound for Europe. For nearly two weeks the scandal, while rumored, was kept from the public; but it broke into print on Sunday, November 7th, on the front pages of every Chicago newspaper. There was general consternation and speculation, but Chicago heard nothing more from Wright for almost two years. All that was really known was that he and Mamah Cheney, after a sojourn in Berlin, were living quietly in a small villa above Florence, at Fiesole.[5]

Manson goes on to explain that Wasmuth was already at work on the elephant folio of Wright's work and that Wright's presence in Berlin had become a necessity—"Thus, even under emotional duress, his flight to Europe was not wholly irresponsible; it was conditioned by the practical considerations of his career."[6] Manson wrote these words with Wright's sympathetic cooperation, many years after the events in question were taking place; at that time, Wright was very far from feeling much concern for "the practical considerations of his career," and neither was Catherine Wright in Oak Park, where, with a minister at her side, she issued a statement to a small army of newspaper and magazine reporters. They had been hounding her for such a statement ever since the Berlin correspondent of the *Chicago Tribune* had telegraphed the news that a "Mr. Frank Lloyd Wright and wife" were registered as staying at the Hotel Adlon, in Berlin, and were receiving mail from home at that address. The correspondent had had the feral wit to look over the mail arriving in Wright's name at the Wasmuth offices and had discovered there a picture postcard from Catherine Wright (the picture was of Unity Temple), reading, "My Dear: We think of you often and hope you are well and enjoying life, as you have so longed to. From the children and your wife, Catherine L. Wright."[7]

One notes that the signature isn't merely "Catherine," but "your wife," and that the "marital slavery" Wright complained of is hinted at here, in this instance quite justly, by Catherine's taking care to sign her full name: she is the only wife he has and his name is also hers. She will not give him up if she can help it.

That was the burden of Mrs. Wright's message to the reporters filling the little house in Oak Park. Difficult as the event must have been for her—few women in America at that time had ever been obliged to face reporters in large numbers, especially when the reporters' purpose was to stir up the nastiest possible sexual scandal—Mrs. Wright was characteristically clear-headed and dignified. Her words:

> My heart is with him now. He will come back as soon as he can. I have a faith in Frank Lloyd Wright that passeth understanding, perhaps, but I know him as no one else knows him. In this instance, he is as innocent of wrongdoing as I am. These cablegrams and bits of verification do not change my position in the least, nor alter my feelings. Why, this is simply the publicity part of a struggle that has been going on for a long time. . . . He is honest in everything he does. A moment's insincerity tortures him more than anything in this world. Frank Wright never has deceived me in all his life. . . . His whole life has been a struggle. When he came here as a young architect, he had to fight against every existing idea in architecture. He did fight, year after year, against obstacles that would have downed an ordinary man. He has fought the most tremendous battles. He is fighting one now. I know he will win.[8]

Cleverness as well as courage is manifest in these remarks; in Mrs. Wright's version of the elopement, Wright hasn't cravenly run away from his personal and professional obligations but has bravely chosen to battle for his soul against Mrs. Cheney by going off with Mrs. Cheney. His heroism in the battle is apparently to be measured by how long it lasts—that is, how long he stays with her. The reporters must have been impressed by this ingenious advocacy in Wright's behalf; nevertheless, it was rage and spite that they were seeking to provoke in Mrs. Wright, and they had further questions. Would Mrs. Wright seek any action in court? Again she outwitted them:

> Whatever I am as a woman, aside from my good birth, I owe to the example of my husband. I do not hesitate to confess it. Is it likely then that I should want to commence court action? I shall make no appeal whatever to the courts. I stand by my husband right at this moment. I am his wife. He loves his children tenderly and has the greatest anxiety for their welfare. . . . I feel certain that he will come back when he has reached a certain decision with himself. When he comes back, all will be as it has been.[9]

The reporters saw an opportunity to shatter Mrs. Wright's irritating self-control. "When Mr. Wright comes back," one of them asked, "how will Mrs. Cheney fit into the picture?" Mrs. Wright gave way a little to their base hopes, but only a little:

> With regard to Mrs. Cheney, I have striven to put her out of my thoughts. It is simply a force against which we have had to contend. I never felt that I breathed the same air with her. It was simply a case of a vampire— you have heard of such things. Why must the children suffer for things they are unaccountable for? They cannot think of a separation. They worship their father and love their mother. If I could only protect them now, I would care for nothing else.[10]

The interview was a long one and filled several columns in the newspapers. Mrs. Wright had given a masterly performance, not telling the truth as she knew it but not actually lying. She had left the door open for a reconciliation with her husband and she had avoided calling Mrs. Cheney anything worse than a creature possessed by the devil. Still, the situation was more desperate than she had admitted; she and Wright had quarreled bitterly over the past several years and although the children might well worship their father, they were nearly always ready to take their mother's side. The chance of a reconciliation was remote. Moreover, Mamah Cheney, far from being a vampire, was a strong, intelligent, and attractive woman, far better educated than Mrs. Wright, and with notions about "free love" and other then revolutionary practices very appealing to a man bent on abandoning the conventions within which he had established his career. Mamah Cheney was not only the woman he was making love to—she was the source of the not very substantial philosophical propositions by means of which he hoped to justify a new life.

In his autobiography, Wright attempts to define these propositions, which in a mangled form contain some of the notions that Wright and Mrs. Cheney had been picking up from one of Mrs. Cheney's favorite writers, Ellen Key, author of *Love and Marriage* and a daring feminist of the period:

> First: Marriage not mutual is no better, but is worse than any other form of slavery.
> Second: Only to the degree that marriage is mutual is it decent. Love is not property. To take it so is barbarous. To protect it as such is barbarism.
> Third: The child is the pledge of good faith its parents give to the future of the race. There are no illegitimate children. There may be illegitimate parents—legal or illegal. Legal interference has no function whatever in any true Democracy. . . .[11]

Mamah Borthwick Cheney. Mamah Borthwick had grown up and attended school in Oak Park and it was Edwin Cheney's willingness to establish a home for her there that was an important factor in her consenting to marry him. When several members of her family died in rapid succession, a wish to escape from the scene of so much sorrow (to say nothing of a wish to escape from the harmless, unexciting Eddie) may have helped to inspire her reckless "spiritual hegira" with FLW.

© SUSAN WOLDENBERG

Wright claims to have worked hard at these definitions of what he calls an "honest" life, but one sees at a glance that they are, in philosophical terms, gibberish. (Ellen Key would have been appalled by his lack of intellectual rigor.) What does he mean by "mutual"? If we do not know that, plainly we cannot compare marriage to "any other form of slavery." But even here he has stacked the deck with "other," which silently defines marriage as a form of slavery whether it is mutual or not. How has he dared to omit the possibility that marriage can be many things, both pleasant and unpleasant, without being a form of slavery? How does he define "decent"? Where has the concept of "love" suddenly emerged from, when what he has been talking about is marriage? Does he assume that love and marriage are synonymous? How does he define "barbarous"? And so on and so on, until his argument loses itself in a swamp of plays on words regarding "legitimacy" and "Democracy," and we throw up our hands in despair of ever pinning him down. Plainly, his "honest" life amounts to the life that he wishes to lead, and the arguments that he adduces in favor of that life exist in order to mitigate the guilt he feels at his selfishness.

In Wright's place, only a monster could have failed to feel a large measure of guilt, and Wright was far from being a monster.

The one truly inexplicable aspect of Wright's hurly-burly flight from Oak Park was the handing over of his architectural practice to an almost total stranger, a young German-born architect named Hermann von Holst. Wright had only recently been introduced to von Holst by Marion Mahony, who was engaged in preparing her exquisite drawings for the Wasmuth folio. In the rambling and angry autobiography that she composed in her old age, Marion Mahony notes that she was offered the job and turned it down. Drummond had already left Wright after a dispute over money that Wright owed him, and so was unavailable. Byrne and other young architects who had worked in the Studio were offered the job and proved no more eager to assume the responsibility than Miss Mahony herself was. There may have been another element in Wright's search for a substitute: looking to the future, he may well have feared that one or another of his gifted colleagues would usurp his practice so successfully that there would be no hope of his ever regaining it. Whatever the reason, he turned to von Holst, whose own practice, then largely residential, was in its Beaux-Arts point of view wholly at odds with Wright's. With Mahony's assistance, von Holst carried to completion the Wright projects that were then in their preliminary stages. Commissions that were almost ready to go out for bids were dealt with at the Studio by Isabel Roberts and John van Bergen. For one or two of the current designs that had captured Wright's attention, he sent back from Europe, clandestinely, a few additional drawings. When these jobs were finished, Miss Roberts and van Bergen closed and locked the Studio door.

13

WRIGHT AND MAMAH CHENEY spent a year abroad, the first few months of their stay being devoted in large measure to the preparation of the Wasmuth folio. For newly united lovers, their living arrangements were peculiar: Mrs. Cheney rented a flat in Berlin and Wright rented a flat in Florence, where, sometimes with the assistance of his son Lloyd and with other helpers, he completed the drawings and floor plans begun in Oak Park by Marion Mahony. As often as possible, he joined Mrs. Cheney in Berlin, from which they undertook a number of hasty sightseeing jaunts throughout Germany. It was during this period that Wright sought out examples of the recently deceased Olbrich's architectural handiwork in Darmstadt; characteristically, he pretended that Olbrich had had no influence upon him, dismissing him with a witticism about the color of the nursery in Olbrich's house (a peculiar shade of purple). The remainder of their stay in Europe was given over to a pleasantly idle pseudo-honeymoon in Fiesole, "far above the romantic city of cities Firenze, in a little cream-white villa on the Via Verdi."[1] There they are said to have been engaged in translating excerpts from Goethe; if so, the effort was mainly Mrs. Cheney's, since Wright had scarcely any German beyond *"Lieber Meister."*

In his autobiography, Wright describes the months in Fiesole as an idyll. His words are those of a lovesick Romeo: "Walking hand in hand together up the hill road from Firenze to the older town, all along the way in the sight and scent of roses, by day. Walking arm in arm up the same old road at night, listening to the nightingale in the deep shadows of the moonlit wood—trying hard to hear the song in the deeps of life."[2] Many years later, that was how he remembered their days and nights, but there were other days and nights, when his mood was dark and even despairing. Here is a letter to his friend Ashbee, written from the cream-white Villino Belvedere in the spring of 1910:

I have intended to write you for some time past and the kind invitations from Mrs. Ashbee which have reached me here at Florence only sharpen the pain with which I must let you know why I cannot come to see you— why I have not come—why I passed your little home in Chelsea with a longing and a disappointment hard to bear.

I think you will believe that I would do nothing I did not believe to be right—but I have believed a terrible thing to be right and have sacrificed to it those who loved me and my work in what must seem a selfish, cruel waste of life and purpose. I have never loved Catherine—my wife—as she deserved. I have for some years past loved another. She was married also and had three children [two of her own and her dead sister's child]. For a short time only was there anything furtive in it. It was open to all whose real concern it was and with their knowledge I took her with me when I sailed for Germany to carry out the publication of my work, upon which I am now engaged.

There seemed no real life for anyone in any other way. She is with me now.

I cannot ask others to countenance the thing I believe to be right when I know it may, yes, it *must* seem wrong to them. So I will not go outside the necessary contact of everyday life among strangers.

I am sure you will credit me with what good it is possible to credit me and will give me the benefit of any doubt. Still, I know what a blow this will be to you—to all who have believed in me. What a traitor I seem to the trust that has been placed in me by home, friends, and not least the cause of Architecture. I know the bitterness of it all and know that life in the larger sense in which I dared conceive it and the hope that I might somehow save what was good in the life that had been and carry it to a truer, nobler fruition for all in a life to be—I know now that cannot be—that life is broken—maimed at best.

I wanted to square my *life* with *myself*. I want to do this now more than anything else. I want to *live* true as I would *build* true, and in the light I have I have tried to do this thing. Advice has been of little use. The necessary light must come from within. Life is *living* and only living brings the light. If I can live, I will see the true way through the stress and wreck, and whatever that way is I shall follow it. . . .[3]

Ashbee wrote an admirable letter in reply, assuring Wright that whatever he had done, or thought he ought not to have done, would make no difference to their friendship. In a consolatory vein, he added that he had come to the conclusion that there were only two sins in the world— the sin of cruelty and the sin, reserved to artists, of wantonly destroying what they know to be a beautiful thing. A few months later, Wright had unhappy news to convey to Ashbee:

Your kind—you can never realize how welcome—letter has awaited an answer longer than I expected, when I delayed it in order that I might know what to say. The fight has been fought—I am going back to Oak Park to pick up the thread of my work and in some degree of my life where I snapped it. I am going to work among the ruins, not as any woman's husband but as the father of the children, to do what I can for

Oak Park as it looked at the time of FLW's return from Europe.

them. . . . Your gentle word came like balm upon my aching spirit—gave an uplift to a self-respect struggling for its very existence. The struggle is not over. Its basis has shifted, however, and I hope I will win usefulness and some measure of peace and rest in time, for all. I have been thinking over your moral code, and it is a difficult one for me. It is enough for any man, too much for all but a few; to live up to it would make the world beautiful—as beautiful as we would have it. But I have been cruel. I have hardness in my soul. I have destroyed many beautiful things—in the hope of putting better things in their place, it is true—but realizing many times, too late, that I must fail. . . . I am cast by nature for the part of the iconoclast. I must strike—tear down—before I can build. My very act of building destroys an order, established with much that is virtuous embalmed or at least embedded in it, and it is hard to keep what was best in the life that was and [find a place for it in] the life that is to be.[4]

Whatever the iconoclast may have been feeling in his heart, he returned to Oak Park with a characteristic display of bravado. We behold him in a letter that W. E. Martin wrote to his brother in Buffalo, on October 10th, 1910:

It's true this time. He has returned . . . and I have seen him in the "flesh."

He called me by phone yesterday about 8 A.M. in almost as matter-of-fact way as though it was but yesterday that he had seen me. Said he thought the best way to test my affection for him was to ask me to go down with him for his "luggage," as it failed to come on his train and it was very valuable and [he] wanted to get it out right away. His nerve was staggering and I could not for the moment know what to say, but told him [I] must take the folks to church and would have company for dinner, etc., and in my embarrassment told him would call for him as we went to church and so would go on down for his "luggage," but Winnie [Martin's wife] positively refused to be seen with him in the auto and I didn't know what the deuce to do for I have not been able to decide for myself what my attitude should be. I let it drop until just in time to start for church and then called him up. Mrs. W. answered the phone. Her voice was "cheery" and I asked if she was happy this morning. She replied "Partially so." I asked for him and she said he was somewhere about the house and [I] said tell him to meet me at the station and I would bring him and his stuff home.

He arrived promptly at the station with Llewellyn. W. was dressed to closely resemble the man on the Quaker Oats package. . . . Knee trousers, long stockings, broad-brimmed brown hat, cane and his lordly strut. We shook hands and he proceeded to apologize for putting me to the trouble and said he really forgot for the moment when he phoned me what his position was in Oak Park, and I said, "Well, what is your position?" "Well, you know and I may as well admit that I am a social outcast and of course no one wants to be seen riding around with me, and I called you up as soon as I received your message to tell you I wouldn't come down, but you had gone and so I am here, not as a prodigal son or a repentant sinner, but I am here to set up my fences again, not as they were—that perhaps will not be possible—but will do it the best I can. I admit I have done wrong, but I am not sorry for myself. I am only sorry for my family, my children, and my clients. Your poor brother and Mr. Heath, they must have had to swallow humble pie in large quantities for my misdoings. People have been saying undoubtedly, "I told you so." Well, I am sorry for them all and now all I ask of society is to let me work. If they will only do that, let me work and do one more grand work before I die, I shall be content."

He is as winning in his ways as ever, when he wants to be nice. . . .

Yes! I have seen him and his hair is much grayer, but he evidences but little signs that he himself is ready to eat any humble pie. . . . I tried to drive streets home where I was least known. Mr. Heath's brother-in-law, Mr. Andrews, was walking down Washington Blvd. as we went by, but I didn't toot my horn for him to look up. Perhaps he did not see us.

His homecoming might have been one of joy and pride to all of his friends instead of making one feel sneaking to be seen with him. Who will win out? Society, as it is called, or Mr. W.? I will bet on him.[5]

Another glimpse of the unrepentant sinner, in a letter from Catherine Wright in Oak Park to Janet Ashbee in Gloucestershire:

Mr. Wright reached here Saturday evening, Oct. 8th, and he has brought many beautiful things. Everything but his heart, I guess, and that he has left in Germany.

I believe I could be more brave if I felt any justice in the present arrangement, but as near as I can find out he has only separated from her because he wishes to retain the beauty and ideality of their relationship and feared by staying with her that he would grow to loathe her.

Each morning I wake up hoping it to be the last and each night I hope may prove to be eternal.

We are all well and I ought to be thankful for that. The children are doing well in their work and play and study and I must be thankful for that.

But to feel that an upstart should have come along and so easily have drawn out my account of love with the many years of interest and left me penniless with the banker's consent and protection is pretty tough. And he seems to be so anxious to be sure I have no doubts about it.

Womankind seems to be so moveable a feast, easily sold and easily bought and passed around and tossed away and no mercy except from outsiders.

Since to get rid of me costs so dearly the new article is of course proportionately greater in value, I suppose.

But it is all beyond me and I am so foolish to cry over spilt milk. I thought I had conquered my feelings better than this, so I will brace up and try not to have it occur again. You help me and distance gives me a chance to overflow, which I dare not do here to anyone.

It is bad for the children and I know it has been very brave of Frank to return as he has and I can at least do my share. He is happy to be with the children and oh! how happy they are to have him back.[6]

The letter is charged with contradictions. Catherine's desperate "Each morning I wake up hoping it to be the last" is followed at once by the seemingly tranquil commonplace, "We are all well and I ought to be thankful for that." Understandably, she is furious with Mrs. Cheney—"an upstart . . . the new article"—and although she is furious with Wright as well, she takes care not to say so, dwelling instead upon his happy reunion with the children. Her fate is a miserable one; not only is the once passionate sexual relationship between Wright and her now permanently at an end but she is daily made aware of his eagerness to renew his passionate sexual relationship with Mrs. Cheney. She may write of wishing to die, but she wishes far more ardently to live, and the hardness of soul that Wright detected in himself and commented on to Ashbee may be perceived in Catherine's soul as well, for although she consents to many of Wright's demands, she adamantly rejects his demand for a divorce. If necessary, she will go on living year after year in a kind of sexual limbo, never being free to fall in love with and marry someone else because she will never set Wright free to marry Mrs. Cheney. But nothing as simple as mere hardness of soul is being manifested in this instance; the fact of the matter is that Catherine loves Wright as much as she has ever loved him, and no number of upstarts will make her love him less.

On Wright's part, the situation, though painful, had the advantage of being temporary. He had returned home, which in the terms he had used when writing to Ashbee meant that he had lost his "fight" for liberty, but the loss was not to be a lasting one. Reluctantly, he was back in Oak Park and under the family roof; reluctantly, he would unlock the Studio door and seek to reestablish his architectural practice—a practice that he began at once to suspect his former associates and disciples of having stolen from him in the course of his year away. (Von Holst and Marion Mahony were soon to design a house for Henry Ford—a monstrous mess of a house, which Ford eventually decided not to build. Wright appears to have felt that the commission should have gone to him instead of to von Holst and Mahony; conveniently, he had forgotten the unfavorable impression he had made on Ford.) Within a few weeks, Wright was planning a new fight, in this case with his mother's assistance. Anna Wright, living next door to her son and daughter-in-law, invariably sided with her son in any family discussion; the fierce temper with which she had been accustomed to assaulting her husband and stepchildren had by no means diminished with age, and she is said to have taken pleasure in quarreling not only with Catherine but with Catherine's mother and grandmother as well. According to family accounts, which exist in a number of contradictory versions, Anna had acquired a couple of hundred acres of choice farmland in "the valley of the God-Almighty Joneses," in the township of Hillside, close to Spring Green. She was happy to make a gift of this land to Frank, in order that he be able to build a house there that would mark the beginning of a new life for him. Whether Anna Wright was aware at first that this new life would include a mistress is uncertain; when the time came, she accommodated herself to Mamah's presence, as she was later to accommodate herself to the even more unlikely presence of Miriam Noel. For Anna, the art of motherhood consisted of never letting go.

Again and again in describing the process by which he put a distance between himself and Catherine, Wright chose to use the unpleasant metaphor of fighting. He was still using it as late as the nineteen-twenties, when he was occupied with dictating his autobiography; in a passage notable for its hypocrisy, Wright dares to claim that during the period when he was building Taliesin as a hideaway for him and Mamah he was sustained by "the same faith that characterized my forefathers from generation to

The Adams house in Oak Park (1913). FLW's last work in a community that he had turned his back on and that had then indignantly turned its back on him. Save for the charming front door, reminiscent of the Greene brothers, the design harks back to a much earlier period. FLW's cantilevered eaves often sagged with time; in this instance, a cheap and candid solution to the problem has been found.

215

An idyllic prospect from the "shining brow" of Taliesin.

generation." Never defining that faith but with the implication that it has God's blessing upon it, Wright gives his personal vexations a quasi-religious setting:

> I suppose that faith carried them as it now carried me through the vortex of reaction, the anguish and waste of breaking up home and the loss of prestige and my work at Oak Park. Work, life and love I transferred to the beloved ancestral Valley where my mother foreseeing the plight I would be in had bought the low hill on which Taliesin now stands and she offered it to me now as a refuge. Yes, a retreat when I returned from Europe in 1911 [*sic*]. I began to build Taliesin to get my back against the wall and fight for what I saw I had to fight.[7]

Behold the embattled hero ("truth against the world") building his mighty fortress on a hillside at Hillside! In his eyes, the gesture is a superb one; in the eyes of his immediate family, including his Lloyd Jones aunts, uncles, and cousins (his mother alone excepted), it is the gesture of an impudent and irresponsible scamp. How dared this public adulterer, by now a favorite topic of the scandalmongering press from coast to coast, expect the Godfearing citizens of rural Wisconsin to welcome him there? As proprietresses of a respectable school only a few hundred yards across the fields from the newly rising fortress, his aunts Nell and Jane feared the contamination of his presence, and they were right to do so; in order to protect the reputation of the school, Wright eventually signed and published an affidavit to the effect that he had no official or unofficial connection with it. Strangers came to gawk at the structure he was preparing as a refuge from conventional society; they poked about amidst the piles of stone, sand, and timber, hoping for a glimpse of the devil himself, in his wanton riding breeches and leather puttees.

216

© SUSAN WOLDENBERG

© SUSAN WOLDENBERG

Left, FLW dammed the little stream that flowed below Taliesin partly in order to create a couple of ornamental ponds and partly in order to generate electricity at the dam site. Over the years, the dam kept washing out and the electricity kept going off. Right, FLW's emblematic gatepost at the entrance to Taliesin.

And because Wright was a genius as well as a scamp, the house he designed and built proved to be a work of art that, in one form or another, has enchanted tens of thousands of visitors for over seventy years. Deservedly, it is one of the most celebrated houses on earth; in the United States, it is rivaled by perhaps eight or ten other houses, among which one would wish to include Wright's Fallingwater and Taliesin West. The Lloyd Joneses had been accustomed to giving Welsh names to their homesteads, and even as Wright was building his refuge he decided to call it Taliesin, after a legendary Welsh bard whose name Wright had encountered in a masque of that name by the American writer Richard Hovey. (A pastiche of Tennyson's *Idylls of the King,* with a few sorry echoes of Swinburne, the masque is a trashy cabinet drama; it may have appealed to Wright because it contains a reference to "the prairies of man's heart," though prairies were surely a rarity in Camelot.) According to Wright, the name meant, in Welsh, "shining brow," and he intended his house to serve as the shining brow of the little hill on which it stood. "Not *on* the hill but *of* the hill," he would say throughout his life, pointing out how the stone walls and wood-and-plaster siding of Taliesin seemed to grow out of the slope of the fields and how its long, low, silvery, cedar-shingled roofs and broad chimneys provided a natural crown to the hill.

If Wright's running off to Europe with Mrs. Cheney was a well-publicized scandal and seemed to put an end to a professional career of exceptional brilliance, his return was also, in a sense, a scandal, because he made it clear that he was preparing the way for a new stage of his relationship with his now celebrated mistress. That being the case, it was no simple matter for him to resume his career at the point at which he had chosen to break it off. In the past, his clients had tended to be moderately unconventional people, ready to take a chance on the untried, but many of these clients had been women; risky as it was at that time for men to associate themselves with an unrepentant philanderer, it was even riskier for women to do so. Commissions were therefore slow to reach Wright, and all the more so because, his reputation aside, he was immured for much of the time at Hillside, supervising a small army of carpenters and masons. Lying deep in the Wisconsin countryside, Hillside was by no means as easy of access as Oak Park, to say nothing of Chicago.

Picking at random almost any portion of the long roller-coaster of Wright's life, one wonders how, at just that moment, he was managing to survive financially. In his autobiography, Wright speaks with candor (though never with as much candor as he pretends) of his constant indebtedness,

A portion of the original Taliesin, which three times escaped destruction by fire.

from the moment of his marriage onward; sometimes he blames his plight on the cost of supporting a wife and family and sometimes he confesses that it is his personal fondness for luxurious living and for the acquisition of beautiful objects that has kept him perennially insolvent. Over the years, this insolvency begins to assume the look of a fate pursued rather than imposed, and I will be returning later to the question of why this should be so; suffice it for now to note that I am baffled to understand the means by which Wright paid his bills during the period between 1909 and 1914.

Several big commissions—the Coonley house, the Robie house, and the project for the McCormick house—had been completed a year or so earlier and several smaller commissions were either just about complete or would be completed after Wright's departure with Mrs. Cheney in the fall of 1909, but the fees in all these instances would have gone to pay past debts and to pay the staff for a short time at the Studio and afterward, when the Studio was shut, at von Holst's office. During the year abroad,

Wright had his usual expenses at Oak Park to deal with, along with the rental of apartments in Berlin and Florence and the villa in Fiesole, the cost of sightseeing jaunts, and the cost of printing the Wasmuth portfolios (he was purchasing the entire edition and would have to wait many years to recoup his investment). Having returned to the United States, almost at once he began work upon Taliesin, which from the beginning was planned on a lavish scale, far more appropriate to the purse of a millionaire than to that of a penniless architect. The stream in the valley below the house was dammed in part to create a lake of pleasing aesthetic effect and in part to generate electricity and provide, by means of a hydraulic ram, a supply of water for a stone reservoir at the top of the hill; from there water fell by gravity to the house, with its pools and fountains, to the nearby barns and other farm buildings, and then to vegetable gardens on the lower slopes. Like Jefferson's Monticello, Taliesin was to be a miniature kingdom, self-sustaining and self-delighting, with the hope, as Wright said, of its becoming "a recreation ground for my children and their children perhaps for many generations more." (Children, grandchildren, great-grandchildren, and great-great-grandchildren of Wright are scattered around the country, but none is currently in residence at either of the Taliesins.) How could Wright afford to build so extravagant a country estate at so impoverished a moment? Apparently by plunging ever deeper into debt, always with the expectation that something wonderful was just about to happen. But what of his creditors? Why did they go on lending him money, as all his life men who in other cases exercised tightfisted prudence in money matters appeared willing to do? The fact is that he was a confidence man of infinite charm, and nobody could refuse him anything for long.

Mamah Cheney had remained in Berlin for several months before returning to the United States. She and Cheney were divorced in the summer of 1911, on the grounds of her having deserted him; Cheney received custody of the children, with the proviso that they were to be permitted to visit their mother at appropriate intervals. (Cheney, cool as ever, took his second bride the following year. He and his wife raised three children; he led a tranquil and successful family and professional life, dying at last in St. Louis. It was said of him that he never missed a college reunion.) By the fall of 1911, Taliesin was sufficiently complete for Wright and Mamah—now using her maiden name of Borthwick instead of Cheney—to make it their residence. Wright's intention was to divide his professional life between Taliesin and an office in Chicago, with sizeable drafting rooms in both locations. Indeed, he drew up plans for a delightful little combined house and office to be built on Goethe Street, in the Near North Side district of Chicago, which would have given Mamah and him the best of both worlds, city and country. Never has a narrow urban plot been more ingeniously manipulated to provide ample space within a single structure for two altogether separate functions, and we have reason for regret—a regret to be felt literally scores of times in studying Wright's career—that it was never built.

Forty years later, Wright would prepare drawings for a building not unlike the Goethe Street house but even more ravishing in its delicacy—the Masieri palazzino, which he had been given the opportunity to design on the Grand Canal, in Venice. The building had been commissioned by the parents of a young Italian architect who had been killed in an automobile accident in Pennsylvania, shortly after paying a visit to Wright at Taliesin North. It was perhaps the most graceful act of homage that Wright ever called upon his genius to pay—homage not only to the young architect who had died but to Venice itself, where Wright's building would have been exquisitely at home. A great brouhaha was stirred up not by the civil authorities in Venice but by travel agents and others, who claimed that the integrity of the architectural heritage of Venice had been placed in jeopardy by an American maverick. As Bruce Pfeiffer tells the story in his book, *Treasures of Taliesin,* an Oak Park neighbor of the Wright family,

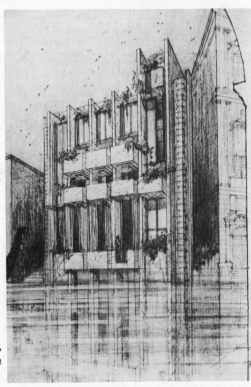

A rendering of the Masieri palazzino, intended for the Grand Canal in Venice. [WF]

Ernest Hemingway, was encouraged to enter the discussion; Hemingway, then living in Africa, told the press that he would rather see his beloved Venice burn than allow a Frank Lloyd Wright building to be erected there. When reporters asked Wright for his reaction to Hemingway's harsh remark, he replied, "Reaction? Why, none whatsoever. After all, that was nothing but a voice from the jungle." But the amateur critics prevailed; the little marble palace was never built.

As 1911 drew to a close, one might have thought that Wright had made an unexpectedly agile recovery from the disarray into which he had thrown his life in 1909. He and Mamah were living together in the most beautiful house he had ever designed, in a setting that was itself of exceptional beauty—a setting that had the advantage of having been both an ancestral possession and the scene of many happy childhood memories. They were on their way to finding a comparatively inconspicuous place for themselves in the community; they were not, after all, as one must take care to remember, daring youngsters bent on shocking their elders. They were in their early forties and therefore entering upon middle age. Quietude and hard work ought to have become them, and these were the conditions of life that Wright claimed to be seeking; nevertheless, some self-aggrandizing, self-destroying demon in him insisted on his making sure that such conditions would be impossible to attain.

Whether Mamah Borthwick egged Wright on in his folly there is no longer any way to know. On the one hand, it is likely to have been at her urging that he had abandoned his family two years earlier, as she had hers; on the other, her obvious decency had been making a favorable impression on the profoundly skeptical inhabitants of Spring Green. What is certain is that Wright announced the holding of a press conference at Taliesin on Christmas morning, 1911—Christmas, of all days in the year!—and when the reporters had gathered, he read them a statement defining Mamah's and his relationship to each other and to the world. At best, it was an amateurish exercise in public relations, certain to fail; at worst, it was an exposure of Wright's ego so obviously self-serving that it threatened to make enemies of everyone present. The *Chicago Tribune* headed its front-page article on the Wright statement with SPEND CHRISTMAS MAKING 'DEFENSE' OF 'SPIRIT HEGIRA.' Datelined Spring Green, the *Tribune* article began:

If the first Christmas of the second "spiritual hegira" of Frank Lloyd Wright and Mrs. E. H. Cheney was not a happy one that fact was not apparent to any caller at the bungalow in which they have placed their household gods, defying society and leaving Mrs. Wright at her home just west of Chicago. . . . Apparently Mr. Wright did not feel any regret he was not present in the Oak Park house where his lawful wife and their six children were spending their Christmas and Mamah Borthwick seemed to have forgotten the Christmases of the past which she had spent with her husband and children.[8]

Wright sketched for the reporters present the circumstances that had led to his and Mamah's being so unjustly made subjects of continuous newspaper gossip. He and Mrs. Wright had married too young; their marriage was a mistake that they ought not to have been allowed to commit, and the marriage had turned into a tragedy. He had learned to find his life in his art and Mrs. Wright had found her life in her children. The divergence of their interests had made it impossible for him to continue his work as an artist while living with his family. He had hoped to fulfill himself as an artist in the companionship he had found with Mamah Borthwick; it was none of the public's business how he and she, loving each other, chose to work out their destiny together. The fact was that laws and rules about love and marriage are made for the average and not for the exception. "The ordinary man cannot live without rules to guide his conduct," he said. "It is infinitely more difficult to live without rules, but that is what the really honest, sincere, thinking man is compelled to do. And I think when a man has displayed some spiritual power, has given concrete evidence of his ability to see and to feel the higher and better things in life, we ought to go slow in deciding he has acted badly."[9]

As anyone could have predicted, the statement was a total failure, opening the door to a hundred questions that Wright had not counted on being obliged to answer. The press was delighted by this unexpected Christmas gift to them: the public discomfiture of an internationally celebrated American, talking publicly about the forbidden topic of sex. Dismayed by the consequences of the conference and the give-and-take that followed for several days thereafter—at one point, Wright summoned a second press conference, at which he called the reporters who attended it "mutts" and "boobs"—Wright (with Mamah presumably working alongside him) prepared a written statement, which he distributed on December 30th. As a specimen of English prose, the statement was Wright at his most bombastic. It read, in part:

> Here we are, four people—a wife and a man and a husband and a woman, who each assumed earlier in life the responsibility of marriage and children. Then the thing happened that has happened since time began. There was the usual struggle with conscience, the usual concession to duty but not the usual clandestine relation furtively continued to save the face of the situation. As soon as the situation developed its inevitable character, a frank avowal to those whose lives were to be affected by a readjustment was made. Time was asked and the man and the woman agreed to make it plain that their love was love. The wife characterized the matter as

mere infatuation that would pass. For a year the wife continued in her household separate from the man. All was wretched and false. At the end of a year the man was called abroad for a year. He made no secret of the fact that he would take the woman with him, but he neglected to inform the newspapers and it was said he had eloped.

It is hard to say who suffered the most. There was the breaking of established ties. but against them was the passion of man for woman and woman for man. The man returned not as husband but as father to insure his family's comfort. Friends thought he came to re-establish the old order, that he had seen the light.

The man knew that only with the woman could he carry out life's purpose. A place was found for the woman. It is this place. There are no family obligations, no family deserted, no duties undone. But the hue and cry of the yellow press was raised, the man and the woman defamed. The prurient consciousness of a great city was turned loose upon the innocent and defenseless. . . .[10]

Wright called this statement his "last word," which proved overly optimistic. For two years, he had been furnishing reporters with excellent copy, and they sensed correctly that he would be supplying them with excellent copy, scandalous or otherwise, for the rest of his life.

In the midst of this self-induced commotion, a few welcome commissions were on Wright's drawing board: the Coonley playhouse, in nearby Riverside; the Angster house, in Lake Bluff; and the Sherman M. Booth house, in the Chicago suburb of Glencoe. If the Booth house had been built according to the original designs, in Hitchcock's opinion it would have been one of Wright's major domestic masterpieces. Hitchcock compares it favorably to the unbuilt McCormick project, which was to have consisted of a series of pavilions and terraces flung along the bluffs bordering Lake Michigan, in the wealthy suburban town of Lake Forest. In the renderings, the McCormick house looks, from the lake side, rather like a Tibetan lamasery, and it may have been this exoticism that prompted Mrs. McCormick to reject Wright's designs and turn instead to the fashionable New York architect Charles Platt, who provided the McCormicks with a tastefully academic Italianate villa. Though far smaller in scale than the McCormick house, the Booth house was every bit as adventurous; in its original form, it took even bolder advantage of its site than the McCormick house did. Approaching the lakeshore, the gently rolling terrain of Glencoe is cut by a number of small but very steep ravines. Wright intended the main block of the house to be placed on a roughly triangular knoll, with ravines falling away from it on all three sides. A concrete bridge would carry a driveway over the ravine lying between the public street and the knoll and then through a porte cochere, by means of which one could gain access to the main block and, across the way, to a wing containing, on the ground floor, a laundry and servants' bedrooms and, on the second floor, a dining room, dining porch, pantry, and kitchen. Other wings of the house held, on two levels, bedrooms, bathrooms, and sleeping porches; in the main block was a two-story-high living room and a music room.

Booth was a lawyer, who at a later and exceedingly troubled time in Wright's life made strenuous efforts to straighten out his tangled financial affairs. Perhaps because what Booth had commissioned from Wright in 1911 was a mansion that proved, on being sent out for bids, too expensive for Booth's means, a much reduced version of the design was built in 1915, on a small portion of the land then in Booth's possession. On the rest of the land, Booth built several small houses as a real-estate speculation. The designs were by Wright, who silently plagiarized a number of his own domestic designs. Some of these had been prepared for his friend the real-estate developer E. C. Waller, Jr., others for the Richards brothers of Milwaukee—in the latter case, making use of a system of partial prefabrication ("Ready-Cut") for the production of low-cost housing.

The Glencoe houses of 1915 are aesthetically a step backward for Wright. They appear to have mattered so little to him except as embodying a favor to Booth or as discharging a financial obligation to him that Wright failed to supervise their construction. By 1913 and 1914, Wright had two of the most important commissions of his life within his grasp, and houses (always—and rightly—his main concern) for the time being had lost their importance. In 1913, Mamah and Wright made a trip to Japan, purportedly at the invitation of the Emperor (though one doubts that the Emperor was issuing many invitations to individual Americans at that point in Japanese history) and more certainly in order to earn some money by purchasing Japanese prints for sale to American collectors. During the course of that

A street ornament designed by FLW; it marks a real-estate development called Ravine Bluffs, in Glencoe. The Perry house in Ravine Bluffs (1915). Like several other houses in the development, it was designed by FLW for an earlier, unrealized project in River Forest.

© SUSAN WOLDENBERG

© SUSAN WOLDENBERG

The Sherman M. Booth residence in Ravine Bluffs (1915). Booth, who for a time handled FLW's tangled legal affairs, was the developer of Ravine Bluffs; he commissioned a large and complex mansion from FLW, which proved too costly to build in its original form.

visit, Wright was approached by representatives of the Emperor, who informed him of the Court's intention to replace the dowdy old Imperial Hotel, built many years earlier by German interests, with a new hotel—one sufficiently de luxe to appeal to foreign visitors to Japan.

Then and there, Wright must have set about spellbinding the Emperor's representatives. It appears that he was successful, for upon his return to America he began work on plans for the hotel. (Why did he trouble to invent, for his autobiography, a wholly different account of how he secured the Imperial Hotel commission? Perhaps because it suited his vanity better than the truth did. According to the autobiography, a committee of distinguished Japanese scoured the entire world for an architect worthy to undertake the Imperial Hotel commission and, arriving at last at Taliesin, unanimously chose Wright. The glory of Wright's whoppers is that they pay no heed to mere pedestrian verisimilitude.)

In the midst of Wright's labors upon the hotel project, E. C. Waller, Jr., came to him brimming with excitement over a project much closer to home—the building of an open-air restaurant and place of entertainment of the sort that was then common throughout central Europe and that, given Chicago's very large German population, was unaccountably missing from its sweltering summertime streets. Wright instantly embraced the notion and expanded upon it. In order to help make it profitable, it should be kept open all the year round, with a winter garden, a bar, and an indoor dance floor. Far loftier in its ambitions than a mere beer garden, it should be a well-built, permanent structure; food, drink, and entertainment would all be of high quality—Pavlova dancing, Caruso singing, the Chicago Symphony Orchestra giving concerts. There was ample land available for such a garden on Cottage Grove Avenue, at 60th Street, just off the Midway. All that appeared lacking was money, and Waller brushed this defect aside as a trifle—money, he said, was always the easiest part of any project.

In a few days, Wright had the plans ready: "The thing had simply shaken itself out of my sleeve," he wrote afterward, as he would often write of projects that particularly pleased him. The budget called for an expenditure of three hundred and fifty thousand dollars. Waller and his friends raised a total of sixty-five thousand dollars; the remainder of the cost depended upon credit, with Wright, among others, taking most of his fees in stock in the Chicago Midway Gardens Corporation. The stock eventually proved to be worthless. (Years earlier, Stanford White had made the same mistake in respect to designing Madison Square Garden, which had in common with Midway Gardens the fact that it was too splendid for its own good and always ran at a loss.) Wright was happier with the creation of Midway Gardens than with any other project up to that time. His personal life was finally what he had struggled to make it be: he and Mamah were contentedly presiding over the green fastness of Taliesin, to which he traveled on weekends while the preparation of drawings and blueprints for Midway Gardens and the daily supervision of its construction proceeded at a breakneck pace in Chicago. Wright's old colleague at Adler & Sullivan, Paul Mueller, who had put up the Larkin building for Wright, was again the contractor in charge, and John Lloyd Wright, now twenty, had joined his father's makeshift office and was serving not only as a tireless assistant clerk-of-the-works but was painting murals for the project as well. The sculptors Richard Bock and Alfonso Iannelli contributed works both figurative and abstract in a variety of materials; Wright claimed that he originated the designs that Bock and Iannelli carried out, though Iannelli later vehemently denied that this was the case. Whatever the truth of the matter, Wright rejoiced at the opportunity to play God in every department: the buildings, the furniture, the lighting fixtures, the crockery, the napery, the glassware.

Midway Gardens was a fantasy on a prodigious scale, unprecedented in Chicago or indeed anywhere else in the country. It sprang up out of its commonplace location like the battlements of some castle in Graustark; within its stout walls of brick and patterned concrete blocks was a vast open space on several levels, at one side of which rose a stage with an

Midway Gardens, Chicago (1913). A masterpiece of joyous pagan fancy, providing food, drink, and entertainment in an Arabian Nights setting. Never a financial success, Midway Gardens was dealt a death blow by Prohibition. Within a few years, it was demolished, portions of it ending up as riprap along the shores of Lake Michigan. [CCL]

elaborate overhanging acoustic shell (an accurate recollection of one of Dankmar Adler's celebrated shells). The interpenetration of exterior and interior spaces was so adroitly manipulated that a visitor could scarcely tell whether he was outdoors or indoors—an effect of magical uncertainty much heightened by ingenuities of artificial lighting, which left the visitor equally uncertain of whether it was night or day. The bizarre angular finials that crowned the pylons on the upper terraces have been compared to the Froebel blocks that Wright played with in childhood and to the Cubist forms then being experimented with by Picasso and his colleagues in Paris; whatever their source, they embodied a promise of merry times within the walls.

Oddly and sadly, Midway Gardens survived for but two years in the form intended by Wright and Waller. Its cultural aspirations may have been too high for the Chicago of that time, its location may have been ill-chosen, or its Viennese "wine, women, and song" antecedents may have proved prejudicial after the outbreak of the First World War, when Germans were suddenly transformed into Huns. Having begun in debt, it continued in debt, and in 1916 it was sold to a brewing company, which hoped to turn it into a successful working man's beer garden. That prospect was dashed by Prohibition, enacted in 1920. In 1929, Midway Gardens was razed, and Wright is said to have gained some measure of sorry satisfaction from the fact that it had been so well built that a wrecking contractor went broke in the course of tearing it down. (Many years later, Wright gained a similar satisfaction from the difficulty encountered in the tearing down of the Larkin building.) Portions of the Gardens were purchased by admirers of Wright and placed in the garden of their home near the Wisconsin Dells; other portions were dumped into Lake Michigan, to help build a breakwater along the right of way of a railroad line. Wesley Peters remembers having glimpsed, from a train window, a twisted pylon finial rising grotesquely out of the waters of the lake.

To PASS IN A FEW HOURS from the happiest moments of one's life to the most despairing is a rare occurrence; it is what befell Wright in the summer of 1914, while he was hard at work at Midway Gardens. Although the Gardens had officially opened a few weeks earlier, much work remained to be done. It was both exhausting and exhilarating to be in command of an army of artisans—and a goodly company of artists as well—as they struggled night and day to complete their assigned tasks; reluctant to leave the scene, Wright would often curl up for a few hours of rest on a pile of wood shavings in some comparatively quiet corner of the grounds. Mamah was at Taliesin, where her children had joined her for a holiday visit. On the advice of John Vogelsang, the restaurateur who had the contract to supply food and drink at the Gardens, Wright had recently hired a couple to serve as butler and cook at Taliesin: Julian Carleton, a native of Barbados, and his wife, Gertrude. Also in residence at Taliesin were William Weston, Wright's favorite carpenter-craftsman; Weston's thirteen-year-old son, Ernest; two draftsmen, Emil Brodelle and Herbert Fritz; and two handymen, Thomas Brunker and David Lindblom. It was just such a little kingdom as Wright had planned to bring into being in that snug green valley of the Lloyd Joneses, practicing "truth against the world."

There are many accounts of the events that took place at Taliesin on August 14th. In his autobiography, Wright states that at noon on that day as he and his son John "were sitting quietly eating our lunch in the newly finished bar, came a long distance call from Spring Green. 'Taliesin destroyed by fire.' But no word came of the ghastly tragedy itself. I learned of that little by little on my way home on the train that evening. The newspaper headlines glared with it."[1] He goes on:

> Thirty-six hours earlier I had left Taliesin leaving all living, friendly, and happy. Now the blow had fallen like a lightning stroke. In less time than it takes to write it, a thin-lipped Barbados Negro, who had been well

recommended to me by John Vogelsang as an ideal servant, had turned madman, taken the lives of seven, and set the house in flames. In thirty minutes the house and all in it had burned to the stonework or to the ground. The living half of Taliesin was violently swept down and away in a madman's nightmare of flame and murder.

The working half only remained.

Will Weston saved that.

He had come to grips with the madman, whose strength was superhuman, but slipped away from his grasp and blows. Bleeding from the encounter, he ran down the hill to the nearest neighbor, Reider, to give the alarm, made his way back immediately through the cornfields only to find the deadly work finished and the home ablaze. Hardly able to stand, he ran to where the fire hose was kept in a niche of the garden wall, past his young son lying there in the fountain basin—one of the seven dead—got the hose loose, staggered with it to the fire and with the playing hose stood against destruction until they led him away. . . . She for whom Taliesin had first taken form and her two children—gone. A talented apprentice, Emil Brodelle; the young son of William Weston the gardener [How can Wright have written "gardener"? Weston was never a gardener]; David Lindblom; a faithful workman, Thomas Brunker—this was the human toll taken by a few moments of madness. The madman was finally discovered after a day or two hidden in the fire-pot of the steam boiler, down in the smoking ruins of the house. Still alive though nearly dead, he was taken to the Dodgeville jail. Refusing meantime to utter a word, he died there.[2]

Carleton had attempted suicide shortly before he was captured by swallowing a large amount of hydrochloric acid. According to his death certificate, he died of starvation in the Dodgeville jail seven weeks later. The acid had burned his throat so badly that he was unable to eat or speak; he left no explanation of his crimes.

In his memoir, *My Father Who Is on Earth,* published in 1946, John Lloyd Wright offers a few salient additions to the horrifying story. These additions include the fact that Edwin Cheney took the same slow train to Spring Green that the two Wrights did, and that John Lloyd Wright managed to secure a private compartment for them, thereby avoiding the ordeal of interviews with reporters who had already been assigned to cover the story. Cheney exhibited his usual stoical good manners, consoling Frank even at the moment that he had to confront the murder of his two children, to say nothing of the murder of the woman with whom he had once been so much in love. According to the *Chicago Tribune,* the bodies of Mamah and the children were brought to the nearby house of Frank's sister, Mrs. Porter. Wright and Cheney spent the night there and had breakfast together. After breakfast, the *Tribune* reporter interviewed Wright.

Though the dispatch carried no byline, the reporter was almost certainly Walter Noble Burns, the famous star reporter of the *Tribune*, whose last name Charles MacArthur and Ben Hecht bestowed upon the irascible city-desk editor in their play *The Front Page*. Burns's byline was affixed to several later dispatches from Spring Green; he was a master of journalistic fustian, much admired by newspaper readers of the day. Burns wrote:

> Bareheaded, his long gray-sprinkled hair tangled, and in the suit in which he hurried away from his Chicago office, Wright pursued his inventory of loss.
>
> "I will rebuild it all, every line of it, as it was when she—"
>
> His voice died and he stood musing . . .
>
> Late in the afternoon Cheney and Wright drew together on the broad lawn at the Porter home. Two automobiles were waiting, one for the body of Brodelle, the other for Mr. Cheney and his dead.
>
> "I'm going away."
>
> "Goodbye, Ed."
>
> There was no trouble in their voices at the farewell. They spoke as men with an understanding. Cheney stepped into his automobile beside the small wooden box that held the bodies of his children and rolled away without a backward glance back at the place where the woman who was once his wife lay dead.
>
> At the station in Spring Green Mr. Cheney personally saw to the placing of the bodies on the train and read a pile of messages of condolences from Oak Park friends.
>
> "You are not remaining for the burial of Mrs. Borthwick?" he was asked.
>
> "No," he answered slowly. "I am only here to take the bodies of my children home for cremation. . . . Concerning Mrs. Borthwick you must talk to—to someone else."
>
> He deliberated and did not utter the name of Wright.[3]

This account demonstrates that contemporary TV reporters are no harsher in their dealings with bereaved persons than their newspaper predecessors were; one would hesitate to believe the *Tribune* reporter except that John Wright tells approximately the same story in his book and Wright himself was content to let it enter history over his son's signature.

Burns begins his account of Mamah's interment with a patch of exceptionally purple prose:

> A man, firm-faced, pale, strained with anguish beyond tears, stood tonight at the head of an open grave in Hillside Valley.
>
> Cloud rack of a passing storm splattered drops of cold rain. At open spots blue moonlight filtered through, lighting the gravestones against

the shadows of the wooded hills. Fireflies gleamed in the thickets and the chirps of the insects arose in chorus.

Frank Lloyd Wright was there to bid farewell to Mamah Borthwick. The builder of the love bungalow in the hills of Spring Green stood alone at the end of his "spiritual hegira." The woman, slain by a frenzied negro axman and incendiary, was laid to rest in the hills where she made herself an exile for an unconventional love.[4]

Wright's own account is more touching and more veritable:

A primitive burial in the ground of the family chapel. Men from Taliesin dug the grave, deep, near Grandfather's and Grandmother's grave. Uncle Enos had come to say it would be alright. But I felt that a funeral service could only be a mockery. The undertaker's offices—too, his vulgar casket— seemed to me profane. So I cut her garden down and with the flowers filled a strong, plain box of fresh, white pine to overflowing. I had my own carpenters make it.

My boy, John, coming to my side now, helped me to lift the body and we let it down to rest among the flowers that had grown and bloomed for her. The plain box lid was pressed down and fastened home. Then the plain, strong box was lifted on the shoulders of my workmen and they placed it on our little spring wagon, filled, too, with flowers—waiting, hitched behind the faithful Darby and Joan. . . .

Since Taliesin was first built Darby and Joan were the faithful little sorrel team that had drawn us along the Valley roads and over the hills, in spring, summer, autumn, and winter, almost daily.

Walking alongside the wheels now, I drove them along the road to the churchyard where no bell tolled. No people were waiting. John followed. Ralph and Orrin, two of my young Hillside cousins, were waiting at the chapel gate. Together we lowered the flower-filled and flower-covered pine box to the bottom of the new-made grave. Then I asked them to leave me there alone.

I wanted to fill the grave myself . . .

And no monument yet marks the spot where she was buried.

All I had left to show for the struggle for freedom of the five years past that had swept most of my former life away had now been swept away.

Why mark the spot where desolation ended and began?[5]

Many years later, Wright had a simple marker placed above Mamah's grave. That perennial reminder of the great love of Wright's life may have been among the factors that led Olgivanna to have Wright's remains dug up and joined with hers at Taliesin West.

The events at Taliesin shared headlines with the outbreak of the First World War in Europe. When the events themselves could no longer be made to yield a pretext of news, the newspapers did what they could to stir up excitement by stirring up the moral indignation of an assortment of Mrs. Grundys, male and female. Ministers and other self-appointed custodians of public morality denounced Wright and his late mistress and expressed the opinion that the deaths of seven people (eight, if one included Carleton) and the simultaneous fiery destruction of Taliesin amounted to an appropriate divine punishment for Wright's and Mamah's transgressions. If the punishment was appropriate, why had Wright himself not suffered the same fate as Mamah? The Mrs. Grundys had an answer for that: death had been too good for Wright; what he needed was to be tortured forever by a sense of his infinite sinfulness.

Desolate as Wright was, he had no intention of accepting this version of the tragedy. As he later wrote, "Waves of unkind, stupid publicity had broken over Taliesin again. The human sacrifices at Taliesin seemed in vain. Its heroism was ridiculed, its love mocked."[6] Characteristically, Wright prepared a statement for the local press, a war cry thinly disguised as a message thanking his Spring Green neighbors for their kindness to him. "To you who have rallied so bravely and well to our assistance," he wrote, "to you who have been invariably kind to us all—I would say something to defend a brave and lovely woman from the pestilential touch of stories made by the press for the man in the street."[7] His statement went on:

> In our life together there has been no thought of secrecy except to protect others from the contaminating stories of newspaper scandal; no pretense of a condition that did not exist. We have lived frankly and sincerely as we believed and we have tried to help others to live their lives according to their ideals. . . . The circumstances before and after we came here to live among you have all been falsified and vulgarized—it is no use now to try to set them straight—but there was none of the cheap deception, the evading of consequences, that mark writhings from the obligations of the matrimonial trap. . . .[8]

To this statement Wright added a poem of Goethe's that Mamah and he had translated together and that had been saved from destruction in the fire because Wright carried a copy of it around in a jacket pocket. Since Wright knew so little German, the literal translation must have been by Mamah; the degree to which Goethe has been made to sound like Whitman is no doubt Wright's contribution to their joint effort. The poem is called "A Hymn to Nature," in which Nature ("Nature with a capital 'N,'" as Wright would be telling the graduating class at Sarah Lawrence almost half a century later) is apostrophized as a female principle: "Mankind is all in her and she in all. . . . Whoever follows her confidently—him she presses as a child to her Breast. . . . She pours forth her creations out of

Nothingness and tells them not whence they came nor whither they go; they are only to go; the Road she knows."[9]

Twenty years after the destruction of Taliesin I, Wright asserted that he had never been able to understand the distance that seemed to establish itself between Mamah and him after her death: "Something strange had happened to me. Instead of feeling that she, whose life had joined mine there at Taliesin, was a spirit near, she was utterly gone. . . . Gone into this equivocal blackness near oblivion for several years to come was all sense of her whom I had loved as one having really lived at all. This was merciful? I believe the equivalent of years passed within my consciousness in the course of weeks. Time, never very present to me, ceased to exist. As days passed into nights, I was numb to all but the automatic steps toward rebuilding the home that was destroyed by hateful forces."[10] Taliesin II began to rise out of the ruins of Taliesin I, not so much as a monument to Mamah as to manifest his defiance of the criticism that had been unjustly directed at him. The second Taliesin was to be even grander than the first; he would build a wing for guests, as well as a wing for his mother and his aunts Jane and Nell, threatened in age with the loss of their Hillside School properties. "There was to be no turning back nor any stopping to mourn. What had been beautiful at Taliesin should live as a grateful memory creating the new, and, come who and whatever might to share Taliesin, they would be sure to help in that spirit. So I believed and resolved."[11]

In that passage from his autobiography, Wright is indirectly preparing us for the introduction of a new and different sort of catastrophe—a woman who was to make his life miserable for years to come. Plainly, he is aware of the awkwardness of juxtaposing the grievous loss of his mistress Mamah Borthwick with the almost immediate acquisition of a new mistress, Miriam Noel. He tells us that as a consequence of the ugly publicity generated by the tragedy at Taliesin hundreds of letters had come to him from all over the country, which he had tied up into bundles and burned without reading. This was not quite the case; in order not to miss letters from friends, he had assistants screen the mail as it arrived, and the assistants would sometimes hand along to him an especially appealing letter of sympathy, even if it happened to have been written by a stranger. One such letter came to him from Miriam Noel, who described herself as an artist and who said that as an artist she could well understand his suffering. Wright acknowledged her letter, which led to a response from Mrs. Noel; soon they had arranged to meet, and all too soon he found himself enchanted by her.

Mrs. Noel was a good-looking woman in her mid-forties—Wright himself was forty-seven—who dressed with elegance and possessed a pleasantly sophisticated accent. According to her story, she had been married to and

Mrs. Noel was often publicly praised for her good looks, which eluded the camera and may have been mostly a function of her intelligence and seductive Southern manners. [PF]

divorced from a wealthy Tennessean, had two married daughters and an unmarried son, had moved to Paris and undertaken a career as a sculptress (she had shared a prize there with Gertrude Vanderbilt Whitney), and had been forced to return to the United States because of the war in Europe. Like Mrs. Darwin D. Martin, Mrs. Coonley, and many other women of Wright's acquaintance, she was a Christian Scientist. Mamah Borthwick had been noted for her hearty laugh and open spirit; Miriam Noel had a tantalizingly mysterious manner, at once spiritual and sensual. In no time at all, Wright had installed her at Taliesin II, to the cost of which she contributed a good many thousands of dollars—as usual, Wright had no difficulty accepting money from any convenient source. As for his mother and aunts, the plan to move them into Taliesin was quickly abandoned. Anna Wright, who had been capable of quarreling with her genial daughter-in-law Catherine and who had certainly deplored Mamah, must have been horrified by Miriam Noel, who, Christian Science aside, appeared in every respect to be a classic adventuress. Still, Frank could do no wrong; she would bide her time until he was ready to return to her.

The Midway Gardens commission was behind him; the task had been thrilling at first and, at the end, frustrating, because there had never been money enough to finish anything as he had envisioned it: no scarlet and green glass to be fitted into the patterned concrete walls, no garlands of vines and flowers to bedeck the so-called sky frames crowning the winter garden towers, no hundreds of multi-colored balloons floating above the lighted terraces. But the other great commission of this period was already on the boards: the hotel to be built in Tokyo, for which the budget was downright munificent. (His fee was to be between three and four hundred thousand dollars—by far the largest amount he had ever been able to command.) He would shake the design out of his sleeve, as he had done with Midway Gardens, and it would be neither Japanese nor American, making obeisance to no known style save that of its creator.

The Imperial Hotel commission was to usurp a far greater proportion of Wright's life than he had expected it to, or wished it to. Professionally, it was a great feather in his cap; moreover, it offered him an opportunity to design on a scale that would challenge him aesthetically as, up to then, he had been challenged only by projects that had remained obdurately unbuilt—the McCormick mansion, in Illinois; the Como Orchards Summer Colony, in Montana; and the skyscraping Press building, in California. Personally, it offered him an opportunity to begin life afresh, as he had begun it a few years earlier with Mamah. Many of the conditions that he had sought to escape from then hovered little changed in the background: he was still married to Catherine, he was still helping to support her and the younger children in Oak Park (the studio was remodeled to serve as quarters for the family and the house was rented out to provide income for Catherine), and he was still helping to support his mother and aunts at Hillside. His attempt to impose himself upon the world as a man entitled by genius to ignore the trammels of convention was by no means a success, even among his friends; the bloody consequences of Carleton's madness had tainted his claim to having acted unselfishly in breaking up two families. A stay in Tokyo would establish a firm caesura between tragic past and promising future. It would also provide Miriam Noel and him with the equivalent of a honeymoon—one fortunately many thousands of miles distant from where, a few years earlier, among the nightingales of Fiesole, he had honeymooned with Mamah.

Miriam Noel must have been even more eager to substitute Tokyo for Taliesin than Wright was. Beautiful as were the newly finished house and its accompaniment of gardens, fields, streams, and ponds, the setting was an uncomfortable one for her. She was an ambitious, neurotic woman, eager to be counted among the artistic elite; the city and not the countryside was her accustomed habitat. Mamah's knack for acquiring friends among her Spring Green neighbors would have made it all the harder for the fastidious Miriam to do so, but the problem was avoided, as the problem of ingratiating herself with Wright's innumerable Lloyd Jones relatives was avoided, by the simple act of decamping. There were other reasons for seeking a change of scene: Wright and she had managed to embroil themselves in a particularly nasty public scandal. Not content with conduct-

ing their affair in private, Mrs. Noel had argued in a newspaper interview
that she and Wright were manifesting their superiority over ordinary, non-
artistic mortals by living together in proud disregard of law and custom.
(Wright must have imprudently filled her with the lofty views about "love's
freedom" that he and Mamah had acquired from the writings of the pioneering Swedish sexologist Ellen Key. Mamah had translated Key and in doing
so had indirectly made available to her successor more arguments against
marriage than Mrs. Noel knew what to do with.) Meanwhile, she and Wright
quarreled incessantly, with Miriam now and again taking up residence
alone in the apartment Wright maintained in Chicago.

Some letters that Miriam Noel had written to Frank—letters accusing
him, among other things, of torturing her as he had tortured Mamah
and of cheapening their love by flirting with other, younger women—
were intercepted by a housekeeper, Nellie Breen, whom Wright had dis-
charged; this busybody passed the letters along to the newspapers for
publication and then instituted an action in the Federal courts asking that
Wright be indicted for violating the Mann Act—a statute (passed by Congress in 1910 under the sponsorship of a Chicagoan, James Robert Mann)
prohibiting the transportation of women across state lines for immoral
purposes. Wright retained as counsel his friend Clarence Darrow, one of
the most celebrated criminal lawyers of the day, and Darrow succeeded
in getting the case dismissed, but by then the press had enjoyed its accustomed field day at Wright's expense. Noel's letters made juicy reading
("How can I ever trust you again? . . . I will not be just a wear-and-tear
thing that can be battered and bruised and found right side up when
wanted"[12]), and Wright was prompted to make a number of public statements, all certain to do more harm than good. Burns of the *Tribune* dyed
his prose in its richest purple:

> Over Frank Lloyd Wright's bizarre and beautiful country seat near here
> the shadow of Mrs. Nellie Breen falls like a curse.
>
> Seated in the living room, looking out over the silver loops of the
> Wisconsin River, Mr. Wright today discussed the motives that led his former
> housekeeper to threaten him with prosecution under the Mann Act and
> to make public love letters written to him by Mrs. Maud Miriam Noel,
> now living at the architect's villa. . . .
>
> While Mr. Wright was in the midst of his discussion of Mrs. Breen,
> Mrs. Noel appeared in a clinging gown of shimmering white. "I have
> prepared a statement," Mrs. Noel said, "which embodies all I care to say
> about this affair. Mr. Wright and I have smoothed out all our little misun-
> derstandings. I am here at Taliesin to stay. . . .[13]

Wright himself may have been of two minds about that. He praised Mrs.
Noel in public ("Mrs. Noel is one of the most brilliantly intellectual women

I ever knew"[14]) and went on quarreling with her in private. It was approximately at this time that Wright was introduced by his friend Henry Sell to a Pennsylvania oil heiress named Aline Barnsdall, who wished him to design for her a house and theatre in Los Angeles. He agreed to do so, though well aware that most of his time would be given over to the Imperial Hotel.

In December, 1916, enjoying a momentary truce, Wright and Mrs. Noel set sail from Seattle for Tokyo. In those days, the voyage by steamer between the West Coast and Japan took an average of fourteen days, during which Wright, a poor sailor, was resigned to feeling continuously seasick. Wright was to spend much of the next six years either in Tokyo or crossing the Pacific, on hasty journeys to and from the States. It was a period of physical and intellectual isolation that threatened at the time to destroy his career; out of it emerged the great work of the hotel, but at what a price!

This isolation had far less to do with geography than with a self-destructive impulse that had begun to manifest itself after Wright's return from Europe and appears to have increased even during his happiest times with Mamah. The early symptoms may be found in Wright's conviction that his disciples and colleagues had turned against him during his "spiritual hegira" abroad, stealing his clients and stealing his ideas as well. Like authors and composers, architects are quick to detect plagiarism even where it cannot be proved to exist; Wright correctly regarded himself as the chief source of inspiration for the so-called prairie style of architecture and he correctly observed that the houses designed by Griffin, Elmslie, Purcell, Drummond, and the rest would certainly not have looked as they did if he had never lived. Nevertheless, it is understandable that once Wright had left Oak Park and Chicago, the younger men neglected to pay him the homage he had learned to expect. But from pique to paranoia is ordinarily a considerable distance; Wright's violent denunciation of his erstwhile "boys" in the issue of *The Architectural Record* for May, 1914, strikes a shockingly abusive note even today.

First, Wright in praise of Wright:

> At the expiration of a six-year apprenticeship, during which time Louis Sullivan was my master and inspiration, twenty-one years ago I entered a field he had not, in any new spirit, touched, the field of domestic architecture, and began to break ground and make the forms I needed, alone, absolutely alone.
>
> These forms were the result of a conscientious study of materials and of the machine which is the real tool, whether we like it or not, that we must use to give shape to our ideals; a tool which at that time had received no such artistic consideration from artist to architect. And that my work now has individuality, the strength to stand by itself, honors

Mr. Sullivan the more. The principles, however, underlying the fundamental ideal of an organic architecture, common to his work and mine, are common to all work that ever rang true in the architecture of the world.[15]

Then Wright in dispraise of his former associates:

But the boy who steals his forms—"steals" them because he sells them as his own for the moment of superficial distinction he gains by trading on the results—is no artist, has not the sense of the first principles of the ideal that he poses and the forms that he abuses. He denies his birthright, an act characteristic and unimportant; but for a mess of pottage, he endangers the chances of a genuine forward movement, insults both cause and precedent with an astounding insolence quite peculiar to these matters in the United States, ruthlessly sucks what blood may be left in the tortured and abused forms he caricatures and exploits, like the parasite he is.[16]

Given the reception that such remarks were sure to invite, Wright's intention must have been to make himself unwelcome in the very circles where he had once been the leading figure. At the very least, it would have been difficult for him to set about renewing a practice in Chicago after attacking his local colleagues in a national publication. When he left for Japan, it was surely with a sense of cutting his ties to a city that, perhaps more than any other city on earth at that time, provided the most stimulating challenge to architects. Why did he choose this curious course? Why become a vagabond at the very moment when he had claimed to be putting down roots at the newly completed Taliesin II? Wright would have disliked the comparison, but a similar vagabondage had been undertaken by his father, with this notable difference: that the father moving on from place to place in his middle years carried with him the admiration and affection of everyone he had left behind, while the son carried with him in his middle years the heavy burden of an almost universal disapprobation.

As for Tokyo—"Yes," Wright wrote in his autobiography, "I was eager to go, for again I wanted to get away from the United States. I still imagined one might get away from himself that way—a little. In spite of all my reasoning power and returning balance, I was continually expecting some terrible blow to strike. The sense of impending disaster would hang over me, waking or dreaming. This fitted in well enough with the sense of earthquake, from the actuality of which I should have to defend the new building. But at this time I looked forward to Japan as refuge and rescue. The lands of my dreams—old Japan and old Germany."[17]

Wright had paid his first visit to Japan in 1905, with the Willitses. During that trip and on the trip that he took with Mamah, in 1913, Wright had immersed himself in the study of Japanese prints, on which he was eventually to become recognized as a leading authority; he had purchased

FLW had a gift for sartorial self-expression that sometimes produced exquisite results and at other times approached buffoonery. Here he gains height—always a sensitive point with him—by dint of wearing exceptionally high heels. [PF]

the beginnings of a collection that, at its peak, contained many thousands of distinguished works, in bronze and ceramics as well as on paper. "Their art," he noted, "was nearer to the earth and a more indigenous product of native conditions of life and work, therefore more nearly modern as I saw it, than any European civilization alive or dead."[18]

Wright had prepared plans for a temporary annex to the hotel, for guests in need of accommodation before the hotel proper was ready for occupancy. This annex had been completed by the time Wright and Mrs. Noel arrived in Tokyo and they were invited to take up residence there, in quarters that included a penthouse studio-workshop for Wright. They met and were entertained by many new friends and Wright was invited to design a little "School of the Free Spirit" for the Japanese Hanis. As the months and years passed, Miriam grew increasingly ill, with what appears to have been, according to Wright's description of it, a classic case of schizophrenia: "All would go happily for some days. Then strange perversion of all that. No visible cause. . . . The mystifying reactions became more violent until something like a terrible struggle between two natures in her would seem to be going on within her all the time and be tearing her to pieces. Then peace again for some time and a charming life."[19]

For Wright, the Imperial Hotel was always to be counted among the most memorable commissions of his career, for reasons having about equally to do with the scale of the work and with the many personal and professional problems that clustered themselves around the commission and awaited

Dressed to call attention to himself, FLW (cross-legged) visits a Buddhist shrine in the company of his engineer Paul Mueller and his architectural assistant Antonin Raymond. [PF]

The old German-designed and German-owned Imperial Hotel. It burned to the ground as the new Imperial was going up. Today there is still another "new" Imperial Hotel, waiting to grow old and out of fashion. [PL]   *FLW's rendering of the new Imperial Hotel. At first glance, it appears to be a product of the turn-of-the-century offices of McKim, Mead & White.* [AR]

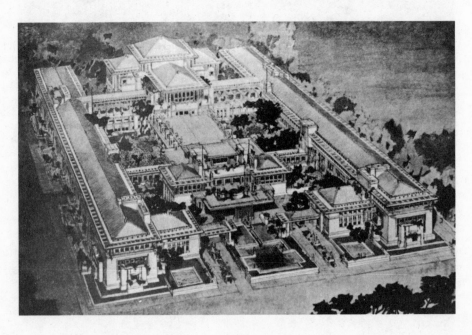

solution in the course of the several years that it took to build the hotel. Wright may have hoped that a prolonged stay in Japan would help to mitigate if not cure Miriam's madness; he certainly hoped that, if he could meet successfully the greatest architectural challenge yet presented to him, the financial rewards would free him at last from those sordid quicksands of debt in which he had felt himself to be drowning; moreover, he had reason to expect that the celebrity accompanying this success would open the door to a hundred other major commissions. Taliesin would remain his retreat, but the world, and not merely the United States, would become his theatre of operations. Satisfactory as it had been for him to design Midway Gardens, the structure as built had proved a disappointment and the enterprise itself had gone bankrupt, leaving him close to bankruptcy as well. It was a moment at which, reaching the peak of his powers, he ought to have been able to address himself in disciplined tranquility to the carrying out of a set of chosen tasks; instead, and characteristically, he found himself in a state of exhausting discomfiture.

It is a failing common among architects to take on more work than they should, and their excuse for doing so is usually that they are haunted from one month to the next, or even from one week to the next, by the fear that the commissions they have been counting on will suddenly be cancelled—that they will find themselves with a sizeable office staff to maintain and not a single project on their drawing boards. Some of the most eminent of our contemporary architects confess to never having refused a commission in their lives; the courage to practice such a refusal is what they continually assure themselves they will attain tomorrow, or the day after tomorrow. With more justification than most of his colleagues (for Wright was often as much in want of work as other architects only nervously dream of being), he said "Yes" to every prospective client who found his way up the steep hill to Taliesin. Once the Imperial Hotel contract had been signed, Wright ought to have devoted himself solely to that immense task; instead, he accepted a multiple set of commissions from Aline Barnsdall, a millionairess with lofty cultural ambitions and a spectacular building site in Los Angeles, upon which she intended to see those ambitions embodied. He also accepted a commission to build a small warehouse in his native town of Richland Center, Wisconsin; unimportant as that project may appear to be, it is worth glancing at as being representative of Wright's lifelong knack for making a client overextend himself as radically as Wright himself was nearly always quick to do. The episode was sufficiently embarrassing to Wright to prompt his omitting it from his otherwise garrulous autobiography.

Albert Dell German, who like Wright was of Welsh descent (the family name was pronounced "Jarman"), was born in Richland Center in 1875 and prospered as a businessman dealing in coal, hay, grain, cement, and other building materials. In 1916, he announced in the local newspaper that he was planning to put up a structure designed by Frank Lloyd Wright. In addition to providing storage for wholesale goods, the structure would contain a restaurant, retail shops, a gallery for regional artists, and space for exhibitions of Wright's handiwork. It was estimated that the cost of the building would be thirty thousand dollars. Nothing on so grand a scale had ever been contemplated in Richland Center, and one may safely assume that Wright had talked the ordinarily hardheaded German into building a far more extravagant structure than he had initially intended; one may also assume that the estimate was Wright's and was, as usual, optimistically low. How did Wright come to be offered this commission in the first place? The tradition in Richland Center maintains that Wright owed German a large sum of money for supplies he had purchased over the years and that he had volunteered to draw up plans for the new building as a way of discharging the long overdue debt. Hoping to salvage a portion of his losses, poor German consented to Wright's proposal and thus fell into a trap from which there was to be no escape. The building was— and is—exceptionally ugly and must have been an occasion for astonishment and dismay to the citizens of Richland Center and the surrounding country-side. Because they were acquainted with Wright's fame throughout the country, they may well have struggled to find beauty in the lumpish cube

The German warehouse in Richland Center, begun in 1917, remains unfinished. It is perhaps the most depressing work ever to come from Wright's hand. The mushroom-capped concrete column commonly used in loft construction lent itself to "organic" decoration.

of concrete, brick, and steel that slowly rose on their main street, defying every other building in town to make peace with it. According to Margaret Scott's charming little history of the German warehouse (1984), it echoed in shape and appearance the Temple of the Three Lintels, in Chichén Itzá, Yucatán, and she quotes Wright as saying of Mayan architecture in general that it is "greater than anything remaining on record anywhere . . . a kinship of elemental nature and natural forms of the material."[20] Writing of the warehouse, Vincent Scully cannot resist the infection of Wright's rhetoric. Whatever "a kinship of elemental nature and natural forms" may mean, its obscurity is matched by Scully's description of what Wright was seeking in the design of the warehouse: "A monumentality even more dense and earth-pressing than he had achieved before—and one more primitive, separate from his earlier culture, exotic to his eyes, and deep in time."[21]

Year after year, German went on building the warehouse, as the money to do so became available to him. By 1919, his expenditures had reached a total of one hundred and twenty-five thousand dollars, or more than four times the amount that Wright had estimated. In 1921, German finally gave up on the unfinished building; the scaffolds surrounding it were taken down and all but one of the entrances was bricked up or boarded up. Like almost all of Wright's clients, German continued to have faith in him despite the innumerable anxieties he had been forced to undergo. In the thirties, German asked Wright to prepare drawings for a remodeling of the derelict interior, but financing proved impossible to obtain. German died in the forties and the building has since passed through a number of hands. To this day, it remains in an unfinished state, with a gift shop occupying the ground floor and a makeshift exhibit of photographs of Wright buildings occupying an upper floor; and to this day it emanates a profound gloom.

15

The Barnsdall story is also in large measure an unhappy one. Aline Barnsdall was fifteen years younger than Wright and resembled him in seeking—far earlier than he did—to free herself from the conventions in which she had been brought up. A pretty, plump-faced woman of high intelligence and formidable energy, she had read Bernard Shaw and was a Shavian "new woman" to the life, bent upon improving the world according to her own strong convictions. She and Wright were at once natural allies and natural adversaries; they were both hot-tempered, arbitrary, and elusive, and Miss Barnsdall, being rich, had the incomparable advantage over Wright in respect to these attributes that she could always indulge them without hesitation. The least rebuff to her plans, and she would take off on a voyage to some distant place, where, as she liked to say, she would "freshen her mind" before returning to the fray or beginning a new one.

Miss Barnsdall was goodhearted and generous and her imperiousness was but the means, in Shaw's terms, of obtaining that equality of opportunity which women had hitherto sought in vain in the obstinacy of a world ruled by men. (In this aspect of her life, she bore a close resemblance to Wright's earlier client, Susan Lawrence Dana, and to his later client, the Baroness Rebay.) There was much that was feminine in Wright's nature and that felt drawn to women who assumed an embattled posture vis-à-vis accepted rules of male conduct—not only Mrs. Lawrence, Miss Barnsdall, and Hilla Rebay but Marion Mahony, Mamah Cheney, and Miriam Noel, to say nothing of his third wife, Olgivanna Milanov.

Shortly after the fire and slayings at Taliesin, Barnsdall had come to Chicago and taken charge of a small theatre there. Wright, always a devotee of the theatre, was still deeply involved with Midway Gardens. As we have seen, a friend in common, Henry Sell, then working as a press agent for a number of advanced theatre groups in Chicago, brought Barnsdall and Wright together, perhaps with the hope that Wright would be tempted to substitute the ebullient Barnsdall for the terrifying Noel. (Like Wright,

Sell was born in Wisconsin, was the son of a minister, failed to gain a formal education, and cultivated mildly raffish companions in the arts. Unlike Wright, he made money at everything to which he turned his hand, from editing magazines to inventing a liver paste that was once an indispensable amenity at cocktail parties. Sell and his wife wrote a book called *Good*

© SUSAN WOLDENBERG

Left, like FLW, Aline Barnsdall was intemperate and ambitious; unlike him, she was very rich. In theory an ideal client, in practice she was an unpredictable adversary. Many years later, the child in her lap became an apprentice at Taliesin. [LA]   At right, the grim Hollyhock House.

Taste in Home Furnishings, which incorporated a number of Wright's ideas on interior decoration.) In his autobiography, Wright says of Barnsdall exactly the opposite of what he evidently intended to say—one more proof that he never troubled to read what he had dictated to an inept or sleepy amanuensis: "Her very large, wide-open eyes gave her a disingenuous expression not connected with the theatre." As if to demonstrate that he was by no means so confirmed a champion of the Shavian woman as Barnsdall would have liked him to be, he adds, ". . . her extremely small hands and feet somehow seemed not connected with such ambition as hers."[1] Barnsdall having found Chicago less receptive to her views on theatre than she had hoped, with characteristic vigor and impatience had decided to seek a more adventurous milieu. She had purchased a large parcel of land in Los Angeles, in a still largely open section of the city; the parcel consisted of a steep, cone-shaped hill rising abruptly out of a level plain, and she commissioned Wright to design for that agreeable site a house for herself at the top of the hill, looking out over olive trees and citrus groves to the Pacific, and on the slopes of the hill a theatre and a number of smaller buildings to serve for the training of actors and dancers. In her impetuous fashion, she gave the property as a whole the name of

Olive Hill and her future residence the name of Hollyhock House, after her favorite flower.

Barnsdall was encouraged in her endeavors by a newly acquired friend named Geddes, to whom she had been introduced in the course of observing the handiwork of a theatrical group in Detroit. At the age of twenty-three, Geddes had just married a young woman named Bel Schneider and had encapsulated her first name in his; as Norman Bel Geddes, he was to become one of the most celebrated designers of the twentieth century, working with equal success in the world of the theatre and in that of industry. Barnsdall was interested in the experiments that Geddes was then conducting with novel forms of stage lighting; at Barnsdall's invitation, on their honeymoon trip to California Geddes and his bride stopped off in Chicago, where Barnsdall had arranged for Geddes to meet with Wright and look over Wright's plans for her new theatre in Los Angeles. With Paul Mueller temporarily in charge of the Imperial Hotel job, Wright was paying one of his brief, hectic visits home and cannot have been eager to make the acquaintance of a young and perhaps meddlesome stranger.

In his autobiography, *Miracle in the Evening,* Bel Geddes gives an amusing account of this introductory meeting, which quickly assumed the form of a papal audience. Because we are used to reading of Wright's top-lofty demeanor in old age, we must bear in mind that at the time of his introduction to Bel Geddes, Wright was just under fifty—perhaps too young to play God convincingly in the presence of a potential rival of twenty-three. Barnsdall was understandably nervous about bringing the two men together; on the way to Wright's office, she impressed upon Geddes how necessary it was to the success of her theatre that it be an architectural masterpiece from Wright's hand, and she added, "Now, be tactful."

"Tactful?" Bel Geddes said. "Me?"

"Well," he records her as replying, "try, anyway. You two will make a wonderful team."

Geddes then goes on to describe the occasion:

Mr. Wright looked kindly and important. . . . He spoke at length about his hotel in Tokyo, saying that it would be his greatest monument. . . . It was some time before he mentioned Miss Barnsdall's theatre or house. It may have been her disappointed expression that reminded him. He went into another room and returned with a roll of blueprints. There were four of the theatre and the house. Miss Barnsdall looked at them eagerly, but then glanced up at the architect in surprise. "Aren't these the same plans that you showed me five months ago?" she asked. Wright admitted they were, his jaw set defensively. . . . Miss Barnsdall brightened considerably when Wright said that he would have new drawings in a couple of weeks that would clarify his ideas on the theatre.

It will be a new kind of theatre," she said to me, smiling. "Won't it be wonderful?"

"It certainly will," I said. "Tell me, Mr. Wright, in what basic respects will your theatre differ from others?"

"At the right time, young man, at the right time," he said.

"When I saw 'Sumurun,'" I persisted, "it struck me how much more effective the play would have been in a theatre permitting a freer type of lighting and staging. Did you see it?"

"Never heard of it," said Wright.

"Oh. Well, in European theatres—"

"It isn't necessary for me to see other theatres in order to design better ones," said Wright.

"Well, it just seems to me that people who have ideas but no real experience in the theatre can learn a lot from what they are doing in Europe. Have you seen Moderwell's book 'The Theatre of Today?'"

"We can't learn anything from Europe. They have to learn from us. Europe is a dying civilization. The theatre in Europe died in Athens in 500 B.C."

It sounded drastic . . .

His personality and conversation had a grand and romantic flavor. Most interestingly and almost without pause, he expounded his theories on philosophy, art, morals, and other architects. He appeared to be more intelligent than instinctive artistically, more ingenious than inspirational, and he discussed his work as if Aline and I could not understand even the rudiments. "I prefer to answer questions before they are asked," he would say. His enthusiasm was exciting in itself. It swept him along and us, too. Sometimes he forgot what he was talking about, but he kept right on with something else, and all of it was stimulating.[2]

Many months later, while Geddes was engaged in lighting a show for the Little Theatre, in Los Angeles, Barnsdall prevailed upon him to meet for a second time with Wright, who had come to town for a few fleeting moments of consultation on the Hollyhock project. By then, Wright had done a good deal of work on the design of the theatre, but in Geddes' eyes the work had made matters worse instead of better. The sight lines were faultier than ever and no provision had been made for lighting equipment, curtains, or scenery. Geddes and Wright argued at length about what was essential in staging productions of plays in a contemporary theatre and Wright fell back upon his usual argument that nobody need design a stage more complicated than that which had satisfied the Greeks. Angrily, he said to Barnsdall, "If left alone, I will give you the finest theatre in the world. If you are unable to leave me alone, I will not waste my time going any further with it." Barnsdall assured Wright that she and Geddes

would restrain themselves, and Geddes reports that he said—unhappily—
"I will be happy not to say another word."

Geddes goes on:

> Aline had such faith in him, and he was so persuasive, that there was
> nothing I could do. She was as eager for her theatre to proceed as for
> her house, but both dragged on and on. She knew he was wrong, and
> once, at least, told him so. In that instance, he ignored her for months.
> . . . She decided to let him complete the Tokyo hotel so he could again
> become interested in working in America. I pleaded with her to get the
> opinion of progressive theatre people and not wait. But she would not
> even show the plans to Richard Ordynski, a director in the company with
> whom she was very close. [Barnsdall had a daughter by Ordynski.] Nor
> would she build the theatre Wright's way and leave the alterations until
> later. . . . Despite Wright's orations to the contrary, I came to the conclu-
> sion that he was not genuinely interested in the theatre. He certainly
> knew next to nothing about it. Yet he loved it, as a child loves posies
> without knowing how to make them grow. His love for it never grew to
> the extent that he would marry it to his architecture. Years later, when I
> had plays rehearsing, he would motor from Taliesin to New York and
> stay for a week or more attending all rehearsals, and then drive back,
> the day before the opening. . . .
>
> In spite of Aline's doing everything possible to appease him, their
> relationship terminated unhappily. She had selected the finest architect
> she knew of, and had written into his contract an expression of confidence
> and faith few other clients had ever done. In return, he treated her with
> a total lack of appreciation; felt in fact that she was the one lacking in
> appreciation. As for cooperation, she gave him everything he asked for,
> while he, though employee, granted no request involving a difference of
> opinion. His stubbornness in return for her generosity had a discouraging
> effect upon her regard for all creative people. After five years of trying
> to get her theatre, she finally gave up all her hopes and plans. The house
> was indeed finished, but it recalled for her so many unpleasant moments
> that she lived in it for only short periods over a few years and then gave
> the entire hilltop property to the city as a park. Frank Lloyd Wright, by
> behaving as he did, was responsible in my eyes for thwarting what might
> well have been the greatest creative theatre organization this country has
> ever seen, or ever will see.[3]

Recklessly, greedily, Wright had accepted the Hollyhock commission. He
had known that he would be spending most of his time for a couple of
years at least (actually, it turned out to be five) in Tokyo, designing and
supervising the construction of the Imperial Hotel; he had also known
that his impromptu methods of designing, which led to his continual failure
to prepare complete working drawings, made it necessary for him to be

on the site as often as possible during the time that a building was under construction. Moreover, he must have perceived from the start that Barnsdall would prove a temperamental client and that no "clerk-of-the-works" appointed by him to serve in his place would satisfy her needs for long. During the years that the Hollyhock House was being built, Wright's son Lloyd was sometimes in charge of the job, though with no authority to speak in his father's behalf and serving often as the scapegoat for errors committed by Wright. At other times, Rudolph Schindler, a young Viennese who had come to America as an avowed disciple of Wright and was for a period Wright's favored "Jesus," was placed in charge, but Wright in far-off Japan became increasingly convinced that Schindler was usurping his place as the designer of the project. (Wright had felt the same conviction in respect to his office staff when he ran off to Europe with Mrs. Cheney, leaving much unfinished work behind. It is a suspicion that many great men find it difficult to resist feeling, though it should be added that in respect to a knack for questionable dealing Wright may well have met his match in Schindler.) Under the circumstances, it was remarkable that anything of value emerged from the commission, as Wright himself was eventually to acknowledge. In a letter written to Barnsdall in 1921, at the height of a quarrel between them that was already of several years' duration, Wright said of the Hollyhock House, "You will marvel then, perhaps, as I do, that a thing so harmonious, strong, and unlike anything of its kind in the world should be there at all. That this creative thing should have survived the petty personal strife that 'dogged' its growth, step by step, is a miracle, as you will feel this yourself, perhaps, as the echoes reach you before you reach its threshold.

"Order shall come out of chaos for you—because the principle at stake is dearer to me than my humiliations are bitter; and because your devotion to it was stronger than your own resentment or the power of misrepresentation and the alarmist advice of unwilling, unfaithful amateurs that threatened it during construction and are crowding in upon it even now."[4]

Architectural historians are by no means immune from the infection of psychobiography, but in their case manifestations of the disease are likely to prove especially unlucky; it is certainly possible to find broad hints of autobiography in the writings of poets and playwrights and in the canvases and bronzes of painters and sculptors, but such hints are far less broad and far less frequently to be found in the form of brick, stone, glass, and steel, in structures that are the sum of a thousand accidents over which the designer, or designers, have had no direct control whatever. Behind which of the hundreds of façades of buildings in a score of styles can we discern with confidence the soul of the eminent nineteenth-century American architect Richard Morris Hunt? Could anyone guess from the classical impersonality of the J. Pierpont Morgan Library, in New York City, that Charles Follen McKim was a man who signed personal letters to his old friends Augustus Saint-Gaudens and Stanford White "K.M.A.," short for "Kiss My Ass"? At first glance, Wright's oeuvre makes a rich feast for explorers of the Wright psyche, but the feast invariably proves less nourishing than it has promised to be. It is the case, for example, that the sheer oddity of the Hollyhock House in relation both to its setting and to the client for whom it was intended has led to much injudicious speculation concerning Wright's emotions at the time he was designing it.

It is certainly a perverse building—perverse in terms of the architectural conventions of those days and perverse in Wright's own unconventional terms. Today the vast bulk of the house is hidden behind substantial sixty-year-old plantings of eucalyptus and pine, but in the early twenties it imposed itself upon the naked crown of Olive Hill with a tyrannous blatancy, seeming to crush the land beneath it. In scale, shape, and color it stood in total contradiction to Wright's eloquent argument in favor of an accommodation between architecture and nature, exemplified in the design of Taliesin: "I knew well that no house should ever be *on* a hill or *on* anything. It should be *of* the hill, belonging to it. . . . I wanted a natural house . . . a broad shelter seeking fellowship with its surroundings. A house that could open to the breezes of summer and become like an open camp if need be."[5] But in Hollyhock House he created an exotic Mayan fortress, as forbidding as his grim, almost windowless warehouse in Richland Center and all too plainly descended from it. The rooms of the house opened, not without a seeming reluctance, upon walled garden courts; the enormous living room had but a single exterior window-opening, and access to the living room fireplace (always the heart of a Wright house) was rendered difficult by the presence of a small, shallow pool. The sleeping quarters for Barnsdall and her infant daughter were raised well above the ground and were cramped and ill-lighted; views of the surrounding landscape and of the nearby Pacific were obtained from balconies and rooftops.

As Wright had used a stylized version of sumac leaves in the decoration of the Dana house, so at Barnsdall's request he had decorated the exterior of the Hollyhock House with stylized versions of her favorite flower, cast in concrete in the form of friezes and finials. Wright claimed to have conceived of the house as what he called, in musical terms, a *romanza*, or short, lyrical piece, and the concrete hollyhocks were for him an embodiment of the romantic, though he was careful to justify them as "integral ornament." They are perhaps less playful to our eyes than they were to Wright's or Barnsdall's; they do little to lessen the essential harshness of the structure as a whole.

In his autobiography, Wright confesses that the Hollyhock House is full of mistakes; after scattering buckshots of blame in all directions, he consents at last to hold himself chiefly to blame, in part because he had flouted his client's wishes and in part because he had lost control of the project through his many absences abroad. And yet somehow, he says, "by way of the downright brutality, insolence, and persistence of the architect and the client's desire, too, though both architect and client were torn to tatters—'form' got into the building in spite of all the folly."[6]

If it would be hazardous to seek clues to the nature of Wright's emotional life in the sorry history of Hollyhock House, how much more hazardous would it be to attempt a similar search in respect to the Imperial Hotel! The building itself is, of course, a major episode in his professional career. Its success in withstanding the great earthquake of 1923 is one of the most conspicuous threads in the legend that Wright wove to accompany and, often enough, to replace the facts of his real life. Moreover, Japan and its culture had had a profound influence on Wright as a young man, and this influence was one that he would sometimes deny and sometimes exaggerate throughout his life. (As we have seen, of the other great influence upon his youth—the arts and crafts movement in Great Britain and Europe, and especially the Secessionist movement in Vienna—he took great care to feign ignorance.) He certainly came to know a good deal about Japanese prints, which he began to collect in the course of his first visit to Japan, in 1905, and which he later took to dealing in as a business sideline, particularly when he was in acute financial trouble. "Wrieto-San," as the Japanese called him, appears never to have acquired more than a smattering of the Japanese tongue and his knowledge of Japanese history was that of a sympathetic amateur. Antonin Raymond, the Czech-American architect who became a protégé of Wright's, accompanied him to Japan to assist in the preparation of the working drawings for the Imperial Hotel, and subsequently spent most of his professional career in Japan, was amused to discover that Wright was not above attempting to "improve" his Japanese prints with the help of colored pencils and crayons.

Scholars ceaselessly worry the bone of how many visits Wright may have paid to Japan. The voyage by steamer across the Pacific took approximately two weeks; though a poor sailor, Wright endured the round-trip journey at least half a dozen times, accompanied on different occasions by Catherine Wright, Mamah Cheney, Miriam Noel, and Anna Lloyd Jones Wright. (Given Wright's passion for Japan, it is ironic that, with the possible exception of Mrs. Cheney, whose response is unknown, Wright's women companions all found their visits to Japan unpleasant.) Once he had arrived in Tokyo, Wright was able to communicate with the States only by mail and by telegraph; the isolation he was bound to feel during the weeks and months that he devoted to his labors on the hotel was much heightened by Miriam's madness.

Wright was a notoriously hot-tempered man, quick to take offense and quick to heap abuse even upon close friends and relatives. In Miriam's periods of dark violence, he was unable to keep from making bad matters worse; he would strike back at her (sometimes physically as well as verbally), and each would be driven to higher and higher pitches of exacerbation. They were an ideally unsuitable couple, and yet they had much in common, including an instinct for the most effective means of punishing each other. In a typical instance, Miriam accused Wright of having sexual designs upon a Russian woman with whom they had become acquainted; in retaliation, Wright informed the Russian woman that Miriam was a morphine addict. After a frenzied exchange of vituperation, Miriam withdrew to a mountain inn at Ikao, some distance from Tokyo. Distressed by her absence, Wright felt remorse taking the place of anger; in a state of extreme agitation, he wrote her within a period of a few weeks in the summer of 1919 a series of letters unprecedented in his correspondence for the degree of self-abasement they profess. Evidently dashed off at high speed, with errors of grammar and spelling unusual with Wright, the letters portray a man at the end of his tether, acknowledging a guilt greater than the immediate circumstances seem to call for. He denounces himself (" 'The Work of Frank Lloyd Wright' has a new and sinister look to me now. I shall wince when I see it on the drawings and books") and describes the conflict between them as "like ascending one's own funeral pyre, and, like Hercules, destroying oneself with one's own hands." Taken together, the letters amount to a confessional cry more agonized than any that Wright had ever uttered before or would ever utter again—a flagellation that has purged him of almost every trace of his accustomed self-importance. His words are worth setting down at length:

Dearest Miriam,

I must take my medicine. I have read your long, heartbroken letter and I understand—too well, too late. I wanted to come to Ikao just to be near you for a little while but I can't now.

You are quite right: I have no true personal culture. My talent has come between me and the things that bring it [culture] usually by personal sacrifice. Instead of making the sacrifices myself I have been taking them from others as my *right*. And I see how it has hardened and roughened the points of contact—how I even handle my prints as though they are waste paper—and have hardly patience enough to hear a voice, any voice, besides my own. [My] pride in my work has served to give me the self-respect that enabled me to *keep on* when it were best that I should fail— for my own soul's good . . . I am younger than you know—so young that I can *see*—still detached from "*me*." So young that all is negligible except the hurt and sorrow and pain I give to others—my own counts only until I have swung the sword and burned the house. What lives in my heart today and brings the groan to my lips at night, the sweat to my face, is what I have done to others—"Conscience-stricken," you say, and I am. That is partly my *unease* of soul—my chafed and chafing spirit, my fretful angry impotence. But even that is not to my credit. I am a creature of warm animal instincts with something born of heaven thrown in—to sink or swim and but for you it would have sunk . . .

Let me tell you, Miriam dear, the truth. I had not loved you much until I began to understand my hungry need at first and your gifts came to me in the dark like a ray of hope. I was, like you, in love with love, or [with] the quest for it and, as I know now, I had never found it. I took you as I take everything and then came reaction. So awful it was under those circumstances because conscience still had me in toils and I could not escape. But then came the self-deception I have practiced always with myself to slip and slide and cheat and what I did to escape is past belief, but it is a matter of record. You see I distrusted what I didn't want to understand and knowing so little of human feelings—even my own—I did not hesitate to slay or betray or desert their every right in every aspect. I have told you often how I despised myself even then for the crookedness of those days. But you had shown me something even then that stayed by me and kept coming up through all that baseness and treachery and confusion . . .

I did not love you then enough. I wanted to, but my weaknesses and my pet vanities and special pretensions were all antagonized by you— no matter what they were. You have explained them all. And I had never realized what terrible depths of despair, and to what extremity a sensitive, neurotic woman, highly developed and nervously disorganized by internal change could be. I was shocked and troubled and afraid night and day. I loved you enough to want to save you through it all but I looked at you for the solution instead of at myself—and when I brought you to Taliesin I had hardened to a situation that was awful enough for you. . . .

I watched you for the cause. I was told that after-effects of morphine left one subject to depression and hate. That violent hatreds and antipathies were the result . . . I have never known much of hatred—malicious and vindictive as I can be in a hot flash. And I came to believe that if I was ever going to save you for myself, I must find a hidden cause and treat it . . . Your very look in those days—the unnatural pallor—all seemed to make me suspect—and I am quick to suspect—as quick as I am to forgive, and both so facile because I have been so ignorant of the consequences to others of the use of words, which I have learned now are deeds. I have taken for granted the indulgence of others to myself and repaid it by what I considered indulgence to them. It didn't make me love you any less (rather more), and I think in your extremity as I saw it then I came to really love you.

Oh, Miriam, you call it treachery—it was not. A nightmare, you say, yes, a terrible one—for me too. But as you say I had my work and [was] still kept up by it while you had nothing. Blinded by natural desires I have never learned the meaning of my share in the iniquity and never having lived before with anyone so proudly sensitive, so well versed in human feeling, so strong and so superior to myself in every way but one. I did not know how to treat a companion as an equal; and that led to your assumption of superiority which I punished characteristically . . .

I thought I saw hypocrisy. I am skilled in the arts of hypocrisy, I see and can detect it in others quickly, having the tests all well within myself . . . [Here in Tokyo] it began all over again—the sore spots were flicked and chafed continually for now *you* were down and wouldn't change— probably because you said I hadn't really.

But I had. The beginning of the change had come. And this winter our struggles have gone deep into my soul. The degradation of experience every time I committed excesses with you and upon you showed me what I was . . . As I have gone down, strange to say my love for you has gone up . . . Love and compassion and sorrow came between-while to sit in my heart—and the whole aspect began to change and you became more beautiful. An unearthly sweetness shone from you often.

Long ago there ceased to be any other face for me. No one ever seemed able to wear clothes; no one ever seemed so worth coming close to or doing things for as you. And yet see how I neglected you when you turned on me. But I took you, Miriam dearest, when I didn't love you much—anyhow, not enough—and your prophecy that I would come to want you and realize the need of you so much that I would cry to God to give you to me has come true.

Of course you don't love me now. I don't see how you could. The finest, strongest women have sometimes, I know, loved the weakest men. But I do not want to be loved that way. All my conscious life I have been seeking love—the right kind of love. Drowning myself in sexual intercourse would not be, never was, good enough for me. But I have never realized that I have to put my house in order with some true culture before taking a bride into it. This inner chamber I call my heart has been very long neglected—the prospects are not beautiful, the air is not sweet. And in spite of the commotion the dust is on everything and blood stains are on the floor. The pictures are turned to the wall in regret and shame and what would a bride do there? A sorry place for earth's fairest gift to man! What a mess, my dearest, what a mess! . . .

Ah, Miriam, if only you might be what I should gain! How gladly I would go to the stake! Disgrace is nothing to me now, [any] more than [it was] then—something to be overcome. [Disgrace] I can *overcome,* but the loss of you I feel I never can *overcome.*

Frank[7]

For a time, they were reconciled, but only for a time; there was many a bitter quarrel yet to come.

•

Wright was quick to invent mysteries, some of which were self-protective and others of which appear to have been gratuitous—feats of obfuscation performed for the pure pleasure of the performance. The mystery of how he gained the commission to design the Imperial Hotel is probably in the former class; like any architect, and far more often than he was usually willing to admit, Wright fought hard to get commissions, and the hotel isn't likely to have been an exception. More important than the question of how Wright got the commission is the question of when. If he had begun work on the project in the studio workshop at Taliesin as early as 1913, then the thought that he had been devoting to the disposition of the very large spaces of the hotel property would help to explain the unusual speed—a matter of days—with which he was able to draw up plans for the comparatively large spaces of the Midway Gardens property. At that stage, the two projects would have had a good deal in common, and it is indeed a fact that the designs for the Imperial that Wright prepared in this country and carried with him to Japan were more playful in feeling and less exotic in appearance than the designs he prepared in Japan, according to which the hotel was actually constructed. Americans visiting the hotel (demolished in 1967) used to assume that it had been Wright's purpose to design a building in the Japanese style, but of course it was nothing of the kind; the hotel had no more to do with Japan than it did with Colonial New England, and if the Japanese took pride in it at all, it was on account of its strangeness. Like Midway Gardens, the building was a freak, the offspring of genius.

It appears to have been at some point after the building of Midway Gardens that Wright began his curious flirting with Mayan themes. They manifested themselves in a dismayingly heavy-handed fashion in the Richland Center warehouse and in a slightly gentler fashion in the Hollyhock House. They were to be found in the Imperial Hotel as well, having the advantage there of a seeming plausibility derived from the archaic-looking speckled lava-stone out of which much of the detailing was carved. (This lava-stone—*oya* in Japanese—was embraced by Wright for aesthetic reasons, though he was warned by the Japanese that it was highly porous and incapable of being waterproofed; the Japanese themselves rarely made use of it for building purposes. Characteristically, Wright brushed the warnings aside.) The public rooms of the Imperial were vast and bizarre, and some travelers found them overpowering and more than a trifle foreboding, as if some ancient bloody sacrifice were just about to take place in them; the bedrooms were small but because much of the furniture was built-in, they struck the snug, cheerful note of a ship's cabin.

The chief fame of the hotel springs from its having survived the great earthquake of 1923. From the beginning, Wright was aware that earth-

The reflecting pool before the main entrance to the Imperial Hotel. The pool was threatened with being dropped from the plans because of its high cost; FLW argued for saving it as a ready source of water in case of fire. When the great earthquake and fire of 1923 devastated Tokyo, the water in the pool was put to good use. [AR]

quakes were common in Japan and that Japanese builders in earlier times had accommodated themselves to the likelihood of recurrent destruction by erecting structures of light wood and paper, fragile and readily combustible, but also readily rebuildable. Such an accommodation to the caprices of nature was impractical in a city bent upon aping the great masonry cities of the West; in his designs for the hotel, Wright would have to confront what he later described as "this terrible natural enemy of all building whatsoever—the temblor!" In his autobiography, he wrote that "the terror of the temblor never left me while I planned the building nor while, for more than four years, I worked upon it. . . . I studied the temblor. Found it a wave-movement, not of sea but of earth—accompanied by shock that no rigidity could withstand." He goes on:

> Because of the wave movements, deep foundations like long piles would oscillate and rock the structure. Therefore the foundation should be short or shallow. There was sixty to seventy feet of soft mud below the upper depth of eight feet of surface soil on the site. That mud seemed a merciful provision—a good cushion to relieve the terrible shocks. Why not float the building upon it? A battleship floats on salt water. . . . Why not, then, a building made as the two hands thrust together palms inward, fingers interlocking and yielding to movement—but resilient to return to original position when distortion ceased? . . . Why fight the quake? Why not sympathize with it and outwit it? . . .

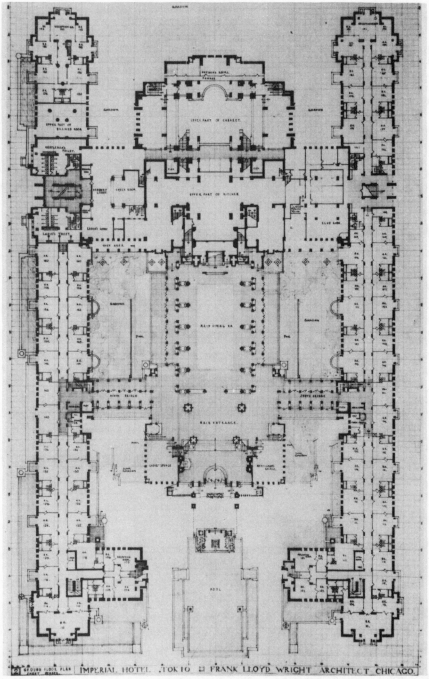

Despite the exotic detailing of the hotel—as mysterious to the Japanese as to any American or European visitor—its basic plan was rigorously axial; it could have been mistaken for a successful projet *at the Beaux-Arts.* [WF]

The manipulations of volumes of space in the Imperial Hotel were to be echoed in a diminished form in the lobby of the Arizona Biltmore Hotel, in Phoenix. [CJ]

> The great building . . . became a jointed monolith with a mosaic surface of lava and brick. Earthquakes had always torn piping and wiring apart where laid in the structure and had flooded or charged the building. So all piping and wiring was to be laid free of construction in covered concrete trenches in the ground . . . independent even of foundations. . . .
>
> Last but not least there was to be an immense reservoir or pool as an architectural feature of the entrance court—connected to the water system of the hotel and conserving the roof water.[8]

With the invaluable assistance of Paul Mueller, who had helped him bring into existence the Larkin building, Unity Temple, and Midway Gardens, Wright set about floating his vast structure on a couple of thousand close-set stubby concrete fingers ("like a waiter," he said, "carrying a tray"). Raymond claimed that the fingers never really worked and that what Mueller and Wright wound up with was an immense concrete slab resting on mud. Whatever the truth of the matter, the project continued year after year, with Wright constantly changing his plans according to the capabilities of the local work force and his ever-increasing knowledge of what the hotel would have to consist of in order to serve adequately both its foreign and Japanese clientele. It was to be a symbol of Japanese prominence in the world as well as commercially profitable. Was the hotel not being funded, after all, to a considerable extent by the royal exchequer, allied with many eminent Japanese businessmen? And would they not lose face, to say nothing of money, if the hotel were to fail as a result of having been put so entirely in the hands of a single American—an American, moreover, known professionally to be an outsider if not an eccentric and known personally to have been guilty of immoral conduct? With every delay in construction and with every additional item of expense, some of them running into tens of thousands of dollars, Wright was made to feel that the burden of responsibility rested upon his shoulders alone. Added to this burden was that of the mercurial Miriam, who oscillated between being in his arms and at his throat. Not that the fault was altogether hers; Wright was not mad but he could feign madness when he found it useful. In the autobiography that Antonin Raymond wrote in age, he recounts what he calls a "painful and ludicrous incident" that involved him and his wife, Noemi, Miriam's closest confidante. The old Imperial Hotel had burned to the ground as the new hotel was rising; Wright, Mrs. Noel, and the Raymonds were occupying quarters in the so-called Annex, which had been hastily thrown up to provide temporary shelter for guests. Raymond writes:

> In the middle of a cold night, Mme. Noel in nightclothes burst into our bedroom crying and lamenting about the cruel treatment she was subjected to by the master, who accused her of ignoble crimes in coarse language. She could stand no more. We offer her an armchair; Noemi kneels at her feet. The door opens again. Frank, in an old-fashioned short-sleeved nightshirt, strides in, takes an impressive pose, and pointing a finger at me calls me a "traitor," giving "this creature" comfort and plotting against his master, and on and on. Then he gets into our bed, throws the bedcover over his shoulder in a most dramatic gesture à la Mussolini, and keeps up his accusations of all three of us in a sarcastic voice. I beg him to cease. We could surely better discuss all this in the morning. Whereupon Miriam looks down upon Noemi. "My dear! You are shaking! What can be the matter?" Shortly after, Frank gets out of our bed, and they walked back to their room together.[9]

Word having reached Oak Park that Wright had come down with the dysentery that then afflicted most foreign visitors to Japan, nothing would do but that his eighty-one-year-old mother must hasten across land and sea to nurse him back to health. It was the first time she had traveled abroad since her arrival in the United States as a child. She came down at once with the same complaint as her son; the cure called for spending several weeks in bed on a diet that consisted entirely of a flavorless boiled rice. Mrs. Wright made a rapid recovery and undertook the usual tourist outings; she had learned something about Japanese prints from Wright and, according to Raymond, would supplement her meagre Japanese vo-

When FLW fell ill in Tokyo, Anna Lloyd Jones Wright insisted on crossing the Pacific to nurse him. She, too, fell ill, but enjoyed herself sightseeing and quarreling with Mrs. Noel. [RA]

cabulary by filling in gaps with the names of Japanese artists, e.g., "Please call Hokusai and tell him to hurry up with my breakfast. I am dying to go for a ride in my Hiroshige."[10] Humorous as the old lady may have been, her presence in Tokyo proved unendurable to Miriam. In Wright's words, "The fact that she came blew the remnant of my relationship with Miriam Noel back across the Pacific with an insane fury."[11]

To the burden of that failed relationship was added the further burden of an awareness of the impoverished family Wright had left behind him, the elder members of which were beginning, to his dismay, to initiate in youth many of the mistakes he had reached early middle age before making. (His son John had been employed by him for a time in Japan; they had quarreled, and John had been sent back in disgrace to the United States.) It was no wonder that Wright often fell ill, blaming the humid climate rather than his circumstances for this uncharacteristic response to adversity. He grew increasingly touchy as Raymond, for his part, grew increasingly bored with his duties as draftsman:

> The principal cause . . . was the endless repetition of Wright's mannerisms, his grammar, as he called it, to which I could add nothing and which seemed to me so devoid of content, particularly in Japan. It was not long before I began to feel that the design had nothing in common with Japan,

its climate, its traditions, its people, and its culture. I do not believe that this ever occurred to Wright, whose thoughts were entirely concentrated on the expression of his own personal imaginings. The hotel finally turned out to be a monument to himself.[12]

Raymond decided to resign his position with Wright and form an architectural partnership with a young American architect then living in Tokyo. When he announced his decision, Wright again accused him of being a traitor and returned a rendering that Raymond had been working on for some weeks with the following hot-tempered note:

My dear Antonin:

The rendering was brought to me yesterday. I am disgusted. I find it hopeless.

After waiting something over one month more for something to make good your facile promises—I find this—a greasy photographic print with about ten hours work upon it intended to resemble nothing so much as a dunghill in a mud puddle.

Such "slavery" it is evident is across the grain, and I realize that no satisfactory rendering of my work can be done out from under the instant touch of my own hand—even were you at your "best."

So we will give it up. You may pay back your travelling expenses to the Hotel and we are quits. . . .[13]

To which Wright, evidently growing angrier as he wrote, furnished a stinging postscript:

And to this I want to add that from now on I prefer your honest enmity to any friendship you have or may profess for me and my work. You are now a fatuous member of a guild that preys upon Architecture and Architect everywhere. . . .

It is agreeable to record that when the two men met again, at Spring Green in the late nineteen-thirties, Wright was the soul of cordiality, his fury forgotten or blamed upon his ever-convenient ancestral Welsh temperament. Though the hotel was not yet finished, Wright left Tokyo for the last time in 1921. According to Raymond, Wright was dismissed on the grounds of his having so continuously and outrageously exceeded the construction budget, but there is no hint of dismissal in Wright's account of his departure. On the contrary, he claims to have been much honored, not least by an unexpected increase in the size of his fee (a large portion of which he spent on the purchase of many hundreds of Japanese prints for his collection), by several farewell banquets, and by an army of loyal workmen, who followed his car through the streets to the railroad station shouting, "Banzai, Wrieto-San, banzai!"

The famous sequel to the building of the Imperial Hotel came two years later, when Tokyo and Yokohama suffered unprecedented devastation in the greatest earthquake in Japanese history. For days, American newspapers were filled with headlines describing the effects of the quake, and it was assumed by many—but not by Wright, staying for the moment in Los Angeles—that the Imperial Hotel would be found among the ruins. Finally, a telegram was received at Taliesin, signed by Baron Okura, Chairman of the Board of Directors of the corporation that financed the building of the hotel. The telegram was forwarded to Wright in Los Angeles; it read: HOTEL STANDS UNDAMAGED AS MONUMENT OF YOUR GENIUS HUNDREDS OF HOMELESS PROVIDED BY PERFECTLY MAINTAINED SERVICE CONGRATULATIONS OKURA.[14]

That happy ending to his Japanese commission is so welcome that one hesitates to diminish its charm by raising questions about its accuracy. For one thing, the telegram that Wright took care to publish in his autobiography and elsewhere is datelined as from Spring Green and not Tokyo. The original document is not to be found in the archives of Taliesin and there is at least a possibility that Wright himself wrote the telegram and arranged to have it sent to him in Los Angeles. According to Raymond, the hotel did suffer some damage (comparatively minor, it is true); what is more important to history is that an overwhelming majority of the steel-framed buildings in Tokyo readily survived the earthquake and that Wright's "floating" foundation was no more successful in resisting the earthquake than the conventional foundations of other steel-framed buildings. Moreover, the great weight of the hotel caused it to sink continuously on its unstable concrete mat over the years, in some places to a depth of four feet; the high cost of maintaining the basic utilities of the hotel in the face of this subsidence was one of the chief reasons for its demolition. The hotel was a gorgeous confection, but it was by no means the engineering marvel that Wright professed it to be.

16

WRIGHT HAD ACCEPTED the Imperial Hotel commission in the early, happy days of his liaison with Mamah Cheney; by the time the first set of plans had been prepared and the backers of the hotel were ready to begin construction, Mamah and her children had been murdered, Taliesin had been burned, and Wright had been pitched headlong into an altogether different stage of his life—one that was to be marked by incessant emotional turmoil and frequent despair. He set off for Japan in the brave hope of emerging from ruins actual as well as metaphorical. By bad luck the companion with whom he chose to open this chapter in his life was a woman unconsciously bent upon destroying herself and everyone around her.

The years in Japan embraced the carrying out of one of the greatest of Wright's architectural feats; it also embraced his amassing of a much-admired collection of Japanese screens, prints, and ceramics, and his success as a dealer doing business with the Metropolitan Museum, in New York City, the Spaulding brothers, in Boston, and other wealthy collectors. (Most of the fee he earned from the Imperial Hotel—said to have been upward of half a million dollars—was spent upon art works.) When he returned to the United States, it was again with the expectation of making a fresh start, but by now he faced an accumulation of burdens that, for most men in their middle fifties, would have seemed daunting indeed. He was still married to Catherine Wright and was helping to support her and a couple of the younger children, as well as his elderly mother. He was still paying taxes and making mortgage payments on the Oak Park house. He was still involved with Miriam Noel and he was still quarreling with his client Barnsdall.

Fortunately, Wright possessed an unquenchable optimism about the future—this was among the many useful attributes inherited from his father—and an energy exceptional both in amount and in its capacity to renew itself from one day to the next; he confronted his burdens with his usual uncanny mask of debonair composure. In writing to Darwin D.

Martin, his perennially bewitched benefactor, he would occasionally lower the mask and confess how much it cost him to wear it. And to his daughter Catherine, who never forgave him for the breaking up of the family, he wrote from Japan of his loneliness. In a speech given to a women's group in Chicago, in 1918, during one of his brief visits back to the States, Wright asserted his public persona, speaking, like Whitman, as the man he would choose to be and not as the man he was: "The artist's needs are as other men's, intensified. He is broad, strong, resourceful, typified by a love of life that survives great trials and comes through with a song in his heart, resilient, however his spirit be outraged or his body broken."[1]

Wright used to say that the Middle West having been tilted up on end, all of its prosperous layabouts had slid down into the southwest corner of California. Despite this mocking view of the populace, in 1922 Wright was ready to throw in his lot with that singular, sunburned corner of the land. Exhausted by his arduous labors in Japan, he could perceive advantages in California at that particular moment which he might have scorned a few years before. Taliesin would remain his ever-to-be-cherished retreat, but his son Lloyd had become a permanent resident of Los Angeles and it was obvious that the state as a whole would be enjoying a long-range growth in population, which would lead in turn to ample professional opportunities for architects. "The newcomer from the fertile midwestern prairies," Wright wrote in his autobiography, "came here to make sunshine his home. But at first his home did not know how to bask any more than he himself did. Shirt sleeves were his limit and his home had no shirt sleeves nor anything at all 'easy' about it."[2]

The so-called Spanish mission style had been adopted with some unease by the newly transplanted Middlewesterners, and Wright hoped to be able to devise an altogether new style of architecture, as suitable to the climate as to the emerging culture. A key aspect of this new architecture would be the humble and inexpensive concrete block, which was easy to manufacture, easy for unskilled labor to erect, and easy to maintain without paint or other preservative. It was also capable of embodying a variety of interesting shapes and patterned surfaces. Wright spoke of it as making possible the housing, at a reasonable cost, of millions of Americans from coast to coast; California, being more open to experiment than most of the states, would be an ideal place in which to launch the new architecture. For several years, Wright had been seeking to develop a concrete wall-slab that would have tensile as well as compressive strength, and to this end he and his son Lloyd worked out over several years a method of linking blocks together with steel rods extending both horizontally and vertically from one block to the next to any required length or height. One set of these linked blocks made up the exterior face of a wall, the other set made up the interior face, leaving a hollow space between them. The rods lay in channels running along the tops and sides of the blocks; once the rods had been fastened together, they were sealed in place by concrete grouting. The result was a reenforced wall-slab thin but strong, which thanks to its hollowness would help to keep a structure free of damp, as well as cool in summer and warm in winter. Because a wall of such blocks could be composed of a variety of repeated patterns, much as an Oriental rug is, Wright described himself as a "weaver" of what he called "textile" blocks.

Other people had been experimenting with reenforced concrete blocks of this general nature; among them was Wright's former disciple and employee Walter Burley Griffin, who developed what he called a "knit-lock" system several years before Wright did. Wright has been accused of "borrowing" elements of Griffin's and other inventors' concrete-block designs, and he may well have done so. It was certainly the case that he never understood the so-called weaving of his textile blocks as thoroughly as Lloyd did and it was Lloyd who had to solve a number of the problems that arose in the course of learning how to build with them. The fact is that, because of his fame, Wright was in a position to champion the textile block more effectively than anyone else. He hoped, for example, to employ concrete block in the enormous real-estate development that the oil millionaire Edward H. Doheny commissioned him to design for a tract of land in the Sierra Madre mountains, north of Los Angeles. To judge by Wright's renderings, this would have been one of the most romantic of all his major projects, rivaling the Baghdad fantasies of his old age; unfortunately for Wright (and for the world), Doheny proved to be one of the leading figures in the Teapot Dome oil-leasing scandal that came to light during the administration of President Harding and the project was cancelled. A similar fate befell a project for Desert Valley and for a cottage colony to be built on the shore of Lake Tahoe. The cottages were designed to resemble tepees; houseboats equally bizarre in appearance were to float upon the surface of the lake. (In the renderings, the top-heavy houseboats look far more like houses than boats and might well have proved hazardous to their occupants in any weather save a dead calm.) Subsequently, it turned out that the promoter of the Lake Tahoe project had employed Wright simply in order to be able to make use of his name in the selling of lots in the development; by then, Wright's celebrity was sufficient to make him a possible victim of—and a seeming accomplice in—many forms of real-estate chicanery.

The first textile-block project to achieve reality was "La Miniatura," a house designed for Mrs. George Madison Millard in Pasadena, in 1923. Seventeen years earlier, Wright had designed a house for the Millards in Highland Park, Illinois. Mr. Millard had been one of the country's best-known dealers in rare books; now Mrs. Millard was a widow, who was carrying on her husband's book business and selling antique European furniture as well. Wright describes her as a sunny-spirited woman, blue-eyed and with unruly hair, and plainly she was of an adventurous disposition. She wished to build a small, romantic house that would serve as both a shop and a home and she had but ten thousand dollars to spend. (In a comparatively modest mood, Wright wrote in his autobiography, "I was proud now to have a client survive the first house and ask me to build a second. Out of one hundred and seventy-two buildings this made only the eleventh time it had happened to me."[3])

Wright described his textile blocks to Mrs. Millard, pointing out that they would provide fireproof quarters for her books and antique furniture. Mrs. Millard said that as long as the house had an old-world atmosphere, the blocks would be fine. Wright wrote of her that at that moment "she didn't fully know that she was to be lightly but inexorably grasped by the architectural fates and used for high exemplar."[4] Mrs. Millard had already purchased a treeless lot in Pasadena, but Wright and she discovered "a ravishing ravine nearby, in which stood two beautiful eucalyptus trees." "Ravine" is the word commonly used in and around Chicago for what is called an "arroyo" in the Southwest; dry much of the year, arroyos carry off large quantities of floodwater in the rainy season and are much more dangerous to live by than the comparatively harmless ravines of Illinois. For obvious reasons, they are not thought desirable as building sites, so Mrs. Millard, having disposed of her original lot, was able to acquire the arroyo property at a low price. Flying in the face of conventional prudence, Wright and she decided to build at the very bottom of the arroyo, where a small pool would be dug to reflect the house.

Partly because the narrowness of the arroyo precluded the long, ground-hugging horizontals of the Prairie House style (which Wright in California had temporarily lost interest in) and partly because the concrete block by its cubical form invited the design of houses as multiples of cubes, La Miniatura is an exquisite little box, or more accurately—given that the attached garage is very much a part of the composition—two boxes. (Years later, Lloyd Wright doubled the size of the garage to hold two cars instead of one and added still another cube to his father's composition, in the form of a studio placed a short distance behind the garage and at right angles to the house.) The patterned blocks of which the house is constructed are square, but the effect of the house as a whole is one of an intensely concentrated verticality. As its name implies, it is not so much a small structure as a miniature, with each of its parts so perfectly in scale with one another that, at first glance, it defies being accurately measured—it could equally well be a toy or a palace.

La Miniatura is assuredly among the most beautiful houses to be found anywhere in the world, regardless of size. The interior is as exquisite in its shapeliness as the exterior and has a plan of remarkable ingenuity, comprising three full floors and terraces at four levels, with easy access to its surroundings and to the street. The living room is only eighteen feet wide by twenty-eight feet long, but being two stories high, with a mezzanine suspended above a handsome chimney breast and with high French doors opening upon a cantilevered balcony, it gives the impression

"La Miniatura," in Pasadena (1923), is surely one of the prettiest small houses ever built. It is also—and still more remarkably—one of the most intensely exploited three-dimensional objects that any architect has ever devised: a cube packed with cubes, every square inch of which yields pleasure and use.

of being on a grand scale. The polished concrete floor has the sheen of tawny marble; beams of sunlight fall across it through the crosses that pierce the patterned concrete blocks of the outer walls. Richly stained dark wood covers the ceiling and the parapet of the mezzanine; one could more easily imagine oneself to be in some secret mountain lodge in the heart of Europe than in conventionally upper-middle-class Pasadena.

As was so often the case with Wright, the design of the house enchanted the client; it was only in the course of building the house that troubles arose. The contractor putting up La Miniatura turned out to be a light-fingered scoundrel, engaged in building a house of his own and "borrowing"

One thinks of "La Miniatura" as sequestered in a narrow ravine, overhung by giant eucalyptus trees. It possesses as well a broad, level lawn cunningly shut away from the world.

many of the necessary materials from the Millard job. In the best of circumstances, the house was certain to have exceeded Wright's characteristically optimistic estimates—already far beyond the ten thousand dollars initially stipulated by Mrs. Millard—but the crookedness of the contractor used up the last penny of the funds that Mrs. Millard was able to scrape together. Rather than see his first experiment in concrete-block design left unfinished—he was by then, he admits in his autobiography, thinking of himself as a sculptor in concrete as Palladio, Bramante, and Sansovino had sculpted in stone—Wright himself managed, he says, to contribute six thousand dollars toward the completion of the house, which a sequence of contractors carried out in a storm of lawsuits, builders' liens, insults, and general ridicule.

"But the Gods," Wright goes on to say, "will allow no creative effort of man's to go untested. The Japanese themselves believe them jealous, purposely leaving some glaring fault in a conspicuous place to placate them."[5] Wright had neglected to follow this tradition, and the consequences proved costly:

> And just for that came an unusual cloudburst concentrating on that ravine.
> . . . No one in fifty years ever saw the culvert that now took the street water away below the basement of the house, overflow. But the heavens opened wide, poured water down until it got to the level of the pretty concrete dining room floor, determined to float the house if the thing

could be done. . . . Failing utterly to move it, [the heavens] left a contemptuous trace of mud on the lower terraces, put out the fires in the sub-basement, burying the gas heaters beneath solid mud. And went away. Mrs. George Madison Millard's spirit, faith, and pride went out with the fires. She wept.

But soon we got this little matter fixed up by aid of the city of Pasadena. Even this was not to be enough to add to what had already been. Depths of misery were yet to be plumbed. . . . Yes—let no one imagine that because this region is perpetual sunshine the roof is any more negligible a feature of house-happiness than back there in rain and snow and ice. The sun bakes the roof for eleven months, two weeks, and five days, shrinking it to a shrivel. Then giving the roof no warning whatever to get back to normal if it could, the clouds burst. . . . I knew this. And I know there are more leaking roofs in Southern California than in all the rest of the world put together. I knew that the citizens come to look upon water thus in a singularly ungrateful mood. I knew that water is all that enables them to have their being there, but let any of it through on them from above, unexpectedly, in their houses and they go mad. It is a kind of phobia. . . . I had seriously taken precautions in the details of this little house to avoid such scenes as result from negligible roofs. . . . But what of it? What defense when any roof chooses to leak? It subsequently was found that our builder had lied to me about the flashing under and within the coping walls. . . . You may feel that by confessing this shameful incompetence in this manner I am making light of a bad matter. But really I am doing penance here. Maybe I am only making a bad matter worse. However that may be, Mrs. George Madison Millard's spirit, though dampened, was not one to be broken even by this last trial. Enough of this left-handed confession. I finally fixed the house when I found out about it.[6]

Alas, for Wright's boast that he had "fixed" the house! Like a hundred other houses that Wright designed, in a variety of climates, La Miniatura was always to leak and presumably leaks to this day. So famous did Wright become for his leaky roofs, including the roofs of Taliesin in Spring Green, that he developed a number of defensively humorous responses to his clients' complaints. A well-known anecdote concerns a long-distance telephone call to Taliesin made by Hibbard Johnson, owner of Wingspread, the great country house that Wright designed for Johnson in Racine, Wisconsin, in the nineteen-thirties. Johnson to Wright, indignantly: "Frank, we're just sitting down to Thanksgiving dinner and your damned skylight is leaking. What are we to do?" Wright to Johnson, suavely: "Move the table." On other occasions, when a client complained of a leaky roof, Wright, with an irritating absence of embarrassment, would reply, "That's how you can tell it's a roof."

La Miniatura survives with unaging grace its reckless siting in an arroyo, its leaky roof, and the ravages of more than sixty years of constant family use. One recognizes it at once as the building to which Wright himself provided the happiest tribute:

> "La Miniatura" stands in Pasadena against blue sky between the loving eucalyptus companions, and in spite of all friction, waste, and slip is triumphant as Idea. . . . Alice Millard lives in it. She says she would have no other house she has ever seen. She fought for it and finally won—whoever may think she lost. It is her home in more than ordinary sense. It is the reward anyone has a right to enjoy in any sincere high adventure in building. . . . As for me . . . I would rather have built this little house than St. Peter's in Rome.[7]

The building of La Miniatura had been a painful experience for Wright. His hope of settling down in California and establishing a new career there was beginning to seem illusory; if he had expected that the eccentric personality he had taken care to cultivate from his teens would be more likely to flourish in that tropical forcing-house of eccentricity, his expectations were meeting with disappointment, often enough at the hands of people even more eccentric than he. Three local commissions came to him in quick succession: the Storer house, the Ennis house, and the Freeman house. The order in which they were constructed is subject to debate. Eric Wright, grandson of Frank Lloyd Wright and son of Lloyd Wright, the long-suffering supervisor of the construction of the houses, believes that the Storer house came second after La Miniatura, the Ennis house third, and the Freeman house last. (Eric Wright is an architect in Los Angeles and has been in charge of the recent sympathetic restoration of the Storer house, currently owned by the movie producer Joel Silver. Eric Wright's reckoning in respect to the dates of the three houses is based on structural differences in the casting of the concrete blocks; in any event, all were designed in 1923 and were completed late in 1924.)

Like La Miniatura, each of the three houses began with the pleasure of its design and ended in frustration, aesthetic and financial. The house Wright designed for Dr. John Storer, a dentist practicing in Los Angeles, occupies a steep hillside plot on Hollywood Boulevard; in direct contradiction to everything that Wright had earlier preached about the natural, nearly invisible joining of structure and site, the Storer house, small as it is, asserts its presence with a surprising degree of arrogance—an arrogance far more obvious in the nineteen-twenties, when the hillside lacked the softening effect of foliage, than it is today. A high wall of concrete blocks supports a terrace from which rises a severely vertical pavilion of two stories, with a flat roof and adjoining wings. A visitor enters the house not by a conventionally indicated front door but by any of five identical

Like the movie set of a Pompeiian villa, the Storer house rises out of the naked, unpopulated hills of Hollywood in the twenties. [ELW]   The automobiles parked in front of the Storer house offer a jaunty contrast to its dignity; in fact, the house is smaller and less dignified than it looks, having (for example) a back door but no front one. [ELW]

French doors, which open into a combination reception hall and dining room. One wing contains a kitchen, a servant's bedroom, and a bathroom, along with a rear entry giving access to a semi-detached garage and driveway; the other wing contains four bedrooms and two baths, ingeniously stacked on two levels that link the lower hall and dining room with a handsome, high-ceilinged upper living room, lit by windows that appear at first glance to be unbroken continuations of the five French doors immediately beneath them. Eric Wright thinks that his grandfather intended the floor of the upper living room to "float" as if unattached to the adjacent walls, thus permitting the fenestration to be truly continuous; either the engineering required for this structural sleight-of-hand was beyond the competence of the builder, or Wright, by then back at Taliesin, had neglected to send the necessary working drawings to his son Lloyd, with whom he constantly, maddeningly, failed to keep in touch except when blame was to be assigned.

The problems that Lloyd Wright faced in supervising the Storer project were matched by similar difficulties in respect to the Ennis and Freeman projects. Mr. and Mrs. Charles Ennis were wealthy and could afford the additional expense that Wright's arbitrary tardiness imposed on them, but in the case of the Storers and Freemans every penny counted and every delay caused them not merely the irritation that the Ennises felt but outright indignation. Eventually, Wright consented to an arrangement—highly imprudent and therefore characteristic of his flair for financial bungling— by which he would assume a share in the final cost of the Storer and Freeman houses, should that final cost exceed a certain level (which of course it did). As with La Miniatura and a hundred other houses, what mattered to Wright was that they be brought into existence as he wished them to be; how to pay for them was another matter.

Lloyd Wright as a go-between found himself continuously rebuked by clients and architect alike—a fate rendered all the more painful to him because the architect was his father. Of the difficulties so often attendant upon the father-son relationship Frank Lloyd Wright appears to have learned little from his own filial experiences. In his autobiography, he wrote harshly of William Cary Wright, who was, in fact, a far more sympathetic and affectionate parent than his son would ever prove to be. With little formal education, Lloyd Wright had been trained as a landscape architect in the offices of Olmsted & Olmsted, the leading landscape architects in the country, and had begun to receive commissions for the design of houses as well. In 1923, he was thirty-three years old, which is to say that compared to his father and grandfather he was making a very late start on a career. That start was made no easier by the tasks he was called on to perform as his father's surrogate. Lloyd was a proud and gifted

© SUSAN WOLDENBERG

The doors on the ground floor lead into a combination entrance hall and dining room; the windows above light a lofty living room. One wing of the Storer house contains, neatly stacked on two levels, four bedrooms and two bathrooms; another wing contains a kitchen and servants' quarters.

man, and he fought back hard against his father's bullying; nevertheless, the bullying went on and the son continued to give way to it.

The letters and telegrams that passed back and forth in the early nineteen-twenties between Lloyd in Los Angeles and his father at Taliesin make unhappy reading; more than half a century later, one wonders how Lloyd resisted the temptation to walk away and leave his father floundering. In one letter, Wright criticizes his son in terms that Wright's mother must often have employed in criticizing him; the words of the indictment are so clearly applicable to Wright himself that we wonder how he could have failed to hear the minatory voice of Anna Wright ringing in his ears as he wrote them:

> . . . You are "spongy" and you don't know just why. But I will tell you why. It is because you are not really *reliable*. You will say a thing *is* so when you only *think* it is so. You will promise and not keep it. You will buy when you can't pay. You will attempt anything and blame failure on others. . . . You are sentimental but not kind. . . . I think you would carelessly do wrong to anyone when you ought to be more careful. You are quick to impute to others the quality that is rankling in your own soul. . . . You are absolutely the worst-mannered young man I know. . . . I enjoy being with you for a while, but soon I find myself vulgarized somehow by the lack of consideration or whatever it is that emanates

from you. . . . The value of a dollar is a blank to your mind. Your sense of time is loose. Your step is loose. Your grasp of your work is loose. Your sense of justice is loose. . . . Your eye is on me and my acts as you see them. . . . Turn it upon your own soul for your own good. I have been your *"excuse"* for too long, my son! Too long! You will answer for your own sins. I will answer for mine. Tighten up the essential screws till they hurt. They are nearly all loose. Now, this is all in no other than a spirit of would-be helpfulness. . . . It is written out of a full and understanding heart, for what it may be worth, in time, to you. . . .[8]

Harsh son of a harsh mother! That side of Wright's character which revealed him to be the lovable son of a lovable father was little in evidence when Lloyd was most in need of it. A grown man, Lloyd was being scolded like a child, and however painful that must have been for him, it can scarcely have been less painful, seeking to acquire a good reputation on the coast, to be blamed for the grossly negligent professional misconduct of an absentee architect who happened to be his father.

A typical telegram of the period:

FRANK LLOYD WRIGHT
SPRING GREEN WISCONSIN

STORER STOPS WORK SEARCHES FUNDS ENNIS PATTERN FACE NOT HERE YET MUST STOP WORK UNLESS FORWARDED IMMEDIATELY POST BY AIRPLANE

LLOYD[9]

Telegram in reply:

LLOYD WRIGHT
5417½ HOLLYWOOD BLVD
LOS ANGELES CALIF

BLUEPRINTS PATTERN FACE BOUND IN WITH SETS FILED AT BUILDING DEPARTMENT OTHER COPY SOMEWHERE THERE SENDING ORIGINAL KEEP ME ADVISED REGARDING STORER DID NEEDHAM FALL DOWN IMPOSSIBLE FOR ME TO ASSIST HIM UNTIL AFTER MAY FIRST AND DOUBTFUL THEN LOUIS SULLIVAN BURIED LAST WEDNESDAY

FATHER[10]

From a sheaf of increasingly frantic telegrams from Lloyd Wright, the first two addressed to his father's factotum at Taliesin:

WILL SMITH
TALIESIN
SPRING GREEN WISCONSIN

CALL MR WRIGHTS ATTENTION TO WIRES VITAL

L

276

WILL SMITH
TALIESIN
SPRING GREEN WISCONSIN

GIVE IMMEDIATE ATTENTION WIRE 28 UNANSWERED MATTER IMPORTANT
WIRE

L

FRANK LLOYD WRIGHT
TALIESIN
SPRING GREEN WISCONSIN

HAVE CARRIED ON AS FAR AS POSSIBLE E [ENNIS] DEMANDS ACCOUNTING
BALANCE FIFTEEN HUNDRED DUE AT ONCE AND CONTROL OF ALL PAYMENTS
GREATLY EXERCISED OVER COST OF BLDG STOP I DESIRE TO RESIGN POSITION
UNTENABLE BUT WILL CONTINUE IF YOU THINK ADVISABLE AND I RECEIVE
YOUR SUBSTANTIAL SUPPORT AT ONCE UNDER ANY CIRCUMSTANCES DO NOT
FAIL ME I HAVE DONE MY BEST SPARE US FURTHER HUMILIATION

L[11]

Poor Lloyd in his extremity manages within the confines of a single telegram to threaten resignation and then to withdraw the threat. In letters to Lloyd, the father treats the son as a child, a servant, a colleague, an adversary, then, without warning, as a confidant, worthy to be accepted as a true native of the Wright country:

Dear Lloyd:

. . . work is not so far forward as I had imagined. But I've no doubt you are doing your best and that is good. Color would help the Storer house. The awnings especially should go on at once. Color if judiciously applied to the piers would help a lot. I think what you say is probably true as to its lacking joy. We'll see, however, before we finish. . . . The Ennis work looks backward. How is it possible that the surveys on that work and on Freeman should have been so far out? Suit might be brought against the surveyors? As to Mrs. Ennis not being [allowed] on the job, I think you are entirely wrong. If the job is all right, she would be better off. If it is wrong, she would help straighten it out. To stave her off would only arouse her suspicions and be bad for the result. Keep her in touch patiently. She and he are in the right spirit, I am sure. I shall write to them to stick close to you and hold up your hands and not do anything to weaken them. Of course, pioneers—that is what we are— take pioneers' fare and no dessert. . . . Freeman et al. are the usual difficul- ties, no more. Do not chafe too much, the stake is large for which you are playing?

As to my affairs, I have yet only the contract for tentative sketches for the office bldg in the middle of which I am [the National Life Insurance Company skyscraper, in Chicago, which was never built]. I have a couple of good commissions at Madison and one at Washington, Maryland, which are good but slow. There is nothing immediate—all is on long lines, with "cash" as scarce as ever, only more so. . . . I have less than none by forty-seven thousand dollars. . . . I am learning to be alone by degrees. It is a long time since anything warm and human has transpired in my life with M [Miriam]. She left about May 5th but for years before that, really. Life requires technique, as does any other expression, if art. Let us learn it. In our relations as a family we have been pretty raw—savages, rather. Punishment is certain and ought to be valuable. That is really all there is to a true education—profiting by the experience of joy and punishment. . . . Have a good word and a fine thought for everyone you touch. Cut out rough stuff and avoid anger as you would a house afire.

Affectionately,
Father[12]

Probably to Lloyd's surprise, Wright wrote to the Ennises as he had promised to do. The letter reads in part:

My dear Mr. and Mrs. Ennis:

The time is approaching when things always look darkest, in the building of a building. It is about now that you need your architect's counsel and moral support and I am sorry not to give it in person.

Lloyd has kept me pretty well informed of the progress of events. The work is slower than I anticipated; the city has interfered in points wholly unnecessary, arbitrarily adding some to costs, but I suppose the wonder is they let it happen at all, because it is so far from the stock of their shop.

However, they have not really hurt it and something is coming to Los Angeles worth seeing and thinking about. . . . Don't let any influences or uneasiness of your own minds as to costs or conduct alienate you from Lloyd or Lloyd from you. He is very sincere and earnest in behalf of your work, and while he may make mistakes they will be less than anyone else, no matter how experienced in building, would make, although not the same ones, perhaps; and those he does make will not hurt the final result of your building. . . .

You see, the final result is going to stand on that hill a hundred years or more. Long after we are all gone, it will be pointed out as the Ennis house and pilgrimages will be made to it by lovers of the beautiful. . . .[13]

In respect to the possible longevity of the Ennis house, Wright's prophecy promises to prove accurate. It is now well over sixty years old and like the nearby Barnsdall house it is indeed an object of continuous pilgrimage. Most of the pilgrims are not, however, as Wright hoped they would be, lovers of the beautiful; rather, they are students and admirers of Wright, who find the house of interest because it so obviously defies his often enunciated theories of architectural beauty instead of embodying them. Half a century of landscaping and irrigation have helped to conceal the brute force with which the Barnsdall house dominates Olive Hill, but no amount of planting can diminish the barbaric arrogance with which the Ennis house imposes itself between earth and sky. Nor does the structure strike us as a mere unlucky specimen of misplaced high spirits, like, say, San Simeon; no, the house appears to assume that it belongs precisely where it is and that we should be grateful for the bizarre vehemence with which it calls attention to itself. Trying to say a good word for it in Wright's own lifetime, Hitchcock wrote that its "monumentality suits the site, but is rather undomestic." The fact is that the monumentality of the structure, far from being suitable, threatens to crush the hilltop upon which it sprawls and that one might better look for traces of domesticity in Richardson's Allegheny County Jail.

In fairness to Wright, it should be noted that his description of the house as a thing of beauty was written before the Ennises and he came to a parting of the ways. Tiring of Lloyd's presence and his father's absence, the Ennises took matters into their own hands and finished the house as best they could. In 1940, long after the Ennises had departed, the house was sold to the Hollywood producer John Nesbitt, who at once sat down and dashed off a charming letter to Wright. Nesbitt expresses his happiness at being in possession of the house, for which he has had to pay only twenty thousand dollars, and his bewilderment "as a man of moderate means" over how to furnish a house composed of such rich materials— teak, marble, and bronze. Nesbitt asks for a copy of the plans, in order that he may set about making repairs to "a hundred-foot-long bulge" in the retaining wall to the south of the house. Wright replies that he will be glad to send the plans "if I can find them," that Nesbitt has no reason to fear the "slight" bulge in the retaining wall, and that to Wright's dismay he had been obliged to turn the house over to ignorant clients before he had finished it. "Much is needed to be done to put your house in proper condition for living in it the way it was designed to be lived in. The elaborate iron work—fixtures—marble sills and floors and such were all put in over the architect's head by Ennises' friends in the business. I would love to see that dignified place come into its own, finally."[14]

The usual romantic interlude began, with Wright at his most winning and the client bewitched. Nesbitt asked Wright not only to undertake the restoration and improvement of the Ennis house but also to design for the Nesbitt family a seaside house at Carmel, farther up the California coast. By a little over a year later, the romance had faltered; Mrs. Nesbitt was apparently growing tired of the difficulty of improving the house (which Wright had taken to calling "the Glendower opus," 2607 Glendower Avenue being its proper street address) and the Carmel project was having to be postponed by the prospect of a war with Japan. If such a war were indeed to break out, the government would be likely to restrict the building of private houses; in any event, the last place to build a house in case of war was Carmel, whose rocky headlands were no doubt already being eyed favorably by the Japanese High Command.

Wright wrote reassuringly to Nesbitt about the Glendower opus: "Don't be scared. Believe me, I can do wonders with that house."[15] If necessary, Wright might get Aline Barnsdall to buy it, once she saw how beautiful it was certain to become. Meanwhile, although Lloyd, once again a go-between and whipping boy, had shown signs of walking off the job, Wright stood ready to send a couple of additional whipping boys along from Taliesin to finish the job. Wright promised Nesbitt that he wouldn't run him into debt and—rather eerily, since he had promised the same thing to the Ennises—that the house would make him and his family proud for a hundred years. By late December of 1941, the United States was at war with Japan, and Wright and Nesbitt were at daggers drawn. Wright accused Nesbitt of failing to pay for the labor he had expended upon the Carmel project; Wright was in desperate need of a thousand dollars to help buy

Windows in the Freeman house, with mitred glass corners.

© SUSAN WOLDENBERG

Perched high among pines and looking out over Hollywood, the Freeman house is an experiment in vertical cubage. When new and without its present tethering of greenery, it must have seemed an experiment in cubical vertigo. The concrete blocks of the Freeman house have begun to crumble with time— a consequence of the poor quality of concrete employed.

© SUSAN WOLDENBERG

food and shelter for the Fellowship at Taliesin. A week of intense skirmishing, then truce and a settlement of their differences, but the love affair was over. The Carmel house, which Pfeiffer describes as one of the most imaginative of all Wright's designs, was never to be built, and the Glendower opus continued to be bought and sold, bought and sold, with its battered Mayan outer walls still bulging and its interior still formidably grand and uninhabitable.

As for the Freeman and Storer houses, they, too, marked for Wright the dashing of hopes both personal and professional. One would have supposed Samuel and Harriet Freeman to be ideal clients; they were Easterners who had come West with some means, with advanced sociological and political views (they were commonly accused of being Communists), and with a sophisticated admiration for Wright. They had purchased a small, exceedingly steep plot of land on Glencoe Way, from which one gained a sensational view of Los Angeles; close as the property lay to the heart of Hollywood, it felt curiously remote and even rural—a feeling that it conveys to this day, thanks in part to the welcomely unkempt plantlife that has sprung up all round it. The house that Wright designed for them is, like La Miniatura, intensely vertical, with sleeping quarters in a basement that emerges onto grade level as the hillside falls away and with a laundry

Left, defying FLW's own precepts, the Ennis house crowns a hilltop instead of embracing it and is better suited to sheltering a Mayan god than an American family. Right, an awesomely long corridor in the Ennis house; at its end one encounters not a bloody sacrificial altar but a conventionally pleasing bedroom and bathroom.

on the opposite side of the house, also at once a basement and a perch. Inside and out, the house is built of concrete blocks, some plain and others patterned; pierced blocks in the high clerestory of the living room bring sunlight into what would otherwise be a shadowy space around the open hearth. Opposite the hearth, wide glass doors and fixed sash look out over the city; where the fixed sash turn the outer corners of the room, Wright for the first time has joined mitred panes of glass at right angles to one another without the aid of stiles to support the horizontal mullions in which the glass is set.

The Freemans lived for over half a century in the house. At one point in what appears to have been a troubled marriage, they were separated, but they went on living in the house, since each of them felt too fond of it to move away. Mrs. Freeman fell in love with Rudolph Schindler (as what woman in Los Angeles in Schindler's time did not?) and much of the ingenious built-in furniture in the house is by Schindler; with equal ingenuity, he turned the laundry into a charming small apartment. As one might expect, the roof of the house leaked and Schindler did his best to repair it, cheaply and ineffectually. Wright once paid a visit to the house and if he lost his temper on catching sight of the mutilated roof, he approached apoplexy when he saw Schindler's furniture. Mrs. Freeman always loyally chose to champion Schindler over Wright. On being told in her nineties that certain electric fixtures in the house had been designed by Wright and were therefore extremely valuable, she shook her head. "No," she said. "Schindler." Freeman died in 1980; at her death, in 1986, she bequeathed the house to the University of Southern California. Given the irresponsibility that universities nearly always manifest in respect to houses of architectural and historic value that have been placed in their custody, one hopes that the Freeman house will be preserved and cherished as it deserves to be.

The Freeman house ought to have been a delight to build, but again there were quarrels among the clients, the contractors, and Lloyd as the clerk-of-the-works. From distant Taliesin Wright wrote to Lloyd, "I am sorry for the impasse in L.A., but sorry is no help." Heavily in debt as he was, he would be going still further into debt because of the Ennis, Freeman, and Storer houses; he blamed Lloyd for much that was going wrong and Lloyd blamed his father for blaming him. As the triple fiasco drew to an end, Wright arrived at last in Los Angeles; in the course of discussing the Storer project, it appears that the two men lost their tempers and exchanged insults. A few days later, Wright mailed the following semi-apology to Lloyd:

> I've just come from the Storer house. It's a tragedy from my standpoint, but I can see how hard you've worked to pull it out and I approve many things you did. I have been thinking things over and I guess in the heat and shame of the failure and loss I've been thinking more of myself than of you, more heedless than I ought to be. You've got to stay here and the thing ought to be fixed up for you as well as may be. I took that stand with the Doctor [Storer], who broke out bitterly against you. I did

3 PHOTOS © SUSAN WOLDENBERG

Concrete blocks were part of an attempt by FLW and his son Lloyd to develop a method of low-cost construction. The block was already a commonplace; FLW's notion was that by giving it a richly modeled surface it could serve both aesthetic and economic ends. Some of the blocks are solid, some pierced to admit light and air, and others are glazed, admitting only light. Left to right, Millard, Freeman, and Storer houses.

what I could to show him where he came in and I came in—as well as for *our* share of the blame.

And I shall be so with Ennis and Freeman. I think we should not try to work together any more but that needn't prevent getting this awful mess into as fair shape for you as can be done by our cooperation. I shall forget your break with me and if in this spirit you wish to see the matter to a conclusion I am with you. If not, I'll do the best I can along these same lines anyway.

I guess you've had about enough. A session with old Doc makes me realize a few things—at least you did your damndest. Angels can do no more.

Father[16]

17

THE "AWFUL MESS" that Wright encountered and sought to deal with in California was no worse than the assortment of messes confronting him during approximately the same period back home at Taliesin. Few men of genius, possessing the high intellect that accompanies genius, have contrived to invent a life as recklessly entangled as Wright's had become by the early nineteen-twenties. He was well into his fifties and presumably at the height of his powers; his opportunities ought to have been unlimited, and yet it was his fate to see them vanish again and again into thin air or be seized by others far less capable than he of satisfactorily fulfilling them. Once he had liked to boast that the Lloyd Jones motto was "truth against the world," with the unspoken proviso that "truth" was, in fact, a synonym for Frank Lloyd Wright; now he began to fear that the family motto meant that the world was against him and not that he was against the world: a dangerous fear to entertain, since it might well lead to a retreat from reality and the eventual paralysis of his talent.

Writing of age, Henry James described it as a slow, reluctant march into the enemy country—the country of the general lost freshness. James argued that by preserving one's freshness one need never grow truly old. "We are all young to life," he said, and it was certainly the case with Wright that he remained invincibly youthful in spirit and that this youthfulness sustained him through many a dark passage. He would leap out of bed in the morning convinced that some unlooked-for good fortune was just about to provide a single happy solution to his multiplicity of problems; if by nightfall the solution had not yet arrived, tomorrow was another day. Meanwhile, there was the inescapable Protestant obligation to keep oneself busy. "I don't know where to turn at present," he wrote Lloyd, during a particularly bleak period, "but I know I've got to work like hell. That's all I ever really know."[1]

Among the problems that Wright failed to resolve was that of his wife. By law, he was entitled to seek a divorce on the grounds of voluntary separation for more than five years; in 1918, he had arranged with his attorneys to file a complaint against Catherine Tobin Wright in the circuit court of Sauk County, Wisconsin, alleging that the Wrights had been separated for the required number of years and that Wright wished "the bonds of matrimony now subsisting between the parties be wholly dissolved and that each of them be freed therefrom." For some reason, this action hung fire until the autumn of 1921, when Wright's attorneys undertook a new action, which led to the granting of an absolute divorce on November 13th, 1922. It is noted on the decree that Catherine was fifty-one, was employed as a social worker in Chicago, had not contested the divorce, and would be paid alimony.

Wright was forbidden by law to marry again until a year had passed. Since the relationship between Miriam and him had been deteriorating steadily throughout most of the six years that had passed since she had arrived at his doorstep to console him for the loss of his beloved Mamah, it was strange indeed that as soon as it became possible for him to marry Miriam he did so. In his autobiography, Wright claims that the wedding took place at midnight in late November, at the middle of the bridge that crosses the Wisconsin River just upstream from Taliesin. According to their marriage certificate, the wedding did indeed take place in Spring Green, on November 19th, 1923; it was presided over by his friend and attorney, Judge James Hill.

Why on earth did Wright marry Miriam? Perhaps in part and in some fashion that he took care not to examine, it was a response to the death

FLW's mother was buried in the Jones family graveyard. Her ambiguous epitaph echoes the family motto, "truth against the world."

of his mother, which took place in February of 1923, at the age of eighty-four. She had been in failing health, mental as well as physical, for a considerable period, and spent the last months of her life at a sanatorium in Oconomowoc, Wisconsin; the physician attending her there gave the cause of her death as "old age and anemia." She was buried in the little Lloyd Jones graveyard in Hillside; Wright failed to attend the service, as he had failed to attend his father's. His mother had been a termagant, in almost every respect unlike the heroic and lofty-spirited woman whom Wright depicted in his autobiography; still, he had been her favorite and he saw nothing unnatural in her insistence upon remaining physically close to him, forgiving him every transgression of the moral and social standards to which she had sought to bind him. The loss of so powerful a force in his life was bound to leave Wright feeling untethered and ill at ease; at that moment, he may have turned for reassurance to Miriam, as he had turned to her after Mamah's death, and it may be that Miriam herself became at that moment a convincingly sympathetic surrogate for the lost loved one.

Wright claimed that he had hoped by marrying Miriam to help their relationship, but "with marriage she seemed to lose what interest she had in life at Taliesin . . . the circumstances becoming more than ever violent, even dangerous, I consulted Dr. William Hixon, a famous psychiatrist of Chicago."[2] Dr. Hixon informed Wright that Miriam's case was hopeless and that Wright would be in constant physical danger if he were to remain in her presence—all the more reason, therefore, for Wright to be grateful when in April, 1924, Miriam left Taliesin in order to set up housekeeping in Los Angeles. Once more in single possession of his kingdom, Wright in spite of mounting financial problems played to the hilt his favorite multiple role as host, high priest, artist, flirt, and patriarch:

> Young people had come from all over the world attracted by Taliesin's fame abroad to share its spirit; to learn, I suppose, what message the indigenous United States had for Europe. And, evenings, after good work done, the piano, violin, and cello spoke there the religion of Bach, Beethoven, and Handel. William Blake, Samuel Butler, Walt Whitman, and Shelley often presided. Carl Sandburg, Edna Millay, and Ring Lardner, too, had something to say or sing. And life in the hills revived for the little cosmopolitan group eager to know this "America," for Taliesin was at work quietly Americanizing Europe while American architects Europeanized America.[3]

In the fall of that year, Wright announced that after January 1st, 1925, his architectural practice would be conducted out of an office in Chicago at 19 East Cedar Street, a couple of doors away from where he had once rented an apartment. He filed plans with the building department for the remodeling of the premises there, but his intentions appear to have been thwarted by a number of adverse events, including a fire in April, 1925, that for the second time threatened to burn Taliesin to the ground. Wright tells the story with such relish that one cannot help suspecting him of a primordial admiration for fire—fire as being equally a source of life and its destroyer. A fireplace served as the sacred central place of every house he designed; fires burning on broad stone hearths were for him metaphors of the warmth generated by the gathering-in of family life. One kindled a fire out of love; at the same time, one feared fire, as a perhaps uncontrollable adversary. There were to be several outbreaks of fire at Taliesin over the years and according to local gossip at least one of them was begun by Wright himself, acting on an unlucky impulse. Out for a stroll, he saw that a hayfield adjacent to Taliesin had been left too long unmown; having made sure that the wind was blowing away from the house, Wright struck a match to the dry grass, which readily caught fire; all too soon the wind changed direction and the burning field threatened to consume the house. Farmhands and volunteer firemen from nearby Spring Green were summoned, hoses were laid, and the fire was doused. On another occasion, Wright ordered an apprentice who had been heaping some dead brush to dispose of it by burning it. Again the adjacent field caught fire, again Taliesin was threatened, again the local volunteer firemen were summoned, and as the fire was being quenched Wright, striding up and down in front of the crowd of onlookers that had gathered, began sketching with his cane in air the new barns that he would build if the old barns were to be consumed. In New York City to oversee the building of the Guggenheim Museum, he once managed to fill his suite at the Plaza Hotel with smoke when he attempted to start a fire in a blocked-up fireplace; the blaze was quickly extinguished, leaving him little excuse for rebuilding or redecoration. In describing fire, Wright's prose always gains a genuine eloquence:

When about a year after I had finally separated from Miriam, one evening at twilight as the lightning of an approaching storm was playing and the wind rising, I came down from the evening meal in the little detached dining room on the hill-top to the dwelling on the court below to find smoke pouring from my bedroom. Again—there it was—Fire!

Fire fanned by that rising storm meant a desperate fight. My heart was sad as I realized all had gone from the place for the evening but two besides myself. Mell, the driver, and Kameki, a Japanese apprentice.

I called for water. And water came to the constant cry of "Water!" for two hours. I thought I had put out the fire when an ominous crackling above the bedroom ceiling indicated fire had got into the dead spaces beneath the roof. I sent alarm out again, and again the people of the countryside came in and turned to fight flames at Taliesin.

The rising wind blew the flames—raging now beneath the roof surfaces—out above the roof in a dozen places. "Let us save what we can of the things inside," they cried.

"No, fight the fire. Fight. Fight, I tell you. Save Taliesin or let all go!" I shouted. I was on the smoking roofs, feet burned, lungs seared, hair and eyebrows gone, thunder rolling as the lightning flashed over the lurid scene, the hill-top long since profaned by crowds of spectators standing silent there. . . . I could not give up the fight. . . . Suddenly a tremendous pealing roll of thunder and the storm broke with a violent change of wind that rolled the great mass of flame up the valley. It recoiled upon itself once as the rain fell hissing into the roaring furnace. But the clouds of smoke and sparks were swept the opposite way. . . . In that terrible twenty minutes, the living half of Taliesin was gone—again! . . . Everything I had in the world, besides my work, was gone. . . .

A few days later clearing away still smoking ruin to reconstruct, I picked from the debris partly calcined heads of the Tang Dynasty, fragments of the black basalt of a splendid Wei-stone, soft-clay Sung sculpture, and gorgeous Ming pottery that had turned the color of bronze by the intensity of the fire. All sacrificial offerings to whatever gods may be, I put the fragments aside to weave them into the masonry fabric of Taliesin III. Already in mind it was to stand in place of Taliesin II. And I went to work again to build better than before because I had learned from building the other two.[4]

The fire was estimated to have caused a quarter of a million dollars' worth of damage; Wright had something like thirty thousand dollars' worth of fire insurance and, as usual, no readily available assets except his Japanese prints. (It was at about this time that he finally disposed of his Oak Park house, which Darwin D. Martin had been helping him carry for a number of years; Catherine Wright, her children grown, by then was occupying a small apartment in Chicago.) How Wright managed to rebuild Taliesin and keep adding to it, making it one of the grandest country estates in America, when he was continuously in debt and often enough at a loss to find the wherewithal to buy groceries, remains more or less his secret; it is hard for ordinary mortals to run up large debts in comparatively small communities, where people are likely to estimate accurately how long they will have to wait for payment. From his earliest days in Oak Park, Wright had earned a reputation for being either "slow-pay" or a deadbeat, and with every passing year his extravagances and his inability to support his extravagances marched hand in hand; he was as irresponsible and, at times, as unethical as a Mississippi riverboat gambler, and yet he was so incomparably charming a self-promoter that in a crisis he could always count on a few friends to stand by his side, attempt to impose order on his affairs, and plead with him (of course in vain) to reform.

As careless—or, to put it more accurately, as unscrupulous—as Wright was in financial matters, he was equally careless or unscrupulous in sexual matters. At the time of his running off with Mamah Cheney, Catherine Wright informed the press that her husband was "as clean as a baby," but nearly everyone else in Oak Park was skeptical of the degree of fidelity that this figure of speech implied. When he and Catherine paid their long visit to Japan with the Willitses, there is some reason to suppose that Wright was agreeably surprised by the nature of the sexual customs he encountered there. (Richard Bock, the Wrights' close friend, reports in his unpublished autobiography that Mrs. Wright did not enjoy the trip, though she subsequently enjoyed lecturing about it to her fellow clubwomen in Oak Park.) Even with Mamah, Wright devised a life in which she remained immured at Taliesin while he spent most of every week in Chicago. He and Miriam became lovers within a few weeks of Mamah's death; less than a year later, she was accusing him of sleeping with younger women. Miriam is by no means a reliable witness, but he was certainly involved with other women during the course of their turbulent, long-drawn-out misalliance; indeed, at one point he was sufficiently in love with someone—her name known to a few scholars but as yet unpublishable—to propose marriage to her, not once but several times. When he fell in love with Olgivanna, in the late fall of 1924, he was eager to install her at Taliesin as soon as possible, but he had to make sure that Miriam, by then his wife, was out of the way; according to rumor, there was also a young woman, an undergraduate at the University of Wisconsin, to be gently removed from the premises.

Given Wright's knack for turning fact into fiction, one is bound to be skeptical of his account of the first meeting between him and Olgivanna. It amounts to what he would call a *romanza,* and it is possible, if not likely, that, at a moment in his life when he was in need of an agreeable surprise, life in its indiscriminately blundering fashion provided him with one. Feeling "lower down in my own estimation than I had ever been in my life," Wright and a male friend had decided to while away a Sunday afternoon in Chicago by attending a matinee performance of a Russian ballet company. Just after the performance began, "a dark, slender gentlewoman . . . unobtrusive but lovely"[5] was shown into the seat beside Wright's friend—the only empty seat in the house. In the darkness of the auditorium, Wright secretly observed the new arrival. To his friend, Wright volunteered a rebuke of both the performance and the audience: "They are all dead. The dead are dancing to the dead." As he had intended, the remark was overheard by their neighbor, who threw him "a quick, comprehending glance," and "the glance went home: a strange elation stole over me." At the intermission, the two men scraped acquaintance with the dark-haired gentlewoman and invited her to have tea with them after the performance. She accepted the invitation in a low, musical voice, "with perfect ease and without artificial hesitation. I was in love with her. It was all as simple as that."[6]

Over the next few days, Wright and the young woman became friends. He learned that her name was Olga Ivanovna Milanov Hinzenberg, that she was called Olgivanna for short, and that she was (or said she was) twenty-six years of age. She had been born in Cetinje, in what had been, before the First World War, the mountainous little independent kingdom of Montenegro and was now one of the pieces in the newly created jigsaw-

Olgivanna and baby Iovanna. [EWI]

puzzle of a nation called Yugoslavia; her father had been a judge and one of her grandfathers had been a well-known Montenegrin general and patriot. She had been educated privately in Russia and Turkey, had married in her teens a Russian architect named Vlademar Hinzenberg, and had had a daughter by him, born in 1917 and named Svetlana. Hinzenberg was a naturalized American citizen, living in Chicago. Olgivanna had been separated from him for several years; she made her home at the Gurdjieff Institute for the Harmonious Development of Man, in Fontainebleau, where she helped to teach the principles of the then much praised philosopher-magus, Georgi Gurdjieff. (The Gurdjieff cult still flourishes, especially in New York City.) Olgivanna had come to New York City with Gurdjieff and a group of his disciples to put on an exhibition of dances at Carnegie Hall; she and her daughter stayed with her brother Vladimir and his family in Hollis, a suburb of New York. She had journeyed to Chicago in order to settle certain family matters with Hinzenberg and had been planning to return in a few days to New York, pick up Svetlana in Hollis, and return to Fontainebleau.

Wright wooed Olgivanna ardently throughout the late fall of 1924 and by early in the new year they were lovers, happily at home at Taliesin. (Not that Wright was admitting it; to his son Lloyd in February he writes dolefully, "I have been alone now a couple of months, but I've been alone really for many years, so there is no great hardship in the fact, although

291

I need help.") Soon enough Olgivanna had managed to secure an uncontested divorce from Hinzenberg and had brought little Svetlana on from Hollis. For his part, Wright was hoping soon to obtain a divorce from Miriam, whose financial demands varied from one day to the next, more because they were a means of punishing Wright than because they were important to her. The divorce became all the more necessary to Wright when it turned out that Olgivanna was pregnant; in December, she gave birth to a daughter, whom she and Frank named Iovanna. Miriam took advantage of the birth of the baby to engage in further dithering over the terms of the divorce and to grant many interviews with the press—interviews providing a notoriety that was the next-best thing to fame. She pictured herself as a tragic figure fighting for survival against high odds, while Frank and his young mistress reveled in their sinfulness at Taliesin, Miriam's rightful home.

Vexed by Miriam's publicity-seeking, in early summer Wright cancelled negotiations for a divorce. Miriam responded by attempting to break into Taliesin, which caused Olgivanna and the baby to go into hiding and led Wright to garner some publicity of his own. In his usual guise of seeking only to pacify everyone, Wright published a letter in the Spring Green weekly newspaper, calling on his neighbors to understand his version of "truth against the world," which included his "honest" relationship with Olgivanna (his neighbors may have recalled hearing from him how "honest" his relationship with Miriam had been in the years before he married her, how "honest" his relationship with Mamah had been in their unmarried state) and his desire to remain at Spring Green, "working until I die. I want to mind my own business and not be subject to public question if I can help it."[7] The letter is indeed a touching document; it is addressed "To the Countryside," which is very much in the manner of a grand seigneur addressing his peasants, but it is signed, "Such as I am, with affection, your Frank Lloyd Wright," and in those words a genuine emotion of contrition and lonely self-doubt is evoked.

"Not be subject to public question if I can help it"—what extraordinary words these are, when spoken by a man who from his twenties to his nineties sought always to be at the center of public attention and behaved in a fashion so determinedly outrageous as to be bound to produce a continuous avalanche of questions from friends, neighbors, total strangers, and even from members of his own family. Something in him courted failure as ardently as it courted success, and it was indispensable to him that the courtship should take place in the presence of as many people as possible. In international politics after the Second World War, the term brinksmanship became a common descriptive term; before the word existed, Wright embodied the activity not only throughout his middle years but—at least in respect to his finances—on into old age as well, with a perverse

Above, this newspaper photograph was accompanied by a juicy caption, which read in part, "Love-nest of F. Lloyd Wright and Dancer. Here is the bungalow on Lake Minnetonka, near Minneapolis, into which the long arm of the law reached and dragged forth Frank Lloyd Wright, internationally-famous architect, and his affinity, Mrs. Olga Milanoff, Montenegrin dancer. . . ." [MPL]   *Right, Olgivanna and Iovanna at Lake Minnetonka.* [MJ]

skill born of long practice. So great was his virtuosity in repeatedly risking disaster that we must be on our guard against supposing that the suffering he underwent in the course of his chosen ordeals was not every bit as authentic as the suffering that ordinary mortals would have felt in the same circumstances. He *did* suffer, and perhaps, given his genius, more than the rest of us would have done, but he suffered with a kind of relish, and the source of that relish remains one among his many secrets. Behind the mask of anguish lies, perhaps to our surprise, a true anguish, but why has he invited it, and not once but many times?

In his brisk precis of Wright's "time of troubles," Twombly compares the events of the period to a Horatio Alger novel, though in the case of Alger's heroes conventional virtue can be counted on to triumph over evil and in Wright's case Miriam and he were about equally at fault. In late August Miriam filed a suit against Olgivanna for alienation of affections, asking one hundred thousand dollars in damages, despite the fact that Wright was not known to have met Olgivanna until after he had left Miriam. Acting, so he was later to claim, on the advice of his attorney, Wright went into hiding with Olgivanna, Svetlana, and Iovanna. He tells the story in his autobiography; characteristically, though he was short of money, their means of transportation was one of the costliest cars on the market: "My little family and I . . . set out in the Cadillac for somewhere. Why not go to Minneapolis? [Lake] Minnetonka was beautiful. . . . We found a charming cottage at Minnetonka owned by a Mrs. Simpson. I persuaded her that she needed a vacation and she let us take the house as it stood. . . . We were to be the Richardsons or something. We kept forgetting to remember who we were."[8] Meanwhile, Olgivanna's ex-husband, Hinzenberg, was persuaded by Miriam's lawyers to join in her mischief-making. First, he secured an injunction against Olgivanna, in order to prevent her from taking Svetlana out of the country; then he obtained a writ of habeas corpus by means of which he hoped to secure custody of Svetlana, on the not very logical grounds that Olgivanna's giving birth to a baby proved her unfit to be a mother. Finally, Hinzenberg sought the arrest of Wright and Olgivanna as fugitives under the Mann Act—the same act that the infamous Mrs. Breen had unsuccessfully invoked many years earlier in respect to Wright and Miriam.

In that same crowded month of September, the Wisconsin Savings Bank foreclosed a twenty-five-thousand-dollar mortgage that it had long held on Taliesin. Wright owed the bank eighteen thousand dollars over and above the mortgage; to protect its interests, the bank took possession of the property and made plans to auction it off, along with its contents. By then, Miriam had won a court order granting her joint access to the property; the bank therefore took care to secure an injunction forbidding either Wright or Miriam from entering the grounds of Taliesin. Two or three more suits sprang up in imitation of the earlier suits and Hinzenberg posted a five-hundred-dollar reward for Wright's arrest on the charge of having abducted Svetlana. Late one evening, a sheriff, accompanied by lawyers, reporters, and photographers, arrived at the Simpson cottage, arrested Wright, and hauled him off to the Hennepin County Jail, in Minneapolis, where he spent the night. The next morning, he appeared in court, where the charge of abduction was dismissed. He and Olgivanna were then conducted to a Federal court, to deal with the Mann Act charges. It emerged that, shortly after Iovanna's birth, Wright had taken Olgivanna on a holiday to Puerto Rico; this amounted to a technical violation of her status as an alien resident, and it took Wright a second night in jail and several weeks of litigation before "the little family" was free to leave Minne-

FLW being led off to jail. [MPL]

sota. On the eve of their departure, Wright must have been astonished to receive a friendly salute from a local newspaper. In a leading editorial, the *Twin City Reporter* wrote:

"Morally we are right, legally we are wrong."

This statement has become more or less famous in Minneapolis since Frank Lloyd Wright, internationally famous architect, and his companion, Mme. Olga Milanoff, were arrested in a cottage at Lake Minnetonka a week ago.

The case of Wright and his companion is indeed a strange one so far as the feelings of the people in this part of the country are concerned. Sympathy seems to be all with Wright and the woman whom he swears he loves and who is the mother of a child born out of wedlock as the result of her association with Wright. Most everyone in discussing the case expresses the wish that Wright and Mme. Milanoff succeed in "beating" the charges, grave in nature, brought against them by the State of Wisconsin and the United States government.

Wright is a famous man. He is one of the foremost architects in the world. Monuments to his skill are many. Genius that he is in his chosen profession, his life so far as the married side is concerned has been one blunder after another. Perhaps it is the obvious mercenary attitude the former Mrs. Wright, Miriam Noel, of Chicago, is taking in her attitude toward Wright that has aroused so much sympathy. . . . If he loves Mrs. Milanoff [sic], is willing to marry her and provide a home for her and the children . . . then why not make the road to happiness . . . easy for him?[9]

This editorial appears to have been in response to an "open" letter that Wright had distributed to the press, in vehement protest against the indignities he had undergone:

My work secured my fame. Therefore, notoriety has been thrust upon my life industriously for fifteen years past, until now it seems to swamp the fame. Why? I could explain and insult my country. I could justify myself and disappoint almost everybody. I will do neither. . . . On the one hand, a poor, deluded woman . . . vowing that she would "hound him to the ends of the earth." On the other hand, a man trying for nearly a year to shield his baby girl and her frail mother from these lusts, seeking in many places retirement to work and get her well again and let the baby girl grow strong. That name of mine would pursue them wherever we would go.

And tapped wires, intercepted telegrams, detectives, reporters everywhere. Photographers, lawyers, Kikes [sic] and shysters who played upon an outraged father, beyond his knowledge and drew him into their scheme as a tool. Prosecuting attorneys and process servers. Attacking parties of newspapermen, led by the suffering "wife." Bailiffs, courts, police, reward claimers, venal servants, blackmail. . . . Sheriffs led by newspaper parties, and jail, and newspaper parties led by sheriffs. Immigration officers and now investigators of the Department of Justice of these United States. . . .[10]

In his usual fashion, Wright has worked himself up from a vivid description of the facts as he sees them in a particular situation to a description of himself as the innocent hero-victim of a corrupt society:

Regardless of morality or manhood or justice, they would break him now because he dared to be true. Because he asserted his right to love and work and life as greater and stronger than the empty title any selfish, scheming, heartless woman might unfairly bring against him with malicious intent, because divorce laws are what they are.

Yes, he has sinned, this man. The deadly sin in a democracy such as ours, for he has allowed his fellows to get the idea that he thinks he has ideas, and would stand upon their shoulders to save those ideas for them if he can. . . . To keep true individuality inviolate is the real business of our country.[11]

This preposterous identification of his personal problems with American democracy must have been highly irritating to a number of his friends,

FLW and Olgivanna in court, accompanied by their attorney. [MJ]

who, precisely because they were among the leading figures in that democracy, had been persuaded by Wright to publish in his behalf an open letter to the Federal District Attorney in Minneapolis, urging him "not to permit your high office to be used as an instrument of persecution and revenge."[12] The signers of the letter included Ferdinand Schevill, professor of history at the University of Chicago; Robert M. Lovett, editor of *The New Republic;* and the poet Carl Sandburg. How eager they must have been for Wright to keep his mouth shut on that occasion! But it was his nature never to be content with keeping silent, especially if he had been told that it would be prudent to do so. As for keeping silent as a gesture of gratitude to the friends who had risked their reputations in his behalf, nothing could have been less like him: family, colleagues, friends, clients, employees, and strangers encountered at random all served as the fuel that the fire of his ego wantonly consumed. Wright had an acute sense of humor, which failed him utterly when his selfish interests were at stake. Darwin D. Martin, who lent Wright many thousands of dollars (few of which were ever repaid) and upon whom Wright poured a continuous shower of insults, referred to him once as "a sassy debtor," and indeed he was sassy in every aspect of his life. His earliest reputation had been that of a spoiled child granted exceptional privileges by a doting mother; having been sassy from the cradle, he would go sassy to the grave.

Because Taliesin was forbidden to them, Wright, Olgivanna, and the children spent the winter of 1927 in a little rented cottage on the beach at La Jolla, California. In February, a third fire at Taliesin, blamed on faulty electrical wiring, did several thousand dollars' worth of damage to

Wright's books and architectural renderings. At the insistence of creditors, much of his large collection of Japanese prints—one of the finest in the country and valued by Wright at over a hundred thousand dollars—was sold at auction in New York City for less than forty thousand dollars. (Wright habitually overvalued his prints, but it was generally conceded that the sale was an unexpected financial disappointment. The proceeds went to the auction house, which had advanced at least that amount of money to Wright in the form of loans.) In May, Wright was in Madison, where the Wisconsin Savings Bank, with a total of forty-three thousand dollars in claims against him, offered him a year's grace in which to pay off his debts and regain possession of Taliesin. Meanwhile, Miriam, after weeks of negotiation, finally agreed to a divorce, which was granted to Wright in August. According to the terms of the divorce, she was to receive six thousand dollars in cash and an income of two hundred and fifty dollars

A strange love-hate postcard from FLW to Miriam Noel. [PF]

a month from a trust fund of thirty thousand dollars, provided by Wright (he being penniless, the actual money was provided by friends of Wright, working behind the scenes). Miriam went on making trouble on ever higher levels of irrationality, at one point breaking into Wright's house in La Jolla while Wright and Olgivanna were away and destroying several hundred dollars' worth of furniture. After falling ill in Hollywood, she died in Milwaukee, in 1930, of what was officially described as "exhaustion following delirium." Under "occupation," her death certificate recorded "none of late," followed by "formerly sculptress"—a sufficiently sad obituary for a woman whose early life had been so charged with promise. In her will, she left one dollar apiece to each of her blood relatives and all her jewelry and other personal possessions to a friend, Helen Raab. The jewels were thought to be of high value; on being put up for sale, they proved to be mostly of paste and brought a total of fifty-six dollars and fifty cents. Wright was reported in the press to owe her estate six thousand dollars; as far as the record shows, the sum was never collected. A couple of years after her death, the *Milwaukee Journal* published portions of her autobiography, in which she tells (in a prose that is at least a match for that of Walter Noble Burns) of the happy beginning and sad end of her affair with Wright. Some if it may be true; all of it was true for her:

> In that one long moment [of their first meeting] while I stood on the threshold trying desperately to regain my poise, Frank Lloyd Wright looked into my face with eyes that became strangely, subtly, brilliantly alive and magic happened to me. I felt my heart, which I had long thought dead, wake and glow and live. I lowered my lashes to veil the unbidden response I knew my eyes were making to his. But it was too late. . . .[13]

Miriam is soon quoting Ibsen to the effect that self-fulfillment is the highest attainment possible to a human being. She mourns the fact that most of us fall short of that attainment. Wright agrees with Ibsen and her:

> "How true!" he sighed, looking into the fire with eyes whose wistful pathos went to my heart as an arrow to its mark. "How wretchedly true of me."
>
> "You?" I exclaimed in surprise. "Surely you of all people have least cause to say that. Wherever you go you can see the story of your own success told in the enduring language of mortared brick and chiseled stone. Wherever art is appreciated, your creations are pointed out as examples of original beauty. You are at the very zenith of fortune and of fame."
>
> "Fame," he repeated bitterly. "What is fame but a circle in the water? In this tangled adventure called life, I have achieved fame, it is true. But what of it? Even while I wear my laurels thick upon me, I find them turned to a crown of thorns upon my brow. Fame has brought me pleasure, but it cannot bring me happiness."[14]

Many thousands of words later, the autobiography comes to its sorry end:

> When the divorce decree became final on August 25th, Frank and Olga were married.
>
> On the day they were married I had thought I could go no further into the depths of suffering, but that day was my Gethsemane. I knew there was nothing else in the world for me to live for.
>
> For me the day is done and I am in the dark.[15]

Immediately after Wright's divorce from Miriam, some of the same friends who had arranged to set up the trust fund in her behalf recruited a few more friends and established a corporation known as "Wright, Incor-

A stock certificate in "Frank Lloyd Wright, Incorporated," issued to Darwin D. Martin, who helped to devise the corporation and was well aware that the stock would prove worthless. [UB]

porated" (later to be reorganized as a corporation called "Frank Lloyd Wright, Inc."), the purpose of which was to free him from the Great Dismal Swamp of financial misery into which his repeated extravagances invariably led him. The corporation was capitalized at seventy-five thousand dollars; shareholders in the corporation would, in effect, own the fruits of Wright's professional labors and would distribute these fruits according to their best judgment, gradually paying off Wright's debts and granting him an allowance large enough to live on but not large enough to purchase—as he had been known to do—thousands of dollars' worth of luxuries in a single shopping spree.

Among the incorporators of this risky and peculiar enterprise were Wright's close friends Professor Schevill and Darwin D. Martin; his faithful client, Mrs. Avery Coonley; the designer Joseph Urban; Wright's sisters Jane and Maginel; and the writer Alexander Woollcott. Later investors were Harold McCormick, George Parker, Philip LaFollette, and Ben Page, who with Wright's encouragement was soon to marry Catherine Wright—a marriage that, taking place when Catherine was sixty-one and perhaps not altogether out of love with the husband she had lost twenty years earlier, proved unsatisfactory and soon ended in divorce. In May, 1928, Wright having been unable to earn enough money in the course of a year to discharge the bank's claims on Taliesin, the bank put the estate up for auction. It was known to the corporation that the bank itself was planning to bid in the property, which it did at the low price of twenty-five thousand dollars. Wright, Incorporated, then arranged a deal with the bank, paying off its claims at a favorable discount (the bank was evidently delighted to wash its hands of the troublesome Wright) and so gaining possession of Taliesin in the name of the corporation.

In August, a year after his divorce from Miriam and therefore, according to Wisconsin law, at the earliest opportunity, Wright married Olgivanna. This was exactly the procedure he had followed in marrying Miriam, five years before, and in a repetition of timing that might well have made Olgivanna uneasy, the wedding ceremony is said to have taken place at midnight—not, however, at the middle of a bridge but in the small, fashionable town of Rancho Santa Fe, inland from La Jolla. (Some accounts mistakenly place the ceremony in Santa Fe, New Mexico, thanks to Wright's careless ascription in his autobiography.) They passed their honeymoon in Phoenix, where Wright had spent much of the previous year at work on the Arizona Biltmore Hotel, and in October they were able to return at last to Taliesin.

The long-delayed wedding announcement. [LC]

18

Like most of the projects, realized
and unrealized, that Wright was involved in during the nineteen-twenties,
the Arizona Biltmore Hotel was a mingling of good and ill fortune—at
once an adventure and a misadventure. Among Wright's first clients in
Chicago had been a wealthy businessman named Warren McArthur, for
whom in 1892, while still in the employ of Adler & Sullivan, Wright had
designed one of his so-called bootlegged houses. In an early passage of
his autobiography, describing the confusion attendant upon the raising
of his six strong-willed and undisciplined children, Wright speaks of McArthur's having come to Sunday lunch at the little brown-shingled house in
Oak Park. McArthur "being something of a wag . . . caught one of the
children and called to me, 'Quick now, Frank, what's the name of this
one?' It worked. Surprised by the peremptory request I gave the wrong
name."[1]

A few years later, Albert McArthur, the youngest of Warren's three
sons, was provided with a beginner's job at the Oak Park studio. Young
though he was, he cultivated a beard and was promptly nicknamed "the
Goat." McArthur habitually overslept, and Isabel Roberts, in her unofficial
capacity as den mother of the Studio, found herself obliged every morning
to wake McArthur by telephone and urge him to make haste to his drafting
board. When Wright set off on his "spiritual hegira" with Mamah Cheney,
the Studio was closed and McArthur had to look elsewhere for his architectural training. Eighteen years later, McArthur, by then an architect practicing in Phoenix, was planning to build on the outskirts of the city, in what
was still open desert looking out toward Camelback Mountain, a resort
hotel to be called the Arizona Biltmore. The project was being promoted
by Albert and his brothers Warren, Jr., and Charles; the great economic
boom of the twenties was reaching a peak in 1927 and the brothers were
eager to lure Eastern millionaires to Phoenix during the winter months
with an array of amenities—golf, tennis, swimming, horseback riding, and

FLW and Iovanna at Taliesin North, negotiating a couple of obstacles. It may be that something has gone wrong with the water system; something often did. [EWI]

the like—in a setting equal in luxury to any of the best-known Florida and California winter resorts.

Wright, Olgivanna, and the children were uneasily perched at Taliesin (the Wisconsin Savings Bank was attempting to evict them as morally undesirable) when a letter arrived from Albert McArthur, outlining his plans for the hotel and asking Wright's advice as to the practicality of using concrete blocks in its construction, as Wright had used them in the construction of his houses in Los Angeles. Wright of course replied that his "textile" concrete blocks were a highly practical method of construction and that, if McArthur wished him to do so, perhaps he could come to Phoenix and lend a hand in designing blocks suitable for the Biltmore and in showing the local contractor how to manufacture them. To the Wrights' delight, McArthur reacted favorably to this suggestion, and early in 1928 the Wrights were able to exchange the cold and snow of Wisconsin for the warmth and sunlight of Arizona—to exchange, also, for the general disapproval of the Spring Green community the sympathetic friendship, renewed after many years, of the three McArthur brothers and their widowed mother. A contract was drawn up between the hotel corporation and Wright, giving him a salary of a thousand dollars a month, seven thousand dollars for the use of his method of textile-block construction, and a promise that the McArthurs would use their best efforts to secure a further payment of fifty thousand dollars for the use of the blocks if the hotel were to prove sufficiently profitable.

To this day, the extent of Wright's contribution to the design of the Arizona Biltmore remains a matter of dispute. It was certainly a condition of his employment that he remain behind the scenes and he spoke candidly of having done so (though to speak of being behind the scenes is to hint strongly that one isn't altogether idle there). By the time the main building

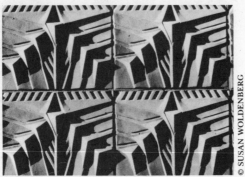

Concrete block that Wright designed for use at the Arizona Biltmore Hotel. The overall pattern varies according to how the blocks are laid up.

and its scattering of nearby cottages had been completed, in 1929, gossip held that Wright and not McArthur had been their designer. Over the years, McArthur was increasingly distressed to discover that the gossip had been given the dignity of publication both in magazines and books. In a letter to *The Architectural Record,* he wrote, "Now that these false statements have found their way into the public record, I am placed in an equivocal position. . . . I have in my possession, besides all the originals of the plans, details, specifications, contracts, and correspondence incident to the project, sufficient other documents to prove that I was the architect of these buildings, and that Mr. Wright's relation to the project was no more than that of a private consultant to me, and to me only, for the specific purpose of the technical application of his invention, the 'Textile-Block-Slab Construction.' "[2] According to McArthur, soon after the building was completed and in anticipation of just such a controversy, he solicited a statement from Wright, confirming these facts. The *Record* printed the statement in full:

> All I have done in connection with the building of the Arizona Biltmore, near Phoenix, I have done for Albert McArthur himself at his sole request, and for none other.

Albert McArthur is the architect of that building—all attempts to take the credit for that performance from him are gratuitous and beside the mark.

But for him, Phoenix would have had nothing like the Biltmore, and it is my hope that he may be enabled to give Phoenix many more beautiful buildings as I believe him entirely capable of doing so.[3]

The more closely this statement is studied, the more peculiar it becomes. The first paragraph leaves open the possibility that Wright did indeed design the hotel, at the sole request of McArthur. The second paragraph gives McArthur official credit for the building, but to people familiar with the profession it would be well known that such official credit is often given to the person who signs the blueprints and not to the person who has actually prepared the design. The third paragraph praises McArthur for giving Phoenix something that it wouldn't otherwise have had, which is a way of saluting the creation of the hotel without addressing the subject of its design. The paragraph ends with a pious hope that McArthur will be able to give Phoenix many more beautiful buildings because he is capable of designing them—not, be it noted, because he has proved capable of designing the particular building under discussion.

The pride of the entire McArthur family became linked to the question of who had designed the Arizona Biltmore for a variety of reasons, among which were the high cost of the buildings (far above the estimate that Wright had given them, based on the presumed cheapness of his concrete block); their consequent difficulties in respect to financing; and finally the stock market crash of 1929, which ended for the time being any prospect of the hotel's securing the wealthy Eastern patronage for which it was intended. After the crash, the McArthur brothers lost control of the project, which was taken over at a bargain price by William Wrigley, the chewing-gum king. In a coupling of financial disaster and personal distress, the brothers had reason to seek a scapegoat and reason as well to choose Wright; the one worthwhile asset remaining out of the debacle of the Biltmore was the distinction of its design, and the McArthurs were not inclined to surrender that asset to their scapegoat.

For his part, Wright behaved well, perhaps because he was indeed partly to blame for much that had gone wrong. Though he may have pretended otherwise to the McArthurs, in fact he had little firsthand dollars-and-cents knowledge of the concrete-block construction that he had designed; in the case of the California houses, that practical aspect of their use had been under the supervision of his son Lloyd, who had been in charge of the building of a total of eleven concrete-block houses, designed either by his father or himself. As soon as the McArthurs had put Wright under contract, he wrote Lloyd for detailed information about the making of the blocks, as well as about their cost, but he lacked Lloyd's daily on-site experience. The building authorities in Phoenix were skeptical of the structural soundness of the blocks and insisted upon far heavier steel framing of the entire building than Wright's specifications called for; moreover, the local contractors, being unfamiliar with the manufacture and handling of the blocks, cultivated their unfamiliarity in order to prove that concrete blocks were more expensive than any conventional method of building.

Wright's unaccustomed benignity in dealing with the McArthurs may have been prompted less by a feeling of guilt over his share in the failure of the hotel (he had shared in many another failure without contrition) than by Olgivanna's newly achieved influence. Wright and she had had their baby, they had been able to live together for the first time as a family with a regular source of income and in agreeable domestic circumstances in Phoenix and La Jolla, and they were looking forward to being married—reasons enough for Olgivanna to begin, in a near-wifely and altogether European fashion, to temper his impetuousness. Let McArthur have whatever credit his professional pride forced him to seek! Let the evidence of the buildings themselves suffice to establish authorship, and all the more so since if they were given to McArthur, he would go down in history as

© SUSAN WOLDENBERG

Façade of the Arizona Biltmore. The architect of record, Albert McArthur, and his backers insisted for financial reasons on making the structure bigger than FLW wished it to be.

one of the most devout, not to say most abject, of the imitators of a great original.

The evidence of the buildings happens to be strongly in favor of Wright. The main building is four stories high and Wright used to criticize it on that account, stating that the building was intended to have but three stories (the added story was for added revenue); if in imagination one removes the top story, one sees how intensely Wrightian the profile of the building against the sky would be. As for the lobby, which even as it was built notably resembles the lobby of the Imperial Hotel, Wes Peters affirms that Wright had wished the level of the mezzanine ceiling above the registry desk to be much lower and that McArthur had insisted upon the present height; as (again in imagination) we drop the mezzanine ceiling by a couple of feet, we see at once the telltale difference between Wright's boldness and McArthur's blandness. But it is in the cottages rising from the velvety lawns of the hotel that one perceives Wright's hand most clearly. The cottages are ravishing little cubes, themselves composed of cubelike concrete blocks, whose patterns are molded in depth to accept and refract the brilliant Arizona sunlight. They remind us immediately of La Miniatura in being toylike and yet ample—palaces playfully so reduced in scale as to strike us at first glance as being scarcely larger than dolls' houses. Surely the occupants, whoever they may be when not on holiday, are here but grown-up children, without a care in the world.

The increasing prosperity of the times fostered scores of other projects for the entertainment of the upper middle classes, and Wright was invited to be the designer of several of the best of them. Besides the soon abandoned Doheny and Lake Tahoe projects, Wright designed for a Chicago business-man named Gordon Strong an oddity intended to crown a mountain in Maryland. What came to be called the tourist industry was just getting under way in this country, thanks to the increasing popularity of automo-biles, and the go-getting Strong was unself-consciously eager to defile his mountain by turning it into an elaborate tourist facility. Dominating a variety of shops and restaurants would be a gigantic spiral ramp, which Wright christened "The Automobile Objective" and which resembled in shape a Brueghel-like version of the Tower of Babel. The interior of the ramp would contain a planetarium, possibly for no better reason than that it was a vast, windowless space unsuitable for any other purpose; from the double lanes of the ramp automobiles would ascend and descend (presumably at a speed moderate enough to discourage accidents), giving drivers and passengers alike a bird's-eye view of the surrounding country-side. Wright and Strong had a falling-out and The Automobile Objective was never built, but, as was so often the case with Wright, once a concept had entered his mind, he never let it go; the spiral emerged again and

Exterior of one of the cottages, whose interiors—like those of "La Miniatura" and, later, the Price Tower—are marvels of three-dimensional manipulation.

One of the pergolas connecting the hotel to cottages scattered seemingly at random in the hotel grounds.

again in the years to come, in a shop (San Francisco), an automobile show-room (New York City), a parking garage (Pittsburgh), and at last, trium-phantly, a museum (also in New York City).

Of the unbuilt projects, Wright nominated in his autobiography as the most nearly flawless in design the resort hotel San Marcos in the Desert, which he was commissioned to build by Alexander Chandler, a successful hotel-owner and promoter. Having begun his career as a veterinarian, Chandler took care to retain the title of "Dr." in the course of accumulating considerable wealth in Arizona real estate. The town in which he had built a small, fashionable hotel called the San Marcos bore his name; now in his late years he was planning to build, on a tract of several thousand acres in the high mountain desert, a new and unprecedentedly lavish hotel. Meeting with Wright, he told him—one master of blarney to another!—that he had been seeking for ten years a man worthy to design a building on such a site. Taken to see it, Wright agreed with Dr. Chandler both as to the beauty of the setting and as to his being the only architect worthy to heighten its beauty with his handiwork. That was in the late summer of 1927; by early October, on his way back to Taliesin from La Jolla, Wright stopped off at Chandler to show the Doctor a set of drawings, to which he gave instant approval.

With the promise of a substantial fee (most of which would go, of course, to Frank Lloyd Wright, Inc., for the continued liquidation of his debts), Wright set to work in his newly restored workshop at Taliesin on the plans for San Marcos in the Desert. In January, he received a telegram from Dr. Chandler, urging him to come out to Arizona and design San Marcos on the spot. At that moment, Taliesin was snowbound; a blizzard was raging and the temperature stood at twenty-two degrees below zero. Wright was quick to accept the Doctor's invitation. He and his family and the handful of young draftsmen—his "boys"—whom he had hired to assist him on the San Marcos project bundled themselves into three or four cars and set out for Arizona. "Held off so long from active creation," he wrote in the autobiography, "I could scarcely wait to begin. . . . After nearly seven years of waste and turmoil here a great opportunity came to me: an ideal site unspoiled, the man promoting it well up to the thing he wanted done. Something like this is the rarest good fortune in any architect's life."[4]

Arriving in Chandler, Wright found that it would cost him several thousand dollars to rent space enough to shelter his family and the "boys." He proposed to Dr. Chandler that if a small portion of land could be provided near the site of the proposed hotel, he and the boys would build a temporary camp there. Dr. Chandler, always as adventurous as Wright, at once agreed to the proposal and chose for the campsite a rocky plateau with a superb view of the entire desert floor. With his usual seemingly

Whether times were good or bad, FLW always treated himself to the best of automobiles. In the Arizona desert, he poses in a 1928 Packard straight-eight touring car, complete even to a tonneau windshield. [AU]

effortless speed, in a couple of days Wright had drawn up plans for the camp—fifteen little cabins with floors and walls of cheap roughly sawn lumber and with roofs and window openings protected only by canvas, rigged like sails and thus capable of being raised or lowered according to need (the temperature of the desert was blazing hot by day, very cold by night). The cabins were joined by a zigzag board fence, forming a compound; cabins and fence were painted what Wright called a dry-rose color, to match the light on the desert floor. The canvas triangles in the gables of the cabins were painted a bright scarlet, like the blossom of the ocotillo plant, after which the camp was named. Wright described the camp as resembling "a group of gigantic butterflies with scarlet wing spots, conforming gracefully to the crown of the outcropping of black splintered rock . . . a human gaiety in the desert is under way."[5]

At first without electricity or conventional plumbing, the Wright party rejoiced in their primitive quarters, eating meals in the open, "in a dining-room sixty miles wide," and going to bed almost as soon as the sun. And at Ocatillo (Wright chose to "improve" the name of the plant by misspelling it as the name of the camp), happier than he had been in many years, Wright worked from late January until early June upon the plans for San Marcos in the Desert, bringing to bear upon them forty years of thought and training. In his autobiography, he writes:

We worked out the "resort" as a great block-system series of intercommunicating terraces facing to the sun of the south. There were three of these terraces, each room [of a total of three hundred] with its own pool and garden, one terrace rising above the other against the mountainside. . . . The block system in this case is genuine reinforced masonry, the same within and without. The block shell here will be integral with the structure. It is the structure itself. . . .

The plan of this far-flung, long-drawn-out building, owing to the placing of the levels of the sun-lit terraces, is such that each room, each bathroom, each closet, each corridor even, has direct sunlight. Every portion of the building to be lived in is free to the sun and also to magnificent views. . . . And the whole structure would approximate what we call permanent—say three hundred years at least. . . .

So, of course, it was all too good to happen. Sometimes I think it was just a dream. But here are the completed plans, there you may see the carefully studied details. Responsible estimates were complete; the contract was signed by Paul Mueller, the good builder, awaiting the Doctor's signature.

Then at that moment as Dr. Chandler took the train to complete the arrangements for coming to build came the crash of 1929. Where was Dr. Chandler? There with the quick "comeback." Now instead of a $40,000 fee, I found myself with a deficit of $19,000 to add to the mounting mountain of debt at Taliesin.[6]

As for Ocatillo, within a couple of months of its being finished, photographs of it were appearing in German and Dutch architectural magazines and later in magazines throughout the world. It had been intended to be temporary—Wright called it an ephemerid—and indeed it vanished within a year. The Wrights had returned to Taliesin for the summer and were planning to return to Ocatillo the following winter; the stock market crashed in October, 1929, and Dr. Chandler was obliged to put off—temporarily, as he then thought—the building of his hotel. (The Wrights continued to admire and feel a strong affection for Dr. Chandler despite the added financial burden that his own financial difficulties had placed upon them. In the nineteen-forties, the irrepressible Doctor, then in his late eighties, was still eager for Wright to build a dream-palace for him in the desert and Wright, knowing that it could never be, cheerfully walked over the site with Chandler and promised to prepare plans.) The Wrights remained at Taliesin during the winter of 1930, while in far-off Arizona the local Indians pillaged Ocatillo, presumably using much of it for fuel. "Yes," Wright noted ruefully, "the Indians carried it all away. But I have learned not to grieve long now that some work of mine has met its end; has had short life, as we say, even though it happens that a better one cannot take its place."[7] He was consoled, he said, by the thought that the machinery of publicity, otherwise in many ways so odious, helped to preserve representations of his designs, if not their actuality.

The boom of the twenties had been of little direct benefit to Wright. Had he not abandoned his promising career in Chicago, no doubt he would have prospered as a host of less gifted, more conventional architects were able to do; nor would his unconventionality as an architect have prevented the gaining of a number of important commissions in those

Interior of FLW's quarters at Ocatillo, the name FLW gave to a temporary camp in the Arizona desert; here he drew up plans for a luxurious resort hotel, San Marcos in the Desert. In FLW's view, no structure was so temporary as not to deserve a grand piano. [AU] A sample section of concrete block wall as designed for the San Marcos project; unbuilt, the hotel became one of what FLW called his "office tragedies." [AU]

boom times. The national impulse in the presence of seemingly unlimited amounts of easy money was toward experiment; it is in hard times that men grow cautious intellectually as well as in respect to their pocketbooks. Chicago was riding high, and Wright might well have ridden high as well; instead, he set out on a course that had for him the illusory advantage of appearing to be a fresh start, personally and professionally. Unluckily, it turned out to be neither; or, rather, it turned out to be a series of false fresh starts, begun with high hopes and ending in despair. When the crash came, Wright was in his sixties, deeper in debt than he had ever been and with little executed work to show for a decade of incessant striving. If the world thought of him at all, it was as an unruly old maverick who had thrown away his chances through arrogance and flagrant sexual misconduct.

The irony of Wright's position at the time of the crash was that he had never been fitter to accomplish works of genius than at the very moment that the opportunity to do so was taken from him. The bitterness of the loss of the masterly San Marcos project he sought to mitigate by a charming backward glance at his Japanese experience: "I have found that when a scheme develops beyond a normal pitch of excellence, the hand of fate strikes it down. The Japanese made a superstition of the circumstance. Purposefully they leave some imperfection somewhere to appease the jealousy of the gods. I neglected the precaution. San Marcos was not built."[8] But there were other projects, not quite so nearly perfect in his eyes, that the crash and not the jealousy of the gods brought to an abrupt halt. The most important of these projects was an apartment-house tower that he had been commissioned to design for land contiguous to the ancient church of St. Mark's in the Bouwerie, in New York City.

The rector of the church, the Reverend William Norman Guthrie, was an Episcopalian with notions about divine worship that were strikingly at odds with those of William Manning, the tightly buttoned bishop of the diocese; to the Bishop's distress, Guthrie believed that worship could readily embrace theatre, eurhythmic dancing, and other pagan practices. Guthrie was a superb amateur actor, in the pulpit and out of it, and had been a friend of Wright's for twenty years. Wright had designed a house for him in his native Tennessee; Guthrie having moved on to New York, the house was never built. It was Guthrie who had commissioned Wright, in 1926, to design another project fated never to be built—a steel cathedral in New York City that was to be over two thousand feet high (by far the highest structure on earth) and that was a source, thirty years later and on a much reduced scale, for the design of the Beth Sholom Synagogue, in Philadelphia.

Guthrie's powers of persuasion must have been almost equal to those of Wright himself; he was able to convince the vestry of St. Mark's that this scandalous figure out of the Middle West—an architect who had never built anything in the East and, affecting to despise New York City, had used it as a hideout in the midst of his extramarital legal difficulties—was the very man to design at least one and (if the one succeeded) perhaps three or four apartment towers of a revolutionary nature within the sacred precincts of the stern old church and its adjacent graveyard. In retrospect, it is easy to see that the towers would have been ideally unsuitable for that location, crowding in upon and effectively destroying the open, eighteenth-century setting of the church. One of the towers would have leaped straight up out of the graveyard tomb of many long-buried Stuyvesants, the church and the graveyard having been once a part of Peter

Another "office tragedy": the apartment-house project for St. Mark's in the Bouwerie. Not a tragedy to New York City, since the building would have effectively destroyed St. Mark's church and its ancient graveyard setting. [AU]

Stuyvesant's farm. Such considerations counted for little with Wright. Like most of his contemporaries and like many architects today, Wright felt an irritated impatience with the past; the Greeks with their tiresome dependence upon post-and-lintel, the Renaissance with its highfalutin misreading of Rome and Greece—there was scarcely a structure built later than Nineveh that Wright wouldn't have rejoiced to knock down in order to put one of his own in its place.

The thrilling oddity and elegance of the St. Mark's tower were never to be surpassed in Wright's oeuvre. The design sprang from studies that Wright had made earlier for still another unbuilt project of the twenties— the National Life Insurance Company skyscraper, on Water Tower Square, in Chicago, which Wright designed for the wealthy chief owner of the company, Albert M. Johnson. In his own way, Johnson was almost as great an eccentric as Wright. He was a fundamentalist in religion and a romantic in social relationships. For years he secretly financed the maintenance of a castle in the California desert, presided over by a paid puppet and publicity-seeker who called himself "Death Valley Scotty", and who pretended to be in possession of an inexhaustibly rich gold mine. Wright said of Johnson that he belonged to the type ordinarily called conservative "who, tempted, will sneak up behind an idea, pinch it in the behind, and turn and run." Sexually inhibited but intellectually adventurous, Johnson used to say, "Now, Mr. Wright, remember! I want a virgin. I want a virgin." The building that Wright produced for Johnson (and that Johnson failed to build, at first perhaps out of shyness in the presence of more virginity than he had counted on and later because of overwhelming financial reverses) was designed like a tree, with great steel-and-concrete masts rising from deep foundations and supporting floors that were cantilevered out from these masts as branches spring from a tree trunk. The floors grow thinner in section as they approach their outer edges, which support screening walls composed of panes of glass and lightweight, insulated copper spandrels. Wright tells of having brought the elevations and plans for the building to Louis Sullivan shortly before his death; according to Wright, Sullivan said, "I had faith that it would come. It is a work of great art. I knew what I was talking about all these years—you see? I could never have done this building myself, but I believe that, but for me, you could never have done it."[9] Wright agreed with his dying mentor, and why not? Sullivan's remarks paid an equal compliment to both of them. The engineering principles employed in the National Life Insurance building were also made use of in the St. Mark's tower, which, being intended for apartments instead of offices, had a far more intricate plan: forty interlocking duplex apartments, with four apartments on each of ten floors, all supported by a pinwheel-shaped central core containing four tiny, six-sided elevators, plumbing and electrical connections, and chimney flues.

Though the stock market crash no doubt deserves the chief blame for the abandonment of the St. Mark's tower project, the Reverend Dr. Guthrie was simultaneously engaged in a series of battles with Bishop Manning. Guthrie would have been hard put to it to carry through an unprecedented real-estate speculation like the tower unless he had had the full backing of his vestry and congregation; this he lost, and he and eurhythmic dancing and other advanced notions were politely ushered into exile. Nevertheless, as we have seen, no design that Wright believed in was ever truly abandoned; it was only postponed. San Marcos in the Desert might well find a builder today; as for St. Mark's in the Bouwerie, it emerged just over a full decade later, in the form of the grand Crystal Heights project in Washington, D.C., in 1940, which remained unbuilt, and, after another ten or twelve years, in the Price Tower, in Bartlesville, Oklahoma.

A project of the depression years that Wright was convinced would make him and his backers many millions of dollars (and that actually might have done so) was his design for a standardized, prefabricated gasoline filling station, which he hoped to sell to Texaco or Shell or one of the other big national companies. Filling stations of the time often imitated past styles—half-timbered Tudor and the like—just as private houses did. Wright called his design the "Overhead Service Station." Instead of gasoline pumps cluttering the ground level of the station, gasoline was stored inside a cantilevered, gable-roofed structure, with hoses hanging down at intervals, within easy reach of a large number of cars. Seeking partners in this new enterprise, he wrote to William R. Heath, of the Larkin Company, for whom he had designed a house in Buffalo almost thirty years earlier:

> Ye Gods! Driving up to the door of a sweet-pea cottage to get an engine-tank refilled with petrol! Why not put a white apron, clocked hose, and high heels on the attendant, let his hair grow to an attractive bob-length, and put a rose in his hair, to go with it. . . . I want to get a gas-station born that lives up to the nature of the affair as I see it. . . . Something that will grow by the roadside to meet the demand and acknowledge it as the trees and flowers do. . . . The major part should be machine-made and kept in stock to be assembled with variety to suit the occasion. . . . I am tired of camouflage and nasty-nice. The gas-station is rapidly taking the place of our old railway stations. . . . It has a future but not as a pseudo-colonial cottage, mind you, or anything like it. . . . Give me a chance, dear man![10]

Wright wrote in a similar vein to the most generous and forgiving of all his benefactors, Darwin D. Martin, Heath's colleague in the Larkin Company. Heath and Martin were both understandably leery of attempting any business relationship with Wright. Lacking their help, he was unable to build a prototype with which to tempt one or another of the big companies; reluctantly, Wright found a place for the service station among other unrealized ideals in his Utopian concept, Broadacre City. Many years later, he was given the opportunity to design a gas station in Clocquet, Minnesota; it was, and is, a grotesque affair, and to the degree that it embodies some of the attributes of the earlier station one breathes a belated sigh of relief on behalf of Heath and Martin.

Though Martin refused to back the gas station, his affection for Wright continued to withstand the many strains to which Wright habitually subjected it. To do this kindly man justice, we ought to glance back at the middle twenties for a moment, observing that it was Martin who managed by dint of one awkward financial feint or another to preserve Wright's remaining interest in the Oak Park property (this largely for the sake of Catherine Wright). It was Martin who consented to purchase a large block of stock in Frank Lloyd Wright, Inc., knowing that Wright would be sure to disregard his legal commitments to that corporation; and it was Martin who in his double role as client and soft touch bestowed many thousands of dollars upon Wright even as Wright was making him the object of almost continuous verbal abuse.

As we have seen, Martin and Wright had much in common; each had undergone a troubled childhood, had been forced at an early age to make his own way in the world, and had acquired a remarkable mastery of English literature and the art of letter-writing. Luckily for their friendship, they could find humor in unlikely situations. As Wright was seeking to separate himself forever from the tenacious Miriam, one of his lawyers had written to Martin, mentioning that Wright was unable to discover Miriam's whereabouts. In the certainty that Wright would be shown his reply, Martin wrote, "It is entirely of a piece with Wright's usual carelessness to have mislaid his second wife." At once Wright fired back at Martin:

> If you knew anything at all about wives (which of course you don't, having had only one), you would know they are not so easily mislaid as their husbands are misled. Mrs. W is in Los Angeles. . . . The confusion arose over her being in transit—literally. I am glad to see you haven't lost your punch, any more than I have my wife. . . . And let me tell you in this matter of being laid (mislaid or otherwise) they either do it themselves or it isn't done at all, among gentle people.[11]

A more characteristic letter from Wright to Martin, written in the same year (1925):

> This is my "bread and butter letter" to thank you for the bread and butter I did not get. It has since seemed to me such a sad reflection on human life and character—this affair of you and me and yours and mine.
>
> If you would lend me some of your stored-up power [that is, capital] instead of [lending it] to Kansas farmers or stock brokers, see what I could do with it! And you be none the loser except as you would write and write and worry and worry yourself to death for fear you would lose it.
>
> And this because, harassed and all but beaten down by my quarrel with the system or perhaps by ignoring it, I've made you await the course of events for repayment heretofore. Now, if at any time I had felt you were in need of that money or anything I had, you would have had it from me, just as others have had it in such circumstances. You can't believe that, but it is true.
>
> Now I've been struck by misfortune and am trying gallantly to "come back." You push my hands off the gunnel of your boat because I spent the interest I should have paid you "regularly" to pay you "irregularly" in a lump. Look at what surrounds you because you have met and known me and set it against the file of bootless correspondence you so effectively showed Heath at the critical moment. . . . I came to you as a brother in need and really my need was deep and wide, for I am unable to go on

to meet the load this last misfortune leaves upon my shoulders and carry on my work at all. . . .[12]

Wright goes on to say that Heath has described Martin as being worth several million dollars—why will not Martin spend a little of all that money on the purchase of some of Wright's Japanese prints and other Oriental treasures, which are all that Wright has left to dispose of? Wright has uttered this cry before and will utter it again; the patient Martin, already in possession of more Japanese prints than he wishes and having no desire to become a dealer in them, finds some means of tiding Wright over for a few months, and in the spring of 1926, filled with foreboding but once more irresistibly drawn to the grand mesmerizer, the Martins invite him to design a country house for them on the south shore of Lake Erie, fifteen or twenty miles west of Buffalo. At the height of his troubles with Miriam and constantly on the wing, Wright consents to design the house and then procrastinates, both in respect to its design and to visiting the site, which is a spectacular one on a high bluff overlooking the lake. Martin writes with disciplined annoyance, "Your client is Mrs. Martin. She is unable to travel [Mrs. Martin was slowly going blind and as a Christian Scientist was refusing medical attention] and everything must be made as easy as possible for her. . . . If a house is built, it is only for her pleasure and we must make a joy to her of the very planning and building. . . ."[13]

Wright provides his usual combative/embracing rejoinder:

No, Darwin D. Martin, my conscientious attention to any building problems entrusted to me is not dependent upon attitude toward me. As an artist, once I accept a commission the interest of the building as a fine thing as such, according to the human requirements, stands. And anyway I would do my best for Mrs. Martin, or you, either.[14]

Wright then goes on to say, insultingly enough, that Martin has never understood what is rightfully due an architect for his labors because he, Wright, has always spoiled him; and, speaking of money, would Martin please be kind enough to send five hundred dollars at once to Mrs. Catherine Wright, at her apartment in Chicago?

It is commonly said of Wright that in designing a house for a client he would brook no interference with what he believed to be in the client's best interests and that the client was therefore obliged to become the silent victim of Wright's aesthetic tyranny. This was sometimes the case but not always; moreover, in fairness to Wright it ought to be noted that when a strong-willed client collided with Wright the ironic consequence was often a worse house instead of a better. As we have seen, Darwin Martin's brother William and his colleague Heath both accepted with equanimity the houses

© SUSAN WOLDENBERG

"Graycliff," the Darwin D. Martins' summer place on Lake Erie. The clients' requirements included placing Mr. Martin's bedroom at a point where the fewest possible number of people in the household would be obliged to hear him snoring. The living room at "Graycliff," with comfortable summer furniture not by FLW. [UB]

that Wright thought suitable for them, and their houses are among the most satisfactory works of art of his career. But Darwin Martin, despite his near-worship of Wright, constantly proposed improvements to Wright's plans, many of which turned out to be undesirable. Mrs. Martin, who was far from worshipping Wright, also made numerous suggestions, mostly of a practical nature (large enough closets, wall space sufficient for a double bed), and the result of their agitation was the flawed house on Jewett Parkway, in Buffalo, and, in 1927, the oddly conventional house on Lake Erie.

The building of Graycliff, as the house on the lake was called, proved a joyless experience for everyone concerned, not only because of the Martins' incessant revisions ("Mrs. Martin thinks best to center the living-room fireplace," Martin wrote, "or even to move it off-center south as much as it is now off-center north, to enlarge the north chimney-corner") but also because Wright was unable to supervise its construction. And despite all their wrangling, Martin had one more commission to offer Wright: a monument to be placed in the family plot that Martin had purchased in Forest Lawn Cemetery, in Buffalo. In high spirits despite the subject matter, he wrote to Wright, "I never saw your work in this line, but when previously here you said it was your specialty. [Wright would claim anything as his specialty if it meant securing a job.] We want a Wright design for consideration. I much regret that I could not convert Mrs. Martin to cremation and no cemetery lot at all; so having the lot and two graves elsewhere in the cemetery to be moved to it (her father and sister) and room for all the family, we want a design that can be confined to a space of no more than one grave. Isn't this a good time for you to dash it off?"[15]

True to form, Wright produced a design for a monument on a scale that would cover the space of several graves. Nevertheless, it was just what Martin had unconsciously desired to achieve: not a tomb grimly grand, like the many already aggressively elbowing each other aside in Forest Lawn, but a flight of shallow marble steps, mounting the easy slope of the lot and granting a visitor a pleasant retreat for meditation. At the top of the steps a single headstone would bear the family names: Martin, Barton, and Foster. Martin was delighted with the design; he protested without much conviction that it would be "tremendously expensive, à la Wright," but for once expense appeared not to matter—he wanted to be sure that it would last at least a hundred years. Immediately he nicknamed it "The Martin Blue Sky Mausoleum," in witty recognition of the fact that it wasn't a mausoleum, and began pestering Wright for detailed elevations and plans. Alas! The Blue Sky Mausoleum was one of the many Wright projects defeated by the depression. Martin lost the bulk of his fortune over the ensuing years, and when he died, in 1935, the monument was still unbuilt. In a note to Mrs. Martin, written a few days before Martin's death, Wright says, "I only wish I had been less taking and more giving where he was concerned, but character is fate and mine got me into heavy going—and no safe harbor yet in sight."[16] (Even at that tragic moment for Mrs. Martin, Wright could not resist taking center stage and striking the note of self-pity that Martin had always deplored in him.) In a postscript, Wright mentions that the secretary to whom he has been dictating the note had reminded him of the existence of a plaster model of his scheme for the Martin monument, which he had sent on to Martin years earlier and which Wright guesses "is probably around somewhere." He has been criticized for the seeming callousness of this afterthought and even suspected of attempting to drum up business by it, but that is surely too harsh a judgment to pass upon him: he was recalling Martin's happy response to the design and the pride with which he looked forward to giving it substance. By a sad irony, after half a century the plaster model of the monument may still be "around somewhere" but Martin himself lies in an unmarked grave.

The design of the Martin Blue Sky Mausoleum had preceded the crash of 1929 by a scant few weeks. As businesses faltered or collapsed and at first thousands and then millions of Americans were thrown out of work, Wright had the sorry advantage over his fellow architects of an intimate acquaintance with hard times. He had not been poor since childhood, but he had been overextended—sometimes desperately so—since his twenty-first year. Now it was no longer easy to find credit, since everyone was equally in need of it; Wright was still in theory an employee of Frank Lloyd Wright, Inc., but the corporation had nothing to sell except his genius, and the market for architectural genius had been wiped out. If Wright wore a brave mask before the world—continued, indeed, to practice in public his habitual arrogance—he must have known how little it would be able to deceive Martin. In the depths of the depression, he wrote to him, "I won't weary you with prospects. You'd say 'prospects' were all I ever had. 'A fellow who is always just going to have money and never quite does.' As it happens, remember I've actually earned about a million dollars—single-handed. I can't be through, as I was never in better health nor more productive nor so 'famous,' as they say, in my life."[17] And yet the years passed with little of professional value to show for it: lectures for which he would be paid a couple of hundred dollars, magazine articles for which he would be paid even less. With not a shred of evidence on which to base his claim, the old man sat at his desk and composed a proud boast to Martin: "I have my best work yet ahead of me."[18] And so he had.

In an article in *The Architectural Record* published in the late twenties, Wright had spoken with candor about the situation in which he found himself: "I would much rather build than write about building, but when I am not building I will write about building —or the significance of those buildings I have already built."[1] The repetition of the word "building" gives the sentence an air of levity, or mock-levity, but the emotion that prompted the sentence is surely one of repressed bitterness. As we have seen, Wright was granted comparatively few commissions at a time when the profession of architecture as a whole was booming, and to help earn even a scanty living he had turned to writing and lecturing.

Wright's bitterness was heightened by his impression that former acolytes and employees like Rudolph Schindler and Richard Neutra were moving up in the world at his expense. He heard that Schindler, practicing as an independent architect in Los Angeles, had made public certain claims in respect to the amount of original work he had contributed to the Barnsdall and Imperial Hotel projects. Wright wrote to his son Lloyd:

> The pus-bag at Los Angeles that has poisoned the atmosphere there for you and for me is at last where it can be smelled and seen. . . .
>
> That lying duette at Kings Road [Schindler and Neutra] has done underhanded work that has been more harmful than either you or I can even now believe. . . .
>
> Don't row with them unless you have to. But open them up. If not, shut them up. Rudy is yellow, always was. . . . If drawing ideas and schemes of the Master's can make them the draftsman's it is only necessary for the Master to turn his back and his help can steal him blind.
>
> They do.[2]

On the same day, Wright to Schindler:

> Out in front with your naked sentiments in your hand at last. I congratulate you on a little show of your real self. Since you have concluded to deal

openly and aboveboard with me for the first time in your life, probably, I'll be honest with you.

Get this:

Where I am my office is. My office is *me*. Frank Lloyd Wright has no other office, never had one, and never will have one. You know it damned well.

He has never even had a "foreman" in his work. A superintendent only rarely on any job. What "office" then were you in charge of?

You were, officially, superintendent of the Barnsdall houses, and a poor excuse for one, playing both ends against the middle all the time. You were "officially" nothing else.

I left you behind me to finish up certain things I had begun.

If you don't know I would no more dream of building any of your imitations of me than I would those of any one of the forty or more workmen who sought work with me, you are not only yellow but feeble-minded.

No matter if you wrote a thousand letters and made a hundred sketches that never materialized on your own while you were marking time for me. That doesn't put you in charge of Frank Lloyd Wright's office. Get that where you keep your drawings.

You never saw one single drawing or material schedule or anything else that ever entered into the building of the Imperial Hotel. Everything you ever touched or saw I saw fit to throw away. . . .

I want no more communication with you. Anything from you will go back unopened. Lloyd is near enough to take this up.[3]

Many years later, there was a touching sequel—or, rather, two touching sequels—to that miserable episode. The breach between Wright and Schindler had never been healed, but on a visit to Los Angeles in old age Wright was tempted to effect a reconciliation. He had himself driven to Kings Road, got out of the car, started up the garden path toward the house, hesitated, and then turned back, not quite able to make the first move. The second sequel came some time later, when he received a letter from Schindler's wife, Pauline, with the news that Schindler was dying. She assured Wright that Schindler had no idea that she was writing to him; would he be willing, she wondered, to send a note to Schindler in the hospital—a word would mean so much to him. Wright obliged, with a spirited salute to the memory of their early days together. Schindler received the letter a few days before he died and was made as happy by it as his wife had prophesied.

It was in the early thirties that, at Olgivanna's urging, Wright began his autobiography, dictating it at intervals to a succession of stenographers. It is an odd fact that while he took great pride in the book and from time to time fussed over corrections and emendations to be incorporated into later editions, he appears never to have read the text line for line, leaving untouched scores of conspicuous blunders. The carelessness of the author has been all too faithfully imitated by his editors. From one edition to the next, they have failed to notice entire sentences scrambled within themselves or printed out of sequence, along with individual words that the stenographer has either misheard or that the transcribers of the stenographer's notes and of Wright's handwritten interlineation in the original typescript have heedlessly skimmed past. Having had little formal schooling, Wright had educated himself by reading, in indiscriminate fashion, a large number of books that would have been identified in his youth as examples of "the world's finest literature." In a postscript to the autobiography, he notes with a wry bravado: "For the writing of this work I have long ago consulted and occasionally remembered Pythagoras, Aristophanes, Socrates, Heraclitus, Laotze, Buddha, Jesus, Tolstoy, Kropotkin, Bacon, William Blake, Samuel Butler, Mazzini, Walt Whitman, Henry George, Gruntvig, George Meredith, Henry Thoreau, Herman Melville, George Borrow, Goethe, Carlyle, Nietzsche, Voltaire, Cervantes, Giacosa, Shelley, Shakespeare, Milton, Thorstein Veblen, Nehru, Major Douglas, and Silvio Gesell." A formidable list, which Wright has obviously thrown together in order to astonish and impress us, which it does. Few ordinary readers—myself included—would recognize the names of Gruntvig (a nineteenth-century Danish poet and statesman), Giacosa (a nineteenth-century Italian poet), Gesell (a twentieth-century German economist), and Major Douglas (a twentieth-century Canadian economist, much admired by Ezra Pound).

The one person whose writings Wright goes out of his way to boast of not having consulted is Louis Sullivan. It is safe to assume that Wright makes this boast not for the reason given—that Sullivan's thought had been "an open book to me for many years"—but to conceal the extent to which he has modeled much of the earlier portion of his autobiography on Sullivan's autobiography. Yeats defined rhetoric as the will attempting to do the work of the imagination, and rhetoric in this sense was a temptation that Sullivan and Wright were rarely willing to resist. In the same article in *The Architectural Record* that I have already quoted from, Wright mentions that his friend Carl Sandburg had once criticized him for employing so many abstract nouns. "Why," Sandburg asked, "do you use the words 'poetry,' 'beauty,' 'truth,' or 'ideal' any more? Why don't you just get down to tacks and talk about boards and nails and barn doors."[4] Wright was reluctant to take this advice. "I think that is what I should do. But I won't, unless I can get an equivalent by doing so. That equivalent is exactly what I cannot get. Those words—romance, poetry, beauty, truth, ideal—are not precious words—nor should they be *specious* words. They are elemental human symbols and we must be brought again to respect for them by using them significantly if we use them at all, or go to jail."[5]

One notices that Sandburg had not mentioned the word "romance." Wright may have introduced it into Sandburg's list because he was self-conscious about being called a romanticist. "An emotional being imbued with much sentiment," he wrote, "I am therefore called names. A 'new traditionalist' for one. Soon I may be called an 'old sentimentalist.' Indeed, that, I suspect is what the premature historians already hint when they refer to me as a 'romanticist.' At any rate, unashamed, I am searching for this poetic development that I call the sound body of architecture, a search based not upon sentiment but upon principle."[6] Which is to say that Wright, whether writing or speaking, was incorrigible in his failure to perform the feat of thinking hard—of driving his mind past the cozy lowlands of A, B, and C into the comparatively distant and chilly heights of D, E, and F. He persisted in letting the mere sound of certain incantatory words take the place of their meaning, which led to his uttering with perfect self-confidence an evangelical gibberish consisting of words like "search," "sentiment," and "principle," none of which he condescended to define. When he spoke with seeming indignation of "the provincial grandomania of the cultural lag," what on earth was he talking about? A Wrightian shrug would serve him for an answer: what you didn't understand was plainly beyond your capacity to understand. Even in the lectures that he delivered at Princeton University, in 1930—lectures that he was proud to have been invited to give and to whose preparation he devoted some care—he offered as his farewell sentence a characteristic specimen of high-toned nonsense, to wit, "A common sense is on the rise that will sweep our borrowed finery, and the scene-painting that always goes with it, to the museums, and encourage good life so to live that America may honorably pay her debt to manhood by keeping her promises to her own Ideal."[7]

Wright's contented abdication of intellect (which he shared with his hero Whitman) was more readily excusable in his speeches than in his writings. Throughout the depression years, for negligible fees, Wright gave hundreds of talks, ostensibly on architecture but in actuality upon any subject that happened to attract his attention. He discovered all too soon that to play Peck's Bad Boy was profitable; audiences in towns and cities from coast to coast learned to depend on him to say something that would offend the local high muckamucks, the information upon which he based his abusive remarks being furnished to him in most instances by local reporters in pursuit of good copy. (He sneered at Pittsburgh, saying it would be cheaper to abandon it than rebuild it; he offered a similar recommendation in respect to New York City and Washington, D.C., and had harsh words even for harmless little Milwaukee.) Wright had claimed to despise the press and yet had courted it assiduously from early manhood;

in his sixties, he was simultaneously its master and its slave, and by the time he had reached his seventies and eighties, he was repeating with undiminished zest to a new generation of reporters the wisecracks with which he had once entertained their parents and grandparents.

Ignoring the thinness of the content of most of his speeches and interviews, one can praise Wright's skill as an orator—a skill for which his father and his Uncle Jenkin had been famous. They had begun as journeyman preachers and "journeyman preacher" was the phrase Wright used to describe his own speaking career. He commanded an auditorium small or large with an ease that approached witchcraft; it was often said that when he entered a room crowded with people, and long before he was generally known to have entered it, the level of energy in the room could be felt to have been raised by his coming. Uncannily, one gained the impression that a remarkable event might soon be taking place, and often enough it did, the magus deriving much of his power over people from their conviction that he was somehow already in possession of it. This magical aspect of Wright's personality was heightened through the years by Olgivanna's shrewd manipulation of his personal seductiveness. She had learned much from her years of sitting at the feet of Gurdjieff, in the feudal establishment that that fiercely mustachioed old Tartar had created at Fontainebleau; when the time came, in 1932, for Wright and her to found the Taliesin Fellowship, she was able to adapt many of the practices of the flourishing Institute for the Harmonious Development of Man to the needs of the infant organization near Spring Green. One of the practices that she took care not to introduce was Gurdjieff's initiatory sexual revels with young female neophytes seeking transformation. Olgivanna kept Wright on a short leash even when sexual fantasy may be assumed to have taken the place of sexual activity.

The Taliesin Fellowship was a notable social invention, or, rather, re-invention. Its predecessors include not only Gurdjieff's Institute, in Fontainebleau, Ashbee's arts-and-crafts colony, in Chipping Campden, and Elbert Hubbard's Roycrofters, in East Aurora, but also such utopian nineteenth-century experiments in this country as Brook Farm, the Oneida Community, and New Harmony. It must be said that "Fellowship" was an inaccurate name for the system of apprenticeship that the Wrights established at Taliesin. A dictionary definition of fellowship is: "the companionship of individuals in a congenial atmosphere and on equal terms." While Taliesin certainly seemed to promise a congenial atmosphere, the question of equality never arose, whether between the Wrights and the apprentices or, as the years passed, between classes of "insider" apprentices and "outsider" apprentices. Nobody occupying an official position at Taliesin would be likely to admit that followers of Gurdjieff have been more highly thought of than non-followers, or that a Gurdjieff "cell" dominates, or used to dominate, the running of the Frank Lloyd Wright Foundation. Nevertheless, a student of the history of Taliesin comes to sense the existence of a hierarchy there—one based not upon seniority alone but upon a cult within a cult. Since Mrs. Wright's death, in 1985, this hierarchy may survive in a much diminished form. The disciplines, physical and intellectual, that Gurdjieff exacted from his followers were far more difficult for individuals to live up to than the mild social disciplines exacted at Taliesin. Like most leaders of cults, Gurdjieff had devised his own vocabulary, to which ordinary folk had no access; there were occult "ways" by means of which mankind could achieve immortality, but knowledge of the best of these ways was reserved to a few. By "working on oneself," one developed certain bodily skills—gymnastic exercises, dances, and methods of breathing—that led to the development of certain mental skills, which enabled one to outwit the usual confines of time and space and eventually to slip across the threshold of the mundane into eternal bliss. To his followers, Gurdjieff was a latter-day Socrates, who through hard questions and still harder answers hinted at the direction of the "way"; his Plato was the Russian mathematician P. D. Ouspensky, whose book *In Search of the Miraculous* is a not quite impenetrable exposition of Gurdjieffian sense and nonsense.

Gurdjieff visited Taliesin in 1935. In his account of his years as a Wright apprentice, Edgar Tafel gives a vivid sketch of the holy rascal:

> The impressions Gurdjieff left with us were not altogether spiritual. The thing we all remembered most clearly afterward—more than his music or philosophy—was that he had taught us how to prepare sauerkraut. Under his direction, we made sauerkraut with apples—core and all—raisins, cabbage, and herbs. . . . We heaped it on our plates, ate as much as we could stand, and threw the rest in the garbage can as discreetly as possible.[8]

Some time later, in the course of a visit to his family in New York City, Tafel gained a second glimpse of Gurdjieff. The setting was a restaurant in Greenwich Village:

> When I walked in, I saw Gurdjieff, head shaved as always, sitting at a corner table in the back. He spotted me, pointed, and bellowed in his Russian accent, "He played my music like 'sheet'! He played my music like 'sheet'!" (I had tried to play one of his piano compositions when he visited us.) Back at Taliesin, I told Mr. Wright about the encounter. He asked me to tell him the story again and he laughed and laughed. Often as we sat working in the drafting room, he'd call out, "Edgar, what did Gurdjieff say about your piano playing?"[9]

The prospectus for the Taliesin Fellowship strikes us today as being far longer and more complex than it ought to have been, but the Wrights at that period of their lives were still widely regarded as outside the pale of ordinary society and they must have felt the need to present credentials of an appropriate respectability. Wright mentions in his autobiography that a number of young men were constantly coming from around the world to work with him at Taliesin, as once long ago they had come to him at Oak Park. Why not devise a structure to contain this happy circumstance? He and Olgivanna composed and sent out a circular letter to a small group of friends. It was headed, "An Extension of the Work in Architecture at Taliesin to Include Apprentices in Residence," and it began:

> Frank Lloyd Wright together with a number of competent assistants will be in residence at Taliesin and will there lead the work of a new Fellowship of Apprentices to be now established.
>
> Three resident associates: a sculptor, a painter, and a musician, eventually chosen for the work to be done, are contemplated. An inner group of seven honor-apprentices having the status of senior apprentices and three technical advisors trained in industry will also be chosen to assist.
>
> Leaders in thought from many countries may also come to occasionally share for a time in our activities, perhaps temporarily reside there.
>
> We believe that a rational attempt to integrate Art and Industry should coordinate both with the everyday life we live here in America. Any such rational attempt must be *essential architecture* growing up by way of social, industrial, and economic processes natural to our way of life.[10]

So far, so good, but the Welsh bard and journeyman preacher cannot be held long in check; behold him in the next paragraph making a characteristic somersault into woozy polemics:

> Not only must this framework and background of future Democracy be developed in itself as a kind of organic architecture, but the very qualities most basic and worthwhile in Philosophy, Sculpture, Painting, Music, and the Industrial Crafts are also fundamentally Architecture. Principles underlying life and the arts are the same. So it is the Architecture of Life itself that must be the fundamental and therefore the first concern of any true culture anywhere if the world is to be made safe for Science.[11]

"Safe for Science"? The phrase is not merely a crushing anti-climax but an irrelevance as well, perhaps emerging from Wright's unconscious as an echo of Woodrow Wilson's famous slogan to the effect that the world must be made "safe for democracy." Not a word about science has been mentioned up to that point in the statement; moreover, in claiming that architecture embraces all the other arts (to say nothing of philosophy and

In the thirties, the Hillside School buildings that FLW had designed for his aunts were brought back from near-ruin to serve the needs of the apprentices and their increasingly busy master.

industry as well), Wright is riding a favorite hobbyhorse of his, one notoriously of little value. On and on he goes, at last getting down to what Sandburg called "tacks." It is necessary, after all, for him to justify the chosen location of the Fellowship: "The Big City is no longer a place for more than the exterior applications of some cliché or sterile formula, where life is concerned. Therefore the Taliesin Fellowship chooses to live and work in the country. The Fellowship establishment is located on a fine farm forty miles west of Madison, four miles from the nearest village on State Highway 23 in beautiful Southern Wisconsin."[12]

The statement proceeds to announce that a total of seventy apprentices will be admitted to the Fellowship. "They will enjoy the benefits of simple home life, with meals in common and fixed hours for work, recreation, and sleep. In the evenings, entertainment will be provided in the form of music, cinema, literary conferences, and the like. The emphasis will be upon apprenticeship and not upon scholarship." An undertone of puritan severity is detectible: "A fair division of labor in maintaining all branches of work will fall to the share of each member. Especial predilections or idiosyncrasies, although respected, will not be separately encouraged. There will be no age limit for apprentices but the qualifications of each will be decided finally by Mr. Wright after a month's trial in the Fellowship work. The right to reject any applicant at any time is reserved—either before or after being formally received into the Fellowship. The Fellowship, however, is not on trial. The apprentice is."[13] The letter concludes by noting that a fixed fee of six hundred and fifty dollars a year will be charged and that the apprentices will be expected to contribute at least four hours of physical labor a day, whether on the grounds, in the fields, felling wood, cooking, or waiting on table.

It soon turned out that seventy apprentices amounted to too ambitious a target; the number was changed to twenty-three, which not by coincidence matched the number of young men and women who actually began the Fellowship program on October 1st, 1932. (A year later, the annual tuition was raised to eleven hundred dollars, to conform with expenses.) Even to house twenty-three apprentices in makeshift quarters taxed the resources of Taliesin. A number of carpenters, plumbers, and electricians, drawn from the ever-increasing ranks of the unemployed in Spring Green and neighboring towns, were pressed into service, at low wages, to repair and remodel the ruinous buildings of the nearby Hillside School—the sainted teacher-aunts had long since gone to heaven and their celebrated school had long since been abandoned to wind and weather—turning it into dormitories, a vast drafting room, a dining room, a kitchen, and the usual offices and storerooms. The apprentices had been made aware that they would learn by doing, but the amount of doing must have astonished and dismayed many of them, especially those who had come to Taliesin from comfortable upper-middle-class homes. Perhaps it consoled them to observe that Taliesin itself was in a state of conspicuous disrepair, with leaky roofs, faulty plumbing, and unreliable furnaces and electric generators. It may also have consoled them to observe that the Wrights pitched in at every turn and that when Wright claimed to find some sort of primordial virtue in physical hardship, he shared the hardship; if the fires went out, he, too, shivered.

From the start, a chorus of skeptical voices proclaimed that Wright had outdone himself in artful dodging by the invention, in the name of the Fellowship, of a method of acquiring grandeur at no cost to himself. The nerve-wracking difficulty of living beyond one's means had been eased for him by his simply and exquisitely having no more need of means; a small army of robust young folk would serve him night and day, paying him a considerable sum for the privilege of being in his presence whenever he felt inclined to let them enter it. He made no pretext of being a teacher; rather, he was an example, whose usefulness to them had but one undeniable defect: he was a genius and as such by definition inimitable. They could hold his colored pencils for him, they could watch him fiddle with his T-square and triangle, and they could turn his graphic musings into hundreds of pages of working drawings.

The apprentices could also be counted on to punish any adversary of the Master—going so far, in at least one instance, as to take the law

Having been assaulted by a stranger in the streets of Madison, FLW suffered a broken nose. He is seen here in court, pressing charges against his assailant. [AP]

into their own hands. It was a favorite story of Wright's, perhaps because although he was intended to be a victim, he survived as a hero. He and one of the apprentices had driven into Madison to do some shopping for tools. Broke though he was, he was driving what was then one of the most beautiful and expensive cars in America—a Cord. Given that he was engaged in a labor dispute with some workmen who had been helping to prepare the buildings at Taliesin for the Fellowship, and given, further, that he had no doubt run up big charge accounts at a dozen shops in Madison, it was perhaps tactless of him to be seen tooling about in such a vehicle. Shopping completed, Wright was about to step into the Cord when a man he described as an angry farmer struck him several times on the back of his head. (The farmer's son had already seized the apprentice-driver and was holding him captive half-a-block away.) Wright turned to confront his assailant—"assassin" is his word—and received several more blows in the face.

> Instinct warned me not to strike the man [he writes]. So I clinched with him and he went down into the gutter on his back. I held him down there until he said he had enough. But in the split second when getting off him I stepped back to let him up, he kicked backward and up at me with his heavy boot, caught me on the bridge of the nose with his boot heel. I pinned him down again. Blood spurted all over him. This time I had both knees on his chest, his head still in the mud in the gutter. While holding him down there I deliberately aimed the torrent of blood with a broken nose full in his face. His own nose, his mouth too, clotted with

blood, he gagged and gasped for breath. . . . "God damn it, take him off," he shrieked. "Take the man off me, for Christ's sake! He's killing me!" But I had not struck him. I was careful not to. . . . I let him up and he disappeared in the astonished crowd. . . .[14]

Wright was driven to a local clinic, where a doctor congratulated him on the youthfulness of his blood (Wright was sixty-five), set his nose, bandaged him, and sent him home. That evening four of the apprentices drove to the farmer's house and attempted to horsewhip him. The police having been summoned, the apprentices were pursued, captured, and charged with assault. They passed two days in jail, stood trial, pleaded guilty, and were fined fifty dollars apiece. As for the farmer, who had been charged with assaulting Wright—his grievance against Wright was based on the fact that Wright allegedly had long owed his wife money for domestic service at Taliesin—by Wright's account, he was found guilty, fined, and soon thereafter left town.

That Wright's motives in establishing the Fellowship were selfish and impure was an indictment that would often be made, and Wright was not unaware of the measure of truth that it contained. But in his view motives were irrelevant; did he give good value in setting an example or did he not? Nor was he unaware that merely setting an example might prove a reason for subsequent hard feelings; what of the apprentices who, finding after a couple of years that they had no aptitude for architecture, would feel that the washing of a great man's dishes had been a sorry waste of time and money? Wright would probably have answered that question by saying that there were bound to be disappointments on both sides; within a decade, he wrote, "As the plan for the Taliesin Fellowship unfolded itself, I had hoped that apprentices—like the fingers of my hands— would increase not only my own interest and enthusiasm for my work as an architect but would also widen my capacity to apply it in the field. The first came true. But the second, as yet, is a temporarily frustrated hope. We somewhat overshot the mark. But I have not yet given up hope. We are steadily improving."[15]

What Wright meant by saying, "We somewhat overshot the mark" is worth a moment's speculation. As discreetly as possible (for the Fellowship was still a necessary prop to his professional career and to his luxurious style of living), he was placing on record his gloomy opinion of the results that the Fellowship program had produced up to that time. Where were the apprentices who, having drunk at the sacred fount, had gone out into the world and created architecture commensurate with that experience? Who had accomplished work not simply derivative of the Master but embodying the Master's principles? Not to have worthy disciples is to invite the casting of doubt upon one's own worth. "We are steadily improving,"

© SUSAN WOLDENBERG

FLW's bedroom wing at Taliesin North. The bedroom ceiling is a fraction of an inch above six feet. FLW enjoyed having breakfast on this terrace.

he wrote, but we are bound to suspect him of thinking otherwise. More than half a century has passed since the founding of the Fellowship, and of the hundreds of apprentices who have spent a portion of their lives there perhaps six or eight have achieved a considerable reputation. To be sure, fame (though Wright cultivated it with unbecoming ardor) is not an appropriate test of success, much less of self-fulfillment; nevertheless, for historians of architecture to be able to call to mind so few out of so many—!

The Fellowship came into existence because, to put it crudely, there was no other way for Wright to turn Taliesin into the grand country estate that he had always envisaged its being and because there was no other way for him to carry on the practice of architecture in the remote countryside, where draftsmen, secretarial help, and the like were hard to come by. The same reasons apply still more emphatically to Taliesin West, which at the time of its founding, in the late thirties, was even more difficult to get to than Taliesin North. Wright pretended all his life to admire nature, but what he liked was to alter it; for example, there were no ponds at Spring Green when he acquired the property and soon there were several; to procure water at Scottsdale he had to drive a pipe four hundred feet down through the desert floor. He took a millionaire's pleasure in making the uninhabitable habitable, as the Morgans and Whitneys did in the Adirondacks, and his pleasure was all the greater because he wasn't a millionaire— he was an adventurer riddled with debt and without prospects: to him, an exhilarating situation.

If the first batch of apprentices to arrive at Taliesin were puzzled by the disparity between the promises of the prospectus and the reality of ramshackle Taliesin, they must have been still more puzzled by the fact that the world-famous Frank Lloyd Wright—the man whom they were to be privileged to assist as he brought one masterpiece after another into the world—was, in fact, like any ordinary architect, all but unemployed. His last major executed commission had been a house for his cousin Richard Lloyd Jones, in Tulsa; it was a curious structure, flat-roofed and made up of alternating vertical panels of concrete block and glass; the scale of the building is so difficult to make out from a short distance away that it could readily be mistaken for an immense penitentiary, several stories high and hundreds of feet long. It is indeed a big house, with six bedrooms and a library and billiard room along with the usual living room, dining room, kitchen, and servants' quarters, but it is only two stories high and its interiors open into one another in a sufficiently informal domestic fashion.

FLW and the apprentices gathered around the twelve-foot-square model of Broadacre City. [ET]

The plans, elevations, and renderings of a number of breathtaking projects lay furled in the vault at Taliesin: St. Mark's, San Marcos, the Elizabeth Noble apartment house in Los Angeles, and a complex of joined apartment towers in Chicago. On Wright's drawing board were a few active projects: the house he was designing for Malcolm Willey, in Minneapolis; a newspaper plant for the *Capital Journal,* in Salem, Oregon; some prefabricated sheet-steel farm structures for the Walter Davidson Company, in Michigan; and a so-called "house on the mesa," designed to be shown at the exhibition of contemporary architecture held at the Museum of Modern Art, in New York City, in 1932. The instigators of that exhibition were two young firebrands named Henry-Russell Hitchcock and Philip Johnson, who, in the catalogue accompanying the exhibition, coined the term International Style for the work of the European architects they then most admired (Le Corbusier, Gropius, Mies van der Rohe, and the like) and who, at the time, angered Wright by assuming, in Johnson's witty phrase, that he was the greatest American architect of the nineteenth century. Though Wright later became friends with Hitchcock and Johnson, he never wholly forgave them for failing to accept his version of architectural history, which asserted that the achievements of the International Style were based upon Wright's pioneering efforts and that the degree to which his later work appeared to echo certain aspects of the International Style was a predictable consequence of his continuing on his own course and of the jackals continuing unsuccessfully to imitate him.

The Willey house is of particular interest, both as it was originally designed, in 1932, and as it was redesigned and finally built a couple of years later. Presumably for reasons of cost, the house shrank from two stories to one; in the course of doing so, it saluted and said goodbye to certain aspects of the prairie style going as far back in time as the Tomek, Robie, and Coonley houses (1907–1908) and presaged the many small houses of the future that Wright was to design in what he called the Usonian style. He said he had taken over from Samuel Butler's novel *Erewhon* the term Usonia for the United States; scholars have been unable to find "Usonia" in standard editions of *Erewhon,* and Wright may well have lifted the word from Herbert Spencer or Edward Bellamy. Be that as it may, the term came to serve as a handy synonym for "Wrightian" and to imply, often quite tiresomely, an improvement over anything that was merely American. The 1932 Willey house was raised above the ground, like the Tomek, Robie, and Coonley houses, with the main living quarters on the second floor, but Wright no longer pretended that this elevation was in order to keep the occupants of the house from the damp of the prairie soil—after all, the bedrooms, bathrooms, and study were on the ground floor—or that it was in order to improve their view over the surrounding countryside. By 1934, for reasons of economy as well as aesthetics, he was eager to place the occupants of his houses as close to Mother Earth as possible. The fact was that his Tomek and Coonley ground floors had been every bit as gloomy as the subterranean basements they had replaced; moreover, they had been large spaces, expensive to build, that no practical use could be found for. In the Tomek and Coonley houses, as in the Robie house as well, much of the ground floor had been taken up with billiard rooms or children's playrooms, neither of which seemed of importance in the depression. The 1932 Willey house introduced a ship-lapped wooden parapet on its cantilevered upper deck, and this parapet became a favorite Wright motif, appearing in the Johnson, Sturges, Lloyd Lewis, and Pauson houses, among innumerable others.

FLW at a Wisconsin county fair. His chief disciple, Wesley Peters, stands behind him with his first wife, Svetlana, Olgivanna's daughter by her first husband. [EWI]

It was during this period of the thirties that Wright was thinking through the program for Broadacre City, his imaginary substitute for the classic city of the past. In a preliminary work, *The Disappearing City*, first published in 1932 (in a charming, cranky, Wrightian format), he wrote that "to look at the plan of any great city is to look at the cross section of some fibrous tumor. . . . The properly citified citizen has become a broker dealing, chiefly, in human frailties or the ideas and inventions of others. . . . A parasite of the spirit is here, a whirling dervish in a whirling vortex."[16] (Whirling dervishes were among Gurdjieff's earliest teachers, so Wright may here be taking a dig at Olgivanna's revered Master.) He goes on to say that every citizen of Broadacre City, secure in his possession of an acre of land, will manifest true individuality, which Wright defines as "organic spirituality." Easier to define than "organic spirituality" is the physical setting of Broadacre City:

> Imagine spacious landscaped highways, grade crossings eliminated, "bypassing" living areas, devoid of the already archaic telegraph and telephone poles and wires and free of blaring billboards and obsolete construction. Imagine these great highways, safe in width and grade, bright with wayside flowers, cool with shade trees, joined at intervals with fields from which the safe, noiseless transport planes take off and land. Giant roads, themselves great architecture, pass public service stations, no longer eyesores, expanded to include all kinds of service and comfort . . . each citizen of the future will have all forms of production, distribution, self-improvement, enjoyment, within a radius of one hundred and fifty miles of his home now easily and speedily available by means of his car or his plane.[17]

Now, much of this setting has been realized over the years—indeed, much of it had already come true at the time *The Disappearing City* was written. (The Bronx River Parkway, in Westchester County, New York, incorporating most of the desiderata noted above, opened in 1913.) What was unattainable in Wright's utopian vision was not the transformation of city and countryside but the transformation of man; his organic spirituality, far from being heightened by Broadacre City, might well be crushed by it. As usual, Wright's mind was asimmer with unrecognized paradoxes, springing in most cases from the half-remembered snippets of Rousseau, Henry George, Nietzsche, and the like that collided rambunctiously with one another in Wright's mind. As is the case with most utopians, Wright preached a freedom for the individual that could be achieved only by means of mass regimentation. At some point in the governance of Broadacre City a benign tyrant is called for; not in the least to our surprise, that tyrant turns out to be an architect.

The apprentices at Taliesin constructed a twelve-foot-by-twelve-foot model embracing four square miles of Broadacre City; it was exhibited in 1935 at the Industrial Arts Exhibition at Rockefeller Center—by an irony that everyone appears to have enjoyed at the time, precisely the sort of urban setting that the polemics of *The Disappearing City* were intended to destroy and that Broadacre City was intended to replace. (The model is currently on display at Taliesin North.) At first glance, Broadacre City seems to offer its inhabitants the best of several worlds: the fresh air and sunlight of the open country, the convenient shopping and social amenities of the suburbs, the intense cultural opportunities of the central city. At second glance, one perceives that, its formidable political hazards aside, Broadacre City threatens to turn the entire country, from coast to coast—

seashores, deserts, plains, and mountains—into a single immaculate and homogeneous non-city: an incarnation on a monstrous scale of the very suburb that he had become so touchingly eager a resident of at twenty and that had threatened to hug the breath out of him at forty. All his life, Wright had feared great cities and had been attracted to and repelled by their allurements, but to think that he, of all people, would choose a monstrously enlarged Oak Park as an alternative! How can he not have observed, in the course of writing *The Disappearing City,* that this was just about all that his brave new world amounted to?

20

Hismory offers few examples of people achieving a deserved success late in life, especially when that success crowns many years of seeming total failure. In the presence of such an example, we feel a shared sense of triumph, for we, too, inescapably grow old, inescapably confront failure (or the increasing fear of failure), and seek to wrest from life for our individual stories the unlikely boon of a happy ending. That being the case, we have reason to be grateful that the last quarter of a century of Wright's life set such a high standard of implausible good fortune—a good fortune rendered all the more implausible by the fact that Wright attained it without the least sacrifice of his notorious lack of common sense and conventional good manners; he remained as uncomfortably impudent as ever to his fellow citizens, but they came to relish his abuse and, on the rare occasions when his self-proclaimed "honest arrogance" was not on flagrant display, to deplore its absence.

The vividness of the transformation of Wright defeated into Wright victorious was much heightened by its unexpectedness. Approaching seventy, Wright had appeared also to be approaching the end of his career. He was, as usual, deeply in debt and, with the entire nation undergoing a major depression, was far less able than formerly to gain credit by charm and blarney. Though the Taliesin Fellowship helped to keep the Wright family fed and clothed and with a roof (no matter how leaky) over their heads, the apprentices were acquiring the skills of laborers, farmhands, and house servants rather than those of draftsmen and architects. They were unquestionably in the presence of a great man, but one whose discourse owed more to the high spirits of Whitman than to the high intelligence of Whitman's master, Emerson. The talks, concerts, and movie shows held weekly at Taliesin provided a ritual context for a kind of monasticism based not on Christianity but on a sentimental deism, which, though it found God in all things, had little use for godliness. Such reverence as they were inclined to feel they devoted to their resident godling, who took seriously his role as, in newspaper jargon, "a living legend" and who

In fine weather, FLW was quick to call for picnics and was happy to leave to others the labor required to prepare them. Edgar Tafel is the curly-topped young man behind the woman in the white net cap. [ET]

also had the sensual man's weakness for fast cars, going on picnics, and quarreling publicly, at the top of his voice, with his wife. Edgar Tafel remembers the astonishment that he felt, as a gently brought-up young Easterner, at hearing the two Wrights going at it hammer and tongs, with Olgivanna giving back as good as she got and neither of them showing the least embarrassment over the presence of a sizeable audience of apprentices. The Welsh temperament met its match in the Montenegrin temperament; with some pride, Wright announced that he had discovered certain subterranean racial connections between the two peoples.

To make ends meet, Wright accepted as many speaking engagements as he was offered, for fees amounting at most to a couple of hundred dollars. One such engagement led him to Dallas in the winter of 1934; a successful young merchant named Stanley Marcus, whose family department store, Neiman-Marcus, was later to become one of the most famous in the country, had founded an organization called the Texas Book Club, which had the virtuous educational intention of increasing the public's interest in books and the virtuous commercial intention, difficult to accomplish in the midst of the Great Depression, of selling more books. Marcus was himself a collector of books and of art, to say nothing of being a collector of people. He and his wife took to Wright at once and Wright responded, inviting them to visit him at Taliesin. In the course of their visit, Marcus mentioned that he and his wife were thinking of building a house and he asked Wright's advice about the two architects that they had in mind to design it, Neutra and Lescaze. Wright asked, as he had asked many a time before, "Why be satisfied with a substitute when you can get the original?" Marcus replied, "Mr. Wright, we never dreamed that a man of your high reputation would consent to design a house for us—a small house, after all, since we have only forty-five thousand dollars to spend." Forty-five thousand dollars in 1934 would have had the purchasing power of half a million dollars today, so the house was by no means as small an undertaking as Marcus politely pretended.

Wright assured the Marcuses that he was not only willing to design a house for them but would also make sure that it didn't cost more than ten thousand dollars. The Marcuses were enraptured and soon Wright was paying a second visit to Dallas, in order to inspect the site that the Marcuses had chosen. The season was winter, but the weather during the course of Wright's brief stay happened to be exceptionally balmy. "Why, Stanley, you have better weather here in Dallas than they do in Arizona!" Wright exclaimed. Marcus explained that Dallas was enjoying an unusual thaw and that in a day or so the harsh weather of winter would be sure to return. For some reason, Wright clung to his initial impression and in a few weeks there arrived from Taliesin some floor plans for a house that, among its other oddities, had no bedrooms.

Marcus to Wright, by long-distance telephone: "Excuse me, Mr. Wright, but how does it happen that there are no bedrooms in the house?"

Wright to Marcus: "In your climate, you don't need bedrooms. You can sleep out-of-doors."

"But, Mr. Wright, if I sleep out-of-doors, I'll catch a cold. I'm very susceptible to colds."

"If you sleep out-of-doors, you won't catch colds."

Defeated on that flank, Marcus launched a second attack. "Also, Mr. Wright, we notice that there are no closets in the house."

"Closets are rotten. They just accumulate a lot of junk."

"But, Mr. Wright, I'm in the apparel business. My wife and I really do need to have some clothes."

"You shouldn't. They're a damned nuisance." This from Wright, the incomparable dandy!

"Also, Mr. Wright, we notice that you haven't made any provision for screens on the windows. I read a lot late at night and in summer, when the windows are open, I'll have every bug in Texas lighting on me."

"Screens are ugly. Let the breezes blow the bugs away."[1]

After much debate, Wright at last produced drawings of a house that had bedrooms, closets, and screens—indeed, the house and its accompanying decks and terraces were ingeniously encapsulated in screens supported by enormous, harpoonlike, cantilevered brackets attached to the roof. A model of the house was constructed at Taliesin and was later photographed for the issue of the the *Architectural Forum,* published in January, 1938, that devoted itself entirely to Wright's works. (This exceptional journalistic compliment—the *Forum* was then the premier architectural journal in the country—was repeated in somewhat different form when, a few weeks later, Wright achieved that apogee of "establishment" acceptance, a favorable "cover story" in *Time.*) As if to back up Marcus's many arguments in favor of screening out insects, in one of the *Forum* photographs we can observe a fly that has happened to land on the model just as the photograph was being taken; given the scale of the model, the fly, perched on the parapet of a terrace, looks as big as a sheepdog.

In the *Forum,* Wright explains that the house—owner unidentified—had never been built, because it was supposed to have cost twenty-five thousand dollars and the estimates ran to as much as thirty-five thousand dollars; he writes, "We reluctantly laid the plans aside and the job went local." As is usual with Wright, this explanation is partly true and partly false. When Marcus sent the plans out to be bid on, the lowest estimate came to a hundred and fifty thousand dollars. He telephoned the bad news to Wright, who expostulated that contractors never knew how to read his plans and therefore always overbid. Impetuously, Marcus said, "Whose fault is that—yours or theirs?" Wright flew into a rage, shouting that he would undertake to build the house himself, and at a fixed price. Marcus then made matters worse by asking, "Will you go bond to bring it in at a fixed price?" Wright's rage doubled and redoubled; he claimed that his honor had been impugned by Marcus's mention of a bond. (A man who has spent his life in debt is touchy in respect to going bond and becomes all the touchier if, like Wright with Marcus, he has been writing letters to his prospective client, begging him again and again for the loan of a few hundred dollars.) Wright broke off relations with Marcus and refused to speak to him for several years. Even without speaking, he succeeded in getting the last word as far as the house was concerned. Seeking to make a friendly gesture, Marcus sent Wright a photograph of the house that he had had designed for him by a local architect, Roscoe De Witt. Wright wrote, "Dear Stanley: I didn't think you would be satisfied with so little."

Later the two men were reconciled, and after the Second World War Marcus and his friend John Rosenfield, an art and architecture critic in Dallas, introduced Wright to a brand-new Texas millionaire named Rogers

Lacy. A florist with a greenhouse in Longview, Texas, Lacy one day had the unexpected pleasure of seeing an oil well blow out in his backyard, in what proved to be the heart of the richest oil field in East Texas. With more millions at his disposal than he had ever dreamed of possessing, Lacy wished to do something memorable for himself and Dallas; to that end, Wright designed a revolutionary skyscraper hotel for Lacy, which went unbuilt because of Lacy's sudden death.

Many of the apprentices were what later came to be called dropouts—young folk who spunkily decided to give up the usual college education in favor of spending a few years in a manifestly eccentric little community in the Middle West. This community was entitled to bestow no degrees (it still isn't), and thanks to an almost universal professional prejudice against Wright, was more likely to prevent a young person from getting a worthwhile job in architecture than to assist him in doing so. Among the earliest apprentices, William Wesley Peters had dropped out of M.I.T., and Edgar Tafel out of New York University; other dropouts were John Howe and Robert Mosher. They had applied to Taliesin with the intention of learning to practice architecture in the Wrightian fashion, there were others who joined the Fellowship not because they were interested in becoming architects but because they wished to experience living in the Wrightian fashion.

In 1934, an exceptionally intelligent young man of twenty-four named Edgar J. Kaufmann, Jr., was attracted to Taliesin, in part as a result of reading Wright's autobiography. Kaufmann was the son of a wealthy department-store owner in Pittsburgh and had recently been studying art and architecture in Vienna and Florence; he was already fairly sure that he would not be making his career as an artist or architect (in fact, he was to become a well-known architectural historian and teacher), and his stay of less than a year at Taliesin appears to have been an act of spiritual devotion, with Wright as its object. Enigmatically, Kaufmann has written, "So strong and convincing were Wright's principles that after a while—since I was not attuned to the Fellowship routine—it was time for me to leave."[2] As is always the case with its elusive author, the illogical paradox conceals far more than it reveals, but no matter: whatever may have gone wrong at Taliesin, Kaufmann claims that "waking up in that marvellous place still seems one of my most profound experiences,"[3] and from the world's point of view his brief novitiate there had at least one profound consequence: the commissioning of Fallingwater.

Edgar J. Kaufmann, Sr., and his wife, Liliane, came to visit their son at Taliesin. The father was then forty-nine: as his son describes him, "a magnetic and unconventional person" (which happens to be an accurate description of the son as well). "Wright and my father," Kaufmann writes in his book *Fallingwater,* "were both outgoing, winning, venturesome men, and Father quickly felt the power of Wright's genius. Mrs. Wright and my mother were cosmopolitan, and romantic in their taste for poetry; Mother responded to Mrs. Wright's courageous character."[4] The Kaufmanns fell at once under Wright's spell, and to do so was, of course, inevitably to spend money. Within a few months of having met him, Kaufmann had asked Wright to design a planetarium for the city of Pittsburgh (an unexecuted project); a new office for Kaufmann at the department store (which took two years to design and construct; it is now at the Victoria and Albert Museum, in London); and a country retreat for the Kaufmann family. He had also given Wright the funds with which to build the large model of Broadacre City.

These commissions amounted to a first installment on the several hundred thousand dollars that Wright was eventually to cost Kaufmann. Like Darwin D. Martin before him and like his contemporary "Hib" Johnson, Kaufmann could never quite believe the fate to which he had committed himself. He was a clever businessman, who knew a great deal about accumulating money and about prudently preserving it, and yet a self-confessed outlaw in fancy dress was able to entice him into a succession of expensive follies; Kaufmann was dismayed and delighted by this unlooked-for turn of events, and he and Wright remained close friends (not without occasional adversarial skirmishes) until the day he died.

The Kaufmanns had long owned a beautiful tract of wilderness embracing a stream called Bear Run, in the mountains some sixty miles south of Pittsburgh. They were accustomed in summer to roughing it at a camp near the stream and they asked Wright to design for them there an all-the-year-round country house of a more substantial nature. Wright visited the site and noted, among other things, a very large and smooth boulder overhanging the waterfall that was Bear Run's most remarkable feature; he was told that Kaufmann liked to sun himself on the boulder, listening to the waterfall, that the family enjoyed swimming in the shallow pools below the waterfall, and that they enjoyed the view of the waterfall from a point on the opposite bank, a few score yards downstream. A topographical map of the site was sent to Wright during the winter of 1935, along with word that the Bear Run house should be planned to cost between twenty and thirty thousand dollars. To Kaufmann's distress, many weeks passed and no drawings or plans emerged from the studio workshop at Taliesin. Kaufmann had scheduled a business trip to the Middle West for the following September and he telephoned to Wright, saying that he would like to drop in at Taliesin and see Wright's drawings and plans for the house at Bear Run.

We may choose to believe any of several accounts of what happened next; all are equally admiring of Wright's coolness at a moment of crisis. According to Tafel's recollection, Wright "boomed" into the telephone,

Edgar J. Kaufmann, Sr., and FLW enjoying a chat in the living room at Taliesin West before its canvas and wood construction gave way to glass and steel. The furniture is a welcome hodgepodge, with FLW's own handiwork in the minority. [AL]

"Come along, E. J.! We're ready for you." Overhearing the words, Tafel and Mosher at their drafting tables outside Wright's office were aghast, for they felt sure that Wright had not yet drawn so much as a single line on the Bear Run project. The next morning, Kaufmann called again; he was in Milwaukee and would be driving at once to Taliesin. The distance was a hundred and forty miles, and Tafel reckoned that the trip would take the impatient Kaufmann no more than a hundred and forty minutes. Tafel describes the scene:

> [Wright] hung up the phone, briskly emerged from his office, some twelve steps from the drafting room, sat down at the table set with the plot plan, and started to draw. First floor plan. Second floor. Section, elevation. Side sketches of details, talking *sotto voce* all the while. The design just poured out of him. "Liliane and E. J. will have tea on the balcony . . . they'll cross the bridge to walk into the woods. . . ." Pencils being used up as fast as we could sharpen them when broken. . . . Erasures, over-drawing, modifying. Flipping sheets back and forth. Then, the bold title across the bottom: "Fallingwater." A house has to have a name. . . .
>
> Just before noon Mr. Kaufmann arrived. As he walked up the outside stone steps, he was greeted graciously by the master. They came straight to the drafting table. "E. J.," said Mr. Wright, "we've been waiting for you." The description of the house, its setting, philosophy, poured out. Poetry in form, line, color, textures, and materials, all for a greater glory: a reality to live in! Mr. Wright at his eloquent and romantic best—he had done it before and would often do it again. . . . Kaufmann nodded in affirmation.
>
> They went up to the hill garden dining room for lunch, and while they were away Bob Mosher and I drew up the other two elevations, naturally in Mr. Wright's style. When they came back, Mr. Wright continued describing the house, using the added elevations to reinforce his presentation. Second thoughts? The basic design never changed—pure all the way.[5]

Now, what makes this feat all the more astonishing is that Fallingwater stands, or appears to stand, not upon the solid earth of some Middlewestern prairie but upon air. Cantilevered out over Bear Run by means of almost invisible concrete supports—Wright called them "bolsters"—the house and its series of terraces seem to float in saucy defiance of gravity above the waterfall. To the south, facing the view, its walls consist almost entirely of glass; to the north, its walls are of rough sandstone, hewn from a nearby abandoned quarry. Wright said of the house, "I think you can hear the waterfall when you look at the design. At least it is there, and he [Kaufmann] lives intimately with the thing he loves."[6] Looking over the elevations and plans with Wright, Kaufmann proved the old man's equal in coolness.

© SUSAN WOLDENBERG

A view of Fallingwater that shows the anchorage of its cantilevered balconies in solid rock.

He may have been expecting a rustic lodge, on the order of the cabins that Wright had designed for the Lake Tahoe project; he certainly cannot have expected a house composed of vehement horizontal slashes of reinforced concrete, because Wright had never made so great a use of reinforced concrete in a house before; moreover, in a woodland setting Wright was given to singing the praises of wood. Be that as it may, the only mild objection that Kaufmann raised to the bizarre structure that Wright had been imagining for so many months was that he had supposed it would be located on the opposite side of Bear Run, where it would offer a pleasing view of the waterfall. With characteristic aplomb, Wright made no effort to disguise the peculiar fact that the house as he had designed it was the one place from which it would be impossible to gain a glimpse of the waterfall. On the contrary, he emphasized the peculiarity, saying, "E. J., I want you to live with the waterfall, not just to look at it."

A month later, the Kaufmanns received at their Pittsburgh home (a Norman-French farmhouse invention of considerable charm) a set of drawings of the Bear Run retreat. The drawings bore the name that Wright had given the house: Fallingwater. The Kaufmanns accepted the name at once, without giving it much thought; Edgar Kaufmann, Jr., has since said that the family wasn't even particularly struck by the fact that the name simply—and delightfully—reversed "waterfall." "It was an extraordinary moment when the full force of Wright's concept became apparent," Kaufmann has written. "We did not hesitate; whatever the previous expecta-

© SUSAN WOLDENBERG

Engineers hired by Kaufmann never ceased to fear that the balconies would someday pitch headlong into Bear Run.

tions and whatever the problems suggested by the plans, here was an amazing augmentation of our regular refreshment in nature. . . . The prospects were exhilarating."[7] It was only when the actual building of the house began that exhilaration gave way to alarm and sometimes to anguish. For the novel structural engineering that this unprecedented house required, Wright depended upon his right-hand man, Wes Peters, and a brilliant Chicago engineer named Mendel Glickman. Uneasy about hanging a house in midair from the rock-strewn shore of a mountain stream, Kaufmann took care to show the plans to a firm of engineers in Pittsburgh, who filed an extremely gloomy report on the project. And with reason: for example, Wright, ever the romanticist, had decided to make the boulder on which Kaufmann had been accustomed to sunning himself serve as the very heart of the house. With ill-concealed contempt for such amateurish sentimentality, the engineers stated: "We have no information concerning probable stability of the large boulder to be incorporated into the structure."[8] Nor did they have any information on the rate at which the waterfall was eroding and on the risks involved in any future floodings of Bear Run.

When Kaufmann sent his engineers' report to Wright in Wisconsin, Wright hot-temperedly demanded that Kaufmann stop work on the project and return all Wright's drawings, on the grounds that he no longer "deserved" the house. Kaufmann apologized and the work went on, but there were to be further misunderstandings, in part because Wright was rarely present, his apprentice-representative, Bob Mosher, was inexperienced, and the contractor—chosen by Wright—proved less competent than he had represented himself to be. On the advice of the Pittsburgh engineers and without Wright's permission, more steel reinforcing rods were introduced into the main-floor slab than Wright's plans called for. On discovering this (and fearing that the additional weight of steel would jeopardize his cantilever instead of strengthening it), Wright dashed off a furious letter to Kaufmann:

> If you are paying to have the concrete engineering done down there, there is no use whatever in our doing it here. I am willing you should take it over, but I am not willing to be insulted. . . . I don't know what kind of architect you are familiar with but it apparently isn't the kind I think I am. You seem not to know how to treat a decent one. I have put so much more into this house than you or any other client has a right to expect that if I haven't your confidence—to hell with the whole thing. . . .[9]

It is worth noting that the sentence beginning "I have put so much more into this house . . ." is almost word for word the same vexed cry from the heart that Wright had uttered when writing to Darwin D. Martin some thirty years earlier and to Aline Barnsdall some twenty years earlier. And in each case the statement was true, but in each case the client felt the same way and uttered approximately the same cry, reducing it to a poignant irrelevance. Architect and client would become locked in an embrace that neither was willing to extricate himself from, though the possibility of doing so had to be constantly seen to exist. Kaufmann learned quickly how to deal with Wright; his reply to Wright's outburst was masterly, parroting its language in a witty fashion that Wright couldn't fail to be amused by.

> Dear Mr. Wright:
>
> If you have been paid to do the concrete engineering up there, there is no use whatever of our doing it down here. I am not willing to take it over as you suggest nor am I willing to be insulted. . . .
>
> I don't know what kind of clients you are familiar with, but apparently they are not the kind I think I am. You seem not to know how to treat a decent one. I have put so much confidence and enthusiasm behind this whole project in my limited way, to help the fulfillment of your efforts, that if I do not have your confidence in the matter—to hell with the whole thing.[10]

FLW's Gale house (1909), in Oak Park, is thought to have been a source of Fallingwater. Less plausibly, it is also thought to have served as an inspiration to Le Corbusier.

And then a long postscript, which, coming from a man younger than some of Wright's own children, amounted to a series of gentle filial rebukes:

> Now don't you think that we should stop writing letters and that you owe it to the situation to come to Pittsburgh and clear it up by getting the facts? Certainly there are reasons which must have prompted you to write as you have.
>
> I am sorry that you are calling Bob [Mosher] back. He seems entirely wrapped up in his work and in its progress, but this is beyond my control and you must use your best judgment.
>
> It is difficult for me to conceive that a man of your magnitude and understanding could write such a letter. In deference to our past association, I must naturally put it aside as if it had never been written, as it certainly does not conform to the facts.

So the building continued to rise, with Tafel taking Mosher's place as Wright's supervisor and with a constant series of unlucky episodes to be got past. Acting on the advice of still another firm of Pittsburgh engineers, Kaufmann had encouraged the contractor to extend by several feet a stone wall helping to support one of the cantilevered terraces. Discovering this

350

SUSAN WOLDENBERG

© SUSAN WOLDENBERG

FLW determined the height of parapets by his own height, which means that they were nearly always lower than most people would like them to be.

unauthorized "improvement" in the course of a visit to the site, Wright ordered the top four inches of the extended portion of the wall to be secretly removed, leaving the cantilever supported as he had originally intended it to be. When, a month or so later, Kaufmann confessed that he had had the wall extended, Wright led the way to the wall and pointed out the missing four inches. The terrace had shown no signs of failing, and Kaufmann consented to remove the extra length of wall. Edgar Kaufmann, Jr., says that during the course of the construction of Fallingwater both Wright and his father proposed a number of unsuitable ideas. Wright, for example, wanted to cover the concrete parapets of the house with gold leaf, which would have looked very odd indeed blazing away in the midst of a forest; with some reluctance, Wright agreed to the parapets being painted an off-white flecked with mica. (At present, the concrete is painted a faded peach-blow color.) For his part, Kaufmann wanted to turn one of the terraces into a swimming pool. Out of their quarrels and compromises emerged one of the most interesting houses on earth.

As had been the case with the desert camp Ocatillo, Fallingwater became famous even before it was finished. Photographs of it appeared in magazines

Left, a view from among the rhododendrons in the forest that surrounds Fallingwater. Right, an optical illusion created by an adroit marrying of steel and stone; a man appears to be hanging in space behind the windows and is not.

and newspapers throughout the world; in the photograph of Wright that appeared on the cover of *Time,* in January, 1938, a drawing of Fallingwater filled the background. Overnight, it had become a symbol of his oeuvre, as, at the turn of the century, the Larkin building had been a symbol and as the Guggenheim Museum would one day be. Like them, it violated with equanimity Wright's own preachments about the accommodation of structure to site. The Larkin building was totally at odds with its environment and so is the Guggenheim; one comes upon Fallingwater as upon some gorgeous apparition, strongly asserting the implausibility of its steel-and-concrete presence in a fold of the ancient Appalachians. It defies not only gravity but comity; it is a feat of architecture that prompts in a visitor approaching it for the first time a temptation to applaud, as in astonishment one might applaud an exceptional feat of magic onstage.

Its appearance aside, Fallingwater is of interest for the part it played in helping to revive Wright's reputation as our greatest living architect and for revealing the degree to which he had been keeping abreast of his contemporaries in the profession. He had made a lifelong practice of mocking the handiwork of any possible American rival; as for rivals abroad, especially the more celebrated members of the International School, he was childishly rude in his dismissals of them. Le Corbusier was always a favorite target; he was a poor painter, Wright would say, but he ought to go on with his painting and forget about architecture. Gropius and his Bauhaus jackals he swept away with the back of his hand. If he saw some hope for Mies van der Rohe, it was to the extent that Mies was an admirer of Wright and was attempting to carry out Wrightian principles. (In his late eighties, Wright would refer to Mies, almost twenty years his junior, as "old" Mies, as a way of slighting him with an appearance of affection.) Any hint that Wright had borrowed for use in Fallingwater certain aesthetic principles of the International School would have aroused his instant wrath, but the hints were there and they were inerasable.

The risks assumed in the siting and construction of Fallingwater were amply justified by its appearance and by the pleasure the Kaufmanns and their troops of guests took in being able to "rough it" so luxuriously between stream and sky. (A combined guesthouse, garage, and servants' quarters was added in 1939, located on the steep slope above the house and connected to it by a winding stone pathway sheltered by a canopy that looks at first glance as if it might be fashioned out of ribbon candy but is, in fact, of reinforced concrete.) Nevertheless, the risks had been real and there was never to be a time that Kaufmann himself felt sure that the building was safe. Cracks would appear and be mended and reappear; deflections of the cantilevered terraces could be detected by the naked

Few architects can match FLW at making concrete behave in a playful fashion.

More playfulness in concrete: the curving, covered walkway that leads up to the guest house at Fallingwater. Wesley Peters and Mendel Glickman provided the ingenious engineering.

eye, though most of them proved to be minor and to be caused by changes in temperature from season to season. In his book, Edgar J. Kaufmann, Jr., notes that one or two major improvements in the support of the structure have been made, but he is plainly impatient with the idea that the structure's flaws amount to a serious criticism of Wright's planning. He writes:

> Do these faults impugn Wright's ability? Comparable situations indicate an answer, bearing in mind that the architect and his client knew the design of Fallingwater was an exploration beyond the limits of conventional practice. . . . Some of the great monuments of architecture have suffered structural troubles, precisely because they were striving beyond normal limitations. The dome of Hagia Sophia in Constantinople, the belfries of St. Peter's in Rome, the core of the Pantheon in Paris, all threatened the stability of their structures and required drastic repairs, yet these buildings still stand and add glory to their countries and their art. My father was no monarch and his house was not conceived as a public monument, but Wright's genius justifies these references. No apologies are necessary for what he achieved at Fallingwater.[11]

T HE SAME APOLOGY, denying—and correctly—the need for any apology, might be uttered in respect to the second major project by means of which Wright regained his reputation: the Administration Building of the S. C. Johnson Wax Company, in Racine, Wisconsin. Again, we are in the presence of a superb client, who, again in the position of believing himself to be a hard-headed businessman, becomes infatuated (there is no other word) with Wright the architect and then—reluctantly, wondering what will become of him but helpless not to find out—infatuated with Wright the man. It was the fate that had befallen Kaufmann, as it had befallen Darwin D. Martin many years earlier. Herbert Johnson, informally known as Hib (he was christened Hibbard but took his father's name, Herbert, to ensure a certain corporate as well as familial continuity), was the third generation of his family to run a company that is often described in the press as one of the largest privately held companies in America. Today it is said to be worth billions and back in the thirties it was presumably worth many hundreds of millions, but the Johnsons have always cultivated what we call nowadays a low profile, and in seeking out Wright to design an administration building Johnson was proving himself to be even more adventurous than Martin had been in his day and than Kaufmann was being at the very same moment.

Hib Johnson, a year older than the century, had been president of the company since the death of his father, in 1928. Under the father's direction, the company had become well known for its interest in the welfare of its employees; it had been a pioneer in introducing paid vacations, the eight-hour day, and profit-sharing. Hib Johnson said that people might call it "enlightened selfishness," but he believed in it and practiced it, and by 1936, when it became obvious that the company, constantly expanding, was in need of a new administration building, he wished to make sure that the employees would gain improved working conditions as well as more space. He visited Hershey, Pennsylvania, the model town of the

Hershey Chocolate Corporation, where a windowless, air-conditioned administration building had recently been completed, and he returned to Racine with the intention of putting up a structure that would set a higher than usual aesthetic standard for industrial architecture. An amateur artist and collector of art (and later to be the donor of an art museum at Cornell), Johnson had much in common with Martin and Kaufmann as a client: a respect for the profession of architecture, a willingness to experiment, and a hunger for intellectual companionship beyond what he had found available to him in the course of his business life.

Johnson commissioned a local architect named Matson to design an administration building for the company; it proved to be a conventional exercise in the Beaux-Arts manner and as such was disappointing to Johnson and to his lively and intelligent general manager, Jack Ramsey. Having heard strong indirect recommendations of Wright, in mid-July of 1936 (just when the company had been hoping to break ground for the new building) Johnson authorized Ramsey and a couple of colleagues to visit Taliesin, where Wright put on a grand display of hospitality and made an informal presentation that shocked and thrilled his visitors: he proposed that the company abandon all of its present buildings in downtown Racine and move out into the countryside, a few miles west of the city, where a new community might be established—a community that would embody in its design the aspirations of Broadacre City. Ramsey was bowled over by Wright, as W. E. Martin had been long ago, and on his return to Racine he wrote a letter to Johnson, then at his summer cottage in northern Wisconsin, that often paralleled word for word the letter that W. E. Martin had written to his brother Darwin some thirty-five years earlier:

> Regarding the new building, I had a day Friday that so confirmed and crystallized my feeling about Matson's present offering and that at the same time so inspired me as to what *can* be done that I was on the point of sending you wild telegrams Friday night when I got home, or getting you out of bed on the telephone. . . . Honest, Hib, I haven't had such an inspiration from a person in years. And I won't feel satisfied about your getting what you want until you talk to him—to say nothing of not feeling justified in letting $300,000 be clothed in Matson's designs.
>
> He's an artist and a little bit "different," of course, but aside from his wearing a Windsor tie, he was perfectly human and *very* easy to talk to and most interested in our problem and understood that we were not committing ourselves, but, gosh, he could tell us what we were after when we couldn't explain it ourselves.
>
> About Matson's sketch, he was decent but honest. About the strongest remark he made was a bit of gentle sarcasm concerning the niches, something to the effect that they "memorialized the defunct windows," meaning that Matson evidently could not forget that windows *had* to be in a building

whether it were windowless or not. [Matson's design called for the building to be lighted from above, by skylights in the roof.]

I believe he got the greatest kick, and understanding of our desires, when I showed him a copy of that note you wrote Matson about what you would like to symbolize on those niches and medallions, telling him it was not definite but would probably give him an idea of the "flavor" of your thought on the building. He wants to talk to "the young man." The young man has some sentiment he wants expressed, but he'll *never* get it that way by adding isolated details to such a plan, etc. . . .

And he asked about what we thought this building would cost us. I said, when we got through with the building, landscape, furnishings, etc., we'd be investing around $300,000. He asked how many people it would house. I said about 200. He snorted and said it was too damn much money for the job and he could do a better functional job in more appropriate manner for a lot less. . . .

. . . He is very easy to talk to, much interested in our job whether he has anything to do with it or not, because it hits his ideas of modern building, because it is a Wisconsin native proposition, and because it seems to hurt his artistic conscience to see so much money spent on anything ordinary. . . . *Will you see him?*[1]

The ravishing little Hardy house in Racine (1905), which clings to a bluff high above Lake Michigan and which most of the local citizens regarded as an architectural freak.

© SUSAN WOLDENBERG

Plainly, Wright's performance had been masterly, for Ramsey was not a man easily deceived. And in a sense he hadn't been deceived on the level that mattered most—the perception that Wright was a serious artist and was capable of producing a masterpiece. It was on the snake-oil salesman level (that level in the practice of architecture which so often gains the architect his commissions) that Ramsey fell for the greatest snake-oil salesman of them all. The famed eloquence of a Richard Morris Hunt or a Stanford White resembles the tongue-tied diffidence of a schoolboy compared to that of Wright at his most winsome. One notes in Ramsey's letter Wright's collegial gentleness toward the handiwork of the benighted Matson, whom he was able to express a sufficient degree of contempt for by a single witticism; one notes, too, his selfless interest in the job "whether he has anything to do with it or not," though we know from Tafel's memoirs that he was, in fact, desperate to get the job and had put the apprentices to work prettying up Taliesin in order to give the Johnson delegation the most favorable possible image of the Wrightian way of life. And, finally, one notes his usual absolute confidence in being able to build the structure more cheaply than anyone else could do; he "snorted" at the extravagance of the sum that poor Matson had reckoned on spending, despite the fact that Wright himself was notorious for underestimating the cost of almost every project that he had been associated with, often exceeding his budget by a factor of four or five to one.

The admiration for Wright expressed by Ramsey and a couple of his colleagues in the Johnson Wax Company had to confront and outweigh the adverse opinion of him long held in Racine. The only local example of Wright's architecture—the pleasing little Thomas Hardy house, of 1905, suspended like an exquisite, symmetrical toy on the edge of the bluff above Lake Michigan—was held to be an unfortunate urban accident, totally at odds with the conventional houses facing it across South Main Street. In an interview with the architectural historian Jonathan Lipman, in 1981, Hib Johnson's sister, Henrietta Louis, reported that their father always laughed at the house, which the family thought of as "kooky." She added, "Frank never went over in Racine very much." And that was the case, of course, throughout much of his native state, where to this day he is remembered largely for having failed to pay his bills, for wearing outlandish clothes, and for conducting an irregular married life.

Although Hib Johnson had passed the Hardy house hundreds of times in the course of driving back and forth between his house and his office, and although Wright pointed it out to him on the occasion of a visit to Racine in 1936, at the beginning of their friendship, no record exists of Johnson's view of its supposed kookiness. Having read Ramsey's letter, Johnson made haste to pay a personal visit to Taliesin. The Wrights and he had lunch together, and the mettlesome asperity they displayed (Johnson complained at once of the food he was being served and Mrs. Wright at once rebuked him, while Wright launched an attack on Matson's plans) reflects great credit on all three of them. Given that the only commission being worked on at Taliesin at the time was Fallingwater and that the Johnson Wax commission promised to be a lucrative one, the Wrights proved valiant in their disputatiousness; as for Johnson, he was scarcely more than half the age of his host and was supposed to be playing the role of a mere businessman in the presence of a man of genius. Johnson wrote afterward, "He insulted me about everything, and I insulted him, but he did a better job. I showed him pictures of the old office, and he

Wesley Peters, FLW, and "Hib" Johnson watching with confidence as the test column for the Johnson Wax administration building is heaped with sandbags up to its prescribed load-bearing capacity and then well beyond it. [WMF]

said it was awful. I came back from Spring Green and said, 'If that guy can talk like that he must have something.' Everything at Spring Green was run down. He had a Lincoln-Zephyr, and I had one—that was the only thing we agreed on. On all other matters we were at each other's throats."[2]

"He must have something." Hib Johnson's father had been famous for his hunches, on which he acted with notable success; Hib, too, had hunches, and within a couple of days he was prompted to write a letter offering Wright the commission for a two-hundred-thousand-dollar office building and enclosing a check for a thousand dollars, as an advance on his total fee of ten percent of the cost of the building. So began an adventure that must have been equally thrilling for both Wright and Johnson—an adventure that consisted, for Wright, of a succession of near-miraculous improvisations on an essentially simple theme, and that for Johnson consisted of a succession of surprises, some joyous and some (the greater and more poignant portion) despairing. On his first visit to Racine, Wright again vigorously championed his contention that the entire plant should be moved out into the countryside, with a model town for employees to be built encircling it. In vain: Hib Johnson was willing to take chances, but not such a chance as that, especially in a depression and with a board of directors mostly of his father's generation and fearful of Hib's unbusiness-like leanings. According to Lipman, on his return to Taliesin and on report-ing to Olgivanna that he had failed to convince the company to move, Wright heard Olgivanna speak the words that architects' wives have spoken to their husbands for uncounted centuries: "Give them what they want, Frank, or you will lose the job."

The building emerged not out of long months of planning, after much study of the company's needs and a minute examination by many hands of hundreds of pages of detailed working drawings; on the contrary, it emerged as a big canvas by Picasso might have emerged, at feverish speed, as the consequence of a pell-mell ransacking of the artist's unconscious. In his autobiography, Wright describes the receipt of Hib's letter in dionysiac terms: "The birds began to sing again below the house at Taliesin; dry grass on the hillside turned green, and the hollyhocks went gaily into a second blooming. . . . What a release of pent-up energy—the making of those plans! Ideas came tumbling up and out onto paper. . . ."[3]

Whether in respect to design or construction, speed is rarely an aspect of architecture that deserves praise. Johnson and his colleagues were hoping to put up the Administration Building almost as quickly as conventional factory buildings went up, and this hope was strengthened by the rate at which ideas did indeed come tumbling up and out of Wright's mind (working night and day, Wright and his apprentices prepared the basic drawings for the building within ten days). Soon enough, however, it became obvious that the new building would fall victim to Wright's time-consuming and expensive practice of refining his ideas in the very act of carrying them out. The building was scheduled to be completed within a year; in fact, it took three. As for expense, at the beginning Wright spoke glibly of providing a building, furnishings included, for a quarter of a million dollars; in the end, the building and its furnishings cost closer to three million dollars. Disparities of time and money on such a scale are ruinous to companies (to say nothing of individuals) of limited means, and the Johnson Wax Company, being rich and privately owned, was probably among the few in the country that could have afforded to back Wright in what increasingly appeared, as the years passed and the millions were spent, to be a colossal and perhaps unusable folly.

The approximate configuration of the building was borrowed from a newspaper building that Wright had designed five years earlier for his friend George Putnam, publisher of *The Capital Journal*, in Salem, Oregon. (Hard times caused the project to remain unbuilt.) The most notable borrow-ing from that project was a forest of concrete-and-steel columns that Wright had designed to support duplex apartments and a roof garden above a vast, two-story-high room; half a city block long, this room contained the newspaper's printing presses at ground level and offices on a glass-enclosed mezzanine overlooking the presses. Wright called the columns dendriform, or "tree-shaped," though they could be more accurately defined as "upside-down-tree-shaped," since they are at their narrowest at the base and increase in girth as they rise until, spreading out like a vast circular root system and attaching themselves lightly but firmly to adjacent circular root systems, they serve, in the case of the Johnson Wax building, not so much to support the roof as to become it.

In the newspaper building, the mushroom columns were an ingenious and efficient means of providing the maximum amount of floor space for cumbersomely large printing presses; moreover, the narrow bases of the columns rested upon foundations separate from the foundations that bore the weight of the presses, thus ensuring that the considerable vibration caused by the printing of the newspaper wouldn't be transmitted to offices and living quarters on the floors above. In the Johnson Wax building, what Wright liked to call "the great workroom" would contain nothing but desks, chairs, and other clerical gear, so there would be little difficulty with vibration; as for the columns, in the great workroom they would support only themselves and the exquisite latticework of glass that filled the interstices between their not quite contiguous lily-pad tops, while else-where in the building they would be supporting conventional built-up roofs. (It is worth observing that all the terms commonly employed to describe the columns are drawn from nature: forest, tree, root, branch, mushroom, lily pad. Wright would say, "But of course! My vocabulary and nature's are one. To be in the Great Workroom is to be among pine trees, breathing fresh air and sunlight.") From the start, the Johnson Wax building was based upon aesthetic and sociological considerations and not upon practical ones, and it is marvelous—though largely irrelevant to its design—that it has managed to function as well as it has over the past half-century. The Johnson Wax Research Tower, designed and built a few years later, is, as we shall see, another story.

Wright had insisted that a contractor be chosen who would put up the Administration Building on a cost-plus basis; his experience had been that, because of the novelty of his designs, most contractors who bid on them either bid too low or too high, in either case out of ignorance. Johnson had a friend in Racine, Ben Wiltscheck, who had been trained as an architect and had chosen instead to become a builder; he was introduced to Wright, on whom he made a favorable impression, and Johnson was delighted when Wiltscheck agreed to undertake the job. And with reason, for Wilt-scheck, like Mueller before him, proved able to accommodate himself to Wright's importunate demands and to his no less importunate acts of irre-sponsibility, now failing to deliver a promised drawing, at other times failing to keep a long-scheduled appointment. Johnson, Ramsey, and Wiltscheck respected Wright for his genius and, resigning themselves to the Foxy

Grandpa aspect of his nature, came to cherish his faults almost as if they were virtues; they would often be angry with him, but they could never stay angry with him for long.

Everyone was eager to start excavating the site and pouring the concrete foundations for the Administration Building before winter, which tends to come early in Racine. Characteristically, Wright urged them to proceed without waiting for the necessary permissions of the local building department and the Wisconsin Industrial Commission, saying that if either official body wished to prevent construction, "Let them call out the militia!" Together, Wright and Johnson succeeded in outwitting bureaucratic opposition to Wright's unconventional methods of creating foundations for the building: in emulation of what he claimed were ancient Welsh principles, he would dig a shallow trench and pour concrete over a bed of loose broken rock and gravel. Equally unconventional was his way of constructing the walls of the building; he invented a sandwich made up of a single thickness of brick on the exterior, a filling of insulating cork and concrete grout, and a single thickness of brick on the interior, strengthened at intervals by transverse copper straps. As for heating the building, he planned to force hot air through ceramic tiles in the concrete floor slab—a method of heating that Wright had admired in Japan and that Johnson and his colleagues were all profoundly skeptical of. In the publicity generated by Wright's designs and by his reckless quarrels with bureaucracy, it came to light that he had never been granted a license to practice architecture in his native state, where he had been fruitfully at work for over fifty years. Lipman reports that bureaucracy, its feelings hurt, was tempted to challenge Wright on this point, but when he offered to take a public oral examination at the state capital, bureaucracy prudently backed down.

The speed with which the project began soon faltered, thanks not only to Wright's innumerable second thoughts but also to the fact that he was simultaneously engaged upon Fallingwater—a project every bit as important to him (and, as it turned out, to the world) as the Johnson Wax building was. Kaufmann and Johnson were like two mistresses, each of whom Wright felt an equal ardor for and was bent upon keeping permanently in his embrace; to that end—and in a hectic fashion not unfamiliar to him in his earlier sexual life—he was striving to keep each of them as little aware of the other as possible. To make matters still more hectic, a large number of smaller commissions were arriving on the doorstep at Taliesin, none of which, after his long years of enforced idleness, Wright felt inclined to refuse. Of the apprentices on hand, only a few—Peters, Tafel, Mosher, and Howe among them—had sufficient professional competence to be sent out on jobs as Wright's lieutenants, and being in their twenties they found it hard to imitate successfully their master's dictatorial ways.

In December, Wright came down with pneumonia, which in the days before antibiotics was often enough a fatal illness, especially for the elderly. Work on the building came to a standstill during Wright's convalescence; meanwhile, his doctors were urging him to spend his winters in a climate that would prove easier on him than Wisconsin's ice and snow. With the

The test column early in the process of being loaded. Many members of the press were on hand, hoping to observe a disaster. FLW helped to mitigate their disappointment by showing off; from time to time, he would stride forward and give the column a kick. [JW]

alacrity of any patient hearing from his doctors the advice he wishes to hear, he took the first steps toward the establishment of a camp in the desert outside Scottsdale that would eventually become Taliesin West, his russet-and-ocher kingdom "on the rim of the world." Convalescing in Phoenix, familiar to him from the days when he had "ghosted" the Arizona Biltmore, he looked about for a parcel of land where he could establish a permanent base; on a remote and inaccessible mesa overlooking Paradise Valley, he found just the sort of site that he always urged upon clients—that is, a site that no reasonable person would consider building upon. The desert floor was covered with boulders; one had only to build wooden forms, gather up boulders and dump them into the forms, pour in enough concrete to fill the interstices between the boulders, and one had the foundations and walls of a camp that might well last as long as the mesa itself. Perishable wood and canvas would serve to create roofs and windows and could be replaced as the fiercely hot and fiercely cold seasons passed and rotted them; and everywhere there would be, as one knew them back at Spring Green, great stone hearths upon which Promethean fires would be kept constantly ablaze.

The two major innovations of the Johnson design—the hollow reinforced-concrete dendriform columns and the Pyrex glass tubing used in place of conventional skylights in the windowless building—were a cause of further delays. Lipman has written of the columns that "they remain one of the most remarkable structural designs in twentieth-century architecture. In their unprecedented structural and aesthetic success they were the supreme example of Wright's dictum, 'Form does not follow function. Rather, form and function are one.'"

The members of the Wisconsin Industrial Commission thought otherwise. The state codes required that a twenty-one-foot-high concrete column with a design load of six tons be thirty inches in diameter; Wright's tapering column was but nine inches in diameter at the base. After much wrangling, in late March the commission agreed to let Wright build a single column and test-load it; by the end of May, a steel form had been fashioned and the column poured, and on June 4th, 1937, the test was begun, with four cross-braced timbers helping to stabilize—but not support—the column. In the presence of the commission and other state and city bureaucracies, of representatives of the companies that had manufactured the cement and steel mesh with which the column was reinforced, of a host of press photographers, of Johnson and his staff, and of a dozen Taliesin apprentices (to say nothing of the two engineers, Peters and Glickman, who had actually calculated the design and who were survivors of the perils encountered in the design of Fallingwater), Wright ordered the loading of the round petal at the top of the column. With the help of a crane, workmen began piling heavy sacks of sand on the petal; Wright stood confidently in its shadow, drawing for members of the crowd of onlookers sketches to illustrate the engineering principles involved. Once a weight of twelve tons—twice the weight that the column was expected to bear—had been reached, the commissioners were ready to call off the test, but Wright jubilantly commanded, "Keep piling!" When there was no room left on the petal

A passageway fashioned of the Pyrex tubing that took the place of ordinary glass throughout the building. It had the grievous defect of leaking—no compound had then been invented that would successfully seal the joins between the tubes. Having leapt ahead of the available technology, FLW quixotically blamed technology for having failed him.

© SUSAN WOLDENBERG

for sand, pigs of iron (much heavier than sand) were lifted into place. By late afternoon, the column was supporting sixty tons, or five times the necessary amount. Wright ordered the four timbers to be pushed aside and down fell petal, sand, pig iron, and column, with the column remaining unbroken as it hit the ground.

Next came the aesthetic question: what sort of glass should fill the skylights and the clerestories (Wright called them sunbands) that were to pierce the brick screening walls of the building? At first, Wright had thought of employing the prismatic glass for which he had prepared and patented designs back in the nineties, but as usual he was looking for something better than what had served in the past, no matter how successfully; for him, from youth into extreme old age, the lure of the new and untried was always very great. After a year's search, he began conducting experiments with a heat-resistant Pyrex glass tubing manufactured by the Corning Glass Company and hitherto used for test-tubes and other chemical purposes. Wired into place on aluminum racks set horizontally in the sunbands, the tubes would strengthen the building's emphasis upon streamlining, already manifested in its low profile and rounded corners, and it would transmit light without revealing to the occupants what Wright considered to be the inimical small-town environment in which Johnson and his colleagues had insisted upon constructing the building.

Corning sent the first shipment of glass to Racine in the spring of

1938, when, according to Lipman, Wright was still trying to figure out how to join the four-foot-long tubes together by means of smaller tubes fitted into their ends; he was also striving to locate a mastic that would serve as a watertight caulking between the tubes. From the moment the tubes were chosen, nobody doubted the beauty of their appearance in the roof and walls, and except when the sun struck them at an angle that produced a blinding glare, the quality of the light they transmitted was

The entrance lobby of the Administration Building. Here, too, the Pyrex tubing failed and a conventional skylit roof was built above the original roof.

much admired. But—and what a fantastically expensive and pertinacious "but" it proved to be!—the tubes were in every other respect a failure: the problem of glare in fine weather was never solved, nor was the problem of leakage in rainy weather. Over the years, innumerable attempts were made to solve the problem on Wright's terms, always without success; at last, the company resigned itself to solving the problem by a discreet elimination of its source: the rooftop tubing was covered over by a second roof and artificial lighting was introduced between this roof and the tubes, simulating daylight. Meanwhile, the tubes themselves were replaced wherever possible throughout the building by sheets of glass cast in a form resembling tubes.

The building was erected by fits and starts, thanks in part to the incompleteness of the working drawings that Wright and the apprentices were turning out and in part to the changes that Wright kept introducing. Ramsey protested again and again, never quite so angrily as he was entitled to; on one occasion, Wright replied, "Your 'crab' received—don't be too hard on the boys and me! Will you? They do pretty damned well with a pretty difficult task—you would say if you knew all. You see the building grows as it is built and is none too easy, therefore, to keep up with always."[4] Who but Wright would have dared to use the occurrence of second thoughts (and third and fourth and fifth thoughts) as a reason for failing to fulfill his professional obligations as an architect? It was his lifelong practice to do so, and it cost his clients—Martin, Barnsdall, Kaufmann, Johnson, and scores of others—sums that would eventually total many millions of dollars, and yet they contrived to forgive him as, with the passing of time, irritated incredulity was transmuted into admiration. To have survived Wright was somehow to have been elected members of an immensely distinguished secret honor society—a sort of post-collegiate Skull & Bones, with Wright as its sacred icon.

Many of the Wright buildings produced by this unnerving method are assuredly masterpieces and would perhaps have proved less masterly if produced by more conventional methods; a few (among others one thinks of the Kansas City Community Church) are failures, though blame for failure is always harder to allocate fairly than praise for success. In the case of the Johnson Wax administration building, one marvels at the comparative good nature with which his clients put up with Wright's manifestations of "genius at work." Indeed, so much under Wright's spell was Hib Johnson that, having commissioned the building, he proceeded to commission a private residence as well, to be erected on a stretch of open fields that he owned not far from the shore of Lake Michigan. Johnson had been married and divorced and was now marrying for a second time; he and his wife would be bringing a couple of children apiece to the new house, which must therefore be ample. The house, of which there will be more to say later, was a simpler matter to design and build than the Administration Building, but was subject to the same provoking delays and consequent increased costs, and Johnson was finally driven to writing a letter of protest to Wright.

By the age of seventy, Wright was accustomed to receiving such letters and had become an adroit placater of indignant clients. Lipman quotes from the letter that Wright sent Johnson from his new quarters in the Arizona desert—quarters that, ironically enough, Johnson's steady flow of fees was helping to make possible:

> You seem to feel you've paid your old architect an awful lot and the work costs an awful lot more. . . . No architect creating anything worth naming as creative work ever made or ever can make any money on what he does. . . . I have, as you know, given my personal attention to every little matter of minutest detail in both buildings. To me, neither structure is just a building. Each one is a life in itself, one for the life that is your business life, and one for your personal life.[5]

Wright goes on to explain why he considers his fees highly reasonable and why he believes that the Administration Building will pay for itself on the strength of its advertising value to the company. Without apology, he passes from the defensive to the offensive; surely to Johnson's astonishment as he read the letter, Wright abandons justifying what may have seemed past extravagances and boldly asserts his right to further financing. The right is not put in the form of a tentative request; one notes the absence of a question mark: ". . . to help get started in the desert . . . you could send me quite a check without too great a shock to good business sense, and no very real tax on friendship, either."[6]

Johnson's reply was a cry from the heart, almost word for word matching the cries uttered under similar circumstances by Martin and Kaufmann, and is worth quoting at length:

> As I have told you on many occasions, I am pleased with the work, the buildings are going to be beautiful and practical and true creations, but the cost and time element make things embarrassing for me, to say the least. I know it does no good to complain, as you are an artist so in love with your work that nothing will make you change your ideas of what the two buildings ought to be, even though it works a hardship on your client. You would rather tell the client whatever comes into your head as to the cost and the time to construct, at the start, just to sell the job and give satisfaction to your art to create something worthwhile, rather than to be accurate in cost estimates. Why didn't you put me wise long ago as to the true costs and the time to construct? Would that be unreasonable to ask? That is water over the dam now and I am going to have to take it, but I will never like it. That is, the way you have handled me; the buildings I am going to love.[7]

Later on in the letter, Johnson, in a tone of mingled affection and exasperation, addresses Wright as "Frankie," and we perceive that Wright has managed to establish a relationship with Johnson in which he is at once Johnson's

father (which at seventy he was certainly old enough to be) and his son—
a Peck's Bad Boy, a truant, an ineradicably mischievous Huck Finn. And
so we have no reason to be surprised when, at the end of the letter, Johnson
notes that he is enclosing a check for three thousand one hundred dollars,
as the amount due Wright according to the latest reckoning of the fees
he has earned on the office building and house—fees that keep increasing
in size as the office building and house increase in cost.

Months passed, and the work of building went on. A torrent of complaints sped westward to Wright in Arizona, begging him to come to Racine
and solve the many problems daily arising there; an equal torrent of mes-
sages begging for money and saying little or nothing about the problems
sped eastward to Johnson in Racine. A typical Wrightian telegram: DEAR
HIBBARD MUST HAVE MONEY OR MUST SHUT DOWN WILL YOU HELP ME OUT
WITH PERSONAL ADVANCE FIVE THOUSAND DOLLARS PAYING YOURSELF BACK
OUT OF MY EARNINGS IF YOU WIRE THE SUM TO THE VALLEY BANK SURE WOULD
BE NICE COMING EAST SOON BUT IMPOSSIBLE UNTIL FIXED HERE THAT SUM
WILL DO FAITHFULLY FRANK.[8] Johnson to Wright: SURE SORRY CANNOT AD-
VANCE MONEY AS MY CREDIT HAS BEEN EXTENDED AS FAR AS POSSIBLE. . . . YOU
NEED EDGAR [TAFEL] HERE TO SPEED CONSTRUCTION TO EARN COMMISSION
STOP GOOD LUCK HIB.[9] Back and forth, back and forth, with Ramsey step-
ping in to defend Johnson against "Frankie" by means of a generous ges-
ture: CAN SEND YOU FIFTEEN HUNDRED DOLLARS STOP WILL THAT ENABLE
YOU TO GET AWAY AND IF SO WHEN SHALL WE EXPECT YOU IN RACINE STOP
ANSWER RAMSEY,[10] which evokes still another fusillade from Wright:
JACK THERE IS A WELL HERE MUST PAY IMMEDIATELY THOUSAND DOLLARS SUIT
BEGUN BUILDING MATERIALS FIFTEEN HUNDRED NECESSARY FOOD DURING AB-
SENCE FOUR HUNDRED CARLOAD LUMBER TRACK ON DEMURRAGE SIX HUNDRED
CANNOT TURN MY BACK KINDLY TELEGRAPH VALLEY BANK PHOENIX TWENTY
FIVE HUNDRED CAN THEN COME ALONG RIGHT AWAY.[11] Ramsey
telegraphed the twenty-five hundred dollars and sooner or later—but later
rather than sooner—Wright arrived in Racine.

In the 1938 all-Wright issue of the *Architectural Forum,* particular attention was devoted to Fallingwater and the Johnson Wax administration
building, and this national—indeed, international—publicity, which delighted Wright beyond measure, helped to mollify Johnson and his colleagues in the company. Though far from finished, the building was already
famous and was drawing visitors in large numbers to remote and much
astonished little Racine. The summer of 1938 was spent installing the glass-
tube skylights and the completion of the building was scheduled for the
first of October. That deadline passed, and it was announced that the
building would be opened the following February. Wright came down
with pneumonia for the second time in December, was nursed back to
health by Olgivanna and the apprentices, and was then bundled off to

Arizona to recuperate. A new date—late April—was proposed for the opening. The guerrilla warfare of telegrams continued. In midwinter, Ramsey to Wright: SCORES OF LEAKS IN GLASS TUBING AND NEW ONES DEVELOPING WITH EVERY CHANGE IN WEATHER AND RECAULKING ONLY TEMPORARILY EFFECTIVE STOP ALSO WOODWORK CONTINUES WARPING STOP SINCE THOSE TWO FAULTS RENDER WHOLE BUILDING RIDICULOUS AND UNUSABLE MUST HAVE IMMEDIATE PERMANENT SOLUTION.[12] Wright to Ramsey, in a pacifying mood: ALL REPORTS FROM WILTSCHECK AND EDGAR EXTREMELY FAVORABLE HAVE COMPLETE CONFIDENCE IN SUCCESS OF BOTH GLASS WORK AND WOOD WORK CERTAIN MINOR LEAKS AND WARPAGE ARE INEVITABLE BUT GUARANTEE TO OVERCOME ANY THAT APPEAR FAIR PLAY AND GOOD FELLOWSHIP ARE BEST EVEN IN MONEY TROUBLES WE ARE HEADING INTO TREMENDOUS FAVORABLE PUBLICITY WHY THROW IT AWAY EXPECT TO COME EAST ABOUT [MARCH] FIFTEENTH.[13]

Meanwhile, furniture for the Administration Building was being constructed according to Wright's designs. As he had done in the case of the Larkin building, Wright had persuaded Johnson that the building and its contents must be seen to be of one nature. The furniture that he designed, mostly of metal, shared the same streamlining as the building: desks and chairs were either rounded or curved and in their emphasis upon horizontality somewhat resembled the biplanes and triplanes designed by aeronautical engineers early in the century—heavy as the furniture might be, one suspected it of being capable of flight. Despite much advice to the contrary, Wright insisted on designing a chair with three legs, remarkable for its instability. With his usual gift for employing any argument, however implausible, in order to have his way, Wright claimed that the chair would improve the alertness and efficiency of the employees by forcing them to adopt a correct posture in order not to tip over. The chair having spilled enough people unceremoniously onto the floor (Wright himself is said to have been one of them), he was at last obliged to approve the design of a comparatively normal four-legged chair.

The Administration Building officially opened in May, 1939, after almost three years of construction and at a cost approaching three million dollars. Neither time nor money mattered—the building was an instantaneous triumph, both with the executives and employees of the company and with the world at large. To this day, it gives delight and no amount of criticism, whether of its oddity in aesthetic terms or its elitism in philosophical terms, is likely to diminish that delight. As far as I know, few writers have concerned themselves with the question of Wright's sudden and unexpected espousal of streamlining, which he carried to such extraordinary lengths in the Administration Building and, later, in the Research Tower. (In the *Capital Journal* project, upon which the Administration Building was based, the shell of the building was severely rectilinear.)

Streamlining was known to be of practical value in the design of automo-

© SUSAN WOLDENBERG

An exterior view of the Johnson administration building. FLW was determined to keep occupants of the building from looking out at their (to him) distastefully humdrum surroundings.

biles, airplanes, and trains, but in the nineteen-thirties it became the fashion to design stationary objects whether large or small (refrigerators, furnaces, electric toasters, and even pencil sharpeners) with so-called aerodynamic contours; the fashion spread to architecture, colliding with the weaponlike zigzags of Art Deco and sometimes marrying them. But what has streamlining to do with architecture, except as an expression of meretricious faddishness? The Administration Building wasn't going anywhere and had no need for reduced wind resistance; in its relentless multiplicity of suave roundnesses, it embodied some playful whim in Wright's unconscious—one that was wholly at odds with the no less playful whim that led to the vivid angularities of Fallingwater, designed at precisely the same time. It is tempting to find a clue to Wright's streamlining of the Johnson Wax building in the fact that Hib Johnson and he, both devotees of fine cars, owned Lincoln Zephyrs, which have entered history as among the most handsomely streamlined cars ever designed. Wright claimed, without adducing proof, that he was the first to apply the term "streamlining" to buildings—the first use of the term, according to the Oxford English Dictionary, goes back to the early years of the present century—and he certainly took pride in the virtuosity with which he manipulated it. He was delighted when *Life* magazine described the interior of the building as "like a woman swimming naked in a stream," and he himself hit upon a robust sexual analogue, saying that the Johnson building was the feminine descendant of the masculine Larkin building. In his autobiography, he wrote, "It was high time to give our hungry American public something truly 'streamlined,' so swift, sure of itself, and clean for its purpose . . . that *anybody* could see the virtue of this thing called Modern. . . . Organic architecture designed this great building to be as inspiring a place to work in as any

371

cathedral ever was in which to worship. It was meant to be a socio-architectural interpretation of modern building at its top and best. . . . Let's say here that it is technically, and in the entire realm of the scientific art of Architecture, one of the world's remarkably successful structures. I like it. They like it. Let it go at that."[14]

During the long-drawn-out anguish of bringing the Administration Building and his house to completion, Johnson frequently asserted that he would never again employ Wright on any project, but in much the same fashion as Darwin D. Martin many years earlier, no sooner was he free of Wright's vexatious trammels than he found himself missing them. When a new laboratory building was needed, he turned to Wright for its design, concealing (perhaps even from himself) his eagerness to place himself at Wright's mercy by laying down a barrage of provisos concerning the need for an accurate budget and for the timely delivery of complete working drawings. Having blithely agreed to these provisos, Wright set about preparing a design that boldly contradicted several of the principles

© SUSAN WOLDENBERG

© SUSAN WOLDENBERG

Right, the Johnson laboratory tower. As the company's laboratory needs changed, the tower became increasingly inefficient; it has stood idle for many years. Left, interior of the tower, which FLW called a "helio-lab," and which often proved sunnier—and hotter—than its occupants wished.

of efficiency and aesthetics that he had enunciated in respect to the Administration Building.

Where the Administration Building seeks to convey an impression of extreme horizontality, what came to be called the Research Tower is obviously intended to provide a strong vertical contrast; sturdily square in plan but with rounded corners, it rises with the dignity of a miniature skyscraper. It is clad in alternating bands of brick and obscure glass tubing; through the glass, one is able to detect that the building consists of a central mast, from which seven square shelflike floors project, each of them of sufficient height to contain a circular mezzanine level. The floors extend to the cladding, while the mezzanines, which are in effect free-standing, permit, by Wright's reckoning, an ease of oral communication between workers on the two levels). Fitted within the mast are a circular elevator, fire stairs, and utilities.

Like so many of Wright's works, the Research Tower succeeds as an aesthetic object, but from the beginning it presented an almost endless series of difficulties. Wright nicknamed it "the helio-lab," but *helios* proved an enemy instead of a friend, overheating the building and threatening to parboil and blind its occupants. Wright had as little use for awnings and shades as he did for screens; he also refused to permit the use of sprinklers throughout the building, on the grounds of their ugliness. The result was that fire insurance on the building could be secured only by the payment of higher than ordinary premiums. Chemical experiments involving combustible materials had to be carried out in another building, and when with the passing of time the number of workers employed in the tower increased, the single set of fire stairs was deemed inadequate. Eventually, the building had to be shut down. No practical use has yet been found for it, though Wes Peters would like to turn it into executive offices. To this end, he has prepared a design that would affix an additional set of fire stairs to the exterior of the building; so far, the Johnson company has proved reluctant to make the change, in part because a tower by its nature discourages ready communication between offices and in part because they rightly fear to tamper with a world-renowned masterpiece.

Wright, whose literary talent included a knack for naming houses, called Johnson's house Wingspread because it consisted of four wings extending in pinwheel fashion from a high-ceilinged, many-sided open space—to Wright the "Wigwam"—centering upon an immense chimney with five fireplaces on two levels and with a small glass observatory clinging to its southern face at the point where the chimney emerges from a sloping tiled roof. (The observatory was intended to serve as a sort of "tree house" for the Johnson children.) Wright called Wingspread the last of his Prairie

Houses, but he must have done so tongue-in-cheek, in the same sly fashion that permitted him to pay himself a stupendous compliment ("one of the world's remarkably successful structures") and immediately follow the compliment, in seeming modesty, with, "Let it go at that." True, the setting of Wingspread is a landscape of rolling meadows, interrupted here' and there by adroitly planted clumps of pines, while the settings of most of Wright's turn-of-the-century Prairie Houses were comparatively cramped suburban lots and therefore not authentically of the prairie at all; nevertheless, "Prairie House" evokes a sense of ground-hugging simplicity of form and, within that form, the prospect of an equal simplicity in the conduct of life. Wingspread evokes something very different; it is an exceedingly large mansion, having a floor area of fourteen thousand square feet and shouldering the sky with the self-important eccentricity of some mock-Gothic castle in the Thousand Islands. A true folly, it imposes itself upon

The living room at Wingspread.

its site instead of accommodating to it. Wright may well have sensed this (to him) unwelcome fact, since he took care to praise Wingspread for the opposite reason: he boasted that its presence improved the site, giving it a charm that it lacked when it was merely so much untampered-with nature.

When Wingspread was under construction, Johnson's wife died and Johnson was tempted for a time to abandon the project. At Wright's urging, both for the sake of the children and as a memorial gesture to his dead wife, Johnson finished the house and occupied it for twenty years, accepting with good humor the fact that it leaked as profusely as the Administration Building did and that its scale was far too grand for the family shelter he had had in mind. Johnson was an ideal client in his willingness to forgive the defects that Wright's buildings almost invariably possessed—defects that Wright managed in most cases to turn into proof of his high aesthetic intentions. (At the beginning of the Administration Building project, Johnson visited the house that Wright had designed for his cousin Richard Lloyd Jones, in Tulsa; innumerable tubs and canning jars were scattered throughout the house to catch water leaking through the roof. Mrs. Lloyd Jones apologized to her guest with a kindly witticism: "This is what happens when you leave a work of art out in the rain." In spite of the leaks, Johnson expressed admiration for the house.)

In 1959, shortly after Wright's death, Johnson decided to turn Wingspread over to a philanthropic foundation that he had established in its name. The Wingspread Foundation would occupy the house and make use of it as a conference center. Three years later, after the house had undergone the minimum amount of alteration necessary to turn it from a private residence into an efficient center (the five-car garage, for example, became staff offices, while what had once been the children's playroom became one of the larger conference rooms), the Wingspread Conference Center was opened in Johnson's presence. In the course of the ceremonies, he took care to keep Wright in the foreground:

> There seems to be unanimous opinion, among those best informed, that this building of Mr. Wright's carries with it a quality—rare to conference centers generally—of inspiration and of a relaxed atmosphere. Mr. Wright, whom I always considered a close friend, was of the opinion that environment was one of the great factors which influenced the fuller development of human beings. I am sure he felt environment influenced their behavior towards the ultimate in being creative and as distinguished from being imaginative.
>
> A creative man, however, has to use his imagination to create, and in every sense of the word Wright was a great creative man. He showed me how a creative architect works and how valuable he can be toward the development of individuals or toward a society's culture and science. . . . In the spirit of Frank Lloyd Wright, we will . . . seek to stir and foster the creative nature of a free people, which is so enjoyable, and at the same time so essential, to their continued and expanding freedom.[15]

More than a quarter of a century has passed since the Wingspread Center was dedicated. Today it flourishes under the direction of William B. Boyd, husband of Johnson's daughter Karen (for whom Wright designed, in 1954, a pleasantly romantic house on a bluff above the Racine River). It was to Karen that Wright once extended a remarkable invitation. Visiting Wingspread, he fell ill after lunch and mistook indigestion for a mortal heart attack. He lay down on a couch in the living room, composed himself, beckoned to Karen, and said splendidly, "Come and watch how a great man dies."

It may be unjust for a commentator who never knew the house when it was occupied by the Johnson family to say of it that it appears to serve its present purpose better than it did the purpose for which it was designed; nevertheless, rightly or wrongly, one guesses that Wingspread is one of those cases—common enough in architecture—where too free a hand and too liberal a budget have led to an over-ample opulence rather than to refinement. The grand wigwam of Wingspread rises more gently out of the landscape than it did when it was new, thanks to the profusion of grapevines that cling to its pergolas and walls and to the high trees that share its sky, but even today it bespeaks a technical bravado (one thinks of that preposterous ship's-prow cantilever on the second floor of the bedroom wing, defying gravity out of mere prankishness), instead of the cozy domesticity that Wright was so eloquent a champion of in his small houses.

22

THE YEARS 1936 AND 1937 were little short of miraculous in respect to the number of commissions that, after the desolate years of the Great Depression, suddenly flooded in upon Wright. The wonder is not that he should have accepted these commissions so eagerly (and, in view of the amount of professional assistance available to him at Taliesin, so recklessly) but that, having accepted them, he was able to give so much of himself to their execution. At seventy, how many individuals have preserved undiminished that combination of attributes—talent, intelligence, energy, discipline—by which substantial works of art are brought into the world? Among a handful of others, one thinks of Yeats, Wright's near-contemporary, and of how in age he learned to express in a kind of joyous frenzy feelings that in his youth he had kept hidden behind a scrim of exquisite pre-Raphaelitish fancy. In the last weeks of his life, Yeats wrote, "Man cannot know the truth, but he can embody it." For Wright, the embodiment of truth in architecture was a perennial goal, to which he devoted himself with especial passion during the fruitful decade and a half of his life between seventy and eighty-five. He was never intellectually rigorous enough to set this truth down in coherent form in words (a hortatory Welsh eloquence kept getting between him and the logical pursuit of an argument); again and again, however, he was able to set it down in his designs, in a seemingly inexhaustible number of variations.

In 1936, Wright was simultaneously at work on, among other projects, Fallingwater, the Johnson Wax administration building, the Hanna house, and the Jacobs house. Every bit as remarkable as the number of projects on his drawing board was the diversity of the designs that he was providing his newfound clients from coast to coast—clients who were themselves so diverse in nature and circumstance that of the best of them it might be said that they had nothing in common except their ability to stand up to Wright. They admired him and with time they came to feel affection for him, but they also fought him; when, testing their resolve, he chose to

377

bark at them, they barked back, to his delight. He was contemptuous of so-called yes-men, and a client who said yes too readily might wind up with a house as uninteresting as he deserved.

High in Wright's regard were Paul and Jean Hanna, who commissioned one of the most beautiful and, in terms of its accommodation to their needs, one of the most satisfactory of all Wright's houses—"Honeycomb," in Palo Alto, named by Wright after the hexagon module upon which its plan is based. As young newly married academics at Columbia University, in New York City, the Hannas as early as 1930 were clipping and filing newspaper accounts of the lectures Wright delivered at Princeton that year; later, they secured a copy of *Modern Architecture,* the published version of the lectures, and sat up all night reading it. Possessing exceptionally lofty ideals in regard to the kind of life they intended to share and the kind of house that would help to make such a life possible, they perceived in Wright's words what long before (according to Wright) Mrs. Avery Coonley had perceived in his works: "the countenance of principle." They wrote a fan letter to Wright and Wright responded, inviting them to visit him at Taliesin; in the summer of 1931, the Hannas passed a happy twenty-four hours in Wisconsin with the Wrights and their cluster of apprentices. In a book vividly describing their long relationship with Wright, the Hannas recall his having mentioned even then his desire to design a house whose shape would be derived from a honeycomb instead of a box. On parting, the Hannas asked Wright if he would consent to design a house for them some day. Of course Wright said yes—how could he not have said yes to that ardent and knowledgeable young couple, and particularly in the dark days of the thirties, when the question was rarely being put to him?

In 1935, Hanna was invited to join the faculty at Stanford University. He and Jean and their three small children set out on the long drive from New York City to Palo Alto, stopping off at Taliesin for three days. In the course of their stay, the Hannas, with Wright's help, drew up a sort of prospectus for the house they longed to build. Given that they were in their early thirties, that they had limited means, and that they had three children to raise, it was indeed an ambitious document; as a summary of the joint intentions of the architect and his clients at that fleeting, fortunate moment before the problem of a budget has to be faced it is worth quoting in full:

> Land on the brow of a hill, with view and drainage, large enough for gardening, playing, and privacy;
> a house nestling into the contours of the hill;
> a house enclosing enough space for a variety of human activities without crowding three young children and their parents;

a house warm and dry in inclement weather, but thrown open to the breezes of terrace and garden when desired;

walls of glass so that we could always be visually conscious of sunrise or sunset, the fog banks rolling over the hills, or trees and grass in the fields;

a house so equipped that electricity, natural gas, and labor-saving devices would do the drudgery, leaving time and strength for the more creative aspects of life. We wish to be free of tending the furnace, regulating room temperatures, washing dishes, carrying out garbage;

furnishings that carried out the simple, unified pattern of the house as a whole; little decoration as such; only the honest use of materials;

a house accommodating art objects that had a special meaning for us and reminded us of great events, great people, or great experiences;

a house sheltering indoors up to thirty guests at dinner parties; up to one hundred guests for musical evenings, receptions, cocktails, or teas; overnight guests or relatives; seminar groups of students or colleagues;

a house with terraces and gardens that would accommodate up to two hundred guests for informal functions, sunning, or relaxing in sunshine or shade, and children's activities, such as rollerskating, games, dancing;

a house that could be remodeled easily as changing family composition and function required.[1]

In late March of 1936 the Wrights and their daughter Iovanna came on from Arizona to visit the Hannas in Palo Alto. Hanna showed Wright three possible building sites, including the property that the Hannas were eventually able to secure on a long-term lease from the university—a hillside looking west over the university campus and with a pleasing southern exposure as well. In April, a set of plans and elevations arrived from Taliesin. Although Wright in the course of his visit had again spoken of laying out a house in hexagons, the Hannas were astonished to discover that he had actually done so. Wright wrote of the plans, "I imagine they will be something of a shock. . . . I hope the unusual shape of the rooms won't disturb you, because in reality they would be more quiet than rectangular ones and you would scarcely be aware of any irregularity. The furniture [to be designed by Wright] works into the scheme naturally enough. You have contrasting high and low ceilings in every room. . . . The house itself is built upon prepared ground—precast hexagonal tiles laid down on concrete and the house erected on the intersection lines. The outside walls are only 2¾ inches thick of redwood insulated with aluminum foil. The walls inside just the same and the ceiling all wood. . . ."[2]

Bravely the Hannas studied the plans, which even today, to a person familiar with the house, are sufficiently difficult to comprehend: what can be walked through with perfect ease has the look, on paper, of being a labyrinth. The Hannas wrote to Wright, expressing their delight with his honeycomb and proposing a few slight changes—the first of scores of "slight changes" by means of which the house became a true collaboration between architect and clients. Hanna spent a couple of days at Taliesin, going over the sketches with Wright and the apprentices, and receiving from Wright, written in pencil, an impromptu "memo of agreement":

> It is hereby agreed that Paul Hanna retains the services of Frank Lloyd Wright as architect in the erection, furnishing + planting of a dwelling at Stanford University, California, on a plot of ground to be decided upon for the purpose. The terms of employment are as follows—
>
> For preliminary sketches payable when accepted or rejected by Mr. Hanna, 3% of proposed cost of dwelling.
>
> For plans and specifications, payable when plans are ready, 5% of price of estimates.
>
> For superintendence arranged to mutual satisfaction of parties hereto—2% of projected cost payable when building is [completed].
>
> Total fee to be adjusted at completion of building.[3]

As the Hannas have pointed out, the memorandum was neither signed nor dated, but it amounted to as nearly a true legal contract as the parties concerned felt they would ever need. When, on May 31st, Wright rendered his first bill, the Hanna's trust in him received its first test. At the beginning, the Hannas had made it clear to Wright that fifteen thousand dollars was the absolute limit on the amount of money they could afford to spend on the house; moreover, they assumed that the fifteen thousand dollars would include the architect's fee. Now they discovered that Wright was projecting an eighteen-thousand-dollar house, which, with an architect's fee of eighteen hundred dollars, would bring the total cost of the house to almost twenty thousand dollars, or more than twenty-five percent above budget. (Moreover, Wright had silently raised the percentage on the first fee they were being asked to pay, from three to three and one-half percent.) Understandably, the Hannas protested and Wright applied the verbal emollients he had learned to count upon during a lifetime of answering protests: "I appreciate your dilemma. Everything gets down to a money matter so quickly. . . . About the preliminary fee you must have misunderstood me, or I misunderstood myself. But don't you worry. . . . It will come out right in the end. . . . If the sum due . . . inconveniences you at the moment, take your time. . . . I got tossed off the road-grader making a new road to Hillside. Wrenched neck and leg—couple of ribs knocked in—damn'd painful as I sit here writing, but worse when I try to lie down. . . . My best to Jean and the babies. . . ."[4]

In July, the Hannas learned that Stanford would permit them to build on the hillside they coveted and Wright sent along a new batch of plans, embracing a number of the Hannas' suggestions. In September they had still further suggestions to make (a hallway between the children's playroom and bedrooms was only nineteen and a half inches wide and the Hannas pleaded that it be increased to a minimum of thirty-two inches), along with an urgent request for working drawings complete enough for local contractors to be able to estimate costs and make bids on, and an even more urgent request that Wright himself be present in Palo Alto when the building contracts were let. No answer. They wrote again in October, to learn from Eugene Masselink, Wright's secretary, that the apprentices— "the boys," as Masselink called them—would have the working drawings ready in another ten days; they would be mailed to the Hannas as soon as Mr. Wright had had a chance to look them over upon his return from a short lecture tour in the East. (Wright was certainly in the East during that period, inspecting Fallingwater and its newly poured concrete cantilevers; he was also in Racine, working on the Johnson Wax job. He was fortunately past having to earn pittances on lecture tours.)

The delays caused by Wright's prolonged absences from Taliesin distressed the Hannas, and with reason, because Hanna had arranged to be excused from his duties at Stanford during the months of November and December in order to help build the house. So far not a spade of earth had been turned. The ten days promised by Masselink having passed, the Hannas wrote again, truly vexed. They pointed out that the agreed-upon date for the completion of the house was April 1st, 1937, and that the landlord of the rented house in which they were then living was unwilling to extend their lease beyond June; if the house were not finished on schedule, the Hanna family would be homeless. In late November, they sent Wright a telegram, begging him for the information they had sought in their letters; the next day, they received a characteristically unilluminating reply: OKAY COMPLYING WITH REQUEST. They had survived the first rite of passage of all Wright clients: they had proved themselves capable of being at once victors and victims and of choosing not to discriminate between one condition and the other.

In December, Wright came to Palo Alto to seek approval of his plans from the Stanford comptroller. Ever the prankster, Wright took care first to insult the comptroller and then to make him laugh, charming him to the point where the comptroller burst out, "Mr. Wright, if Hanna wants you to design his house, I will approve your plans without even looking at them." During that visit, Wright informed the Hannas that their house would probably cost them twenty thousand dollars; after having talked with their contractor, in January he raised the probable sum to twenty-five thousand dollars, adding, to heighten their confusion, that they would be getting what amounted to a fifty-thousand-dollar house for that price. The Hannas were aghast. They assumed that to build the house would be to place themselves in debt for the rest of their lives; nevertheless, their pride in the unbuilt house was so great that there could be no turning back. In fear and trembling, they signaled to their contractor to begin work.

In late January, over the Hannas' vehement objections, Wright's plans continued to call for two-foot-wide doorways and bathtubs, a hallway less than twenty inches wide, and beds thirty inches wide. IMPOSSIBLE LIVING CONDITIONS, they wired him. COMPLETE REDRAWING OF BATHROOMS HALLWAY AND BEDROOMS MUST BE DONE IMMEDIATELY. . . . Wright replied, defending his specifications on the grounds that the Hannas, like the Wrights, "are not so big." To this, the Hannas hotly rejoined, "We may be small people but hardly pygmies. . . ." The quarrel continued for weeks, and in their book the Hannas are at pains to point out that, although Wright is commonly described as having been arrogant and intolerant, it is they who were arrogant and intolerant at that point in their relationship with Wright and he who was a patient father-figure to a pair of "brattish" clients. In a long letter to them, he writes, "The door to my own bathroom opens to one foot, nine inches. It has not occurred to me that it was narrow. I am sure there are no impossible living conditions anywhere, even in the narrow gallery leading the little girl to her bedroom. . . . I have studied this thing

© SUSAN WOLDENBERG

The Hanna house, Palo Alto (1937). Paul and Jean Hanna, a young academic couple at Stanford University, fought what seemed to them at the time a life-and-death struggle with FLW to create their ideal house. And an ideal house was what they and he achieved.

all the later half of my architectural life, with the idea of the eventual prefabricated house. I *know* what I am talking about. It is no matter of taste but, if it were, good taste is all on the side of more human proportions for articles of human use. . . . Try to get hold of this in feet and inches of structure, as I have. . . . If you feel it necessary, I will send a superintendent to stay with you while you need him. I don't want to promise anything about my own advent. [Wright was suffering from phlebitis after recovering from pneumonia.] Whatever gods may be take umbrage where there is too much presumption. I hope this lets in light and restores confidence. If it doesn't, why, then those same gods have mercy."[5]

The house was under construction for several months, and scarcely a week passed without an unexpected crisis. Carpenters, electricians, plumbers—nobody had ever undertaken to work with a hexagon module before, and to be always confronted with a 120-degree angle instead of the conventional 90-degree right angle caused problems psychological as well as practical. Mistakes were made and corrected and again made and corrected, always at the Hannas' expense; some mistakes were made that were not correctable. The copper-foil roof, for example, was supposed to be laid with ridged horizontal seams, paralleling the rooftree and eaves; instead, the roofers laid it with vertical seams, paralleling the rafters. Wright had neglected to send the Hannas a copy of his specifications for the roof, so they had no way of knowing what his design intentions were. (A composition roof has since replaced the copper.) Costs kept rising day by day. The Hannas reminded Wright that he had promised them a twenty-five-thousand-dollar house and that they had estimated on their own hook that it might come to as much as thirty-five thousand dollars; as the end of construction approached, they found that they had already spent more than thirty-seven thousand dollars. "We are going to be heavily in debt," they wrote. ". . . the events are irrevocable, and we are glad that we have the house, but you should know at what a price this has been achieved. When you come, you can say where we have made errors. . . ."[6]

Wright was able to point out in reply—as he had done with other clients over the years—that he, too, would be likely to suffer as a consequence of the high costs of the house: "We shall probably never build another house in Palo Alto. . . . You know I would not have let the thing go on at all if I hadn't seen in you a more than ordinarily capable client and in Turner a good builder whose judgment I had no reason to doubt. . . . As for the details, we did pretty well considering the break of my illness. . . . The only consolation I can offer you for being in debt—like me—is that it is a spur to action and that unlike most homeowners you have something worthwhile to show for your indebtedness. However, that doesn't satisfy me. I feel badly about the whole business and almost wish we hadn't gone on with it. My best to you both."[7] The letter had the desired effect; the Hannas found the seeming sadness of their father-figure too much for their tender hearts to bear. They wrote at once, "Please forgive our childish wailing from time to time. You know that we love this house regardless of the delays and financial sacrifices. It is the loveliest shelter we have ever seen. . . ."[8]

What was true for the Hannas at that moment was soon to prove true for the world at large: many tens of thousands of people have visited this loveliest of shelters over the decades and will go on visiting it for uncountable decades to come. Wright added a guesthouse and workshop in the early nineteen-fifties; in 1957, the Hanna children being long since grown and dispersed, a large-scale reorganization of the space within the original house was undertaken, granting the Hannas in their professionally busy middle years fewer but larger rooms for both work and entertaining. For the new master bedroom and library, Wright had designed fireplaces with the usual floor-level hearths; Jean Hanna flew to Taliesin West to ask Wright for raised hearths. She was warned by the apprentices in the drafting room that Wright would never consent to such a change, but when she explained to him that a raised hearth in the library would enable her husband and her to watch a fire from their desks and in the master bedroom a raised hearth would enable them to watch a fire from bed and also enable an occasional visiting grandchild to do so from an adjoining

The garden of the Hanna house.

guest room, Wright said, "That sounds like a perfectly legitimate reason. You'll have your raised hearths."

Wright paid his last visit to Honeycomb in 1958, a year before he died. By then, the Wrights and the Hannas had been friends for over thirty years; they had shared not only the house (as we have seen, all the houses that Wright designed remained, in a sense, "his") but the good fortune that had attended both families. From the days of his impoverishment in the Great Depression, when it appeared that the world of architectural fashion had passed him by, Wright had risen in his self-delighting old age to become the most celebrated architect on earth; as for the Hannas, they had become celebrated within the compass of academe and, thanks to the long-continued high sales of Hanna's textbooks on child education and to wise investments, they had acquired considerable wealth. The days when they had feared that the Honeycomb would crush them under a weight of unpayable debt were long passed; those days were by no means forgotten, but they could be jested about as proving the soundness of Wright's thoroughly unsound maxim, "Give me the luxuries and let the necessities take care of themselves."

During the course of that last visit to the house, the Hannas had the pleasure of hearing Wright, in a tone of lilting boyish wonder, exclaim over how well "it all came together." After his death, the Hannas, by then in their late fifties, began to ponder a suitable disposition of the house—one that would ensure its preservation and would give it a purpose worthy of the man who had designed it. (Worthy, too, though the Hannas were too modest to speculate in such terms, of the couple who had commissioned the house, had chosen its site, had helped to build it with their own hands, and had contributed so much to its air of playful repose.) With the encouragement of their children, who had residences elsewhere, they decided to donate the house to Stanford, promising at the same time to help raise an endowment for its maintenance. Their hope was that the house would be put at the disposal of visiting lecturers and other distinguished guests of the university. (Instead, and to the Hannas' regret, the university has chosen to house its provost in Honeycomb, thus saving itself the expense of providing him with adequate quarters elsewhere.) The Hannas deeded the house to Stanford in 1974 and moved out of it a year later. In 1977, thanks in part to the prompting of the Hannas and their Japanese friends, the Nissan Motor Company gave five hundred thousand dollars toward the endowment of the house. The gift was a gesture of homage toward Wright for his lifelong advocacy of Japanese culture. A gesture similar in purpose can be found in the hillside garden of the Hannas' house, where a visitor is likely to happen upon a large and unexpected object: one of the grand carved oya-stone urns that Wright designed to stand high on the porte cochere of the Imperial Hotel. Just before the hotel was demolished, its owners offered the urn to Hanna as a souvenir. Since the urn weighs two tons, a more timid man might have refused the offer; not Hanna, who with characteristic resourcefulness managed to bring it intact all the way from Tokyo to Palo Alto. The urn looks perfectly at home in the Hanna garden, and why should it not? For it is, in fact, neither Japanese nor American; it is an outward and visible sign of the Wright inscape, whose boundaries are not to be measured in rods and chains.

An urn from the Imperial Hotel, which Professor Hanna acquired at the time that the hotel was demolished, arranged to have shipped across the Pacific, and placed on the lawn of the Honeycomb house.

© SUSAN WOLDENBERG

In the *annus mirabilis* of 1936, a fourth wonder, even more important to Wright's career (though not to his artistic development) than Fallingwater, the Johnson Wax administration building, and the Honeycomb, emerged in the form of the Jacobs house, commissioned by a young couple in Madison, Wisconsin. Herbert Jacobs was a reporter on the Madison *Capital Times;* he and his wife, Katherine, had a small daughter and were in need of a house. Having almost no money, they were nevertheless determined to possess a house worthy of their ambitions; their ideal at the time was something in the Dutch Colonial style, made of white-painted brick. No such house happened to be available in Madison. A cousin of Katherine Jacobs—an artist who had spent a summer at Taliesin—urged them to build a house of their own and to have Frank Lloyd Wright design it for them. The Jacobses thought of Wright as an architect for millionaires, but the cousin persisted in recommending him and at last made an appointment for them to meet with Wright at Taliesin. On the forty-mile-long drive west from Madison to Spring Green, the Jacobses nervously wondered how to put the problem of their poverty versus their ambitions before the great man. They decided to assume a totally false air of bravado, and upon meeting Wright Jacobs blurted out a mocking paraphrase of a then well-known statement by an American politician ("What this country needs is a good five-cent cigar"), saying, "What this country needs is a decent five-thousand-dollar house. Can you design one for us?"

In his usual buoyant manner, Wright said at once, "Would you really be satisfied with a five-thousand-dollar house? Most people want a ten-thousand-dollar house for five thousand dollars." The Jacobses assured Wright that they were aware of what they would have to do without in a house built at that price. Merrily quoting a line of verse that he had been taught in childhood and had uttered to a hundred clients over the years— " 'Will you walk into my parlor?' said the spider to the fly"—Wright led the Jacobses into his private office and set about weaving the web that was to hold them contentedly entrapped until he died. For twenty years, Wright said, he had been eager to design a low-cost house. He had thought long and hard about the difficulties to be faced and he would be glad to undertake the adventure with them. To keep the cost of the house down to five thousand dollars, it would have to be built for forty-five hundred dollars; that would yield him a fee, reckoned at his usual ten percent, of four hundred and fifty dollars.

As Jacobs was later to write (for Wright would become the subject of many books and articles by Jacobs), he and his wife began the adventure in a state of highly disadvantageous innocence. They supposed, for example, that the magical figure of five thousand dollars would include the price of the land on which the house would be placed. Wright let them encounter on their own the shock of discovering otherwise, saying only that he couldn't begin to design their house until after they had purchased a site. He urged them to find a location in the open countryside; instead, they settled for a plot in the suburbs of Madison that measured sixty feet by one hundred and twenty feet and cost them eight hundred dollars. That sum was exactly half of all the capital they had available; the rest of their expenses would be dependent upon a mortgage. A further proof of their innocence was that they expected the house to be designed and built within three months; in the event, it took well over a year before they were able to move into a house that, even by that time, was still far from finished.

The Jacobses' impression that Wright was an architect for millionaires had led them to suppose that his drafting room was continuously chock-a-block with major projects; they were astonished to discover that, on the contrary, they had come to him with their tiny commission at the very moment that he was at last beginning to receive a few big ones—was, indeed, for the first time in many years, working for millionaires. Little by little it became clear to the Jacobses that Wright had been eager to accept the designing of their house not only because he was truly interested in the problem of low-cost private housing but also because he saw that their house would serve as a useful working model on a small scale for certain experiments that he intended to carry out on a large scale with his other commissions. Earlier, he had convinced the Johnson Wax people to heat "the great workroom" of their new administration building by simply heating its floor. Pipes were to be embedded in a concrete slab laid over gravel, and heat in one form or another passed through the pipes, which by gravity would rise to warm the floor; a warm floor underfoot would provide greater comfort at less expense than the heating (and, in America, habitual over-heating) of an entire room. Wright had observed this method of heating in Japan, where heated air from an underground furnace wended its way back and forth through clay flues under the floor before escaping upward through a chimney. The Japanese had borrowed this technique from the Koreans; two thousand years earlier, it had been a commonplace throughout the Roman Empire.

With his usual vivacity, Wright had managed to persuade a skeptical Hib Johnson in Racine and the skeptical Hannas in Palo Alto that this ancient method of heating was, as modified by Wright in the nineteen-thirties, far ahead of its time. At one stroke, save the heavy expense of deeply excavated foundations and basements by the pouring of a monolithic concrete slab! Obliterate the uncleanness and cumbersomeness of either radiators or hot-air ducts by means of pipes hidden in the slab! Who would not find the prospect irresistible if it was also practical? The fact was that Wright had no way of knowing whether the method would work, especially in the cold climate of Wisconsin. He had come to suspect that the circulation of heated air would not suffice in the slab, but whether steam or hot water would prove an adequate substitute was a question to which the Jacobs house would be able to supply a discreet answer. The house would also serve to test the practicality of the thin board-and-batten sandwich out of which he intended to build its walls, the practicality of its almost flat roof (in a climate marked by heavy snowfalls), and the practicality of its replacement of a garage with a mere cantilevered shelter—what Wright christened a carport—and its omission of gutters and downspouts.

The Jacobses were willing to have their house serve as a laboratory; they were also willing to serve as guinea pigs in that laboratory. If they were innocent in regard to money and property, they were sophisticated in regard to the sort of society they wished to bring up children in; they expected always to be servantless and hardworking and to live as close as possible to the land. They were accustomed to building furniture and stitching clothes and planting gardens, and they welcomed in the design of their new house an open workspace instead of a kitchen, an informal mingling of labor and leisure, both indoors and outdoors. And the house that Wright designed for them was a marvel of accommodation to their needs and to the aspirations that he was helping them to discover in themselves. The first step had been to persuade the Jacobses that their newly acquired lot was too small; they returned to the real-estate agent from whom they had purchased it and he agreed to take it back and to sell them two lots on the opposite side of the street, which not only provided them with twice as much land but with a far more agreeable view, dropping gently downhill over open land. (So confident had Wright been that they would follow his dictates that he had designed their house to be sixty feet wide—the exact width of the original lot and therefore, according to local setback requirements, incapable of being legally fitted into place upon it.) The two lots used up all their available cash, but the Wrightian attitude toward money was beginning to have an effect on them: they were afraid not to take chances in the presence of a man who had spent a lifetime doing so. When, to their dismay, the Federal Housing Administration refused to grant them a mortgage (a flat roof was against F.H.A. rules), the Jacobses were rescued by another chance-taker and admirer of Wright— a Madison banker who, as a young man in Chicago, had enjoyed visiting Midway Gardens. With a skeptical cheerfulness rare among bankers, he lent them the necessary forty-five hundred dollars.

Small as the house was—fifteen hundred square feet in all—the many ingenuities of its plan made it seem at least twice that size. In the shape of an L, with the base of the L parallel to the street and embracing the living room, workroom, bathroom, and entry, and the upright of the L paralleling the northern boundary of the property and embracing the three bedrooms, it presented a harsh, even a forbidding, aspect to the street, having only a narrow band of clerestory windows at the point where the blank house wall and the overhang of the flat roof met. The family car would occupy most of what in conventional houses would be a front porch, while the front door, being set at right angles to the street, was nearly invisible. If the street façade of the house was uninviting (and must have distressed the Jacobses' neighbors, who were used to glancing into one another's windows), the inner façade was an unexpected and delightful expanse of high glass doors, opening from the living room onto a sunny eastern terrace; the bedrooms looked south through matching high glass doors and shared with the living room a view of the ample garden.

The house gained an almost instant fame, in part because of the publicity aroused by its low cost (emerging from the Great Depression, hundreds of thousands of Americans were eager to possess a house in the five-thousand-dollar range), in part because of its unprecedentedly open design, and in part because of the curious nature of its construction—nobody

The Jacobs house presents an uninviting front to the passerby. At the rear, the garden is all light and air—a reward to the passerby who has had the good fortune to become a guest.

had ever tried living on a slab before or had ever tried cooking in something called a workspace, lit from above and scarcely to be distinguished from the adjacent dining space. It was all very odd and perhaps, given the past history of the architect who had designed it, faintly scandalous; so great was the number of people who came to peer and poke about and shake their heads as the house went up that, once the Jacobses had moved in, they decided to charge admission to the premises: twenty-five cents.

Among the visitors to the house when it was still under construction was Walter Gropius, who had been lecturing at the University of Wisconsin and arrived in the company of an officious local architect. Wright happened to be making a hasty, unannounced tour of inspection, as he often did on his way to the Johnson job in Racine; according to Jacobs, the local architect invited Wright to meet Gropius and show him around, and the usually gracious Wright refused. The refusal may have had more to do with the local architect's having neglected to ask Wright's permission to bring Gropius to the site than to any personal disregard for Gropius, whose Bauhaus principles Wright had often vociferously condemned. After all, Gropius had done Wright the favor of becoming one of the original "Friends of the Fellowship" when it was founded at Taliesin in 1932. (Also a Fellow was Mies van der Rohe, with whom Wright was on cordial terms despite their professional differences.) The all-Wright issue of the *Forum* having given a prominent place to the Jacobs house, the crowds increased to the point where, in hopes of controlling them and of thus securing at least a measure of privacy for themselves, the Jacobses raised the price of admission to fifty cents—a welcome means of helping to pay for the house.

From youth, Wright was shameless in begging for materials from manufacturers either at no cost to himself or at a substantial discount. Wood,
glass, steel, stone, plumbing fixtures, roofing materials—he was always in
need of them and it was true that he was often bent upon experimenting
with them in such a way that a deal, however unbusinesslike it appeared
at the start, might eventually show his benefactor a profit. In the case of
the Jacobs house, he hoped to gain the assistance of a large plumbing-
supply company in New York, which for the sake of discovering whether
Wright's new-old heating principles would perform as successfully in North
America as in Asia (and in doing so open the door to an entirely new
source of revenue for the company) would underwrite the cost of the
equipment and its installation. The company's engineers looked over
Wright's blueprints and pronounced the system unworkable. Later, when
the system was in operation, some of the engineers came to the house,
saw that the system worked, and returned to New York to issue—apparently
out of wounded pride—a second negative report.

Wright called the Jacobs house Usonia One, and the first of anything
is likely to contain flaws. The heating system, although it worked, proved
less efficient than Wright had counted on its being. Steam failed to heat
the pipes adequately in cold weather, and after a year or so, on Wright's
recommendation, continuously circulated hot water took its place, to good
effect. Storm windows, which the Jacobses couldn't afford and which Wright
detested, would have made the house more weatherproof; as for screens,
indispensable in the Wisconsin summer, Wright "forgot" about them entirely, no doubt because they would have made the house look less like
an open-air pavilion. The Jacobses insisted upon his designing screens
for them and Wright consented to do so; at his suggestion, they paid for
them with the last portion of his architect's fee.

One might quarrel with Wright and say of the Jacobs house that it
was Usonia Three, having been preceded by houses designed in the Usonian
vein for the Hoult family, in Wichita, Kansas, in 1935, and for the Lusk
family, in Huron, South Dakota, later in the same year. Both houses, which
never got beyond the planning stage, owed a good deal to the Willey
house of 1934, which must then be categorized as ur-Usonian, or even
Premature Usonian. All such labels, creating boundaries in a process that
by its nature is without boundaries, are nonsensical; nevertheless, Wright
himself was willing to establish periods and affix dates—on occasion, to
alter dates—whenever it served a sufficiently advantageous (and sufficiently
devious) purpose. He invented the term Prairie House for a kind of house
that had little to do with the prairie and much to do with the suburbs,
and he invented the term Usonian in order to impose an American name
on a style of house having far more to do with the structures that Mies

van der Rohe and other architects in Middle Europe were designing than it did with the design of houses in Middle America.

As we have seen, Wright plucked the word Usonia from some as yet unidentified source; what matters is not where the word came from but the weight that Wright meant it to carry, and why. He was always placing his literary and oratorical gifts at the service of his profession; often, he wrote things and said things that were mere repetitious bombast and yet they were the means—clumsy, indirect, too high in pitch—that enabled him to accomplish something of value in his career. "Usonian" staked a claim on behalf of the work that was far more than a mask for whatever foreign strains may have entered into it. So in its time did "Broadacre City," which if Wright hadn't stamped it as his own would have struck us as a wisecracking book-title by the sour likes of Sinclair Lewis.

Throughout his entire career, Wright was determined to place an authentic American stamp upon his work. Drawing inspiration, as well as certain major principles of scale and volume, from a score of foreign sources (Austria, Scotland, Japan, Mexico), he sedulously covered his tracks with allusions to an American past drawn not from history—Wright was shaky on American history—but from American letters. On his mother's side, he was a first-generation American; it was his father's side of the family, largely snubbed by Wright, that arrived here in the seventeenth century and entitled him to speak grandly of his American heritage. So convincing was he that few of his readers or auditors took the trouble to challenge his credentials as a spokesman for America. He found a number of ways to elude this challenge, mild and infrequent as it nearly always was; one of them was to speak Usonian—a tongue so lyrical that larks tumbled out of the sky to listen to it.

23

ONE OF WRIGHT's favorite quips—
that the apparent ease and speed with which he produced his designs
was a consequence of the fact that "I simply shake them out of my sleeve"—
came close to being the truth about the Usonian houses. Between 1936,
and 1941, when the Second World War put a stop to nearly all construction
except for military purposes, Usonian houses sprang up all over the country;
after the war, scores of variations on the basic theme sped from the drafting
rooms of one or the other of the two Taliesins. The popularity of Usonian
houses was such that Wright's task in designing them threatened to reduce
itself to an infinitely repeated process of self-plagiarism; it became obvious
in many cases that people who requested a house from him were seeking
not an ingenious Wrightian solution to the challenge of their particular
domestic requirements but an instantly recognizable Wrightian object. For
that reason, they were rarely distressed to discover that the house they
had commissioned was almost identical to half a dozen other houses designed during the same period, usually in some other part of the country.
Points of resemblance among these houses amounted to a guarantee of
authenticity and therefore, indirectly, to a guarantee of one's prestige as
an aesthetically advanced member of the community.

In commissioning a Usonian house, one could expect it to have but
a single story; to have a masonry chimney core, either of stone or brick;
to have wings extending out from the core, often at an angle of from
sixty to a hundred and twenty degrees and with a cladding of either cypress
or redwood; to have a carport instead of a garage; to have large expanses
of glass facing south and slitlike clerestory windows facing north; to have
bedrooms as small and snug as ships' cabins; and to have a large living
room, with a fireplace that announced itself unmistakably as the heart of
the house. One might have a servant, or servants, in a Usonian house,
but they were not the inescapable presences they had been in the days of
the Prairie House. The kitchen having been transformed into a workspace
and in most cases being open to the rest of the house had also shrunk

markedly in size; a uniformed servant would look as odd in it as a dinosaur. (Wright had little or no firsthand experience of kitchens; he had been waited on at table since infancy, either by women members of his family, by servants, or by apprentices, and he found it hard to take seriously the complaint that his workspaces were too small.)

Wright laid out his plans on a grid, which was readily adaptable to whatever module happened to strike his fancy; the module could be of any size or shape, whether rectangular, triangular, circular, hexagonal, or octagonal. The geometry of the grid in two dimensions was usually easy enough for a layman to perceive; what Wright possessed and was able to exploit with dazzling results was the gift of imagining the geometry of a grid in three dimensions. In the course of working out the manifold relationships of the length, breadth, and height of a house, his mind's eye would be roving at liberty through its constantly altering volumes and calculating the psychological effect that these volumes, once they had reached proportions satisfactory to him, would have upon the future occupants of the house—an effect that no layman could be expected to deduce from a network of pencil strokes appearing on a flat sheet of paper. Wright liked to make the entering of his houses a matter of surprising twists and turns (we picture our ancestors as having penetrated their cave dwellings in something like the same zigzag fashion), but it was in respect to our perception of height that Wright manipulated our senses most cunningly. He joked about having employed his own comparatively short stature as a measure of the norm, but this was less of a joke than he pretended: even a casual visitor to a Wright house is almost certain to feel an expansion of spirit that goes beyond any mere expansion of one's physical scale. Perhaps it isn't an exaggeration to say that one feels in a Wright house that one has gained, at least for the time being, what Henry James called the sense of an "increased fitness to live."

Wright was able to experience his unbuilt designs every bit as fully as a composer experiences a work written but as yet unperformed; indeed, the labor of drawing up plans was undertaken chiefly in order to provide a document—one that not only satisfied the requirements of clients but became in Wright's hands an actual, verifiable work of art, independent of its utility. As such, it might be described as a thought transformed into a thing and therefore able to outlast its maker and enjoy the chance, available to every work of art, of entering history. But the document is not a necessary part of the artist's satisfaction in creating whatever precedes the document; to that extent, the document is gratuitous. Perhaps that is the reason that Wright was so much less distressed than one might have expected him to be over the great number of his projects that remained unbuilt; for him, the creative act had already been completed twice—once in his mind and once on paper—and its third completion, in stone, wood, glass, and the like, was sometimes, thanks to the compromises that had accompanied its execution, a vexatious anti-climax.

Even with the many commissions that Wright was accepting for private residences from coast to coast, the problem of money remained a paramount concern; his correspondence continues to be filled with complaints over what appears to be an ever-escalating indebtedness, and at first one is puzzled to understand how this can be so. Wright has recovered his high place in the world's regard and the burden of the Great Depression is beginning to lessen; surely this hardworking man should be setting foot at last upon the approaches to Easy Street. Not so, because he pursues poverty with the same zeal that other men pursue wealth. Moreover, poverty on the high level that Wright's ambition dictates can be achieved only by a superlatively careless extravagance, practiced tirelessly around the clock. Luckily for his ambition, Wright was as great a prodigy in the mismanagement of his financial affairs as he was in the profession of architecture. No matter how much money he earned, he saw to it that his expenditures exceeded it. Money in the hand, to say nothing of money in the bank, rendered him lightheaded and irresponsible, a condition that could be cured only by his taking an immediate plunge backward and downward into insolvency.

The most vivid account of Wright's attitude toward money is to be found in his son John's agreeably eccentric memoir, *My Father Who Is on Earth*. In telling of that time of troubles when he was working for his father in Chicago on the Midway Gardens project, John writes that a sheriff turned up at the office one day, seeking immediate payment of a debt of fifteen hundred dollars for back rent. Having not a penny available, Wright was face to face with just the sort of challenge he relished. He smiled at the sheriff asked John to show him around the drafting room, and slipped away. John kept the sheriff occupied with blueprints of Midway Gardens, meanwhile assuring him of Wright's greatness. At last Wright returned, bearing aloft a check for ten thousand dollars. A Bostonian collector of Japanese prints, with whom Wright had done business in the past, had happened to be in Chicago that day and Wright had just succeeded in selling him a portion of his own collection of Japanese prints. Off to the bank went the sheriff and the Wrights to cash the check; the sheriff was paid off and then, as John Wright tells the story, his father proposed that they make the rounds and pay some more debts:

. . . It was fun, but a glance from the corner of my eye showed me that an expensive mood was descending upon him. At Marshall Field's he saw a chair that struck his fancy.

"One hundred and twenty-five dollars," read the salesperson from the ticket that dangled from the arm.

"I'll take a dozen, send them up to Taliesin." Next he ordered a dozen Chinese rugs. At Lyon and Healy's he saw a concert grand piano. He caressed its keys with his Beethoven-like fingers, then ordered three. . . . Dad was now into his never-failing credit again. A gong somewhere sounding six times stopped him. Soon we were seated comfortably in the Pompeian Room of the Congress Hotel. The dinner Dad ordered was the envy of a gourmet who sat and stared at us. We ate slowly, luxuriously enjoying the music of the famous Pompeian orchestra. The inner man satisfied, Dad leaned back in his chair—the picture of serene contentment. It had been a perfect day, he had succeeded in plunging himself in debt again and everything was normal once more.[1]

Along with the many Usonian houses, two major projects engrossed Wright during this period: the campus that he was designing at Lakeland, Florida, for Florida Southern College, and what might well be called the campus of Taliesin West, in the desert outside Scottsdale. The two projects were linked financially as well as aesthetically; they were also linked by an almost comically exact resemblance between Wright's personality and that of Ludd Myrl Spivey, the President of the college. A short, thin, bald, handsome, bespectacled go-getter, Dr. Spivey was an ordained Methodist minister and, curiously enough, a lifelong disciple of the philosopher John Dewey. Spivey was determined to make his college prosper, and the fact that it had little endowment, few wealthy alumni, an unimpressive academic reputation, and a student body consisting of five hundred girls and two hundred and fifty boys (most of whom were without funds and had to work their way through school) presented no substantial obstacles to him. Like Wright, he was a spellbinder with unbounded energy and self-confidence and with an incomparable knack for talking people out of sums of money greater than they intended to spend.

Ludd Myrl Spivey—the name (pronounced "spy-vee") is out of Dickens at his most exaggerated—had taken over a ramshackle institution, Southern College, in 1925, with the intention of giving it a new nature as well as a new name. By 1935, it was called Florida Southern College and, having weathered the worst of the Great Depression, was ready to improve its perennially debt-ridden lot. Founded in the middle of the nineteenth century as a Methodist seminary and still devoted in part to the manufacture of Methodist preachers, it maintained the disciplines of a Puritan culture in a pagan Mediterranean setting: some sixty acres of orange trees on a hillside falling away to a large, shallow lake. A building program is the classic way of attracting attention to an institution and in a devout Christian institution one might as well begin by raising money for a chapel. It appears to have been the case that Dr. Spivey was unfamiliar with Wright's work— indeed, for some time he had him confused with a then popular novelist named Harold Bell Wright. No matter; once he had it fixed in his mind that many people considered Wright the greatest living architect, the gifted promoter residing within the college president hit upon the notion that the world's greatest architect was just what poor little Florida Southern, possessing no superlatives of any kind, was most in need of.

In April, 1938, Spivey sent Wright a telegram, care of the inn where Wright was staying in Arizona while Taliesin West was being laid out and its first walls poured. The words of the telegram provide an early clue to the likeness between the two men. Spivey to Wright: DESIRE CONFERENCE WITH YOU CONCERNING PLANS FOR GREAT EDUCATION TEMPLE IN FLORIDA STOP WIRE COLLECT WHEN AND WHERE I CAN SEE YOU.[2]

"Great education temple"—is that not the high-flown and deceptive phraseology with which Wright himself would have sought an introduction to an ideally impressionable stranger? And if Spivey's harsh financial circumstances were unknown to Wright, Wright's harsh financial circumstances were equally unknown to Spivey. Like so many of Wright's clients before him, Spivey was unaware of how readily Wright's services could be obtained. Wright answered with a cordiality based upon his usual optimistic assumption that a big fee was just around the corner; he invited Spivey to come to Taliesin in Spring Green a few days later, and there a true cordiality sprang up, even as the question of the funding of the great temple emerged. To Wright's credit, the question appears not to have troubled him; Spivey

Two dudes. FLW conferring with Dr. Spivey, the go-getting little president of Florida Southern College, in Lakeland, Florida. [WMF]

was offering him the opportunity to design a master plan for an entire campus, of which the chapel would be the centerpiece and chief source of fund-raising, and in the presence of that opportunity money scarcely mattered. Wright consented to lay out a plan that would eventually embrace a total of eighteen buildings, of which ten were actually built; he would be paid thirteen thousand dollars for the plan and for each of the buildings, according to his usual ten-percent fee. As for when he would be paid—well, Spivey must promise to do his best. And Spivey, about equally delighted by having secured Wright's services and by the looseness of the financial arrangements, promised his new-found friend that he would do so.

So began the forging of the first financial link between them. From that moment on, over a period of years, their correspondence can be divided into four categories: Spivey's urgent protests over Wright's habitual tardiness in the delivery of plans; Wright's apologies for his tardiness, nearly always with the assurance that the plans are just on their way; Wright's urgent solicitation of funds from Spivey, lest the Wrights and their army of apprentices starve to death; and Spivey's apologies for his tardiness, nearly always accompanied by a small check. The truth was that Wright needed Spivey's money not to keep from starving to death but to keep on building Taliesin West and to keep on altering Taliesin North; he was living far beyond his means and enjoying the melodrama of near-catastrophe with his accustomed zest.

As for the aesthetic links, they are visible at a glance when one compares the complex at Lakeland with the complex at Taliesin. Long, straight axes are interrupted here and there by powerful diagonal axes, which are sufficiently arbitrary to impose a substantial degree of tension on the plans—

© SUSAN WOLDENBERG

Bell-tower at Taliesin West.

398

© SUSAN WOLDENBERG

FLW planned a campus at Lakeland whose strong diagonals resembled those on which Taliesin West, pictured above, was being laid out at approximately the same time.

a tension unlooked for in the light of their non-urban settings. (A similar tension, also in a non-urban setting, may be noted in the plan for Hadrian's villa, which Vincent Scully, eager to endow his heroes with his own astounding breadth of knowledge, thinks may have been Wright's source of inspiration for both Lakeland and Taliesin West.) At Lakeland, Wright designed a long axis that was to run straight downhill through the orange grove, past a large amphitheatre, and out into Hollingsworth Lake in the form of a pier; this axis was never completed, and it is doubtful whether the city of Lakeland would have permitted the pier to invade the lake. A similar long axis at Taliesin—more readily detectable in reading the plan than when one is actually strolling about the grounds—runs along the mesa and directs the eye to the distant horizon. To connect the main buildings at Lakeland and protect the students from the heat of the sun, Wright designed a series of covered "esplanades"—a fancy Wrightism for sidewalks. At Taliesin, the walks and terraces are left open to the sky, since it was designed to be a winter residence, when the sun is welcome.

Alike as the college and Taliesin are in many respects, the impression they make upon visitors is that of a radical disparity. One thinks of the college as an assortment of white Mediterranean buildings rising against a background of profuse green foliage and a blue lake and sky; the air one breathes is humid and sensual and the pressure of a contemporary culture feels close at hand. At Taliesin, contemporary culture appears to have been commanded to keep its distance; passing through its gates, we enter a time-warp that carries us back no telling how many thousands of years, to an era when hunters stalked such prey as they could find among the sunburnt rocks—those purple and ocher and umber rocks, rocks crudely shaped and hot to the touch, that lie scattered over the desert floor and out of which Taliesin is built. The air is dry and threatens, as summer approaches, to become pitiless; one might be consumed in it without the need (the mercy?) of flame.

One last similarity between Florida Southern and Taliesin deserves to be noted: they were built with the help of unskilled labor, provided in one case by students of the college and, in the other, by members of the Taliesin Fellowship. Students at the college earned a portion of their tuition by mixing and pouring concrete for floor slabs and walkways and by manufacturing the tens of thousands of concrete blocks that Wright designed to serve as the basic module for the buildings of the college. (They also generously contributed their urine; collected daily and mixed in a carboy with salt and muriatic acid, it made a brew that, on being applied to the copper used as a decorative element throughout the college, hastened the process by which its bright orange hue oxidized into a permanent soft blue-green.) The concrete blocks are pierced and the apertures filled with glass of various rich hues—contemporary equivalents of stained glass, which in the tropical sun wink and glitter and blaze as if afire.

In the name of economy, Wright tried using sand excavated from the site as an ingredient in the concrete. When the first of the blocks to employ this concrete immediately crumbled, Wright learned that the fertilizer spread for years among the orange trees had rendered the sand valueless for construction purposes; reluctantly, the college had to truck in sand from elsewhere. At Taliesin, the walls, also built with unskilled labor, look immemorially old—the handiwork of some long-vanished race of brawny supermen. The initial superstructure of Taliesin consisted of rough-cut redwood posts and rafters, with adjustable canvas blinds; in subsequent years, the wood was replaced by steel and the canvas by glass and plastic.

Students at Florida Southern laying concrete. [FS]

Wright's master plan for Florida Southern was never carried to completion. After his death, one of his former apprentices, Nils Schweizer, gradually assumed the role of college architect; he has added several buildings to the campus that are understandably more in his vein than in Wright's. An immense circular fountain that Wright called a waterdome—it was supposed to hurl a globe of scintillating water some fifty feet into the air—stood beside the Administration Building at the top of the hill. Ideally, it was to dominate the campus and prepare us, in a subliminal fashion, for the circular library building farther down the hill. (A building that may be said to have prepared us, again subliminally, for the Guggenheim Museum.) The waterdome never functioned correctly, drenching passersby instead of delighting them; an attempt was made to control its exuberance by reducing it to three small pools, and when that solution to the problem failed, the fountain was filled in and came to be mistaken for a helicopter landing pad.

The most interesting building at Florida Southern is Wright's enchanting Annie Pfeiffer Chapel. Its auditorium is a late and more exquisite version of the auditorium of Unity Temple, providing a similar intimacy between speaker and audience and promising an even greater intimacy between earth and heaven (or, at second best, sky). The glass in the pierced blocks of the side walls of the chapel strikes a note of pagan joy—a note more pagan, indeed, than the go-getting ministerial Dr. Spivey may have counted on. A skeletal steel tower supports a lattice of slanting skylights but is itself seemingly without support, being cantilevered out from piers having no visible connection with it. Wright intended the open armature of the tower, like the finials at Midway Gardens, to be covered with a profusion of blossoming plants; in neither case was the intention able to

Concrete block at Florida Southern, with many-colored glass inserts that transmit and refract the sun.

© SUSAN WOLDENBERG

be realized. During construction, one portion of the tower was leveled by a high wind. Wright blamed faulty workmanship for the accident and other people blamed Wright's engineering; when the tower was rebuilt, it contained far more steel bracing than had been called for in the original plans.

Beautiful as the Pfeiffer chapel is, at the time of its completion it cannot be said to have pleased everyone. Many people had been under the impression that Spivey was raising money for a conventional Georgian building with a Wren-like spire; a modified Erector Set caught them by surprise. At the dedicatory ceremonies, Mrs. Pfeiffer stepped forward and revealed her opinion of the building by words that may have perturbed Spivey but must have charmed everyone else and would certainly have charmed Wright and sent him into gales of laughter. "They say it is finished," she said, and sat down.

The First World War had had comparatively little effect upon Wright's personal and professional life; during much of the time that the war was raging in Europe, Wright was at work in Japan on the Imperial Hotel and a handful of smaller commissions there, and it was perhaps just as well that he was out of the country as the moment approached, in 1917, when the United States would declare war upon Germany. The events of

© SUSAN WOLDENBERG

The Pfeiffer chapel and its steel spire. Florida Southern occupies the site of an orange grove; riskily cutting corners as usual, FLW sought to use the sandy soil under the orange trees to manufacture concrete, but without success.

the Second World War have tended to obscure for most of us the degree of anti-German feeling aroused in the United States by the propaganda that accompanied the First World War. The fiercely mustachioed Kaiser was depicted in the press as being even more diabolical than the authentically diabolical Hitler was later discovered to be. A large proportion of American citizens were of German origin and much of our culture sprang from German sources, whether in music, art, architecture, philosophy, medicine, or theology (to say nothing of folklore, including most of our Christmas customs), but almost overnight it became necessary to repudiate that cultural inheritance and, in the case of German-Americans, to deny one's ancestry as well. In the Middle West, in cities like Indianapolis, Cincinnati, Milwaukee, St. Louis, and Chicago, all of which had very large German populations, such enterprises as banks, insurance companies, singing societies, social clubs, and the like took care to alter their names, and so did many tens of thousands of families.

Wright had always been pro-German, and his addressing Louis Sullivan as *"lieber Meister"* may have been, as suggested earlier, a hint of the affinity that both he and Sullivan felt for things German. Among his earliest architectural influences had been Olbrich and other Viennese architects; moreover, he had reason to be grateful for the fact that a German publisher, urged on by a German professor, had helped him to attain an international reputation in his early forties. Nothing in Wright's nature would have permitted him to denounce Germans on the basis of anything so simple and arbitrary as their having become the acknowledged enemy of the United States; his mischievous (and often insensitive) tactlessness on public occasions would have been bound to keep him in hot water if he had been able to exercise it. In Japan, he was kept harmlessly busy denouncing Americans for their artistic boorishness; he was not invited to express opinions on American military strategy.

The Second World War was a different matter; he took it hard and for a number of reasons. Foremost among them, though not the one that could be most readily mentioned, was the damage that it was certain to do to his career. After so many years of neglect, some of it self-invited and some of it a consequence of the times—the near-cessation of construction during the Great Depression, the obtuse preferences of a society that Mencken mockingly identified as the "booboisie"—Wright was again (in Frost's phrase) "at the top of steeple, where only one person at a time can hope to be." He grew daily in fame and productivity. Never had he enjoyed a greater appetite for work and pleasure, never had he possessed a more passionate imagination, and to foresee that a war should stand between him and the fulfillment of that imagination—! The prospect was literally intolerable, and his indignation provided the fuel for a repeated public denunciation of the threatened war.

As early as 1938, Wright wrote to Dr. Spivey, apologizing in case something he had said at a Rotary luncheon in Tampa had proved an embarrassment. Spivey had asked Wright to address the luncheon as a way of helping to raise funds for the building program of the college; as Wright explained in his letter, he had a facetious imp in him that prompted him to say inappropriate things, and one such thing was his urging the Rotarians not to assume the right to criticize Fascism and Communism abroad when we had so many political evils at home that we were failing to deal with. As the war approached, Wright, like so many Middle Westerners an isolationist by conviction, became increasingly vocal in his opposition to it. He joined the leading isolationist organization, America First, along with General Robert Wood, Charles A. Lindbergh, and hundreds of other prominent citizens. In the revised version of his autobiography, published during the Second World War, Wright inserted a cryptic salute to Lindbergh—one that may be difficult for contemporary readers to understand. (A favorite newspaper nickname for Lindbergh at the height of his popularity was "the lone eagle." Hence Wright's reference, in the following passage, to American coins.) The salute reads:

TO THE AMERICAN EAGLE

If you must have a skyscraper—he is a flyer. You will see his symbol on the back of most of our coins. And he is a square American. I sent him the following telegram: "We knew you could fly straight, but now when everywhere is equivocation and cowardice you not only think straight but you dare speak straight." You know whom I mean. And this goes for his brave little wife.[3]

The occasion for this message must have been a notorious speech that Lindbergh gave in Chicago, in 1941, which was widely assumed to be anti-Semitic in tone if not in substance. Lindbergh blamed wealthy Jewish-Americans for using their power in the press and elsewhere to force us into war because of their sympathy with the plight of European Jewry. Lindbergh was accused of being a champion of the Nazis and an enemy of the British, whom the United States, though it was still technically neutral, was engaged in helping to wage the war; to the President of the United States, among many others, Lindbergh, once our greatest hero, had become a traitor. Given the opportunity to take a bold and unpopular stand, Wright manifested in this instance an uncharacteristic timidity. Nevertheless, it might be argued that, at the time, it took courage to set down in print even so obscure a signal of loyalty to Lindbergh.

Be that as it may, the passage is also of interest as a proof of the extreme informality with which so much of the manuscript of the autobiography was dictated. Speaking as if with a confidential wink to the reader, Wright says, "You know whom I mean." Then he adds, with the grammatical carelessness of the spoken word, "And this goes for his brave little wife." What is the meaning of the "this" that is being uttered here? For although Anne Morrow Lindbergh served as a close adviser to her husband in his "America First" activities, she refrained from making speeches. Ironically, Wright was never to learn that she had pleaded with her husband before he gave the speech to remove all references to Jews; Lindbergh was so confident of his being known to be a man of virtue and therefore incapable of embracing anti-Semitism that he refused to do so.

If Wright could not dwell publicly upon the professional catastrophe with which the war threatened him—what was one man's artistic and financial success or failure compared to the slaying of millions of his fellow human beings?—it was also the case that he could no longer speak freely of his admiration for Germany and Japan, the two foreign countries by which he had been most highly revered. It may have been a consolation to him that, though an isolationist, he was able to cultivate at least a moderately soft spot in his heart for Great Britain, especially since in 1939 he had been invited to lecture on architecture in London and to become an honorary member of the Royal Institute of British Architects. In 1941, King George VI awarded him the Gold Medal of the Royal Institute and Wright dispatched an unusually modest cable: YOU PROPOSE A GREAT HONOR. I ACCEPT GRATIFIED THAT DURING THIS TERRIFIC WAR ENGLAND CAN THINK OF HONORING AN ARCHITECT. In 1942, in the midst of the Battle for Britain, a London newspaper cabled Wright for fifteen hundred words of suggestions for the eventual rebuilding of the city. Wright was quick to reply with a host of facile suggestions (have no rich, have no poor, have no idle land, have no real-estate exploiters, have no traffic problems), most of which could be reduced to a single suggestion: make the rebuilt London a duplicate of Broadacre City. The newspaper thanked Wright and sent him a check for twenty guineas.

Before the United States entered the war, Wright was able to design and Oversee the construction of an ever-increasing number of projects. Well over a dozen superb houses came from his drafting table, including the Rosenbaum house, in Alabama; the Schwartz and Pew houses, in Wisconsin; the Goetsch-Winkler and Affleck houses, in Michigan; the Sturges house, in California; the Baird house, in Massachusetts; the Christie house, in New Jersey; the Sondern house, in Missouri; the Stevens house, in South Carolina; the Pope-Leighey houses, in Virginia; the Pauson house, in Arizona; and the Lewis house, in Illinois. One forces these houses into a group because of their relationship in time, but not the least interesting thing about them is their exceptionally wide geographical span. That Wright's Usonian houses function so well in so many different climates and in such a variety of settings establishes the authenticity of his claim to have invented something new in the world—something worthy, therefore, of possessing its own name.

The Goetsch-Winkler house is thought by many architectural historians to be the most elegant of all the Usonian houses; it is interesting also as revealing the strong influence that Mies van der Rohe was having upon Wright, though Wright would have taken pains to deny it. His tiresomely reiterated view of the matter was that all the major architectural influences of the twentieth century could be traced to his doorstep; he would certainly have mocked Scully's suggestion that hints of the Barcelona Pavilion can be detected in the Goetsch-Winkler house and that hints of Le Corbusier's Villa Savoie can be detected in Fallingwater. Perhaps even less welcome to him would have been the notion that the Sturges house owes something to the Liebknecht-Luxemburg monument, which Mies designed in Berlin, in 1926. Plunging outward from a steep hillside in Brentwood, the cantilevered Sturges house at first glance gives the impression of being as windowless and uninhabitable as a mausoleum; entering the house, one discovers that the shiplapped redwood parapet of the balcony was designed to conceal from neighbors and passersby in the street below an ample rank of French doors, which open onto the balcony from the living room and two bedrooms. The workmanship in the Sturges house was defective—it leaked more deplorably than most Wright houses—and the correspondence between Sturges and Wright is notable for the authenticity of its vituperation. How angry Wright could get! In the end, he volunteered to take over the house, repair it, and find a new purchaser for it; he also came close to offering an apology:

> I've been asking too much of my boys and expecting too much of my clients because the "hellments" [the continuous rains] are no sympathizers with ideas right or ideas wrong.[4]

From another letter, a few months later:

I have admitted that the apprentice system hasn't worked out very well. But you were happy and satisfied with apprentice John [Lautner] and cooperated with him enthusiastically in building the house. I did not see it until it was practically done. Why you assume now that *I* was all that was the matter with it remains to me, in the circumstances, a little puzzling and no little unjust. But . . . if I am responsible for successes, so I must no less be responsible for failures. I think your house is a failure, but only so far as that part of it carried on by you and John is concerned.[5]

Like any architect, Wright adopted a convenient elasticity of opinion in regard to his handiwork. If it was rare for him to admit that he could fail—accepting responsibility for the failure of the Sturges house, he made it clear that the responsibility really lay elsewhere—it was equally rare for him not to praise his successes in terms more generous than those employed by his admirers. To pay him a compliment was to wait to hear him top it. When reporters asked him which was his favorite project, he would always glibly reply, "The next one." In the presence of a client, it cost Wright no pangs of conscience to assert that the client's house was especially close to his heart, but in fact he had a number of genuine favorites, like the Winslow, Coonley, Roberts, Kaufmann, and Hanna houses. Of this company was the house he designed for Lloyd Lewis, a newspaperman and historian in Chicago and one of Wright's closest friends. The site was a low-lying woodland on the banks of the Des Plaines River, in Liberty-ville, north of Chicago—a site not unlike that of the Coonley house, in Riverside. Because the land was subject to flooding and was likely, in winter, to be damp as well as cold, Wright set the house upon brick piers, with a bedroom wing at a level halfway up the broad flight of stairs leading to the main living quarters. Much as Wright disliked screens—he considered them an affront to the purity of his designs and sometimes, as in the Jacobs house, "forgot" to include them in the specifications—the profuse insect life of the flood plain required him to fashion a screened porch

The Pope-Leighey house, Virginia (1939). Left, front elevation. Right, rear elevation. An inexpensive Usonian house, now requiring—and deserving—a second restoration at perhaps twenty times its original cost.

© SUSAN WOLDENBERG

for the Lewises; in fine weather, the porch and living room could be thrown into one, providing space for the big parties that the Lewises were accustomed to giving and that Wright himself often attended. (Other frequent guests, also close friends of Wright's, were Alexander Woollcott, Charles MacArthur, and Carl Sandburg.)

Despite their friendship, Lewis and Wright bickered back and forth, by mail and telegram, over things that went wrong in the course of building the house—things that, had Lewis but known it, usually went wrong in the course of building a Wright house. In most cases, they were things that could have gone wrong with houses by other architects, but Wright was touchy on the subject; he was well aware of his reputation for tardiness in the preparation of working drawings and for failing to make personal tours of inspection as often as promised. To put the blame for errors on faulty superintendence was of little use, because the superintendent was generally of Wright's choosing. At one stage of construction, dismayed to find that the cypress-clad parapets of the screened porch were so high that he couldn't look out upon the river when in a seated position, Lewis wired Wright that "the parapets must come down," adding, "Why don't you?"—a joking reference to an opening night in Chicago that the Lewises had invited the Wrights to "come down to" from Taliesin. Wright dashed off a telegram, furiously threatening to abandon the job altogether, on the grounds that Lewis had insulted him by seeming to consider himself a greater architect than Wright.

In a letter replying as temperately as possible to Wright's threat, Lewis wrote:

> What was "insulting" about my discovering that the balcony was so high we couldn't see the river? That seems to me to be a very natural mistake and not a serious one, being one wholly of angles that couldn't have been made in advance without a most elaborate use of surveyors, etc. What was so awful about suggesting the lowering of the parapet by one board? . . .
>
> Now, if you want me to have faith in you, you have simply got to go 50–50 and have faith that I am for you today exactly as I have always been. I am not going to have an argument about the angle on a river spoil our friendship. Frankly, you are worth more to Kathryn and me than the whole God-damned house. You should remember this, know it, and not suddenly be insulted at a detail in the give-and-take you and I have always enjoyed.[6]

Lewis's letter had the desired effect. The volcanic Wright temper was reduced to the merest simmer. Wright to Lewis:

> I see you don't exactly know what an architect is for or why. So let's leave it there. In that, the insult consisted. . . . You cannot realize what

careful adjustment inch by inch of proportions of wood to brick and both to space go into making a finely proportioned house. A sense of proportion can't be taught. You have it or you haven't got it, that's all. Your house has it now and wouldn't have it if I obeyed your whim.

The parapets at Glen Lloyd are exactly the glass height at Taliesin. You liked Taliesin and said so. Well, we can't see the ground nearby, either—why should you? I see no reason that you should see the river while sitting down except at the dining table, where I did let it in. . . . I could (and will if you say so) perforate the top boards as I have in your study, where I lifted the parapets to give you privacy from people entering from the road. . . .[7]

The friendship was safe; perhaps it had never been in danger, though Lewis had obviously feared that it might be. He writes with relief to his hot-tempered old comrade:

Your letter was swell. Your letters are always swell. It's your telegrams that are lousy. I guess mine are, too. . . . As to the parapet height, we'll do without the river if you say so. . . . I've seen the Mississippi, the Seine, the Thames, the Danube, the Rhine, the Missouri, the Platte, so we can get along without the Des Plaines between meals.[8]

In his autobiography, Wright genially recalls the building of the house and, probably out of affection for Lewis ("my beloved most intimate friend"), goes so far as to confess that his designs for the house had flaws:

Lloyd Lewis is not only my own client after my own heart [still another example of the carelessness with which the autobiography was edited and proof-read. Wright must have dictated ". . . is not only a client after my own heart . . ."] but he is one of my warmest and most faithfully insulting and insulted of friends. . . . He employed me to build him a house. He was a hard client. But not hard enough.

Having been there myself, often, I knew it was so damp and hot out on the prairie by the Des Plaines River that I set Lloyd well up off the ground to keep him high and dry in Spring, Fall, and Summer, his domicile winnowed by the wind . . . beneath! Thereby I exposed him in Winter not unnecessarily, but somewhat expensively. For the good of his health? Yes. But more for the good of his soul. . . . So, up there off the ground, the beautiful river landscape coming in through three sides of the beautiful house and the woods showing beneath, it was hard to keep Lloyd warm in Winter. Kathryn, his wife, didn't cool off so readily as Lloyd did, but the sixty-five degrees we set for normal in a floor-heated Usonian house just didn't jibe by about twenty degrees with the Daily News office where Lloyd worked. . . . With usual bravado, pretending to make light of the thing, I thought of various ways of keeping the writer warm. I thought of wiring him to an electric pad inside his vest, allowing lots of lead wire so he could get around. But he waved the idea aside with contempt as a passing of the buck. No patience at all, so we dropped that. Then I suggested we appeal to Secretary Knox to turn down the heat at the Daily News from eighty-five gradually to sixty-five, so he could become acclimated. But Lloyd said the cold-blooded "Daily News" men couldn't get their stuff out at that temperature. Anyway, he didn't want to be educated; he said he *was* educated. So we dropped that one, too.

There was nothing left for me to do, since I had made the house part of the landscape and the landscape all around it came in on three sides (and underneath as well) but put on some double windows at Lloyd's expense just like the other folks do, in hiding around there in those fashionable woods. . . . Still in the same spirit of bravado, knowing that it is not at all in my own interest I now refer to the unkindest ordeal of all. The innocent very simple little fireplace I built for Lloyd to sit by when he writes just refuses to draw . . . too simple, I guess, to know how. We have built some three thousand fireplaces that do draw and a few that didn't know how at first but that do know how now. This particular one, though, Lloyd's own, doesn't know how yet. It will. We haven't given up.[9]

Two major, non-domestic projects were launched in the shadow of war, the first of which—the Community Church, in Kansas City, Missouri—was brought to a mangled completion, with Wright indignantly refusing to list it among his works, and the second of which—the enormous Crystal Heights complex, in Washington, D.C.—was rejected by the local planning commission before so much as a shovelful of earth could be turned. The Community Church was presided over by a popular preacher of the day, Burris Jenkins, whose intention was to create a liberal, non-ritualistic "church of the future." That was the term Wright used to describe the structure on his blueprints and renderings, and in many respects the design, being truly novel, lived up to and surpassed its designation. The floor plan closely resembles that of the Annie Pfeiffer Chapel in Lakeland, which Wright had designed a year or so before and which was itself a refinement of the Unity Temple of thirty-odd years earlier. (Marcel Breuer appears to have borrowed the plan for the auditorium that he designed for Sarah Lawrence College, in Bronxville, New York, in the nineteen-fifties.)

A gently squashed hexagon containing a raked auditorium with a balcony, upholstered theatre seats, a so-called chancel that might readily serve as a stage, several capacious "social" rooms, a kitchen, and, above the chancel, a shallow pierced dome, through which spotlights were to be aimed in order to form a cone-shaped spire of light against the night sky, the building struck many Kansas Citians of the time as being shockingly irreligious in appearance, both inside and out. Most shocking of all was its being, in effect, a drive-in church. Wright had been among the first of American

© SUSAN WOLDENBERG

The Community Christian Church, in Kansas City (1940). The local building authorities raised so many objections to FLW's plans that he angrily abandoned the project.

architects to acknowledge the fact that automobiles had become an indispensable part of our civilization and therefore deserved to be dealt with by architects without embarrassment or compromise. (Lutyens in England was similarly a pioneer in embracing the automobile.) The site sloped steeply downhill toward Brush Creek and Wright took advantage of the slope to provide a multilevel garage, conveniently linked at different levels to the church; members of the congregation could park their cars and stroll straight into the church in happy disregard of the weather.

Every bit as unconventional as the design of the church were the methods and materials that Wright wished to employ in its construction. Speed and economy were of the highest importance: the new church was being built because the old one had burned down and the congregation was homeless. To build a church out of the usual brick or stone would be expensive; moreover, raising money enough to build such a church would be unduly time-consuming. As always, Wright was optimistic about costs; he assured the Reverend Doctor Jenkins that he could provide a church for a hundred and fifty thousand dollars that Jenkins would have to pay anybody else five hundred thousand dollars for. According to his autobiography, "the scheme was therefore the simplest thing that we could imagine. . . . And, if I do say so myself, a damn good scheme." He would make use of his favorite rock-ballast foundation instead of heavy foundations going down below the frostline; he would make the walls of the church and garage out of Gunite, a concrete mix sprayed out of a gun onto a sandwich of paper and steel wires fastened to a light steel skeleton. These walls are thin but strong and require little maintenance, and Wright was looking forward to using them in future low-cost projects.

At once Wright ran into difficulties. Local builders were so reluctant even to bid on the bizarre project that Wright had to fall back upon Ben Wiltscheck, the contractor who had built the Johnson Wax building in Racine, to take on the Kansas City church. Then the local authorities refused to issue a building permit; their codes called for poured concrete foundations and plenty of them. (Tom Pendergast, the notorious political boss of Kansas City, was in the concrete business. In a classic feat of crookedness, he paved over the entire bottom of Brush Creek with concrete in the name of flood control. This disposed of a great deal of concrete; by ill luck, it also made sure that the soil of the creek bed could no longer absorb flood waters and thereby greatly heightened the risk of flooding in the areas adjacent to the creek.) Little by little, Wright and Wiltscheck had to give way to local customs, legal and illegal, and to the machinations of local lawyers. Finally, Wright and Wiltscheck abandoned the project, sustaining a loss of many thousands of dollars in fees by doing so. To this day, the church remains a sorry-looking white carcass on the hillside (Wright had intended it to be painted a faded-rose color, to blend with the buildings in the nearby Country Club Plaza); yet enough of Wright's intentions remain discernible within its walls to make one share the indignation that Wright must have felt in being forced to walk away from it. Fortunately, much that was good in its plan emerged years later in the Kalita Humphreys Theatre, in Dallas, and in the Beth Sholom Synagogue, in Elkins Park, a suburb of Philadelphia.

What would have been the largest and most lavish project of Wright's career was a proposed real-estate development in Washington, D.C., known sometimes as Crystal City and sometimes, still more romantically, as Crystal Heights. It was the brain child of an able and lively young entrepreneur named Roy S. Thurman, who formed a syndicate to purchase a ten-acre tract lying between Connecticut Avenue and Florida Avenue—the last unbuilt-upon land in downtown Washington. It had been for many years the estate of a prominent lawyer, Mills Dean, and was celebrated for its stand of ancient oaks, said to date back to Indian times. Thurman, who had an eye for architecture—he was later to commission the only building in Washington by William Lescaze—and an eye for publicity as well, announced that the project would cost somewhere between ten and fifteen million dollars, a sum of formidable magnitude in that time and place. Thurman also announced that Wright was the only person worthy to prepare the plans.

Having agreed that he was indeed the man for the job, Wright set to work and in a short time had produced a masterly solution to the problem of how to place upon a beautiful wooded hillside in the heart of a busy, traffic-racked city a linked procession of exquisite towers of white marble, glass, and bronze. The towers were a refinement of the unbuilt St. Mark's in the Bouwerie towers of 1929, and of the Chicago apartment towers of the following year, also unbuilt. The Crystal City towers were to stand on an immense terrace, which also served as the roof of a five-story-high garage that would contain—depending upon which newspaper story one read—anywhere from fifteen hundred to four thousand cars. With his usual showmanship, Wright boasted that a line of cars eight miles long could be parked in the garage within twenty minutes. How did he ever arrive at this preposterous calculation? In looking over his bills from Wright, Hib Johnson used to exclaim, "The man can't add!" If he had overheard this Wright boast, Johnson might have emended his exclamation to read, "The man can't divide!"

Crystal City was to consist of a hotel and private apartments totaling twenty-five hundred rooms, a thousand-seat movie theatre, a cocktail lounge, and a score of retail shops, along with the garage. To newspaper reporters, Wright asserted, "Versailles won't look like much compared with this when it is finished."[10] Because one of the towers was a hundred and thirty-five feet high and the height of buildings in Washington was limited by law to a hundred and ten feet, a zoning variance would have to be secured for the tower; other variances would be required for the retail shops facing Connecticut Avenue. Thurman and the money-men behind him grew impatient as weeks went by and the variances weren't granted; when he pressed hard for action, the variances were refused him, and he erupted in language worthy of Wright himself:

> This decision obviously was made without reference to the record. If hidden selfish interests have not dictated it, I can only say that the entire proceeding has been marked by crass stupidity, blundering, and mental myopia. If this moronic bureaucracy continues, all of the new private construction that may legally go on here can be described as "substituting the slums of today with the slums of tomorrow."[11]

Wright jumped into the controversy with his usual relish. In a long article headed "A Genius Fights With the D.C. Government to Save His Crystal City" and bearing the sub-head "But the Pillars of Ancient Rome Are Against Him," Wright argued that "the same nobility of architectural expression characterizes Crystal Heights that characterizes the Washington Monument, with the immense advantage to the Heights of serving to make the lives of Washington citizens richer in every way, while the monument serves only to awaken memories or instill awe in the beholder."[12] A reporter described him as "a saintly-looking man with the acidulous tongue of a Richelieu," and quoted him as calling Washington's assortment of public buildings in Roman and Greek styles "huts and hovels" and as saying that of all relics of the past unworthy of preservation the newly

Left, FLW with the developer of the Crystal Heights apartment-house project in Washington, D.C. (1940). [RT] *Above, rendering of the project, which the Washington authorities rejected in part because it wasn't "classical."* [RT/ WF]

rebuilt Williamsburg was the silliest of all. It happened that Williamsburg was a favorite project of Fredric A. Delano, uncle of Franklin D. Roosevelt and Chairman of the National Capital Park and Planning Commission, the body that would have the final say on the Crystal Heights project. In the course of happily lashing out against his opponents, Wright was goaded by reporters into saying that the trouble with Washington was that its architectural decisions were made by "a bunch of Beaux-Arts graduates and goddamn fairies." One of that "bunch" was no less a person than Mr. Delano, who cherished the classical Beaux-Arts tradition and who remained implacable in his opposition to the project. The syndicate that had been formed by Thurman withdrew its support and Wright rolled up his beautiful drawings and retreated to the sunburnt desert stronghold of Taliesin West.

24

Т<small>HE WAR YEARS</small> amounted to a pro-
longed irritation to Wright and the Taliesin Fellowship. Wright appears
to have felt none of the moral fervor that President Roosevelt wished the
country at large to manifest in regard to the war being waged against
powerful adversaries in Europe, Africa, Asia, and on the high seas. Instead,
Wright engaged in a number of bitter quarrels with old friends, who in
some cases had relatives facing possible death in combat. The historian
Lewis Mumford, long one of the chief champions of Wright's genius, was
an ardent interventionist and had a son, Geddes, who was to die in the
course of the war; after an angry exchange of letters, Mumford and
Wright broke off relations altogether and mended them only with difficulty
when the war ended. Again and again up to within a year or so of his
death and with a touching urgency unusual in his correspondence, Wright
kept pleading with Mumford to come to Taliesin for a visit, but Mumford
never did. Alexander Woollcott, Archibald MacLeish, Carl Sandburg, Edward Steichen—a host of old comrades were distressed not only by Wright's
increasingly conservative political views (although he claimed to be an anar-
chist, vis-à-vis Roosevelt and the New Deal, he sounded more and more
like a Hoover Republican) but also by his seeming callousness in placing
his philosophical dicta ("There never was a just war") and personal interests
above those of his fellow citizens. Another genius, Matisse, who happened
to be almost the same age as Wright, spent most of the Second World
War in Nice, contentedly painting pictures of the Bay of Angels and of
sloe-eyed, voluptuous odalisques, but he had the good sense to ignore
the war rather than to respond to it with heated bluster.

Despite the fact that there was little new work to be done, Wright
wished to keep the Fellowship as nearly intact as possible. The fees paid
by the apprentices were a source of income more necessary to him than
ever; it was also a matter of considerable importance that the apprentices
by their bodily labors ensure the maintenance of the two Taliesins and
the preservation of the lordly style of living to which Wright had been

accustomed since youth. Wright eagerly defended the principle of conscientious objection; many of the apprentices became C.O.'s, and several of them ended up in prison. Wright enlisted the aid of colleagues and famous acquaintances in an attempt to persuade the authorities in Washington that the Fellowship was at work upon a project indispensable to the future well-being of the country and that the apprentices should therefore be exempted from the draft. To this end, he drew up a grandiloquent document called the Broadacre City Petition, which, submitted to the White House in the darkest moments of the war, rivals in grotesque self-importance the letter that James Joyce is reputed to have sent to the King of England during the First World War, asking His Majesty to put aside less important tasks in order to locate a pair of trousers that had been mailed to Joyce from Dublin and that, passing through enemy territory, had failed to reach him in Zurich. Wright's petition:

> We, the undersigned, respectfully ask that the Administration of our Government authorize Frank Lloyd Wright to continue the search for Democratic FORM as the basis for a true capitalistic society now known as Broadacre City. We believe that work should immediately be declared a worthy national objective and the necessary ways and means freely granted him to make such plans, models, and drawings as will enable our citizens and other peoples to comprehend the basic ideas the plans, models, and drawings represent and which, without political bias or influences will be invaluable to our people when peace is being considered.[1]

Astonishingly enough, Wright was able to accumulate hundreds of distinguished signatories to this petition, including Thomas Benton, John Dewey, Albert Einstein, Buckminster Fuller, Carl Milles, Charles A. Beard, Joseph Brewer, Norman Bel Geddes, Mies van der Rohe, Georgia O'Keeffe (the only woman), Walter Gropius, Henry-Russell Hitchcock, Thornton Wilder, and Wright's cousin by marriage Robert Moses. The petition fell upon deaf ears, and the Fellowship dwindled to a scant four or five apprentices.

Eccentrics attract eccentrics, and one of Wright's new friends during the war period was the musicologist and promoter Carleton Smith, who somehow or other had achieved a close personal relationship with many of the great ones of the earth, or boldly claimed to have done so. (In the late nineteen-seventies, Smith talked the Pritzker family of Chicago into setting up the Pritzker Architecture Prize, partly on the basis of a discussion he said he had once had with the King of Sweden, in which they had both lamented the absence of a Nobel Prize in architecture. In fact, Smith had no particular interest in architecture; he had fallen back upon it alphabetically as a field of endeavor worthy of receiving a prize when he could find nobody willing to set up a prize for agriculture. If the Pritzkers had not bit on architecture, Smith had planned to take his chances with astronomy.) In an unpublished autobiography, Smith tells of his friendship with President Roosevelt's mother, Sara Delano Roosevelt, and of how she introduced him to her son with the admonition, "Franklin knows nothing about music. You must teach him what he ought to know." According to Smith, on one occasion Mrs. Roosevelt was indignant with her son because a speech he made at the launching of a battleship interrupted a Saturday afternoon Metropolitan Opera broadcast to which she had been looking forward. She asked the butler to get her son on the telephone, in order to give him a good scolding; after a brief delay, the butler reported that the battleship wasn't picking up.

When the government was in need of housing for workers at the atomic energy plant in Oak Ridge, Tennessee, Smith recommended Wright to the President, saying that Wright would be able to design half a dozen basic houses that could then be prefabricated by the thousands. Roosevelt expressed interest in seeing Wright's designs, but when weeks passed and no designs appeared, he urged Smith to bring Wright to Washington to talk things over face to face. Smith's memoirs contain a vivid description of the encounter (which, like so many of the encounters described in Wright's autobiography, may never have taken place):

> . . . so I took him [Wright] to Washington and he wore a cloak over his shoulders and had a big cane and never took his hat off when he came into the Oval Room and he stopped at the door with great drama and said, so the President could hear, "You know, Carleton, I've always told you I would rather be Wright than President," and then he wheeled around and came up to the President's desk and shook hands with him and he said—and I will never know whether he thought this out in advance or whether it came naturally—he said, "Franklin," or "Frank," he called him, "Frank," he said, "you ought to get up out of that chair and look around at what they're doing to your city here, miles and miles of Ionic and Corinthian columns!"[2]

Rarely do we hear of two consecutive feats of tactlessness in which the second so convincingly—and so shockingly—surpasses the first. Roosevelt had an aristocratic distaste for being addressed in an over-familiar fashion, and to be called by his first name, or, still worse, by a diminutive of his first name (making it a duplicate of Wright's) must have enraged him, but to be urged in his paralyzed condition to get up out of his chair and look around—! Smith's memoirs are, alas, silent in regard to what followed; it is certainly the case that Wright had no part in the housing of workers at Oak Ridge.

Sensitive as he was, Wright often misread the nature of an occasion and alienated people with whom he had intended to make a lighthearted connection. (Once, meeting Philip Johnson in a seminar at Yale, Wright exclaimed, "Why, little Philip! I thought that you were dead!" It happens that Johnson is a tiger, well able to give as good as he gets; a lesser man might have been offended by this gratuitously cruel wisecrack.) If Wright had behaved properly with Roosevelt, they would surely have become friends; Roosevelt's ego was a match for Wright's and his confidence in his talent as an architect (he designed his hideaway cottage at Hyde Park in what he believed to be the Dutch Colonial style) might well have led him to consider himself Wright's peer.

News of the German surrender, in May, 1945, reached Wright at Scottsdale; when the Japanese surrendered, a few months later, he was at Spring Green. By then, he was seventy-eight years old, in rude health

© SUSAN WOLDENBERG

The glass prow of the Unitarian Church in Madison (1946–1951).

and tearing high spirits. At a time when most men putter about, setting their affairs in order, Wright was characteristically bent upon keeping his affairs in disorder; he was giving talks, writing articles, and tirelessly stirring up excitement in any community that, to his practiced eye, was threatened with contentment. Although he had been able to build little or nothing during the war, he had been drawing plans for a variety of projects, and with peace and the renewal of construction he was ready to go to work on a scale of sheer busy-ness greater even than that which he had enjoyed during the late thirties.

A meeting house for the First Unitarian Society of Madison, Wisconsin, was among the early projects to be undertaken after the war. It is constructed of rough-cut limestone, carted to the site by members of the congregation, and is dominated by an immense sheltering roof of welted copper, rising to a gable over the pulpit and choir loft and so steeply angled as to put one in mind of—in Wright's phrase—"hands joined in prayer." It is always risky to use architecture as a metaphor for something else (except as an eye-catching advertising prank, as when a restaurant that is to be called the Brown Derby is built in the shape of a brown derby). "Hands joined in prayer" is a Gothic image, echoing Dürer's famous drawing, and not a Unitarian one. Given the Unitarians' skepticism about the Holy Trinity, the triangular module on which the meeting house is laid out may also be suspected of deviational tendencies. As originally designed, a stone spire with insets of stained glass was to be built *under* the roof instead of above it, at the point behind the altar and choir loft where the roof achieves its highest elevation; when the building was under construction and Wright saw what an agreeable prospect the open end of the auditorium provided, he chose to replace the stone spire with windows of plain glass. The extreme

© SUSAN WOLDENBERG

The copper roof of the church swoops out over the hillside as if in flight.

overhang of the roof above this glass "prow" was designed to shelter a bell, suspended from a chain; the bell was removed when it was discovered that in stormy weather it swung back and forth and threatened to smash the windows. The meeting house contains some perennially incorrigible Wright flaws: a choir loft too small for any choir to sing in (it now contains organ pipes) and too extreme a cantilevering of a portion of the great roof. Where it swoops down over the front entrance as a daringly unsupported porte cochere, the roof's supports have sagged and for any member of the congregation more than six feet tall it hints not at a cozy welcome but at decapitation.

Forty members of the Taliesin Fellowship helped to complete the meeting house in time for its dedication in August, 1951. From the stone pulpit, Wright gave an address on "Architecture as Religion," and a few weeks later members of the Fellowship contributed a program of "Gurdjieff Movements," under the direction of Mrs. Wright. On the face of a balcony at the rear of the auditorium Wright arranged to have lettered a quotation from (according to Wright) a Persian poet, who may well have been Wright himself:

DO YOU HAVE A LOAF OF BREAD BREAK THE LOAF IN TWO
AND GIVE HALF FOR SOME FLOWERS OF THE NARCISSUS
FOR THY BREAD FEEDS THE BODY INDEED BUT THE
FLOWERS FEED THE SOUL

A heady cultural cocktail for the godly Unitarians of Madison: Wright, Dürer, Gurdjieff, and a nameless Persian poet! And for over thirty-five years the meeting house has proved its worth in the community as what Wright, in describing his early Unity Temple, had called "a good time place."

Another project, this one small in scale and comparatively low in cost but important in any account of Wright's exploration of new forms, was a house that Wright designed for Herbert and Katherine Jacobs—the same couple for whom he had designed his first Usonian house, in Madison. After five pleasurable years in Usonia One, the Jacobses decided that they and their three growing children should undertake the experiment of moving to the country. They bought a ramshackle farmhouse, capable of being lived in until the time came when Wright would provide them with plans for a new one; they invited Wright to help them choose a site for the new house, and together they hit upon a nearby hilltop overlooking the open Wisconsin countryside, exposed to bitter winds in winter and the hot sun of summer. Wright proposed what he called a solar hemicycle house, which would nestle in a scooped-out garden area a couple of feet below grade, with a façade largely of glass facing south and a solid earth berm at its back. All winter long the sun would shine into the half-circle of ground-floor living and dining areas and into the bedrooms that shared a mezzanine above those areas; in summer, the broad overhang of the roof would keep the glass in shadow. The walls would be of stone, drawn from a nearby quarry (Taliesin North, Fallingwater, and the Madison Unitarian meeting house had all similarly profited from the proximity of quarries), and the entrance to the house would be from the north, by way of a romantic, dungeonlike tunnel cut through the berm.

Throughout the final years of the war, Jacobs pleaded with Wright for working drawings and specifications, and Wright kept putting him off with what Jacobs later described in his memoirs as "masterly one-liners . . . variations on the theme that he would be over to see us as soon as he could find the time and that he greeted us affectionately."[3] It wasn't until the late summer of 1946 that Wright dropped in unexpectedly at the Jacobses' farmhouse and after a meal in which he downed no fewer than seven biscuits dripping with homemade butter, helped them to stake out the foundations for the new house. With the Jacobses themselves mixing and pouring concrete, laying up stone, and putting down floors, the house reached a habitable stage by the end of 1948. They had hoped that the house could be built for five thousand dollars, especially with all the "sweat equity" (as it later came to be called) that they had contributed, but knowing Wright they were not surprised when the total cost amounted to something over twenty thousand dollars. The house did indeed accommodate itself well to extremes of heat and cold, as Wright had assured the Jacobses it would, and he took pride in driving friends and clients over from Taliesin to have a look at it, arriving without warning at any hour of the day or night. As the Jacobses well understood, a house that Wright designed remained everlastingly his, and the owners of it were in practice mere custodians.

Most of the small domestic commissions of the postwar period were carried out under Wright's supervision by senior members of the Fellowship, like John De Koven Hill and John Howe, the latter being celebrated among his Taliesin colleagues for being able to turn out a perfectly satisfactory Usonian house in a matter of hours. Occasionally, Wright took a particular interest in a house whose site interested him; for example, when Mrs. Clinton Walker asked him to design a little cottage for her on a rocky stretch of beach at Carmel, he visited the beach and was captivated by the opportunity it would give him to build at last, though on a much reduced scale, a house similar to those he had designed for several earlier clients possessing similar sites—houses that for a variety of unhappy reasons had remained on paper. (For an architect, it is one of the compensations of age that nothing in a lifetime of work need go to waste; Wright at ninety would be "shaking out of my sleeve" design ideas that he had cherished for seventy years.) The Walker house had a broad roof supported largely by the stone mass of a central chimney; an almost unbroken band of casement windows looked out over the Pacific, with the horizontal mullions of the windows ingeniously corbelled one above another in such a way as to permit sections of the windows to be opened downward rather than outward, thereby admitting air but not high winds and blown sea water.

Once Wright had sent the plans to Mrs. Walker, she evidently showed them to a number of friends, who like all friends in such circumstances were eager to suggest improvements. In the case of the Jacobses, who built their two Wright houses more or less with their own hands, Wright permitted certain minor changes in his plans in order to simplify their labor, but suggestions by ignorant strangers did not sit well with him. In his book, *Letters to Clients,* Bruce Pfeiffer prints Wright's reaction to Mrs. Walker's helpful friends:

> Again we are up in the air. Looks very much as though the "Cabin on the Rocks" was on the rocks in more senses than one. You were once of my mind about the cabin. You gave me reason to think so and I was happy to build it as I put my best mind and heart into producing a little masterpiece appropriate to the unique site.
>
> An ordinary little door and window house on that site would look as foolish as a hen resting where you ought to find a seagull.
>
> I am unwilling to spoil my charming sea-bird and substitute the hen. You don't need me for that. Anyone can do it.[4]

Mrs. Walker quickly made amends and the project proceeded. A few months later, she again transgressed, seeking an alteration in the plans that Wright disapproved of. Sternly he admonished her, as if she were a naughty child: "Please be good." The house got built largely as Wright had wished it to be built and on visiting it in 1952 he sent her a grateful letter. Among other things, the letter demonstrates that there has been no lessening in the quality of his intellect at eighty-five:

> . . . I hope this tiny aristocrat among the Carmel bourgeois, so exciting in itself, is not only a domestic experience giving you the joy you, its progenitor, deserve, but a spiritual uplift.
>
> To build anything in these ambiguous times is bound to be either a foolish or heroic event. But your heroism is on record now at Carmel. The place should be grateful to you for this all too rare kind of patriotism, a fine thing to do with money. . . .[5]

The letter also demonstrates that Wright is as clever as ever at getting out of a difficulty. It appears that a fireplace he added to the house at her pleading has proved not to work well. Wright has an explanation: she has mistaken its nature. It is designed to burn pole wood and not cordwood. One sets the pole wood vertically in the fireplace and permits the poles to blaze all the way up to the top; the blazing poles will encourage the draft and very little smoke will come down the flue to annoy Mrs. Walker and her guests. He writes, "Of course treated as an ordinary fireplace it is bound to smoke." One wonders why he hadn't tried explaining Lloyd Lewis's smoky fireplace in the same fashion. Perhaps he did, and perhaps Lewis as an old friend simply laughed at him.

Proof of Wright's lifelong interest in solving the problem of low-cost housing for individuals is the fact that the largest file of drawings in the

Taliesin Archives is devoted to the nine hundred drawings that Wright prepared for the American Readi-Cut System of prefabricated houses, which Wright worked on between 1911 and 1917 and which came to nothing. He maintained an interest in the problem of low-cost multiple housing as well. A residential land development competition was held by the City Club of Chicago, in 1913, under the auspices of the local chapter of the American Institute of Architects. As we have already learned, Wright didn't believe in competitions, on the grounds that a jury by its nature is bound to award the prize to the least controversial—and therefore the least interesting—entry; nevertheless, and characteristically, he submitted a plan *hors concours,* in which he proposed the division of plots of land in such a way that four houses occupying the center of a block would enjoy an exceptional degree of privacy. By means of what he called a quadruple-block plan, "each householder is automatically protected from every other householder. He is the only householder upon the entire side of his block. His utilities are grouped to the rear with his neighbors' utilities, and his yard, front and rear, is privately his own. His windows all look out upon open vistas and upon no one's unsightly necessities."[6]

Wright returned to the problem in his grand design for housing in his utopian Broadacre City; in a project known as the Suntop Houses, in Ardmore, Pennsylvania, only one unit of which was built; and in a Federally funded project in Pittsfield, Massachusetts, begun during the war and cancelled before construction could begin. In these projects, Wright fitted four separate houses into a single whole, with each house enjoying the privacy that Wright had described in his 1913 Chicago plan. The three-dimensional intricacy of the design requires multiple stories instead of the one story commonly employed in the Usonian houses and reminds us of a similar intricacy in Wright's design for the St. Mark's in the Bouwerie apartment-house tower (unexecuted), in New York City; the Kaufmann apartment-house tower, in Pittsburgh (also unexecuted); and the Price mixed-use tower, in Bartlesville. All of these designs depend upon Wright's uncanny ability to make his way—one might almost say, to *feel* his way— in three dimensions as he moves, pencil in hand, through the process of resolving a problem that few ordinary architects or engineers ever confront, since it doesn't occur to them that such a problem is capable of being posed, much less of being resolved. (The same gift for creating a certain volume of space by means of structure and then seeming to dissolve the structure, leaving the volume intact, is detectable in the disciplined sensuality of the baroque architecture that Wright affected to despise.)

Still another category of low-cost housing that Wright remained preoccupied with throughout his life was that of communities formed by people of like interests (and usually of like incomes), who for reasons of economy and aesthetics as well as of friendship pooled their resources, purchased a substantial amount of property, and called upon Wright to design houses for them at appropriate sites on the property. An early example of such a community design was the Como Orchards Summer Colony, at Darby, Montana, commissioned in 1910 by a number of members of the faculty of the University of Chicago. (A clubhouse and fourteen cottages were built, though without the benefit of Wright's supervision; he and Mamah Cheney were by then in Europe.) Another academic enclave was inaugurated in 1937, by professors on the faculty of Michigan State University, in Lansing; Wright designed seven houses for the project, of which only one—the exquisite Winkler-Goetsch house—was actually built, in 1939.

The other houses in the project were unable to secure financing, in part because the Federal Housing Authority refused to approve Wright's plans. Wright had gone to Washington to submit the plans to the FHA in person and he was understandably indignant at being turned down. In the *Architectural Forum* for January, 1948, devoted entirely to Wright's work (as the January, 1938, issue of the *Forum* had also been), Wright took particular pleasure in publishing the Lansing project, with a caption calling attention to the fact that these Usonian houses had been "repudiated" by the U.S. government. He went on to say that "many other [Usonian houses] have been built in some twenty-nine states since, embodying precisely the same construction as then proposed and with perfect satisfaction to all concerned. Government expert opinion reported 'the walls will not support the roof; floor-heating is impractical; the unusual design makes subsequent sales a hazard.'"[7] So much, one hears Wright crowing, for the U.S. government and its damned experts!

In the same issue of the *Forum,* Wright published a scheme for low-cost housing that he devised for a workers' cooperative in Detroit, in 1942; after much bickering among the workers, the scheme came to nothing, and Wright headed the double-page spread of drawings, "BERM HOUSES FOR COOPERATIVE WORKERS DETROIT MICHIGAN ABANDONED FOR LACK OF COOPERATION." Also depicted in the *Forum* were two not-for-profit cooperative projects in which a true cooperation was practiced: Parkwyn Village and Galesburg Country Homes, both located near Kalamazoo and both embracing a ground plan of meandering roads and a Wright innovation—plots of land laid out in circles, which Wright with his knack for neologisms called discs and of which he wrote, "The center of each disc of ground once located by survey and diameter given, any house owner can tell where his lot limits are. No lot line touches another wherever the scheme is perfect. All interspaces are to be planted to some native shrub like barberry or sumach, throwing a network of color in pattern over the entire tract."[8]

The largest cooperative designed by Wright is the Usonia Homes project, in Pleasantville, New York, begun in 1947 and still flourishing. Headed by an engineer named David Henken, who had spent a year at Taliesin, a group of young New Yorkers, politically liberal and with moderate financial resources, purchased just under a hundred acres of second-growth woodland within an hour's drive of New York City and asked Wright to lay out a road system and begin designing houses for them. Though so close to New York and at no very great height above sea level, the property resembles an Adirondacks wilderness, with steep hillsides and handsome outcroppings of rock. Wright took admirable advantage of the topography in planning the curves and grades of the roads, along which he placed his one-acre discs. He designed three Usonian houses, which made ample use of the local stone and hugged their difficult sites as readily as his Usonian houses in the Middle West hugged the prairie.

The press of work at Taliesin made it impossible for Wright to continue designing houses for the Pleasantville project—a task that, in any event, he had always expected local architects to complete, subject to his approval. Wright was past eighty and faced unflinchingly—indeed, faced with joyous high spirits—the fact that so little time remained in which to fulfill himself.

During the war years and in the years immediately after the war, Wright undertook some of the most important projects of his life—projects that for one unfortunate reason or another failed to be realized. It is a mark of his greatness that these unbuilt structures make up a sufficiently remarkable body of work to justify our calling him our greatest architect on the basis of that work alone. One would be hard pressed to nominate any other architect for whom so seemingly extravagant a claim could be made. Is not architecture built work and not mere taking thought? To ask the question in harsher terms by reversing it, can ink and crayon on paper be called architecture? Ordinarily, the answer is no; in Wright's case, the answer is bound to be yes. For what he has put down on paper are real buildings. Pretty—and even beautiful—as the renderings that accompany his plans and elevations often are, they are not simply pretty, not simply beautiful; nor are they what we devote the larger part of our attention to. Our admiration for Wright is based upon structures that have existed in his mind, that are capable of existing in the world at this very moment, and that in many cases have already come to exist in the world, in the form of more or less successful imitations. For it is yet another mark of Wright's greatness that his unbuilt projects have had almost as profound an influence upon twentieth-century architecture as his built projects have had. As I have mentioned, his houses are today a quarry for scavengers. His mind, too, has been—and is—a quarry and has had, and will always have, its scavengers.

Of the imitations of Wright that have made other architects famous, the most conspicuous are surely the numerous hotels designed over the past twenty years by John Portman. In Atlanta, in 1967, Portman designed the first of them, the Hyatt Regency, which boasted a vast, deliberately wasteful interior space of prodigious height known as an atrium (a word borrowed from Roman architecture and now so universally applied to any undifferentiated interior space that few office buildings dare to admit they are without one). In the Hyatt Regency, playful, glass-walled elevators glide up and down the interior walls of the atrium; access to the hotel's bedrooms is gained by way of corridors whose parapets, hung with vines, overlook the busy floor of the atrium. A drum-shaped restaurant, also glass-walled, surmounts the roof of the hotel and slowly revolves, giving diners a bird's-eye view of Atlanta and its not very interesting red-clay countryside.

Many of the aspects of contemporary hotel architecture that we tend to attribute to Portman are derived from a hotel project that Wright planned, in 1946, for the Dallas oil millionaire Rogers Lacy. In the traditional Texas fashion, having become richer by accident than he had ever expected to be, Lacy had been persuaded that a big hotel, designed by the world's greatest architect, would serve admirably as a monument to himself and to Dallas. He was introduced to Wright, who within a few months had prepared his revolutionary designs for a block-square, sixty-four-story hotel—a building twice as high as any then standing west of the Mississippi River. In Wright's own words:

> This is a design for an urban hotel without interior corridors, regular windows on the street [for once tactful, Wright omitted to say that he had found nothing in downtown Dallas worth looking at], or stores below, to add to congestion and deprive the hotel of its best asset: the comfort and entertainment of its guests. . . . The structure is as completely organic as we can make it, weighing about one-tenth what skyscrapers of the Rockefeller Center type weigh, stabilized at this great height by a great single feature lacking in most similar buildings. This is the impressive mass of an adequate air-conditioning intake and exhaust, to which all parts of the great hotel have direct access.
>
> All supports are set back from the property lines to allow clear glass surface all around the street frontage, the entire ground floor being transparent from side to side of the entire ground area. Because the building is in the form of an open court, the center of this space will be on bright light and become a large water basin over the service features below.
>
> Various parts of the lower stories and mezzanine protrude as pergolas into this central court. From one corner of the interior court the tall shaft rises, placed to cast no shadow on the court. In plan, the life of the hotel is in the patio. By this simple means, its to-and-fro, ordinarily humdrum, is here dramatized and made interesting in spite of itself.[9]

Wright goes on to speak of further novelties in the hotel's design: off-street access by car to the hotel's entrances, ample basement parking facilities, an exterior cladding of metal and translucent panels filled with fiberglass insulation, and sun balconies overlooking the profusely planted court. The hotel was a modification of the St. Mark's in the Bouwerie project of the nineteen-twenties, which was finally to be realized in the Price Tower, in Bartlesville, in the early fifties; that it was an excellent model for Portman to follow is proved by the immense popularity of his hotels throughout the country and the degree to which they, too, are imitated, providing us with hundreds of imitations of an imitation of an original that happens never to have been built.

Wright was correct in predicting the success of the Lacy design, but he was overly optimistic in respect to the good it could do a given community. "If our cities are to continue habitable," he wrote in the *Forum*, "something like this turning inward . . . is absolutely necessary." Which is to say that Wright was praising his hotel as the solution to a problem that, in almost the same breath, he was ready to describe as insoluble. Not for a moment did he believe that our cities would continue to be habitable; he had already violently denounced them on many occasions as being uninhabitable. But "this turning inward" has proved the worst possible way of saving a city from itself; indeed, the forty years that have passed since Wright wrote those words have shown that "turning inward," as Portman's fortresslike hotels invariably do, serves to hasten a city's death. Not turning inward but turning outward, embracing street life instead of repudiating it, is our best means of restoring vitality to urban areas. It is, as we shall see, an oddity and a misfortune that all his life Wright disliked and distrusted the street.

An enchanting unbuilt Wright project of the nineteen-forties was a funeral parlor (as Wright would have called it; now "home" is the conventional term, though a place less like home it would be hard to imagine). The design was commissioned by a San Francisco undertaker (now "mortician") named Nicholas Daphne, who is said to have run an undertaking establishment as bizarrely vulgar and successful as the Forest Lawn Cemetery in Los Angeles, celebrated in the fictions of Aldous Huxley and Evelyn Waugh. Daphne had purchased a choice hilltop site, where he wished to erect a cluster of chapels for his numerous clientele, along with what is known in the trade as "work areas." Wright is at his best in telling the story of this adventure:

> Nicholas P. Daphne called me after midnight a year or so ago to say that because he had bought the finest lot in San Francisco he wanted the best architect in the world to build a mortuary on it. Nick asked me

if I had ever built one. I said no, and I thought that was my very best qualification for doing one. So he gave me the job. Of course I had to "research" a good deal and that nearly got me down. I would come back home, now and then, wondering if I felt as well as I should. But Nick had a way of referring to the deceased always as "the merchandise," and that would cheer me up. I pulled through. . . .

This series of chapels (seating seventy-five to a hundred people), each chapel with its own garden (all gardens in a garden) stands elevated upon the mass of shale now composing the unique site. The plan of the whole was an attempt to take some of the curse off the customary undertaker's official proceeding. I didn't expect to make even the funeral of one's enemies exactly cheerful, but I did think I could give the obsequies some beauty without destroying their integrity.

Here five simultaneous funerals may be so conducted that one is not too aware of another. All preparation and disposal of the deceased is from down below in chambers independent of the ceremonial arrangements for special mourners. The place of mourning for the families called the "slumber room" caused most trouble, as the chief mourners do not care to be seen, though they do want to see. And inasmuch as for some time before the funeral the deceased must lie in a private room at their convenience as mourners, the processes of one funeral immediately following another, the proper allocation of this space became a major problem. Here the synthesis is fairly complete and the business of the undertaker's funeral arrangements, choice of caskets, flowers, etc., is located in an independent building at the entrance to the chapel yard . . . a colorful, happy environment abundant with music . . . has been provided . . . the emphasis is here laid not on Death but on Life.[10]

One readily detects in Wright's words the pleasure—the almost boyish glee—that he took in working out a puzzle worthy of him. To keep five totally immobile articles of "merchandise" from bumping into one another as they rose and fell from the chambers below to the chambers above, and to bestow on the mourning relatives of that merchandise the near-miraculous capacity to see without being seen—! Only the supreme master of three-dimensional thinking could have brought it off, and only a master ironist (a peer of Waugh himself) would have dared to claim that in doing so he had produced "a colorful, happy environment" in a veritable sea of coffins and corpses. Alas, the cost of this necrophiliac fantasy proved too much for Daphne's purse; if it had been built, it would surely have rivaled in popularity the Wee Kirk o' the Heather, in Forest Lawn Cemetery, in Los Angeles, where happiness in the presence of the dead loved one is the only emotion that one is expected to feel.

25

ONE OF THE GREAT WORKS of Wright's seventy-year-long career is the Solomon R. Guggenheim Museum, in New York City. Architecture is a profession celebrated for accommodating itself to age—indeed, for granting age an opportunity to flower in a way that goes far beyond accommodation. Like many men of genius, Wright as he grew older was able to draw up out of the deep well of his unconscious an ever richer (and ever more mysterious) assortment of fantastic structures. They are structures that elude being satisfactorily catalogued as of a certain time and place, although in every instance time and place are known to us; like the Church of the Sagrada Familia, in Barcelona, by Wright's contemporary Gaudí, or the Chapel of Notre-Dame-du-Haut, at Ronchamp, by his despised younger rival Le Corbusier, the masterpieces of Wright's old age emanate an air of having always existed, of having been shaped out of the earth itself, by members of a race who have left us no other sign of their existence.

What could be odder and less expected than the primordial apparition of the Guggenheim Museum, coiled ready to spring skyward from its block-front on upper Fifth Avenue? It is a freak that astonishes passersby as readily today as it did the passersby of almost thirty years ago; it bears no relationship to its self-aggrandizing bourgeois neighbors, from whom it fastidiously shrinks back in the very act of asserting its superiority over them. Surely, one thinks, it would be better suited to a steep hillside in Himalayan Tibet, in the shadow of that immense lamasery of which Wright (so wary of saluting any architectural work except his own) kept a photograph above his desk; surely Fifth Avenue with its street wall of neo-Renaissance and neo-Gothic pastiches is the least sympathetic place upon which to set this gigantic wind-up toy. And one would be right to think so: the only reason that the Guggenheim stands where it does is that no other site for it could be found in the early nineteen-forties, when the three chief figures in the adventure of designing and building it were impatient to see it begun.

The Guggenheim Museum.

These figures were Solomon R. Guggenheim, Baroness Hildegard Rebay von Ehrenwiesen (more commonly known as Hilla Rebay), and Wright. Guggenheim, who was born in 1861 and died in 1949, a decade before his museum was completed, was a member of the celebrated copper-mining family; like any American millionaire of the period, having proved himself in the world of business, he started to prove himself in the world of culture by collecting Old Masters. His wife, Irene Rothschild Guggenheim, preferred collecting contemporary art. (So did other wives; it was in large part the taste of millionaires' wives that led to the founding of the Museum of Modern Art.) In 1927, Mrs. Guggenheim purchased some collages by a young German artist named Rebay (1890–1967), who was having her first American show at Marie Sterner's gallery on Fifty-seventh Street. Later, Rebay met the Guggenheims at the home of James Speyer, a banker, philanthropist, and patron of the arts. Rebay and Irene Guggenheim became friends. The following year, Rebay painted a portrait of Solomon Guggenheim—a realistic likeness of an elderly, pleasant-faced man in knickerbockers and knit hose. As Joan M. Lukach says in her biography of Rebay, "Convincing Guggenheim to sit for a vivacious, witty, sophisticated European noblewoman cannot have been difficult." Rebay took advantage of the sittings to interest Guggenheim in a genre of painting that she had first encountered among her artist-colleagues in Europe and that she was determined to introduce to the New World; she called the genre "non-objective" and distinguished it from "abstract" painting as being conceived

430

by intuition within the mind of its maker and not abstracted from anything in nature.

In a small studio that Rebay rented in Carnegie Hall were hung works by such painters as Kandinsky, Klee, and Rudolf Bauer (Bauer was for many years her lover; Lukach is able to demonstrate that a more disagreeable and demoralizing companion can scarcely ever have lived). Soon enough, Guggenheim became a disciple of non-objective art—indeed, the most eager and generous of disciples, addressed with affection by his newfound artist friends as "Guggi." Under Rebay's vigorous tutelage, Guggenheim put together an assemblage of paintings that, besides the artists mentioned above, came to include Chagall, Moholy-Nagy, Gleizes, Mondrian, Delaunay, and Balcomb Greene. Within a couple of years, Guggenheim and Rebay were faced with the problem of finding appropriate shelter for his ever-expanding collection. According to Lukach, Guggenheim thought at first of bequeathing it at his death to the Metropolitan Museum of Art. This solution to the problem would have angered Rebay, since the collection would then have passed out of her control; luckily, it didn't appeal to Guggenheim for long, as he glanced about and noticed how many of his fellow millionaires—Freer, Frick, Huntington, and Mellon—were taking care to provide monuments to themselves in the form of museums. Why shouldn't he do the same, and all the more so because of the little-appreciated nature of his collection? When it came to the buying and selling of art in the early thirties, his artists were more or less orphans; he had reason to wish to protect their handiwork after his death, as well as to protect the joyous, eccentric, and sometimes irascible Rebay.

By coincidence, in 1930 some of Rebay's artist-colleagues contemplated founding a utopian artists' colony in a village outside Paris. The colonists would build a museum to contain their works, and the designer of the museum would be Le Corbusier, whom Rebay had already met. Le Corbusier wished to design his museum in the shape of a spiral within a square; its galleries would be connected by ramps and would have moveable walls, and it would omit the grand entrance and grand staircases that museums of an earlier day had found indispensable. The little colony never came into existence, thanks in large part to the Great Depression, but Rebay continued to speculate on the design of an ideal museum building—a temple or dome of non-objective art (Lukach assumes that Rebay wrote "dome" in English as a translation of *Dom*, German for "cathedral"), where space would be found for a library, a movie theatre, a shop for the sale of educational materials and reproductions of paintings, and where the music of Bach and other classic composers would provide a continuous accompaniment.

On trips abroad, Rebay discussed her ideal museum building not only with Kandinsky and other artists but with a veritable anthology of architects,

Left, Hilla Rebay at the age of forty-five. Right, Solomon R. Guggenheim, as painted by Rebay. [RF]

including Le Corbusier, Gropius, and Breuer. She also consulted an enchanting gnome of a man, Frederick Kiesler, who had been born in Vienna and had been living for some time in New York City; among his innumerable unbuilt projects was a windowless museum fourteen stories high, by which Rebay was much impressed. (Kiesler's visionary architecture was based on organic shapes—an egg, say, or a snail—that he called "endless" because of their curving configurations and that were equally applicable to all kinds of buildings, public and private.) Rockefeller Center was under construction in the thirties, and the Rockefeller family was eager to establish within the precincts of the Center a cluster of cultural activities, including a new opera house—the replacement of the old Metropolitan Opera House, on Seventh Avenue, had provided the initial impetus for the Center—and much enlarged quarters for the recently founded Museum of Modern Art. Young Nelson Rockefeller proposed that a building for the Museum of Non-Objective Art be built adjacent to a Museum of Modern Art building, and he had his friend and associate, the architect Wallace K. Harrison, prepare a master plan for this purpose. Guggenheim and Rebay discussed the project with Rockefeller, Harrison, and Kiesler in New York and with several architects abroad, among them Edmund Korner, Mies van der Rohe, Le Corbusier, and Gropius, but for reasons having to do with the Rockefellers' inability to purchase the necessary amount of land the project fell through. (Many years later, the Rockefellers' hoped-for cluster of cultural activities was realized at Lincoln Center, with Harrison again in charge of the master plan.)

Throughout the thirties, in the continued gloom of the Great Depression, Guggenheim with the prudence of the rich took care to keep Rebay's audacious acquisitiveness within bounds; even so, the collection was enhanced by the many bargains—Légers, Feiningers, Nicholsons—that the depression made possible. Rebay was tender-hearted as well as shrewd; if she bought pictures cheaply, she also gave away to impoverished artists as much of Guggenheim's and her own money as she dared. She was at once the curator of a collection, a benefactress, and a messiah: when the collection went on public exhibition in Philadelphia, she wrote in an introduction to the catalogue, "Non-objectivity is the religion of the future. . . . Non-objective paintings are prophets of spiritual life." Guggenheim would not have gone so far, but he felt strongly that the general public would profit from being able to see his six or eight hundred paintings at first hand. In the late thirties, he considered sponsoring a pavilion at the New York World's Fair of 1939, which would be devoted to a history of art and for which examples of non-objective art drawn from his collection would provide a climax. Rebay designed the pavilion—an ingenious one-story circular structure with a dozen wings extending from a central garden. Because the collection still lacked a permanent home, the World's Fair project was abandoned as an extravagance. Faced at last by the likelihood of a world war (and a consequent ban upon all peacetime construction) and by his own increasing infirmities, Guggenheim rented quarters on East Fifty-fourth Street, in New York City. Rebay and a young architect named Muschenheim remodeled the quarters, and as great a portion of the collection was hung as Rebay could find room for upon its elegant gray walls. On May 1st, 1939, the Museum of Non-Objective Art—"The Art of Tomorrow"—threw open its doors.

In May, 1943, Rebay renewed her campaign to achieve a permanent home for the collection. She wrote to Moholy-Nagy, asking him to recommend an architect, and he drew up a list that included Le Corbusier, Gropius, Neutra, Breuer, Keck, Aalto, Lescaze, and himself. Moholy-Nagy was aware that Rebay had already discussed the project with Kiesler, Korner, and Mies; given that the United States was waging a great war against Germany and that Rebay herself was still a German citizen, Moholy-Nagy's list seems a singularly tactless one. Rebay must have sensed, however belatedly, that a native-born American architect was called for, and her choice fell upon Wright. Why had she not thought of him in the first place, especially in the light of the high esteem in which he had always been held in Germany? The answer is simple. It appears that she had assumed that Wright was dead. Astonished to discover, through members of the Guggenheim family, that he was still alive and in vigorous health at seventy-six, she purchased his books, found in them ideas about architecture (and life) very like her own, and sent off a characteristically urgent invitation, which read in part:

Dear Mr. Wright:

Could you ever come to New York and discuss with me a building for our collection of Non-objective paintings. I feel that each of these great masterpieces should be organized into space and only you would test the possibilities to do so. . . . I need a fighter, a lover of space, an originator, a tester, and a wise man. . . . I want a temple of spirit—a monument, and your help to make it possible, especially with our trustees and president. May this wish be blessed.

Hilla Rebay[1]

Wright countered with an invitation to Taliesin. Under the misapprehension that Rebay was a man—a misapprehension hard to understand, since her letter was written in an extremely feminine hand, on blue notepaper—he asked, "Why don't you run down here for a weekend? Bring your wife. We have room and disposition to make you comfortable. Of course I feel I should have no difficulty in giving the Foundation what it desires and needs."[2] More was contained in these words than a simple offer of hospitality, though the offer was genuine enough. Wright had long made use of Taliesin as a form of sales pitch; few visitors could resist its charm or fail to accept it as proof of the talent of its designer. Moreover, the scale of its operation as a country estate of seemingly unlimited resources aroused a becoming awe even in the rich. This awe heightened Wright's sense of his puissance—like any magus, he performed miracles because he was thought capable of performing miracles. When Rebay's letter arrived, Wright was particularly in need of psychological as well as financial reenforcement. As Bruce Pfeiffer notes in his book, *The Guggenheim Correspondence*, "The summer of 1943 was a very lean time for the drafting room at Taliesin. The nation was two years into the war. Most of Frank Lloyd Wright's apprentices had either enlisted or been drafted into the armed forces, and those remaining devoted their time to working the farm. Architectural commissions had dropped off sharply; there was little work on the boards."[3]

Rebay wrote back to explain, almost by way of apology, that she was not a man but that she had been in charge of forming the collection and that the kind of building she had in mind would take endless thinking, planning, and testing. She added that Guggenheim ("a great man, full of vision, courage, and understanding") was eighty-two years old, would soon be leaving New York for the summer, and was rarely in New York in winter; therefore "we have no time to lose." That there should be no further confusion over her gender, she took care to sign the letter "Baroness Rebay." The note of urgency that she struck on that occasion is ironic, given that Wright and she were at the start of an undertaking that would require sixteen years to complete. The irony is increased by the fact that the start was unusually brisk; Wright came to New York, met Rebay and Guggenheim, captivated them with practiced ease, and in late June signed a contract to design a museum for the Solomon R. Guggenheim Foundation. The contract stipulated that the museum was to cost no more than seven hundred and fifty thousand dollars, exclusive of the cost of whatever site might be chosen.

By the middle of July, Wright and Robert Moses, the New York Parks Commissioner, were surveying possible sites for the museum. (Wright was always proud to claim Moses as "Cousin Bob," Moses's wife being a distant cousin of Wright's.) One site was in the Riverdale section of the Bronx, another a hilltop on the northern tip of Manhattan, still another on West Fifty-fourth Street, next to the Museum of Modern Art garden. Other sites were on Park Avenue and Madison Avenue, north of the Pierpont Morgan Library—one of Charles Follen McKim's finest works, which Wright characteristically described as "a graveyard." When Rebay objected to the hilltop site as being too remote, Wright with his usual bravado replied, "I do not doubt the drawing power of an architectural masterpiece," and the implication was that Rebay would also do well not to doubt it.

Wright's letters to Rebay are sometimes tiresomely preachy—"Architecture (there is none in New York City) is the mother-art of arts. Where she really *is* she is not likely to murder her infants or frustrate her sons and daughters"[4]—and sometimes affectionately avuncular—"We [Olgivanna and Wright] enjoyed our visits with you more than anything that has happened to us that we can remember."[5] Plainly, he admired her as much as he had once admired Aline Barnsdall, with whom Rebay had much in common, including a plump, rosy-cheeked, bouncy presence, a hot temper, and a high intelligence. With her continuous expenditure of energy, she seemed, Wright told her, "a superwoman . . . a human projectile." She had deeply loved her parents, now long dead, and the Wrights became substitutes both for her parents and for the children she had never had. She fussed over them and spoiled them and tried to make them over, especially in regard to the preservation of their health. Rebay was a demonic amateur physician, with many crackpot notions about dead teeth and bloodletting. Under her influence, Wright consented to have his teeth removed and replaced by dentures. More radically, both the Wrights consented not once but several times to have big black leeches applied to their throats, in order to drain poisonous "old" blood from their bodies and prompt the manufacture of pure "new" blood. Despite his age, Wright was able to survive this treatment (which once upon a time had helped to kill George Washington); when the Wrights noticed one day that Rebay appeared to be casting clinical glances at the healthy teeth of their young daughter, Iovanna, they ceased to pay serious attention to her medical advice.

Months passed in the search for an appropriate site. The businesslike Guggenheim urged Wright to design a museum first and fit it onto a site afterward and Wright replied that this was not how great architecture—his architecture—was achieved. Nevertheless, he began preparing tentative sketches for a low, horizontal building, not unlike the Johnson Wax building. When it became obvious that land in Manhattan was too expensive to permit a sizeable horizontal building, Wright hit upon what he considered an ideal solution to their problem: a vertical building instead of a horizontal one. On the last day of 1943, Wright wrote to Guggenheim, "I can see a tall building of a new type perfectly appropriate to our purpose, having monumental dignity and great beauty, requiring about half the ground area we have been looking for."[6] So excited was Wright by this inspiration that he volunteered to come to New York and resume "prospecting" sites at no cost to Guggenheim except for his traveling expenses. He was not in the habit of looking for sites on behalf of a client, and it is a measure of his eagerness to build the museum that he should have made such an offer, which Guggenheim, on his way to South Carolina for the winter, appears to have rejected. Despite the rejection, Wright wrote Rebay that he would have come to New York anyway, but he was simply too hard-up.

As he often did in order to heighten a client's interest in a project (and so help to ensure its eventual acceptance), Wright pretended to Rebay that she might find the novelty of his design for the museum shocking or offensive—"the whole thing will either throw you off your guard entirely or be just about what you have been dreaming about."[7] In late January, Wright sent Rebay his first sketches for a vertical museum, which turned out to be in the shape of a spiral. He labeled a drawing of it "Ziggurat," and pointed out to her that, as far as engineering was concerned, they could choose a ziggurat that was "either top side down or down side up." The ziggurats of ancient times had necessarily diminished in size as they rose, because of the inert, compressive building materials—stone, brick, earth—available to their builders; with reinforced concrete and steel, an upside-down ziggurat would be as easy to build and would possess even greater strength than a down-side-up one.

Wright had been designing projects in the shape of spirals at least as early as the unbuilt Gordon Strong planetarium and "automobile objective" of 1925. The Guggenheim spiral was followed in the late forties by a couple of immense spiral designs for Pittsburgh—a civic center and a public garage, both commissioned by Edgar J. Kaufmann and both unbuilt— and by comparatively tiny spiral designs for the V. C. Morris Shop, in San Francisco, and the Hoffman Jaguar salesroom in New York City, both of which are still standing. The ramped spiral appears again and again in the projects of Wright's old age, including a house that he designed for his son David, built in Phoenix, in 1952, and a cluster of three houses designed for Helen Donahoe, near Phoenix, in the spring of 1959, a few weeks before his death. (The drawing of what Wright called "The Donahoe Triptych"—Wright bestowed names on houses as if to bestow on them the magical gift of life—was the last that Wright ever signed; as for the three houses, perhaps because the magical giver of life was himself no longer alive, they were never built.) More than the triangle, the hexagon, or the circle, the spiral struck Wright as a thrilling architectural form because it exists in three dimensions and because an expanding spiral—what he dubbed in the case of the Guggenheim "an optimistic ziggurat"—seems to defy gravity.

As Wright was sure to have known, the spiral appealed to Rebay on grounds that went well beyond architecture. She had spoken to him of Le Corbusier's unbuilt spiral museum outside Paris (which some scholars believe Le Corbusier borrowed from Wright's Strong project) and of Kiesler's "endless" structures, but for Rebay the spiral in architecture was simply the outward and visible sign of the spirals that existed for her and for her fellow champions of Non-Objectivity in the spiritual world. She and her colleagues were all members of a sort of undeclared secret society, based in part on theosophy and in part on other more arcane Eastern cults. Representational painting reflected the gross materialist world that surrounded them; non-objective painting represented the purity of what Yeats called the self-delighting soul. (Yeats himself had been at least temporarily fascinated by theosophy and Rosicrucianism, and into old age wrote passionately of "the gyres, the gyres!"—that is, "the spirals, the spirals!") Rebay accepted Wright's plan for a spiral building almost without taking thought, because it fitted so exactly into her concept of a temple, in which art would be celebrated as a higher form of religion. Though Wright took care at the start to assure her that his design was highly practical, at the start she gave practicality but half of her attention. He wrote:

A museum should be one extended expansive well-proportioned floor space from bottom to top—a wheel chair going around and up and down, *throughout.* No stops anywhere and such screened divisions of the space gloriously lit within from above, as would deal appropriately with every group of paintings or individual paintings as you might want them classified.

The atmosphere of the whole should be luminous from bright to dark, anywhere desired: a great calm and breadth pervading the whole place. . . .

There should be no "stuffs"—either curtains or carpets. For floors, either cork or rubber tiling, etc., etc.

Much crystal, much greenery about. No distracting detail anywhere.

In short, a creation which does not yet exist.[8]

Soon enough, Rebay, having omitted to have first thoughts, began to have second ones. Her former lover, the pernicious Bauer (who had been sedulously spreading the rumor that Rebay was a Nazi), damned the design as being of no use whatever, and Moholy-Nagy was equally adverse in his opinion. Wright's riposte to the latter: "Moholy-Nagy has the nerve to suggest to us what a museum should be like? I never did respect him for brains."[9] The comparative feebleness of this riposte may have been thanks in part to the fact that Wright himself, at this late stage of his career, had never been called on to design a museum; the design of the Guggenheim was indeed revolutionary in many respects and therefore untested, and Wright may have felt a defensiveness that emerged, as it so often did with him, as bluster. (After almost thirty years, the appropriateness of the design for museum purposes remains a legitimate topic of debate, though the design as an expression of architectural genius does not.)

Guggenheim also appears to have been provoked by well-meaning friends into expressing some skepticism in respect to the design, but Wright took care not to lose his temper with the source of the commission. His reputation as an architect was at stake; so was his financial position, which was as usual desperate. He excoriated Rebay directly and arranged for Guggenheim to learn of the state of his feelings at second hand:

I wonder to whom you have been listening again. I can imagine, of course. Surely you have not failed so completely to grasp the essential idea with which you were so completely delighted when presented to you as you now pretend.

I foresee I am to have no client but am to have instead only a group of small critics whispering to you concerning something about which they can really know nothing and about which you now say that you know nothing either. *That is rather terrible for me?*

. . . No great good thing in building ever happened where the client was at the mercy of the passing suggestions of this one and that one, no matter who they were. . . .

But I shall do nothing further with the plans until I hear from you as to what in the changed circumstances of your mind you now desire.[10]

And to this letter he added the canny postscript, "Since you mention that Mr. Guggenheim is in the same 'nervous' state of apprehension as yourself I have sent a copy of this letter to him." The letter gained the end he had sought; within a couple of weeks, he received from Guggenheim a note saying, "Your preliminary sketches are entirely satisfactory, and we are now authorizing you to proceed to make detailed plans. . . . Enclosed find check for $21,000.00 in payment for the first stage of your contract. . . ."[11] Wright made a dash east to visit his patrons, who were summering in the White Mountains of New Hampshire; a day or so later, he wrote Rebay in high spirits from Taliesin, "The model [of the museum] is in work and so are the plans. Please give my best to Mr. Guggenheim. He is a grand man—and do you take good account of yourself and get a good rest. I noticed a great improvement in you."[12]

For most of the following eighteen months, Wright and the Fellowship worked on the drawings for the museum, making constant changes to accommodate what Wright called Rebay's "hunches"—a high-ceilinged sanctum separate from the main ramped gallery, for the display on a permanent basis of the museum's masterpieces; a theatre for the showing of non-objective films; and a restaurant. Some of Wright's own hunches met with Rebay's veto. For example, he had a lifelong, nineteenth-century predilection for roof gardens and wanted one on the Guggenheim; Rebay wrote sharply, "New York's air is too dirty to sit outside much and so roof gardens sound nice but are useless, as I know from experience."[13] Nor did she approve of Wright's suggestion that the exterior of the building should be a mixture of red brick and red marble: "I do not like red," she wrote, "as it is of all colors the most materialistic. . . . Red is a color which displeases S.R.G. [Guggenheim] as much as it does me."[14] Wright had stumbled unawares upon one of Rebay's many irrational spiritualist convictions, but he was prepared to defend red, at least for a time:

When I was a cub-architect, I once declared in a public lecture that blue was not an architect's color. It did not substantiate whatever it was applied to, I said. Well, I've lived to laugh at that dictum. It was a mere personal idiosyncrasy. I use blue now for what it may be worth. And you, too, Hilla, will live to laugh at your fancy dictum that red is carnal (your personal idiosyncrasy)—(or affliction). . . . But *just what red?* is a matter for careful choice. See samples we send you. But if you are unable to overcome your own "idiosyncrasy"—then how about Black Montana [a kind of granite]? See sample—warm black—because a strong contrast is necessary if the walls are to be bright with light and the main footing adequate and firm.[15]

439

Wright eventually decided to clad the building in a rich, cream-colored marble; for reasons of economy, he consented to what he hoped was a temporary makeshift—painting the naked concrete a warm beige. We have to remind ourselves that Wright rejoiced in color and that his wish to cover the parapets of Fallingwater in gold leaf was no temporary aberration. Back at the turn of the century, he saw to it that gold leaf was applied to the mortar between the bricks on the interior of the Darwin D. Martin house, to handsome effect, and for more than half a century his palette grew brighter and brighter, culminating in the many-colored fantasia of the cultural center in Baghdad, commissioned by the King of Iraq in 1957.

As the Guggenheim project developed, a difference of opinion arose between Rebay and Wright that was to continue until the museum was built and may be said (at least indirectly, as a topic of debate on a theoretical level) to continue up to the present day: in general, the proper hanging of pictures in a museum and, in particular, the proper hanging of the Guggenheim collection in the building that Wright designed for it. Rebay had been hanging pictures for decades and had strong convictions about how best to show them off; moreover, she was familiar with the practices of innumerable museums throughout the world and was familiar with the desires of most of the artists whose works she had purchased for the Guggenheim and for her own collection. Wright talked big—one can

Interior of the Guggenheim.

scarcely cite an occasion on which he didn't talk big—but the fact was that he had never designed a museum, had little or no familiarity with the nature of non-objective art, and had a low opinion of the painters whom Rebay praised to him. His fixed ideas about the exhibition of works of art were based on traditional methods of exhibiting Japanese scrolls and prints. For several clients (as well as for himself) Wright had designed tables upon which prints could be shown, resting against a slightly tilted easel; he wished the walls of the Guggenheim to be slanted in an easel-like fashion and to have light come in through a narrow band of glass tubing above the pictures, much as light entered the Johnson Wax building. Further light would be supplied from the great domed skylight at the top of the quarter-mile-long ramp. Rebay thought of the collection as nearly complete and therefore ready for enshrinement; Wright, disliking what he knew of the collection, wanted his museum to accommodate itself to works of art that might be purchased at some future time, long after Rebay and Guggenheim and he were dead. Rebay was concerned to have the pictures in her "temple" permanently hung—"built into the walls," as she put it. Wright was eager to have them hung in as temporary a fashion as possible, with sliding screens and moveable partitions.

The more they quarreled over this problem, the more uneasy Rebay became. Her friends kept telling her that because Wright was notorious for his dislike of paintings of any kind she would do well to leave the exterior of the museum to Wright and have an architect more sympathetic to the collection—Mies, say, or Kiesler—design the interior. Wright indignantly rejected this proposal, though he said he was willing to have Mies or Breuer or Mendelsohn or Gropius (all of them what he called "fairly capable" architects) look at a model of the museum and make whatever suggestions they liked. Rebay heightened his indignation by writing, "While I have no doubt that your building will be a great monument to yourself, I cannot visualize how much (or how little) it will do for the paintings. . . ."[16] Wright replied, "What is this inimical fury over 'the monument to myself'? Silly, Silly! What could a building be to me if its work was not done superbly well?"[17] Almost thirty years later, critics of the building continue to echo Rebay's doubts; the mildly scolding tone of Wright's answer implies that he had heard such doubts expressed before (perhaps as early as the Larkin building) and that they gave him little distress. He was content to leave undebated the principle that every work that came from the hand of a genius was, by definition, a monument to that genius. "I need no monument," he wrote Rebay, meaning not that he had chosen in modesty to do without one but that he had already created many hundreds of them.

The war ended in 1945, but Guggenheim appears to have been under the impression during the next few years that building costs, inflated by the war, would eventually drop back to earlier levels and so he put off breaking ground. One of two remaining parcels of land facing Fifth Avenue was purchased, giving the museum the entire blockfront except for a house on the Eighty-ninth Street corner. The length of the façade of the museum was able to be increased from one hundred and sixty feet to one hundred and eighty feet, and by being able to embrace the Eighty-eighth Street corner the museum avoided the appearance of being squeezed breathlessly—this curious object from outer space—between two conventional neo-Renaissance limestone housefronts. Meanwhile, Wright and an assortment of different engineers considered various methods of constructing the building; at one time it was to have been composed entirely of Gunite, like his Kansas City church; at another time, it was to have been of pre-stressed concrete. In the end, the cheapest means of building it turned out to be reinforced concrete, and even this cheap method was, by Guggenheim's standards, extremely costly. He and Wright had expected, in 1943, to build the museum for $750,000. By 1946, the ever-optimistic Wright had raised its estimated cost to $1,500,000, and in early 1949 Wright estimated that he could build the museum for $2,500,000. Rebay reported that this sum was out of the question. Mr. Guggenheim, by then approaching ninety, had named a certain sum in his will—it was said to be two million dollars—to be devoted to the building of the museum and to the future maintenance of the collection; every penny taken from this capital sum for the construction of the museum building would leave that much less income for the maintenance of the collection, and so Wright and Rebay found themselves with still another reason to be at odds, Wright favoring maximum expenditure on the building, Rebay favoring the preservation of the maximum amount of income.

Late in 1949, Guggenheim died. He had turned out to be less impatient than most rich old men to erect a monument to himself in his own lifetime; indeed, by the time the monument was built he had slipped into history as just one of many Guggenheims, of whom his brother Simon, his niece Peggy, and his nephew Harry were all more famous. His will bequeathed the promised two million dollars for the museum building, but left open the possible time of its construction and even left open, to Wright's dismay, the question of who its architect should be. It soon became obvious that the directors of the Solomon R. Guggenheim Foundation were doubtful of the worthiness of the collection that they had been placed in charge of, were doubtful of Rebay's worthiness to direct the collection, and were doubtful of Wright's ability to put up a building for a reasonable sum. After years of wooing Guggenheim and Rebay, Wright had to set about wooing the Board of Trustees of the Foundation, of which Harry Guggenheim was soon elected Chairman. Luckily, Wright and Harry took to each other, and Harry's wife Alicia, a lively and enterprising Middlewesterner born in Chicago, at once became a close friend of the Wrights.

Little progress was made in 1950 and 1951, except to revise plans for the museum when, at Wright's urging, the trustees of the Guggenheim Foundation acquired the last parcel of land on the blockfront—what Wright called "the hangnail." After literally hundreds of revisions, the working drawings for the museum reached their final form. Once built, the museum would be able to assume its rightful posture on Fifth Avenue as a free-standing object; if the world were to consider it bizarre, at least it would be bizarre upon its own terms.

26

At Taliesin, as the Guggenheim Museum struggled to be brought to birth, the number of new projects increased markedly from one year to the next. It was a time of regained activity, of a busy-ness not unlike those happy and frantic early days in the Studio at Oak Park, when Wright and half a dozen gifted assistants found themselves working night and day, seven days a week, turning out so much work that afterward it was hard to tell who among them deserved praise for a particular accomplishment. Back then, William Drummond boasted of having single-handedly executed two house commissions over a single weekend (none of his colleagues corroborated the boast), and it was certainly true that work got done with remarkable speed. Marion Mahony devoted much of her time to making exquisite renderings based on hurried Wright sketches, while on at least one occasion, reversing the process, Wright is said to have "ruined" a Mahony drawing in a rash attempt to improve it. The Studio in its prime was a spinning top, which skittered to a halt with Wright's sudden, unlooked-for decampment to Europe with Mamah Cheney.

At Taliesin in the forties and fifties, the Fellowship came to number between fifty and sixty—young (and afterward not quite so young) men and women from all over the world, who gladly paid substantial fees for the privilege of being in Wright's presence and serving him in the role of draftsmen, household servants, and field laborers. Thanks in large part to his indefatigable showmanship, Wright was by now the most famous architect on earth. Having achieved this lifelong goal was certainly agreeable, and he was by no means willing to surrender an iota of that fame or consent to the approach of any rivals, even worthy ones. He continued his childish sneering at "old" Mies (almost twenty years younger than Wright), Le Corbusier ("He should have been a painter. He was a bad one, but he should have kept on"), the internationally successful architectural firm of Skidmore, Owings & Merrill ("Skiddings, Own-more, and Sterile"), and at other imaginary adversaries.

No profusion of honors from universities and professional arts organizations, including the tardy bestowal upon him, in 1949, of the Gold Medal of the American Institute of Architects, could make up for the neglect to which he felt (or pretended to feel) he had been subjected for the previous half-century: the most famous architect on earth was content to assert again and again that he had been shamefully ignored, and there was not always a merry twinkle in his eye when he made that preposterous assertion. Even the tardiness of his being offered the Gold Medal was a result not of his ever having been found unworthy of it; rather, it was a result of his decades of harsh mockery of the Institute, prompting a suspicion that he would use a highly publicized occasion like the bestowal of the medal to launch still another gratuitous attack upon it. Instead, for once, he behaved comparatively well.

From coast to coast, and from many points abroad as well, people wrote in to Taliesin, begging Wright to grant them the boon of a house from his hand. As the commissions streamed across Wright's desk, the Taliesin drafting room threatened to resemble the kind of big architectural offices that Wright had always affected to despise. Although he denied that any such resemblance was possible, the world outside Taliesin's gates thought otherwise and, not without malice, began to say so. With Wright's increasing prosperity it was difficult to defend on an intellectual basis the income he derived from the Fellowship (Wright's defense was that the cost of maintaining the Fellows at Taliesin far exceeded the fees they paid). It was also difficult for him to claim simultaneously that he was not a teacher and that Taliesin was a teaching institution, entitled to every available tax-exemption. One way to avoid the issue of his personal affluence was to argue, as Wright often did, that he earned nothing for himself— that every penny of his income went to the Frank Lloyd Wright Foundation. But if this was true, it was equally true that the chief beneficiary of the Foundation was Wright himself, who lived on a level of luxury that many of his millionaire clients had reason to envy.

The practice of architecture on a large scale is ill understood by the general public; it may be worth glancing at for a moment in order to make clear the resemblance, or (in Wright's view) lack of resemblance, between it and Taliesin at the height of Taliesin's post-war prosperity. For generations, the public has been invited to accept the romantic notion that architects work as artists are reputed to work, in a kind of divinely inspired solitude. The highly unromantic role of the architect as a businessman presiding over a complex commercial enterprise that is sometimes profitable and sometimes not is an unfamiliar one to most of us. Many architects have reckoned that ninety percent of the time and energy that they devote to the practice of architecture must be spent upon the "nuts and bolts" of contracts, working drawings, specifications, and the like; ten percent is spent upon actual design. That Wright was obliged to practice architecture in such a fashion is a fact that makes some of his admirers uncomfortable. They find it hard to realize that over a long lifetime he had to write many hundreds—perhaps thousands—of letters devoted entirely to the subject of money, nearly always either pleading for it as his due (which in some instances it was and in most instances it wasn't), or begging for it as a loan, or apologizing for not having enough of it to pay back a loan or settle an account.

If Wright was a businessman at all, he was one with a knack for spending money instead of accumulating it; moreover, he possessed a rarer and more dangerous knack, which was for outwitting those friends of his who, having already demonstrated their competence in the world of business, sought to put his tangled financial affairs in order. Again and again, by one device or another (turning him into a corporation and issuing stock in him, later making him an employee of a not-for-profit foundation), they plotted to save him from a succession of fiscal follies, always in vain. Though he claimed to suffer agonies over his debts, the fact was that he seemed to draw strength from them; they were the natural element in which he frolicked and he felt weakness only when—mercifully, never for very long—some harsh twist of fate cast him up helpless upon the beach of solvency.

If the public continues to think of the architect as a romantic figure, Wright himself is at least partly responsible, having from his teens adopted the romantic concept of striving to be several people at once. One of the masks he wore was that of the artist-architect, with his unconventional philosophy (a mingling of hand-me-down Emerson and hand-me-down Nietzsche), his unconventional personal life, and his unconventional, dandified dress (cape, pork-pie hat, and cane—a garb as distinctive as Charlie Chaplin's). Despite his theatrical garb, Wright contrived to turn Taliesin from an atelier, with its attendant and often charming inefficiencies, into a machine that was able to process, like any conventional architectural office of a certain size, thirty or forty substantial projects a year. Taliesin remained in appearance a one-man show, although it was by no means a one-man office; a few of Wright's faithful acolytes gained a limited degree of recognition in the world, but only in relationship to Wright and Taliesin. As Wright liked to boast, they were the fingers on his hand, and for them it was an accepted and even welcome state of affairs—a condition not of employment merely but of a way of life: for as long as Wright was alive, they would be judged as appendages of a great man and not as individuals. The question of their receiving adequate credit for their accomplishments never arose, and this was less surprising then than it would strike us as being today, for the system of apprenticeships out of which the profession of architecture developed made no provision for giving—much less for taking—credit.

For well over a hundred years, it was the custom for the name-partners in an architectural firm to be credited with all of the work carried out by the firm; only in comparatively recent times have individual partners been given such credit, in whole or in part. For example, when Wright was getting his start as an architect, McKim, Mead & White was the leading architectural "factory" in New York City, employing many architects and dominating the profession there; at the time, either McKim or White was invariably identified as the person who had designed one or another of the hundreds of buildings to which they had affixed their names. (Poor Mead, the middle partner, confessed that he had been reduced to the role of "keeping my partners from making damned fools of themselves.") The fact was that dozens of McKim, Mead & White buildings were scarcely glanced at by McKim and White in the course of their busy careers. White visited Europe at least twice a year, which amounted to four weeks on the water, along with several additional weeks on the Continent; he also spent time salmon-fishing in Canada, visiting his brother in New Mexico, and entertaining at his country place on Long Island. Though superhumanly energetic, how much work could he accomplish in the course of a given year, especially when that year had also to embrace constant attendance at the opera, the theatre, and fashionable dinner-parties, to say nothing of the pursuit and conquest of innumerable ambitious soubrettes?

Even in respect to some of McKim, Mead & White's most important commissions, it was the case that they were handed about the office as cavalierly as a box of cigars. The commission for the Villard houses—in 1882, the biggest the firm had yet received—came to McKim, who, on unexpectedly going abroad, passed it along to White, who, also going abroad, passed it along to a young colleague, Joseph Wells. Seemingly without the knowledge of the partners, Wells made the momentous decision to design the exterior of the building in imitation of an Italian Renaissance palazzo. The design was a great hit and led the firm to specialize in such imitations, of which many proved to be more interesting than their originals. As for Wells, on being offered a partnership in the firm, he refused it on the grounds that "I wouldn't want to sign my name to so much damned bad work."

A bureaucratic hurly-burly of the same magnitude was familiar to Wright in the architectural "factories" of Chicago. "Uncle Dan" Burnham, of Burnham & Root, had once offered Wright a position roughly akin to that of Wells at McKim, Mead & White, and Wright had turned it down, out of an authentically virtuous determination to remain his own man. When Burnham died, in 1912, there was said to be seventeen million dollars' worth of business in the office; his was the biggest factory in the country. The success that Wright enjoyed in old age inevitably altered the nature of his practice; certain conventions that he had spent a lifetime avoiding were forced upon him and not the least of these was his having to sign his name to so much work that, if it was not "damned bad," was at the very least unlike him at his best. As almost every architect known to history has consented to do, in times of prosperity he found irresistible the temptation to accept far more work than he could devote his finest efforts to; the remarkable variety of designs that one encounters in riffling through any photographic record of Wright's work in his eighties and nineties at first fills one with awe and then with a measure of skepticism. Is the variety a function of a multiplicity of ideas in a single mind, or simply that of a multiplicity of minds? How much of what we see is from Wright's hand, how much from other hands?

When Wright's sister Maginel Barney asked him in his late eighties, "How do you think of it all?" he replied, "I can't get it out fast enough." It is a statement more revealing than either Wright or Mrs. Barney may have perceived it to be: for one thing, it takes care not to answer her question and, for another, it implies that volume of work and even speed of production have taken precedence over quality. He had always been able to respond quickly to a given task—one thinks of Fallingwater emerging on paper overnight like the feat of some master prestidigitator—but the initial burst of creative activity was usually followed (a luxury of lean times) by weeks of revisionary tinkerings. The hundred or so houses designed at Taliesin during the nineteen-fifties ring innumerable changes on the few basic forms of the Usonian houses of a decade or so earlier—changes that have to do with the cladding of a house, with minor (and often ingenious) manipulations of floor plans and rooflines, and with siting, which had once been a matter of extreme importance to Wright and was now often subject to the offhand decisions of clients and builders.

Some houses were built on the tops of hills, violating a cardinal Wright principle, "Of the hill, not on it." Other houses were shifted from one portion of a site to another, perhaps on the advice of a builder who had happened to hit rock in the course of preparing foundations, or who wished to lower the steep grade of a driveway. Wright had always taken pains to relate his houses to the sun, though he was quick to disobey his principles whenever he found it convenient to do so. For example, the first Jacobs house was built on a plot of land across the street from the plot for which it had been designed. Wright casually "flipped" the floor plan to accommodate the new site. The serendipitous result was that the house as it stands gains the benefit of many hours of morning sun; if the house had been built on the original plot, it would have faced west, into the murderous late-afternoon light. Many of the houses of Wright's old age display a capricious orientation, which is probably to be blamed on a lack of that close supervision which the early houses had almost always enjoyed.

If the domestic commissions of this period, like the commissions of the Oak Park period, cannot all be said to bear the stamp of Wright's genius, it should also be noted that while most of the twenty thousand drawings of one sort or another that are stored in the archives at Taliesin are likely to have passed under Wright's eye, hundreds and perhaps thousands of them are not likely to have felt so much as the lightest touch of his fistful of colored pencils. (Say he prepared a drawing every day of every year for seventy years; he still could not have amassed the collection of drawings now at Taliesin. In fact, there were periods in his life, some of them lasting for months, when he made no drawings at all.) Again, we face a confusion between what the public believes about the practice of architecture and what that practice actually is. Because the price of drawings and paintings in the international art market has risen in recent years to such unprecedented heights, many young collectors have begun purchasing architectural drawings, as being comparatively inexpensive and comparatively varied in style and abundant in supply. What some of these collectors appear not to realize is that drawings prepared in the offices of most of the major architectural firms of the twentieth century have only the most tenuous connection with the architects who have been the "name" partners in these firms. One could list half a dozen famous American architects who have never made a drawing in their lives—who are, indeed, unable to draw above a kindergarten level of skill. For these (and related) reasons, architectural drawings can be a risky field of connoisseurship, to say nothing of their being a risky field of investment.

Wright's greatness as an architect and his ability to choose clever renderers have led him to become a leading figure in an area of enterprise that scarcely existed at the time of his death. In order to maintain its extensive holdings in Wisconsin and Arizona, the Fellowship has permitted a large number of drawings from the archives at Taliesin to be offered at public sale. These drawings sell for from a few thousand dollars up to two hundred thousand dollars apiece, which is to say that the Taliesin collection as a whole may be estimated to be worth several hundreds of millions of dollars. But if the vast majority of the drawings are the handiwork of generations of gifted apprentices—if only a few hundred out of many thousands of the drawings bear so much as a pencil stroke by Wright—what is being sold?

The profusion of domestic commissions in the decade following the war included a couple of especially pleasing family projects: houses for those two of his four sons who were not architects. David, who was born in 1895, has been a successful businessman, employed by a company that

The roof-deck of the David Wrights' house in Phoenix (1950), which looks out over a grove of orange trees; FLW called the tops of the trees "David's lawn."

manufactured concrete blocks; in the early nineteen-fifties he and his wife purchased a large plot of land in an orange grove on the outskirts of Phoenix. They asked Wright to prepare a design, which turned out to be a modified version of a house that had been commissioned by a client in New Jersey. The house had never been built, and it was characteristic of Wright, then in his middle eighties, to be stubbornly resolved to see it realized. As we observed with the Jester-Pfeiffer house, built after Wright's death, he would offer a favorite design again and again, to as many as half a dozen clients in half a dozen different localities, before gaining acceptance of it; he was therefore in David's case by no means fobbing off on a member of the family a house of doubtful value. On the contrary, the house was of particular interest to him, being closely related in concept to his main preoccupation at that time, the Guggenheim Museum.

The plan of the David Wright house consists of a spiral ramp leading at an easy grade to a curved and cantilevered one-story structure, from whose elevated entrance deck a second ramp winds upward onto a flat roof; from the roof, one looks out over what Wright called a vast "lawn" of orange trees to the wrinkled, rust-colored mountains.

The house had been intended to be built of wood; given David's occupation (and Wright's own preference), it was decided to build it of concrete block instead. With Wesley Peters's help, David Wright (who says of himself, "I'm a pretty good amateur engineer") redesigned the house to that end, introducing a large quantity of steel that he took care to conceal from his father. David Wright also acted as the general contractor for the house. While the wooden roof was in the course of being framed, Wright dropped in for a visit, glanced up at the short cross-pieces that conventionally stiffen rafters, and, pointing with his cane, said, "Those braces must go." David Wright looked at his father and said coolly, "I don't think so." And the braces remained.

When the house was finished, Wright drove over from Taliesin with his then resident photographer, Pedro Guerrero, to take pictures of it for *House Beautiful.* David and his wife, Gladys, had planted some bougainvillaea vines along the ramp leading up to the entrance of the house. Wright was dissatisfied with the look of the vines on the parapet of the ramp and—as usual acting as if any house that he had designed was his—began to tug and pull at them in order to create a more artistic effect in Guerrero's photographs. David Wright asked his father to leave the vines alone. The father persisted in adjusting them and David again objected, this time angrily. Wright attempted to stare down his sixty-year-old son. "I guess you'd rather I wasn't here," he said. "That's right," David said, and Wright and Guerrero got into Guerrero's car and drove away.

A year or so later, Wright designed a house for his youngest son, Robert Llewellyn Wright (1903–1985), an attorney who practiced in Wash-

© PEDRO E. GUERRERO

The David Wright house as it looked in FLW's lifetime; today it is deep in greenery. The ramp winding upward at the left serves as an awning for the round kitchen window.

ington, D.C. Standing on a wooded hillside in Bethesda, Maryland, the house is a two-story-high solar hemicycle built of concrete block and wood siding—a refinement of the design that Wright had begun experimenting with many years earlier, in the second Jacobs house. It is agreeable to note that he gave his sons almost identical fireplaces in the living rooms of their houses and that he took particular pains with the design of the furniture for their houses. Both houses are, in a sense, airborne, and it is tempting to imagine that the father has designed for his middle-aged sons tree houses reminiscent of those that they clambered up to in the deep woods of Oak Park.

A couple of years before his death, Wright designed an enchanting rug for the living room of the David Wright house, echoing the circles and curves of the structure and reminding us of the many-colored, joyously childlike windows of the Coonley playhouse, which he had designed almost half a century earlier. The house provided an escape from what was sometimes for Wright an oppressive sense of being under too close a scrutiny at Taliesin West. Recruiting an apprentice to serve as a chauffeur and fellow conspirator, Wright would steal away from his benign imprisonment, drive to Gladys and David Wright's, and knock on their door. "May I come in?" he would say, wearing the expression of a truant who knows that sooner or later he is sure to be punished for his wickedness. Before Olgivanna's death and after, Gladys and David Wright kept themselves— and keep themselves—at a tactfully calculated distance from the administration of affairs at Taliesin. At ninety-two, David (a Lloyd Jones in physique) is big and bluff, with merry blue eyes and a head shapelier even than his father's. Looking back over his life, he says of his extraordinary family that while he is proud to be a member of it, the cost of membership, in terms of wear and tear on the emotions, can be very high. And then he smiles and proposes lunch at the club, followed by a round of golf. But first a libation must be poured in the form of an ice-cold dry martini; in spite of everything, there is much to be thankful for.

Along with the many domestic commissions (some of the latest of which are not worth serious scrutiny) came several important commissions for buildings of a public nature. For both personal and professional reasons, the most pleasing of these commissions was for the Price Tower, in Bartlesville, Oklahoma. It is a story that defies every normal expectation by having a happy beginning, middle, and end and is unlike a fairy tale only in lacking a villain. If Wright was a charmer, so in his different way was Harold C. Price; between them they succeeded in bringing into the world a work of art that is itself the embodiment of charm. The Price Tower is in some ways an absurd structure, especially given the purpose for which

David Wright playing golf in 1986, at the age of ninety. A drive straight down the fairway, to the dismay of an eighty-year-old golfing rival.

© SUSAN WOLDENBERG

it was designed and the place in which it was built, but a critic seeking to attack it on rational grounds would be accused, and quite rightly, of having humorlessly missed the point; as simply and clearly as the Romeo and Juliet water tower, and more simply and clearly than its rival, the Guggenheim, it needed only to be in order to give delight.

In an introduction to a book, *The Story of the Tower,* to which Wright contributed a text that he and the publisher of the Horizon Press, Ben Raeburn, assembled from earlier Wright dicta, Harold Price describes the origins of the project, beginning with his arrival in Bartlesville, in 1915, as a penniless young chemist with a job in one of the local zinc smelters. It is a classic American "rags to riches" success story of the period a generation later than Wright's and helps to explain the rapport that sprang up immediately between the two men; Wright was always inclined to feel a simplistic admiration for what used to be called in his day "titans of industry," though he denounced the economic system that had produced them. He was, after all, seemingly in spite of himself and in spite of the system, an American success story on a colossal scale. Besides, the two men saw themselves as pioneers: members of a small brotherhood that was entitled to practice its own version of "truth against the world."

Price's introduction deals with the first question that people always asked him:

Why did we build the Tower? The answer goes back to a day in October, 1915—forty years ago, when I first came to Bartlesville . . . then a town with a population of less than ten thousand. . . . There were two brothers, Frank and L. E. Phillips, running the town's largest bank. The town's foremost surgeon, Dr. Webber, was drilling oil wells and raising cattle and refusing to bill most of his patients. . . .

The First World War brought on changes. The Phillips brothers started their oil company. . . . After the war, during the depression of 1920, two of the smelters shut down permanently, and I was out of a job, and with borrowed capital started one of the first electric welding shops in the Southwest. . . .

All of this over thirty years ago. The little town grew steadily. The people with big, fine ideas remained there. As their enterprises prospered, they did not pick up and move to larger cities. Instead, they made every effort to make their town a better place in which to live. . . . The little electric welding shop developed into a construction company that welded and built pipe lines all over North and South America.

Now, how did we come to build this Tower? We wanted a building of our own. We agreed to build a three-story building, with another company taking the entire first floor. My two sons, Harold and Joe, recently graduated from the University of Oklahoma, suggested we get Frank Lloyd Wright to design the building. They argued that it would cost no more to get a building with a beautiful, outstanding design than it would be to get the usual box-type design. . . . However, I did not believe that Mr. Wright would be interested in such a small building. My sons telephoned him and made an appointment. We went to Taliesin. I told him I wanted a three-story building with about 25,000 square feet of floor space. He said immediately that three floors was most inefficient and suggested ten floors of 2,500 square feet each. We finally compromised on nineteen floors, and included apartments with the offices.[1]

One's first thought is, "Some 'compromise'!" A client wishes a three-story building and his architect talks him into a nineteen-story one; moreover, the architect does so in part by claiming that a tall, slender building is more efficient for office purposes than a low, broad-based building, which is not the case. Indeed, a tall, slender office building would be justified only in an intensely built-up large city, where land values were extremely high; Bartlesville in 1952 had a population of perhaps twenty thousand people and possessed many hundred acres of low-cost land on which to build.

What had happened was more complicated—and even more agreeable—than what Price recalled in his introduction. Harold Price, Jr., had graduated from the University of Oklahoma, but Joe Price was still an undergraduate there. He was a friend and admirer of Bruce Goff (1904–

1982), Chairman of the Department of Architecture at the university. One of the few architects whom one can speak of in the same breath with Wright, Goff was apprenticed to an architectural firm in Tulsa, Oklahoma, at the age of twelve, was designing buildings for the firm at the age of fifteen, and was made a full partner at the age of twenty-five. Goff had become a friend and protégé of Wright's in his teens. Joe Price mentioned to Goff that his father was thinking of putting up a new office building in Bartlesville and that his brother Harold and he wanted the building to be something beyond the merely utilitarian; would Goff be interested in designing it? Goff replied that of course he would be delighted to design the building but that if they wished a truly beautiful building they should find out whether the greatest architect alive—Frank Lloyd Wright—would be interested in designing it for them. With his father's permission, Harold Price, Jr., telephoned Wright in Spring Green, and Wright said at once, as Goff must have known he would, "Come on up!"

Mr. and Mrs. Price and their sons arrived at Taliesin and were welcomed by Wright at the top of his form—the white-haired wizard superbly holding court in his incomparable kingdom, which by the nineteen-fifties struck most visitors as being more like a medieval village than a single country residence. The Prices were extremely proud of a house that they had just finished building in Bartlesville, designed for them by the celebrated California designer of ranch houses, Cliff May. (May, now in his late seventies, has designed hundreds of Southern California ranch houses all over the world, including such unlikely locations as Ireland and Switzerland.) Strolling about Taliesin, the Prices perceived that many of the attributes of their May house had been anticipated by Wright forty years earlier—a simple, natural use of stone and wood, the low horizontals of the wings of the house running along the earth and seeming to grow out of it, the cedar-shingled roofs with their broad overhangs. Already convinced of Wright's genius, they stated their modest needs; with a gesture which implied that modesty was but a form of meagreness, Wright began to sketch in words a building that would prove worthy of their aspirations. "It will be a needle on the prairie," he told them, "a tree that has escaped from the forest." Those were his actual phrases, and how could the Prices fail to be impressed by them? Was this not how a great man was supposed to speak? Were they not fortunate to be in his presence, and did it not begin to look as if he might condescend to take their little project under his capacious wing?

Price was a hard-headed businessman, but (like Darwin D. Martin before him) he was also a romantic; to a romantic, the patter of a superlative confidence man is a kind of poetry. A deal was struck, and a few weeks later the first drawings were ready; the Prices returned to Taliesin and were given a glimpse of their exquisite tower. They were aghast with admiration. What they didn't know at that moment was that their needle on the prairie, their tree that had escaped from the forest, had nothing to do with either prairie or forest; it had come into existence as a proposed apartment-house tower that Wright had tried to erect on Second Avenue, in New York City, almost a quarter of a century earlier, in the churchyard of St. Mark's in the Bouwerie. Among other factors, the Great Depression had given that project its quietus, but Wright had correctly believed it to be among the best of his creations and had never stopped seeking an opportunity to build it in one form or another, whether in Chicago, Washington, D.C., or Pittsburgh. Now at last, thanks to the wealthy and bewitched Prices, it would rise, to general astonishment, among the domestic roofs and chimneys of Bartlesville. The local press reported that from the top of the tower the view would embrace up to eight hundred square miles of Oklahoma. That was far more of Oklahoma than most Oklahomans had ever seen at one time, or had perhaps ever wished to see; the townsfolk of Bartlesville were understandably awed.

Price's younger son, Joe, took the admirable photographs that illustrate *The Story of the Tower* and that let us see what an exceptionally adroit feat of engineering it is; we see, too, that Wright's metaphor of the escaped tree is not, after all, a mere grandiloquent figure of speech. In his brief text, Wright hints (as he occasionally did in respect to the Guggenheim as well) that the tower stands in its own park; what it really stands in is a large plot of land covering a quarter of a city block, every foot of which is occupied by the tower and its accompanying parking lots. That small, obligatory fib aside, Wright's account is an accurate one:

> This skyscraper, planned to stand free in an open park and thus be more fit for human occupancy, is as nearly organic as steel in tension and concrete in compression can make it; here doing for the tall building what Lidgerwood made steel do for the long ship. The ship had its steel keel; this concrete building has its steel core. A composite shaft of concrete rises through the floors, each slab engaging the floors at nineteen levels. Each floor proceeds outward from the shaft as a cantilever slab extended from the shaft, similar to the branch of a tree from its trunk. The slab, thick at the shaft, grows thinner as it goes outward in an overlapping scale pattern in concrete until at the final outer leap to the screen wall it is no more than three inches thick. The outer enclosing screens of glass and copper are pendent from the edge of these cantilever slabs. The inner partitions rest upon the slabs.
>
> There are three offices to each floor and one double-decked to every alternate floor; each apartment is unaware of the other or the offices, as all look outward. The structure throughout eliminates the weight and waste space of masonry walls. The supporting members stand inside, away from day-lighted space and carry elevators and the entrance hallways well

within themselves. Two of the exterior walls of every apartment and office are entirely of glass set into metal framing. But the building is so placed that the sun shines on only one wall at a time and narrow upright blades, or mullions, project nine inches, so that as the sun moves, shadows fall on the glass surfaces and afford the protection necessary for comfort.

The building increases substantially in area from floor to floor as the structure rises, in order that the glass frontage of each story may drip clear of the one below, the building thus cleaning itself. . . . The central steel reinforced masonry shaft extending well into the ground may carry with safety a greatly extended top mass. This building is earthquake-, fire-, and soundproof from within by economics inherent in its structure. The structure weighs less than half the usual tall masonry-encased building and increases the area available for living by more than twenty percent . . . the skyscraper comes into its own on the rolling plains of Oklahoma.[2]

In the course of constructing the tower (a task undertaken by an excellent local contractor named Haskell Culwell), Wright visited Bartlesville and, it is agreeable to learn, found it possible to admire the house that May had designed for the Prices. Earlier, he had promised to "liberate" the Prices from their house; now he admitted that the liberation would be unnecessary. (May and Wright were friendly acquaintances. On the occasion of their last meeting, at Taliesin West, May brought all of his Wright books to be autographed; Wright signed them at top speed, then tossed them one after another through the air to May, who scrambled to catch them as if they were so many basketballs.) The tower rose with a more and more improbable delicacy against the sky, and before the rigid window framing had been put in place young Harold Price would walk to the outer edge of one of the concrete slabs ten or twelve stories above the ground and jump up and down. The slab, being at that point but three inches thick and highly flexible, would respond to his weight like a diving board; on the ground far below, veteran construction workers would scatter for their lives, assuming that the entire structure (to say nothing of Harold) was about to collapse on them.

So happy was the relationship between Wright and the Prices that long before the tower was completed they had offered him two more commissions—a house for the senior Prices, to be built in Phoenix, and a house for Harold, Jr., and his family, to be built in Bartlesville. The Phoenix house, no longer in the possession of the family, is very large and, in the view of critics unsympathetic to much of Wright's late work, of a theatrical showiness totally at odds with the principles that Wright had spent a lifetime defining and defending. (At odds, too, with the cozy "pioneer" simplicity that the Prices enjoyed in their May house, in Bartlesville.) The Price

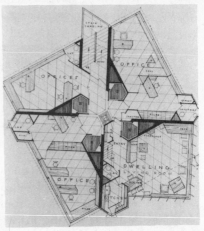

Left, the Price Tower, in Bartlesville (1952). In the distance, a church spire more characteristic of the local architecture. Right, space in the tower is divided between offices and duplex residences. The beehivelike shapes toward the center are tiny elevators, tucked into the quadruple core of the building. [JP]

house in Phoenix perches on an outcropping of rock and is approached by a steep blacktopped driveway. Its most striking feature is an immense, pillared atrium, vaguely prehistoric in ambience; one is tempted to suppose that its builder, far from being a twentieth-century American millionaire, was a bearded Assyrian king, well guarded by lions.

The house for the young Prices is in the true Usonian vein: long and low, with cantilevered balconies that, like so many Wright balconies, have sagged alarmingly with the years. (They had begun to sag before Wright's death; young Harold asked Wright what to do about the problem, and Wright replied that, while the cantilevers would never give way, for their peace of mind the Prices might install some steel Lally columns under the low places. The telltale columns are there to this day.) Wright liked designing houses for young people; one can think of fifty couples whom Wright worked with and befriended, including the Hannas, the Jacobses, and the Reisleys. Like their predecessors, the Prices found that Wright's reputation as an architect-ogre, one who insisted that every square foot of every floor plan remain just as he had originally laid it out, was highly unfair; they asked for many changes, especially in the size of children's bedrooms and the like, and Wright consented to all of them. (When Roland Reisley, looking over the plans for the house that he and his wife were building in Chappaqua, apologized for his temerity in daring to ask for certain changes, Wright said, "My dear boy, I'm your architect. An architect exists to serve his client the best way he can." Reisley, then in his twenties, could scarcely believe his ears; if he had been ten years older and twice as self-confident, no doubt he would have elicited a very different response.

The Price Tower was completed in 1956, at a cost of approximately two and a half million dollars, or something like a million dollars more than Harold Price, Sr., had been led to hope it would cost. No matter—it was an immediate success and like the Johnson Wax building provided an amount of free publicity for the Price Company in magazines and newspapers from coast to coast that was beyond reckoning in mere dollars and cents. Wright caused a characteristic fleeting crisis by going on a popular TV show of the time, presided over by Tex and Jinx McCrary. Seated before a photographic blow-up of Bartlesville, Wright pointed out his exquisite, slender Price Tower and then indicated the big, chunky Phillips Petroleum Company office buildings in the neighborhood. Said Wright: "Bartlesville is a very presentable little modern town. . . . And in it the Phillips Oil people have these large business buildings. To me, they're, of course, boxes and ugly. . . . [The Prices] wanted to build another building like the Phillips people. And I said, why not do something to grace your own town? Why not take the skyscraper, make an ideal thing of it, plant it there as beautiful as a tree, and enjoy it yourselves." A newspaper account of the TV interview came to the attention of the head of the Phillips Company, who was a close friend of Harold Price's. In better temper than might have been expected, he wrote to Price, "I wonder how many floors the size of yours we would have to have to take care of our organization here in Bartlesville. It would be some building, wouldn't it?"[3] Price wrote back, "In answer to the question . . . 190 floors. I am glad you have a sense of humor. You need one if you are going to be within range of F.L.W.'s verbal arrows. Never a dull moment."[4] He then fired off a rebuke to Wright: "Please have a heart. Remember Bartlesville is a small town and we have to live in it. Quit picking on my friends. Save your 'shots' for Zeckendorf, Skidmore, and the New York building authorities. You are getting along fine in Bartlesville. Phillips may want to build a building some day, and I may need a pipeline from them to pay for the one I've got."[5]

Wright's friend Bruce Goff, who had so generously recommended Wright for the Price commission, was able to take refuge for a time in one of the apartments in the tower; embroiled in a homosexual scandal at the University of Oklahoma, he resigned from the faculty, and the Prices put him up in Bartlesville until he succeeded in reestablishing a career elsewhere. For Joe Price, he designed two or three structures of a near-magical nature. One of them, intended to display Price's collection of Japanese art, is a richly carpeted pavilion (visitors are required to take off their shoes before entering it) and has a domed ceiling composed solely of feathers; an adjoining tower study has cabinets—and a bar—fashioned of solid onyx: in puritan Oklahoma, it embodies the sensuality of an Ottoman harem.

Wright had designed all of the furniture for the Price Tower, and it must be said that he outdid himself in the ugliness of the pieces and in their dangerousness. The chairs, coarse in appearance, were even more unstable than the chairs he had designed for the Johnson Wax administration building. One had to seat oneself with great care in order not to find oneself flung backward, head over heels, onto the floor. The senior Price had a simple, hearty sense of humor; apparently it amused him when visitors to his delightful office on the topmost floor of the building found themselves undergoing this undignified and sometimes painful experience. One victim of Wright's incompetence as a designer of furniture was the Governor of Oklahoma. Unabashed as usual, for tippy chairs were almost as great a commonplace in his career as leaking roofs, Wright sent a note to Price:

Dear "Hal the Great" Senior:

I learn by grapevine, from Mary Lou [Mrs. Price], that as your architect I got the governor down on the floor. Well, Hal, he can't be much of a governor if the poor devil can't even negotiate a Price Tower official chair?
. . . Happy landings, always, always—

Affectionately,
Frank[6]

Wᴴɪʟᴇ ᴛʜᴇ Gᴜɢɢᴇɴʜᴇɪᴍ Mᴜsᴇᴜᴍ commission continued in a state of agitated limbo, scores of domestic commissions and several major non-domestic commissions passed through the drafting rooms of Taliesin North and Taliesin West. By the early nineteen-fifties, the Wrights were occupying on an annual basis a suite at the Plaza Hotel, in New York City, apparently at Harry Guggenheim's expense. They decorated the suite in a hideous fashion, which surely owed more to Olgivanna than to Wright: heavy draperies and dark furniture and draperies, perhaps echoing some long-defunct Montenegrin vogue for gloom. This suite came to be known as Taliesin East and must have astonished many a visitor bent upon paying homage to the designer of Taliesins North and West.

Some of the domestic commissions were of considerable personal interest to Wright, because they consisted of remodelings of houses that he had designed many years earlier. This was the case, for example, with the Hanna house, designed in the nineteen-thirties to accommodate a young married couple with small children and redesigned in the fifties to accommodate the same couple in middle age, with their children no longer in residence. In other cases, where families had expanded instead of contracting, Wright would add a wing to a house; in still other cases, he would undertake the restoration of a house that had fallen upon evil times, at the same time improving it (in the Isabel Roberts house, Philippine mahogany paneling took the place of plaster and pine). Wright was never averse to making alterations to buildings in order to adapt them to new conditions; as Jefferson before him had tinkered with Monticello for half a century, so Wright tinkered with his Taliesins until the day he died.

One of the most important events in Wright's career was the designing of the Beth Sholom Synagogue. It was under construction at the same time as the Guggenheim Museum and it remained in the Guggenheim's shadow then as it does today. Nevertheless, it is certainly the Guggenheim's equal as a work of art and far surpasses it as a work of architecture. Given the circumstances, the shadow I speak of was a perfectly natural one. Wright had been working on the plans for the Guggenheim over a period of many years and had gained much publicity both for the museum and for himself in the course of carrying out activities that most architects would have sought to carry out in private but that the superb old trouper, dressed to the nines, was eager to carry out on center stage, under a dazzling spot: now seeking a site for the building, now seeking variances and permissions from a number of city agencies in order to get the building put up, and now seeking to still the objections of neighbors to its unusual appearance and of artists to its suitability for hanging the works of their great predecessors and contemporaries.

It was the case, moreover, that the Guggenheim was being built on Fifth Avenue, in the heart of the most publicity-conscious city on earth; the synagogue would be built in the near-anonymity of Elkins Park, a wealthy, predominantly Jewish suburb of Philadelphia. For decades, Philadelphia had been a rival of Brooklyn as the butt of wisecracks. (First prize in such-and-such a contest, one week in Philadelphia; second prize, two weeks in Philadelphia. Or W. C. Fields, speaking of death: "On the whole, I prefer Philadelphia.") The shadow cast by the Guggenheim was also in part of Wright's making. He was quick to accept the commission and spoke of coming to Elkins Park whenever it might prove necessary, but New York City was where he rejoiced to be, lunching at Voisin, dining at "21," and entertaining the press as he strolled along Park Avenue. He journeyed to Philadelphia with reluctance, sometimes traveling by air to and from New York and Philadelphia in order to make the short distance between the two cities seem shorter than it is.

Even today, though the synagogue draws visitors from all over the world, they come in comparatively small numbers: Elkins Park is still Elkins Park; Philadelphia, Philadelphia. It must also be said that from the point of view of tourists wishing to take pretty pictures, or from the point of view of students of architecture dependent upon photographs in books for their knowledge of buildings, Beth Sholom is nothing like as photogenic as the voluptuously roly-poly Guggenheim. Its aggressively angular shape, both inside and outside, is sufficiently difficult to comprehend in three dimensions, as the human eye confronts it, and all but impossible to reproduce photographically, in two dimensions. Wright said of the rounded Johnson Wax building that it was a female counterpart to the brusque maleness of the Larkin building; in something like the same fashion, the synagogue is the male counterpart of the female Guggenheim. It is awesome but not winsome. We earn our delight in it by stages, while in the Guggenheim delight is instantaneously bestowed upon us.

Of all Wright's buildings, Beth Sholom probably comes closest to being a collaboration between the individual who commissioned it and the architect who carried out the commission. One would not have looked for a collaboration of this intimate nature in the old age of an artist who had had only the most fleeting experience of partnership, but then one wouldn't have looked for an architectural gift in Mortimer J. Cohen, the rabbi of the congregation of Beth Sholom. At fifty-nine, Cohen had long since attained a national reputation as a scholar, speaker, and author; he was sympathetic to the arts, but had never been known to draw or paint and his knowledge of architecture (and especially of the architecture of synagogues) was based not upon aesthetics but upon his study of Jewish history. And yet Wright consented to call him the co-designer of Beth Sholom and to put Cohen's name beside his own.

Cohen was born in New York City, in 1894, and attended Townsend Harris High School, the City College of New York, and the Jewish Theological Seminary. In 1920, he was called to become the rabbi of the newly organized conservative congregation of Beth Sholom, in Philadelphia. (The congregation had chosen its name—The House of Peace—to celebrate the end of the First World War.) The congregation dedicated its first synagogue—a red-brick and limestone building vaguely Georgian in style—in 1922. Beth Sholom flourished under Cohen, who, being extremely short, came to be known with affection as "the little rabbi." As the years passed, the increasingly prosperous members of the congregation began moving to the suburbs and Cohen saw that it would soon be necessary for the synagogue itself to move. In the early nineteen-fifties, land was purchased in Elkins Park, a school and community center was built, and Cohen was told that the congregation would undertake to raise as much as half a million dollars more for a new synagogue. Elated, he set down on paper, in precise detail, his notion of what an ideal synagogue should be.

First of all, Cohen wished a building that would owe nothing to the styles—Gothic, Moorish, and the like—that architects of European and American synagogues had fallen back upon in the recent past. Secondly, he wished his synagogue to take its inspiration from Mount Sinai, where God had instructed Moses to build a tabernacle for the wandering Israelites. Jewish historians had written that "The Tabernacle is a moving Sinai," and Cohen decided that his new synagogue must somehow contrive to embody that image. For the first time in his life, he made some sketches, which he took to his friend Boris Blai, Dean of the Tyler Art School at Temple University. Blai had been teaching at Florida Southern College in the forties, had met Wright there, and had become a good friend (in tribute to Blai's tireless gusto, Wright had nicknamed him "The Burning Bush"). Blai assured Cohen that Wright was the only man in the world who would be able to transform his sketches into reality. He urged him to get in touch with Wright, and Cohen, having gained the permission of his building committee, in late 1953 sent off the following letter:

Dear Mr. Wright:

To introduce myself to you, may I say at the outset that I write to you at the suggestion of Dean Boris Blai of the Tyler Art School of Temple University, Philadelphia, known better to you as "The Burning Bush."

I am Rabbi of Congregation Beth Sholom of Philadelphia for the past 34 years. We recently purchased 4 acres of ground in the suburbs and are planning to build a Synagogue. . . .

There is a dream and hope in my heart, of erecting a Synagogue . . . that will be an inspiration for generations to come, so that people will come from all over the country to see it and find here a *"new thing"— the American spirit wedded to the ancient spirit of Israel.*

[Dean Blai] and I are especially thrilled to feel that *we shall have the opportunity of bringing your gifts into Philadelphia, the cradle of our free civilization and our democratic way of life.* We hope that this will inspire you as it does us. . . .[1]

The Rabbi added a P.S.: "On separate sheets, I try to expound my philosophy of the Synagogue I would like to see created. . . . I have also made a rough sketch of its interior." Ordinarily, Wright would have snubbed anyone who presumed to send him a sketch, with its implication that Wright's task would be simply to reduce Cohen's "inspiration" to a workable form. But the letter was so obviously sincere and the sketch was so obviously remarkable—the Rabbi really *had* been thinking hard about what he wished his synagogue to be—that Wright replied in a genial vein, setting a date for a meeting with the Rabbi at the Plaza, in New York City, on December 3rd.

At the appointed hour, Cohen, Blai, and Herman Bornstein, of the Building Committee of Beth Sholom, knocked on the door of Room 223 at the Plaza. Wright, who must have been pleased to discover that Cohen was even shorter than he was, told his visitors that he would be happy to take on the synagogue job, with the proviso that he would deal only with the rabbi—committees and boards of directors were a damned nuisance. For the time being, no contract would be necessary; he and the rabbi would content themselves with a gentleman's agreement and he would avoid dealing with the congregation until the time came to show it his plans and elevations. On December 14th, Cohen wrote to Wright:

On behalf of the Board of Directors of the Congregation of Beth Sholom, I am privileged to inform you that, at a special meeting held this day, they are honored to enlist your services as architect of our new synagogue to be erected in Elkins Park. . . .[2]

To which Wright replied at once that he was sure that Cohen and he would prove "congenial workers in the vineyards of the Lord" and that

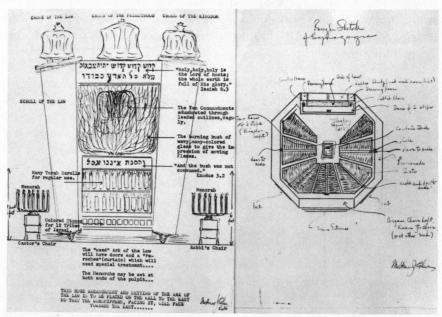

Rabbi Cohen's sketches. Left, at first he was eager to have a burning bush among the symbols displayed in the synagogue; by the time he changed his mind, FLW had become an ardent champion of the bush. A fierce tug-of-war ensued, and for a wonder the rabbi won: there is no burning bush in Beth Sholom. Right, the rabbi's seating plan. [HM]

he would be sending along some sketches within a few weeks. Throughout the years of struggle that followed, with "the little rabbi" constantly pleading with Wright to carry out the task he had undertaken, Wright makes disarming use of the Biblical lore and lingo that he had picked up in childhood from his ministerial antecedents on both sides of the family tree. Cohen supplied him with endless quantities of information about Jewish religious practices and symbols, which Wright ingeniously worked into the fabric of his design, but there was never a time when Wright couldn't effectively pretend that he, too, was a learned student of the Bible. He had by heart a thousand handy quotations, as no doubt the rabbi had his ten thousand; they batted the quotations back and forth like shuttlecocks, and even when they were at cross-purposes the assumption—sincere on the rabbi's part, playful on Wright's—that they were doing the work of the Lord helped them to maintain a civility of discourse rare in the mass of Wright correspondence.

In March, 1954, seven sketches arrived, with a covering letter from Wright that began, "Dear Rabbi: Herewith the promised 'hosanna'—a temple that is truly a religious tribute to the living God. Judaism needs one in America. . . ."[3] (To Cohen's understandable delight, these were the

465

sketches that bore his name as co-designer.) The plans and elevations revealed that Wright had been able to translate almost literally into a habitable structure Cohen's desire for "a mountain of light, a moving Sinai." Behind the definition of "tabernacle" as a portable sanctuary lies its definition as a tent, and Wright had provided a shape that could be read as either tentlike or mountainlike. Three colossal steel-and-concrete uprights, sheathed in copper (later, aluminum was substituted) and rising a hundred and ten feet into the air, formed a tripod from which hung sloping walls of translucent plastic; these walls were divided into panels that—though no doubt needed for purposes of support—gave the approximately hexagonal exterior a pleasing multiplicity of surfaces, like the folds in drapery. The tripod itself rested on a cradle of reinforced concrete, from which three jutting wings sprang at a reverse angle to absorb the outward thrust of the legs of the tripod. The main entrance, modest in scale, faced the street under a cantilevered canopy.

On the interior, a ground-level vestibule gave access downward to a two-hundred-and-fifty-seat chapel, two lounges (one of which was connected by a sheltered passageway to the nearby school and Center), and bathroom facilities, and upward, by twin flights of stairs to the left and right of the entrance, into the main auditorium. The rabbi's plans had called for ramps, but the building was too small to permit them; the steps of the curving flights of stairs were broad and deep, with exceptionally shallow risers, and would be almost as easy to climb as ramps. Making one's way up the stairs from the vestibule into the auditorium would offer the same optical surprise to visitors that the tunnel-like entrance to Unity Temple in Oak Park offers, but on a prodigiously enlarged scale: one would be entering into the very heart of a mountain of light.

In the elevation drawings, one sees at a glance that Wright has plucked certain ideas not only from Unity Temple (1905) but from the steel cathedral project of 1926. With his usual tenacity, he has found no reason to abandon elegant solutions to difficult problems simply because he has made use of those solutions once, twice, or a dozen times before. What could be more natural than for the oeuvre of a long career to resemble a palimpsest, which scholars can employ in whatever fashion they like and which generations of beneficiaries will remain contentedly unaware of? Still, in Wright's case to be unaware is to miss much of the pleasure of observing his exquisite mind at play; the Wright palimpsest is a three-dimensional toy whose every page has depths that can be plumbed for ravishing scribbles. The steel cathedral is an early version of a mountain of light, the synagogue a late version. Little in either of them need be seen to be wholly original, though everything in them is new.

The Board of Directors of Beth Sholom accepted Wright's plans and Cohen sent him off a check for five thousand dollars, as the first of many

The ground-breaking ceremony, with "the little rabbi" turning the first spadeful of earth as FLW looks on. [HM]

payments. Wright attended a fund-raising dinner in June and gave a rousing sales pitch (the role of snake-oil salesman was one he always enjoyed playing); two hundred and fifty thousand dollars was raised, toward a total sum that had grown invisibly and without warning over the previous few months from five hundred thousand dollars to seven hundred and fifty thousand dollars. All summer long, the rabbi prodded Wright for working drawings, which failed to arrive; the engineering problems involved in the steelwork were complex and Wright kept changing his mind about how to resolve them. A ground-breaking ceremony was held in November, at which Wright again spoke. His remarks were extemporaneous and cannot have been altogether pleasing to the devout Jews who had gathered to watch him turn the first spade of earth: "I . . . share your Rabbi's faith and enthusiasm in the future of America. Call it Jewish, call it Methodist, call it any name you please, what's the difference, and those differences are going to grow smaller, more insignificant as the great significance of faith in beauty pays off." There are hazards in extemporaneity, but Wright had never troubled to learn them. Methodist? Faith in beauty? What on earth was the old rascal talking about? Luckily, he managed to arrive at an appropriate peroration: "I hope you will find when you sit in your new edifice that the Torah not only burns but the faith of Judaism has found illumination."[4]

In spite of that hope, a year passed in which Wright fiddled with the plans and the Building Committee of Beth Sholom sought in vain a builder who would be willing to undertake its construction within the proposed budget. Cohen peppered Taliesin with sketches of details of the interior, since Wright, for all his Biblical blarney, knew little about the nature of the symbolism that his designs were supposed to encompass. Aware by then of how impetuous Wright could be and of how clever he was at improvising a precedent where no precedent existed, Cohen wrote, "I am always fearful lest some Jewish layman (architect, artist, or personal friend) may offer information that may not be up-to-date in a scholarly sense or accurate; or it may be of a 'local nature' and not universally Jewish. Remember, Mr. Wright, when you seek advice from two Jews, you are liable to get three opinions."[5]

Not that Cohen didn't have some fairly peculiar ideas of his own to offer. In a letter containing much praise for Wright's plans ("This design is so exquisite that absolutely no change dare be made"), he nevertheless dares to propose a change:

> At present, at the very top of the building, there is a plain copper cap. . . . I have been told that buildings of certain heights must carry a red light because of airplane traffic; our building falls within that necessity. Hence, I advance my suggestion the more cheerfully, because what I have in mind could both complete the building . . . and provide a place to nest the red light.
>
> I have conceived this grand design as the "wandering Mt. Sinai" where God and man communed. It is an eternal symbol of God's revelation to man in terms of the light of freedom after the dark slavery of Egypt. Hence, at the very apex I would have in large, artistically designed Hebrew letters the opening words of the Ten Commandments (Exodus 20.2): "I am the Lord Thy God. . . ."[6]

Wright must have had a lively sense of the mixed feelings with which people flying at night over Philadelphia would have regarded this message; also of the feelings with which the Federal authorities would have regarded it, as the precursor of a hundred other religious messages blinking away in the darkness from the tops of a thousand church spires from coast to coast.

If "the little rabbi" failed to gain his wish in that instance, he had other and more serious concerns to deal with. He was especially worried about the design of the Ark and the Bimah. He reminded Wright that the Ark, which contains the scrolls of the Torah, must be made of wood, because metal, as a symbol of war, was a forbidden material, and that it must always be approached by steps, never less than three but permissibly by as many as twelve, as in the ancient temple in Jerusalem. As for the Bimah, it was the platform on which the rabbi and cantor conduct the service and therefore should be at a low place in the middle of the auditorium, in order to fulfill the words of Psalm 130, "Out of the depths have I cried unto thee, O Lord!" Cohen enclosed with his dicta some sketches, with a provisional apology, "I trust you will look upon my pathetic efforts as an amateur drawer with friendly human and fatherly indulgence." Wright evidently did so, but he was never to give Cohen the Bimah that he sought, arguing that the lowest point in the middle of the auditorium was needed for seats and that every seat he provided meant that much more income for the synagogue.

Haskell Culwell, builder of the Price Tower, was persuaded to undertake the building of Beth Sholom, and actual construction began in the summer of 1956. By then the Guggenheim was also under construction and Wright was spending a good deal of time in New York City. (On June 8th, his eighty-ninth birthday, he preached a sermon at the Universalist Church, on Central Park West.) Wright was designing all the furniture and symbolic accoutrements of the synagogue and was in constant touch with Cohen in respect to their correctness. (The ceremonial chair that he designed for "the little rabbi" had such short legs that a chair of similar design but with legs of a normal length had to be manufactured for Cohen's successor, Rabbi Landes, who happens to be over six feet tall.) Wright was determined to place in the synagogue a representation of the Burning Bush—perhaps to honor indirectly his friend Blai—as a feature of the lighting and the Rabbi was no less determined to prevent it, not an easy thing to do, because the initial suggestion in respect to the Burning Bush had been his. He had come to prefer a representation of seraphic wings, which, gaining confidence in his ability as an artist, he was prepared to design. He wrote to Wright, in 1957:

> I am not happy about the Burning Bush concept, as I have stated in earlier letters, because it is so hackneyed throughout the land. Furthermore, the idea of the Wings—properly done in reds and gold with flaming lights behind them—has not been used and would be more in the spirit of the unique edifice you are creating.[7]

To the rabbi's surprise, Wright capitulated; he wired, WHAT YOU SUGGEST SHALL RECEIVE OUR VERY BEST ATTENTION AND MY LOVE TO YOU AND YOURS.[8]

Months passed, and then years. There was difficulty over the plastic for the sloping walls of the great "squashed hexagon," difficulty over the number of seats and the kind of seats, and difficulty over water leaks everywhere. Again and again, the rabbi would utter a cry from the depths, "To the many letters I have sent you I have received not one response," and Wright would send back word, "My dear Rabbi. Do cheer up. All is not lost. . . ." Or he would say, "All in good time, my dear Rabbi," while

Cohen was beside himself with unanswered questions, an irritated congregation, and an ever-mounting budget. The synagogue would eventually cost something over a million and a half dollars: twice the original estimate, which by Wright's standards amounted to a moderate overrun. It was no consolation to the rabbi to know that a similar set of difficulties was confronting the Director of the Guggenheim at the same moment and for the same reasons. What it might have consoled him to know (Cohen died in 1972) is that the building that he struggled so hard to bring into existence has served the purposes for which it was designed incomparably better than has the more famous Guggenheim.

Standing in the Guggenheim, one is conscious of the formidable ego of the designer, present at every turn of the ramp. Standing in Beth Sholom, one senses that the ego of the designer has been subsumed into the work, which in Wright's case amounts to a near-miracle. Even to visitors who, like me, hold no formal religious beliefs whatever, the structure conveys the sense of an immanent collective sacredness, purged of individuality. Wright had promised the congregation of Beth Sholom that their temple would be a "Mount Sinai cupped in the hands of God," and for once his outrageous rhetoric amounted to a truth.

In asserting this transcendent and unprovable claim on behalf of Beth Sholom, I find myself introducing an old and vexatious distinction between architecture, defined as having a function, and art, defined as being functionless. Since any substantial work of architecture is also a work of art, one feels obliged to judge it by two sets of standards, employed simultaneously even when they are bound to be at odds with each other. In responding to a certain arrangement of forms in three dimensions, why should we care whether the Taj Mahal, the Getty Tomb, and the Medici Chapel have or haven't functions: whether they are mausoleums or comfort stations? Nevertheless, it turns out that we *do* care. The essential impurity of architecture as an art—the impurity of its being charged with a stated purpose—seems to force us, half against our will, to take into account the degree to which it succeeds or fails in carrying out that purpose. Bluntly, we ask of the Guggenheim (or of any of the scores of museums that have been built all over the United States in the past quarter of a century), "Well, but does it, as a museum, *work*?" and if the answer is in the negative, that fact surely tends to lessen our opinion of it as a work of art. There are those who would say, "Be content with the Guggenheim as an interesting feat of sculpture. Say that it succeeds as a work of art and that it fails as a work of architecture." But there are others who would protest at once, "That would be to beg the question. If it fails as a work of architecture, it fails as a work of art."

Putting this unresolvable dispute aside, we are free to marvel at Beth

Sholom as one of the greatest of Wright's works. Over a period of seventy years, Wright designed many houses of worship, few of which may be said to show deep religious feelings. It was characteristic of him to find room for fireplaces in his houses of worship—Beth Sholom has two—and I see this as an attempt to establish what he saw as a primordial link between the houses of God and the houses of men; such a link would have less to do with religion than with family. In his teens, under Silsbee, he may have had a hand in the Lloyd Jones family chapel near Spring Green—a charming little shingle and stone box, like a thousand others throughout the Middle West—and he designed an unbuilt chapel in the same style for a site in Sioux City, Iowa (which long afterward he disowned, saying that Cecil Corwin and he had devised it as a parody of Silsbee's Richardsonian "boulder" style). Also unbuilt was a church project for his preacher uncle, Jenkin Lloyd Jones, in Chicago. Unity Temple was among his early masterpieces, but it was the building itself and not its purpose that interested him. Although for the sake of gaining favorable publicity, he may have paid lip-service to the premature ecumenism of the steel cathedral (a million worshippers of all denominations were to gather under its two-thousand-foot-high tower), in his heart he was bent upon producing a colossal work without regard to its function: feat first, function after. Indeed, the project had begun not as a cathedral but as a post-Victorian crystal palace intended to house a commercial festival of the arts that, as it turned out, nobody was reckless enough to supply funding for. Wright's

Beth Sholom, "the moving mountain of light."

471

own professed religion was a kind of maudlin Whitmanesque pantheism: "Nature," as he kept saying, "with a capital 'N.'"

Of temples that were on a more realistic scale and that Wright succeeded in getting built, one thinks of the only partially realized Community Church, in Kansas City; the superbly realized Pfeiffer chapel, at Florida Southern College, in Lakeland; the Unitarian Church, in Madison; the First Christian Church, in Phoenix; the very late (and still unfinished) Pilgrim Congregational Church, in Redding, California; and the Greek Orthodox Church, in Wauwatosa, Wisconsin (which, however, in execution I am tempted to let Wes Peters share the credit for). In most of these structures, we sense a marked resemblance between their interiors and the interiors of theatres; Wright manipulates the volumes of space at his disposal to create an effect that is first of all dramatic and then, perhaps rather grudgingly, reverential. His personal fondness for theatre was bound to be reflected in his designs; he might well have argued, moreover, that the note of theatre sounded in his churches ought not to be an occasion for surprise, since once upon a time temple and theatre were one. Altar and stage are designed to accommodate certain ritual activities that, after two or three thousand years, appear to have little in common and yet elicit—or are intended to elicit—roughly similar responses. His own theatres, built and unbuilt, often came close to sharing floor plans with his temples: the blueprints for the Dallas Theater Center, for example, would fit quite snugly over those of the Kansas City church.

In the Wright ecclesiastical oeuvre, the Beth Sholom Synagogue is unprecedented for the extent to which the reverential takes precedence over the theatrical. One would not guess this, however, from its exterior, which (like so many of Wright's buildings) flies in the face of his own teaching: instead of being *of* a hill and not *on* it, the synagogue leaps aggressively skyward from its site at the top of a steep hill, and by its great height and peculiar tepee shape dominates an otherwise low-roofed suburban environment. As one approaches it, the building impresses one as a successful if somewhat grotesque feat of technology, carried out in materials—concrete, aluminum, and industrial glass—that lack both intrinsic richness and refinement of detail. That Wright saw this tepee as "a traveling Mount Sinai, a mountain of light," is an interesting iconographical fact, but it is by no means evident to the casual passerby.

It is only when we enter the modest vestibule of Beth Sholom that the building ceases to intimidate us. (Wright invariably employs his entrances to assert a human scale: we all become, like him, persons of unremarkable stature.) As we mount the easy, carpeted, curving stairs, the building seizes us and, in effect, will not let us go. Whether voluntarily or involuntarily, we are subjected to that uncanny overthrowing of conventional expectations that is the hallmark of Wright's genius. The rigid heavi-

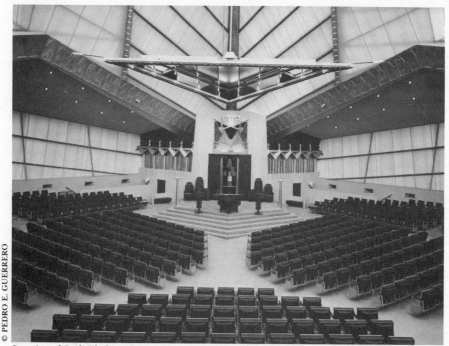

© PEDRO E. GUERRERO

Interior of Beth Sholom. From a few square feet of level space in the center of the synagogue, the floor slopes upward in a continuous, gentle thrust to the side walls, which transform themselves as they rise into a polygonal translucent roof.

ness of the exterior yields to a lyrical dissolving of structure: spaces that seem not to be bounded by walls invite us simultaneously in and down and up and across. We feel a sense of exhilarating disorientation, as if we were postulants about to undergo initiation into some unknown rite. The floor of the auditorium, with its thousand or more seats set in blocks facing the Ark at different angles and at different heights (no seat is at quite the same level as its neighbors), floats under and around us like an immense, shallow dish, over which rises to an incalculable height a pyramid that continuously brightens and darkens according to the amount of light that is available outside. (A bird flying over the synagogue casts a shadow visible to the congregation inside.) Walking from one side of the auditorium to another, we cannot be sure whether we are ascending or descending, or even whether we are moving in the direction that we had originally intended to move. We are in an open space that has, nevertheless, the feeling of a labyrinth. We entered the building from the west, but the entrance is no longer visible; the points of the compass have been expunged by a sweep of the hand of the old magus. We are only where we are, wherever we are, in the presence of a Presence.

28

Even in those passages in Wright's career when, as he would say, he was taking a worm's-eye view of life, some irresistible capacity for joy sustained him. Nor was it anything less than joy; he would not have troubled to put on the mere clumsy mask of cheerfulness in order to help ease the way for those caught up with him in his predicaments. Which is to say that the cheerfulness that played over the surface of his life was real and so was the joy that lay beneath the surface and released its energies in action. Observing him in age, I was amused but puzzled by his ebullience. To be so old and so intelligent, and yet so merry! For I, being young, assumed that age, if it taught us anything, taught us (as Newman said) that we are all implicated in some vast primordial catastrophe. Wright held a different view. In his eyes, man was not a fallen creature, either theologically or psychologically. His grandfather Lloyd Jones's favorite prophet had been the baleful Isaiah, upon whom the grandfather liked to preach hellfire-and-brimstone sermons; Wright claimed to have distrusted Isaiah even as a child. Certainly it was the case that the innocent young Frank leapt out of bed every morning eager to discover what sorts of wonders—he never doubted that they would be wonders—the day would bring; the boy persisted in the man, and a boy's merriment shone out of the old man's eyes.

The merriment had been earned, and at a price that Wright fumbled the task of telling us in his autobiography. All his life, he was more gifted at posturing than at revelation, and in the grand triumphal march of his last years it was prudent to leave unasked any question as to the high price he had paid. The anguish of past decades was well buried; his step was light because he had taken care to make his private burdens light. He was becoming, and would less and less resist the process of becoming, an entirely public man. He was looked up to and pursued and made much of when architects were still twenty or thirty years away from being the rivals of movie and television stars, and yet he was himself a TV star. Appearing on such highly regarded TV cultural programs as *Omnibus*, he outwitted his famous host, Alistair Cooke, by continuously out-talking him.

The amount of work being accomplished at the two Taliesins was astounding. Beth Sholom and the Guggenheim were both under construction; a Jaguar automobile salesroom was being fitted into the ground-floor corner of a skyscraper on Park Avenue. (Small and low-ceilinged though the space was, Wright managed to squeeze in a ramp as its major feature— a ramp that had the scandalous architectural defect of leading nowhere.) The owner of the showroom, Maximilian Hoffman, commissioned a small house on Manursing Island, in Rye, New York; a classic rich man's weekend retreat, it looks serenely out over Long Island Sound toward West Egg and Gatsby's blue gardens. Other private houses were going up in Missouri, Arizona, Washington, Minnesota, Iowa, Ohio, California, Wisconsin, Oregon, Texas, Montana, Michigan, and Utah. The Marshall Erdman Company had begun offering for sale prefabricated Wright houses, the buyers choosing among four basic plans and the houses being erected anywhere in the United States. (So much for Wright's former insistence, in designing a house, upon the primary importance of site and orientation.) In Cloquet, Minnesota, in 1956, he designed a modified version of the Broadacre Service Station—Wright's only service station and, as I have mentioned, an exceptionally disheveled-looking structure.

Marilyn Monroe, newly married to the playwright Arthur Miller and eager to carry out an ambitious program of self-improvement, came by appointment to the Plaza and asked Wright to design a house for Miller and her on some country property that Miller owned in Connecticut. Enchanted with Monroe, Wright soon presented her with plans for a lavish house that, in somewhat different form, he had designed for a couple in Texas and, when they had failed to build it, had offered to a Mexican political figure, who had also failed to build it. Miss Monroe was hoping to have children and Wright provided an elaborate nursery suite in the plans. Before the project had reached the point of being bid on by contractors, the Millers had separated and the house was abandoned. When I asked the laconic Miller about the episode and in particular about his impressions of Wright, he startled me with his reply. "Wright reminded me," Miller said, "of W. C. Fields."

Meanwhile, there were several public projects on the boards as well. The most important of them—indeed, one of the most important of the long list of unbuilt projects that Wright was to accumulate throughout his lifetime—was the Monona Terrace Civic Center, in Madison, Wisconsin. Wright worked up at least three versions of the project between 1938 and 1955 and Wes Peters (almost as optimistic as Wright himself) went on tinkering with a fourth version after Wright's death. The city of Madison is laid out on an isthmus between Lake Monona and Lake Mendota; its main streets radiate out from a central square occupied by the state capitol building. In Wright's youth, his family lived in a little house overlooking Lake Mendota, and Wright retained a sentimental attachment to the city, mingled with a feeling of bitterness over the fact that the University of Wisconsin had never offered him an honorary degree and that the state had never commissioned a building from him. The bitterness was, of course, an expression of his sentimentality; he persisted in urging the Monona Terrace project not because the politicians who ran the city were eager to have it but because he was determined to make them have it.

Monona Terrace was to be a seven-and-a-half-acre park extending fanwise into the lake from an already existing embankment along the shore; between the shore and the embankment ran a broad span of railroad tracks. The park with its accompaniment of fountains and gardens would be constructed on the highest of five decks rising from shore-level and entered by way of a pedestrian mall built high above the tracks. The lowest deck, occupying the outer rim of the structure, would be a marina, with docking facilities for pleasure boats; on the decks above would be glass-walled cocktail lounges and restaurants and, in the windowless interior of the structure would be auditoriums, art galleries, courtrooms, a jail, a railroad station, and extensive parking facilities. It was a mega-building in the thirties, before the word "mega-building" existed, and even in the fifties the concept seemed to many architects and city planners an acceptable one. No one appears to have wondered why it was a good thing to bring large numbers of people, all bent upon different errands, into a single space, thereby ensuring the distress of overcrowding and of traffic jams impossible to unsnarl. For a few years, the portmanteau mega-building became a fad, and Wright was not above embracing a fad, provided that he could claim to have originated it. It was true, moreover, that Wright had a lifelong weakness for the colossal. Knowing better, he could not resist fantasizing on a Napoleonic scale.

The Mile High Illinois building is a case in point. If Wright felt that he knew what was good for Madison as a city and for Wisconsin as a state (though city and state might disagree with him), he felt that he knew what was good for Chicago and Illinois as well. As far back as 1933, so he tells us in his autobiography, he had been summoned to New York City, to attend a meeting in Town Hall; there a host of admirers had gathered to protest his exclusion from the roster of architects chosen to design the buildings for the Chicago "Century of Progress" World's Fair. Wittily, Wright had protested the protest, saying that it was surely better to have one architect unemployed in such parlous times than to have the eight or ten or fifteen architects already employed at the Fair, whom he could neither work with nor work against, be thrown out of work.

Called on to speak in the course of the meeting, Wright good-humoredly offered three suggestions for the design of the Fair. (He boasted—unconvincingly—that all three suggestions were improvised on the spot.) The boldest of them called for a single vast building that would be half a mile high and would contain within its walls the entire Fair: "a great skyscraper in which the Empire State Building might stand free in a central interior court-space. . . . Instead of the old stage-props of the previous fairs, the same old miles of picture buildings faked in cheap materials, wrapped around a lagoon, a fountain or theatrical waterfall in the middle—to be all eventually butchered to make a Roman holiday— let there be, for once, a genuine modern construction. [After the Fair] the business of the city itself might move into it with all its multifold minor branches. . . ."[1]

In 1956, Wright unveiled at a press conference in Chicago his design for a building twice as high as the one he had proposed for the Fair. He called it the Mile High Illinois, because he intended that all the official departments of the state of Illinois be brought together in it, as in 1933 he had intended all the departments of the city of Chicago to be brought together. A rendering of the building, painted on canvas and twenty-six feet high, was set up in the ballroom of the Sherman Hotel, along with photographs and drawings of other Wright buildings and projects. Some years earlier, Wright had written, "Vertical is vertigo, in human life. The horizontal line is the life-line of humankind."[2] Now he was saying that a single building over five hundred stories high, holding a hundred thousand people, fifteen thousand automobiles, and a hundred helicopters was the best thing for humankind. "No one can afford to build it now," he said, "but in the future no one can afford *not* to build it."[3] And further: "The Mile High would absorb, justify, and legitimize the gregarious instinct of humanity. And the necessity for getting together would mop up what now remains of urbanism and leave us free to do Broadacre City."[4]

In engineering terms, the Mile High is an extravagantly elongated version of the Price Tower; it is capable of being built, but whether it is capable of being occupied is another question. In New York City, there are towers of comparatively moderate height—forty stories or so—that in a high wind veer out of true by as much as two feet, setting off fail-safe mechanisms in the elevators and so bringing them to an abrupt halt. For this reason, when high winds are predicted, people employed in the buildings must be sent home. In a city notorious for its high winds, a couple of hundred stories in the exquisitely narrow upper reaches of the five-hundred-story Mile High might well prove uninhabitable during much of the year.

On the presentation drawing of the Mile High, Wright set down a list of men that he admired and evidently thought of as professional colleagues, though only the first of them had actually filled that role. It is a list interesting enough for the names and still more interesting for the aphoristic summaries that Wright affixed to them:

Memorial To:

Louis Sullivan, son of Chicago
First made the tall building tall

Elisha Otis
Inventor of the upended street

John Roebling
First steel-in-tension on the grand scale:
the Brooklyn Bridge

Lidgerwood, naval architect
First ocean liner keel.
Makes it what it is today.

Coinget and Monier of France
Reinforced concrete.
The body of our modern world.

And to this list he added salutations to certain contemporary engineers who had been of assistance to him, whether directly or indirectly:

Eduardo Torroja, engineer, Spain

Professors Beggs & Cross, science of continuity

Professor Pier Luigi Nervi, engineer, Italy

Dr. J. J. Polivka, engineer, University of California

Maillart, engineer, Switzerland[5]

Wright's offer of Mile High as a state office building fell, as he had plainly expected it to do, upon deaf ears. A year later, he was making another handsome offer, this time to the state officials of Arizona, who were planning a new capitol building in Phoenix. He told a reporter for the *Phoenix Gazette* that he had enjoyed living in Arizona for twenty-five years and regretted never having had the opportunity to design a building for the people of the state. At the reporter's urging, Wright agreed to make some sketches of an ideal capitol building and preside over a public presentation of them. On the appointed day, Wright described "Pro Bono Publico" (his name for the project) in characteristically eloquent terms:

These preliminary drawings indicate a high, wide, sheltering, crenelated, copper-plated, concrete, self-supporting canopy of modern open construction like a great tree filtering sunlight over subordinate copper roofs over beautiful buildings, gardens, pools, and fountains. . . . Created like a true oasis in the desert . . . no vertical jam, no time lost, but all on one level.[6]

The nerve of the old wizard! A year earlier, he had been championing the efficiency of his vertical Mile High; now he is championing the efficiency of his horizontal capitol. His drawings show a linked series of gaudy structures, the central one of which is girded round with stone columns at ground level and is sheltered by an enormous shallow dome, whose hexagonal shape is repeated in the domes of the adjoining structures—not, of course, the dreary, conventional columns and domes of other state capitols but Wrightian columns and domes that have floated earthward out of the Arabian Nights to come to rest near the reddish-purple moonscape of Papago Park.

It was literally from the Thousand and One Nights of Scheherazade that Wright and the Fellowship drew inspiration for a gorgeous complex of buildings commissioned by the King of Iraq, in 1957. In the spring of that year, Wright flew to Baghdad to meet the King, with whom he appears to have got on well (Wright condescended to treat heads of state as his equals). Here again was an opportunity for designing on a prodigious scale, since the complex was intended to include an opera house, a civic auditorium, a planetarium, two art museums, several university buildings, a grand bazaar, and a colossal monument to the great caliph, Haroun al-Rashid. To judge by the published drawings, the complex marked a degree of fantasy so extreme that not even the romantic setting—an island in the Tigris River—can justify it. (As the project was about to get under way, the King was assassinated; the blueprints lie furled, probably forever, in the Taliesin archives.)

What is seen to be romantic or unromantic in a given setting is, of course, something that we determine for ourselves, out of who knows what accumulation of received ideas; to Americans of Wright's generation the very word "Baghdad" was charged with romance, but I doubt if Wright in his prime would have consented to design an exotic building simply because the setting struck him as exotic. He rejoiced to be challenged by settings of exceptional difficulty, like those he encountered and outwitted in the Ennis house or in Fallingwater, but the settings for some of the greatest of his creations—Unity Temple, the Johnson Wax administration building, the Price Tower—rose out of flat city lots of an ordinariness that might have been expected to paralyze his hand. Would Wright in his prime have considered the huge, many-colored, curiously effeminate toys of the Baghdad project a suitable tribute to the King and the culture that had produced him? Would they not have seemed, rather, a Disneyland parody of that culture, patronizing the royal client in the very act of paying homage to him?

In the baublelike works of Wright's final years, I detect a Wright so unlike his past self as to raise in my mind the question of his share in them. I am quick to say that I have no documentary evidence whatever for suggesting that the works, while approved by him, had not been designed by him; my suggestion is based largely on intuition, but I would add that when it comes to matters of art, intuition legitimately aspires to anticipate knowledge and, ideally, to be confirmed by it. In the history of a large architectural firm like McKim, Mead & White, the documentation needed to attribute buildings with certainty to one or another member of the firm is remarkably scant; in the case of a so-called one-man office like Wright's, the difficulty, which might be assumed to be less than in a big office, perversely proves to be far greater, because everything that passed under Wright's eye is by convention attributed to him, while the actual maker of a design remains more or less permanently anonymous. That said, I would argue that in Wright's last years something more radical than a mere change in "style"—a word (and a concept) that Wright was, in any event, loudly scornful of—can be sensed to have taken place; the change is either a direct consequence of Wright's failing powers or, less directly, of his being increasingly subject to the influence of others. This influence need not be related to failing powers; Wright's busy life in New York City, where he had become something of a social butterfly, is enough to account for the delegation of much daily donkey work of supervision to the faithful staff in residence at both Spring Green and Scottsdale.

What I have described as the toylike and baublelike aspect of late Wright is deplorably manifest in the Marin County Civic Center—a single, radically overextended beached whale of a structure, which defies several of Wright's cardinal precepts and in doing so exemplifies the arrogance for which he was famous and for which, in this case, he may deserve little or no blame. After sixty years of preaching "of a hill and not on it," we find Wright not only placing a building on a hill but on two hills and with brute force filling up the valley between them. The building echoes the assertive multiplicity of arches and vaults, structural and decorative, of the Greek Orthodox Church in Milwaukee, which can be accounted for (if not excused) by the fact that the plan of the church comprises a single grand circle; in the Marin County Civic Center, the circular plan of the auditorium and of certain other interior spaces is mostly buried within the length of the megastructure. The arches visible as one approaches

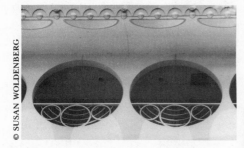

The Marin County Civic Center marches over a couple of hills with a Roman disregard for obstacles. However Roman in principle, the Center's detailing owes more to Fabergé than to Caesar.

the Civic Center, and through which at ground level vehicular traffic flows back and forth, put us in mind, bizarrely, of the ancient Pont du Gard, in southern France. What on earth is a Roman aqueduct doing in the brown bubble hills of Marin County? Which is to ask, what has become of the Wrightian principle of accommodating to nature instead of defying it? To make matters still more unlike Wright, one is constantly aware of being in the presence (as in the case of the Arizona state capitol project) of an immense dome—Wright's despised symbol of public authority.

The unexpected reminiscence of the Pont du Gard in the Civic Center has to do with its arches, diminishing as they rise tier upon tier, and not with the finicky amusement-park ornamentation that takes the place of a cornice and that, stretching some eight hundred and fifty feet along the façade, comically resembles the frilly paper-lace border of a valentine. In discussing the Center, Michael Graves and Charles Jencks have agreed that it gives the impression of being a shopping mall instead of a succession of grim government facilities (including courthouses and a jail), and that the intention of the building was evidently to humanize activities that most of us find intimidating; in that case, the sky-blue roofs, the red flooring, and the silly gold aluminum balls that are a repeated decorative motif are supposed to lift our spirits and put us, as good Americans, in a mood to buy; how frustrating, then, that little is for sale there except in the post office (among the stamps on sale is one bearing a handsome likeness of Wright).

The Civic Center was Wright's only realized government commission. Ironically, it was constructed after his death, being opened to the public in 1962. Still more ironic is the fact that it should be so uncharacteristic of him: a compendium of what he had spent a lifetime denouncing. Beth Sholom and the Guggenheim Museum, both of which he observed under construction and which were opened a few months after he died, are much more nearly appropriate monuments to his genius than either the Civic Center or, for that matter, the Grady Gammage Memorial Auditorium, at Arizona State University, in Tempe, Arizona: in the canon of Wright works, the last of his non-residential commissions. Wes Peters supervised the construction of the auditorium and his hand is everywhere visible in it. Despite its great size—it holds three thousand people—it has the unexpected peek-a-boo daintiness of a boudoir; one wonders what can be holding it up and whether one ought to knock discreetly before entering.

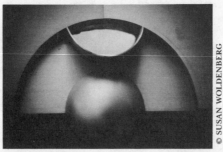

A burnished pendant, which FLW may have intended as a lighthearted tribute to the Golden West.

The opening of the Guggenheim and the dedication of Beth Sholom were happy occasions—in the case of the Guggenheim, not less happy because of the absence of its architect. The ceremonies marked the end of sixteen years of rancorous travail, of compromises aesthetic and financial, of disputes intellectual and personal. The director of the museum, James Johnson Sweeney, was every bit as hot-tempered as Wright, and, moreover, often had reason on his side; when I happened to be a direct or indirect observer of the quarrels between them, in most cases I tended to side with Sweeney. Olgivanna Wright scornfully described Sweeney in print as "doubting Thomas" Sweeney, but his doubts were well based. For example, the ribbons of glass that Wright intended to have pour their light into the galleries from a point just above the tops of the paintings were blacked out on Sweeney's orders and correctly so; the very glass itself was an experiment that Wright had conducted to his satisfaction at the Johnson Wax building, in Racine, but on several counts it had already proved a failure there and it would certainly have proved, as Sweeney knew, a failure at the Guggenheim as well.

The building has never been used as Wright wished it to be used, but that is a fate that has befallen almost every museum in New York City in our time, except perhaps for the grandly unacquisitive, imperturbable Frick. Few New Yorkers foresaw the transformation of its museums from sequestered repositories of art, devoted to the identification and preservation of their treasures and visited largely by scholars and connoisseurs, into Buffalo Bill circuses, whose blockbuster shows of fashionable artists and sculptors draw tens of thousands of paying customers annually. Museums have become an uneasy cross between theatre and boutique, seeking to achieve "selling" reviews and lines at the box office and to sell costly souvenirs in the form of replicas of real objects of art; for the upwardly mobile they have supplanted opera as a place to be seen and of zoos as a place to take the children. Against high odds, the Guggenheim has managed to accommodate itself to the new museumgoer without becoming a circus. It has also managed to survive the restrictions placed upon it by the eccentricity of its architecture, and in the course of doing so it has outlived the early jest that it would make an ideal mausoleum for Wright, with his sarcophagus dominating the rotunda as that of Napoleon dominates the rotunda of the Invalides.

The dedication of Beth Sholom took place within a few days of the opening of the Guggenheim. Olgivanna Wright had been invited to give the principal address at the synagogue and she had graciously consented to do so. (Her gracious consent was followed almost immediately by a brisk note demanding the twenty-seven thousand dollars that she said the synagogue still owed her husband's estate.) After Cohen had paid a suitable tribute to Wright ("His so-called arrogance, I am convinced, was a mask to shield himself against a world that often did not treat him kindly"), Mrs. Wright was introduced and spoke on the text, "Give Us the Temple in Which to Worship." She congratulated her late husband on having been "a man who daringly built a synagogue through which the voices of God and Moses were called again to life in visible form."[7] This statement irritated many members of the congregation by its implication that the voices of God and Moses had been silent until Wright happened along; they were also irritated by the fact that she failed to mention the "co-designer," Rabbi Cohen. Ignoring this slight, Cohen wrote a note of thanks to Mrs. Wright:

And so we come to the end of our project, but I hope not to the end of our association with each other. To me this has been a most difficult and arduous task that has taken out of my life six full years. But my reward has been rich—knowing your wonderful husband, Mr. Wright, you, yourself to me also a very remarkable and admirable person, Wes Peters, and Taliesin. I shall cherish this experience for the remaining years of my life.[8]

But it turned out, as it did in so many Wright projects, that the end was not quite the end. The rabbi had enclosed with his note a check for twelve thousand, five hundred dollars, in partial payment of the fees still owed to Wright and with a promise to pay the remainder as soon as certain critical defects in the design of the building had been remedied. The roof leaked incessantly, despite innumerable attempts to repair it, and in a spirit of acrimony on both sides (the sorely beset "little rabbi" wrote to Peters, "Each time we plan a service or a wedding, I am a nervous wreck"), the final payments were made late in the following year. The roof of Beth Sholom still leaks—gently now, instead of torrentially—and the main auditorium is so expensive to heat that in cold weather services are usually held in the basement chapel, but the pride of the congregation in its "wandering Mount Sinai" remains undiminished.

Wright in old age—which is to say the Wright that I encountered first as a reporter and afterward as a friend—had put on by then the latest of the many masks that he had spent a lifetime inventing and discarding. He had become a professional great man, with the few advantages and the numerous drawbacks of that position. One of the most conspicuous of these drawbacks is the extent to which a celebrity becomes a sort of walking and talking automaton. As friends of such a celebrity, we find ourselves bearing reluctant witness to the repetition of clockwork utterances and gestures, which by their familiarity ensure the celebrity's immediate recognition. An act of will is required to discern behind the mask of the professional great man the man who is genuinely great, as Wright was; we remind ourselves that other great men—Yeats, Picasso, Einstein—responded much as Wright did to the temptations of fame. In Wright's case, it may be that he enjoyed playing the role of great man more than he ought to have let us see; the relish with which he took center stage and held it struck many people, including members of his family, as unbecoming. In 1957, John Lloyd Wright wrote, "When people prostrate themselves at his feet and he sits in his king chair absorbing it and when he freely informs the public that everything good in architecture was done by him first, I am thoroughly embarrassed."[1]

For my part, I found it easy to forgive Wright his public showing off, in part because I was experiencing it for the first time, in part because it made good copy, and in part because my admiration of him was of long standing and would readily have survived the discovery that he was *only* showing off. But of course there was always much more to him than that, up to the very moment of his death. It was never necessary to fall back upon piety as a reason for being grateful to be in his presence. As for the good copy, at least once a year in those days the "Talk of the Town" department of *The New Yorker* would welcome a piece about him. Quotations from these pieces have appeared in earlier biographies of Wright, and I feel an uneasy sense of self-cannibalism in mentioning them here: still, they portray the living Wright at the top of his self-dramatizing bent and so at least one of them deserves a place in this narrative. The variety of topics that Wright and I discussed was, as usual, happily hopscotch, in execution; here it begins with his praise of the Plaza:

"I've stayed here on my visits for forty years," he said. "A beautiful hotel. They started to remodel it downstairs a few years back, but thank God I got here in time to stop them. The little devils had already wrecked the Palm Court, but I saved the Oak Room and the dining room." On a table between Wright and us were stout pots of tea, a plate of stout sandwiches, and a scattering of magazines and papers. As we talked, the tablecloth was slowly darkened by an assortment of Wright graffiti, ranging from floor plans and elevations of houses, churches, and factories to a sketch of his Jaguar, which is currently his favorite car and is, he said, capable of reaching ninety without a tremor. Wright himself is so plainly capable of reaching ninety without a tremor [he was then eighty-six] that we couldn't help asking how he had managed to outwit age. At that moment, the telephone rang, and he bounded to his feet to answer it. "Damned thing rings all day!" he said with pleasure. Over the telephone, he made an appointment for nine the next morning, and then he returned to his tea. "I have seven children and ten grandchildren and three great-grandchildren, so I must be old, but I don't feel old, I feel young," he said. "I draw and I build and teach my apprentices and send them out into the world, not to be like me but to be themselves. At last count, a hundred and sixty-eight practicing architects had been trained by me at Taliesin, in Wisconsin. When can I ever have been readier to do good work? When can I ever have been fitter to be alive, to help build an American culture? Not a civilization, because we already have a civilization, but a culture. And you can't have a culture without architecture."

The telephone rang again, and Wright, racing to it, exclaimed, "*Damn* the thing!" He made an appointment for ten the next morning, hung up, ruffled his bright-blue flowing tie, took a deep breath, and asked us please not to consider him a member of the architectural profession. "I'm not a member of any profession," he said. "I'm a one-man experiment in democracy, an experiment that worked. An individual who rose by his own merits, beholden to no one. When Sullivan and I came to architecture, it had been slumbering for five hundred years. We woke it up. We gave it a fresh start. We made it organic. We said architecture was space to be lived in, not a façade, not a box, not a monument. Wallie Harrison says the slab's the thing. I say the cemeteries are full of slabs, but who wants to be in a cemetery? Does all this sound arrogant? Let it sound arrogant, then! I defy anyone to name a single aspect of the best contemporary architecture that wasn't done first by me. Or a single aspect of the worst contemporary architecture that isn't a betrayal of what I've done. Like those awful U.N. buildings. Or that Corbusier thing in Marseille.

Massacre on the waterfront, I call that. Or any of those skinny glass boxes! Why, I wouldn't dare walk on the same side of the street with them. Fool things might explode. There! That's from a fellow who knew what architecture was when all these glass-box boys were just so many diapers hanging on the line. . . ."[2]

On and on Wright went, seeming to gain strength as my own strength ebbed. He ticked off a number of the projects he had under way, estimated that up to that moment six hundred and forty projects had "come true" over the length of his career, went to the window of his suite, looked down over the traffic on Fifth Avenue, cheerfully shook his fist at it, and wound up the interview with, "I'm flying home to Taliesin tomorrow afternoon. We have thirty-five hundred acres out there. My family followed the Indians onto that land. The name of our town is Spring Green. Spring Green, Spring Green! Out there, chickens give eggs, cows give milk, and old Wright he rides his Tennessee walking horse."[3]

One chooses a mask in youth in order to move about freely behind it, taking the measure of who it is that one has the capacity to become. To the amusement of his fellow Dubliners, young "Willie" Yeats chose correctly the mask of a Parisian poet—broad-brimmed velvet hat, beribboned pince-nez, and cape—and grew to be a true poet behind that more or less comical disguise. Hemingway, who ought to have chosen the mask of a poet, chose instead the mask of a tough guy hunter-killer and eventually

Professing to despise New York City, FLW in age rejoiced to visit it, turning his suite at the Plaza Hotel into a third home—Taliesin East.

broke down under the strain of its falseness. Wright chose the mask of an artist-writer-dandy, oddly combining elements of Whistler, Richard Le Gallienne, and William Morris. In the small town of Madison in the eighteen-eighties, and even in the metropolis of Chicago, he must have seemed an exotic bird of paradise, and he remained an exotic bird of paradise in New York City in the nineteen-fifties. The key to wearing a mask successfully is, of course, to be aware at every moment that it is indeed a mask, and

FLW at Taliesin North posing successfully as a grand old man. Note the low chairs that visitors were required to occupy.

Wright never faltered in that respect; the adornment of his person, like the eloquence of his speech, was simultaneously who he was and who he pretended to be.

I was made aware of Wright's superlative self-awareness one evening at Taliesin North, when I was enjoying dinner with the family—Frank, Olgivanna, and Iovanna, along with three teen-aged Gill children. Iovanna and I got into a vehement discussion—characteristic, no doubt, of both of us—concerning the nature of the relationship between God and man.

As the argument grew more intense and, I suspect, more nonsensical, Frank attempted to calm the disputants with a few words of his own. Iovanna wheeled on him and, like any daughter to any father, exclaimed, "Oh, Father! You don't know anything about it!" He accepted the rebuke quietly, and we went on to discuss other topics, including a theory of mine that all the great men of that period—Franklin Roosevelt, Churchill, and the like—had some taint of the charlatan in their makeup. Frank said instantly, "Brendan, do you consider me a charlatan?" I was unprepared for so direct a challenge and mumbled some weaseling reply, in the course of which I substituted for the harsh term "charlatan" the somewhat less harsh "mountebank."

After dinner, Wright walked me up and down the living room and, accepting the likelihood of the fact that words like "charlatan" and "mountebank" might well be applied to him, gave an explanation that satisfied me at the time, though I realized with reluctance that it was precisely what any authentic charlatan/mountebank would have been certain to give. "I had to make a noise in the world, in order to gain as much of the world's attention as I could," he said. "Otherwise, I would have had a lot of work on paper and only a little of it coming up out of the ground in bricks and mortar." It was an argument based on nothing more complex— and nothing, alas, more moral—than that the end justifies the means, but then his entire life had been based upon that argument, and there superbly he stood, the erect handsome old man, defying me to say that he had made use of it in vain. For of course it had not been in vain, and how well he knew it!

In Manhattan, over tea or drinks at the Plaza and on a basis less serious (and less perilous-seeming to me) than that occasion at Taliesin, we would talk of the relationship between the maker and the thing made as it had been manifested throughout his life. For over sixty years he had been seeking extravagant praise and had been expressing, in exceptionally rude terms, contempt for the only people whose praise ought to have mattered to him, including architects, architectural critics, and historians of American culture. In that case, what was his celebrated arrogance but the puerile combativeness of the schoolyard, rendered more and more gratuitous and unappealing by every masterpiece that he achieved? This was the question that, uttered in circumlocutions intended to mitigate its harshness, lay between us and that he returned to again and again, not so much to answer it as to play with it and be amused by it. A few years earlier, he might have been angered by the question; the mask he wore for me forbade those hot-tempered outbursts that even the idolatrous Olgivanna wrote of with awe. ("At times when he turned white with fury, his eyes were molten steel. His whole face and body became saturated with a force beyond human. He was terrifying to behold. . . ."[4]) He had survived and triumphed by dint of strategies that he had no need to examine; in high spirits, he spoke of Truth with a capital "T," as he spoke of Nature with a capital "N," but in neither case did the words bear any weight of authentic meaning. They were Welsh tarradiddle, useful in getting from one point to another in a discussion, and one knew that, backed into a corner, Wright would say simply, "Well, there you are!" and so escape the irritating tether of mere common sense.

In the dining room of the Plaza, under faked wooden ceiling beams that Wright much admired, we would drink Irish whiskey, always with the same difficulty in ordering it. Wright would tell the waiter, "Old Bushmill's neat, please," and then add, with emphasis, "That means I want no ice." "Of course, sir," the waiter would reply. As the waiter went off to the bar, Wright would lean toward me and say, "They never listen. Watch, now. There will be ice." Back would come the waiter with the Irish whiskey, in a glass filled with ice cubes. Wright would pick up a spoon and, lifting out the ice cubes one by one, proceed to flip them across the green-carpeted floor, to the astonishment and pleasure of other patrons of the Plaza: Foxy Grandpa on a rampage. Sometimes we would meet in the ground-floor bar at "21," whose preposterous decor—its dusky low ceiling hung with model airplanes, model buses, and the Lord knows what—was again a source of admiring comment from Wright. One day a tiny figure whose head was topped by a dark velvet beret waved to us from a distant banquette. "Oh, God!" Wright exclaimed in dismay. "Ayn Rand!"

Rand's novel *The Fountainhead,* published in 1943, has been one of the leading best-sellers of all time (over four million copies have been sold), and its hero, an architect named Howard Roark, is widely supposed to have been based upon Wright, though Rand denied it many times and so, with reason, did Wright. Rand was bent upon preaching the gospel of individualism as a political and ethical ideal and denouncing the false doctrine of humanitarianism; to the ancient question "Am I my brother's keeper?" she answered with a ringing "No!" She decided to use the profession of architecture as a vehicle for dramatizing her then generally unpopular right-wing, anti-altruistic principles. As it happened, she knew little or nothing about either architecture or Wright when she began writing her trashy classic, but through friends she was able to persuade the distinguished New York City architect Ely Jacques Kahn to provide her with a "cover" job in his office while she boned up on the nuts and bolts of the profession. (According to Rand's biographer, Barbara Branden, it was Kahn who gave Rand the idea of using a housing project as a major factor in the plot of *The Fountainhead.*) Kahn arranged for Rand to meet Wright at a banquet held in New York. Rand told Wright that she was writing a novel about an architect and would like to interview him; to her disappointment, Wright begged off with some vague words about the uncertainty of his future plans.

Rand sent Wright the first three chapters of the novel and he wrote to her saying that he liked nothing about them. After the publication of *The Fountainhead*, she met Wright in Los Angeles, at the home of his son Lloyd, and on that occasion they got on well. He had not yet read the novel, but he recalled that among the things he had disliked in the first three chapters was the fact that Roark had been described as being tall and with red hair, and he had wanted him to be short, with white hair. Lloyd Wright laughed and said, "Oh, Father, Miss Rand wasn't writing your biography!" Subsequently, Wright read the novel and praised it to Rand but refused to issue a public endorsement of it. He invited Rand and her husband to visit Taliesin North; the shabby condition of the house and the social conditions under which the Fellowship operated were, it appears, a shock to Rand. Individualism as a theory was one thing, but the benign tyranny practiced at Taliesin was quite another. Nevertheless, she commissioned a house from Wright and was delighted with the designs he furnished her; it remained only a project in part because she wasn't sure where she wished to build it and in part because she couldn't afford it. As usual, Wright found these reasons unacceptable. He assured her that with minor changes the house could be built in Connecticut, Texas, Arizona, or Florida. As for affording it, "My dear lady," he said, "that's no problem at all. Go out and make more money."[5] In the end, Rand did indeed make plenty of money but chose to live in Manhattan, which was a site that Wright, possibly to his regret, had neglected to mention.

The producer of the movie version of *The Fountainhead* was eager to have Wright prepare the drawings that Roark, played by Gary Cooper, would be seen at work upon during the course of the movie. One story holds that Wright demanded a fee of two hundred and fifty thousand dollars to perform this task, along with the right to approve or reject the script and the sets—a demand that was promptly refused. According to another story, he demanded his usual fee of ten percent to design the sets; when asked if that meant ten percent of the budget for the sets, which was four hundred thousand dollars, he said that, on the contrary, he wished ten percent of the budget for the entire movie, which was four million dollars. Again, his demand was refused.

At "21," Rand addressed Wright as "Master" and, fixing us with her formidable black eyes, gently lectured us on her political views, which Wright, despite a reputation among conservatives for being a near-Communist, was by no means beyond sharing. He had always talked a great deal about democracy, as Sullivan had talked about it before him, but the word meant whatever they wished it to mean, and in neither case did it imply respect for the masses. Wright wrote sneeringly of the common herd in his book on Sullivan, itself sneeringly entitled *Genius and the Mobocracy*, and some of his words might well have been lifted directly from the speeches that Rand put into the mouth of Roark. "The creator lives for his work," says Roark. "He needs no other men. His primary goal is within himself. . . . The man who attempts to live for others is . . . a parasite in motive and makes parasites of those he serves."[6] And here is Wright on Sullivan and his so-called disciples, really his imitators: "A disciple . . . is a graft. A graft does not support anything. . . . The profession to which Louis H. Sullivan belonged, unable to value him, neglected him. But professionalism is parasitic—a body of men unable to do more than band together to protect themselves. So far as the life of what they profess is concerned they have it by the throat as a jealous husband might strangle an unfaithful wife."[7]

Wright and Rand were both consummately elitist, but by the nineteen-fifties, at a time when Rand was politically active, Wright was no longer interested in politics as a subject of debate, especially in New York City; too many of his friends there deplored his rhetoric, which in any event defied analysis. Even over drinks, what was one to make of a sentence such as, "Spirit is a science mobocracy does not know," when the words "spirit," "science," "mobocracy," and "know" were all left undefined? Like Wright, Rand was a highly intelligent spellbinder and therefore to some extent a rival; that day, he found her—or pretended to find her—tiresome. Perhaps he also found it tiresome that some of his fame was derived by then from his being thought the model for Roark, which amounted in his eyes to serving as a sort of stand-in for Gary Cooper, who was infinitely more famous than he. Though Wright rejoiced to know celebrities and instantly put himself on a first-name basis with them, he did not rejoice to be discovered in their shade.

In the novel, Roark destroys with charges of dynamite the housing project that he had hoped would prove his masterpiece; he does so because the project, having been mutilated by others in the course of its construction, is no longer the expression of his sacred individuality. In an eerie and distressing echo of this gesture, Wright in extreme old age, quarreling with the tax assessors in Wisconsin, threatened to burn Taliesin to the ground, leaving the ruins to serve as a rebuke to the money-grubbing philistines that had shown so little respect for his works. Luckily, the threat was as hollow as it was outrageous, and the amount of tax money in dispute was raised at a benefit dinner given in honor of Wright: again the sly old fox, this time on an exceptionally rewarding rampage.

Few men and women in their middle and late eighties are physically and psychologically prepared to be as joyous as Wright was during his late New York period. He was still living beyond his means, on a scale that might daunt a minor millionaire, and a score of professional difficulties continued to vex him as certain major projects—Beth Sholom, the Guggenheim, the Kalita Humphreys Theatre—approached completion, but his zest for life remained undiminished. Meanwhile, an ever-increasing number of new commissions arrived at the gates of Taliesins North and West and were parceled out among the Fellowship. There were times (surely for the old master the best of times) when it was possible for him simultaneously to pursue his career, enjoy his earned fame, and revel with friends. One such friend was Joseph Brewer, who in his youth had been a partner of the publisher George Putnam and had edited Henry-Russell Hitchcock's first book. Formerly President of Olivet College, Brewer had moved East and was occupying the post of deputy chief librarian at Queens College. He and his wife were eager to have Wright design a country house for them on a remote hillside in East Fishkill, an hour or so north of New York City.

One morning in the fifties, Brewer drove to the Plaza in his little Simca, picked up Wright, and drove him up the Taconic Parkway to the site, which from Wright's point of view was an ideal one, being almost impossible to build upon: a couple of immense, mossy escarpments emerged from a steep, thickly wooded slope, down which plunged an icy mountain brook. At the foot of the slope lay a pretty meadow and pool, but Wright had no interest that day in pretty meadows and pools; the two escarpments ran parallel to each other and Wright saw at once that with his usual ingenuity he would be able to fit a long, canoe-shaped house into the high cleft between the escarpments, with cantilevered decks floating in space at either end (a house not unlike one he had designed some years earlier for a client named Charoudi, which had remained unbuilt). Wright clambered with delight up and down the damp and slippery rocks, exclaiming that he would be able to give the Brewers a house even more beautiful than Fallingwater. At last he could no longer contain his boyish glee; climbing to the top of one of the escarpments, he proceeded to slide down its rounded surface to the meadow grass some twenty feet below. What were old age and old bones and the threat of a broken neck in the face of such an opportunity? Once he had landed safely in the grass, it was discovered that his trousers had been wet through by the slippery rocks; in order to dry him out, newspapers were fetched, rolled into tubes, and thrust up inside Wright's trousers. And so he was returned to the Plaza, where—one suspects—he received a severe scolding from Olgivanna, whom Wright in such circumstances always took care to address as "Mother."

Another merry occasion (one that may also have ended in a scolding by "Mother") was a consequence of Wright's meeting with one of the leading real-estate developers of the day, William Zeckendorf (1905–1976). The story is told in Zeckendorf's lively autobiography, published a few years before his death:

> Wright I met as a supposed antagonist on a TV discussion panel where I (the builder) was supposed to be his meat. All I knew about Wright was that I liked his work. When my aides compiled a dossier of his speeches and writings, I discovered the man made profound good sense. As a result, during the TV show we sang in duet and had a great time. After the program, in order to further admire each other and ourselves, we went out to my place in Greenwich for dinner and a few drinks. The company was so excellent that we had a few more drinks, but in the course of maneuvering down into my wine cellar for a fresh bottle of brandy, Wright caught his heel on a step and fell, giving himself a nasty gash on the scalp. The next stop was the emergency ward of the hospital, where this fierce old man, refusing an anaesthetic (he already had enough in him), sat on the operating table swinging his legs and singing bawdy songs as the intern stitched his scalp.[8]

It was uncharacteristic of Wright to drink to the point of getting tipsy, but the story—and Wright's condition—is vouched for by Zeckendorf's son, William, Jr., who was present on that remarkable occasion. Moreover, the reference to Wright's swinging his legs on the operating table is a convincing detail; it was his habit throughout his life to hoist himself lightly onto any convenient horizontal perch and sit there kicking up his heels as he talked. He had a strong prejudice against the very idea of people sitting in chairs, arguing that the human body was to be seen at its most graceful in a reclining position. Critics of Wright's furniture would say that his prejudice against chairs was self-evident, and Wright himself confessed that his shins were often rendered black and blue through unlucky encounters with chairs of his design.

The generous-hearted Zeckendorf became a good friend of Wright's. In 1957, the Board of Directors of the Chicago Theological Society, owners of the Robie house, made plans to tear it down and replace it with a high-rise dormitory. The board had hoped to carry out a similar act of vandalism in the early nineteen-forties and Wright had led the successful fight against them. Now he took up the struggle for a second time, and with his incomparable gift for making enemies he attacked the board in the press, saying, "It all goes to show the danger of entrusting anything spiritual to the clergy." At a critical moment, Zeckendorf arranged to purchase the house—the price was one hundred and twenty-five thousand dollars—with the intention of using it as a temporary headquarters for the Chicago branch of his real-estate company; as soon as the company no longer needed the space, the house would be turned over to the Frank

Lloyd Wright Foundation. Before this transfer could be carried out, Wright died, and Zeckendorf was obliged to fall back upon a second-best solution to the problem of preserving the house: he presented it to the University of Chicago and it now serves the university as its Office of Alumni Affairs. Though preserved, the house has been so harshly dealt with over the years that the historian Donald Hoffmann describes it as being today an inauthentic fossil.

At Taliesins North and West, Wright in his last years debonairly tried on his ultimate mask—that of a resident deity, imparting his beatitudes from within the shelter of those gorgeous temples of his own making.

Perhaps for Olgivanna's sake, FLW assumes here the mask of an august conventionality. Even the Weimaraner has put on an appropriately respectable expression. [AP]

Like most deities throughout history, he contrived to remain present even when he was absent—indeed, his absence amounted to an intensified presence, since the degree to which he was missed was precisely the degree to which he was credited by true believers with being indispensable. The orchestration of the order of worship was in Olgivanna's hands and Wright consented to her semi-ecclesiastical arrangements without losing a sense of humor about them and about himself; he was grateful for them because, like her household arrangements, they left him free to work and play without undue interruption.

Young as Olgivanna had been during her period of discipleship under Gurdjieff, she had learned much from him about the organization of a cult and about the discipline required to make a cult prosper. In Oak Park in his early twenties, the charismatic Wright had had no difficulty gathering about him a group of devout acolytes, but in Yeats's phrase, "they came like swallows and like swallows went." It was Olgivanna's powerful character that helped to hold the acolytes at the two Taliesins in benign bondage. Many of them had come to the sacred door as dropouts, and so it was only to be expected that among their number there would be still further dropouts; nevertheless, enough of the faithful elected to spend years of their lives there—in some cases, to spend the whole of their adult lives there—to ensure that the cult survived. Moreover, the death of the founder, far from scattering the cult, in a perhaps unexpected way strengthened it, for Wright had passed from mortality to immortality and was no longer subject to the frailties inherent in human nature. Crudely put, he was beyond doing injury to his own image, and Olgivanna and the inner circle of worshippers had already seen to it that a wealth of evidence of his long and fruitful stay upon earth was close at hand and would, with care, prove imperishable.

What I have called Wright's beatitudes were sayings about architecture that he had accumulated over seventy years and he saw no reason to abandon them simply because he had been encouraged to repeat them on so many occasions. The truths he perceived them as embodying had been reenforced for him by repetition; unselfconsciously and with professional gusto he uttered them not only at the Taliesins North and West but at college campuses across the country, at press conferences, and at forums social, political, and religious. Catching sight of a pulpit, he was soon in it, as generations of his ancestors had been before him, but a picnic in a meadow would provide a no less suitable setting. Dozens of these sermons were recorded in Wright's old age and continue to be played on a regular basis at the two Taliesins and at lesser shrines. Herewith a representative sample:

"Organic architecture is a natural architecture. It means building for and with the individual as distinguished from the pseudo-classic order . . . mainly derived from survivals of ancient military or monarchic orders. Or that later attempt at elimination and classification now grafted upon organic architecture called 'The International Style' by ambitious provincials. Or as distinguished from any personal preconceived pertinent or impertinent formula for mere appearance. Organic architecture is informal architecture, architecture in the reflex, architecture seeking to serve man rather than to become, or be becoming to, those forces now trying so hard to rule over him. Here is one good reason why we may say organic architecture is the architecture of democracy."[9]

"Who founded New York City? It was Cain, wasn't it? Cain was the founder of the city after he murdered Abel. He had incurred the displeasure of the Lord and he went out and founded the city and here it is yet. Here is the city founded by the man who murdered his brother and is still murdering his brother. . . ."[10]

"Man's moral nature dwindles as his machines increase in power. . . . He has possession now of a means he has not been educated to exercise. He is more deadly now and no more competent morally than he was in the days of the Egyptians."[11]

"Jesus himself was the greatest promulgator of an organic architecture! Why and how? When he said, 'The kingdom of God is within you!' And that's where the kingdom of architecture is! It's within the nature of your situation! The nature of your environment! The nature of your site!"[12]

As befitted a deity, certain high holy days were given over annually to honoring Wright; two of them—Christmas and Easter—he was obliged to share with his Christian predecessor and (according to Wright) fellow architect, Jesus Christ; the third—his birthday, which fell on June 8th— was entirely his own. In one of her autobiographical books, *Shining Brow,* Olgivanna describes how the apprentices would devote weeks to the design and making of unusual Christmas gifts for the Wrights; how Wright would always object to the presence of a traditional Christmas tree at Taliesin West ("It is ridiculous to have a Christmas tree in the desert"), and then grudgingly consent to it; and how everyone would gather in the living room on Christmas night to sing carols. Olgivanna also describes the Easter festival at Taliesin West, to which hundreds of their friends were invited. The main dish on this occasion was the Russian Easter bread called baba, which took many hours to prepare under Olgivanna's supervision.

In *Shining Brow,* Olgivanna writes that Easter, 1959, was "the happiest one of all our thirty-seven years together. It was a beautiful morning, full of sunlight. We both dressed in white. I went early to Mr. Wright's room to wish him a Happy Easter. We walked out to greet our young people and our guests. Balloons flew everywhere. Tables were spread with flowers, Babas rose from circles of multi-colored eggs, the pascha cheese shimmered white in garlands of blossoms and leaves. . . . We ate gaily and like children broke the eggs end to end. Happy and free we laughed, immersed in purity of spirit. . . . Four of his children were there—Lloyd and his wife, Helen; David and his wife, Gladys; Catherine and her husband, Kenneth Baxter; Iovanna, of course; his granddaughter, Anne [Baxter]; his grandson, Eric—the last Easter with their father and grandfather."[13]

Having worked hard to gain celebrity, FLW was happy to meet and mingle with other celebrities. He had reason to be pleased when one of his grand-daughters, actress Anne Baxter, became famous. [WMF]

Several years later, Catherine Baxter wrote to Grant Manson about that Easter visit, saying that she and other members of the family had had the feeling that Wright "had grown suddenly very old and very tired. Tired of the burden he had shouldered for so many extra years of productivity and as a superman was expected to keep on creating and producing as a one-man production line. It must have been enervating to his soul at times."[14] This was a view of Wright more sympathetic than Catherine was accustomed to expressing. From the moment that Wright had left the house in Oak Park, Catherine had taken her mother's side and, though consenting to reestablish a family relationship with her father, had refused to forgive him. Lloyd Wright and John Lloyd Wright, being young men at the time of the separation, had silently taken their father's side; Llewellyn was too young to take in what was happening to the household, while Frances was divided in her loyalties (at times living with her mother, at other times she served briefly as her father's official hostess at Taliesin). It was David among the boys who had to shoulder much of the mother's grief and prolonged distraction, and he retained a measure of bitterness against Wright to the very end. When the mother died, a day short of her eighty-eighth birthday and only a couple of weeks before Wright himself died, David waited a full day before driving over from his house in Phoenix to Taliesin, to break the news to his father. Wright's eyes filled with tears and he said to David, "Why didn't you tell me as soon as you knew?" David stared at his father, unable to resist exacting some small measure of revenge on behalf of his mother. "Why should I have bothered?" he asked. "You never gave a god-damn for her when she was alive."

On April 4th, 1959, a few days after that happiest of Easters, Wright complained of stomach pains. He was taken to a hospital in Phoenix, where he was operated on for an intestinal blockage, accompanied by hemorrhage. He survived the operation in a manner that the doctors considered remarkable in a man of ninety-one and appeared to be making an excellent recovery. Wes Peters believes that the post-operative medication prescribed for Wright was imprudent and may have hastened his death instead of preventing it; be that as it may, late on the evening of April 9th the nurse attending him heard him breathe a sigh and a moment later he was dead. The next day, Peters and an apprentice loaded Wright, embalmed and coffined, into a pick-up truck and drove steadily, sleeplessly, through the night to Taliesin North, where on April 12th, in the living room of the house, a Unitarian funeral service was performed.

Following the precedent established by Wright in the burial of Mamah Borthwick almost half a century earlier, his coffin was placed on a flower-strewn farm wagon drawn by a pair of sturdy farm horses. With forty or so family members and friends and employees of Wright walking behind it, the wagon was driven to the little family burial ground at the foot of the hill a few hundred yards from Taliesin. Under Olgivanna's watchful eye, Wright's body was interred not far from the graves of two of the other powerful women—Anna Lloyd Wright and Mamah Borthwick—who had helped to shape his life. When her time for dying came, Olgivanna would secure possession of whatever was left of him and mingle those remains with hers.

The cortege at Taliesin, April, 1959. [MJ]

30

I HAVE SPOKEN of the relationship between the maker and the thing made and of how Wright and I would discuss the means by which, over a long lifetime, he had succeeded in welding the two into one. It is this feat among others that prompts us to identify him as a genius—a gross and unsatisfactory label (though Wright was not above applying it to Sullivan and himself, on the grounds in his case of "not having so much to be humble about"). Behind a succession of masks incessantly put on and taken off, Wright achieved his unity of person and purpose not in the traditional way, by withdrawal from the world and a disciplined suppression of individual identity, but, on the contrary, by a flagrant exploitation of his identity, carried out upon the most prominent platforms available to him.

The world learned to salute Wright upon his accomplishments, but never so early and so often as he saluted himself; disconcertingly, he was discovered to be as great as he said he was. Moreover, he appeared eager to tell us precisely how his greatness had come about. Shocking as his immodesty was, it proved all the more shocking because it was based upon

© SUSAN WOLDENBERG

FLW's grave-marker in the Jones family cemetery; the design is reminiscent of the Coonley playhouse windows. The epitaph reads, "Love of an idea is love of God."

501

an authentic merit and was therefore, by our usual standards of decorum, uncalled-for: tooting one's own horn was thought to imply that there was nothing to the horn but its toot. Wright's case was the mighty exception. Though we might make fun of his bravado, the content of the bravado remained intact; when we called his bluff, to our embarrassment it proved not to be a bluff at all.

Wright left us not only his hundreds upon hundreds of works, built and unbuilt, but thousands of pages of documentation as well, covering nearly all of his not quite ninety-two years. If the works are unchallengeable in the actuality of their bricks and mortar, the exceptionally abundant documentation that Wright bequeathed to us ends by arousing our suspicions. Seeming to contain so much, it contains remarkably little of value concerning the key episodes of his life. Putting aside its artful obfuscations, we arrive at its no less artful omissions, among them the near-saintliness of the father, the near-madness of the mother, the excision from his life of the half-brothers and half-sister, the womanizing, the relentless taking advantage of family and friends, the borrowing of funds from clients, the non-payment of taxes. . . . The list begins to assume the character of an indictment, as if before our reluctant eyes the genius-hero were being exposed as the epitome of a genius-villain. But for all Wright's crafty toying with us, that dour accusation is more than he deserves to be confronted with. Whatever his career may have cost others in suffering strikes us now, almost thirty years after his death (and with most of the sufferers' voices muted by death), as producing a gift to the world that far outweighs the persistent, outrageous selfishness of the giver—a gift that transforms his selfishness into generosity.

It is a commonplace that nobody, and least of all a genius, achieves greatness except at a price, and it is no less a commonplace that history, year by year and at an accelerating rate, silently reduces that price. We accept the notorious fact that a genius ransacks and uses up with a greater or less degree of ruthlessness everyone within reach of him, but what a glib and inappropriate belittlement this is! For it is equally a fact, though it passes unnoticed, that vast numbers of people who are not geniuses ransack and ruthlessly use up everyone within reach of them; moreover, these ordinary mortals, unlike geniuses, are apt to take far more out of the world than they give back. From the point of view of history, they strike a bad bargain with the world; people like Wright, as Wright would be the first to tell us, strike a good one.

Wright learned early in life to waste little energy upon regret or— what is more debilitating—remorse. At the nadir of his relationship with Miriam Noel, he wrote to his son Lloyd that there were techniques for dealing with the miseries of life that were not unlike those by which one

The grand seigneur practices a lifelong skill.

© PEDRO E. GUERRERO

was enabled to create art. The statement has a cold-blooded ring to it, and I doubt if Wright ever contrived to practice any of these techniques for long; certainly in respect to family life, whenever a crisis threatened to erupt in his presence his usual procedure was simply to walk away: a response too instinctive to be described as a technique. The energy that he saved and spent elsewhere by dint of eliminating (or perhaps only diminishing) remorse had superlatively fortunate consequences for the rest of us; there they stand, the wondrous works, and our spirits are quickened by their presence.

At the moment, Wright appears secure in his claim to being the greatest of American architects. Even the most ardent champions of Jefferson, Latrobe, Davis, Richardson, Hunt, McKim, and the like are wary of placing their candidates on a higher plane than Wright. It may be that this wariness springs in part from a sense that Wright has not yet consented to become a mere laureled shade in the pages of history and, at the first glimpse of an approaching rival, will prove eager to demonstrate his prowess as an adversary. But of course there is more to the matter than the imagined combativeness of a ghost. Outside the world of sports, the question of rankings trivializes the so-called contestants. Opinions on the attribute of greatness in the arts are especially subjective and therefore not a fruitful topic of debate, but if the attribute of "American" is capable of being discussed, then it is fair to ask whether any architect in our history can match Wright in that respect.

Frost's famous poem "The Gift Outright" begins, "The land was ours before we were the land's" and ends with the haunting lines

> Such as we were we gave ourselves outright
> (The deed of gift was many deeds of war)
> To the land vaguely realizing westward,
> But still unstoried, artless, unenhanced,
> Such as she was, such as she would become.[1]

Presumably, it was to be the task of American architects to carry out a just share of that hoped-for enhancement. The architects I have mentioned above were certainly aware of this responsibility and assumed that they were fulfilling it; having come into possession of a thinly furnished country in an almost empty New World, when it came to choosing models it was natural for them to look back again and again to the Old World. In the course of doing so, they manifested, not for the first time and not for the last, the essential irrationality of architecture as an art. For if architecture, which Wright insisted on calling the mother-art, were based upon anything as rational as the need for shelter, then any country, or any portion of a country, would develop within a readily measurable span of time an indigenous style, ideally suited to the climate, topography, and economic conditions of the region. Nothing so rational ever happens; on the contrary, the art of architecture imposes, not without great hardship, a literary or aesthetic ideal that is often almost laughably inappropriate to its setting.

As Wright himself confessed, the profession of architecture keeps producing styles instead of a style. Jefferson, for example, happened to admire French architecture as much as he deplored that of the British. Having chosen as a site for his home a remote and inaccessible mountaintop, he spent the rest of his life fiddling with Monticello in order to make it resemble the stylish one-story-high pavilions that he had watched his French friends building in the outskirts of Paris. A pavilion that functioned well in Paris could scarcely function at all when perched high on the edge of a primeval forest in the Blue Ridge mountains of Virginia. Jefferson's guests froze in winter and baked in summer and although there was plenty of wine, water was always in short supply. What matter? Jefferson in his green fastness was à la mode du Faubourg St. Honoré. The parallels between the overextended Jefferson struggling in the eighteen-twenties to keep up Monticello and the overextended Wright struggling a hundred years later to keep up Taliesin are very close and would strike us as comic if they were not at the same time, on a domestic scale, so touchingly heroic.

© SUSAN WOLDENBERG

Midsummer at Taliesin. Ripening corn fills the valley of the "God-Almighty" Joneses.

Wright railed against styles in architecture ("We do not choose the style . . . style . . . will be what we are"[2]) and mocked the degree to which architects were the puppets of fashion, but in doing so he underestimated the power of fashion to alter our lives, by no means always for the worse. The fact is that fashion has no more to do with common sense than architecture does; they are equally absurd and equally irresistible, and for the same unreasonable reason: they nourish us and make us happy. Nor should it distress us that happiness can be derived from anything so apparently insubstantial as fashion. Fashion is not insubstantial, though it is fleeting and unpredictable. It is as hard as steel and not to be eluded by timidity on our part, much less by our adopting a touch-me-not air of superiority to it. We do not embrace fashion; fashion embraces us. Among its many other uses, it serves to keep us looking outward as well as inward; a change of fashion is always an occasion of promise. (One thinks of Tennyson's defense of change as being necessary "lest one good custom should corrupt the world.") It seems to assure us of an opportunity to make a fresh start, and behind all the changing fashions in architecture that we consent to— and are right to consent to—that grandly primordial fact continuously emerges and justifies our otherwise silly and sheeplike pursuit of novelty. Wright misread the nature of fashion, seeing it as frivolous instead of fundamental; ironically, in the course of attacking it he established a fashion of his own, in dress, manner, and architectural design. It was shrewd of his uncle, Jenkin Lloyd Jones, to refer to Wright's earliest works as his "Oscar Wilde houses." Oak Park was not known for its fin-de-siècle decadence, but Wilde and Wright had more in common than mere dandyism.

We read the architectural history of our country in terms of the fashions that have dominated it from one decade to the next. Throughout much of the nineteenth century, despite repeated efforts to break free, it was to England that we turned for guidance; the Victorian period marked the height of the power and glory of the British Empire and we reflected the fashions of that Empire in the absence of any popular homegrown alternative. Aside from the log cabin, which is about equally owed to the Irish and the Swedes, what native product had we to boast of? From Victorian England came a succession of models, many of them derived as much from literature and ecclesiology as from architectural precedent. Popular English Gothic novels led to a vogue in this country for English Gothic castles, the best of them designed by Alexander Jackson Davis; humble indeed was the American city or town whose leading citizen did not attempt to imitate an Abbotsford (and in many cases bankrupted himself in the process).

By the late eighteen-seventies, Victorian Gothic had had its way with us from coast to coast, in houses, churches, colleges, hospitals, power stations, railroad stations, armories, and jails. Our architects and their clients were enjoying certain other flings as well, in the so-called Italianate style, the French Empire style, and the château style lifted by Hunt from the French Renaissance. The hard-bitten, self-made millionaires who commissioned these châteaux may well have gained the impression, glancing out over their stone moats, that Fifth Avenue, in New York City, and Prairie Avenue, in Chicago, were convenient American versions of the Loire, much improved by having been drained and paved. If you could not afford a château, a style arrived from England in the eighteen-eighties that almost anyone could afford in one size and shape or another. For no very clear reason, the style was called Queen Anne, and it gave architects an opportunity to avoid monotony in design by embracing a calculated chaos. Wright's first architectural employer and mentor, J. L. Silsbee, was a master of the style, and in gaining the romantic effect admired by his clients he depended less upon chaos than most of his contemporaries. The Hillside Home School, which Wright is supposed to have designed under Silsbee's guidance, was a big, breezy, self-confident structure, putting more emphasis (as befits a school) upon the hygienic advantages of cross-ventilation and open porches than upon romance.

The Queen Anne style is to be seen at its best in the small cities and suburbs of America; there the rising middle class realized its boyhood dreams of making good by acquiring a house with a round tower, a pillared front piazza, and big bay windows that stared blindly across a narrow strip of grass at their neighbors' equally big bay windows. It was houses in this style that Wright in the eighteen-nineties found himself designing for ambitious businessmen in the suburbs of Chicago, and it can be said in his behalf that, perhaps because of his training under Silsbee, he managed to find something of interest in a style that, as a brash young man in a hurry, he might well have been tempted to parody.

Queen Anne, neo-Colonial, Tudor—Wright plunged headlong through what he would afterward think of as unavoidable preliminaries. (In old age he called the dining room of his charming little Oak Park cottage "a youthful indiscretion," but he was far from feeling that way about it when he drew the plans). Then came a succession of houses—the Heller, the Husser, and, among unbuilt projects, the McAfee and Devin houses—that, as Manson points out, owe a good deal to Sullivan but that are also, to my eye, much in debt to European sources. If Wright was indeed working his way toward the horizontal Prairie House, why these experiments in the vertical, which was also the most conspicuous dimension in the Furbeck, Fricke, and W. E. Martin houses? I suspect that they are the fruit of that incessant, wide-ranging observation and study of the practice of his fellow architects abroad that Wright kept up throughout his life and was always at pains to disguise; do we not observe in them hints of

German and Austrian originals? It appears to have been a necessary aspect of Wright's high self-regard to boast again and again of an absence of precedents in his work. When he admitted a precedent, it would usually turn out to be either Sullivan (his chosen surrogate father-brother-son) or some remote figure such as Froebel, talk of whose delightful, trifling "gifts" would be likely to throw us off the track of the real sources of his inspiration. Just as, early in his career, Wright pretended not to understand why he was addressed in Germany as "the American Olbrich," so later he pretended not to have been influenced by Mies, Le Corbusier, or any other contemporary. One ends by feeling sorry that, though he was capable of learning and absorbing so much, the demands of his ego prevented him from acknowledging that he possessed this capacity to the nth degree in the field of architecture. Plainly, he possessed it—and rejoiced to possess it—in the fields of literature and history: as a college dropout who had managed to educate himself through the reading of scores and hundreds of stout volumes, he would always pay grateful tribute to his sources, but in architecture he sought to establish himself simply and implausibly as the Prime Mover.

The very catholicity of the precedents on which Wright drew is part of his claim to being considered the greatest of *American* architects. And it is worth noting that this title (so important to him and otherwise so irrelevant) doesn't in the least imply that he has provided us with an American style. There is no such thing as an American style, much less *the* American style, and there is no such thing as a Wright style, much less *the* Wright style. We are a polyglot nation and the fact that Wright's work is polyglot should not be perceived as a mere coincidence; nevertheless, its multifariousness owes far more to Wright's having passed through many stages of development in the course of a long life than to his seeking to be representatively American. Not that Wright himself would have consented to this lessening of the scope of his intentions. He wrote endlessly, in book after book, about the nature of the architecture that America deserved and that he was the man best fitted to present it with, but his writings and his architecture are often enough at odds. He was an evangelist, with the unreliability of all evangelists in the presence of hard facts. The hortatory rhetoric with which he described Broadacre City or the Usonian house has no necessary connection with his designs for them. The ideal America that he wrote about and talked about might have been realized— unluckily, might yet be realized—as a coast-to-coast, bumper-to-bumper Levittown.

Playfully, Wright would sometimes devise connections between one Wright structure and another—for example, the Larkin as the male lover of the feminine Johnson Wax—but the only serious connections that exist between his buildings are those related to the purpose for which they were designed, the period in which they were designed, and his emotional state at the time that he designed them. We cannot examine seven or eight hundred Wright structures and projects for structures and detect in them a characteristic American motif or theme. Even the greatest of American architects is no more likely to perform such a feat than the greatest of our novelists is likely to write what will be universally hailed by critics as the great American novel. The country is too big and too complex to lend itself to such sterile parlor-game simplicities. Still, there *is* a sense in which Wright may be said to be more thoroughly American as an architect than most of his predecessors and contemporaries, and that is in respect to the astonishingly wide geographical distribution of his work. There are Wright buildings in thirty-six states, and although thick clusterings of them exist, as one might expect, in Wisconsin, Michigan, Ohio, Indiana, and Illinois, examples of his handiwork are also to be found in Florida, California, Texas, and Connecticut. New York, in Wright's day the most densely populated state in the union, is notorious for the scarcity of Wright works that it possesses: fifteen in all. Thinly populated Utah understandably possesses but one, and of the states that possess none the most surprising to me are Maine, North Carolina, and Rhode Island, upon whose coasts clients of the kind that might have been counted on to appreciate Wright's work have built many a cantilevered imitation-Wright pavilion but never the genuine article.

When we glance about at the imitations of Wright, we find that they, too, in their deplorable profusion, amount to a measure of his Americanness. For what other American architect has been imitated so often in the past hundred years? And not in one style only, like Cliff May with his sensual Southern California ranch houses or Royal Barry Wills, with his chaste little Cape Cod cottages; Wright has been imitated in the Prairie House style, the Usonian house style, and even the troglodytic house style of Taliesin West, winding serpentlike along its rosy concrete-and-stone revetments. Wright claimed to have invented the carport as a substitute for the garage (an early example of its use is in the first Jacobs house) and the hundreds of thousands of maladroit carports scattered across America today may be said to be indirect imitations of Wright, as are the high clerestory windows, the tiny, open-ended kitchens, and the broad-eaved roofs that have served as symbols of contemporary domestic architecture for a couple of generations of diligent Wright copyists. On that low aesthetic level and on the much loftier aesthetic levels of Romeo and Juliet and Fallingwater and Beth Sholom, elements of Wright's designs and of the reasoning process that they embody have become a part of our national consciousness. He is a highly visible presence among us; he is also a potent invisible one. We do not let him go and he does not let us go.

●

Thanks to the great age that Wright attained, he may be said to have encompassed within his immediate family something like four centuries of American history. His grandfather Wright was born in 1788, a year after the Constitutional Convention; he himself flourished throughout much of the nineteenth and twentieth centuries; and his grandchildren, whom he knew well, will presumably live far into the twenty-first century. (Two of the grandchildren are architects: Elizabeth Wright Ingraham, practicing in Colorado Springs, and Eric Lloyd Wright, practicing in Los Angeles.) Wright relished the sense of participating in so broad a span of time; with his usual cockiness, he looked forward to a place in history among a small company of his peers: Lincoln (for whom, after all, he had been named), Emerson, Whitman, Twain, and the like. These are figures so remote from us in 1987 that it is hard to recollect that Emerson—who had rubbed shoulders in Boston with Charles Bulfinch (1763–1844), our first native-born professional architect—had lived on into Wright's boyhood, that Whitman had lived on into Wright's manhood, and that Twain had lived on into Wright's early middle age. It was into their lonely continent, their time of bloody Indian and fratricidal wars, their rural and politically corrupt culture, that Wright was born; it was an America violent, disputatious, and untender that provides the background against which Wright deserves to be judged.

Only rarely does it occur to us to examine that nineteenth-century background of Wright's because he encouraged us during his lifetime to treat him as a prankish contemporary, a Peck's Bad Boy bent upon shocking us even in his eighties. Thanks to our recollection of him in this role, he may strike us as being too insistently outrageous, too demanding of our attention, too eager to be a star of the "media" to measure up to the standard that we are accustomed to setting for our great men. (Perhaps it was this aspect of Wright that caused Arthur Miller to compare him to W. C. Fields.) The Wright of the eighteen-seventies was a bewitching boy, growing up before the advent of electric lights, telephones, automobiles, aircraft, radios, and television, to say nothing of indoor plumbing, central heating, and buildings of steel and glass that rose ten or fifteen stories above the street and that, borrowing from sailors' slang, would soon come to be called skyscrapers. Overnight, the penniless Wisconsin rube, a runaway from home and mother, found himself blinking with delight under the white arc-lights of Chicago. Nothing had prepared him for the urban wonders of the Loop: theatres, cabarets, saloons, a deafening cacophony of songs and cries. At that moment, he had everything to learn.

The speed with which the rube transformed himself into a dude, the dude into a fashionable young bachelor, the bachelor into a bridegroom, and the bridegroom into the ill-prepared father may well account for, if not justify, the alternation of indulgence and privation that he inflicted upon his bewildered first wife and their six children. How charming he was to them and how cruel! Late in his life, John Lloyd Wright was to recall that the relationship between his father and him had been one of a continuous lacerating oscillation between being spoiled and being bullied. It was a pattern that Wright imposed not only upon members of his first family but upon his mistresses, his second and third wives, his seventh child, his apprentices, and even upon his clients. And nearly always it was the case that each of them in turn forgave him, because of the degree to which their lives had been heightened and intensified by him. He was

Beret jauntily in place and suspenders askew, the old wizard surveys his beloved kingdom. [EWI]

an elixir, delectable and addictive, and if, as Stanley Marcus has said, "Frank could make you feel like a moron," he could also make you feel like the chosen companion of a god.

In his last decades, Wright consented with a saving humor to his role as a divinity, the machinery of the cult being (or so he pretended) out of his hands; it was Olgivanna who had taken charge of that aspect of his life and who assumed responsibility for the day-to-day manipulation of his comings and goings. After the resurrection, Christ said, "In a little while, ye shall not see me and again a little while and ye shall see me," and it was by no means sacrilegious on the part of the faithful at Taliesin to have felt that Wright's unpredictable appearances and disappearances had a similar element of the miraculous about them. Nor did it strike

John Lloyd Wright as unnatural to call his biography of Wright *My Father Who Is on Earth*. He was being mildly facetious as well as mildly blasphemous, but an authentic awe (and an authentic anguish) was concealed within the title as well.

In an unpublished memorandum, John Lloyd Wright wrote, "Placed on a pedestal in Rome is an equestrian statue by Bernini of the Emperor Constantine, who had his father-in-law hanged, his brother-in-law strangled, his nephew's throat cut, his wife smothered in a bath, and his favorite son beheaded. All through ancient history sons of great men were beheaded, hanged, thrown into dungeons, and pitched into the sea. The more tender-hearted of the great fathers just quietly smothered them. In the words of Genghis Khan, 'There cannot be two suns in the heaven nor two Khans on the earth.' "[3] He struggled to see his father clearly as both his rival and his champion: "At one time his disinterest in my work depressed me. But I soon realized that he was so engrossed in himself that there was little left for me, except as I might be useful to him in attaining his aim. . . ."[4] At the same time, with a mingling of resentment and gratitude: "Since I understand him, his insistent reiteration that I am an ass and that all that is good stems from him loses much of its ominous sting. If enemies pursue, the cacophony blossoms into a herald call, 'John, I'm coming down and clean them up!' "[5]

Unlike his elder brother, Lloyd, who throughout his life chose a course of blind loyalty to their father, John Lloyd Wright was genuinely eager to come to grips with Wright as a phenomenon. He wrote:

> My father's domestic life has posed many problems for this son. There was a constant struggle between the head and the heart. I first remember him as the head of our household, owned by the family. Second, I remember him owned by a lady love he desired to marry but could not because my mother would not let him. Third he was owned by a poetess from Paree, or some place, whom he inadvertently married when my mother let him. Fourth, he was owned by a beloved object whom he married after adjudication of unique complexities and by whom he has, I thought, remained owned. The fifth shock was when he told me he was owned by a Foundation.[6]

With wit and sadness, John Lloyd Wright ended by imagining the epitaph on his tombstone: "Here lies John Lloyd Wright, accidentally shot as a mark of affection by his father."[7] John sent his father an early copy of *My Father Who Is on Earth*, which his father had gently urged him not to write. Wright's response to the book was kindlier than might have been expected. He returned the book with a number of emendations scribbled in pencil in the margins. The son transcribed these annotations in still another copy of the book and then added his annotations to the parental annotations, often impishly correcting them. "There is some truth in it," Wright wrote, of the book. ". . . Dad hopes you will get some money out of this (on the whole) well-written washing of family linen—soiled, but not so dirty as one might think?"[8] And among Wright's tiny penciled annotations is a description of himself as he suspects the reader is bound to see

Left, John Lloyd Wright. Right, Lloyd Wright, FLW, and Eric Lloyd Wright, son of Lloyd. [ELW]

him: "The man apparently was a sort of clever confidence-man, winning by sheer dexterity over those of more solid worth and greater attainments. . . . Many suffered in silence that he might glitter—I know! I know!"[9] So the man-god himself was capable of being wounded, if not brought down; there was blood in him and he could bleed.

So resourceful was Olgivanna in the carrying out of the rituals associated with Wright's divinity that what amounted to a feat of sleight-of-hand took place after his death: the funeral once successfully got past, the preparations that had been begun much earlier for the celebration of Wright's ninety-second birthday (officially his ninetieth) were continued with unabated energy and good cheer. Indeed, the funeral came to seem like an interruption and not a full stop to a life that, having largely outwitted old age, appeared capable of outwitting death as well. The birthday party in June at Taliesin West was every bit as happy an occasion as the Easter party in April that Wright had sauntered through a few days before being taken away to the hospital. Uncannily, he was no less present for being absent, and this quasi-religious, quasi-magical feat continued to be performed year after year on the appointed holy days.

The last Easter party that I attended at Taliesin West, in 1984, boasted the traditional parabolas of many-colored balloons against the brilliant Arizona sky, the traditional festive food and drink (including those arduously prepared high babas), and the traditional army of guests. "Young" Harold Price was there—young in his late fifties—and Orme Lewis, Wright's attorney, and Jean and Howard Lipman; among the Fellowship were Wes Peters, Bruce Pfeiffer, Dick Carney, Charles Montooth, and a dozen others. Although Olgivanna was in her late eighties and almost totally deaf and blind, in her indomitable fashion she pretended to hear and see as well as ever. Under a hat broad-brimmed to ward off the sun and in a garb that may have owed something to Montenegro and certainly owed much to her imagination, she sat with me at lunch, smiling, dark-eyed, and handsome. As we chatted, I sensed her determination to preside with a show of undiminished strength and grace over a springtime ritual that now, after almost half a century, was being gently wrested from her grasp. She had served as the priestess of a shrine whose god had steadily gained in puissance over the years; now she was failing, now against her will she was slipping away (had already, in respect to her sight, slipped away into a first darkness), but the god remained.

It was true that many people had found Olgivanna difficult to deal with in the long years of her proprietorship of Wright. Others had felt a sympathy for the woman who, like so many men and women living within range of Wright's irresistible magnetism, fought hard to achieve a separate identity. At one time or another, she was to attempt dancing, composing, writing—they were all but patchwork. The daughter she had by her first husband died young, in an automobile accident; the daughter she had by Wright was fated to lead a life unworthy of her gifts. Olgivanna's vocation proved to be a narrow one, though not because she had intended it to be. Long ago, she and I had quarreled, perhaps for no better reason than that we both found quarreling an acceptable form of social intercourse. Be that as it may, on that last Easter afternoon, embracing her fragile body in goodbye, I could think only of her gallantry. She had lived under Wright's spell and had done more than anyone else to keep that spell alive by means of the Fellowship and the Frank Lloyd Wright Foundation. "God help them when I am gone!" Wright had exclaimed, and it was Olgivanna who for almost thirty years had struggled to keep the two Taliesins more or less intact, both physically and (as she would have said) spiritually.

It was—and is—a task hopeless by nature, one capable of achieving only a temporary appearance of success. For sooner or later the best-kept shrine is bound to be seen as empty, the god as no longer in residence and therefore no longer in a position to dispense either charity or wrath. Something like this is what one already observes with sadness, visiting either of the Taliesins. They are monasteries that, despite their unrealized material wealth (the hundreds of acres of land, valued in the millions; the thousands of Wright drawings, valued in the tens of millions), have grown impoverished through the inexorable, punitive attritions of age, loss of energy, and lack of purpose. The more elderly votaries dye their hair to keep themselves looking as young as they were when "Mr." Wright flourished among them, but they primp in vain. The Wright they speak of with deferential ardor will not be rounding the corner, cane in hand, to greet them; he is dust, somewhere on the desert floor.

It is another Wright who flourishes today, far beyond the boundaries of his life and time. His fame multiplies at a rate that even he would find satisfactory. Admiration of his handiwork approaches the universal. Who complains any longer that his roofs leak, that his chairs draw blood, that he never used to pay his bills? Old scamp, old teller of lies, old maker of wonders! How do you manage to go on performing this feat of hypnotism upon us? For it is the case that we are all more or less continuously under Wright's spell, sometimes when we would least expect to be, or wish to

be. Again and again, a moment comes when in our imaginations we find ourselves crowding about the young-old wizard. We fall silent, sensing that something is about to happen. In his low, melodious voice, he begins to describe what he has it in mind to set down upon the white sheet of paper that lies before him. A tray of colored pencils is at his elbow. A fire crackles on a nearby stone hearth. "An open fire is an aid to creative effort," he likes to say. And then, with his usual twinkle, "And so is a baked onion."

We watch in awe as from a hand moving lightly and swiftly across the drafting table there leaps into being something never seen before.

For photographs (as keyed) I am grateful to the following:

AI	The Art Institute of Chicago
AL	Avery Architectural and Fine Arts Library, Columbia University
AP	Associated Press/Wide World Photos, Inc.
AR	Reproduced from *Architectural Record*
AU	Reproduced from *An Autobiography* by Frank Lloyd Wright, Longmans, Green and Co. (copyright Frank Lloyd Wright Foundation, 1932)
BEC	Buffalo and Erie County Historical Society
CCL	Commission on Chicago Landmarks
CJ	Reproduced from *Imperial Hotel* by Cary James, Charles E. Tuttle Co., Inc. of Tokyo, Japan
DB	Reproduced from *Herkimers, Holsteins & Cheese* by Judith Redline Coopey, courtesy Donald Brace
ELW	Eric Lloyd Wright
ET	Reproduced from *Years With Frank Lloyd Wright* by Edgar Tafel
EWI	Elizabeth Wright Ingraham
EWJ	Elaine Wright Jones
FA	Felicity Ashbee
FS	Reproduced from *The First Hundred Years*, courtesy Florida Southern College
HM	Hedy C. Margolies
HR	State Historical Society of Iowa, Iowa City, courtesy Hope Rogers
HS	Frank Lloyd Wright Home and Studio Foundation
IL	Reproduced from *Olbrich* by Ian Latham, Academy Editions, London
JP	Reproduced from *The Story of the Tower*, photographs by Joe Price
JW	Johnson Wax
LA	Los Angeles Public Library

LC	Library of Congress
MJ	*Milwaukee Journal* Photo
MPL	*Minneapolis Journal* Photo, courtesy the Minneapolis History Collection, Minneapolis Public Library
NY	The New-York Historical Society
PF	Phil Feddersen
PL	Philip Lyman
RA	Reproduced from *Antonin Raymond*, Charles E. Tuttle Co., Inc. of Tokyo, Japan
RF	Hilla Rebay Foundation
RT	Roy Thurman
SA	Stanford University Archives
TS	Tim Samuelson
UA	University Archives, State University of New York at Buffalo
WF	© Frank Lloyd Wright Foundation
WH	Reproduced from *The Prairie School Review*, courtesy Wilbert Hasbrouck
WMF	Frank Lloyd Wright Memorial Foundation
WS	Walter Bill Schmidt
WW	William Walker

Photographs by Philander Barclay, courtesy The Historical Society of Oak Park and River Forest; photographs by Grant Carpenter Manson, courtesy Oak Park Public Library; photographs by Richard Nickel, courtesy Richard Nickel Committee; photographs by Obma Studio, courtesy Frank Lloyd Wright Memorial Foundation.

FLW jacket photo (which appears also on final page of text), courtesy FLW Home and Studio. Photo montage at the end of Chapter 11: Unity Temple, © Susan Woldenberg; Secessionist Art Gallery, [IL]; Larkin building [BEC].

NOTES

CHAPTER 1

1. F. Schumacher & Co., catalogue, 1986.

CHAPTER 2

1. Frank Lloyd Wright, *An Autobiography,* second edition (Duell, Sloan and Pearce, 1943), p. 11. (Hereafter cited as FLW, *Auto.*)
2. FLW, *Auto,* ibid.
3. Elizabeth Wright Heller, "The Story of My Life" (unpublished manuscript, Iowa State Historical Society Iowa City), pp. 8–9.
4. FLW, *Auto,* p. 12.
5. Pamphlet, courtesy Elaine Wright Jones.
6. Correspondence, courtesy Elaine Wright Jones.

CHAPTER 3

1. Heller, "Story of My Life," pp. 18–19.
2. FLW, *Auto,* pp. 13–14.
3. FLW, *Auto* (first edition, 1932), p. 12.
4. Ibid.
5. FLW, *Auto,* p. 14.
6. Ibid., p. 16.
7. Ibid., p. 19.
8. Ibid., p. 25.
9. Heller, p. 45.
10. FLW, *Auto,* pp. 48–49.

CHAPTER 4

1. FLW, *Auto,* p. 50.
2. Heller, "Story of My Life," p. 111.

3. William C. Wright vs. Anna L. Wright Divorce File, Circuit Court for Dane County, Wisconsin, 1884–1885.
4. FLW, *Auto*, p. 51.
5. Ibid., pp. 59–60.
6. Tim Samuelson, "Sullivan and Adler" (unpublished manuscript), p. 1.

CHAPTER 5

1. *Western Architect*, June, 1924, p. 64.
2. Louis H. Sullivan, *The Autobiography of an Idea* (American Institute of Architects, 1924; Dover Publications, 1956), p. 9.
3. Ibid., pp. 9–10.
4. Ibid., p. 14.
5. Ibid., pp. 15–16.
6. FLW, *Auto*, p. 49.
7. Sullivan, *Auto*, pp. 186–190 passim.
8. Ibid., pp. 191–192.
9. Ibid., p. 196.
10. Carl Condit, *Macmillan Encyclopedia of Architects* (Macmillan, 1982), volume 2, p. 494.
11. Sullivan, *Auto*, pp. 234–235.
12. Ibid., p. 240.
13. Ibid., p. 251.
14. Ibid., p. 256.

CHAPTER 6

1. FLW, *Auto*, p. 104.
2. Sullivan, *Auto*, p. 56.
3. Ibid., p. 64.
4. FLW, *Auto*, p. 271, as quoted in David S. Andrew, *Louis Sullivan and the Polemics of Modern Architecture* (University of Illinois Press, 1985), p. 13.
5. Andrew, *Louis Sullivan*, p. 13.
6. Ibid., pp. 88–89.
7. FLW, *Frank Lloyd Wright on Architecture* (Duell, Sloan and Pearce, 1941), p. 183.
8. FLW, *Auto*, p. 97.
9. Ibid., p. 101.
10. George Elmslie to FLW, 6/12/36, Northwest Architectural Archives, the University of Minnesota (William Gray Purcell Collection). Reprinted, *Journal of the Society of Architectural Historians*, Vol. XX, Number 3 (October, 1961), p. 140.

CHAPTER 7

1. FLW, *Auto*, p. 105.
2. Ibid.

3. Ibid., p. 104.
4. Ibid., p. 106.
5. Ibid., p. 109.
6. Ibid., p. 107.
7. Grant Carpenter Manson, *Frank Lloyd Wright to 1910* (Van Nostrand Reinhold Company, 1958), p. 27.
8. FLW, *Auto,* pp. 110–111.

CHAPTER 8

1. FLW, *Auto,* pp. 113–114.
2. Manson, Frank Lloyd Wright, p. 62.
3. Henry-Russell Hitchcock, *In the Nature of Materials* (Duell, Sloan and Pearce, 1942), caption to Plate 28.
4. FLW, *Auto,* p. 128.
5. Ibid., p. 129.
6. Ibid., p. 128.
7. Ibid.
8. Ibid., p. 118.
9. Ibid., pp. 135–136.
10. Ibid., pp. 137–138.
11. Ibid., p. 136.

CHAPTER 9

1. FLW, *Auto,* p. 139.
2. Ibid.
3. Leonard K. Eaton, *Two Chicago Architects and Their Clients: Frank Lloyd Wright and Howard van Doren Shaw* (M.I.T. Press, 1969), p. 96.

CHAPTER 10

1. Letter from W. E. Martin to Darwin D. Martin, 10/2/02 (University Archives, SUNY Buffalo).
2. Letter from DDM to John Larkin, 3/20/03 (SUNY Buffalo).
3. Ibid.
4. DDM to his wife, 8/14/03 (SUNY Buffalo).
5. WEM to DDM, 5/20/04 (SUNY Buffalo).
6. FLW to DDM, 7/14/04 (SUNY Buffalo).
7. DDM to FLW, 9/16/04 (SUNY Buffalo).
8. Ibid.
9. DDM to FLW, 9/29/04 (SUNY Buffalo).
10. FLW to DDM, 10/13/04 (SUNY Buffalo).
11. FLW to DDM, 7/28/05 (SUNY Buffalo).

12. WEM to DDM, 9/12/05 (SUNY Buffalo).
13. FLW to DDM, 9/19/05 (SUNY Buffalo).
14. WEM to DDM, 9/19/05 (SUNY Buffalo).
15. Ibid.
16. DDM to FLW and WEM, 9/21/05 (SUNY Buffalo).
17. DDM to FLW, 12/30/05 (SUNY Buffalo).
18. FLW to DDM, 1/2/06 (SUNY Buffalo).

CHAPTER 11

1. FLW, *Auto,* p. 152.
2. FLW, *Larkin Idea,* issue of November, 1906 (reprinted in *Prairie School Review,* first quarter, 1970).
3. FLW, unpublished letter to *Architectural Record,* 1908 (reprinted in *Journal of the Society of Architectural Historians,* October, 1982).
4. Edgar Tafel, *Years With Frank Lloyd Wright* (Dover Publications, 1979), pp. 86–87.
5. FLW, *Auto,* p. 154.
6. FLW and Dr. Rodney F. Johonnot, *The New Edifice of Unity Church* (privately printed brochure, 1906).
7. George Elmslie, letter to FLW, 10/30/32 (Northwestern Architectural Archive).

CHAPTER 12

1. Donald Hoffmann, *Frank Lloyd Wright's Robie House* (Dover Publications, 1984), p. 34.
2. Ibid., p. 94.
3. FLW, *Auto,* p. 507.
4. Janet Ashbee's journal, 1908 (Ashbee Journals, King's College Library, Cambridge, England; courtesy Felicity Ashbee).
5. Manson, *Frank Lloyd Wright,* p. 212.
6. Ibid.
7. Finis Farr, *Frank Lloyd Wright* (Scribner, 1961), p. 117.
8. Ibid., pp. 117–118.
9. Ibid., p. 118.
10. Ibid., p. 119.
11. FLW, *Auto,* p. 163.

CHAPTER 13

1. FLW, *Auto,* p. 164.
2. Ibid., p. 165.
3. Letter, FLW to C. R. Ashbee, 3/10/10 (Ashbee Journals).
4. Letter, FLW to CRA, 7/8/10 (Ashbee Journals).

5. Letter, William E. Martin to Darwin D. Martin, 10/10/10 (University Archives, SUNY Buffalo).
6. Catherine Lloyd Wright letter to Janet and C. R. Ashbee, 10/12/10 (King's College, Cambridge, England).
7. FLW, *Auto,* p. 167.
8. *Chicago Tribune,* 12/26/11.
9. Ibid.
10. *Wisconsin State Journal,* 12/30/11.

CHAPTER 14

1. FLW, *Auto,* pp. 184–185.
2. Ibid., p. 185.
3. *Chicago Tribune,* 8/17/14.
4. Ibid.
5. FLW, *Auto,* pp. 185–186.
6. Ibid., p. 188.
7. *Weekly Home News,* Spring Green, 8/20/14.
8. Ibid.
9. Ibid.
10. FLW, *Auto,* p. 187.
11. Ibid., pp. 189–190.
12. *Chicago Tribune,* 11/17/15.
13. Ibid., 11/8/15.
14. Ibid.
15. FLW, *Architectural Record,* May, 1914.
16. Ibid.
17. FLW, *Auto,* pp. 193–194.
18. Ibid., p. 194.
19. Ibid., p. 204.
20. Margaret Scott, *Frank Lloyd Wright's Warehouse in Richland Center* (Richland County Publishers, 1984), p. 128.
21. Vincent Scully, *Frank Lloyd Wright* (Braziller, 1960), p. 24.

CHAPTER 15

1. FLW, *Auto,* p. 224.
2. Norman Bel Geddes, *Miracle in the Evening* (Doubleday, 1960), pp. 155–157.
3. Ibid., pp. 163–164.
4. *Letters to Clients: Frank Lloyd Wright,* edited by Bruce Brooks Pfeiffer (California State University Press, 1986), p. 31. FLW to Aline Barnsdall, 6/27/21.
5. FLW, *Auto,* pp. 168, 174 passim.
6. Ibid., p. 230.
7. Unpublished letter, FLW to Miriam Noel, June, 1919.
8. FLW, *Auto,* pp. 214–216 passim.
9. Antonin Raymond, *An Autobiography* (Charles E. Tuttle, 1973), p. 76.

10. Ibid., p. 70.
11. FLW, *Auto*, p. 223.
12. Raymond, pp. 71–72.
13. Ibid., p. 77.
14. FLW, *Auto*, p. 222.

CHAPTER 16

1. *Frank Lloyd Wright on Architecture,* edited by Frederick Gutheim (Duell, Sloan and Pearce, 1941), p. 88.
2. FLW, *Auto*, p. 239.
3. Ibid., p. 241.
4. Ibid.
5. Ibid., p. 249.
6. Ibid., pp. 249–250.
7. Ibid., pp. 251–252.
8. Letter, FLW to Lloyd Wright, 6/26/21 (courtesy Eric Lloyd Wright).
9. LW telegram to FLW, unspecified date, just prior to 4/13/24 (courtesy ELW).
10. FLW telegram to LW (courtesy ELW).
11. LW telegrams to Will Smith and FLW, 4/24, undated (courtesy ELW).
12. Letter, FLW to LW, 9/15/24 (courtesy ELW).
13. Letter, FLW to Mr. and Mrs. Charles Ennis, 9/4/24 (courtesy ELW).
14. *Frank Lloyd Wright: Letters to Clients,* edited by Pfeiffer, p. 218. FLW to John Nesbitt, 4/24/40.
15. Ibid., p. 220. FLW to John Nesbitt, 8/3/41.
16. Letter, FLW to LW, undated, ca. 1925 (courtesy ELW).

CHAPTER 17

1. Letter, FLW to LW, undated (courtesy ELW).
2. FLW, *Auto*, p. 260.
3. Ibid.
4. Ibid., pp. 261–263 passim.
5. Ibid., p. 509.
6. Ibid., p. 510.
7. *Weekly Home News,* Spring Green, 6/10/26.
8. FLW, *Auto*, p. 280.
9. *Twin City Reporter,* Minneapolis, 11/5/26 (University Archives, SUNY Buffalo).
10. Undated typescript by Frank Lloyd Wright (ca. 11/5/26), accompanying typed copy of editorial from the *Twin City Reporter* of 11/5/26 (SUNY Buffalo).
11. Ibid.
12. *Philadelphia Ledger,* 10/28/26 (SUNY Buffalo).
13. *Milwaukee Journal,* 5/8/32 (SUNY Buffalo).
14. Ibid.
15. Ibid.

CHAPTER 18

1. FLW, *Auto,* p. 112.
2. FLW, *Architectural Record,* June 1941, p. 7.
3. Ibid.
4. FLW, *Auto,* p. 307.
5. Ibid., p. 310.
6. Ibid., pp. 313–315 passim.
7. FLW, *Auto,* p. 312.
8. Bruce Brooks Pfeiffer, *Treasures of Taliesin* (California State University Press, 1985), Plate 16a.
9. Ibid., p. 259.
10. Letter, FLW to W. R. Heath, 10/4/27 (University Archives, SUNY Buffalo).
11. Letter, FLW to DDM, 2/5/25 (SUNY Buffalo).
12. Letter, FLW to DDM, 11/1/25 (SUNY Buffalo).
13. Letter, DDM to FLW, 5/5/26 (SUNY Buffalo).
14. Letter, FLW to DDM, 5/16/26 (SUNY Buffalo).
15. Letter, DDM to FLW, 1/3/27 (SUNY Buffalo).
16. Letter, FLW to Mrs. Martin, 12/6/35 (SUNY Buffalo).
17. Letter, FLW to DDM, received 8/21/30 (SUNY Buffalo).
18. Letter, FLW to DDM, 1/10/31 (SUNY Buffalo).

CHAPTER 19

1. *Architectural Record,* Volume LXIV (December 1928), p. 512.
2. Letter, FLW to LW, 6/19/31 (courtesy ELW).
3. Letter, FLW to Rudolph Schindler, 6/19/31 (courtesy ELW).
4. *Architectural Record,* Volume LXIV (December 1928), p. 507.
5. Ibid.
6. FLW, *Frank Lloyd Wright on Architecture,* p. 130.
7. FLW, *Modern Architecture* (Princeton University Press, 1931), p. 115.
8. Tafel, *FLW,* p. 139.
9. Ibid.
10. FLW, *Auto,* p. 390.
11. Ibid.
12. Ibid., p. 391.
13. Ibid., pp. 392–393.
14. Ibid., pp. 432–433.
15. Ibid., p. 399.
16. FLW, *The Disappearing City* (William Farquhar Payson, 1932), pp. 26, 3.
17. Ibid., p. 44

CHAPTER 20

1. Stanley Marcus, conversation with author.
2. Edgar F. Kaufmann, Jr., *Fallingwater* (Abbeville, 1986), p. 39.

3. Ibid., p. 38.

4. Ibid., p. 36.

5. Tafel, *FLW,* p. 3.

6. Donald Hoffmann, *Frank Lloyd Wright's Fallingwater* (Dover Publications, 1978), p. 18.

7. Kaufmann, *Fallingwater,* p. 41.

8. Hoffmann, *FLW's Fallingwater,* p. 23.

9. Letter, FLW to Edgar J. Kaufmann, Sr., 8/27/36 (courtesy Avery Library, Columbia University).

10. Letter, EJK, Sr., to FLW, 8/28/36 (courtesy Avery Library).

11. Kaufmann, *Fallingwater,* pp. 51–54 passim.

CHAPTER 21

1. Jonathan Lipman, *Frank Lloyd Wright & the Johnson Wax Buildings* (Rizzoli, 1986), p. 12. Letter from Ramsay to Johnson, 7/19/36.

2. Ibid., p. 13. Interview with Johnson by Edward Wilder, 1940.

3. FLW, *Auto,* p. 469.

4. Lipman, *FLW,* p. 73. Letter from FLW to Ramsey, undated.

5. Ibid., p. 75. Letter from FLW to Johnson, 12/30/37.

6. Ibid.

7. Ibid., p. 76. Letter from Johnson to FLW, 1/6/38.

8. Telegram, FLW to Hibbard Johnson, 3/38 (Johnson Archive).

9. Telegram, HJ to FLW, 3/38 (Johnson Archive).

10. Telegram, Jack Ramsey to FLW, 3/38 (Johnson Archive).

11. Telegram, FLW to JR, 3/38 (Johnson Archive).

12. Telegram, JR to FLW, 3/38 (Johnson Archive).

13. Telegram, FLW to JR, 3/1/39 (Johnson Archive).

14. FLW, *Auto,* pp. 471–474 passim.

15. Wingspread Dedication Speech by HJ, 6/24/61 (Johnson Archive).

CHAPTER 22

1. Paul R. and Jean S. Hanna, *Frank Lloyd Wright's Hanna House* (MIT Press, 1981), p. 18.

2. Ibid., pp. 20–21. FLW to P. and J. Hanna, 4/7/36.

3. Ibid., p. 23. FLW contract, undated, spring 1936.

4. Ibid., pp. 24–25. FLW to P. and S. Hanna, 6/17/36.

5. Ibid., pp. 47, 48, 51 passim. FLW to P. and S. Hanna, 1/27/37.

6. Ibid., p. 68. P. and J. Hanna to FLW, 8/15/37.

7. Ibid., p. 70. FLW to P. and J. Hanna, 8/18/37.

8. Ibid., p. 72. P. and J. Hanna to FLW, 8/23/37.

CHAPTER 23

1. John Lloyd Wright, *My Father Who Is on Earth,* pp. 77–78.
2. Pfeiffer, *FLW: Letters to Clients,* p. 166. Spivey to FLW, 4/11/38.
3. FLW, *Auto,* p. 500.
4. Letter, FLW to George Sturges, 3/15/41 (courtesy Stanford University Archives).
5. Letter, FLW to GS, 8/4/41 (courtesy Stanford Archives).
6. Pfeiffer, *FLW: Letters to Clients,* p. 206. Lloyd Lewis to FLW, 9/3/40.
7. Ibid., p. 207. FLW to Lloyd Lewis, 9/4/40.
8. Ibid., p. 208. Lloyd Lewis to FLW, 9/5/40.
9. FLW, *Auto,* pp. 496–497.
10. *Times-Herald,* Washington, D. C., 9/40.
11. Ibid., 1/17/41.
12. Ibid., 1/12/41.

CHAPTER 24

1. Broadacre City Petition (courtesy Avery Library).
2. Carleton Smith, unpublished memoirs, pp. 64–65.
3. Herbert Jacobs, *Building with Frank Lloyd Wright* (Chronicle Books, 1978), p. 88.
4. Pfeiffer, *Letters to Clients,* p. 265. FLW to Mrs. Walker, 2/27/51.
5. Ibid., p. 269. FLW to Mrs. Walker, 12/8/52.
6. *City Club Competition* (The University of Chicago Press, 1913), p. 96.
7. *Architectural Forum,* January, 1948, p. 79.
8. Ibid., p. 84.
9. Ibid., p. 123.
10. Ibid., p. 116.

CHAPTER 25

1. Joan Lukach, *Hilla Rebay* (Braziller, 1983), p. 183. Letter, Rebay to FLW, 5/30/43.
2. Ibid., pp. 183–184. Letter, FLW to Hilla Rebay, 6/10/43.
3. Pfeiffer, *The Guggenheim Correspondence,* p. 1.
4. Ibid., p. 18. Letter, FLW to HR, 8/16/43.
5. Ibid., p. 15. Letter, FLW to HR, 7/23/43.
6. Ibid., p. 25. Letter, FLW to Solomon R. Guggenheim, 12/31/43.
7. Ibid., p. 41. Letter, FLW to HR, 1/20/44.
8. Ibid., p. 40.
9. Ibid., p. 47. Letter, FLW to HR, 7/5/44.
10. Ibid., pp. 47–48. Letter, FLW to HR, 7/6/44.
11. Ibid., p. 49. Letter, SRG to FLW, 7/27/44.
12. Ibid., p. 49. Letter, FLW to HR, 8/4/44.

13. Lukach, *Rebay*, p. 191. Letter, HR to FLW, 6/19/45.
14. Ibid., p. 191. Letter, HR to FLW, 6/19/45.
15. Ibid., p. 191. Letter, FLW to HR, 7/25/45.
16. Ibid., p. 195. Letter, HR to FLW, 1/13/45.
17. Ibid., p. 195. Letter, FLW to HR, 1/18/45.

CHAPTER 26

1. Frank Lloyd Wright, *The Story of the Tower* (Horizon Press, 1956), pp. 7–9.
2. Ibid., pp. 16–17.
3. Letter, K. S. Adams to Harold Price, 5/3/56.
4. Letter, HP to K. S. Adams, 5/4/56.
5. Letter, HP to FLW, 5/4/56.
6. Letter, FLW to HP, 11/20/57.

CHAPTER 27

1. Letter, Mortimer Cohen to FLW, 11/16/53 (courtesy Hedy Margolies).
2. Letter, MC to FLW, 12/14/53 (courtesy HM).
3. Letter FLW to MC, 3/15/54 (courtesy HM).
4. FLW speech at groundbreaking, 11/14/54 (courtesy HM).
5. Letter, MC to FLW, 12/54/1/55.
6. Letter, MC to FLW, 4/8/54 (courtesy HM).
7. Letter, MC to FLW, 8/23/57 (courtesy HM).
8. Telegram, FLW to MC, 8/24/57 (courtesy HM).

CHAPTER 28

1. FLW, *Auto,* pp. 353–354.
2. Ibid., p. 547.
3. Pfeiffer, *Treasures of Taliesin,* Plate 64-b.
4. Ibid.
5. Ibid.
6. Ibid., Plate 67-b.
7. Courtesy Hedy Margolies.
8. Letter, Mortimer Cohen to Mrs. FLW, 9/22/59 (courtesy HM).

CHAPTER 29

1. John Lloyd Wright, "Special Problems That Befall a Son of a Great Man" (eighteen-page unpublished typescript, dated 7/5/57, Avery Library, Columbia University; courtesy the Judge Welsh Collection of Avery Library).
2. Author, *New Yorker,* 9/26/53.

3. Ibid.
4. Olgivanna Wright, *Shining Brow* (Horizon Press, 1960), p. 299.
5. Barbara Branden, *The Passion of Ayn Rand* (Doubleday, 1986), pp. 140, 172, 189–191, 208–209.
6. Ayn Rand, *The Fountainhead* (Bobbs-Merrill, 1943), p. 738.
7. FLW, *Genius and the Mobocracy* (Duell, Sloan and Pearce, 1949), p. 4.
8. William Zeckendorf, *Autobiography* (Holt, Rinehart & Winston, 1970), p. 242.
9. Patrick J. Meehan, *The Master Architect* (John Wiley & Sons, 1984), p. 122.
10. Ibid., p. 137.
11. Ibid., p. 160.
12. Ibid., p. 177.
13. Olgivanna Wright, *Shining Brow*, p. 118.
14. Letter, Catherine Baxter to Grant Manson, 10/10/66 (courtesy the Grant Manson Collection, Oak Park Public Library, Oak Park, Illinois).

CHAPTER 30

1. Robert Frost, "The Gift Outright" (courtesy Henry Holt & Company).
2. FLW, *Auto*, p. 156.
3. John Lloyd Wright, Addendum to *My Father Who Is on Earth* (courtesy Avery Library).
4. JLW, "Special Problems That Befall the Son of a Great Man," p. 7.
5. Ibid., pp. 7–8.
6. Ibid., p. 2.
7. Ibid.
8. FLW's handwritten annotation on JLW's *My Father Who Is on Earth* (courtesy Avery Library).
9. Ibid., p. 117.

INDEX

ABOUT THE AUTHOR

In 1936, shortly after graduating from Yale, **Brendan Gill** joined the staff
of *The New Yorker* and has been there ever since, writing poems, short stories,
Profiles, and book, movie, and theatre reviews. He recently revived "The
Sky Line," the architectural department of the magazine long written by
Lewis Mumford. Gill is the author of some fifteen books, including his mem-
oir, *Here at The New Yorker*, three works of fiction, and biographies of Cole
Porter, Tallulah Bankhead, and Charles Lindbergh.